ROME IN THE ANCIENT WORLD

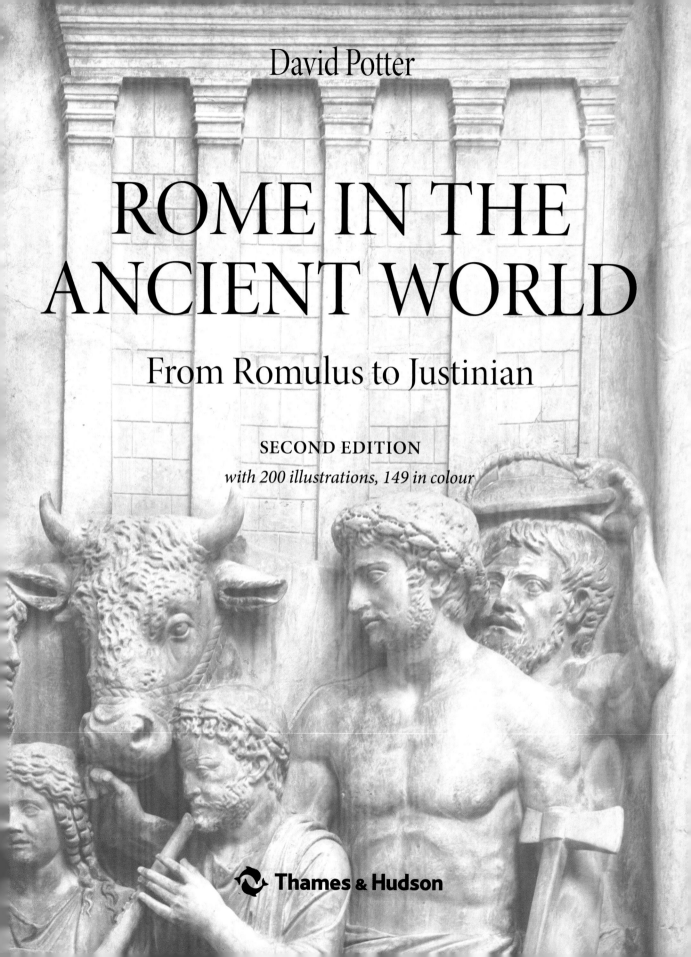

David Potter

ROME IN THE ANCIENT WORLD

From Romulus to Justinian

SECOND EDITION

with 200 illustrations, 149 in colour

Thames & Hudson

To the memory of
W. G. Forrest and P. S. Derow

Title page: In this marble relief, which may once have adorned an
arch at Rome, the emperor Marcus Aurelius makes an offering to
the gods in front of the temple of Jupiter Optimus Maximus (Musei
Capitolini, Rome).

First published in the United Kingdom in 2009
by Thames & Hudson Ltd, 181A High Holborn,
London WC1V 7QX

Second edition 2014

Rome in the Ancient World © 2009 and 2014 David Potter

British Library Cataloguing-in-Publication Data
A catalogue record for this book is available from the British Library

ISBN 978-0-500-25197-3

Printed and bound in China by C&C Offset Printing Co., Ltd

To find out about all our publications, please visit
www.thamesandhudson.com. There you can subscribe to
our e-newsletter, browse or download our current catalogue,
and buy any titles that are in print.

Contents

Notes to the Reader

Classical Sources

Following common conventions, Classical texts are cited by author, the title of the work (when more than one by the author has survived, or where confusion could arise from the fact that authors have similar or the same names), and the book number within the work as a whole, followed by chapter and sub-chapter numbers (these divisions are all the work of modern editors). For convenience, standard English translations for the title have usually been used. This means, for example, that Tacitus's *Annals* appears as Tacitus, *Annals of Imperial Rome*, as it does in Michael Grant's Penguin translation.

Documentary texts, such as inscriptions and papyri, are conventionally cited by the primary publication, by the number assigned in a major published collection, or by the number assigned in an annual survey of publications. Thus, for example, the text establishing a festival in the city of Oenoanda in southwestern Turkey is cited as *Supplement of Greek Epigraphy* 1988 no. 1462 C, which means that the text is the third item (C) in an extended dossier of letters (text number 1462) as presented in the volume for 1988. *Roman Statutes* 7 means that the text of a Roman law concerning land distribution is text 7 in Michael Crawford, *Roman Statutes*.

Roman Names

In the developed system of nomenclature, which was in common use by the mid-Republic, all Roman males had at least two names. These were the *praenomen* or "first name," which was derived from a relatively short list of seventeen *praenomina* in regular usage, and the *nomen* that identified the group of families (*gens*) to which a person belonged. For women, the use of *praenomina* was more restricted than for men. They tended to be known by the feminine form of the family *nomen* (e.g. the daughter of a Julius was Julia), and they might be distinguished from their sisters by the addition of an adjective indicating birth order—the second daughter of a Julius might be either Julia Secunda or Julia Minor.

By the mid-Republic, aristocratic Roman gentes tended to adopt a third name or *cognomen*, to which additional names (*agnomina*) might be added to commemorate substantial achievement. For example, in the case of Publius Cornelius Scipio Africanus, the *cognomen* Scipio identifies his family line within the *gens*, and the *agnomen* Africanus commemorates his victory over Hannibal in north Africa. This relatively straightforward system predominated into the third century AD, when elaborate combinations of names (something that does have parallels earlier) became commonplace, especially as *nomina* came to be used as indicators of social status after the emperor Caracalla's grant of near-universal citizenship in 212 AD.

Introduction:
Methods and Sources

In order to write the history of Rome, or indeed of any society, we must rely on two quite different processes. One is the development of models that will help us explain why things happened. The second is the close reading of the evidence that enables us to test those models.

Models for ancient history (or any other sort of history) are ideally based upon questions that arise from the study of the evidence, evolving from questions about sources to broader questions about society. For example, from such questions as "Why did this person say this?" and "What relationship does this statement bear to actual events?" we progress to "What is the significance of the fact that a person should think that way?" and to "What made it possible for people like this to exist?" The central question that drives the analysis in this book is: "How did the community of the Romans develop from a small number of people living on the banks of the Tiber to a community encompassing some sixty-four million people spread from one end of the Mediterranean to the other?" Allied with this question are two more: "How did the Romans themselves understand this development?" and "Did the Roman understanding of their community change over time?" These three questions will be addressed in the chapters that follow.

Early Rome

The sources for Roman history vary over time. For the early period, covered in Chapter 1, we have very little reliable evidence. Archaeological study has revealed some things about the communities that lived around the Latin plain from the eighth to the sixth century BC: this allows us to see something of the urban development of Rome, as the villagers living in settlements clustered on what would become the seven hills of Rome drained the marshes in the valley that would become the Roman forum, and began to build in the area they had created. Earlier evidence reveals something of the lifestyle of people before the development of the urban community. There are, however, no texts of great significance before the middle of the fifth century BC, the date of the Twelve Tables (Rome's first law code, which is known only through quotations in later authors). Much else that we think we know depends upon the principle that Roman institutions were deeply conservative, and thus preserved some traces of earlier institutions into the period for which we have better sources. This is the same principle that Roman writers used when they tried to reconstruct their own history.

The first Roman historian of Rome was Fabius Pictor, who wrote in Greek, at the end of the third century BC. After Fabius, the first significant historian of Rome—writing this time in Latin—was Marcus Porcius Cato. The work of both historians, and indeed of all other Roman historians before the first century BC, is known only through quotations in later authors. The reason for this is probably that later generations found their history far less interesting than that written by Livy between the 30s BC and (so we are told) AD 17. Livy's *Books from the Founding of the City* consisted of 142 books, and covered Roman history from its foundation down to 9 BC. Much of Livy's history does not survive intact—we must rely on later summaries of what he had to say for all but 35 books. The surviving books are 1–10, which give the history of Rome from the foundation to 293 BC, and 20–45, which cover 219 to 167 BC.

One thing that set Livy's account of early Rome apart from those of his predecessors was that he was able to exploit the work of Marcus Terentius Varro, writing a generation earlier, who composed a massive work on Roman institutions known as the *Human and Divine Antiquities*. In so doing, Varro appears to have scoured whatever earlier records survived, including those owned by priests, legal texts, and treaties. For this reason, although we do not have the actual documents, we may be reasonably certain that we have a fair idea of the legislative history of Rome from the fifth to the third century BC. Varro's work, while better than anything else, does not, however, seem to have been a radical break from earlier tradition, which had used similar material. Sallust, a contemporary of Varro, knew that Roman history before the beginning of the wars with Carthage in 264 BC was dominated by the tale of the conflict between the patrician and plebeian orders, and that this was reflected in the history of Roman law. In Chapter 1 we will consider whether there was indeed a "struggle between the orders." It may also be a projection of second-century views about the nature of the legislative process back onto an earlier era (in other words, an explanatory model devised by the Romans themselves).

Latin writers are not the only witnesses to Roman history. Much of what we know about Rome at all periods comes from the pens of Greek writers. Dionysius of Halicarnassus, a contemporary of Livy, wrote 20 books on the *Antiquities of the Romans* from the foundation of the city to the outbreak of war between Rome and Carthage; 11 of these books survive intact, giving the story down to 441 BC. Another witness to early Roman history is the historian Diodorus Siculus, whose 40-book *Universal History*, linking Greek with Roman history, was completed in the 50s BC: 15 of his books survive intact, covering the fifth and fourth centuries BC.

Although it may seem that such writers as Livy, Dionysius, and Diodorus wrote a prodigious amount—and by some standards that is true—we need to keep in mind that an ancient book was constrained by the size of papyrus rolls; the typical "book" by a prose writer fills a little more than 70 pages in a standard modern edition. If we had all that Diodorus wrote we might then have something like 2,800 pages, no small achievement, but still not masses when we consider the fact that his history covers some 600 years. Livy is more detailed—we might have close to 10,000 pages for 750 years—but that calculation is somewhat deceptive, since Livy did not divide his space evenly. Instead of offering 7.5 pages per year from 753 BC (Varro's date for the foundation of Rome) onwards, he covered the first 243 years in 75 pages, and the next 220 in around 650 pages, while offering an enormously detailed treatment of the history of Rome from the end of the second century BC onwards. Still, by trying to understand how such authors as Livy and Dionysius reasoned, we can gain some impression of what could be known in their lifetimes about earlier Roman history, and have some confidence that there was at least a thin documentary foundation for what they wrote extending back into the fifth century.

Ancient books were traditionally written out on scrolls made from sheets of papyrus, a thick, paper-like material that can be seen in these frescos from Pompeii and Herculaneum. To make a papyrus roll was a labor-intensive process: the stem of a papyrus plant was stripped, its inner pith was cut into strips and pressed together into sheets, and these were glued together to make a scroll.

To say that there was a thin documentary foundation for what Livy and Dionysius wrote does not begin to tell the whole story behind their work. Ancient authors felt free to embroider their accounts with rhetorical compositions to bring out the "true meaning" of events. For the early period, they also drew upon myths and legends that had become part of the folk memory of the Roman people through stage performances, holidays, and simply seeing old monuments (ancient Rome was also ancient by Livy's time). They therefore worked into their histories episodes that to us are largely (or wholly) invention.

The Early Republic

By about 400 BC, the starting point for Chapter 2, the type of evidence we have for Roman history begins to change. For the history of the war with Pyrrhus in the late 280s BC we have sources that drew upon books written by Pyrrhus and at least one contemporary. These works are quoted by later writers—chiefly Plutarch, who lived towards the end of the first century AD and composed, along with very many other books, the *Lives of Famous Greeks and Romans*, which preserves a great deal that is not covered by other sources. From the beginning of the war with Carthage in 264 down to 146 BC we have the work of Polybius, a Greek who was taken to Rome as a hostage in 167 BC and wrote a forty-book *Universal History* to explain how the Romans had come to dominate the world in which he lived (the narrative fills thirty-nine books; the fortieth acted as a sort of table of contents). Again, we do not have everything that Polybius wrote—only books 1–5 survive intact—but he was extensively quoted by later authors (including Livy) so that we have a reasonable idea of what he had to say for much of the period in question. Another historian whose work becomes increasingly important at this point (and especially for the period covered by Chapter 3, from 133 BC) is Appian. A Greek who composed histories of Rome's wars in the second century AD, Appian preserved material from many sources, including books of Livy that have not survived. At this period also we begin to get more contemporary documents, inscribed on bronze or stone.

Inscriptions on bronze or stone are absolutely crucial to our understanding of Roman history (and the history of Greece for that matter), and readers will see that

I have tended to quote them as evidence of what was said or done. Since inscriptions were usually carved at the time that a public statement was made or the moment that an individual decided to commemorate something, they are absolutely contemporary witnesses (although there are some cases where inscriptions were recarved at later times). All of the literary evidence we have was filtered through copyists from antiquity through the Middle Ages, and its survival is largely the result of their tastes (which is why so many books by authors I have mentioned do not survive). That is not true of inscriptions, whose survival is due to random circumstance. But that does not mean that their use as evidence is entirely straightforward. By their very nature inscriptions shed an intense spotlight on one moment of time. If one is interested in the specific point that is dealt with in the text of an inscription—the terms of a law, for instance—then this spotlight is intensely valuable. But it is often the case that inscriptions were broken between the time they were carved and the point at which modern scholars began to catalogue their information. Since the language of inscriptions often follows precise formulae, it is sometimes possible to "restore" or fill in missing bits of text on the basis of parallels. At other times efforts to fill in the blanks are conjecture. When I quote inscriptions in this book, I have used certain conventions to indicate the nature of the translation. If text is within square brackets [ ] it is restored. Text within parentheses ( ) is my own intervention to explain terms or other aspects of the text that might seem peculiar. Text within angled brackets < > is text restored by a modern editor where it was erroneously omitted by the stone carver. In trying to examine the development of Roman institutions we must often collect and compare large numbers of inscribed texts that deal with similar phenomena to determine what is typical or atypical.

Another stream of documentary information derives from texts written on papyrus plant—mostly, but not entirely, from Egypt. Papyri preserve a mass of documentation about the daily lives of the inhabitants of the empire, many official documents, and a great deal of literature. A third variety of evidence is offered by coins (see box, p. 13).

The Late Republic and Early Empire

From about 133 BC to the mid-third century AD (the period covered by Chapters 3–5) evidence from inscriptions, coins, and papyri becomes increasingly important, but that is not the only change in the evidence available. First, a great deal more art and architecture survives from this period than from earlier years, so we can get a better idea of how people lived. Second, the work of archaeologists in surveying settlement patterns has also given us a much better idea of life outside urban areas, while art historians, working from surviving sculpture, painting, coins, and a wide variety of other objects, can help us gain an impression of Roman aesthetic standards. Third, there is more literature of all sorts. Much of this literature derives from people who participated in the events that they describe. Eyewitnesses can be both intriguing and infuriating: intriguing because they were there, infuriating because their memories are often shaped by their own life experiences, or images that they have of themselves that they wish others to share. Among the great witnesses of this period are Marcus Tullius Cicero, Julius Caesar, and Cornelius Tacitus. Caesar's writings on his own wars are often deeply misleading, but they also offer insight into the mind of the greatest Roman politician of any era. Cicero, who was

COINS AS EVIDENCE

When studied in large numbers, coins offer very important evidence for the structure of the economy. Because they are often encoded with low-level propagandistic messages—much as postage stamps often are today—they can also show how people might be taught to envisage their leaders, some significant events of the past, buildings, or even the jobs of their rulers.

In terms of economic history, the most important use of coins comes through tracking the places in which they are found. People who were in fear for their lives (or simply looking to protect valuables) had a tendency to bury their coins in what we now call hoards. Coin hoards show what kinds of coins tended to be in circulation at any given time, allowing us to gain an impression of the structure of the economy. They can also be a measure of social unrest, as can be seen from the fact that there are almost as many coin hoards known from the period of Hannibal's invasion of Italy (218–202 BC) as from the entire second century BC. (A large number of hoards likewise date from the five years after Sulla's victory in 82–81 BC, and the period of the civil wars between Caesar and Pompey in the early 40s BC.)

When looking at the propagandistic use of coins, we need first to consider who was in charge of minting operations. In the Republic, Roman coins were minted by relatively junior magistrates who were members of a board of three. In many cases these men would issue coins that differed little from those of other magistrates, a favorite pattern being one that represented the goddess Roma on the obverse (front) and the twin gods Castor and Pollux, who were thought to have aided the Roman victory over the Latins in 499 BC, on the reverse (1). At other times, a magistrate might choose a pattern that advertised some moment of family history, or illustrated an important Roman concept. For example, the magistrate M. Herennius (like many Romans of this period, he used only a *praenomen* and *nomen*) illustrates the Roman

concept of *pietas* with an image of the goddess on the obverse and an illustration of the story of one of the Catanaean brothers rescuing his father from an eruption of Aetna on the reverse (2). The image of *pietas*, where a son carries a parent to safety, was later exploited by Caesar in commemorating his ancestor, Aeneas, saving his father, Anchises, at the fall of Troy, and memorably described by Virgil in his *Aeneid* (see p. 22).

1

2

In the first three centuries AD, the authority to mint coins was divided between the emperor, the senate, and individual cities, with the latter two issuing bronze coins, while the imperial mints issued coins in silver and gold. In this coinage the emperor's bust (or that of a family member) was on the obverse, usually with the image of a god representing an imperial virtue, an important building, or another concept, such as the loyalty of the army, on the reverse. It is possible to detect some basic messages about imperial ideology from these coins. There are sometimes sharp breaks, as may be seen in the difference in the portraiture of Septimius Severus (3) and his son, Caracalla (4), or between the individualism of the portraits of Claudius II during his reign in AD 268–70 (5) and the more idealized image of the emperor that predominated in the coins of his successor, Aurelian (6).

3

4

5

6

unquestionably Rome's greatest orator, left not only numerous speeches that enable us to see what sort of arguments a successful orator thought would move a Roman crowd or jury, but also an enormous number of letters to friends, especially to one Titus Pomponius Atticus. These letters can often enable us to follow events from his perspective on a virtually day-by-day basis in the course of the 50s and 40s BC. Tacitus's histories of Rome after the reign of Augustus (27 BC–AD 14) form the basis of our understanding of this period, even though he was not himself a mature witness to events until the reign of Vespasian (AD 69–79). His *Annals*, covering the period AD 14–68 (although the manuscript containing the text breaks off partway through AD 66), and *Histories*, which spanned the period AD 69–96 (though only the first four and a half books, covering 69 and part of 70, have survived), are supplemented by other narrative historians, biographies, and documents. To understand how Romans thought, we must try to combine evidence from as many sources as we can, and for that reason, I will often stress the importance of documents, archaeology, and art. It is also the case that we will rarely, if ever, find a single "Roman" view on anything. Instead, what our evidence will allow us to do is gain some idea of what Romans talked about and how they spoke to each other.

Tacitus, who was probably born in AD 57, died during the reign of Hadrian (AD 117–38). From that time onwards, and for much of the period after 70 BC, we may also rely on the work of a Greek historian, Cassius Dio, to gain an idea of the narrative framework, as well as the value system of a third-century AD Roman aristocrat of Greek heritage. Dio's history, in eighty books, tells the story of Rome from the foundation of the city to the late 220s AD (we surmise from this that he died around AD 230). Again, the greater part of this work is lost. Only books 36–60, covering the period from 69 BC to AD 49, are preserved directly through a manuscript tradition, and even then with some significant gaps; for the rest we are dependent upon summaries and quotations in books from the Middle Ages. But for the period of Dio's lifetime there is again an enormous quantity of other literature, ranging from the vast collection of medical works by the doctor Galen or the equally large quantity of material produced by Roman lawyers of the time, through works of rhetoric, novels, and satire produced by such immensely talented authors as Apuleius or Lucian that help us see how the Romans might have viewed the world around them. For the period beginning with the death of Marcus Aurelius in AD 180 and down to the civil war of AD 238 we also have the eight-book history of Herodian. Although Herodian's access to the upper echelons of government was far inferior to Dio's, his history still offers a vital and interesting (if not always accurate) account.

The Third and Fourth Centuries AD

Chapter 6 begins in the mid-third century just after the death of Cassius Dio, and for the first half of the chapter the narrative relies on accounts that are much later in date. These include a book written in the sixth century by a pagan historian named Zosimus, and a summary of earlier Greek histories written in the twelfth century by an important nobleman named John Zonaras (also the source of a summary of Cassius Dio's history). In fact, the only contemporary narrative for the first thirty years covered in this chapter is an oracular text known as *The Thirteenth Sibylline Oracle*, in which the barely veiled references to contemporary characters allow us to gain some impression of the impact that the political insecurity of these years

This copy of a letter from Eusebius is one of a number of Christian texts collected in a manuscript codex that dates from the sixth century AD. Between the second and fourth centuries AD, pages of parchment bound together into a single volume gradually replaced the papyrus roll as the basic form of the book.

made on contemporaries. Another source is a late fourth-century collection of imperial biographies known as the *Historia Augusta* (*Augustan History*), written in Latin and purporting to be the work of six people writing at the time of Diocletian (the late third century). (The work was once described as *Scriptores Historiae Augustae—Writers of the Augustan Histories*—when it was believed that these people actually existed.) This elaborate forgery has been exposed by generations of modern scholars who have now placed this work in its proper chronological location, and established the fact that there was but a single author. Although deeply unreliable, the *Historia Augusta* preserves some flavor of writings by third-century authors; its contents can be supplemented with some information offered by a group of writers who wrote short summary histories of Rome in Latin in the second half of the fourth century. One of these writers, whose history of the emperors from Augustus to Theodosius I (379–95) comprises slightly more than forty pages as printed in modern editions of the Latin text, is anonymous; another, Eutropius, wrote a very short history from the foundation of Rome until the year 364 (the Latin text is sixty-eight pages); and the third, Aurelius Victor, was an imperial bureaucrat whose history of the emperors from Augustus to AD 360 fills around forty pages. The fourth member of this group, an official named Festus, traced the history of the empire from the Republic to AD 369/370 in half the space (and with minimal coherence).

With the reigns of Diocletian and Constantine (AD 284–337) we fall into a very different pool of evidence. We have numerous speeches in praise of these emperors (or their colleagues, in the case of Diocletian) in Latin, known as the Latin panegyrics. The narrative of the period is built largely from accounts in Zosimus (also useful for the period before Diocletian), and the Latin summaries mentioned above, to which may be added a further summary called the *Origin of the Emperor Constantine*. Two Christian writers, Lactantius and Eusebius, however, supply the vast bulk of new material. Lactantius wrote a bitter denunciation of Diocletian and his colleagues after the initiation of the persecution of the Christians in AD 303. Eusebius's main works are a history of the Christian Church (the *Ecclesiastical History*) and a *Life of Constantine* that is more often panegyric than history.

For the period after Constantine, the sheer quantity of material expands enormously. This is largely due to the survival of masses of Christian material that sheds important light on social attitudes; the vast corpus of speeches and letters composed by the Antiochene orator and teacher of rhetoric, Libanius; the large collection of letters emanating from the late fourth-century senator, Symmachus (a number of whose speeches also survive); and the works of the Emperor Julian. At the end of the fourth century the work of Augustine of Hippo dwarfs that of earlier, non-Christian, authors. In Greek, the huge corpus of the theologian and church leader Athanasius of Alexandria is immensely important, not only for charting the travails of Athanasius himself, but also for understanding the development of Christian polemic.

The influence of Athanasius's discourse is especially strong in the work of a group of early fifth-century historians who saw themselves as extending the *Ecclesiastical History* of Eusebius, especially Socrates, Sozomen, and Theodoret. The work of a fourth historian of this period—Philostorgius, who does not share the confessional prejudices of others—though preserved only in fragments, is often a breath of fresh air. Our main source, however, for the later fourth century is Ammianus Marcellinus, whose history of Rome from AD 96 to 378 in thirty-one books is preserved for the period after 353 (book 14). Ammianus was a splendid writer with a passionate sense of justice, who lived through the events that he narrates. He was the last great historian of the Classical period to work in Latin, even though he was himself born in Antioch, the main city of Syria, and his first language was Greek.

The End of Empire

With the end of Ammianus's history we come to a significant break point in the source tradition. There is no other major narrative historian whose work is preserved intact until the middle of the sixth century. Instead, for the early years of Honorius (from 395), we have poetry by Claudian, a Latin poet whose work enables us to gain the government's perspective on the campaigns against Alaric in 402–3, and on the relationship between Stilicho and the Eastern court.

So far as the Eastern empire is concerned, the works of Synesius offer some insight into the complex negotiations connected with the revolt of Gainas, while the narrative base comes still from Zosimus. Lying behind Zosimus at this point is the work of a historian named Olympiodorus, who was both recorder and actor in many of the events that he describes. Olympiodorus's history was probably completed in the mid-430s. The major historian after Olympiodorus was Priscus of Panium, who wrote in the 470s, though by far the most notable part of his history is his immensely detailed narrative of an embassy to Attila the Hun that he accompanied in 449. He completed his history in the reign of Zeno (*c.* 425–91). The next historian of note (also fragmentary) is Malchus, whose interest in the East is considerable, and who gives us our most detailed account of the year 476 (he seems to have missed the significance of the deposition of Romulus as the "last emperor of the West"). Although his work is said to have run from Constantine to the accession of Anastasius in 491, what we have runs from the seventeenth year of Leo (whom he clearly detested) in 473 to about 480, and offers a great deal of detail about dealings with the Goths before their invasion of Italy.

The dominant historian of the sixth century, from an Eastern perspective, is Procopius, who chronicled the reign of Justinian (527–65). He produced three major works. The largest of these, the *Wars*, comprises three parts, treating the wars with the Persians and Vandals, and the wars in Italy, all of which heap praise upon the emperor and Belisarius, his chief general. The second work (also devoted to the emperor's praises) is about the buildings erected by Justinian. In his third work, the *Secret History*, Procopius—who had clearly become disillusioned with the emperor—tells a very different story, in what is one of the most vitriolic discussions of any ruler at any point in antiquity (it is also highly critical of Belisarius and his wife). At roughly the same time that Procopius was writing, the Italian exile Jordanes was composing his history of the Goths. It was based on an earlier history by Cassiodorus, who was one of the major figures of Ostrogothic Italy, and whose

The Roman forum is viewed here from the temple of Saturn. Like the rest of the forum, this temple passed through many phases. Said to have been dedicated in 498 BC, the remains we see today are of the temple as it was rebuilt in AD 283. Archaeological excavations allow us to reconstruct the history of such sites as this, offering unique perspectives on the past.

voluminous correspondence enables us to gain some insight into the relationship between non-Roman and Roman in the sixth century. Somewhat later in date, but profoundly important, is the work of Gregory of Tours, especially his *History of the Franks*, which traces the development of the Frankish kingdom in the course of the sixth century. For the period between the death of Justinian in 575 and the reign of Heraclius, which began in 610, a narrative base is provided by the (fragmentary) history of Menander the Guardsman and the intact work of Theophylact Simocatta (the "snub-nosed cat"), which ends with the death of the emperor Maurice in 602.

In addition to histories in the Classical style, the fifth and sixth centuries are especially rich in chronicles often presented, in the West, as continuations of Eusebius's chronicle of world history from the Creation to his own time (translated into Latin in the later fourth century by Jerome). In the East, the tradition of chronicles, which descended from a very long tradition within Greek historiography, includes both works of broad focus and those of much more local import, such as that of John Malalas, which, although it concentrates on the city of Antioch in Syria, is a vital source for the history of the Eastern empire in general. Although the quality of the material included in these chronicles varies immensely, there is much that is of great value, such as Malalas's account of the Nike revolt at Constantinople in 532—which reveals many of the shortcomings of Procopius's Classicizing vision—or the account of Heraclius's defeat of Persia in the chronicle of Theophanes.

Sources in Other Languages

From the beginning of the third century AD onwards, much larger quantities of material begin to appear in the languages of the Near East, beginning with the earliest phases of the Jewish Mishnah and extending in the fourth through seventh centuries to a vibrant literature in Syriac (a western Semitic dialect), Armenian, and Coptic (Egyptian). Thus the earliest mention of Mohammed comes in a Syriac chronicle dating to 637 and 640 (A. Palmer, *The Seventh Century in the West-Syrian Chronicles*, Liverpool, 1993, 2: 19); important information about Heraclius's campaigns against Persia comes from the Armenian history of Sebeos, who also provides the earliest extant account of the career of Mohammed (R. W. Thomson and J. Howard-Johnston, *The Armenian History Attributed to Sebeos*, Liverpool, 1999, 95–96); and most of our knowledge of the Arab conquest of Egypt comes from an Ethiopic translation of a chronicle originally written in Coptic by a man named John of Nikiu.

Finally, from the fourth century onwards we find an increasing number of saints' lives in various Eastern languages as well as Greek and Latin. These can provide vital evidence for the way people lived in the rural areas of the Eastern empire, and for relations between urban and rural populations. In many cases these lives contain a great deal of fiction, but even fictions can prove valuable when they reflect the broader patterns of social life and the disputes that informed the lives of their authors or audiences.

None of the evidence that we have explains itself, and the particular value of any passage may be determined by the nature of the questions that are being asked. Nonetheless, whether what they offer is overt fiction, distortions shaped by passion and prejudice, or thoroughly respectable efforts to get at a truth that would have seemed as deeply hidden then as it seems now, our sources enable us to hear the voices and sense the passions of a people who, though long dead, are still very much with us.

The
Formation
of the
Roman
Identity

(800–350 BC)

TIMELINE I THE FORMATION OF THE ROMAN IDENTITY

c. 1000 BC	Earliest signs of settlement on the Capitoline and earliest known tombs in the forum valley
c. 900	Beginning of permanent settlement on the Palatine
753	Conventional date for Romulus's foundation of Rome
730–720	Probable date for the earliest phase of the wall around the Palatine
725–575	Range of possible dates for the draining and paving of the forum
715	Conventional date for the death of Romulus; beginning of the reign of Numa
672	Conventional date for the death of Numa; beginning of the reign of Tullus Hostilius
640	Conventional date for the death of Tullus Hostilius; beginning of the reign of Ancus Marcius
616	Conventional date for the death of Ancus Marcius; beginning of the reign of Tarquin the Elder (Tarquinius Priscus)
578	Conventional date for the death of Tarquin the Elder; beginning of the reign of Servius Tullius
578–534	Conventional date for the introduction of the *comitia centuriata*
575	Approximate date for the first temple building at Sant' Omobono
c. 550	Likely date for the defensive perimeter around the urban area of Rome (the Servian wall)
534	Conventional date for the death of Servius Tullius; beginning of the reign of Tarquin the Arrogant (Tarquinius Superbus)
509 BC	Expulsion of Tarquin the Arrogant; foundation of the Republican form of government; dedication of the temple of Capitoline Jupiter; treaty with Carthage

Earliest Rome

499 **or 496** BC	Romans defeat Latins at the battle of Lake Regillus
494–493	First secession of the plebs; creation of a board of five tribunes
c. 493	*Foedus Cassianum* defines Rome's relationship with the Latin League
457	Number of tribunes increased to ten
452–450	Board of ten (*Decemvirs*) appointed to revise the law code of Rome
450	Completion of the Law Code of the Twelve Tables
449	Reforms of the Laws of the Twelve Tables to protect plebeian rights
445	Plebeian-patrician intermarriage permitted
444	First board of consular tribunes appointed
443	First censors appointed
396	Capture of Veii
391	Exile of Camillus
c. 390	Gauls sack Rome after battle of the River Allia
367	Licinian-Sextian laws on debt, the use of public land, and the admission of plebeians to the consulship
342	Laws passed prohibiting repeated tenure of office within ten years and permitting plebeians to hold both consulships
339	Laws passed on plebeian tenure of the consulship, binding nature of plebiscites and moving the *auctoritas patrum* before bills were put to the vote
287 BC	*Lex Hortensia* confirms legal force of plebiscites

The Development of the Republic

THE FOUNDATION OF ROME was accomplished with a spectacular act of violence. The Romans themselves believed that twin brothers, Romulus and Remus, entered into a contest to see which of them would found a new city. When Romulus won the contest, and was beginning to lay out the boundary of their new community, Remus attacked him, and was killed. For later generations, the murder of Remus served as a paradigm both for the fierce political struggles that shaped the Roman citizen community, and then for the fratricidal strife that reshaped the Roman and Mediterranean communities in the century before the birth of Christ.

The grim tale of murder was not, however, Rome's only foundation myth. In another version, the prime actor was a refugee named Aeneas, fleeing the sack of Troy by the Greeks. In its earliest form, the story of Aeneas offered a model for the integration of Rome into the broader Mediterranean world. In its classic version, composed by the poet Virgil, the story became a message of hope for Romans who had survived the civil wars of the first century BC. Virgil's Aeneas wandered long and far to discover his people's mythical homeland on the banks of the Tiber. There the Trojan refugees encountered the native people: fierce warriors who, inspired by an enraged goddess, engaged them in a great war that culminated in an act of savagery as Aeneas threw down their champion and slew him. In this version too, spectacular death began the process of forging the community from which Rome would ultimately be founded. The difference between this story and the story of Romulus was that Aeneas slew for a purpose. His journey, like that of Rome, would be hard; the point of his suffering, as it was for Romans of the historical period, was often obscure. But there would at least be hope and a new beginning.

Romulus, Remus, and Aeneas are powerful symbols for the development of the Roman community, because deep within the Roman understanding of what it meant to be Roman was a sense that Rome's survival stemmed from the ability to endure, and recover from, acts of violence. Likewise there was a willingness to perpetrate violence. The acquisition of empire was supported by a readiness on the part of the average Roman to fight in war after war, to sustain the loss of friends and loved ones on a massive scale. Appropriately, the legendary founders of Rome were men capable of inflicting death upon their foes, in anger and without remorse, as were the historical Romans who invented them.

Just as the foundation myths were later seen as paradigms explaining the conduct of the Roman people towards one another, two other myths offered paradigms for the way that the Roman community would grow. The stories of how Romulus populated the city include powerful metaphors for two very different ways of defining Roman identity. One of these, as described by Livy (see p. 10), was to draw people in from other places:

> Then, so his large city would not be empty, using an old plan employed by the founders of cities, who gather about themselves a mass of obscure and humble people, pretending that the earth had raised up sons to them, Romulus opened the sanctuary in the place that is now enclosed by two groves as you go up the Capitoline hill. To that place came a crowd from neighboring states, both slave and free, eager for a fresh start, and that was the first advance in power towards greatness. When

The story of Aeneas was not only one of the foundation myths of Rome, but it was also one of the foundation myths of the family of Julius Caesar (see p. 13). This coin depicts Aeneas rescuing his father, Anchises, at the fall of Troy. It was minted to pay Caesar's men during the civil war that began in 49 BC.

THE RAPE OF THE SABINES: WOMEN AND THE CREATION OF ROME

A second story told by Livy about Romulus's role in populating Rome is in many ways precisely the opposite of the asylum story; it is that Rome was short of women and acquired them by force. According to this tale, Romulus invited neighboring peoples to send women to Rome to marry its men. When they refused, he summoned one group, the Sabines, to a religious festival, during which the Romans set upon the female visitors and stole them. This founding myth is known as the Rape of the Sabine Women. Livy asserts, however, that the women were not raped but agreed to accept Roman husbands:

> The young women had no greater hope for themselves or lesser outrage (than their parents). But Romulus himself went around to them and told them that the arrogance of their fathers had been the cause of what happened since they had denied the right of marriage to neighbors, telling them that they would have legal marriages, become partners in all their property and their state, and their children, the most precious thing of all to the human race, if they would just moderate their anger and give their hearts to those to whom Fortune had given their bodies; that injury can give way to affection, and that they would therefore find their husbands better since each man would seek not

This coin depicting the Rape of the Sabine Women was minted during the great war between Rome and its former Italian allies in 89 BC (see p. 129). In this context, the myth served to remind viewers of an earlier conflict between two peoples who eventually united to make Rome great.

> only to be a good husband, but also to console them for the parents they had lost. The wooing of the men confirmed his words, as they excused their deed on the grounds of passion and love, which are the most effective pleas to move a woman's heart.
>
> (Livy 1.9.14–16)

In this story, the Sabine women can be seen as playing two roles. In one interpretation, the women are passive vessels for the transmission of citizenship by biological means—one could become a Roman citizen by being born one. In another interpretation, the Sabine women play an active role in creating the Roman state. When the Sabines showed up to reclaim their women (nearly a year later), the women, many of them now with new babies, begged the men of their old families to make peace with their new. Implicit in this story is validation for the role of women in reconciling antagonistic males through their own bodies.

> he was not now ashamed of his strength, Romulus added policy to power. He appointed one hundred "fathers" [senators], whether because that was a sufficient number, or because that was the total number whom he could call "fathers."
>
> (Livy 1.8.4–7)

The crucial point here is not just the belief that Rome grew because its community was open to outsiders, but also that even the aristocracy of Rome included these newcomers. In broadest terms, this story points to one strand within the Roman tradition: that membership in the Roman community depended upon a person's aspiration to be Roman rather than upon any theoretical biological connection. But another myth, also described by Livy, offers a very different story: suggesting that the Romans acquired the first generation of women for their country by stealing them from their neighbors (see box, above). These myths of asylum and rape remain essential descriptions of two strands that were never fully reconciled within Roman thought. At times, Rome would prove very open to outsiders, usually during periods when the Roman state was ascendant. At other times, Romans would insist more firmly on the narrow definition of membership implicit in the insistence upon a biological connection. The essentially exclusive tenor of this view was often a recipe for serious trouble: it tended to be prominent at times when the Romans were divided against themselves, or their own best interests.

Despite internal conflict and occasional catastrophe in wars with other peoples, the Roman community grew stronger in the wake of each upheaval, recovered from each blow, until, at length, it encompassed the entire Mediterranean world and cast its strength well inland to the lands bordered by the Rhine and Danube rivers, and even to the distant lowlands of Scotland in the north. In the south it would extend down the Nile to the borders of modern Sudan; in the east its outposts would creep as far as the Caspian Sea and the Euphrates river in Iraq.

Throughout all this, the story of imperial Rome remains the story of how the community of Romans reshaped itself through time. The Roman empire was unusual in that it did not so much create new subjects as it did new Romans. By the third century AD, virtually all inhabitants of the empire were Roman citizens, and its emperors were drawn from peoples whose ancestors had once been numbered among the enemies of Rome. The empire survived the loss of its original capital, Rome, and its original heartland, Italy, for centuries. The ideals of Roman civilization were preserved and transmitted by the agents of the Christian Church, a church that had once been seen as a minor, but hostile, force, before it was transformed into an institution of the very state that had put its founder and his closest followers to death. The theme of this book is therefore the way that the diverse communities of Rome were shaped: from the eighth and seventh centuries BC, when Rome began to grow as an urban site, to the seventh century AD when the Roman empire (now ruled from Constantinople) surrendered its ambitions in the face of a new power—that of Islam.

The First Roman Communities

The Roman Story of Early Roman History

Our knowledge of early Roman history comes from writers who worked in the last half of the first century BC. The most important of these writers was Livy. He devoted just one book to the history of Rome from what he thought was the date of the city's foundation, 753 BC, to the end of the period in which it was ruled by kings in 509 BC. In another four books Livy continued his account down to the year 390 BC, when the city had to be rebuilt after its capture by a band of Gauls, Celtic tribesmen from the north who swept through the Italian peninsula to loot and pillage.

The Livian version of Roman history was based upon a tradition that began to take firm shape in the late third century BC, when Romans first began to write the history of their own city. The sources for this narrative are often rather obscure, though it appears that they included myth, explanations of religious rituals, a record of legislation, the fossilized remains of earlier political institutions, and monuments in the city of Rome itself. According to this story—which, as we shall see, is largely a fantasy—the city was founded by Romulus, who served as its first king.

Once the initial community was formed and, again according to legend, the basic institutions of the Roman state were in place, Romulus departed from the earth (some stories have him murdered by the senate, others say that he ascended to join the gods). After Romulus, the tradition held that there were six more kings: Numa, Tullus Hostilius, Ancus Marcius, Tarquin the Elder, Servius Tullius, and Tarquin the Arrogant. In later tradition, Romulus was viewed as the deviser of most of the institutions of Roman domestic life; Numa created the essentials of Rome's religious institutions; Tullus Hostilius began the expansion of Rome throughout the Latin plain; Ancus solidified the work of Tullus; and Servius Tullius laid the foundations for the Roman Republican constitution by reorganizing the citizen body (see p. 43). Little good could be said of the two Tarquins; the second of them was driven from Rome after his son raped the daughter of an aristocratic family, Lucretia, who had previously been identified as a model of domestic virtue (see pp. 35–36). The story about the assault on Lucretia embodies an important feature of the Roman historical tradition: that radical reform is often connected with domestic crimes that prove that representatives of the old order are unworthy; that heroes must be seen to put the state ahead of their families; and that great men must learn to subordinate themselves to the state.

Rome's enemies tend to fall into two categories, prefiguring enemies who existed at the time that the narrative of Roman history began to be written down in the late third century BC. The first of these archetypal foes were the barbarians: either Celts from the north or Samnites from central Italy (both groups, especially the Samnites, were in fact a good deal more civilized than Roman tradition admits). The second enemy was the potent city-state or monarchy, a power that the Romans were able to defeat only through their superior virtues (which were also crucial when it came to dealing with barbarians). In the late third century, the real-world representatives of these "civilized opponents" were the Celtic tribes of Western Europe and the great city of Carthage in north Africa. The type of virtue that enabled Romans to defeat their neighbors was exemplified by young Marcus Curtius, who earned immortal fame (so the story goes) when a chasm opened in the middle of the Roman forum. When the Roman people wondered what this meant, prophets told them that the gods wished them to sacrifice that which was most important to them. Curtius pointed out that Rome's greatest blessing was its weapons and the courage of its people. He then put on his armor, mounted his horse, and rode into the chasm. Romans came face to face with this story every time they entered the forum, and modern visitors can still see the legendary site today: the so-called Lacus Curtius is located in the heart of the forum, opposite the great speakers' platform or rostrum that stood in front of the senate house. Romans were routinely reminded as they read this history that the greatest threat to Rome was internal disunity, usually stemming from certain groups or individuals putting their own interests ahead of the common good.

The stories that resonated with the Romans provided for a most dramatic early history. They believed that a man named Lucius Iunius Brutus led the movement to expel the kings in 509 BC, and that he replaced the king with a pair of magistrates, whom the citizens elected each year. When Brutus's sons then joined a conspiracy to overthrow the young state, Brutus himself presided over their execution. In these years Rome was barely able to hold its own against armies coming south from Etruria (the Etruscans were the classic "civilized opponents"). Two of the most famous heroes of this period were Horatius Cocles and Quintus Mucius Scaevola, who earned their fame for courage in the face of extreme adversity as Rome struggled to hold out against the armies of an Etruscan warlord named Lars Porsenna (a person for whom there is actual evidence in an early Greek history of the city of Cumae, on the Bay of Naples). Horatius was celebrated by a statue near the Vulcanal (the shrine of the god Vulcan) on the slopes of the Capitoline before the end of the fourth century; he had stood his ground against the Etruscans as they pursued the fleeing Roman army at the far end of the bridge over the Tiber, allowing time for the Romans to destroy the bridge behind him before he swam to safety. Gaius Mucius botched an assassination of Porsenna, but when brought before him declared that there were three hundred Romans ready to follow him in the attempt, and showed his contempt for pain by thrusting his left hand into an Etruscan fire. Impressed, Porsenna sent him home and negotiated a treaty with the Romans. Mucius was thereafter given the name Scaevola ("Lefty"), a *cognomen* that survived in his family for many centuries. The most important Etruscan city in this story was Veii (located around ten miles north of Rome), which was finally captured by the Romans in 396 BC under the leadership of M. Furius Camillus. It was just after this great success that disaster struck, when the aforementioned Gauls destroyed the citizen army and captured the city for themselves (although some claimed that they never occupied the Capitoline hill). Camillus, who had been exiled by his jealous fellow-citizens in 391 BC, returned to save the day. He rallied the army, defeated the Gauls, and convinced the Romans to rebuild their city.

Camillus was only one of a number of citizens whom the Romans believed had either been wronged by their fellows or sought to destroy the state by establishing a dictatorship. In the earliest years of the Republic, Roman tradition recalled a man named Coriolanus, who led them to victory before being driven into exile by representatives of a "popular" party that despised his aristocratic arrogance. Coriolanus joined Rome's enemies and would have captured the city had he not been dissuaded at the last minute by an embassy headed by his mother. Another Roman, Spurius Maelius, was accused of seeking royal power by trying to corner the grain supply; while Manlius Capitolinus, who allegedly had been the one to command the defense of the Capitoline against the Gauls, was executed after he was convicted of conspiring to make himself king by championing the cause of debt relief for the impoverished. The Roman law on debt was in fact very harsh, allowing for the enslavement of the debtor. The practice (again according to tradition) only ended after a young boy was raped by his owner after being enslaved to pay his father's debt. He is the third victim (Lucretia was the first) whose appalling treatment led to reform. The second victim was a woman named Verginia, and her story is linked with that of the board of the ten men empanelled in the mid-fifth century BC to write a law code for the city. The first year was a success, but subsequently the board refused to leave office, setting up what was essentially a tyrannical government that lasted until the leader of the group raped Verginia; her family led an uprising that brought about the restoration of traditional magistracies.

Although none of these stories is likely to be completely true—or even true at all—they point to a Roman belief that their state was riven by factional and class warfare until the mid-fourth century. Only after reforms introduced in 367 BC succeeded in settling most points of controversy was the state able to unite, and, in the course of the next seventy years, conquer Italy. These tales, fictional or otherwise, do provide us with important information about the way that Romans thought of themselves: that they were a people under threat from their neighbors; that they should strive to win honor through their deeds; and that even the greatest Romans must subordinate themselves to the will of the community. Romans who refused to do so probably suffered from the sort of deep moral failure that might cause them to commit crimes behind closed doors, revealing them to be lacking the qualities required of a true leader of the state. We will examine the rise of Rome to a regional and world power in the next chapter, but for now we need to look beyond these stories at what we may reasonably believe to be true about Rome in the first centuries of its existence.

Earliest Rome

Our evidence, other than legend, for the earliest period of Roman history, derives from archaeology. This reveals that for centuries before the city began to develop, people had been living on the site of Rome, in a group of settlements nestled on the hills overlooking the great bend of the Tiber river as it descends from the Apennine mountains and pours across the plain of Latium to the sea. A key factor in Rome's success is immediately visible to anyone in Rome today who crosses the Tiber on one of the bridges (the Ponte Garibaldi and the Ponte Palatino) above and below the Isola Tiberina, or across the island itself, where modern bridges replace those of

In the period before the Romans established their dominance, Italy was a patchwork of different languages and distinctive cultures. Using inscriptions and place names as evidence, it is possible to distinguish these different language groups and identify approximately the areas in which they prevailed.

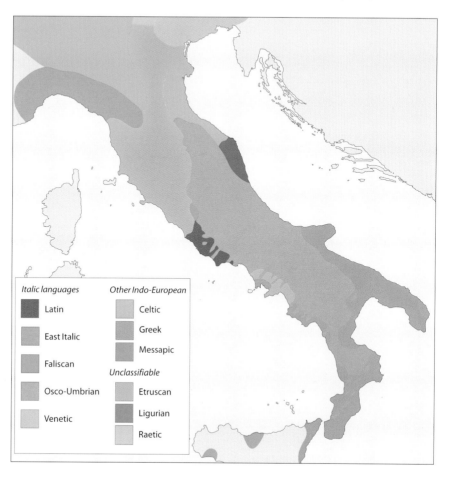

Italic languages
- Latin
- East Italic
- Faliscan
- Osco-Umbrian
- Venetic

Other Indo-European
- Celtic
- Greek
- Messapic

Unclassifiable
- Etruscan
- Ligurian
- Raetic

antiquity. It is here that rapids mark the end of the journey for boats moving along the river from the coast: Rome was quite literally the stopping point for all trade up and down the Tiber.

The people who lived on the site that would become Rome spoke an early form of the Latin language, and were surrounded by many, and diverse, peoples (see map, p. 27). The Etruscans to the northwest spoke a language that did not belong to the Indo-European linguistic group, of which Latin was one branch. The Oscan peoples of the southern and central peninsula spoke languages that were related to Latin, even though they were quite distinct. Greek settlers had begun to colonize the area around the bay of Naples and the southeastern corner of the peninsula in the eighth century BC. Celts held the region of the Po valley in the north. Italy itself was only a unity in the eyes of outsiders. The word *Italia* is Greek, applied to a geographic area with no suggestion that the peoples who lived within it were in any way united. A culturally coherent Italy, dominated by Latin speakers, was only a development of the second and first centuries BC, molded by the fact of Roman domination. The phrase *tota Italia*, "all Italy," is a commonplace to describe an entity that only grew to fruition in the time of Rome's first emperor, Augustus, who rose to power in the second half of the first century BC.

The Tiber crossing that Rome controlled was a crossroads for peoples moving up and down the west coast of Italy. Archaeological evidence suggests that the settlements in the area that would become Rome forged a political union centered on the later area of the Roman forum, a marshy area between the Capitoline and Palatine hills, somewhere around 750 BC. Recent finds reveal that in the course of the later eighth century BC the forum was drained and a palatial structure constructed there, and that walls (which might be seen as symbolic rather than functional) were constructed around the Palatine.

A combination of archaeological and linguistic evidence suggests that early Roman society was highly stratified, and dominated by a powerful aristocracy. It appears that this aristocracy was organized into groups of *gentes* (singular *gens*). A *gens* consisted of a number of individuals, probably all heads of individual *familiae* (see p. 33) who controlled the movement of property into and out of the group. This was most important when the head of a *familia* died without a male heir, because it guaranteed that other members of the *gens* would retain control of property that might otherwise have been given to someone who was not part of the group. The importance of this guarantee may be reflected by the fact that it is also one of the few things that we know about *gentes* from very early evidence—in this case a quotation from the fifth-century Roman law code (see box, opposite).

This inscription from Satricum, dating to around 500 BC, is one of the oldest surviving Latin texts. It reads: "The companions (sodales) of Publius Valerius set this up to Mars." Some scholars identify Publius Valerius with one of the founders of the Republic. Even if this is not the case, the text is evidence for the importance in aristocratic life of language evoking extended family and religion—the sodales are the "brothers" of Valerius.

Terracotta models of huts, such as this one, were used to hold the ashes of the deceased. They stand at the beginning of a long tradition in central Italian culture of using objects evocative of the houses of the living as homes for the dead. Enclosed with other grave goods in funerary urns, they were buried in cemeteries that can be dated to roughly 1000–700 BC.

Archaeology continues to add to our knowledge of Rome's beginnings, and it is at such sites as Gabii (above left), outside the city of Rome, that we can gain a clearer picture of the way that another urban site developed, and also find evidence of competition between aristocratic clans in an urban setting. The current excavations there, and of temples at the site of Sant' Omobono (above right), provide important evidence for Rome's connection with the broader world, and for the use of public resources on massive building projects. In this way the aristocracy spread the state's wealth to those employed in these huge undertakings.

POWER OF THE *GENS*

If a man, to whom there is no heir, dies intestate, the nearest relative on the male side (*agnatus*) shall have control of the *familia* and the property.

If there should not be a relative on the male side, the other members of the *gens* shall have control of the *familia* and the property.

(*Laws of the Twelve Tables*, table 5 lines 4–5; in *Roman Statutes* 2, 641)

The ability to control inheritances may explain why some Roman *gentes* were able to survive, and indeed remain very powerful, for many, many centuries. (There were, of course, many more that did not do so, but our ability to trace the fortunes of some *gentes* for more than five hundred years is one of the remarkable features of Roman history.) In addition to the ability to control property, each *gens* appears to have had a specific geographical base, and to have a specific divine cult, or cults, associated with it.

Although it rapidly became the largest in the area of the Tiber plain—known in antiquity as the Latin plain or Latium (hence modern Lazio)—Rome was not the only city. There were many other Latin communities, some a little older than Rome. The presence of these raises the question of what caused the communities around the Tiber and across the Latin plain—and indeed, many others throughout Italy at this time—to restructure. Is it a mere coincidence that the evolution of urban Italy began at roughly the same period that new city-states began to appear in mainland Greece, on Cyprus, and in what is now western Turkey, or that Phoenician trading stations began to spread from their homeland in modern Lebanon around the western Mediterranean? Probably not. The eighth century saw the first stages of the great military revolution that would transform the political geography of the Near East, opening up new opportunities to the peoples who lived on the fringes of the region, and introducing a new style of warfare based on large armies of heavy infantrymen. The rise of the Greek city-state may be associated with the expansion of economic demand in the Near East, resulting in an increased trade in luxury goods and people to serve in the new armies. It may also be related to the transfer of a style of warfare dependent on massed heavy infantry (hoplites) to the Greek mainland. Increased trade and a new style of warfare appeared in Italy at the same time. Heavily armored warriors, very like the hoplites of the Greek mainland, emerged in Etruria, in Campania, and in Latium around the beginning of the seventh century; the appearance of hoplites presupposes the emergence of a society to support this form of warfare.

Early Political Structures

The infantrymen who wore heavy breastplates of bronze and bronze helmets and carried large shields fought in linear formation. Since warriors were expected to supply their own arms and armor, and since the ability to equip oneself as a hoplite was beyond the means of the average person, the appearance of heavy infantry formations implies a stratified society in which the heavy infantryman is able to draw upon the labor of others to produce the surplus that he needs to arm himself. The *gentes* of early Rome appear to be just the sort of stratified social organizations that could support this style of warfare, with the dominant members of each *gens* serving as the infantry.

The earliest organization of the Roman state provided both a political and military structure: *gentes* were grouped into thirty *curiae*, and the thirty *curiae* into three tribes (the Latin word for tribe, *tribus*, is related to the word *tres*, meaning three). The word *curia* gives us an important clue as to the function of these groups: it is formed from the Latin prefix "*co-*," which indicates joining together, and "*vir*," the Latin word for man. *Curiae* were literally collections of men, and belonging to a *curia* seems to have been required for full membership to the community. The *curiae* met to vote on important matters, such as war and peace or the conferral of overall military authority upon an individual (a *rex*, or king), and formed the basis of the earliest Roman army. The importance of the military role of the *curiae* may emerge from the fact that the Latin word for the citizen body, *populus*, is formed from the verb *populari*, which means "to plunder." The existence of a *rex* in earliest Rome is attested on the first significant Latin inscription, the Lapis Niger (the "Black Stone"), which was erected near the Vulcanal. *Imperium*, the authority of the *rex*, theoretically gave its holder absolute authority over all members of the community and leadership in war. This *imperium* may, even at a very early period, have been separated from religious leadership by the institution of a separate *rex* to oversee the relationship between the state and its gods. It is certain that the institution of the *rex sacrorum*, king of religious rites, outlasted the political *rex*, and we have no real reason to think that the two were ever united.

A single individual wielding supreme authority over human affairs could be a frightening character. At some point it appears that some checks might have been placed on his exercise of domestic authority by the creation of tribunes, probably officials of the tribes from which their title derives, whose role was to ensure that the *rex* did not take arbitrary action within the city. It appears that we may also date to the sixth century BC what was—both in the Roman mind and on the ground that they occupied—the sacred boundary of the city, or *pomerium*. The area within the *pomerium* was "at home," *domi*. All the rest of the world was "abroad," or, in Latin, *militiae*, which really means "at war." In later Roman tradition the ability to exercise *imperium* was limited within the *pomerium* in ways that it was not outside the boundary of the city, and there is no good reason to think that this concept was a later development. The terms of the conceptual division of space between "at home" and "at war" may betray the role that war or the threat of war played in encouraging the political organization that became the city of Rome.

The tribunes and the division of space may not have been the only checks upon the exercise of power by the *rex*. Heads of aristocratic Roman families were, as we shall see, possessed of the power of life and death over all family members, but they were not supposed to use that power unless they had consulted with a council, *consilium*. It seems likely that the *rex* was also supposed to consult a *consilium* before taking any serious action, leading to the creation of an unofficial council of leading men, probably heads of leading families known as *patres* (fathers), that would ultimately become the senate. At no point in its history (at least before the time of Augustus) did the Roman senate have the power to legislate, a fact that may reflect its origins in a royal *consilium*, the function of which was purely advisory. On the other hand, legal authority and actual power were never fully reconcilable in the Roman mind. The head of a household, the *paterfamilias*, controlled all property, determined whom his children could marry, and could even kill children or slaves, but he would be regarded as an unreasonable human being if he used this power without restraint. So, too, we may surmise that the holder of *imperium*, the *rex*, would be very badly advised to do much of anything without taking account of what the leaders of society had to say.

Romans did not believe that the power of a king was hereditary, nor that all their early kings were born within the Roman community. Tradition held that *imperium* was always conferred by vote of the *curiae*, and that no son ever followed his father on the throne. The (legendary) second king of Rome, Numa Pompilius, was said to have been a man from the Sabine hills, and the fifth of the seven kings, Tarquin the Elder, was thought to have been the son of a Greek immigrant to an Etruscan city. An alternative tradition to the mainstream version of seven kings added at least one more with the Etruscan name of Macstarna. The notion that these Etruscan names represent a period of Etruscan domination has now been put to rest by recent scholarship, but the Etruscan names, together with the tradition of kings brought in from other places, remains important. The best analogy for what was happening here is probably provided by the Roman *gentes* themselves. We are explicitly told, for example, that perhaps the most powerful *gens* of all—the Claudii—moved to Rome and was admitted to the community after the end of the kingship. If we allow that this was an ongoing process, and that the role of king was primarily that of a leader in war, then it might make some sense to see these kings brought into the city because of their military skill, and, possibly, because they were outside any disputes between existing *gentes*.

The importation of kings and powerful *gentes* is a feature of very early Roman openness to outsiders. Even at this period it appears that a person could become a Roman citizen by birth (his mother and father were citizens); through emancipation, if he were a slave (he had to be a male to have full citizen rights); or through the action of a magistrate, possibly needing to be confirmed by a vote of the *curiae*. The willingness to admit new citizens enabled the Roman state to grow much faster than other states, which restricted full citizenship to people born of citizen parents—the norm, for instance, in the Greek world. Another aspect of Roman citizenship as it developed into the sixth century was the unequal distribution of the rewards that it brought, inequality in the duties that it required, but the equality of the rights that it conferred. The rewards of citizenship were measured through access to offices and booty won in war. The greater the role a person played in the defense of the community, the greater his access to the rewards. Poorer citizens were not expected to play the same role in the defense of the state as the wealthier members of the community, who formed the core of the heavy infantry and the cavalry. But all citizens had the right to vote, and were due a measure of protection against arbitrary acts by officials. There does not appear to have been a disenfranchised caste of non-citizen members of the community—other than slaves—as there was in Etruscan cities and in many Greek states. Although there were points of tension in this system, the Roman community was nonetheless flexible enough to acquire new members who

ROME AND ITS NEIGHBORS

Rome was one of a number of Latin cities that grew up on the broad plain of the Tiber in central Italy. The Latins were surrounded on all sides by peoples who controlled far larger areas of territory. Among the most important of these neighbors were the Etruscans who bordered them to the north, the Campanians who lay to the south, and the Samnites, who dominated the central Apennines. The Celtic peoples predominated in the Po valley further to the north, and Greeks began settling in Campania and the southern parts of Italy in the course of the eighth century BC, establishing important colonies at Neapolis (Naples) and Tarentum. Rome's relationship with these peoples had an enormous influence on its early history, and many of Rome's institutions would be influenced by the practices of its neighbors.

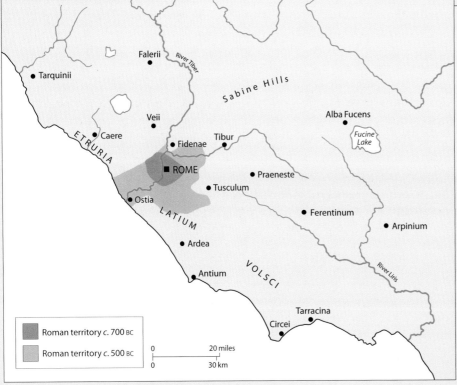

In their own accounts the Romans depicted the early history of their city as one of constant struggle with the Etruscans to the north and the Volsci to the south. The Etruscan city of Veii, only sixteen miles (twenty-five kilometers) from Rome, appears to have been a particular impediment to the growth of Roman power until its capture at the end of the fourth century BC. It is a sign of the aggressively expansionist nature of the Roman state that it succeeded in extending its civic territory even with these obstacles. At the time of the foundation of the Republic in 509 BC, Rome was already one of the most powerful states in Italy.

Roman territory c. 700 BC
Roman territory c. 500 BC

were of varying economic statuses, and thus to grow through the assimilation of new peoples much more rapidly than if it had been dependent upon the sad facts of life in the pre-modern world. It is to those facts, and the structures of the family, that we must now turn.

Domestic and Intellectual World of Early Rome

Definitions

In discussing the *gens* we noted that each *gens* evidently consisted of a number of groups called *familiae*. The Latin word *familia* describes a group of people under the control, *potestas*, of one person. When applied to what we would call a household it means all living beings under the *potestas* of a *paterfamilias*, ordinarily the father or grandfather of the children who resided there. It is worth keeping the Latin term *paterfamilias* in mind as it underlines the difference between the Roman concept of *familia* and our own concept of the family (the English word is obviously related to the Latin, even though the meaning differs). The power of this *paterfamilias* over members of the *familia* was theoretically absolute: he could put any member of his household to death, though he was supposed to take the counsel of other family members before doing so. This power may have emerged in a period where the system of community justice was extremely weak, and the head of a *familia* might have been expected to police the members of his household in the absence of any other authority. If he failed to do so, the result might well be the initiation of a feud with the party that saw itself as wronged. If so, the survival of the absolute *potestas* of the father in the period after the foundation of the state and the emergence of a system of community justice are emblematic of the peculiar conservatism that characterized Roman society. Romans were not unwilling to change, but change in the Roman world was not necessarily accompanied by the rejection of earlier institutions.

Equally if not more important than the power over life and death was the continued control a *paterfamilias* exercised over his children once they had reached maturity. Just how serious a matter was this awesome power? Was the psychology of each Roman conditioned by spending his or her formative years under the despotic rule of a father? Was it this that made Romans such good soldiers, raised to follow their leaders obediently anywhere? The answer to all these questions is "Probably not." The crucial conception that lay behind the *potestas* of the father was *pietas*, a term usually defined as "dutiful respect" towards parents, children, and other relatives. As the examples of *pietas* offered in Classical literature remind us, *pietas* involved obligations to provide support on the part of both the parents and the children. The sense of mutual obligation and devotion that is stressed here is important when it comes to thinking about how members of the Roman community thought and acted. The ideal society was marked by concord and consensus, the ideal marriage by mutual affection, and the ideal relationship with a neighbor by good faith (*fides*). Although Romans may not have been able to attain these ideals with any great consistency, they provided a yardstick against which conduct could be measured.

Life Expectancy, Marriage, and Values

Another question that arises in the context of the power of the *paterfamilias* is just how many multi-generational households there were. Did a Roman male expect his father to be alive when he married? Did a Roman woman expect to find her husband's father roaming around the house that she shared with her husband?

These questions are rather hard to answer. Evidence for average life expectancy at birth ranged between 22.5 years and around 30 years, depending on the population, throughout antiquity. The difference implied by these figures is enormous. An average life expectancy at birth of 22.5 years implies that half of all children die in infancy and that a person who lived to age 10 might, on average, have about 36 more years to live. Thus most adults would die by their mid-40s: only about 21 percent of the population would reach the age of 50 and about 13 percent would live to 60. A population with a life expectancy of around 30 years is one in which the average adult would die in his or her early fifties. The most likely reason why the evidence we have for average life expectancy is so divergent is that it derives from different classes. The evidence for lower life expectancy comes from a sample taken from the lower classes, while that for higher life expectancy comes from wealthier people. This sort of spread is unremarkable in terms of pre-modern demography.

In light of what we know about the demographic structure of the Roman population, it is fair to say that households where the *paterfamilias* was living with his grandchildren were probably fairly rare. Although Roman girls could be married off at the age of twelve, and Roman boys could marry at fourteen, most were not and did not. The vast majority of women married in their late teens or early twenties; the majority of men married in their later twenties, being perhaps seven to ten years older than their wives. In a world where half of all children did not live to the age of five, every woman needed to bear, on average, five to six children if the population was to sustain itself or increase. About half of all households might still have a grandfather alive when the first grandchild was born, but the grandfather would probably be dead by the time his daughter-in-law had borne her last child. The grandmother would be much more likely to survive and exercise some influence over the children as they grew up, but her power was purely social, not that of the *paterfamilias*.

The comparatively low life expectancy in the Roman world, and the age gap between partners at the time of their marriage, might have several consequences. First, it is significant that a Roman who was in a position to seek office would be regarded as a senior statesman in his early to mid-forties; and once he had turned fifty, he would probably be aware that his chances of reaching sixty were not great (see box, right). Second, the fact that women, if they survived childbirth, had a very good chance of outliving their husbands, and could obtain effective control of whatever property their fathers had left them before they turned forty, might tend to make them quite venerable figures in the domestic setting. This was certainly the case from the first century BC onwards, and it may be that women had rather more influence at a much earlier stage in Roman society than our scanty records allow—we simply do not have the evidence we need to be able to say for certain.

What impact did the knowledge that one was unlikely to see one's children grow up past their thirties, or know one's grandchildren, have on a person? And what impact did the fear that one would lose half or more of one's offspring have on parents? These questions are very hard to answer, and the response might be quite

REACHING OLD AGE

Only a small percentage of Roman adults reached the age of sixty, and such a man as the Emperor Augustus, who lived to the age of seventy-six, was a veritable prodigy. Sixty-two was seen as a major milestone for Roman men. Aulus Gellius, writing in Rome in the second century AD, observed that:

> in the long period of human memory … most, if not all, old men experience the arrival of the sixty-third year of life with some disaster or peril either to the body, or of serious illness, death or some mental anguish. Therefore, those who are engaged in the study of words and events of this sort call that year of life the "climacteric."

(Aulus Gellius, *Attic Nights* 15.7.1–2)

different from one class of society to another. Almost all surviving Roman literature was written by men of the very highest social class, and the bulk of our other written evidence comes from those who were able to afford tombstones with inscriptions on them—a phenomenon that appears to have become much more widespread after the end of the first century BC (see pp. 231–32). With such a limited sample it is hard to be certain how relevant any observation we can make was to the experience of the vast mass of people who lived in antiquity. Still, it is worth venturing a few observations. First, there was great stress on the importance of relationships within the family—many texts stress the love of husband for wife, of parents for children. Second, both marriage and divorce were relatively simple undertakings (see box, below).

Even though a married woman might have control of property if her *paterfamilias* had died, she was still expected to play a subordinate role in the household. She managed the accounts, looked after the day-to-day running of the household, and had babies. Lucretia, whose rape by the young Tarquin (son of the last of the seven legendary kings) is said to have precipitated the demise of the monarchy, was identified by her husband as the perfect mate because, when he came home to surprise her, she was minding the house and weaving (the ultimate act of the suitably

MARRIAGE AND DIVORCE IN EARLY ROME

Classical Roman law (which developed between the first century BC and the third century AD) recognized that two people who lived together as man and wife for a year and a day were married. Such unions based on mutual affection may have accounted for the vast majority of families in the Roman world, families that survived at, or just above, the subsistence level.

Where property was involved, arrangements could be more elaborate. There was a religious ceremony to ask the gods if the union would be successful, and a woman was expected to bring a dowry with her that would suffice for her maintenance within the family of her husband.

One of the most striking aspects of Roman marriage is the degree to which a father continued to exercise control over his children's marriages. This control stemmed from the fact that the *paterfamilias* controlled all the *familia*'s property, and technically had to approve the matches made for either son or daughter. A married man with children might own no property other than that which his father permitted him, if his *paterfamilias* was still alive; and a woman's dowry did not technically belong to her while her *paterfamilias* was alive. When he did die, the dowry became the wife's property, although the male assertion of female inferiority required that if a woman's *paterfamilias* had died, her tutor had to approve

her decisions and make sure that she did not behave irresponsibly. (By the imperial period the institution of a tutor for a mature woman was regarded as a quaint formality that could be forgone if certain conditions were met, and there is no reason to believe that the average tutor at any period exercised much actual control over what a grown woman decided to do.)

A woman who married into another *familia* would either pass into the *potestas* of her husband's *paterfamilias* (a form of marriage known as *cum manu* or "with possession"), or remain under the authority of her own (marriage *sine manu*, "without possession"). Thus a woman who remained under the *potestas* of her father at marriage, even if she remained happily married to her husband for the rest of their natural lives, would never become a member of her husband's *familia*. Given the fact that there was a specific form of marriage "with possession" connected with the oldest aristocratic families, it looks as if these forms of marriage were originally related to the interests of *gentes* in regulating the movement of property into and out of the group.

The power of the *paterfamilias* was such that any children whom he recognized as legitimate were members of his *familia*. In the event of a divorce, the woman automatically lost custody of the children.

domesticated Roman woman) rather than going to parties with her friends. Her response to her rape—revealing the deed and then committing suicide—demonstrated that she had, above all, the honor of her husband's family as her aim. A figure both heroic and tragic in the Roman tradition, Lucretia showed how a woman could turn her domestic virtues into matters of public significance through her mastery of her sphere. The pattern of rape and revolution connected with her story and that of others reveals a deep-seated Roman tendency to see public power destroyed by private vices (see p. 182).

A further consequence of low life expectancy may be a great stress on external accomplishment. One's reputation and accomplishment could be left to one's children. Romans have been described as being very "outer-directed," seeking validation of their personal lives through the acclaim and recognition of others. The distinction between the internal and external person seems to have been of little interest: one's self-worth was defined as a father, a warrior, a wife, or a mother. After death, the aristocratic Roman male would be remembered for his accomplishments in the public sphere. His image would be placed with those of other ancestors in the house, and be displayed along with all the others at the funeral of any descendant. It was accomplishment of this sort that linked a man with his ancestors. Women were not entitled to such display until the last century BC, but where we can trace their remembrance in earlier periods it is again through the externals: she may be recalled as the wife of a great man, the mother of many children, or an example to others of the virtues of her gender.

The importance of honoring one's obligations, and intense interest in the record that one could leave for future generations, are central to the value system of the Roman state in the centuries of conquest, the third through first centuries BC. This is the period that begins to give us a substantial amount of information concerning the way that Romans thought about themselves. But there is no reason to think that this value system was a feature of the period of imperial acquisition alone. The evidence that we have from other areas of Roman life, especially that offered by the religious system, the record of public building, and of political institutions, suggests that these fundamental values provided the underpinnings of the Roman community even in its formative years, the seventh and sixth centuries BC.

Religion: Family and State

If the worth of a person was determined not by any inner accomplishments of the soul, but rather by accomplishments that were observable and measurable in the public sphere, then it is perhaps not surprising to find that the religious life of the average Roman was also a matter of very public activity. Classical religious ceremonies involving sacrifice offered an invitation to the gods to show their approval or disapproval. One prayed to the gods in public, speaking out loud, and expected that divine approval would follow from the correct performance of ritual. The *paterfamilias* was charged with maintaining the relationship between his household and its gods, so it was wise to make sure that the gods agreed with him. The notion that the gods should agree with one is a critical feature of Roman religion. The religious system of the Roman people sought to control the natural world, both in the area of private observance and in the area of public cult. The latter was offered on behalf of the state to select gods who were considered to be particularly associated

THE ROMAN CONCEPT OF THE SOUL

The Roman concept of the soul is remarkably complex, involving a tripartite division between *genius*, *manes*, and *lemures*. While we cannot date these developments with any precision, the Roman concept of the *genius*—originally the male spirit of a *gens*, residing in the head of a family during his lifetime, and later the divine or spiritual part of every mortal—looks remarkably like an inherently Roman concept that was altered under the influence of the Greek concept of the *daimon*. It may have developed after Rome established extensive contacts with the Greek world in the course of the eighth century BC.

The *manes* and *lemures* look like nothing in the Greek world, being evidently the kindly and menacing spirits of the departed. There is some question as to just how firm the distinction between these should be, but it is clear that there was something potentially nasty about a *lemur*; however, it is not clear how these notions can be reconciled easily with the existence of a single *genius*. When we cannot reconcile concepts, there is a tendency to explain the contradiction as the result of badly reconciled traditions stemming from different sources.

The very early presence of *manes* and *lemures* in Roman thought may be confirmed by the fact that two archaic family festivals, the Parentalia and the Lemuria, were not readily absorbed into the religious calendar of the Roman state. If it is correct to think that festivals that stress family relationships with departed members are fundamental to the human experience, then it may follow that these were celebrated before the structure of the state religious calendar took shape for the community as a whole.

with the welfare of Rome, the most important of these gods being Jupiter Optimus Maximus ("Best and Greatest"). Rituals were thought to have been approved by the gods, and thus the proper observance of them might be thought to guarantee safety.

The religious duties of the *paterfamilias* on behalf of the household were many and varied. He was charged with maintaining the *familia*'s relationship with the gods who looked after the household, the Lares and Penates. He might form a relationship with other gods outside the household, both those worshipped on a community basis and any others whom he thought important. He also needed to make sure that an orderly relationship was retained with members of the family who had died. The existence of early family festivals, which seem to be related to a complex, tripartite conception of the soul, suggests that this relationship was considered of great significance (see box, above).

On the public side, the relationship between the state and the gods was regulated by the state religious calendar. This calendar, as we have come to know it through much later sources, is an amorphous organism; the Romans added new festivals without eliminating the old. Some of the earliest rites of Roman religion may be those that celebrate agriculture, since they invoke divinities who are most different from the gods that Romans came to identify (not always very easily) with Greek gods in the sixth century. The Robigalia was a festival celebrated in honor of Robigus, the god thought to represent the fungal infection known in English as "rust," which could damage the wheat crop. As part of the ceremony the *flamen Quirinus* (priest of Quirinus, the god sometimes associated with Romulus) would sacrifice a red dog and a sheep near fields of grain. The dog's color evoked the color of the fungus, and the rite is a classic example of the apotropaic aspect of Roman cult, whereby evil was averted through the sacrifice of an object that represented it. Another such festival was the Vinalia, sacred to the god Jupiter. Here the *flamen dialis* (priest of Jupiter, the chief god of the Roman pantheon) opened the season for wine-making: giving orders to harvest the grapes by sacrificing a sheep, and plucking a bunch of grapes between cutting out the sheep's innards and offering them to Jupiter.

The *flamen dialis*, a priest whose life was hedged with restrictions on his conduct, was effectively living as a representative of the god in the city. Similarly, the Vestal Virgins (a group of six women charged with overseeing the cult of Vesta, the goddess of the hearth, in the forum) were supposed to live lives devoted to the service of state cult. Such priesthoods were extremely unusual in that the extent of their service meant that their holders were virtually professionals: the men's lives were dominated by their priestly functions, which prevented them from undertaking any significant public obligations unconnected with their religious role. Others, often serving as members of colleges, were expected to lead lives appropriate to their standing. The actions of these figures are often apotropaic also. For example, the elaborate rites of the Luperci—performed annually on February 15—were plainly designed to protect both the flocks and, by extension, the fertility of the community. The Luperci, whose name derived from their god, Lupercus (whose own name appears to have been connected with the Latin word for wolf, *lupus*), would gather early in the morning in the cave associated with the suckling of Romulus and Remus by the she-wolf (it is likely that the rites were a good deal older than this story, however), which was rediscovered on the Palatine hill in 2007. The festival would begin with the sacrifice of two male goats and a dog. Two of the priests would then approach the altar, where their heads would be smeared with sacrificial blood that would then be washed off using wool soaked in milk. After that, they would strip naked, cover their loins in goatskins, and run around the boundaries of the city striking any woman they encountered. A blow from a Lupercus was thought to promote female fertility, and in later times women who wanted a child would be topless as they awaited the priests. Somewhat less dramatic were the rites of the college of the Arval Brethren, who celebrated for the fertility goddess Dea Dia, whose shrine was at the edge of the early territory of Rome. Although what we know of their festivals comes from texts inscribed between the time of Augustus and the early fourth century, the rites appear to be much older. Celebrations included the singing of a hymn while doing a three-step dance to ward off threats from beyond the boundaries, and feasting to celebrate the security of the harvest.

Other early cults were concerned with the way that Rome dealt with its neighbors, and the resolution of tensions within the community itself. We have no idea how such festivals as the Poplifugia or "people's flight," celebrated in July, and Regifugium or "king's flight" in February came into being, but the very names of these events recall tensions—and that is still the case even if the much later tradition associating the Poplifugia with the rout of Latin armies is true. A similarly opaque festival, the October Horse, held annually, is likewise evocative of strife in that it involved the riotous struggle for the head of a sacrificial horse. In this case the unfortunate beast was always the right-hand horse of whichever pair won a race on the campus Martius on October 15. The rite included the preservation of the horse's blood so that it could be mixed with sacrificial cakes and offered to the god Pales, an agricultural deity whose festival on April 21 would become Rome's birthday. After the race, a fight would break out between the young men of the opposing teams, each representing districts of the forum. The aim was to capture the horse's head and nail it up in a public place. We do not know when this festival began, but the Romans of the third century BC believed it to be ancient, as was the festival a few days later involving a priestly college consisting of a dozen patricians, the Salii. Associations of Salii seem to have been common in cities of the Latin plain, and, like the *fetiales* (also common to Latin cities: see p. 40), were connected with relations between states. In Rome, it was on October 19 and March 24 that they would process through the streets dressed as warriors, stopping at various places to dance and sing a hymn. The dates of their dance mark the opening and closing of the season for war. Likewise, it may be significant that the shrine in the meeting place of the earliest assembly, the *comitium* (p. 42) was dedicated to Vulcan, a god whom the Romans understood to be concerned with matters of state.

Although we cannot date the foundation of any of the activities mentioned above, they appear to have developed before Romans began to associate their gods closely with those of the Greek pantheon. This is supported by the apotropaic nature of these rites, and the connection with priests called *flamines* (a term that later Romans associated with their earliest priestly offices), and with *sodalitates*, "brotherhoods," another habit later Romans assumed was ancient. These associations make it reasonable to think that these rites were all in operation before the end of the sixth century BC (if not a good deal earlier). Likewise, they reflect some important aspects of the Roman psyche—a sense that the outside world was threatening, that Roman society itself needed to be on guard against the forces of internal disruption, and a distinct preference for group action in decisions about public cult. So it would be that as the institutions of the Republic developed, colleges of priests would continue to give the state advice on matters put to them, while the actual decision-making was left to magistrates (though it was often the case that members of these *sodalitates* could and did serve as magistrates also). The reason for this is that the business of the gods was taken extremely seriously, and the collegiate mentality of the Romans did not support a single individual with sole authority to mediate an important relationship.

The evolution of Roman state religion, an amalgam of different practices, parallels the development of the community as a whole. Because Roman religion was open to new gods and festivals of all sorts, to study it is to study a society in constant flux, open to new ideas and practices that appear to us to derive from a wide variety of sources. To a Roman the situation would have looked somewhat different. People learned about the gods from observing the effect of divine action. Natural disasters were a manifestation of divine anger; victories in war were manifestations of divine pleasure. Disease could stem from a god, and so could healing. The internal logic of the cult system in Rome, as in any ancient community, stemmed from the belief that the celebration of the gods was dictated by divine action. Old gods were not formally rejected when new gods were introduced, even if the worship of new gods might seem to duplicate existing ones. There were no books—other than collections of oracles that professed to offer direct divine revelation—to guide the average Roman to an understanding of what the gods meant or did until the first century BC (and even then such books were not readily available to the average person). Books of oracles were themselves often regarded with suspicion, requiring the advice of specialists to determine if they were authentic or fakes. Indeed, the Roman state restricted access to such books, potentially dangerous as they were, by asserting that only prophecies attributed to a woman known as the Sibyl who had lived in the distant past, or others that had been authenticated by the state, were to be taken seriously. The average Roman was supposed to learn about the gods by participating in their worship, and thus be aware that the divine world was remarkably complicated, requiring constant attention if family and community were to survive.

In the period after the end of the sixth century BC the decisions of magistrates were central to the evolution of state religion. Before this, in the eighth and, possibly, the seventh centuries, the various *gentes* probably played an important role in the introduction of new gods to Rome. Some gods worshiped by individual *gentes* could become gods for the community as a whole, as seems to have been the case with the cult of Hercules at the Ara Maxima on the south side of the Palatine hill, and possibly the gods of the Lupercalia, another festival that came to be associated with community fertility and, later, the birth of Romulus and Remus. It may be that through contact with the cults of Greek cities, individual *gentes* became interested in divinities who were visualized in anthropomorphic—human—form. The Greeks appear to have been unique among Mediterranean and Near Eastern peoples in viewing their gods in a predominantly anthropomorphic form, as opposed to animal or a combination of human and animal (or in no visible form whatsoever). The evolution of the Roman pantheon in the direction of gods and goddesses who were visualized in human form may thus be a reflection of profound external influences on the Roman and, more generally, the Latin community.

Religion and Foreign Relations

Divine cult not only offered structure for a family or community's relationship with the gods, but also helped structure relationships between communities. There may be no more powerful symbol of this than the Roman practice of the *evocatio*, or calling out, whereby the gods of a city at war with Rome were asked to leave their native city and come to reside at Rome. Within the Latin community, it appears that relationships were negotiated through joint celebrations of cults. By the sixth century, one of the most important of these associations seems to have been based at Alba, the center of the cult of Jupiter Latiaris.

Religious ritual facilitated communication between Latin states through a protocol of negotiation known as the fetial process (*ius fetiale*). According to the fetial process, a city that felt that its territory or the rights of its members had been violated by members of another community sent an embassy to the offending state to declare its grievance, and proclaim the justice of its case before the gods. A state that received a fetial embassy then had thirty days to make whatever restitution was called for. If restitution was not made, a fetial priest from the aggrieved community would hurl a spear into the territory of the offending city as a declaration of war.

The fetial process established the gods as the notional arbiters of the dispute: if a state made an unsubstantiated claim, the gods would presumably ensure that it suffered defeat in the ensuing war. In an era when human beings lacked the capacity to control their natural environment, the cult system offered an avenue of communication between human and divine, a form of interface between the visible and invisible worlds. If the lines of communication ever failed, the result was potentially catastrophic.

As Rome became more powerful than any other Latin state—or indeed, than all of them taken together—a new political structure came into being in the later sixth century. This was the so-called Latin League, which appears to have been intended to regulate relations between member cities and to offer a structure for collective action against an outsider. Although we cannot be certain about this, it appears that meetings of member cities took place at least once a year, and that presidency of the league revolved among member cities on an annual basis. The implicit connection between religion and political structures was common to both the Greek and Italic worlds, and may reflect an early stage in social development whereby communities that had not yet evolved distinct urban structures for themselves founded regional associations that later broke down into a group of distinct city-states. Certainly the Latin League itself does not seem to have exerted any real control over member states, which could wage war on each other without League intervention, and it is equally certain that by the end of the sixth century Rome not only overshadowed every individual city in the League, but could also mobilize a force equal to or greater than the League as a whole. In 499 (or 496) BC, so tradition has it, the Roman army defeated the Latin League at the battle of Lake Regillus (see box, left) and forced it into a subordinate relationship, regulated by a treaty. The importance of the League structure in providing a model for later Roman expansion will be examined in Chapter 2.

Rome in the Sixth Century BC

Our story so far has been based upon a series of assumptions. One of these is that the essential patriarchal structure of the Roman family goes back to the earliest period of Roman history. Another is that archaeological evidence from the site of Rome suggests that people had settled on the hills that were later part of the city ever since the eleventh century BC. A third has been that it is possible to use the evolution of the Roman state religion the way that a paleontologist uses fossils to provide a map for the evolution of species. As with the paleontologist, the historian of early Rome may get some of the bones in the wrong place, but one has no choice but to use what one has. So the evolution of the religious system of the Roman state suggests a movement from a small rural community, the chief concerns of which were the survival of its members and their flocks, to a more complex society with links to other states, and one that was open to new ideas. With the sixth century we get a fresh cache of material, and it becomes possible to be a bit more definite.

The archaeological record from sixth-century Rome leaves little doubt that the city had become one of the most powerful in Italy. The forum had been paved (the archaeological moment that marks the actual founding of the urban community), and buildings in it are consistent with the structure of a state based upon the thirty *curiae* described earlier. Very substantial aristocratic houses that can be dated to this period have been discovered on the slopes of the Palatine hill, facing the forum along the road that was to become the Via Sacra. Sometime around 550 BC the territory of the city itself was defined by a (new?) *pomerium*, marked by a circuit of defensive walls that encompassed just over a square mile of territory, an area that was more than two and a half times larger than the next biggest cities in Latium and Etruria.

The redefinition of urban space is connected with Servius Tullius. We have some reason to think that Servius was a real person, not a fictional character invented to explain why something happened, in the way that Romulus and other early kings on the Roman king list were invented: this is because his name is inextricably linked

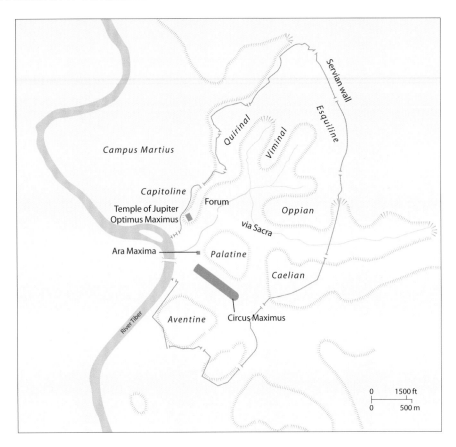

A plan of Rome in the fourth century BC, indicating the city's development over the previous two hundred years. What little we know about the political geography of early Rome is nonetheless very suggestive. The Capitoline and Palatine hills were centers of aristocratic power, and the Roman forum was a focus for aristocratic display, while the Aventine hill was a center for the plebeian movement. Located in the valley that divided the Palatine from the Aventine was the Circus Maximus, where chariot races were already being held by the beginning of the sixth century BC, providing a venue that united the different orders of society.

with a new form of socio-political organization, a form of organization embodied in the constitution of the *comitia centuriata*.

The Latin word *comitia* can refer both to a meeting or assembly (it is the plural of the Latin word *comitium*, which designates a place where assemblies meet; the original comitium is located at the northern end of the Roman forum) and to the voting that could be carried out in such an assembly. *Centuriata* means "centuriate" and refers to the division of the Roman people into centuries. The centuries are connected with the structure of the army, and were so arranged that the bulk of political power was placed in the hands of the heavy infantry. As Marcus Cicero put it in the first century BC, the Servian constitution provided that the majority did not have the most power. But Cicero despised pure democracy, and his understanding of what Servius did may not be quite correct. For the result of the Servian constitution was to provide a framework that enabled more, rather than fewer, people to play a larger role in political life. It meant that primary decision-making power rested with the heavy infantry rather than in the hands of aristocrats. Even if this excluded the majority of citizens from having a real say, it nonetheless drew a clear connection between political clout and the role that a man could play in the defense of the community. An individual heavy infantryman might not have had the same influence as an aristocratic cavalryman, but he still had a voice, and it is very likely that he now had a louder institutional voice than he had before. Full participatory democracy is not something that can be created from nothing: it requires a tradition of expanding involvement behind it.

The Servian Constitution

The box on this page shows how the Servian system divided the Roman people into centuries: 170 infantry centuries split into five classes, divided according to armament, and twenty-three centuries of others. The centuries in the infantry classes were divided into two types by age, the *iuniores* (men aged 17–45) and *seniores* (men aged 46–60). The *proletarii*, grouped in one century, were not awarded any military function. Instead, their theoretical job was to provide children (*proles*) for the state. In the first century BC, the majority of Romans fell into this category.

There are sixty centuries of *iuniores* from the heavily armed classes 1–3, precisely the number of centuries in a traditional Roman legion, and a tripartite division of types is also characteristic of the legion prior to the last century BC. The proportion of heavy infantry to light infantry given by extending this formula to the lightly armed fourth and fifth classes is 3:1.75, also roughly the proportions of the later legion. It thus takes no great leap of imagination to see that the *comitia centuriata* was probably based on the structure of the Roman army.

There are two other significant aspects of the Servian system: voting by collectives, and the further division of the members of centuries into tribes. Collective voting appears to have been a feature of the earlier *curiae* (in the fossilized *comitia curiata* that still met formally to grant *imperium* at the end of the Republic we hear of votes only in terms of *curiae* rather than of individuals). Collective voting works on a principle that is familiar to anyone who has followed the tally of votes in an American presidential election, or for seats in the British parliament. If a presidential candidate, for instance, wins the state of Michigan by one vote, he still gets all the electoral votes for Michigan, and his opponent gets none. In a British parliamentary election, the winner is the candidate who wins the plurality of votes for his or her seat. The opposition parties, no matter how close they come, get no seat, making it possible for a party with less than 45 percent of the popular vote to hold an overwhelming edge in the final parliament.

In a Roman election a person could win a century by a single vote, and receive the undivided vote of the century as a whole in the final tally. All he needed to win an election or to carry a proposal was a majority of the centuries. Unlike an American or British election, where people are organized by location, the centuriate assembly organized Roman voters by social class. The eighteen centuries of cavalry

CLASSES OF THE SERVIAN CONSTITUTION

Infantry Centuries

class	defensive armament	offensive weapons	number of centuries
one	helmet, round shield, greaves, armored breastplate	spear and sword	80
two	helmet, oblong shield, greaves	spear and sword	20
three	helmet, oblong shield	spear and sword	20
four	oblong shield (?)	spear, javelin, sword (?)	20
five		sling, stones, javelin, sword (?)	30
Total			**170**

Other Centuries

century type	number
cavalry (*equites*)	18
engineers	2
musicians	2
proletarii	1
Total	**23**

(wealthy men) voted first, and then the centuries of the next five classes were called, from the first to the fifth.

Romans voted in the centuriate assembly both for magistrates and for laws, which had to be voted on to take effect. In voting for laws, the citizens were given a choice of yes or no. Amendments were not allowed from the floor of the assembly. Citizens simply voted on the text that was presented by the law's sponsor or sponsors, who had to be magistrates. Voting for magistrates worked somewhat differently. Every century had to return a full tally of magistrates for each office, magistracies ordinarily being collegial (there had to be more than one person holding each office). The century reported the vote for the person who had received the majority or plurality, and that person was declared the winner for the century in question. The reports for each century were returned in the order that the centuries had voted (the order within each class was determined by lot). As soon as a person had received the votes of ninety-seven centuries he was declared the victor. The magistrate presiding at the election would then start all over again from the beginning. Votes for the candidate who gained office were thrown out, and the person with the next greatest number of votes in the century was declared the winner of the next position in the college of magistrates that was being elected that day. Votes were only taken for one magistracy on a given election day.

Magistrates ran elections, and the gods watched over them. It was the magistrate's duty to make sure that the gods approved of what was happening, and he did this by watching the heavens. Romans, and many other Italians, believed that the gods sent signs through the flight of birds. If a bird appeared at the right time and in the right place, then everything was fine. If not, public business was cancelled until the gods provided the appropriate sign. If something was going wrong with a ceremony that they had already approved, then the gods might send the presiding magistrate a further sign to stop whatever was going on. The symbolic importance of this procedure is obvious: the magistrate was mediating the relationship between the gods and the community; he was the critical node in the communication network. The system of voting thus reflected the structure of power within the citizen community as well as the relationship between the community and its gods.

The Servian constitution remained in force for the election of magistrates until the first century AD, making it one of the most successful constitutional arrangements in the history of the European continent. Although it was not purely democratic, in that it gave greater weight to wealth and status—the centuries of the first class were certainly smaller than those of the fifth, and there were more of them—it served the Roman state admirably for the election of officials whose primary function would be leadership in war and the adjudication of aristocratic disputes. It was less successful in providing the legislative safeguards that the average Roman citizen may have wanted. The most persistent internal dispute within the Roman community during the centuries after Servius centered on securing the rights of the less well-off members of the community. In the long run this was achieved by creating an alternative way of counting votes, but one that was also based on a Servian institution: the tribes.

As we have seen, the earliest organization of Rome appears to have been based on thirty *curiae*, which were grouped into three tribes. These tribes may have had some geographical significance, joining ten *curiae* consisting of *gentes* that were located

The act of voting symbolized the ideal of consensus upon which the Roman political system was based. Written ballots were first introduced for juries, and they were extended to other forms of voting in the second century BC. This depiction is from a coin minted in the mid-50s BC.

near each other; but there is no way to be sure about this and no real evidence for the distribution of *gentes* between *curiae*. In fact, the earlier tribal structure, which was left intact as far as the *curiae* were concerned, may have had very little to do with the Servian organization. The latter created new tribes and gave them geographical centers either within the city of Rome itself (there were four "urban" tribes) or in other parts of Roman territory. The tribal structure proved extremely flexible, and new tribes were added as Roman territory increased throughout Italy until the number thirty-five was reached in 299 BC, after which no new tribes were created.

The tribes provided local structures for the organization of Roman citizens. Since the easiest way to count people is to do so where they live, and wealth in early Rome was defined in terms of the property that a person had, the status of individuals was determined at the tribal level. Once people were counted and their property assessed, it was possible to assign them to centuries. A glance at a map of Roman territory in the late sixth century (see p. 32) makes plain why a structure of local organizations was needed. By the year 500 BC Rome occupied 320 square miles (822 square kilometers)—just over one-third of the total land in Latium—dominating the length of the Tiber from the Sabine hills to the sea.

The creation of separate structures based on land and wealth is one of the most important features of the Servian system. Where large, ancient city-states were divided by location within their territories, with different groups dominating different areas, local concerns could predominate over those of the community as a whole. By mixing people from different locations into the centuries, the Servian constitution reduced the risk of territorial fragmentation.

The complexity of the Servian system is such that we must wonder if it is proper to see it as the revolutionary product of a single legislator, or as the culmination of a longer process of reorganization. The fact that the Servian system worked suggests that it generally satisfied the perceived needs of the Roman people. No constitutional system can survive if it is not consonant with the existing social value system and political reality. The Servian system, based on the need to rationalize military structure and to build a sense of mutual obligation within the community, seems to have been in conformity with the same values that were central to Roman family structure.

The success of the Servian system may tempt us to see Servius as a political genius. But since we know nothing about him other than the tradition that he was responsible for these reforms, such an assumption is beyond any reasonable chance of proof. It is better to see the system as a communal response to perceived needs. The system worked because the Roman people wanted it to work.

Kings and Magistrates

Servius Tullius was the sixth of the seven kings whom the Romans remembered in their traditions. There is no reason to believe that he was, as later tradition had it, the son of a slave. Such stories of obscure birth tend to attach themselves to famous legislators in later generations. The story of Servius's birth is thematically similar to the tale of Moses in the bulrushes, or the story that Romulus and Remus were exposed in a basket in the Tiber, suckled by a she-wolf, and raised by a shepherd—or any number of other stories that suggest that a person's later greatness was foreshadowed at birth. We should see Servius as one in a series of successful leaders upon whom the *curiae* had conferred *imperium*. Indeed, one of the interesting features of the Servian system is that it supplemented rather than replaced the older *curiae*. The *curiae* continued to meet to confer *imperium*: but the choice of people upon whom they might confer this *imperium* might now be limited by the votes of the *comitia centuriata*. To say this, however, begs the question of whether there were magistrates other than the king upon whom this *imperium* could be conferred.

Given the size of Roman territory in the sixth century BC, the view that the king was Rome's only magistrate is, on the face of it, utterly improbable. It appears that there were still tribunes to protect the interests of the average citizen (see p. 30), and it is likely that there was a college of at least two elected officials known as praetors. One late source tells us that there were two war leaders in addition to the king, and another text, quoting from what appears to have been a text of great antiquity, mentions a *praetor maximus*. The word *maximus* in Latin means "greatest," and is normally used to indicate ranking within groups of three or more. On the other hand, *maximus* can also be used to indicate that one individual is older than another individual, and possibly that one person was elected before another. Even in the later Roman state the person who was returned first in an election to an office where he had just one colleague had some prerogatives simply because he was elected first. It may therefore be that the term *praetor maximus* (see p. 54) refers simply to the person returned first in a college of at least two magistrates.

In any case, it is fair to say that there were probably elected magistrates in addition to the *rex*. The difference between elected magistrates and the king may have been that the magistrate could hold office only for one year, while the term of the *rex* was potentially for life. If the position of the *rex* is seen as being analogous to the tyrants of contemporary Greek cities (in the period when the word tyrant did not have a negative connotation) then the job of the *rex* was to ensure that the constitution of the state functioned smoothly.

If the job of the *rex* was to oversee the political stability of the state, it was entirely possible that the Roman community might decide to do without a *rex*. And so it did, in 509 BC. Annually elected magistrates would thereafter govern the city, a solution that is easier to understand if such magistrates already existed.

Two of the last three kings on the traditional list were named Tarquin. The fact that the name Tarquin is Etruscan led earlier generations of scholars to see the expulsion of the king as a rejection of foreign domination. More recent work has called into question the view that Rome was subordinate to the loosely organized Etruscan federation to the north. Rome was a bigger, more powerful city than any in Etruria, and there is no other evidence for extended Etruscan domination in the Latin plain. There were warlords who raided the area, and some lines from a fifth-century BC Greek historian, quoted by a first-century BC historian, confirm the existence of an Etruscan warlord in Latium for a couple of years around 500 BC. But the career of one warlord, no matter how powerful, is not the same thing as half a century of political and cultural domination. It is safer to see the establishment of the Republic in the context of aristocratic politics at Rome rather than in a hypothetical war of national liberation.

That Tarquin the Arrogant belongs in the context of Roman aristocratic competition is suggested by the fact that he seems to have done a great deal of building. He is said (on reasonably good authority) to have built the great temple of Jupiter on the Capitoline hill (the largest temple in central Italy) and to have laid out some

The François Tomb, discovered at Vulci in 1857, was illustrated with scenes from Greek and Italian mythology painted by Etruscan artists in the fourth to third centuries BC. The scene above presents a number of characters linked with Roman history. These include Caele Vibinnas, who according to one tradition gave his name to the Caelian hill. His rescue by Mastarna, a king of Rome in an alternative version of Roman history linked with Etruria, is depicted on the left.

seating arrangements in the Circus Maximus for chariot racing. From other records of temple foundations in subsequent years it appears that temples were an important feature of aristocratic self-display, possibly a natural development from the connection that some *gentes* can be seen to have had with specific cults. These projects also suggest an increasing connection between political power and ostentatious service to the community. Powerful men showed their power by leaving permanent public memorials of their activity in the urban space of Rome. It is arguable that the presence of a *rex* made it more difficult for other aristocrats to perform in the public sphere, and thus that the end of kingship at Rome was an aristocratic reaction against a form of authority that had come to put an all-too-irksome lid on the boiling cauldron of aristocratic competition.

The Servian constitution itself can be seen in the context of an effort to share power more broadly in Roman society, a royal infringement upon aristocratic power. As such, the Servian constitution may be an opening salvo in a struggle by the office-holding aristocracy to defend its prerogatives against the broader mass of Roman people. But such were the terms of Roman society that this struggle was carried out through the manipulation of institutions rather than violence. Class struggle was endemic to the Classical world, and the Roman experience is remarkable for the absence of domestic violence until the acquisition of a pan-Mediterranean empire in the second century BC radically changed the stakes.

The Emergence of the Roman Republic

The Latin term *res publica* means "public thing," and the name of the political entity that emerged in the wake of the expulsion of the kings was the *res publica populi Romani*, or "public thing of the Roman people." The history of the government of this Republic that an educated person learned in the first century AD went something like this:

> Kings held the city of Rome from the beginning. Lucius Brutus
> established freedom (*libertas*) and the consulship. Dictators were
> employed from time to time, the power of the board of ten for writing
> laws lasted no more than two years, and that of the military tribunes
> with consular authority did not last long either.

(Tacitus, *Annals of Imperial Rome* 1.1)

Freedom (*libertas*) was a central ideal in Roman government. The meaning of the word in this context was essentially passive, meaning freedom from compulsion by a superior authority. The consulship was a collegial office, held by two men each year. A dictator (the Latin word lacked modern pejorative overtones) was an official who could be appointed from time to time in cases of extreme emergency to hold superior *imperium* for a six-month term. (It was considered a good thing if the dictator could solve the crisis for which he was appointed in less than the allotted time.) The military tribunes with consular authority were a board of three, four, or six men who were elected in place of the consuls, possibly in years when anticipated military demand was thought to be more than two men could handle. The first college of military tribunes was elected in 444 BC, the last in 367 BC.

Another view of Roman history in these years offers a somewhat different take on things:

> [t]he abuse of the weak by the strong, and separation of the plebs from the senate, and other civil dissensions were there from the start, nor were affairs managed with equity and justice except when, after the expulsion of the kings, there was fear of Tarquin and a dangerous Etruscan war. Then the senate abused the plebs as if they were slaves, and threatened their lives and bodies as if the senators were kings: they drove them from their fields, and when they had deprived them of everything, drove them by force. The plebs, oppressed by this savagery and by debt, while, at the same time they endured tribute payments and service in constant wars, occupied the sacred mountain and the Aventine in arms, and demanded tribunes of the plebs and other rights for themselves. The second war with Carthage brought an end to discord and contest.
>
> (Sallust, *History of Rome* fragment 11)

Both this and Tacitus's view are somewhat problematic. Sallust, the author of this passage, was interested in a paradigm of history whereby Rome flourished only when confronted by a serious enemy. When that enemy went away, the inherent tensions of Roman society exploded, submerging the good things accomplished in time of crisis in corruption and conflict. Sallust was writing in the midst of the bloody civil wars of the first century BC, and may perhaps be forgiven the extreme pessimism of his outlook.

The view of Tacitus, in the first passage, is complicated by his vision of Republican institutions as the work of a single great legislator, Lucius Brutus. Brutus, whom legend made the instrument of the expulsion of Tarquin the Arrogant, may or may not have existed. What is virtually certain is that, if he did exist, he did not invent the consulship. The early Republic appears to have been governed by magistracies inherited from the regal period, the praetors who held *imperium*, and the tribal officials, or tribunes. The conflict that Sallust describes often comes down to one between magistrates with and without *imperium*, the praetors, and later the consuls (who may first have been so named in 367 BC) on one side, and the tribunes on the other. But there was no single issue that divided the community, and it is inherently improbable to imagine a political struggle that lasted for two hundred years.

The most reliable guide (and it may not be altogether trustworthy) to the political issues of the fifth and fourth centuries is the record of public law. The texts of laws might be preserved even in a society that lacked other means of sophisticated composition in prose. These texts could be important to priests, who could include discussion of them in commentaries on divine matters, and they were important in later years to legal experts who might seek them out. But laws do not ordinarily tell us why they were passed, and the context of legislation can only be reconstructed with difficulty from examination of the matters that were being legislated. The later narrative tradition of Roman history (where this same task was attempted by historians of the second and first centuries BC) is no more than a scholarly reconstruction, and is often based upon assumptions that were plainly erroneous. Roman historians believed that history should provide moral instruction, and might allow moral considerations to overwhelm others when there was no contemporary

CELEBRATING A
TRIUMPH: A FAMILY
AFFAIR

Then the man celebrating
the triumph ascends into the
chariot. The chariot was not
like a racing chariot, or one
used in war, but was worked
into the shape of a round
tower, and he would not be
alone in the chariot, but if
he had children or relatives,
he would place the girls and
infant boys in the car with
him, and put the older ones
on horses—both the yoke
pair and the outer one, and if
there were more, they would
join the procession riding
alongside on warhorses.

(Cassius Dio fragment 23)

narrative that could contradict them. On the other hand, students of Roman institutions who were less interested in moral examples—scholars whom we conventionally refer to as antiquarians, who were interested in the history of Roman institutions that shaped the practices of their own times—could preserve texts of great importance. It is from the traces of their research, preserved through quotations in other writers, including Livy, that we can construct the tale of early Roman history—albeit with some care—since contemporary concerns could shape their exploration of the past rather heavily.

A point that should be stressed at the outset is that the issues that were most often the object of a vote were declarations of war and treaties. Spectacular victories over enemies could be followed by the celebration of a triumph by the successful general. The triumph commemorated the general as the direct agent of the gods in securing the safety of the community (see box, left), and records of triumphs were kept quite independently from other sources. From the record of Roman triumphs and of legislation connected with the declaration of war, it is possible to watch Rome expand to dominate first the rest of Latium, and then Etruria and central Italy. The acquisition of new land, and the increase in the size and power of the state, brought with them new challenges that forced the state to rethink itself on a periodic basis.

Patricians and Plebeians

In the first half of the fifth century BC, the most important development at Rome may have been the division in political society between two groups, known as the patricians and plebeians. Rome after Tarquin was the Rome of the Servian constitution, dominated by a Latin aristocracy that provided the candidates for election to the magistracies. The traditional view of Roman history, promulgated by the Romans themselves, held that the patricians were the hereditary aristocracy established by Romulus, and the plebeians were everyone else. This view is problematic for at least two reasons. The first is that the attribution of any institution to a mythical character (Romulus) raises questions about what the authors of the tradition really knew. There is a tendency among ancient writers to attribute developments for which they have no real evidence to periods or people about which or whom they also have no real evidence. The second reason for doubt is that lists of the Roman magistrates in the first half of the fifth century BC contain the names of magistrates who come from families that were non-patrician in the better attested years of the first century BC, raising the possibility that these early magistrates were not patricians either. Although these lists were all compiled much later than the fifth century BC, they seem to be based on reliable information.

Three lines of argument have emerged to explain the origin of the patrician order. One claims that the lists are not as accurate as they seem, and that the non-patrician names are fakes, added to the lists when they were compiled in the first century BC. The second asserts that the non-patrician names are really patrician, and that the fact that non-patrician families later held these same names results from an aberration of Roman naming practice. The third line of argument is that people whose families were excluded from the patrician class held the office before the patrician class was fully formed.

The first line of argument is unreasonable because there are too many names (sixteen in all, accounting for twenty magistracies). The second line of argument fails to explain why we do not have the same problem with magisterial lists after 445 BC. For the second line of argument to be acceptable (and indeed for the first to work) we should not be able to isolate a break point in 445 BC. This leaves us with the third view: that the patrician order formed after the end of the regal period. Its members were probably heads of leading families in the old *gentes*, because one of the crucial features of the patrician order was a monopoly on religious offices. Since there appears to have been a connection between some cults and the *gentes*, it is reasonable to think that this connection formed the basis for the religious role of the patricians. Indeed, one of the most cherished rights of the patricians was their control of the *auspicia*—the observation of divine signs offered by the flight of birds and other natural phenomena (see p. 44)—which gave members of this order a counter to a tribune's use of the veto: an official in charge of the *auspicia* for some public action could bring a meeting to an end by declaring that the signs were adverse, just as a tribune could halt public business by interposing his veto. Additionally, and perhaps connected with the control of *auspicia*, *patres* had to approve any bill passed by an assembly (this was called the *auctoritas patrum*, "authorization of the fathers"). Initially we cannot be sure just what this meant. Were the *patres* all patricians? Were they patricians who had been magistrates? Were they a group assembled like councils used by magistrates on an ad hoc basis? All we know for certain is that this power remained in effect until 339 BC, when a law was enacted that shifted the moment at which the *auctoritas patrum* was given to the point before a measure was put to the vote. It may be that this power survived into much later periods in the notion that anyone who expected to put a measure before the people needed to get approval first from the senate.

The view that the patrician order was formed after the end of the regal period raises questions about the formation of the plebeians as well. In recent years some scholars have argued that the plebeian order came into existence as a democratic movement that emerged almost as soon as the kingship came to an end. According to this view the plebeians sought to have their rights protected against the aristocrats whose domination of the state was now unchecked by the presence of a king. It is hard to be certain about this. The situation is complicated by the fact that the first firm attestation of the existence of the two orders in opposition to each other comes in the Roman law code promulgated in 450 BC, when marriage between patricians and plebeians was forbidden (a section of the code that was repealed in 445 BC). Plebeians who married into patrician families were presumably rather well off, but they may not have been members of families with connections to older cults, if that is one of the defining features of the patrician order. Thus it is wrong to see the plebeians as the poor.

The best explanation for the plebeian order has less to do with economics than with standard forms of organization in the fifth century BC. Political associations tended to be connected with cults, and the plebeian order may be derived from a cult association that was formed in response to the patricians. One of the most interesting features of the plebeian movement seems to be its connection with the Aventine hill, and the temple of Ceres, Liber, and Libera that had been constructed there, probably in the first decade of the fifth century BC. The Aventine cult, with its express connection to food—Ceres was the goddess of the harvest, Liber the god of the vine, and Libera was plainly his partner—stood in stark contrast with the "patrician" cult of Jupiter Optimus Maximus, Juno, and Minerva, which was expressly connected with the heavens. This may help to explain why the division was relevant in the fifth century, a reflection of current modes of defining groups within society, and why it came to be of no more than formal significance in the fourth century when socio-economic conditions had changed.

While the plebeian movement appears to have been concerned with establishing the rights of citizens in post-regal society, it did not, at first, make use of any new structures to secure its ends. The plebeians appear to have used the old office of the "tribunes of the people" to confront the patricians, since that office did not have *imperium*, or a link to the *auspicia*. The most important tribunician powers were established or confirmed (assuming that the office existed in the regal period) by the *comitia centuriata* in 494 BC. These powers were *sacrosanctitas* and the right to inter-cede on behalf of an individual. *Sacrosanctitas* meant that any person who killed a tribune was cursed. The right of intercession was the prerequisite of the veto power that individual tribunes could use to prevent magistrates from taking any action at all. The right of the tribunes to convene meetings of the people in an assembly known as the *concilium plebis* was established by a law passed through the *comitia centuriata* in 492 BC. The *comitia centuriata* also passed the law of 471 BC that effectively created a new voting assembly for the plebs based on the tribes. The role of this assembly—referred to in later centuries as either the *concilium plebis* or the *comitia plebis tributa*—was to elect magistrates without *imperium* (the tribune and aediles, initially officials of the Aventine cults, were the most important of these).

The law that created the *comitia plebis tributa* may coincidentally have strength-ened the link between tribunes and society as organized in the *comitia centuriata* by providing that there would now be five tribunes, and probably also specified that there should be one from each of the five classes. This was also a feature of the law of 457 BC that raised the number of tribunes to ten, two from each class.

The Twelve Tables

The years 452–449 BC mark a significant break in Roman history. In 452 BC a board of ten was elected to give Rome a new law code. The board took office in 451 BC, and completed its task in 450 BC. The result was known as the Laws of the Twelve Tables. Tradition has it that the behavior of the board in 450 BC was so obnoxious, and its members so abused the fact that they had been elected "without *provocatio*"—that is to say, citizens could not exercise the basic right of *provocatio*, or appeal to the people, against their rulings—that it was forced out by a popular revolution. This may be true, though it is notable that its laws remained in effect despite whatever objections people may have had to members of the board. Certainly the year 449 BC saw the enactment of seven laws that appear to be reactions to perceived defi-ciencies in the Twelve Tables and events of 450 BC. Three of these laws were moved by a tribune. One provided for the election of consuls to replace the board of ten, a second stated that no magistrate should ever again be created "without *provoca-tio*," and the third granted an amnesty to Romans who had refused to serve in the military levy of the previous year. It appears to have been the mass refusal of Romans to respond to the levy that ousted the board of ten.

Four laws were moved through the *comitia centuriata* by a consul of 449 BC. Of these laws, two may have been intended to complement the tribunician program, in that one stated that "decrees of the plebs" or plebiscites should have the force of law, and the other mirrored the tribunician law on the creation of magistrates without *provocatio*. These two consular laws may have been necessitated by the fact that only the *comitia centuriata* had been able to pass laws up to this point. The reference to a specific form of legislation as a plebiscite, however, does confirm that the *concilium plebis* was transformed into an assembly that could pass statutes before the middle of the fifth century. The law-making decrees of the plebs binding on all citizens in 449 BC may, however, not have applied to the future, and may simply have confirmed decrees passed in the crisis surrounding the end of the rule of the board of ten. Two further laws would be passed, one in 339 BC and the other, the *lex Hortensia* of 287 BC (the name comes, as with all Roman laws, from the man who sponsored it, in this case Hortensius), before it was established that all plebiscites had the force of law for all citizens. What is perhaps more important for understanding what happened in 449 BC is that when the Roman people again convened in the *comitia centuriata* to confirm what they had voted for when they had assembled without the patricians, the patricians did not withhold their *auctoritas*.

The other two consular laws of 449 BC dealt with *sacrosanctitas* and the storage of senatorial decrees. The first of these laws is relatively unproblematic as it confirmed *sacrosanctitas* for the tribunes, and extended the privilege to certain other minor magistrates. The other is much more difficult since it implies that there was a body known as the senate that could pass decrees. The fact that there was some sort of formal group with some sort of supervisory role may be taken to be implicit in *auctoritas patrum*, and it may be that the intent of this law was to formalize a structure—an aristocratic council overseeing the actions of magistrates—that was becoming a permanent feature of public life (see pp. 49–50). If so, then we may see it as the first stage in a process that culminated at some point between 318 and 312 BC when a tribunician law known as the *lex Ovinia* ordered the censors—officials who were charged with drawing up a list of Roman citizens and arranging state contracts every five years—to draw up a list of permanent senators (see box, right).

Between 445 and 440 BC, possibly in a sort of tidying-up operation after the promulgation of the Twelve Tables, we hear of four more important laws. One (in 445) rescinded the ban on marriage between patricians and plebeians. The second, in 444, provided for the replacement of the two collegial chief magistrates (still probably called praetors) with a college of four military tribunes with consular power. The other two laws (in 443 and 440) created the office of censor and prefect of the grain supply. The explanation for the creation of the censors was that the chief magistrates were no longer able to do the jobs that the censors were to do, which, at this period, consisted primarily of the assignment of contracts for public services. The creation of the prefect of the grain supply was a temporary arrangement to meet a crisis with the grain supply (bread was the staple of the Roman diet) in that year. The importance of these two laws, and of that creating the military tribunes with consular power, is recognition that the demands of government now exceeded the capacities of the old magisterial structure.

The laws of the first half of the fifth century appear to be concerned with defining the community. They do not necessarily reflect a great deal of strife between different groups, since all significant legislation appears to have been passed through the *comitia centuriata*. The most obvious crisis point is 450 BC, but

PASSED-OVER SENATORS

This term was not originally an insult, because the kings "appointed" and "appointed as replacements" those whom they would have in the public council. After the kings were expelled, the consuls and military tribunes with consular power chose those patricians who were closest to themselves for their public council, and then plebeians—until the *lex Ovinia* intervened, which established that the censors should choose each best man by curia from every order for the senate. When this was done, those who were "passed over" were removed from the senate and held to be disgraced.

(Festus, *Concerning the Meaning of Words* (Lindsay's edition), p. 290)

significant change of the sort represented by the promulgation of the Laws of the Twelve Tables—even if those laws did little more than formalize existing arrangements—would inevitably cause stress. What is perhaps most important is that the Roman people were able to resolve their differences legislatively. By 450 the *comitia centuriata* may have been in existence for about a century, and the Roman people seem to have developed some confidence in their ability to find consensus through the legislative process.

The Licinian-Sextian Laws

The next year of major legislative change was 367 BC. What may have made that year important was the failure of the traditional legislative system to resolve the needs of a very different Roman society. By 367, Rome had accomplished the conquest of southern Etruria (previously dominated by the Etruscan city of Veii) and the land of the Volsci that lay between Latium and Campania. Four new tribes were added to the existing twenty-one in 387; with new land, and new people, came new problems.

As the Roman community grew more powerful, divisions of wealth became more marked. In an agricultural society, where crop failure is a fact of life every few years, debt could become a very serious problem as farmers had to borrow in bad years to survive until the next harvest. The problem of debt was compounded by absurdly high interest rates of around 8.5 percent a month, meaning that a man who borrowed grain to plant his crop would have to return somewhere around 140 percent of what he had borrowed when the harvest came in at the end of the growing season. If a person failed to repay his debt, he became a *nexus*, or temporary slave, of the person from whom he had taken the loan. He could be released from this status only if he paid off the principal and interest in full; if he did not, his creditor could sell him, his family, or his property to get the money.

The brutality of the Roman law on debt was typical of the ancient world. Democratic Athens of the sixth through fourth centuries may have been the only major state to abolish debt bondage. And, just as debt bondage was common, so could the remission of debts become a major social issue for aristocratic politicians breaking ranks with their fellows to seek power and popular favor by supporting such an action. It is in the context of debt legislation that we find the *comitia plebis tributa*—now, if not earlier, operating alongside a second *comitia tributa* that included patricians and was convened by a magistrate with *imperium* rather than a plebeian official—emerging as an important legislative venue. In either form of the *comitia tributa*, where the voting collectives were the tribes rather than the classes, wealth counted for less, and laws aiming to help the poor had a much greater chance of success than in the *comitia centuriata*. Roman political society may have been built on the foundation of mutual obligation, but mass altruism is not the same thing.

The increase in the number of Roman citizens also changed the face and tone of Roman politics. Although we do not have particularly reliable figures, it appears that the number of Romans increased from somewhere around 100,000 to 150,000 in the century after 450 BC. This was less a result of an increased birth rate (highly improbable anyway in a period of endemic warfare) than of immigration from other parts of Italy (especially Latium) and the addition of freed slaves to the population.

One way that the tensions growing within Roman society might be alleviated was through success in war, which brought fresh booty and slaves into the city.

Even if a disproportionate part of this booty ended up in the hands of the command-ers of the victorious army, just a small amount of extra income could help a poorer person. Another way of alleviating pressure was through the foundation of colonies in newly conquered areas of Italy, giving people a chance for a fresh start. But in the twenty years before 367 BC no new colonies were founded, and in the previous decade military expansion seems to have been checked.

The patrician monopoly on magistracies now begins to emerge as yet another issue. In the three generations since the "closing" of the patrician order around 450 BC, new families had emerged whose leaders were increasingly coming to resent the monopoly on power that was maintained by the traditional aristocracy. The cost of this monopoly may have been even more obvious as a consequence of victories won before the Gallic sack. If booty was valuable to the foot soldier, it was even more so to the noble who commanded the army and determined the division of spoils after the victory. Control of magistracies may have had yet another effect, because a standard treaty between Rome and a conquered city usually involved the surrender of substantial territory to Rome that became "public land of the Roman people" (*ager publicus populi Romani*). If our sources are reliable concerning the terms of the legislative program of 367 BC, one aspect of that program was an effort to limit the amount of land that any one man could control. This land could be either in the form of private estates, or of public land (*ager publicus*) that was leased to Roman citizens (and others). Although the land technically belonged to the Roman people, some leases were set up on a long-term basis (there are references in a second-century BC law reforming the distribution of *ager publicus* to inheritable leases), and the rent appears not to have been onerous. The figure in mid-fourth century legislation is a large one (500 *iugera*, the equivalent of 325 acres or just over 80 hectares), suggest-ing that some people were starting to acquire a great deal of land in the course of the conquests. Revenue from landed estates was central to the acquisition of wealth in the upper classes, and as the rules for holding office were changing, it looks like the legislation may have been an attempt to ensure that there would be a level playing field for the future. Ideologically, it also seems to be an extension of such practices as the limitation on ostentatious personal expenditure, which had been in place for some time.

The difference between the legislative programs of 450 and 367 BC is striking, and reflects the new structures of society that had emerged as Rome had acquired large portions of central Italy in the intervening years. The reform program of 367 BC was the work of two tribunes, C. Licinius Stolo and L. Sextius Lateranus. They moved four laws through the *comitia tributa*. The first of these limited payments on out-standing loans to the amount of the principal, from which interest payments already made would be deducted. The second limited holdings of public land to roughly 330 acres or 135 hectares (500 *iugera* in Latin, an *iugum* being about two-thirds of an acre). The third eliminated the office of military tribune with consular author-ity, while establishing instead that the college of two chief magistrates—henceforth to be called consuls—would be supplemented by a third magistrate, of inferior *imperium*, who would manage affairs that they were too busy to look after. The title of this magistrate was now to be praetor (see box, right). The fourth law expanded the college of priests who were in charge of the Sibylline books from two to ten, and ordered that five of the ten would henceforth be plebeian. A final reform that may

THE PRAETOR

There is an ancient law, inscribed with old-fashioned letters and spellings, to the effect that whoever was *praetor maximus* (see p. 46) on the Ides of September would insert a nail; the law was attached to the right side of the temple of Jupiter Optimus Maximus, on the side facing the temple of Minerva. They say that the nail served, in an age when letters were rarely used, to mark the passage of years, and that it was connected with the temple of Minerva because numbers were discovered by Minerva. Cincius, a diligent student of such monuments affirms that nails as indicators of the years are inserted in the temple of Nortia, the Etruscan goddess at Volsinii.

(Livy 7. 3.5–7)

also date to this period was the creation of the office of curule aedile, a patrician equivalent to the old plebeian aedile. Henceforth curule and plebeian aediles would be elected in alternate years (curule aediles in even numbered years by our reckoning). This is also the time at which we can be certain that a further *comitia tributa*, one that included patricians (see p. 53), had come into operation, because at this point we can see that it had a definite function (the election of the curule aedile) that was not accommodated by other institutions. The three assemblies (the *comitia centuriata*, the *comitia tributa* excluding patricians, and the *comitia tributa* including patricians) would continue to exist, side by side, distinguished by their membership and presiding magistrates. It may have been at about this time that the Romans changed the beginning of the official year—the point at which new magistrates took office—to May 1 (it previously seems to have begun in August). This meant that the new consuls would take office at the beginning rather than in the middle of what was already likely to have been the annual period of warfare with Rome's neighbors.

The seventy years after the reforms of 367 would see the completion of the conquest of most of Italy south of the Po valley, and further changes in the structure of the state. There would be three more laws on the subject of debt, in 357, 347, and 326 BC, the latter banning the enslavement of the *nexus*. Tribunician laws of 342 established the principles that there should be a ten-year interval before a man could hold an office that he had already held (this essentially cut down on the repeated tenure of the chief magistracy), that no man could hold more than one office at a time, and that both consuls might be plebeian. In 339 a consul carried a series of laws granting binding authority to plebiscites, transferred the timing of the *auctoritas patrum* (see p. 50) to the point before the passage of a law, and provided that one censor should be a plebeian. In 287 a final law was passed, granting legal authority to all plebiscites. The *lex Hortensia* removed the requirement that the senate first had to agree, which may have been put in place by the law of 339.

The notable feature of the legislation of the second half of the fourth century is that the bulk of it was now carried through the *comitia tributa*. The community of interest between citizens of different classes, apparently reflected by the passage of major reform legislation by the *comitia centuriata* in the fifth century, seems to have broken down, and tribunes had emerged as important authors of social reform. The result was now a state where social status—whether one was born a patrician or a plebeian—still mattered, but that distinction was becoming less important than the issue of whether one had held office. The new rules enhanced competition amongst members of the upper classes, which manifested itself in public service and continued the earlier tradition by which men who had been successful commemorated themselves by commissioning large public projects (especially temples). The members of this class, once they had held the consulship, now came to be known as the *nobiles* ("nobles"). Despite the changes in the wealth and composition of the governing group, it is important to see that the legislative process, and indeed the competitive process within the new office-holding class, albeit very different from that established at the beginning of the Republic, still worked to build consensus. Roman society, for all of its tensions, remained a society based on the rule of law, and the Roman people decided what the law would be, voting through their tribes in the heart of the Roman forum. The Roman people also decided crucial issues of war and peace.

Summary

● Though they may not tell us much about the way that Rome actually developed, myths about the foundation of the city reveal what Romans in the first century BC thought was important about their history. The versions we have of these myths were written down at this time, and give us a vision of a society that was often at war with itself, yet nonetheless remained open to outsiders.

● The archaeology of early Rome, and the study of early Roman institutions—especially religion and the family—reveal a society that was profoundly hierarchical, but placed extreme value on collaboration. Leaders, whether they were kings or fathers of families, needed to consult with their peers before taking action, and needed to ensure that their conduct was in accord with the will of the gods. The earliest political society was based on groupings of families into *gentes*, whose leaders probably formed some sort of council around a king.

● We do not know much about the period before the foundation of the Republic in 509 BC, but it seems reasonable to think that there were kings and that several of the basic institutions of the later Republic came into being. These included tribal officials known as tribunes and quite possibly the magistrates known as praetors who would become the chief executive officers after the expulsion of the last king. Also datable to this period is the development of the *comitia centuriata*, which was based on the organization of the army.

● The key development in the period after the expulsion of the kings was a division between the patrician and plebeian orders, which stemmed from disputes over eligibility for office. Although later Roman historians paint a picture of a "struggle between the orders," similar to the political contests of their own time, the situation in early Rome seems to have been less fraught than that. Later histories stock the period with characters who are thought to be illustrative of important Roman qualities, but these stories are largely (if not wholly) fictional.

● Specific plebeian institutions were created in the course of the fifth century, of which the most important were the *concilium plebis/comitia plebis tributa* and the office of tribune of the plebs. Most reforms were passed through the *comitia centuriata* in the fifth century, suggesting that Roman society put a strong emphasis on reform through consensus. The most important development in Roman society as a whole in the period may have been the creation of a written law code—the Laws of the Twelve Tables.

● In the fourth century BC there is more evidence for serious economic disputes, centered especially on issues of debt and the enslavement of debtors, and continuing disputes over office-holding. The most wide-ranging reforms took place in the 360s—the Licinian-Sextian reforms (named for two tribunes of 367), which ended many disputes over access to office.

● By the end of the fourth century stronger institutions were being formed, and older institutions were formalized—most importantly the senate. Rome was already set on a course that would lead to the acquisition of empire, and a major reason for this was its ability to solve internal difficulties through consensus.

War
and
Empire

(350–133 BC)

TIMELINE II   WAR AND EMPIRE

	350–341BC	Development of the manipular legion
	343–341	First Samnite War
	341–338	Latin War
	334–323	Alexander the Great conquers Achaemenid empire
	328–304	Second Samnite War
	311	Roman levy set at four rather than two legions
The Conquest of Italy	**298–290**	Third Samnite War
	295	Rome defeats Etruscans and Gauls at Sentinum
	284–282	Final conquest of Etruria
	281–279	First phase of the war with Tarentum; Pyrrhus defeats Roman armies at Heraclea and Asculum
	275	Rome defeats Pyrrhus at Beneventum
	272	Tarentum surrenders
	264–241	First War with Carthage (First Punic War)
	241	Carthaginian portion of Sicily becomes Roman province; final expansion of the Roman tribes, which now number thirty-five
	238	Rome seizes Sardinia and Corsica from Carthage
	237–236	Hamilcar Barca of Carthage arrives in Spain
Punic Wars	**229**	First Illyrian War; Rome acquires territory on the east coast of the Adriatic; Hasdrubal succeeds Hamilcar
	228	Four praetors elected for the first time
	226	Treaty of Ebro
	225 BC	Victory over the Gauls at Telamon

	221 BC	Hannibal succeeds Hasdrubal
	219	Second Illyrian War; Hannibal attacks and captures Saguntum
Punic Wars	**218–201**	Second Punic War; Hannibal invades Italy
	217	Hannibal destroys Roman army at Lake Trasimene
	216	Hannibal destroys Roman army at Cannae
The Conquest of the East	**215–205**	First Macedonian War
	202	Scipio Africanus defeats Hannibal at Zama
	201	Carthage surrenders to Rome
	200–197	Second Macedonian War
	198	Six praetors elected for the first time; permanent Roman provinces established in Spain
	197	Flamininus defeats Philip V at Cynoscephalae
	192–187	Syrian War (war with Antiochus III)
The Conquest of the East	**191**	Roman victory at Thermopylae over Antiocuhus III
	190	Scipio defeats Antiochus at Magnesia
	188	Peace of Apamea
	171–168	Third Macedonian War
	168	Perseus of Macedon defeated at Pydna
	149–148	Fourth Macedonian War
Punic Wars	**149–146**	Third Punic War
	149	Lex Calpurnia establishes the first permanent court for trying extortion cases
The Conquest of the East	**146**	Achaean War; destruction of Carthage; portions of former Carthaginian territory become the Roman province of Africa; province of Macedonia established
	133 BC	Attalus III of Pergamon dies; beginning of the establishment of the province of Asia

> Is there any man so stupid or lazy that he does not want to know how,
> and with what system of government, the Romans subjugated the whole
> inhabited world to one rule, a thing never done before, in less than fifty-
> three years?

(Polybius, Universal History 1.1.5)

POLYBIUS, WHO WROTE THESE WORDS in the second century BC, was a Greek. As a young man he had been a successful politician in a league of Greek states that had dominated the northwestern Peloponnese. After a serious failure of judgment on the part of his colleagues, Polybius was taken to Rome in 167 BC as one of several hundred long-term hostages whose presence at Rome would ensure obedience in the future. There he mingled with the leaders of the Roman aristocracy and became a figure of international significance, as well as a historian whose fundamental study of Rome's rise to world power remains one of the most trenchant studies of imperialism to survive from the ancient world.

Polybius's greatness was a product of Rome, and in his person he represents an early phase in the formation of a new cultural idiom that linked the traditions of the Latin world with that of the Greek. At the end of the third century BC, Latin was still a language whose speakers were largely confined to the central Italian peninsula, whereas Greek was spoken throughout the Mediterranean. The resulting Greco-Roman culture that began to emerge in the third and second centuries BC was profoundly Mediterranean, indeed eastern Mediterranean, in orientation. It was this tradition that gave rise to the literary, legal, artistic, and administrative traditions that would become the Roman legacy in Western European history.

The lasting consequences of Rome's acquisition of empire make Polybius's question as important now as it was in the second century BC. It is impossible for us to do more than imagine what the world would have been like without Rome. But how did one state in central Italy alter so profoundly the cultural history of the Mediterranean basin and the lands that bordered it? The assimilation of enemies was the key to Rome's rise. The terms of assimilation change with time, but assimilation remains the ideal result. No less a figure than the great Hannibal, the Carthaginian general who almost defeated Rome in a series of bloody campaigns between 218 and 215 BC, saw the system of Roman relationships with other Italian states as the key to ultimate victory. If these relationships could be destroyed, Rome would be reduced to the level of a local rather than an Italian or Mediterranean power. Hannibal's perception was correct, but he failed to realize his goal and Rome triumphed in the end.

Rome and the Latins

There were three critical developments that enhanced Rome's ability to wage war in the two centuries after the expulsion of the kings, one almost immediately after the foundation of the Republic, and the other two towards the end of the fourth century. The first was a treaty with the other Latin states, probably in 493 BC, known as the Cassian treaty (*foedus Cassianum*). The second was the redefinition of the relationship with the Latins after 337 BC, the creation of a series of bilateral relationships with other states at the expense of pre-existing leagues, and the creation of a new form of citizenship that enabled Rome to acquire direct access to additional pools of manpower without significantly altering its core political society. The third was the replacement of the style of hoplite warfare enshrined in the *comitia centuriata* by a more flexible structure, based on small units, known as maniples: roughly 120 men who were trained to react as distinct elements of the legion. The first of these developments set the formula for future Roman practices of assimilation. The second and third made it possible for Rome to conquer first Italy, and then the Mediterranean.

The Cassian Treaty

According to a traditional Roman chronology, the Latin League went to war with Rome in 499 BC and was defeated at the battle of Lake Regillus. In about 493 BC the Roman magistrate Spurius Cassius concluded a treaty with the Latin League according to which the league agreed to fight in defense of Rome if it were attacked, and Rome agreed to go to war in defense of the Latins. These terms should probably be read in light of the fetial procedure, which presumed that war would only ever be fought if another party had started the trouble, and the treaty might be read as implying that Romans and Latins would take the field together whenever the fetial procedure was invoked. The principle that underlay these relationships was the Roman concept of *fides*, or good faith, guaranteed by oaths sworn before the gods. Other terms of the treaty specified that Rome would provide a commander for the Latin forces, determine the ratio of troops provided by each state, and decide how the spoils of war would be divided. In effect, the army would thereafter be half Roman and half Latin. A further development, in 486 BC, was the admission of a non-Latin people, the Hernici, to the alliance. This set a precedent for the creation of special relationships between non-Latin peoples and the Roman state.

Aside from providing a framework that allowed for doubling the strength of the Roman army, a further result of the Cassian treaty may have been that it formalized a special status for Latins with respect to the Roman state. While not being in any sense "Roman," people with Latin rights were still distinct from others. They had the right to marry Romans, to move to Rome, and to do business there. This invention, through the treaty, of a category of semi-citizen, would enable the community of Rome to grow through diplomacy at a much greater rate than would have been possible if it had had to rely on the two normal demographic modes for population growth: an increased birth rate and immigration.

The Cassian treaty proved to be remarkably successful, and continued to govern relations between Rome and the Latins until 341 BC. In that year the relationship broke down completely and a new war broke out that the Romans were able to win decisively by 338. At that time the Romans decided that a new model was needed, based upon the old one, to govern their relationship with the Italians. This model involved the creation of yet another category of semi-citizen and a new style of alliance.

The Relationship with the Latins after 337 BC

The new elements introduced in 337 were the replacement of a treaty between Rome and the Latin League by a series of bilateral treaties that bound each individual state of the former league to Rome, and the creation of "citizenship without the vote" (*civitas sine suffragio*). Citizens without the vote remained citizens of distinct communities—just like Latins—yet they were Roman citizens in that they had the direct responsibilities of Roman cities to pay taxes to Rome and be liable to the Roman *dilectus* (the call-up of troops), even though they could not serve in the same legions as full citizens. The crucial feature of "citizenship without the vote" was that it could be awarded to anyone, making it possible to create new Roman communities anywhere in Italy.

The new treaties continued to be based upon the Roman idea of good faith or *fides*, a concept intimately linked with the powerful notions of mutual responsibility inherent to Roman society. It is one of the significant features of Roman imperial expansion—not only in the fourth century but also well into the second century BC—that Romans tended to include states they defeated in war, or those that appealed to Rome for aid, in a system increasingly based on the concept of the *deditio in fidem* (a surrender into the "good faith" of the Romans). Ordinarily, Rome responded, in the case of a state that had been defeated in war, by sparing the city from destruction and leaving its essential political structures intact, while sometimes eliminating those members of the ruling class who were held responsible for the outbreak of trouble, and confiscating some portion of the city's territory as *ager publicus* (see p. 70). States that made a *deditio* were supposed to follow Rome's instructions in the future.

This particular feature of Roman imperialism was very different from that of other peoples, who tended to impose garrisons in conquered areas. It was particularly noted by Polybius, who paid much attention to the way that the creation of a zone of "obedient" states defined the growth of Roman power. From a pragmatic point of view, the creation of an "empire of *fides*," which is what gradually took shape in central Italy during the later part of the fourth century, allowed states some leeway to manipulate (usually quite self-consciously on both sides) the Roman ideology to the perceived mutual benefit of both parties. States that felt themselves threatened by stronger neighbors placed themselves within the *fides* of Rome. The Roman state, it appears, was rarely loath to accept offers of *fides*, even from peoples whose own behavior might seem to have merited whatever vengeance angry neighbors were wishing to dish out.

The combination of the new policy towards treaties—bilateral agreements only—and the creation of "citizenship without the vote," gave Rome the ability to control an ever-expanding pool of manpower. States that had come under Rome's control lost their capacity to escape. No city bound to Rome by a treaty could negotiate freely with any other state. States might, of course, choose to do so, but this very act could be construed as an act of war, leaving them open to Roman retaliation well before they were able to organize effective resistance. Communities of citizens without the vote could be placed throughout Italy to keep an eye on their neighbors, and the creation of these communities left the political structure of Rome unchanged: citizens without the vote had to rely on Roman patrons to represent their interests at Rome, thus strengthening rather than diluting the ruling class. Had these people been added to the Roman state as full citizens, their leaders would have been able to stand for office, and their votes might thus have had a direct impact that the governing aristocracy would not be able to control.

Eventually, the inability of Rome's allies to exercise anything other than indirect influence on Roman policy became the single most important issue in Roman

(Opposite) *This fragment of an early third-century fresco from a tomb on the Esquiline hill depicts a meeting between Quintus Fabius Maximus (see p. 82), on the right, and a man identified as Marcus Fannius. Their exchange of greetings illustrates the classic gesture of* fides. *The men behind Fabius are soldiers, and a battle scene occupies the bottom part of the image. The linkage of* fides *and war in this mural is an apt metaphor for the rise to power of Rome in Italy.*

(Below) The equipment of these Samnite warriors, depicted in a fourth-century tomb painting from Paestum in central Italy, is typical of the fighters of their day. Like the Roman soldiers who can be seen in the Esquiline fresco, they are primarily spearmen.

politics, and led to the breakdown of Republican government. But that was only after Rome had acquired an empire. For now, it was seen as a way to preserve the existing system intact, and it provided a mechanism for expansion.

The Doctrine of Decisive Victory

Before the new sources of manpower could be exploited to best advantage, the Roman way of doing battle had to change. The *comitia centuriata* assumed a style of warfare based upon lines of heavily armored infantry (see p. 43). This style was conducive neither to decisive victory—where the losing side was rendered incapable of offering battle again in the same year—nor to efficient use of manpower. Concentration on the encounter between the heavy infantry lines rendered the majority of the manpower pool, which could not afford the requisite armor, superfluous. Moreover, as the battle lines were probably drawn up eight deep (as in the contemporary Greek world), the majority of men in the battle line had no other role than to support those in front of them in the hope that they could force the enemy backwards. Only about a quarter of the soldiers in the line might actually be involved in killing the enemy, unless the opposing line fell apart. A more typical result seems to have been that one side or the other withdrew. If both sides did not commit to battle on a flat plain, there was little that could be done to force the issue.

In 390 BC, according to the Latin tradition preserved by Livy, Rome suffered a spectacular defeat at the hands of a band of Gauls from the Po valley, who destroyed the Roman army at the battle of the River Allia and occupied Rome (see pp. 24–26). It was the worst defeat that Rome had suffered, and it stemmed from the incapacity of the Roman army to handle an unfamiliar style of fighting. Gauls charged in a mass formation. They were physically large men, capable of overwhelming the front of the Roman line at the first rush. They may also have been more mobile on the battlefield, enabling them to outflank the line as they advanced—another recipe for disaster. Fortunately for the Romans, the Gauls accepted a large bribe and went away.

The battle of the Allia proved that the then-current Roman style of warfare, marginally effective against similarly inclined adversaries, was incapable of dealing with an enemy that refused to play by the rules. We have no direct evidence for the point at which the Romans adopted their new style of warfare, but the sudden transformation in the effectiveness of the Roman army after 350 BC shows that the change must fall in the decade prior to the decisive defeat of the Latin League. The full impact of the transformation may be seen in 295 BC, when a Roman army destroyed a combined army of Gauls, Samnites, Umbrians, and Etruscans at Sentinum. The victory secured Roman control over central Italy, brought the series of wars that had begun in 343 BC against the Samnite League of central Italy to an end, and attracted the notice of people living outside Italy. Sentinum is the first Roman victory recorded by a historian—Timaeus—working in Greece. Another early Greek historian of Rome, Philinus, offers the statement that Roman tactics before the outbreak of the first war between Rome and Carthage were modeled on those of the Samnites. Fifteen years after the battle of Sentinum we get our first clear picture of what this new Roman army looked like, from the description by King Pyrrhus of Epirus of the battle of Heraclea (see box, p. 64).

The Roman acquisition of empire may thus be attributed to two reforms in the 340s and 330s. The first of these was the revision of treaty terms with the Latin allies

THE EARLY REPUBLICAN ARMY

Cavalry

Allies

Legion

Legion

Allies

Cavalry

One legion

One maniple

Standard-bearer

Centurion

Standard-bearer

Centurion

The four divisions of the mid-Republican army, illustrated here, were conceived originally as a formation that would wear down an enemy. It was felt that the battle should be decided in the first three divisions, and the engagement of the fourth division was a sign of a particularly difficult fight.

Triarii

Principes   Hastati

Velites

King Pyrrhus of Epirus defeated the Romans with his own professional army at the battle of Heraclea in 280 BC. The description he included in his memoirs provides the basis for later accounts. Pyrrhus reveals that the Roman legion was broken up into maniples: units of two centuries trained to fight independently within the legion. The maniples were grouped in four divisions, the *velites*, *hastati*, *principes*, and *triarii*. The job of the *velites*, the most lightly armed troops, was to open the battle as skirmishers; the *hastati* were to deliver the first attacks. If those failed, the *principes* would be called into action. It was taken as a sign of deep trouble if the *triarii* had to fight at all.

At the point when the new legionary formation was adopted the basic weapon was still the spear, as was typical in central Italian armies of the period. In the course of the next century—we do not know when exactly, but we do know that it was before 225 BC—the spear went from use for hand-to-hand combat to use purely as a missile, and the primary killing instrument became a thrusting sword modelled on a contemporary Spanish weapon.

The manipular formation lent itself to decisive victory. Its strength lay not only in increased flexibility on the battlefield, but also in the ability to relieve troops in the front line. Units could move in and out of direct combat, extending the time that the enemy line could be subjected to actual fighting. It was standard doctrine in the nineteenth century that soldiers could not be expected to sustain the pressure of actual fighting for more than about fifteen minutes, and there is some reason to think that this was also true in the ancient world. Under the old style it was

very hard to replace men in the front rank; under the new, basic tactical doctrine demanded that this replacement would occur on a regular basis (although precise details as to how this was done elude us). Tired men tend to panic more easily, and the longer a battle could be drawn out, the greater the chance of a rout. If one's own troops, in contact with the enemy, could be kept fresher than the people opposite them, then decisive victory was virtually assured.

Perhaps as important as the ability of the legion to launch continuous attacks with fresh men was the fact that the structure of the new legion virtually dictated the tactics that a general would use in battle. Given that commanding generals changed every year in the mid-Republic, and not all of them could be expected to be great military thinkers, the system would seem to have limited the ability of each new general to think creatively, and with men new to supreme command that was not a bad thing. As with the political system, the military system evidently reflected the notion that the rank and file should be able to exercise some control over what the magistrate did with his power.

Finally, there was the issue of numbers. Half the army consisted of Roman allies who were trained, it seems, to fight in the same way as Roman troops. Each allied city was expected, if necessary, to send its entire army to fight for Rome, although in practice the Romans only requested troops according to a sliding scale to spread the burden. Individual allied units were commanded by their own officers, but they were grouped into legions on the Roman model for battle, and it seems likely that the legions of allies were commanded by Romans.

and the development of a novel way of maximizing the human resources needed to sustain war. The second was the evolution of a new style of doing battle. But this is only part of the story. Just as important was the Roman willingness to go to war.

The Wars of the Third Century BC

Rome was at war for eighty of the hundred years of the third century BC. Between 298 and 290 the Romans completed the conquest of central Italy in a war traditionally known as the Third Samnite War. Between 284 and 282 BC the Romans completed the conquest of Etruria (winning a decisive victory over a combined army of Gauls and Etruscans at Lake Vadimon in 284 BC). Conflicts with the city of Tarentum in southeastern Italy escalated into a major war in 281 BC, and the Tarentines called upon Pyrrhus, the king of Epirus (roughly southern Bosnia, Albania, and northwestern Greece), to aid them. The Romans prevailed—but not without great difficulty—in 275 BC. The war with Tarentum seems to have inspired revolts in central Italy that escalated into another major conflict: this only ended with the completion of the Roman conquest of Italy south of the Po river in 264 BC.

In 264 BC war broke out with the great Phoenician state of Carthage in north Africa (the Latin word for Phoenician was *Poenus*, from which we get Punic, the better-known English name for the ensuing wars). The Phoenicians—inhabitants of the modern area of Lebanon—founded Carthage as a trading colony in the eighth century BC. By the sixth century, Carthage, located near the modern city of Tunis, was the preeminent naval power in the western Mediterranean, and appears to have controlled the indigenous Numidian tribes of north Africa through a series of alliances. Carthaginian explorers ranged along the Atlantic coasts of west Africa and Spain, journeying as far north as Britain as well as to the coast of Italy.

In areas where Carthage came to trade, relations with the native peoples appear to have been reasonably peaceful; the earliest document in Roman history may be a treaty concluded with Carthage just after the expulsion of the kings in 509 BC. Carthaginian relations with the Greeks of Sicily were less pacific. By the early fifth century Carthage was attempting to gain control of the island. Wars with the Greek states of Sicily—chiefly the great city of Syracuse—continued with varying success on both sides right down to the third century BC, and it was into the context of those struggles that Rome blundered in 264 BC. The war stemmed from the unstable situation in southern Italy after the defeat of the Tarentines, and the intervention in 264 of one consul, Appius Claudius, who, against the better judgment of his senatorial peers, convinced the Roman people to send him with an army to Sicily.

The First Punic War, as the struggle that ended in 241 BC is conventionally known, was but the first of three wars that ended only with the destruction of Carthage in 146 BC, and the establishment of a Roman province in north Africa. The result of the First Punic War was the creation of the first overseas Roman province in Sicily, and one result of the second was the acquisition of what became two provinces in Spain, previously Carthaginian territory, and an interest in southern France, through which armies would have to pass to reach the new provinces. In very real terms, the emergence of Rome as a Mediterranean rather than merely an Italian power was a result of these conflicts.

THE EXPANSION OF ROME, 390–241 BC

The Roman conquest of Italy was accomplished in three phases. The first saw the establishment of control in the immediate area of Rome, achieved after the capture of Veii in 396 BC and the defeat of the Latin League in 338 BC. The next phase, a series of wars with the Samnites, ended in 290 BC. The final phase, which included the reduction of Etruria and of southern Italy, was completed in the 280s BC.

(Below) The First Punic War began with a series of operations in Sicily; key events were the surrender of Syracuse and the capture of Agrigentum. In 260 BC Roman operations shifted to the sea and to north Africa, but defeat at Utica in 255 BC and the loss of a major battle fleet in a storm moved the focus of the conflict back to Sicily. A new Roman battle fleet was launched in 241 BC and the Carthaginian fleet was destroyed in battle later that year. The Carthaginians agreed after this defeat to withdraw from Sicily and to pay an indemnity of 3,200 talents over ten years to Rome.

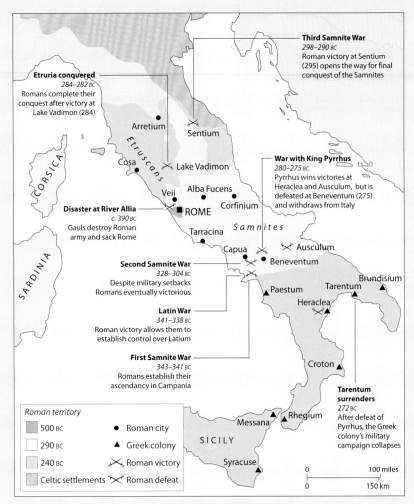

Third Samnite War
298–290 BC
Roman victory at Sentium (295) opens the way for final conquest of the Samnites

Etruria conquered
284–282 BC
Romans complete their conquest after victory at Lake Vadimon (284)

War with King Pyrrhus
280–275 BC
Pyrrhus wins victories at Heraclea and Ausculum, but is defeated at Beneventum (275) and withdraws from Italy

Disaster at River Allia
c. 390 BC
Gauls destroy Roman army and sack Rome

Second Samnite War
328–304 BC
Despite military setbacks Romans eventually victorious

Latin War
341–338 BC
Roman victory allows them to establish control over Latium

First Samnite War
343–341 BC
Romans establish their ascendancy in Campania

Tarentum surrenders
272 BC
After defeat of Pyrrhus, the Greek colony's military campaign collapses

Roman territory
- 500 BC
- 290 BC
- 240 BC
- Celtic settlements
- ● Roman city
- ▲ Greek colony
- ⚔ Roman victory
- ⚔ Roman defeat

0 — 100 miles
0 — 150 km

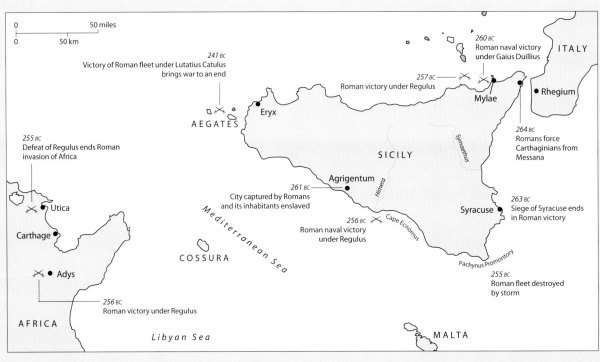

241 BC
Victory of Roman fleet under Lutatius Catulus brings war to an end

255 BC
Defeat of Regulus ends Roman invasion of Africa

256 BC
Roman victory under Regulus

261 BC
City captured by Romans and its inhabitants enslaved

256 BC
Roman naval victory under Regulus

257 BC
Roman victory under Regulus

260 BC
Roman naval victory under Gaius Duillius

264 BC
Romans force Carthaginians from Messana

263 BC
Siege of Syracuse ends in Roman victory

255 BC
Roman fleet destroyed by storm

Eryx (Erice) was the last stronghold of the Carthaginians in Sicily and the base of operations for their general Hamilcar Barca. Besieged by the Romans but never captured, it was finally surrendered as part of the peace agreement with Rome that ended the First Punic War.

That Rome should become a major Mediterranean power seems not to have occurred to the major players when the first war with Carthage broke out. Indeed, the Roman intervention on the island initially had nothing to do with Carthage, but stemmed rather from a request for aid from a community of Campanian mercenaries who had seized control of the city of Messana (modern Messina) and recently been badly beaten by the ruler of the Greek city of Syracuse. In the past they might have sought aid from a similar group of mercenaries who had seized the city of Rhegium (Reggio) on the other side of the straits, but the Romans had recently taken the city and executed those people (former employees of Rome). Deprived of this assistance, the Messenians appealed to both Rome and Carthage for aid.

Hostility with the Carthaginians arose from the unwillingness of the Carthaginian general on the spot to allow that the Romans had any business on the island. In theory peace should still have been possible, if either side had been conditioned to seek it once Appius Claudius had lifted the siege of Messana, even though he had fought both the Carthaginians and Syracusans in doing so. At that point he had done what he had set out to do. None of the parties involved, however, was inclined to see things that way, and after the Romans forced Syracuse to surrender a war began for control of Carthaginian Sicily.

As the violence of the struggle grew, the Romans realized that they needed to command the seas around the island and thus set about building a fleet that could take on the massive Carthaginian navy. The Carthaginians, who were also governed by an aristocratic council with annually elected magistrates, seem to have been no better at long-term planning than the Romans. At no point do they seem to have contemplated the possibility that control of the sea would have allowed them to attack Italy at will, or that they should do everything in their power to prevent the Romans from creating a battle fleet. After four years, during which the Romans captured most of the important cities in the Carthaginian part of the island and compelled the surrender of Syracuse, a Roman navy finally appeared.

The creation of a fleet capable of taking on the Carthaginians moved the conflict into a new phase, in which the Romans sought to win control of the sea and carry the war to Africa. These hopes foundered on the twin shoals of arrogance and incompetence. Arrogance was the chief quality of the general sent to command the expedition to Africa, Atilius Regulus. Once he had established himself in Carthaginian territory and had defeated the first army the Carthaginians sent against him, he offered peace terms so outrageous that Carthage elected to continue the struggle (a decision that resulted in the swift destruction of Regulus's army). Incompetence was the notable characteristic of Roman admirals who allowed their fleets to be caught in storms between north Africa and Italy (see also p. 81). Polybius later noted that Roman magistrates had trouble learning that storms at sea were less amenable to human agency than armies on land (see box, right). Just as telling is an inscription commemorating one of the great Roman successes of the period, the initial victory at Mylae. This document, known to us from a later copy, honors Duilius for his defeat of the Carthaginian fleet at the battle of Mylae in 260: Rome's first victory in a major naval battle. In describing these events Duilius tells how he defeated Hannibal, the "Dictator" of the Carthaginians, and how he had routed all their "most important magistrates," in an earlier encounter on land. The use of Roman terms in this context would seem to reflect the difficulty that the Romans had in envisioning a state that was not structured like their own; hence the trouble they might have had in understanding people who simply did not see the world in the same way as they did.

By 241, both sides had essentially worn each other out. Roman losses by this stage numbered in the hundreds of thousands, thanks largely to disasters at sea, and it is likely that Carthaginian losses were almost as great, for the same reason. When Rome launched a new fleet under the command of the consul Lutatius Catulus, it seems almost to have been a measure of desperation. Carthage was,

ROMAN MIGHT ON LAND AND SEA

In general terms the Romans rely on force in all matters, thinking that it is necessary for them to carry on, and that nothing is impossible once they have decided upon it; they succeed in many cases because of this. In some, however, they fail spectacularly, most of all at sea. On land, attacking men and the works of men they usually succeed because they are matching force against equal force, although they do sometimes fail; but when they encounter the sea and the weather and fight them with force, they suffer great disasters.

(Polybius, *Universal History* 1.37.7–8)

This inscription commemorates Duilius's victory over the Carthaginians. Known to us through a later copy, probably made under Augustus, this fascinating text is one of the earliest surviving pieces of Latin prose.

however, in no better shape. For years it had barely managed to retain a foothold in Sicily, and it only managed to do so largely because its general, Hamilcar Barca, was a man of enormous skill and determination. When Catulus appeared at sea Carthage was stretched to mount any opposition, and the opposition that it did mount proved deeply ineffective. Catulus destroyed the Carthaginian fleet in a battle off the Aegates Islands. Recent work by underwater archaeologists has uncovered wrecks of warships destroyed in this encounter between the islands of Levanzo and Merretimo, suggesting that the Roman fleet waited behind Levanzo for their heavily loaded rivals, and that the Carthaginians had incorporated a number of Roman vessels captured earlier in the war into their force. The discovery of a number of the bronze beaks, or rams (attached to the front of warships, which turned the ships themselves into lethal weapons) has also shown that many of the ships used in this battle were *triremes*—vessels with three banks of oars, one rower to each oar, and a total crew of fewer than 200 men—rather than the larger *quinquiremes*, which had three banks of oars, five rowers to each bank, and total crews of around 500. There is evidence to the same effect in the inscription honoring Duilius, which attests that the losses suffered by both sides (though still horrific) were probably lower than the numbers implied by Polybius, who suggests that the battle fleets in this era consisted entirely of *quinquiremes*.

The defeat of the last Carthaginian fleet meant that Carthage could no longer support its armies in Sicily, and was defenseless in the face of Roman attacks on the coast of north Africa. Catulus recognized the desperate straits into which the Carthaginians had fallen, and also showed that he, at least, had learned from Regulus's fate, taking advantage of his victory to offer remarkably generous terms with Carthage so that the war would end. The terms of the treaty left Carthaginian territory intact outside Sicily, where the recognition of Roman control was by this point no more than an acknowledgment of the status quo, and imposed a relatively moderate financial indemnity—a payment seemingly intended both as admission that Carthage had been in the wrong and to hamper rearmament—without compelling Carthage to submit to Roman control of its affairs.

Roman terms may have been relatively lenient, but Carthage was still in terrible shape. The end of the war left the city with a large, and now redundant, force of

Ancient warships were self-contained weapons. Although they were able to surprise the Carthaginians at the battle of Mylae with a novel boarding apparatus, it appears that, with experience, the Romans reverted to more standard tactics: using the ram attached to the ship's prow to disable opposing vessels (see p. 81). One of the most impressive discoveries of recent years has been a group of rams from ships sunk at the battle of the Aegates Islands in 241 BC. These rams, several of which are inscribed with the names of the Roman magistrates responsible for the construction of the ships, reveal that triremes were mingled with quinquiremes in the main battle line.

mercenaries in its employ. When the Carthaginians refused to pay them, a vicious war ensued that was ended only through the superior generalship of Hamilcar. Still, in 238 BC the Romans used the pretext of a *deditio in fidem* (see p. 62) on the part of the rebellious mercenary garrisons of Sardinia and Corsica, of which Carthage had retained control under the peace agreement of 241 BC, to seize those islands and impose a further indemnity on Carthage. They then turned north to the Po valley, where Roman armies were engaged on a regular basis until the late 220s BC.

The acquisition of significant territory along the Po valley in 232 directed Roman attention to the eastern coast of the Adriatic Sea, especially the region then known as Illyria (roughly modern Bosnia). The prevailing winds on the Adriatic are such that ships sailing north to the Po valley were compelled to sail along the coast of Illyria, where they had a tendency to fall prey to the highly organized pirate fleets there. The consequence was that Rome was drawn into the politics of that area, resulting in an invasion, and the evident acquisition of territory. Control was

DEDITIO IN FIDEM

It is significant that when the Romans began to expand eastwards, they seem to have introduced the same system of control as the one they had developed in Italy. One of the crucial documents relating to Roman expansion eastwards into Illyria is a very badly broken inscription from the island of Pharos, off the coast of modern Croatia. When inscriptions are in such a state we have to piece together the original content on the basis of surviving hints in the text and parallels. In this case the most important parallel comes from a bronze tablet from Spain dating to 104 BC. This text, which is the sole surviving text of a *deditio in fidem*, reads as follows:

> In the consulship of Gaius Marius and C. Flavius
>
> The people of SEANOC gave [… themselves] to Lucius Caesius son of Gaius, the imperator. Lucius Caesius the son of Gaius the imperator after he received [them in *deditio*] referred the matter to his council asking what they thought should be asked from them. He demanded, on the advice of his council [that they should hand over all] captives, stallions and mares that they had taken. They handed all these over. Then Lucius Caesius [the son] of Gaius [the imperator] ordered that they should all be [free.] The fields, buildings, laws and [all] other things that were theirs before [they] handed themselves over which [were then] in existence, he restored to them, for so long as it pleased the Roman people [and senate]; with regard to this matter he ordered those [who were present] to go. The ambassadors Cren[us …] Arco son of Canton.

The crucial lines in the text from Pharos read as follows:

> [Since the senate and] people of the [Romans being] friends [and showing goodwill from the time of their ancestors, returning] to the people of the Pharians, [our] city and [the ancestral] laws, they restored the lands [that belong to the city] on the island […] forty and confirmed the alliance [and friendship] and other privileges …

The clear survival on the stone of the verb "restore," in the context of the land on the island that had been taken from the city and was in Rome's power to return, along with the verb "confirm," shows that we have here the sort of two-part process seen in the text from Spain, that began with a surrender to Rome of everything in the community. This justifies the restoration of the participle "returning." The conclusion that we are dealing with a *deditio* here is based on the surviving words, however, rather than the restoration of the text. This sort of problem with epigraphic evidence is commonplace: often our knowledge of significant developments depends upon such tenuous evidence, and its significance can remain open to question, as here.

The fact that the inscription refers to the city not owning all the land on the island is also interesting: we know that there was a powerful "tyrant" named Demetrius who lived on Pharos, and was placed in overall control of the area after the First Illyrian War ended. The division of the island here may reflect the city's dealing with Demetrius (though we cannot be absolutely certain).

asserted over a portion of the region in 229 BC on the Italian model, whereby cities that entered the *fides* of Rome became members of the Roman alliance system. In this case, it should be noted that the evidence for the extension of the Italian system of control by treaty stems from the battered text of an inscription (see box, opposite).

There is less ambiguity about events four years later. The Gauls had been upset by the Roman seizure of territory in 232, and tensions had reached such a point by 228 that the Roman state offered a very rare human sacrifice to avert an invasion. In 225 BC the Gauls invaded Italy. The Roman army destroyed them at the battle of Telamon (the first battle for which we have explicit testimony that the main hand-to-hand weapon of the Roman infantryman had become a very nasty sword developed in Spain). In the next few years Roman armies campaigned against Gallic tribes north of the Po river. In these cases victory in the field was not accompanied by any comparable conquest of the hearts and minds of the Gauls, whose ultimate response to their treatment was to offer unequivocal support for the Carthaginian general, Hannibal, when he appeared in their midst after a dramatic crossing of the Alps in 218.

Hannibal arrived in Italy from Spain. He was the son of Hamilcar Barca, who held a very serious grudge against the Romans as a result of their seizure of Sardinia and Corsica. Shortly after crushing the revolt of the mercenaries, Hamilcar began to establish a new Carthaginian kingdom in Spain: this would provide Carthage with sources of manpower that could be exploited in place of the mercenaries who had hitherto played a large (and ultimately ambivalent) role in its military structure. Roman concern with Carthaginian expansion appears to have led to two diplomatic initiatives in the 220s BC. One established that Carthaginians would not expand north of the Ebro river in northern Spain, and the second was a treaty with the city of Saguntum, well south of the Ebro. (This seems the most likely order of events, although the situation is so clouded by later polemic that even tenuous evidence— such as that offered by the battered inscription mentioned above for Roman policy in Illyria—would be welcome, in order to cast some light upon what was going on.) What is clear, however, is that in 219 BC Hannibal attacked Saguntum; that the people of Saguntum appealed to Rome for aid; that both the government at Carthage

The citadel at Saguntum in eastern Spain was a powerful fortress in antiquity. It defended a city that was a thriving center of Iberian culture at the time of Hannibal's attack in 219 BC. The appeal of the people of Saguntum to Rome for assistance against Carthage sparked the beginning of the Second Punic War.

and Hannibal rejected Roman claims on behalf of the Saguntines; and that Hannibal captured the city. The result was that the so-called Second Punic War was declared between Rome and Carthage in 218 BC.

Hannibal, whose father had made him—while still a young boy—swear an oath in the temple of Carthage's chief god to be Rome's enemy forever, had devoted himself to the study of Roman institutions from an early age. He had too great a mind to resort simply to imitation of his enemy, and sought rather to build a military force that could take advantage of Roman tendencies on the battlefield. As a leader of men in battle, he had an extraordinary capacity to inspire his troops with his vision—to create a level of military professionalism that was joined to an ideological commitment to his aims. He built what was virtually a private army dedicated to the defeat of Rome in Italy. His plan—revealed through the terms of a treaty that he struck with Philip V, king of Macedon, in 217—did not envisage the total destruction of Rome. Indeed, the treaty with Philip shows that Hannibal hoped for a negotiated settlement, as one of the terms of the treaty makes clear (see box, below right).

In addition to his organizational and motivational skills, Hannibal possessed one of the great tactical minds of the ancient world. He inflicted a number of catastrophic defeats on Roman armies—at Trebia in 218 BC, Trasimene in 217 BC, and Cannae in 216 BC—but, despite his genius, he was unable to break down the system of alliances in Italy. If he had a weakness, it was that he could not understand the moral impact of war upon his victims. Few Italian communities would be inclined to join with him once he had slain their people in battle or ravaged their lands. The two major Italian states that did go over to his side after Cannae—Tarentum and Capua—were both outside the major area of his operations, and their adhesion to his cause was arguably more of a problem than an assistance. Since the two cities are on different coasts of Italy, Hannibal could not support one without abandoning the other, with the result that he could protect neither, effectively handing the Romans victories that they were in no position to win in a straight-up battle with his army. Throughout the years after Cannae, a war of attrition set in between Hannibal and the Roman generals who refused to engage him in a set battle; the Second Punic War took on the shape of a struggle between the will of an extraordinary individual on the one side, and that of a great state on the other (see box, pp. 76–77).

While the war in Italy wore on, Roman armies in Spain were led by Publius Cornelius Scipio, a very young man who owed his command as much as anything to the fact that his father, also Publius Cornelius, and uncle, Gnaeus, had held commands in Spain before him (both of which had ended in disaster). Scipio drove the Carthaginians from their Spanish base, using an army that included thousands of men who seem to have been drawn into service from clients of his family. There is much that links Scipio with Hannibal, for like Hannibal, Scipio studied his enemy, inspired his troops with extraordinary personal devotion, and was able to develop his talents without intervention from a higher authority. In 204 BC Scipio invaded Africa from Sicily, and in 202 he won a decisive victory over Hannibal, who had been recalled to Africa to face him at Zama, effectively ending the war. There is a sense in which the old Hannibal fell victim to the youth and vigor of a pupil, who was thereafter known as Scipio Africanus.

After the Roman defeat at Lake Trasimene in 217 BC, King Philip V of Macedon had entered the war on the side of Carthage. His aim appears to have been to

This coin bears the image of the Phoenician god Melqart. Some scholars have suggested that his features resemble those of Hannibal, but this is impossible to prove. The African elephant on the reverse probably refers to the corps of elephants, two hundred strong, the Carthaginian regime kept in Spain.

HANNIBAL'S TREATY WITH PHILIP V

When the gods have granted us good fortune in the war with the Romans, and if the Romans should ask the Carthaginians to make peace, we will make such a peace as will include you.

(Polybius, *Universal History* 7.9.12)

assert Macedonian influence—challenged by earlier Roman interventions—over the Adriatic. Although this intervention resulted in a decade of desultory fighting between the two sides, ending when Rome made peace with Philip in 205, the Romans did not forgive what they saw as an act of treachery. As soon as the war in Africa ended, Rome declared war on Philip, winning a decisive victory over him at the battle of Cynoscephalae in 197 BC. The victory transformed Macedon into a Roman client state, and made Rome into a major player in the politics of the eastern Mediterranean.

Why Did Rome Fight?

The Militarism of the Third Century BC

A state that seeks to dominate its neighbors, destroying or assimilating all in its path, rarely wins points for civility. But why did the Romans do this? In Thucydides's history of fifth-century Greece, an anonymous character declares that imperial states will inevitably seek to expand their empire. It is not clear that Thucydides himself endorsed this idea, though he does seem to have thought that military success and the possession of wealth stimulated a desire among the Athenians to acquire even more. But Athens notoriously failed to acquire a greater empire after 431 BC and lost the one that it had; it was Thucydides's point that unthinking acquisitiveness was one reason for that failure.

The failure of Athens should put the success of Rome into perspective, for, like Athens, Rome was formally a democracy. Roman militarism cannot be attributed to the ego of a mad monarch who drove the state through fear and the inculcation of some perverted ideology of ethnic or moral superiority. At Rome, as at Athens, decisions about war and peace were voted on by the very citizens who would put their lives and property at risk through their verdict. Polybius suggested at one point that Rome conquered the eastern Mediterranean as the result of a "plan." Yet his own narrative shows that there was no plan, and such long-term planning from one generation to the next is in any case impossible in a state that has no permanent government. There was no established general staff, and there cannot be said to have been much of a bureaucracy even after the empire was acquired.

There can be no simple explanation for a phenomenon as complex as Rome's rise to empire. The factors that explain success on the battlefield—the ability to mobilize manpower on a massive scale and a remarkably effective tactical doctrine—do not explain why Rome engaged in war after war; they do not explain why Roman citizens were willing to vote in favor of war; and they do not explain why war was so often preferable to negotiation as the solution to inter-state conflict. Finally, the factors that led to Roman victory cannot begin to explain why some states should choose to go to war with Rome: Philip V of Macedon was responsible for his own troubles with Rome, and it was Hannibal who started the Second Punic War.

Still, Rome did start many of the wars discussed above, and to explain how it was that the Roman people were willing to engage in war after war several factors need to be considered. Among these may be numbered: an aristocratic ethos prone to warfare; greed; a general culture of militarism in the contemporary Mediterranean; and Roman religious ideals.

Silver coin of c. 190–180 BC depicting Philip V, who became king of Macedon in 221 BC. Through a series of military adventures Philip devoted his reign to trying to extend the power of his kingdom, until his army was finally crushed by the Romans at Cynoscephalae. The terms of a subsequent peace treaty with Rome confined Philip to Macedon, where he ruled until his death in 179 BC.

The aristocratic ethos evolved in the second half of the fourth century when nearly constant warfare made military renown a key component in aristocratic competition. Life was short, and the very brevity of existence may have contributed to a desire for a spectacular achievement, the memory of which could be left to one's descendants. It may also have driven men who had reached their forties to feel that there was not much time left, so that they were predisposed to do as much as they could with a high office that, in all probability, they would never hold again.

It is certainly the case that in the Republican era Roman heroes tended to be successful warriors rather than legislators or intellectuals. The inscriptions on the family tombs of the Scipios reveal much about how highly military prowess was valued (see box, opposite). When Scipio Africanus was brought to trial for misconduct on the anniversary of his victory over Hannibal at Zama, he is said to have led the crowd (who had assembled in the forum to watch his trial) to the temple of Jupiter to offer thanks for his own existence and the salvation of Rome. Scipio was not convicted this time, and his remarkable conduct again allows us to see how tangible were the rewards of martial glory.

In addition to the glory that one could bequeath to one's descendants, the Roman aristocrat may not have been immune to a desire for simple profit. Roman generals decided how the booty they won in war would be distributed after the victory. Some would go to the state, some would be given to the soldiers who had fought for them, another portion would go to the officers, and the rest to the general. The victorious general might also have been in a particularly good position to acquire control over a large portion of the land that a defeated state could be forced to surrender. Often he would also use some portion of the spoils to decorate the temple that the senate had agreed to pay for in fulfillment of a vow to the gods, if the campaign proved successful. The temple would then offer a tangible example to others of the benefits that accrued from generals who were at one with the senate and the gods in furthering the interests of the state.

Greed and the militaristic ethos of the governing class may certainly be factors, but they are not, in and of themselves, sufficient to explain why people voted to fight. One further factor may be a sort of "frontier mentality," stemming from the Romans' division of the world between that portion that was "at home" and the rest that was "at war." Rome developed as one state surrounded by others that were not enamored of it. There may have been a basic predisposition to regard all peoples not bound to Rome by treaty as potentially hostile. The basic facts of life on the frontiers of the Roman state may have contributed to a notion that war was necessary for community survival. But that is not all. The community of Roman citizens may have grown used to the notion that victory in war meant a share not only of the spoils among the men who had served, but also of captured land among all Romans. The Roman people twice voted on motions that led to war that the senate disapproved of. One was the decision to accept the *deditio* of Messana, which precipitated the First Punic War in 264 BC. The other was the bill distributing land to Roman citizens in the Po valley in 232 BC: it was proposed by a tribune against the will of the senate and precipitated the invasion that ended at the battle of Telamon.

Warlike as the Romans were, it is important to see that Rome was not the only state given to violence; it is worth looking at the figure of Pyrrhus and some of the circumstances leading up to the First Punic War. Pyrrhus was a relatively important figure in contemporary Greek politics—politics that were complicated by the struggles for power among former generals of Alexander the Great and their successors. Alexander the Great had died in Iraq in 323 BC and the empire he had conquered began to fall apart almost immediately, as several of his generals sought either to carve out kingdoms for themselves, or to seize control of the whole. Pyrrhus, who grew to maturity during the first round of wars, shared the dream of a new kingdom with other ambitious men of his generation, and at the very time the Tarentines appealed to him, he was reeling from the defeat of his effort to grab the old kingdom of Macedon for himself. War in Italy may have appealed to him—as it had appealed to his father, who had died on campaign in southern Italy a half century earlier—as a way of constructing a broader power base for operations in the East. The important

THE SCIPIO TOMB INSCRIPTIONS

As we have already seen, some of the most valuable evidence for the early Republican period comes from inscriptions, which are particularly useful for providing an insight into the values of those who created them. Some of the earliest texts that we have in Latin are inscriptions on the family tomb of the Scipios, the family of the conqueror of Hannibal. One reads:

Lucius Cornelius Scipio Barbatus, descended from his father Gnaeus, a brave man and wise, whose beauty was equal to his courage. He was consul, censor, and aedile among you, he captured Taurasia and Cisauna in Samnium, he conquered all of Lucania and took hostages.

(Latin Inscriptions of the Free Republic no. 309)

Of his son it was said that:

Most people agree that Lucius Scipio, aedile, consul, censor, was good and the best man at Rome. Son of Barbatus, consul, censor and aedile amongst you, this man took Corsica and the city of Aleria, he dedicated a temple to Storms as a result of a vow.

(Latin Inscriptions of the Free Republic no. 310)

Thus the virtue of the second Scipio was enhanced by the deeds of his father, and was itself memorable for a campaign against the Carthaginians in Corsica, whose god, Storms, aided him in the conquest. Of the son of Scipio Africanus's nephew it was said:

Lucius Cornelius Scipio, son of Lucius, grandson of Gnaeus, quaestor and military tribune, he died at the age of thirty-three. His father defeated King Antiochus.

(Latin Inscriptions of the Free Republic no. 313)

Such texts as these bring us into direct contact with the ideology of the governing class.

A burial ground for one of the greatest aristocratic families of Rome, the tomb of the Scipios was begun in the early third century BC and was still receiving new bodies in the first century AD. Something of a tourist attraction in Ancient Rome, it also served as a sort of family museum.

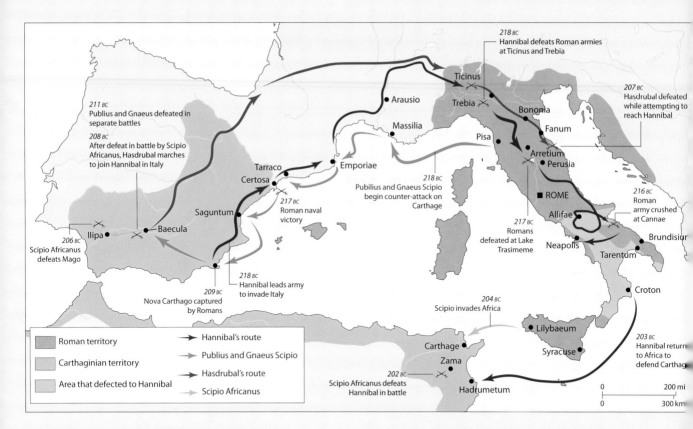

218 BC
Hannibal defeats Roman armies
at Ticinus and Trebia

207 BC
Hasdrubal defeated
while attempting to
reach Hannibal

211 BC
Publius and Gnaeus defeated in
separate battles

208 BC
After defeat in battle by Scipio
Africanus, Hasdrubal marches
to join Hannibal in Italy

218 BC
Pubilius and Gnaeus Scipio
begin counter-attack on
Carthage

217 BC
Roman naval
victory

217 BC
Romans
defeated at Lake
Trasimeme

216 BC
Roman
army crushed
at Cannae

206 BC
Scipio Africanus
defeats Mago

218 BC
Hannibal leads army
to invade Italy

209 BC
Nova Carthago captured
by Romans

204 BC
Scipio invades Africa

203 BC
Hannibal returns
to Africa to
defend Carthage

202 BC
Scipio Africanus defeats
Hannibal in battle

Ticinus · Trebia · Bononia · Fanum · Arretium · Perusia · ROME · Allifae · Neapolis · Brundisium · Tarentum · Croton · Arausio · Massilia · Pisa · Tarraco · Certosa · Emporiae · Saguntum · Ilipa · Baecula · Lilybaeum · Syracuse · Carthage · Zama · Hadrumetum

Roman territory
Carthaginian territory
Area that defected to Hannibal

Hannibal's route
Publius and Gnaeus Scipio
Hasdrubal's route
Scipio Africanus

0 ——— 200 mi
0 ——— 300 km

THE SECOND PUNIC WAR

Hannibal's mastery of the art of war came, in large measure, from his ability to anticipate what his enemies might do and to take advantage of their tendencies. This quality is particularly evident in his massive victories at Lake Trasimene in 217 and Cannae in 216. At Trasimene he was aware that the Roman commander, Gaius Flaminius, was an ambitious politician whose military record was at best ambivalent. Hannibal exploited Flaminius's lack of attention to detail by luring him into an advance along the shores of the lake. Flaminius led his army into the trap, and the Romans were annihilated.

At Cannae, Hannibal was plainly aware that the consuls, Paullus and Varro, had been given an especially large army, which meant that they were expected to take offensive action. When he offered battle on the banks of the River Aufidius, Hannibal did so on a relatively compressed field. This meant that the Romans would have to use an especially deep formation for their infantry—which they did—negating their advantage in numbers, and making them especially susceptible to just the sort of flanking attack that Hannibal had planned, on the assumption that his superior cavalry would defeat that of the Romans.

(Above) The second great war between Rome and Carthage unfolded across the Mediterranean with key battles in Italy, Spain, and north Africa. Among the most important of the war's consequences was the expulsion of the Carthaginians from Spain in 206 BC.

(Below) Hannibal's victory at the battle of Cannae in 216 BC is regarded as one of the greatest tactical achievements in antiquity. Vastly outnumbered, he exploited Roman aggression to emerge victorious.

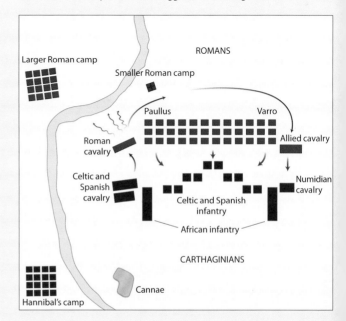

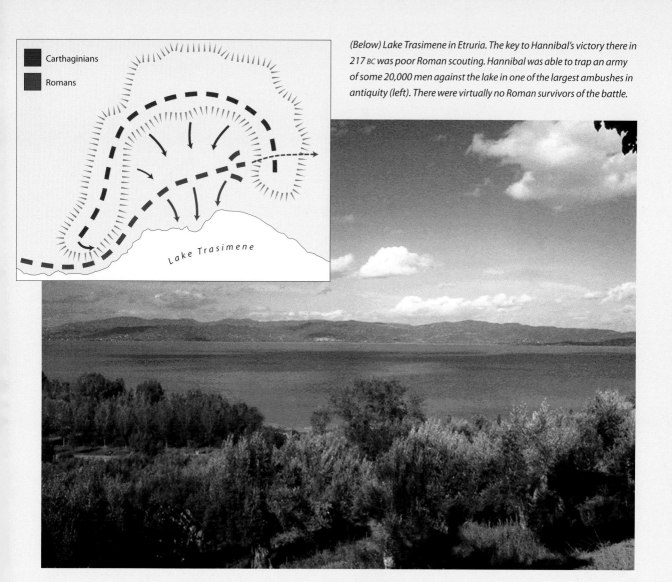

Carthaginians

Romans

Lake Trasimene

(Below) Lake Trasimene in Etruria. The key to Hannibal's victory there in 217 BC was poor Roman scouting. Hannibal was able to trap an army of some 20,000 men against the lake in one of the largest ambushes in antiquity (left). There were virtually no Roman survivors of the battle.

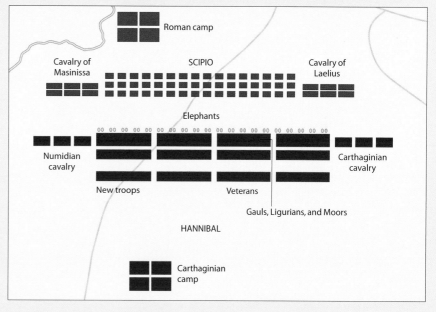

Roman camp

Cavalry of Masinissa

SCIPIO

Cavalry of Laelius

Elephants

Numidian cavalry

Carthaginian cavalry

New troops

Veterans

Gauls, Ligurians, and Moors

HANNIBAL

Carthaginian camp

(Right) In 203 BC Hannibal returned to Africa to defend Carthage from a Roman counter-attack. At the battle of Zama in 202 BC, Hannibal tried to weary Scipio's army by drawing it into action against his elephants and poorer troops while he held his veterans in reserve. This plan might have succeeded had Scipio's cavalry not proved superior to that of the Carthaginians. The Roman horse drove off Hannibal's cavalry and charged to the rear of the Carthaginian battle line, surrounding and destroying the veterans. Hannibal himself escaped the battle.

point here is that Pyrrhus represents a generation of Greek leaders who regarded war as an acceptable tool for the realization of what was essentially a vision of world conquest. Rome was not the only state where empire building was regarded as a legitimate enterprise, and the Roman state was considerably less goal-directed in this regard than were such kings as Pyrrhus.

The events connected with the First Punic War reflect a culture of militarism in a somewhat different way. In a period of intense warfare, such as the fourth and third centuries BC, states may find that their periodic military demands exceed their capacity to meet those needs. There are two possible responses, short of making peace. One is fundamentally to reform the structure of the state in order to mobilize manpower better—effectively the decision that the Roman state made in the 340s BC. The other is to hire professional warriors from somewhere else. This was the choice that the Tarentines made when they appealed to Pyrrhus. The advantage of hiring mercenaries is that a state can acquire "state of the art" soldiers, men who train regularly for war and who may be at the forefront of military developments without having to commit extensive resources to military affairs in times of peace. The disadvantage of mercenaries is that they only fight for as long as they are paid, and they may pursue interests that are different from those of their paymasters. Pyrrhus himself abandoned the Tarentines for several years in the course of their struggle with Rome so that he could fight against the Carthaginians in Sicily. His departure gave the Romans time to collect new armies and train them so that they would be more effective when they met him again in battle in 275 BC.

The Tarentines were not the only people to hire mercenaries, and the employment of Pyrrhus was not their first experience with mercenary armies. They had brought Pyrrhus's father to Italy in 334–331 BC to fight their enemies in southern Italy, and a Spartan general to help them in 304 BC; indeed, the long-term aggression of the Tarentines and their tendency to align themselves with the Samnites may have proved decisive in pushing other states in southern Italy into the Roman alliance. The Greek state of Syracuse had hired mercenary armies earlier and later in the fourth century to fight Carthage, and the Carthaginian army in Sicily was largely made up of mercenaries. Alexander the Great's campaigns against the Persians had resulted in mass mercenary unemployment in the late 320s BC, which created a reserve of manpower that his enemies in Greece employed in a revolt that broke out in 323 BC (and failed two years later). Mercenaries were truly men without a state, living in their own communities between periods of service, and they might occasionally take cities over to serve as their bases. It was just this situation that precipitated the crisis that led to the First Punic War. In (probably) 288 BC the rulers of Messana were the group of Campanian mercenaries who called themselves the Mamertines, "the brotherhood of Mars." It was their example that inspired mercenaries employed by Rome—for even Rome might require the services of such men to garrison areas so that they could concentrate their regular forces elsewhere—to take over the city of Rhegium, opposite Messana on the Italian coast, in 282 or 280 BC (see p. 67).

The widespread use of mercenaries reflects a culture of militarism that extended far beyond the borders of the Roman state. In the Greek world after Alexander, desire to rule the "whole," or the entire empire once controlled by Alexander, appears to have been regarded as a laudable ambition. Skill in war was as much admired and valued there as in Italy. Indeed, the concept of world empire that Polybius attributed

A marble bust of Pyrrhus, king of Epirus. An able general heavily involved in the dynastic wars after the death of Alexander, Pyrrhus transformed his previously weak realm into a powerful state. In 280 he invaded southern Italy but, despite several victories against the Romans, was unable to consolidate his position and withdrew five years later.

ROMAN *FIDES*: ANOTHER VIEW

Hiero said that the Mamertines were rightly besieged seeing as how they had destroyed Camerina and Gela, and they had taken over Messana in complete violation of divine law. The Romans, who always had the word "good faith" (*fides*) on their lips, ought to stay entirely away from these murderers who were utterly contemptuous of "good faith." If they should go to war on behalf of the most impious of men, it would be clear to all the world that they used pity for the weak as a cover for their own ambition, and that they were in truth interested in the conquest of Sicily.

(Diodorus Siculus, *Universal History* 23.2)

to Rome was rather more at home in the Greek world than the Italian in the fourth and third centuries BC. Roman belligerence may thus be seen, at least in part, as a feature of a broader culture of interstate violence.

Finally, there were particular Roman religious ideals, of which the most important in the diplomatic sphere was *fides*. The need to keep faith with an ally under threat could be a powerful argument. States that threatened Rome or its allies were by definition "unfaithful." The justice of Rome's cause in each case could be seen to be proved by success. If the gods were not favorable, then Rome would have lost. This may be the single most important factor of all: success supplied the moral certitude that war was justified, and guaranteed the manifest favor of the gods who routinely supported Roman endeavors.

The prevalence of *fides* in Roman ideology during the third century is perhaps most interestingly revealed in a description of Roman negotiations with Hiero of Syracuse offered by Diodorus Siculus, quoting here from the third-century BC historian Philinus. Philinus's history of the First Punic War had a definite anti-Roman cast, and it enables us a rare glimpse of Rome through the eyes of an enemy (see box, left).

A century later Polybius opens his account of the Second Punic War with an extensive discussion of who really broke the treaty that ended the First Punic War. In this case he reviews all that he feels can be known about relations between the two states, to show that if one regarded the assault on Saguntum as the cause of the war, then the Carthaginians were at fault; while if one felt that the Roman seizure of Sardinia was the cause, then the Romans were responsible (Polybius, *Universal History* 3.30). What emerges from this discussion is not so much clarity with respect to the issues at hand, as the interest that Polybius and his readers had in the question of whether a nation had gone to war for just cause. Again the issue here is, in Roman terms, simply *fides*.

The case with each war is different, and no single cause is sufficient to explain Rome's conduct. Some of the conflicts arose from factors internal to Roman society; others were started by Rome's enemies or waged to avenge actual acts of aggression by outside powers. What is constant, however, is a predisposition by the Roman people to respond to problems with other states with violence.

Technical Prowess

Rome encountered enemies of many sorts during the third century BC, and the capacity of the Roman state to adjust to different military systems made it, by the end of the century, invincible. But Rome was not always superior to its foes, and the wars with both Pyrrhus and Carthage revealed serious weaknesses. Rome's success did not come without enormous loss of life within the Roman community, and Rome had no monopoly on military talent.

At roughly the same period that the manipular legion was developing at Rome, Alexander the Great's father, Philip II of Macedon, conquered Greece by developing a new style of fighting based on lightly armored infantrymen armed with pikes and drawn up sixteen ranks deep in a formation known as the phalanx. The pike phalanx was capable of holding or defeating the old style of hoplite line, and, since its soldiers did not require heavy body armor, Philip could exploit the resources of the peasant population of his realm. He could therefore raise an army that was far larger and more efficient than any other in mainland Greece. His phalanx was supported by a very good force of cavalry and by specialized groups of highly trained light infantry. This army enabled Alexander to conquer the Persian empire, which stretched from western Turkey to Afghanistan, in three decisive battles. The combined arms approach to battle, especially the effective use of cavalry, was thus embodied in the military doctrine of his successors, and it could be supplemented, as it was in Pyrrhus's case, with various add-ons, for example the war elephants that were intended to panic adversaries.

Pyrrhus's army may thus have been technologically superior to that of Rome, based on infantry and employing cavalry as an afterthought. Still, the Roman army fought that of Pyrrhus to a standstill in their first two encounters during 280 and 279 BC. Although technically victorious in that he held possession of the battlefield at the end of the day, Pyrrhus's losses have given rise to the term "Pyrrhic victory," or a victory that is so costly that it is in effect a defeat. In 275 BC, the Romans were themselves able to win a decisive victory at Beneventum. Technological superiority was not enough to win against Roman manpower resources in the long run, and Roman military doctrine proved adequate against the best that the eastern Mediterranean had to offer. This is all the more interesting as Pyrrhus was a professional general who was used to commanding large armies in a way that Roman generals were not. Indeed, Pyrrhus faced three different consular armies, two of which were commanded by men who had not previously held the consulship, and were leading an army for the first time. Individual Roman unit commanders were responsible for the training and discipline of their men, and operations in the field were dictated by strict adherence to a code of conduct that minimized the potential impact of the regular rotation of general officers (see p. 64). The victory over Pyrrhus was thus the victory of a system.

The victory over Carthage may also be seen as a victory of system over technological inferiority. In this case, however, victory was won by a very narrow margin, and in effect came down to little more than the ability of the Roman state to mobilize manpower more effectively than its rival.

When Appius Claudius started the first war with Carthage in 264 BC, Rome had no battle fleet. What ships it did have were drawn from allied states that were required by treaty to provide them when Rome needed them. None of these states seems to have had the main-line battleships of the period—*quinquiremes* and *triremes*—or experience in warfare involving large fleets; the Carthaginians had a huge fleet, and plenty of experience. The only reasons the Romans were able to campaign in Sicily at all were that the straits between Italy and Sicily are narrow, and because it was impossible to mount an effective blockade with oared warships: unable to remain at sea for prolonged periods, these ships crammed too many men into small spaces and were rather unstable (something the Romans would learn to their cost). But what the Carthaginian fleet could do was raid the Italian mainland and resupply Carthaginian forces on Sicily at will. If Rome was to win the war, it needed to defeat the Carthaginian fleet.

The fact that Rome began a war with Carthage without the requisite strategic tool of a fleet is as clear an indication as any that the war was not started as part of any coherent plan of action, and may explain why Appius Claudius was ever after known as Appius Claudius Caudex, or the "blockhead." It is furthermore a sign that Rome had never really taken steps to develop a Mediterranean as opposed to an Italian military organization. The jerry-rigged structure that was put in place to answer the Carthaginian fleet had both the strength of enormous ingenuity, and the weaknesses that stem from inexperience. If the basic structure that Rome had imposed upon Italy had not enabled it to command resources of manpower far beyond those of Carthage, the war would have been lost.

The point at issue very soon became not the ability of the new Roman fleet to fight a battle, but rather the inability of Roman admirals to keep the fleet afloat once the battle had been won. Fleets demanded huge numbers of men: the average *quinquireme* required a crew of 500 men, a *trireme* a crew of 200; a fleet of roughly 200 ships was required to confront Carthage effectively. Even if most of the ships in a fleet were *triremes*, the loss of even 100 ships resulted in staggering casualties. The Romans lost fleets of this size three times, in 255, 253, and 249 BC. The reasons for the losses were the same in each case: Roman admirals, commanding at sea for the first time, sailed into storms.

In battle the Romans were surprisingly effective. After a Carthaginian *quinquireme* had been found washed up on the Italian shore, the Romans had a model for the design of their warships; but realizing that they could not possibly match the experience of Carthaginian admirals, they redesigned the ship by adding a gangplank that enabled their ships to lock on to Carthaginian warships as they approached to ram them (the basic naval tactic of the period). Roman soldiers could then board enemy ships, and, having been placed on ships in far larger numbers than the Carthaginians would have expected, overwhelm them. In the wake of this first victory, the Roman fleet had time to develop, and Roman leaders appear to have had the wisdom to realize that the Carthaginians would not be fooled by the same trick twice. Throughout the rest of the war the Roman fleet fought with traditional tactics, which they seem to have mastered so well that their fleets usually outperformed those of Carthage.

Victory in the war with Pyrrhus and the first war with Carthage may be attributed to the Roman system of alliances in Italy, which made it possible for Rome to sustain losses that would have crushed almost any other state. In neither case can it be said that Roman military organization was superior on the battlefield to that of its opponents, or that its armies were better led. But they were good enough to win through in the end, and the system was flexible enough for the Romans to adopt new tactics as they needed them.

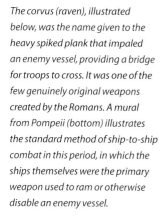

The corvus (raven), illustrated below, was the name given to the heavy spiked plank that impaled an enemy vessel, providing a bridge for troops to cross. It was one of the few genuinely original weapons created by the Romans. A mural from Pompeii (bottom) illustrates the standard method of ship-to-ship combat in this period, in which the ships themselves were the primary weapon used to ram or otherwise disable an enemy vessel.

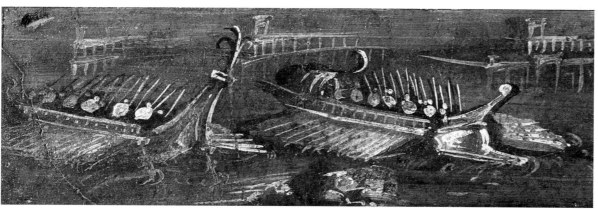

This flexibility was crucial in the war with Hannibal. Hannibal had plainly studied Roman tactics, and he succeeded in inflicting tremendous losses upon the Romans in the opening years of the war. But Hannibal had no great success after Cannae in 216, because the Romans—following the policy of one of Rome's senior statesmen, Quintus Fabius Maximus, "The Delayer"—recognized that Hannibal could be defeated even if he was not beaten on the battlefield. They therefore abandoned their initial strategy of forcing a decisive encounter, as a group of increasingly professional generals, many of them learning their trade from Fabius, took the field. In the meantime, Roman armies proved more competent and were better led than either the remaining Carthaginian forces in Spain or those whom they faced in the minor encounters with Philip V of Macedon.

By the end of the war with Hannibal, the Roman military machine was superior to any in the Mediterranean world. A generation of officers had grown up in those wars, and an enormous fund of experience had been collected that could be drawn upon in subsequent wars against the Greek states of the East. But before we turn to those wars, it is necessary to examine the first tentative Roman efforts to rule provinces outside Italy. The unification of the Mediterranean world would change Rome just as Rome changed those lands that fell under its control.

The Empire: Patrons and Clients

Provinces

Is it conceivable that as Lutatius Catulus watched the last Carthaginian ships surrender or sink off the Aegates Islands in 241 BC, he imagined a brave new world divided into new provinces, each one ruled by a Roman governor? The answer to this question is certainly no. Just before telling the story of the battle of Zama, where Hannibal was finally defeated, Polybius has Scipio Africanus give a speech in which he explains that the consequence of victory will be Roman domination of the "whole." Allowing for the very remote possibility that Scipio ever said any such thing—Polybius was quite capable of making up speeches for characters to stress the major themes of his history—what might his vision of the "whole" look like? Perhaps Polybius's language had betrayed itself here. The concept of the "whole" was a concept that sprang up in the Greek world after the death of Alexander the Great for the area he had once ruled. It had no place in traditional Roman thought.

At the time that Polybius wrote—nearly a century after the victory of Lutatius Catulus—there is no evidence to suggest that the Romans had developed the notion that world domination could be, or should be, the aim of their foreign policy. The language of world domination first appears in the the first century BC, and is given classic expression in Virgil's *Aeneid* as Jupiter promises to give the descendants of Aeneas *imperium sine fine*, "empire without territorial boundaries." Its emergence required that the Romans should first have developed a notion of an empire that actually had fixed boundaries—something that cannot be said to have had much relevance before 82 BC, when the dictator Sulla made it a crime under his treason law for a general to lead his army beyond the borders of his province. What the Romans did have earlier than this was a view of the world that consisted of territory under the direct control of Rome, territory that belonged to subject allies, and territory that belonged to others. The Roman empire that Sulla helped define with his law was one that had provinces with boundaries. In the third century it appears that the Latin word *provincia*, the root of our word province, meant, first, a task assigned to a magistrate, and then the area in which the magistrate exercised his power. It was only in the wake of the war with Hannibal that Rome began to develop a provincial structure. This was very different from the way that kingdoms were defined in the Greek world, and what we can see happening is that the Romans gradually moved away from a system that was based on their previous experience in Italy to one that resembled, to some degree, the system of Greek kingdoms in the eastern Mediterranean.

The Greek kingdoms of the eastern Mediterranean were divided into definable administrative districts known as *eparcheiai* (sing. *eparcheia*) or even, in some cases, *satrapies*, a term descended from the years of the Persian empire. Each *eparcheia* had a governor appointed by a king for what appears to have been an indefinite term of office. The governor might serve until he was needed elsewhere, died, retired, or made a mess out of things. Each administrative district was divided up into civic and tribal territories that would either deal with the governor individually or through a league. Taxes were paid to the king through the governor, and troops were garrisoned throughout the district as the governor saw fit. In order to circumvent the governor's authority, cities or locations might seek patrons who held other important offices in the king's service, or were otherwise sufficiently important in their own right that they might gain access to the king. There might be large tracts of land in a district that belonged directly to the king or that had been given by the king to a favored servant. Indeed, the bulk of land in the empire of the former Persian kings that was not controlled by a city or tribe remained "spear won" land, belonging to the king by right of conquest.

The system of administration in the Greek world is worth keeping in mind as a way of understanding just how the Roman concept of empire began to emerge. The Carthaginian land in Sicily was the first area outside Italy to come under direct Roman rule. At first it was treated as if it were simply another part of Italy. Within this area, some cities were made free allies of Rome, owing no tribute and being allowed to engage in various diplomatic activities so long as they did not conflict with those of Rome. Most cities lost some territory, which became public land of the Roman people and were made liable to tribute payments. There was no governor, and no permanent garrison. The same arrangement appears to have been imposed on Sardinia and Corsica after their annexation in 238 BC, and in Illyria after 229 BC. It was only in 227 BC, when the number of praetors was increased from two to four, that governors were sent to Sardinia and Sicily. This was possibly because the need to adjudicate in disputes between communities in those areas, both with each other and with Roman tax gatherers, had come to require more attention than the existing staff of magistrates (two consuls and two praetors) could provide.

Since Rome did not impose a new system of administration, there is no evidence that there was yet a clear distinction in the Roman mind between land in Italy and land overseas. The fact that no new office (as opposed to new holders of an old office) was created to govern these areas may be evidence that the Roman concept of imperial expansion involved no more than the integration of more territory into the existing system, based on treaties and the concept of *fides*. The Roman overseas empire developed in response to the particular demands of regions taken over from

Carthage. The reason for annexation seems to have been simply to prevent the return of Carthage. It is only in the wake of the Second Punic War that we can see a change, when all the rest of Sicily and former Carthaginian Spain were brought under Roman rule. Spain proved very difficult to govern, necessitating the establishment of a permanent garrison. Otherwise, the most notable feature of the emerging Roman empire is the very low level of government. One consequence, perhaps the most important consequence of the absence of an extensive government structure, was the room that it left for personal patronage.

Patronage

Patronage is an enormously important and complex phenomenon based on personal relationships that exist outside the formal structure of a state. Groups that feel that they have been disempowered under the framework imposed by a state might seek to defend their interests by acquiring a spokesperson from among those who hold power within the state framework. This representative, or patron, is a person who will take an interest in those who seek his aid in return for their support of his interests. On a local level, peasants might seek patrons to protect themselves from landowners, or create local organizations for self-defense against the demands of outsiders. In effect, they create their own informal—but no less powerful for that—administrative structures, with which the authorities must deal.

Bonds of patronage had always been important in Roman society. The Laws of the Twelve Tables had even legislated for the mutual obligations between patrons and clients, possibly institutionalizing bonds that bound less powerful members of *gentes* to a powerful *paterfamilias* within a *gens* in earlier Roman society. The status of a Roman aristocrat depended in large part upon his ability to mobilize the support of large numbers of clients. Struggles between notable aristocrats in early Rome may be seen, in part, as efforts by one man or a group of allied aristocrats to gain clients from others. A man's ability to act as a patron depended in large part upon his ability to hold office, or his personal links with office holders.

The system of patronage inherent in Roman society was exported to the regions that Rome controlled. This is not a particularly surprising development, given that the same patterns of conduct appear to have been commonplace within most Mediterranean societies. What is significant about the spread of Roman patronage is that a shadowy web of relationships between communities and individuals paralleled links between individual communities and Rome.

The first (unwritten) law of the Roman aristocracy was that there should be a rough equilibrium between the most powerful members of the senate. Men whose accomplishments were too great, whose deeds cast those of others into the shadows, needed to be pulled back into line. The aristocracy abhorred the man who obtained clients through some spectacular act that others could not match, a sentiment that created an inherent tension with an ideology that equated worth with achievement.

The acquisition of new territory had the potential to destabilize whatever equilibrium there was in Roman aristocratic society. The aspiring client does not simply seek to make the first Roman who comes along into a patron. Rather, clients tend to gravitate towards those who have the most to offer. An example of the way that this might work is offered by the inscription on a bronze fish discovered in southern Italy, dating to some point between the third and second centuries BC (see box, right).

PATRONAGE AGREEMENT

Through the consensus of the town councilors and of the prefect T. Fa[…] and the whole prefecture of Fundi to make ties of friendship with T. C[…] we hand ourselves entirely and we come into his *fides* in the consulship of M. Claudius, son of Marcus[…].

(*Latin Inscriptions of the Free Republic* no. 1068)

The striking parallel between the language used to describe the relationship between a community and an individual (especially the stress on *fides*) reflects the close amalgamation of private and public power in these years. The expansion of the Roman empire thus led the more powerful members of the aristocracy to become ever more powerful, and acquire more clients. The transformation of the aristocracy into groups of haves and relative have-nots strengthened the division of the senate that had begun to emerge in the wake of the Licinian-Sextian legislation of the fourth century between those whose families had attained the consulship, the *nobiles*, and those whose families had not. Furthermore, while it was entirely possible for a "new man" (a man without an ancestor who had held the consulship in his paternal line) to win the consulship from the fourth century through the first half of the second century, by the first half of the first century this had become virtually impossible. The resources of the *nobiles*, bolstered by clients who had sought their patronage from all parts of the expanding empire, were very hard to beat, and every new acquisition exacerbated the problem.

Taxes

Patronage is a particularly powerful force in societies where the government is weak. At Rome, the structure of government behind the magistrates was virtually invisible. Magistrates had their assistants, but these assistants were not linked to the broader, permanent bureaucracy. Problems that were too complicated for a magistrate to handle on his own were farmed out to private corporations. The privatization of government services is perhaps most obvious in connection with the collection of state revenues—a system which meant that the state would not be able to realize the full amount it might receive from a given tax (see box, p. 86). It had the advantage, however, of allowing the state to know just how much would be available each year, since the specific revenues were guaranteed. It also meant that the state did not have to create a bureaucracy to ensure its ability to collect those revenues: there was no Roman version of the Internal Revenue Service or Inland Revenue. The *publicanus* could profit from the system if he worked with accurate estimates of potential revenue (estimates were usually based on those used prior to Rome's arrival). It was in the interest of the censors to be reasonably flexible with the *publicanus*. If the censors decided that the state should take a bigger cut than the *publicanus* deemed reasonable, the censors might find it hard to get anyone to do the job. It was the taxpayer, or the person renting public land, who could be in trouble.

The rate of taxation within a community was probably set by tradition. We certainly know of cases where the Roman state simply took over preexisting tax structures, and even some cases where taxes were imposed at a lower rate than applied before the arrival of Rome. There was little uniformity from region to region until the overhaul of the imperial tax system in the fourth century AD. But the rate of tax might not always be as much of an issue as either the efficiency with which the tax was collected, or effective surtaxes that could be imposed at random. If a person had to pay a proportion of his grain harvest in tax, the *publicanus* might show up and take it straight from the threshing floor where the grain was separated from the stalk, or he might order the farmer to transport it to an awkward location. In the latter case it might well be worth the farmer's while to bribe the *publicanus* so he did not have to do this. If a person or community could not afford to pay, the *publicanus*

TAX COLLECTION

The Roman state collected taxes either through direct payment from subject communities, or through corporations of tax collectors. The members of these corporations belonged to the equestrian order, a designation that descends from the cavalry force of the archaic republic, and now simply meant people who were admitted to the centuries that had once been reserved for cavalrymen. Those who joined these corporations were also known as *publicani*, and were authorized under a contract that they received from the censors to collect a specific tax or rent, or to provide some other state service (e.g. the supply of tents to the army) for a period of five years.

The corporation that was seeking to win a contract would have to estimate how much revenue it could realize from the tax. It then made a bid to the state, offering to provide a specific amount of money in the course of the contract, and turning over one-fifth of the total each year. If they could not collect enough to cover their bid, then the members of the corporation had to make up the shortfall out of their own pockets; if they collected more than they bid, they kept it for themselves.

might offer a loan (at high interest) to make up the shortfall. Indeed, the opportunity a contract to collect taxes offered for making loans could be every bit as important as the contract itself. The *publicani* became the most important bankers in the Roman world, and their influence was rarely benign.

The individual had little protection against abuse, unless he was very wealthy. Wealthier people, or communities, could only obtain redress by appealing to Roman magistrates. Here again the specter of patronage raised its ugly head. A community with a powerful patron at Rome might be relatively safe, but a community that lacked such assistance had little chance. A Roman magistrate asked to adjudicate a dispute between a community and a company of *publicani* might be influenced by a sense of justice (it happened); but if he was, he had to be ready to deal with the torrent of abuse that would descend from the friends and supporters of the *publicani*. A magistrate might find it easier to listen to the community if the community offered him some further consideration for his decision. A substantial bribe could buy a very nice umbrella with which to deflect the downpour of complaint. Otherwise, a magistrate might be impressed by the power of the community's Roman patron, whom it was even more dangerous to offend than it was to provoke the *publicani*.

The subject communities were not always innocent of wrongdoing themselves. Local magistrates were just as capable of misappropriating funds due to *publicani* as the *publicani* were of trying to get more than was their due. Since the system of patronage opened lines of communication beyond the control of the state, it was open to all manner of abuse. The problem was all the more serious because of the competitive nature of patronage in the Republican system. Under a monarchy, the king was the ultimate arbiter of disputes, and with a certain amount of skill the king could adjudicate between competing interests in the interests of justice. The Roman system lacked the focus provided by the monarch. Disputes were decided in elections and through the courts, both venues where the struggle for personal influence, supported by power gained through patronage, could shape the result. Political power was often more important than the facts of the case. *Fides* was becoming a relative rather than an absolute concept.

The Wars of the Second Century BC

The Defeat of the Macedonian Kingdoms

The consequence of the Second Macedonian War with Philip V of Macedon that followed from 200 BC, upon the end of the Second Punic War, was the establishment of Rome as a power in the eastern Mediterranean. The defeat of Philip was accomplished with the aid of alliances with his rivals in Greece, chiefly the Aetolians, whose league dominated the northwestern corner of Greece above the Gulf of Corinth, and in western Turkey, the home of the kingdom of Pergamon. The war that broke out in 193 BC, four years after the defeat of Philip V, arose from the problems inherent in a series of alliances that were formed for the sole purpose of defeating a single kingdom, and some very profound misunderstandings, on both the Greek and Roman sides, of the obligations that the different parties to these alliances had undertaken.

Our surviving sources are not kind to the Aetolians. Livy, whose account is the most complete that we have, derived his information on affairs in Greece and the East from Polybius. Polybius, whose history is known to us for this period only through quotations in the work of later authors, detested the Aetolians, who, along with the Spartans in the southern Peloponnese, were the principal rivals of his Achaeans. The Aetolians had developed into a power in the late fourth century, as the diverse tribal communities in northwestern Greece developed into cities and formed a league. They had expanded their influence by playing a significant role in the repulse of a Gallic invasion of Greece in 279 BC, and through piratical expeditions throughout the Aegean.

The Achaeans, who were worried by the occasional aggression of Sparta, maintained an ambivalent relationship with the kingdom of Macedon. They joined with the Romans late in the struggle against Philip V, and contributed little to the victory. The Aetolians, on the other hand, had helped Rome in its fight with Philip during the war with Hannibal, and had provided genuine aid to the Roman army throughout the war with Philip that ended in 197 BC. In the final peace the Aetolians had gained very little. The Achaeans, however, gained a great deal. The Roman general who had defeated Philip V left the kingdom of Macedon virtually intact, and then moved to the Peloponnese to assist the Achaeans in the final destruction of Spartan power. This general, Titus Quinctius Flamininus, is a forerunner of later generals who took it upon themselves to dictate the outlines of Roman policy, and only later referred these decisions to the senate for confirmation.

Flamininus's conduct was formally a continuation of earlier practice, but the consequences were very different. Distance from Rome offered greater opportunity for decisive action, and the commands lasted longer. In the wars with Carthage, the Roman senate had become accustomed to extending a general's term in command beyond the term of his magistracy. This process, known as prorogation, was designed to allow for consistency in command, and may be viewed as a military necessity in a period when wars were ever more complicated. But it also meant that generals could exercise extraordinary degrees of patronage. With the expansion of the empire this became all the more serious, as the number of magistrates did not expand to meet new demands. The result was that more men were prorogued in

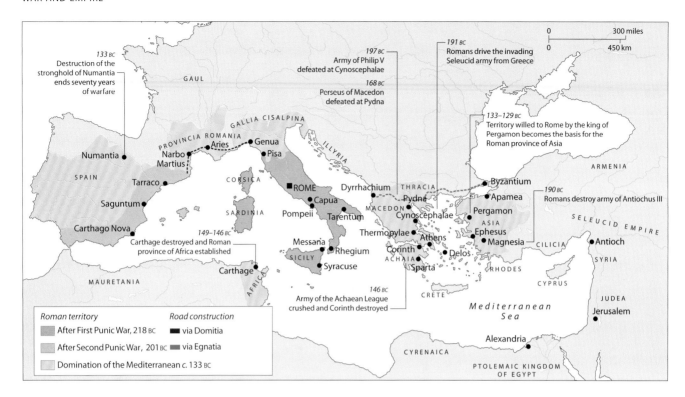

The expansion of Roman power in the second century BC. Victories over Carthage and the kings of the Greek east left Rome the unquestioned superpower of the Mediterranean, but the Romans remained averse to creating new provinces. Before the destruction of Carthage in 146 BC these tended to be established only in places vacated by the Carthaginians, or where peace agreements with client states had failed.

their commands for longer periods, that the pyramids of patronage grew higher, and that the state's control over its generals became less certain.

The best explanation for the failure to increase the number of magistrates is that the only magistracy that could readily be expanded was the praetorship. It was traditional that there could be only two consuls, and there seems to have been no feeling that the old board of military tribunes with consular authority (allowing for a board of as many as six magistrates with the highest power) should be restored. By the end of the third century it had also become traditional (and was soon to become law) to hold the praetorship before the consulship, meaning that an increase in the number of praetors would increase the number of men eligible to be consul. With six praetors, there were already three times as many praetors as consuls, making it more difficult to be elected to the highest office. This situation already worked to the advantage of men from established families when it came to seeking the consulship. There was a great respect for family tradition at Rome, and, of course, the older and more established a family in the highest levels of political power, the greater its base of clients. The political structure of the Roman state could function so long as the playing field was kept relatively even, but by the beginning of the second century, it was beginning to get rather bumpy. The activities of Flamininus set a precedent for others. They also started a new war in Greece.

Even as Flamininus returned home with great fanfare in 194 BC, the Aetolians were looking for an ally to help them overthrow his settlement. They found one in Antiochus III, ruler of the Seleucid empire, which stretched from western Turkey to central Asia and Afghanistan. Antiochus may have been uneasy about the Romans for some time, for the Romans had tended towards alliances with both of his major rivals: the Ptolemaic kingdom based in Egypt (with significant holdings as far north as Palestine, the southeastern Turkish coast, and in the Aegean) and the kingdom of

Pergamon in western Turkey. Antiochus had already made an alliance with Philip V against Egypt in the years before Philip's catastrophic war with Rome, and had aided him in his war (fought in those same years) with Pergamon and the island state of Rhodes. His relationship with Rome had also not been helped by his having given refuge to Hannibal when the latter fled Carthage.

The Seleucid kingdom of Antiochus descended from the realm acquired in the late fourth and early third centuries by Seleucus the Victorious, a general of Alexander the Great, who had managed to wrest control of the bulk of Alexander's empire from various rivals between 311 and 281 BC. The Ptolemaic kingdom was established by King Ptolemy the Savior, another of Alexander's generals, who had taken Egypt as his base after Alexander's death in 323 BC; the kingdom of Pergamon had been established in the chaos that followed Seleucus's murder in 281. Despite losses after the death of the first Seleucus, and under subsequent kings, the kingdom of Antiochus III was the most powerful state in the Greek world, and Antiochus was a natural person to help the Aetolians. He arrived in Greece in 192 BC.

The Roman response to the appearance of Antiochus in Greece was swift and deadly. A Roman army annihilated his expeditionary force in 191 at Thermopylae, and then set about the destruction of the Aetolians. A second army was dispatched under the nominal command of Lucius Scipio, brother of Publius Scipio Africanus, to invade the Seleucid realm. Actual command of the army appears to have been exercised by none other than Publius Scipio himself. Aided by the Rhodians and Pergamenes, the army of the Scipios entered Turkey, and at the very end of 190 destroyed the army of Antiochus III at the battle of Magnesia.

The Peace of Apamea in 188 BC formally ended the war between Rome and Antiochus, and redrew the map of the eastern Mediterranean, depriving Antiochus of all his lands north of the Taurus mountains that form the southern rim of the Anatolian plateau. The consequence of the loss of this important area was to be the gradual dissolution of the Seleucid kingdom. The agent of its demise would not, however, be Rome. Rather, it would be the emergent power of Parthia in northern Iran: shorn of the manpower and financial resources of its western territories, the Seleucid empire fell prey to the geopolitical facts of life in the Near East. For more than two millennia, the area of modern Syria had proved incapable of providing the resources needed to resist a power based in Mesopotamia. Mesopotamia, the land of modern Iraq, was likewise liable to succumb to pressure from powers based on the Iranian plateau. The Seleucid empire had depended for its strength on the ability to mobilize resources from three regions in order to control the Iranian plateau: Syria, Mesopotamia, and the west coast of Turkey. A short-sighted policy on the part of the Seleucid kings, who drew their military forces primarily from Greek settlers rather than from indigenous peoples, made it impossible, in the long run, to stand up to Parthia once the Seleucids were deprived of the resources of western Turkey. Their failure ultimately led to a radical revision of the map of the Near East, which would be divided between Rome and various Iranian regimes until the Arab conquest in the seventh century AD.

Rome created no new provinces as a result of the Peace of Apamea. Instead it handed over extensive territory to its Rhodian and Pergamene allies. They had proved loyal, and, as we have seen, the Roman senate was only interested in creating provinces where they were needed to insure that no enemy could emerge. Loyal client

Antiochus III became ruler of the Seleucid empire after the assassination of his brother, Seleucus III, in 223 BC. Successful in suppressing revolts throughout the empire at the time of his accession, Antiochus took "the Great" as his title, but his military skills proved inadequate when confronting the armies of Rome.

kingdoms could fill this role, their rulers would seek patrons at Rome, and there was no need to strain the apparatus of government further. That apparatus was already strained by the Spanish provinces that had been acquired after the defeat of Carthage.

Spain was not easily subdued. Roman presence upset the balance of power between the local tribes, leading to what the Romans saw as revolt after revolt. The wars in Spain throughout the second century proved challenging. Spanish geography made it very difficult for the Roman army to operate with great efficiency. Large armies could not function easily in the arid regions beyond the major river valleys of the south, and Spanish tribesmen ordinarily refused to descend into the plains to fight set battles where the Romans could annihilate them. Spain thus required a large garrison, and this was a problem. Troops sent to Spain tended not to come home again, making service there extremely unpopular. Furthermore, while the pay of a soldier might be sufficient to allow him to live while on service, there was no insti- tutionalized way to pay for a soldier's retirement. The old system whereby an army was dismissed at the end of a campaign, dividing up the plunder that had been seized from the enemy, was simply inadequate under these circumstances: campaigns went on and on, and the plunder was never very great. Another problem with the traditional system could make the general rather than the state the primary focus of a soldier's loyalty. The soldier's rewards flowed from the general rather than from the government. When troops were regularly being called up and sent home under dif- ferent generals, this was not a major problem. Nor was it an obvious problem, unless one was a serving soldier, when armies were transferred from general to general in a seemingly never-ending cycle. But it was a concern if an army was placed under the command of a successful general who held a command for several years and then returned home at the head of his troops, binding them to him ever afterwards through the distribution of vast quantities of plunder. This could not happen in Spain, but it could, and did, happen elsewhere.

The Scipios returned to Rome before the Peace of Apamea was finalized: Publius faced trial and exile. The case against Publius was particularly interesting, for he was said to have embezzled plunder, thus cheating his own men. These men had not, in any case, returned with him, because the army was taken over by Manlius Vulso, who sought to bind them to him through a campaign of plunder on the Anatolian plateau. More serious may have been Publius Scipio's position within the state. With victories over Hannibal and Antiochus, Scipio was too big a man to be contained within the political system. He was, in the end, a victim of his own success.

Scipio's fate may have been sealed by his preeminence. Manlius Vulso provided a somewhat more attainable model for the average Roman, even though his actions caused some discomfort at Rome. Disagreeable as a human being though he may have been, Manlius understood the system, proving that it was possible to cheat and succeed. In the next couple of decades we hear of several generals who followed the example of Manlius, assailing weak opponents in a quest for glory and plunder. Many of these campaigns took place in Italy, where the tribes of the mountainous northwest, known as the Ligurians, were finally brought under control.

While Roman armies were chasing Ligurians around their mountains, or rav- aging Spanish villages, Rome remained the diplomatic center of the Greek world. Not everyone in the Greek world was particularly happy with the way things were working out. Rome supported its friends, and if local rivalries threatened to work to

Perseus of Macedon was born c. 213 BC, the eldest son and heir of Philip V. As king of Macedon he spent most of his reign developing an alliance of Greek states with which to challenge Rome. After defeat at the battle of Pydna he was deposed, transported to Rome, and paraded in a triumph.

the detriment of those friends, a Roman embassy might show up ordering a return to the preexisting status quo, or ordering the combatants to travel to Rome and explain themselves. It was into this increasingly discontented world that young Perseus of Macedon, son of Philip V, stepped in 179 BC. Perseus was not particularly beloved in Roman society. His younger brother, Demetrius, had been a hostage at Rome for some years, and had acquired a number of powerful Roman friends. After he returned home, Perseus charged him with conspiring against their father, and arranged to have him executed in 180 BC. In the years after his accession in 179 BC, Perseus set about restoring Macedonian influence in Greece, married a Seleucid princess, and generally offered an alternative to those who preferred not to deal with the Romans. By 172 BC this had become intolerable to some groups within the Roman senate, and in 171 BC Rome went to war with Macedonia again. Perseus was defeated in 168 BC, and carried off to Rome where he died in captivity. The Roman senate then decided that it had had enough of the Macedonian kingdom, and divided Macedonia up into four self-governing republics. At the same time it demanded hostages (one of whom was Polybius) from states that had not been particularly dutiful during the war, and took other steps to penalize states whose conduct was regarded as suspect, such as Rhodes. But still there were no new provinces.

The settlement of the war with Perseus lasted for nearly twenty years until, once again, discomfort with Roman control reached a boiling point. In 149 BC a man named Andriscus, claiming to be a son of Perseus, raised the standard of rebellion against Rome in the Macedonian republics. After an initial success, he was defeated and killed. But now the Roman response was more forceful than in the past. All other options having failed, a new province of Macedonia was created. The creation of the new province was accompanied by new orders to the leaders of the Achaean League that they stop trying to force their ancestral enemy—Sparta—into their league. Failing to understand that resistance was futile, or perhaps deciding that life under Roman rule would prove intolerable, in 146 BC the leaders of the Achaean League declared war on Rome. Their army was annihilated, and the city of Corinth, one of the richest in mainland Greece, was destroyed as a brutal lesson in the futility of resistance.

The destruction of Corinth fell in 146 BC, the same year as the destruction of another great city; in the very same year that Andriscus sought the throne of Macedon, Rome provoked a third war with Carthage. The city was besieged for three years, and when it fell, it was destroyed. The territory of Carthage was transformed into the Roman province of Africa. Again, the failure of other options—albeit a failure that was of Rome's making—was the reason for the formation of a province.

The destructions of Corinth and Carthage are emblematic of changes that had been occurring in the course of the previous half century, as the Roman state struggled to get to grips with the consequences of its new status as a world power. Indeed, for students of comparative empire, the Roman Republic had become a classic example of a "conquest state." That is, a state, the resources of which were devoted to the destruction of its neighbors without seeking to build any sort of centralized or coherent bureaucratic structures that would be able to govern new territories. Indeed, Roman behavior became ever more vicious in the decades after the peace of Apamea—and that brought with it new problems. War had now become an absolute necessity for senior politicians, who needed the proceeds of their victories to fund their political careers (or pay back those who had financed them). The Ligurian people of northwestern Italy had been victimized by a series of consular plundering expeditions, all ending in nominal victories and the celebration of triumphs at Rome; the term "Ligurian triumph" gradually passed into common parlance as a phrase designating a minor victory. The conduct of Roman officials in Spain was becoming scandalous: in 150, the governor of Further Spain engaged in the brutal slaughter of tribesmen in the area of what is now Portugal. A survivor of that atrocity, Viriathus, then led a highly organized and successful guerilla war against the Romans that ended (or so he may have hoped) when he compelled the surrender of a Roman army in 140, with the result that the Senate authorized a peace treaty in which Viriathus was named an ally of the Roman people. Two years later he was dead, the victim of an assassination arranged by a new Roman governor, and the wars continued.

At Rome, signs of stress began to appear in the 150s. In 153, for instance, the start of the official year—which had been set as March 1 since some point in the third century—was shifted to January 1, for reasons both practical and ideological. January 1, 153 marked, by a calculation now becoming popular, the end of Rome's six-hundredth year. The change in the calendar, which set the consuls' assumption of office in the midst of a series of winter festivals, also meant that the two men had to find some way to get along before departing for their provinces. A few years later, in the wake of the scandalous massacre that had launched Viriathus's career, the tribune Lucius Calpurnius Piso Frugi passed the *lex Calpurnia de repetundis*, or Cornelian law, concerning recoveries. He established a new standing court as a place to hear complaints of provincial misgovernment, and where people could secure compensation for thefts of money or property by Roman officials abroad. Although the new *quaestio de repetundis*, court concerning recoveries, was little more than a polite gesture—since the senators who formed the jury were loath to convict one of their own—the establishment of a permanent court to hear a specific crime proved to be an extremely important precedent. The number of such courts would expand significantly in the course of the next half century, and the issue of who would sit on their juries would become a matter of intense controversy, once later tribunes passed laws replacing senators with equestrians on these panels. An equally important reform was the introduction of the secret ballot, through a series of laws in the 130s. The first—the *lex Gabinia* of 139—introduced written ballots for elections; the second, in 137, introduced ballots for non-capital trials; while the *lex Papiria* of 131 introduced the ballot for voting on laws. The *lex Papiria* followed rapidly a year in which there had been enormous chaos stemming from the passage of laws proposed by the tribune Tiberius Sempronius Gracchus. Those laws were connected with the use of public land (*ager publicus*), and the final step in Rome's acquisition of the Mediterranean empire.

The kingdom of Pergamon in western Turkey had long been an important Roman ally, and in the year 133, confronted with internal unrest, the last king of Pergamon—Attalus III—died, leaving all royal territory to Rome in his will. The senate was forced to take up the inheritance under a bill passed through the *comitia tributa* Tiberius Sempronius Gracchus. No sooner had the bill been passed than the senate was embroiled in a war that had spread throughout the kingdom of Pergamon. Its instigator was Aristonicus, a man who claimed to be the illegitimate son of Attalus III. Aristonicus acquired some support from the cities of the former kingdom and managed to defeat the first army that Rome sent against him. He had no such luck with the next one. In 129 he was defeated and killed, and Rome established yet another province in the wealthiest region of the old kingdom of Pergamon. This province was called Asia.

The Empire in 133 BC

The acquisition of power did not automatically lead to the creation of more effective administrative structures. In the latter half of the second century BC the characteristic Roman imperial building project was arguably the road. Shortly after 130 work began on the via Egnatia, a road across the Balkans that would link the new province of Asia with the West—Rome elected not to trust its armies to the sea. In 121 work began on another road, this time in southern France, the via Domitia, linking the new colony of Narbo Martius (modern Narbonne) with the city of Arles on the Rhône, and marking the establishment of a new province north of the Alps. It is not improbable that the construction of the two new roads looked back to four great construction projects of the earlier Republic: the via Appia, extended after the end of the Samnite wars in 290 BC to facilitate the rapid projection of Roman force to the south; the two northern roads that linked Rome with the north of Italy in the later third century BC—the via Aurelia on the west coast and the via Flaminia on the east coast; and the via Aemilia, built across northern Italy in the early second century. These roads would seem to be symbolic as well as practical illustrations of a Roman theory of empire, offering physical confirmation of Polybius's point that the Roman empire was conceived of as the area where the Romans could give orders.

But an empire based on roads and instructions was an empire devoid of a purpose that could appeal to its subjects. The result was bitterness and misery, qualities that were abundant around the Mediterranean in the latter half of the second century BC. One of the rare inscribed texts honoring a Roman magistrate that survives from second-century Italy tells us that as praetor in 134, Popillius Laenas restored 900 escaped slaves to their masters in southern Italy. Laenas's action can be seen as a sort of police action in the province within Italy known as "hills and valleys," which was awarded to an official when public safety seemed at threat. But a very different sort of command fell to the consul Lucius Calpurnius Piso when he was sent to Sicily to crush a rebellion the following year (see box, p. 94). The opposition he encountered, and the royal symbols of authority adopted by the rebel leaders, mirrored those of other foes of Rome in the eastern Mediterranean. Andriscus had claimed in 146 BC that he was related to the royal house of Macedon. At about the same time that the Sicilian rebellion broke out, Aristonicus was claiming—possibly with greater justification—that he was the true heir of Attalus III, and allegedly founded a utopian community that he called Heliopolis, or "The City of the Sun."

The reimaginings of kingship in a more perfect and egalitarian world occurred at a time when both the Seleucid and Ptolemaic regimes—especially the Seleucid— were reeling from revolt and, in the Seleucid case, invasion as well. The political order of the century and a half after the death of Alexander had been destroyed by the rising power of Rome, but Rome had, as yet, put nothing new in its place. The fact that there was no guiding principle to Roman expansion other than perceived self-interest meant that the new empire was not replacing the systems of government of the eastern Mediterranean with an ideologically stimulating new regime. Instead, it sent governors whose principal interests were enhancing their own status through

The via Appia, a surviving stretch of which is pictured below, took its name from Appius Claudius, the censor who ordered its construction in 312 BC. The road would eventually link Rome with Brundisium in southeastern Italy, and was a powerful symbol of the new confidence of the Roman state. In the period in which it was built there was no comparable highway anywhere in Europe.

A SLAVE REVOLT

The rebellion in Sicily that the consul Lucius Calpurnius Piso was sent to suppress in 133 BC was perhaps an illustration of the resentment felt by the subjects of the empire. This massive rebellion had broken out in the previous year, centered on the city of Enna. Our prime source for this revolt—Diodorus Siculus, who is here quoting a historian of the first century BC named Posidonius—blames the outbreak on the appalling way that the Sicilians treated their slaves, largely imported from abroad.

Although there is no doubt that slaves played a central role in the initial outbreak, however, the rebellion was not limited to people of servile background. Indeed, we are told that the "common people were not unsympathetic, but rather gloated over" the fate of the wealthy, whose lifestyles they had come to resent (Diodorus Siculus, *Universal History* 33/34.2.48). Once the rebellion had begun, leadership passed to a man from Syria, Eunus, who had been sold into slavery as a household entertainer (he could evidently perform carnival tricks): he now asserted that he had prophetic powers, and took the royal name of Antiochus. His lieutenants included a man called Achaeus (also a frequent dynastic name in the Seleucid kingdom) and another named Cleon, who seems to have been a successful merchant from southern Asia Minor.

This symbolic opposition to Roman rule was symptomatic of uneasiness with the rising power of the empire, which had done nothing to inspire the loyalty that had been felt towards the old dynastic rulers.

war, and promoting peace by supporting vested interests that found their presence congenial. The revolts in Sicily and Asia Minor, while motivated by purely local concerns, nonetheless reflect in their adaptation of Hellenistic symbols the fact that the Roman Republic had yet to offer a coherent symbolic system of representing authority that could replace that of the kings.

The Consequences of Empire

No state can acquire an empire and remain unchanged. We have already seen some problems arising from the acquisition of provinces in the third century, and it is fair to say that these problems were exacerbated by the addition of Africa, Macedonia, and Asia between 146 and 129 BC. But these areas added more than new tribute, new provincial governorships, and the need for new garrisons. Asia and Africa, which were ringed by client kingdoms, required no garrisons, and all were wealthy, urbanized areas, more like Sicily than Spain. The provinces of Macedonia and Asia brought Roman government and Roman patrons ever more deeply into the Greek heartland; their acquisition brought new opportunities to trade, and new links with an ancient culture that Romans seem always to have respected.

Culture

Later Romans, of the second century AD, regarded the Rome of four hundred years previous as a crude, unlettered place devoted to warfare. According to this view, Greek academics changed all this by teaching the Romans how to use Latin in new ways. The view that Roman culture was enhanced through contact with Greece is remarkable not so much because it happens to be somewhat incorrect, but because it asserts that the culture of an imperial power was shaped by that of a conquered people, and because it is a view held by the rulers rather than the subjects. Modern examples of imperialism offer no parallels to the cultural relationship between Rome and the Greek world. Unlike the powers of nineteenth-century Europe, Rome did not seek to export a religion, world view, style of dress, or set of racist attitudes. Rather, Rome assimilated these from its empire.

Despite what some Romans may have believed in the second century AD, the process of assimilation was nothing new to the generation that had conquered Carthage, Macedon, and the Seleucids. Greek culture had exerted an important influence on the tastes of the Roman community from a very early period. Roman gods began to take on the form of Greek gods in the regal period; the early Roman army appears to have been modeled on Greek modes of fighting; and Greek was the language that facilitated communication among the diverse linguistic groups that inhabited the Italian peninsula. The earliest work of Latin poetry that we know of was a translation of Homer's *Odyssey*.

The translator of the *Odyssey*, Livius Andronicus, and his contemporary Naevius, who wrote an epic poem on the First Punic War, are important as the leaders of a new movement in Latin literature. We know that previously Romans had enjoyed a variety of theatrical events, some of them essentially sitcoms, others, possibly, dramatizing events in Roman history. From the end of the first war with Carthage onwards we find quite different Roman dramas, based on Greek plays, with Greek settings, and we have good reason to think that they were popular. Latin literature of all sorts would thereafter be produced in accord with critical canons developed in the Greek world. The production of such work was sponsored by members of the governing aristocracy, people who seem increasingly to have prided themselves on what they saw as their cosmopolitan image.

Fabius's history of Rome, written in Greek, is an exception to the general rule of cultural production in this period. It exists in stark contrast with what was already an identifiable Latin literary tradition and with the expressions of Roman historical consciousness that existed in Latin. Aside from Naevius's poem on the First Punic War, there was also an interesting book (now sadly known only through references in later authors) by a man named Flavius about the Roman calendar. Flavius, a freedman, was an associate of Appius Claudius, and his action was seen as infringing upon the power of the *nobiles*—something that made him so popular that despite his servile origin he would be elected both plebian aedile and tribune in the same year. He established the first chronology of Roman history, taking the foundation of the temple of Capitoline Jupiter as the starting point of the Republican era and seemingly providing a list of magistrates derived from the records of the temple. When the *nobiles* protested his election, he used what must have been considerable diplomatic skills to bring the crisis to an end, dedicating a platform near the *comitium* with an inscription stating that he had done this in the 204th year since the dedication of the temple of Capitoline Jupiter, then believed to be contemporary with the expulsion of the Tarquins.

Flavius's inscription is the earliest—but not the only—sign we have that the Romans did not require written history of the sort that Fabius would write to have a sense of their own history. Fabius himself tells us that a consul of 294 BC had dedicated a temple of "Jupiter the Stayer" just as Romulus had once done (after the battle that broke out when the Sabines came to reclaim their women, whom he had stolen). It seems likely that some of the characters of Rome's earliest history had established places in the public consciousness; for example, there were at this point statues of Horatius and Camillus in the forum. Indeed, one of the things that Fabius seems to have done was to assert the importance of the regal period in Roman history by devoting a good deal of attention to it, before moving on, quite rapidly, to discuss events closer to his own time. His account of the First Punic War is largely known to us through Polybius, and he made the case that the Second Punic War was all Hannibal's fault, pointing out that Rome did not formally declare war until after Hannibal had crossed the Ebro.

Why did Fabius write in Greek? That is not a question that we can answer with certainty, but it is unlikely to be because he imagined that his book would become a runaway success in the Greek world and thus justify Roman policy to outsiders, or to endear Rome to its enemies. Fabius's history seems to have enshrined the importance of aristocratic competition at the heart of its narrative: it was a book by an aristocrat for other aristocrats. The choice of language dissociated history from other popular forms of entertainment—and from such writers as Flavius and Naevius, neither of whom seem to have been especially popular amongst the *nobiles* (Naevius was imprisoned for making a snide comment about the great aristocratic clan of the Metelli). Fabius would be the last Roman aristocrat to write in Greek, and his history seems to have had a good deal less long-term impact than another history that came out a generation later. This history was in Latin, and it was in verse. It was Quintus Ennius's *Annales*.

Quintus Ennius was not originally from Rome. Rather, he was a central Italian who gained Roman citizenship through service in the Hannibalic war. It appears that he came to Rome and was introduced to polite society by a man, the Elder Cato (see p. 98), who was on the verge of becoming a towering figure in the first half of the century. For many years Ennius's fame derived from his Latin versions of famous Greek tragedies. It was only towards the end of his life that he set his hand to his great poem about Rome's history, having at this time discovered a way to make Latin fit into dactylic hexameter, hitherto the meter of Greek epic. What sources Ennius used we can now only guess at, and he seems to have propagated a view of Rome's earliest history that expanded the duration of the regal period enormously; at one point, probably referring to an event around 400 BC, he has a speaker say, "it is now 700 years, more or less, since famous Rome was founded with a divine augury" (*augusto augurio*). The thrust of the poem appears to have been to stress the achievement of the Roman people as a whole, and even though he was not close to the Fabii he was able to praise Fabius Maximus, famously calling him "the man who restored the state by delaying." Although his version of events might at times have offended the pedantically inclined (he gave the province awarded to the consul of 200 BC as Gaul rather than Italy), he gave Romans a thoroughly memorable version of their own history. In so doing, he also made plain his debt to Greece: he opens with an invocation to the Greek Muses and, evidently, with a vision of Homer. In Ennius's vision, to be sophisticated was not to imitate the Greeks, but to learn the ways in which their achievements could be turned to Roman purposes.

Ennius's approach to Greek culture was thoroughly in the mainstream of Roman culture, and with Greek literary forms came new ideas. Rhetoricians with eastern Greek pedigrees began to teach at Rome in the middle of the second century, and doctors with similar pedigrees began to practice there. There is some reason to think

LATIN LITERATURE AND SOCIETY

As literature in Latin begins to emerge in the third and second centuries BC, it is clear that its authors tend to fall into two quite distinct social categories.

Those whom we can identify as the writers of history were men of aristocratic status, as were the authors of published speeches. The leading figures in the development of drama and other forms of poetry were either freed slaves, such as Livius Andronicus and probably the playwright Plautus, or immigrants from other parts of Italy, for example Naevius and Ennius.

Such men were the clients of wealthy senators, and their artistic accomplishments reflected the tastes of their patrons. Latin poetry grew up in this period as an appendage to the aristocratic lifestyle. It is only towards the end of the second century that we find Roman senators turning their hands to various forms of verse, and their teachers tended to be freed slaves or Greeks.

Ennius's *Annales*

Ennius seems to have called his poem the *Annales* (*Annals*) because he organized events on a year-by-year basis, each one opening with the name of the chief magistrates of that year. The poem itself seems to have differed markedly from Fabius Pictor's history not only in choice of language and organization, but also in scope. Whereas Pictor devoted a

The dress and masks of the actors suggests that this third-century AD mosaic, from Sousse in north Africa, depicts a scene from a Roman comedy. Such images as this are evidence of a continuing tradition of performance of Platus's plays, five hundred years after his death.

substantial proportion of his history to the regal period, Ennius put more stress on later events. Three of his poem's eighteen books were about the regal period; the next three he dedicated to the conquest of Italy; three more to the Punic Wars (skipping a detailed account of the First Punic War out of respect for Naevius's poem); followed by three on the defeat of Macedon and early wars in Spain (especially Cato the Elder's campaigns). The final six books dealt with the war against Antiochus (three books), and the most recent wars, ending in 187 BC.

that Greek political theory began to influence Roman attitudes in the later second century, and ideas about what constituted acceptable conduct may have been influenced by Greek moral philosophy. Tastes in art were certainly conditioned by the accomplishments of Greek masters, and a substantial market in the treasures of the East (either plundered or purchased) grew up at Rome.

Greek ideas were often attractive because of their very foreignness. It is telling that plays on Roman themes or with Roman settings seem to have been much less popular than those that were performed in Greek dress, and it is notable that the Roman playwrights Plautus and Terence both openly advertised their debts to Greek authors—they seem to have expected that their audience (and the Roman magistrates who funded the plays) wanted "Greek drama." This interest may have arisen because it was more exciting: certainly, role reversals in Plautus's dramas—with sons and clever slaves fooling strict fathers, love affairs with courtesans, and so forth—were very much at odds with the traditions of the Roman family (see pp. 33–37), suggesting that Roman popular culture was developing a taste for exploring the limits of "traditional values." Nor was it only family values that were challenged on the stage. In one of his plays, the *Amphitryon*, Plautus stars the Greek gods Hermes and Herakles, or, in their Roman garb, Mercury and Hercules. The pantheon of the Roman state had long since been transformed into one with anthropomorphic divinities on the Greek model; and recently founded festivals were thoroughly "modern" in their inclusion of theatrical events, chariot races, and the like. The ludi Apollinares and the Megalensia, for example (the latter celebrating the goddess Cybele, a Greek adaptation of an Anatolian goddess), were both created as the result of oracular instructions in the course of the Hannibalic wars. These events did not mark the limit to the interest in non-Roman forms of worship, however. In 186 BC a major scandal erupted when it was "discovered" that members of the lower classes were turning to the worship of the god Bacchus according to secret rites at night. This was anathema to traditional Roman mores, which dictated that group consultation of the gods be a public event. The language of the subsequent decree of the senate—the earliest senatorial decree that has survived in Latin—reflects precisely these concerns (see box, right).

The decree concerning the devotees of Bacchus is by no means the only example of studied ambiguity with respect to things Greek. At the same time, the very word "Greek" seems to have become synonymous, in the rhetoric of Romans who assumed the mantle of cultural conservatism, with all that was avant-garde and therefore suspect. This is perhaps no more evident than in the oeuvre of the Elder Cato (so called because his great-grandson—known as the younger Cato—was a prominent politician in the middle of the next century). The Elder Cato was born in 234 BC at Tusculum, and is a representative of the non-traditional aristocracy that had been moving into the hierarchy of the senate from Latium and some other portions of west central Italy in the course of the third century. Serving with distinction in the Hannibalic war, he rose to the consulship in 195, and, despite celebrating a triumph for victories in Spain during his consulship, agreed to serve as a military tribune in the army that campaigned against Antiochus III in 192. In this campaign he played a major part in the Roman victory at Thermopylae in 191 because he was able to locate the path around the pass that had once been used by the Persians to outflank the Spartan force that had defended the same spot in 480 BC. In 184 he held the office of censor.

Knowledgeable as he was about Greek history (it is interesting that neither the Scipios nor Antiochus realized the possibility of repeating the Persian attack before he did), Cato's career was marked by extreme public xenophobia, or fear of anything foreign. In the year of his consulship, for instance, he attempted to prevent the repeal of a law limiting expenditure by women that had been passed in the course of the Hannibalic war, on the grounds that it would promote lax morality (represented by expenditure on Greek luxury goods). Despite his service with the Scipios (against both the Carthaginians and Antiochus), he launched vicious attacks on them and others for overt affection for non-Roman customs. Indeed, much of his domestic political career was also tied up in legal cases: he used the courts as a venue in which to assail his political rivals, often on charges that might be connected with lack of "traditional" moral rigor in their lives. He also seems to have disliked Greek doctors and rhetoricians.

Yet at the same time that he was championing an archaizing vision of Roman morality and assailing agents of "modernity," Cato wrote the first major prose history of Rome in seven books—the *Origins*—in a format that was plainly modeled

BACCHANALIA PROSCRIBED

With reference to the Bacchanalia, the senators advised that the following be proclaimed to those who were allies of the Romans: let no one of them plan to hold Bacchanalia in his house. If there are any who maintain that it is necessary for them to hold Bacchanalia, they should come before the praetor *urbanus* in Rome. And then, when their arguments have been heard, our senate shall make the final decision about these matters, as long as there are no fewer than 100 senators present when the matter is discussed. Let no man, whether a Roman citizen or a Latin, or one of the allies plan to associate with a Bacchant woman unless he has come before the praetor *urbanus* … Let no man be a priest. Let no man or woman be a deacon. Let no one plan to establish a common fund … Let no one plan to hold cult ceremonies with more than five men and women present as participants.

(*Select Latin Inscriptions* no. 18)

on contemporary Greek scholarship on city foundations, turning traditions he purported to despise to his own advantage. His other major work, a book on farming, is somewhat different in that it both offers practical advice on farm management and asserts that:

> The bravest men, and staunchest soldiers come from farmers; their occupation is most highly respected and their livelihood is most stable and is viewed with the least hostility, and those who are occupied in this way are least given to revolution.
>
> (Cato the Elder, *On Agriculture,* preface, 4)

A maze of seeming contradictions—on the one hand worldly and sophisticated, on the other bigoted and deeply conservative; deeply committed to preserving the social order, yet a new arrival in that order—Cato sums up in his own person many of the cultural contradictions of the Rome of his day. He died in 149, just as his final policy initiative, a war to destroy Carthage, had finally borne fruit.

Italy and the Empire

The development of Roman tastes was not simply a function of the arrival of more Greeks at Rome. Romans and other Italians were themselves going east in greater numbers. To the Greek resident of a city like Athens, an Italian was virtually indistinguishable from a Roman citizen. There is some reason to think that the problems that were beginning to emerge between Rome and its Italian subjects—and which would burst into flames in the early first century BC—were enhanced by the realization on the part of Italians that they were much better treated in the East than at home. At home they were subjects of Rome. In the East they were members of the people who had conquered the world and mingled with Roman citizens without any obvious differentiation of authority. The creation of the provinces of Asia and Macedonia had opened the eastern Mediterranean up to traders from Italy as never before. Groups of Italians and Roman traders spread eastwards as well as westwards, seeking new opportunities for profit (see box, p. 100).

Significant changes were also taking place in Italy, albeit somewhat unevenly. Legal texts reveal a land dotted with all manner of different forms of settlement, ranging from larger cities, for example Capua or Tarentum, through medium-sized towns to much smaller settlements, such as the prefecture of Fundi (see p. 84). Archaeological evidence suggests that the basic form of settlement in the countryside remained the small farm, and indeed that the density of peasant occupation in the countryside had increased since the unification of the peninsula. Other archaeological evidence suggests that regional differences in terms of wealth and culture were becoming more pronounced. Thus the region extending from Campania along the Bay of Naples to the south, to the southern area of Etruria north of Rome, and into the western slopes of the Apennine mountains to the east, was experiencing a major economic boom. Individuals living in the cities in this region appear to have become extremely wealthy: one late second-century BC house in the city of Pompeii was larger than the royal palace occupied by the king of Pergamon before his demise in 133. The cities themselves were sprouting temples and forums modeled on Roman originals, and stone theaters that may have mimicked wooden adaptations of Greek theaters at Rome.

DELOS AND THE ARCHAEOLOGY OF MEDITERRANEAN TRADE

While the Roman aristocrats who provide the bulk of our written evidence were willing to discuss activities central to their own lives, such as farm management, they were loath to describe the activities of others in any detail (Roman senators were banned from any direct involvement in trade). We are thus dependent upon archaeology to supplement the record, and for the second to early first centuries BC, one of the most important sites is the Greek island of Delos, home to what was perhaps the greatest Italian trading community of the period. Here excavation has revealed a new market place that developed in the latter half of the second century, along with houses occupied by wealthy immigrants from the West, and some hybrid portrait art, which is interesting, if of doubtful aesthetic value.

Some would suggest that the place specialized in the slave trade—one Greek author stated that some 10,000 slaves a day were shipped through Delos—but that seems to be false. Given the fact that the total population of the Mediterranean was probably somewhere between 40,000,000 and 50,000,000 people, such a number would suggest that more than 7 percent of that entire population was shipped through Delos each year!

In fact, the merchants of Delos seem to have dealt in a wide variety of products, illustrative of an increasingly large market for luxury goods throughout Italy. The archaeological record of Italian communities at this period, at least with regard to large-scale public building projects, suggests that the peninsula as a whole was wealthier than ever before.

(Top) The marketplace at Delos. Constructed around 100 BC, and consisting of a collection of shops arranged around a central court, it appears to have provided a social center for the local population of Roman and Italian merchants.

(Left) A striking feature of the art on Delos is the way that idealized Greek forms were combined with Roman "realism." In this statue an ideal body is combined with the face of an older Roman.

Outside this central economic zone, and encircling it from northern Etruria through the central Samnite lands, there are fewer signs of obvious prosperity, though there are some indications that places were beginning to adopt Roman tastes in urban planning. Northern Italy and the east coast of the peninsula at this time show little sign of overt connection with Roman tastes and habits. The evidence from language (chiefly offered by inscriptions) suggests that Latin was becoming more common in everyday usage, but that the pattern of its usage was extremely uneven, and that the rise of Latin might have inspired something of a backlash: we have some texts, for example, inscribed in the Roman way on bronze and in the Latin alphabet, but written in Oscan, the indigenous language of the west coast. These documents—which include a religious text and a municipal code—look as if they may reflect an effort on the part of people in these areas to assert their own traditions, while, at the same time, using Roman tools to do so.

If the development of a unified Roman culture in Italy was uneven (as might be expected, since the adaptation of Roman forms was a matter of local choice), evidence for economic improvement is even more so. Although the wealth of Italians was increasing, especially in the central zone, it paled by comparison with the wealth concentrated in the highest echelons of the aristocracy. The average Roman or Italian participated only indirectly in the evolving culture of the aristocracy. The great luxury of aristocratic houses stood in stark contrast with the dismal poverty of the average city dweller. The language of the aristocrat, the cadences of his speech, and the style of his life all came to mark him apart from the man who hauled grain from the barges on the Tiber to granaries in the city. Inhabitants of Italy east of the Apennines, who were not benefiting nearly so much as those on the west coast, were still living in conditions that had changed little since the period of the Roman conquest.

By the time Tiberius Gracchus compelled the senate to accept the territory willed to Rome by the king of Pergamon in 133 BC, the Roman people had already begun to show signs of rebellion against a political order over which their control seemed to be diminishing. Several times in the two decades before this, consuls had engaged in fierce fights with tribunes over the conduct of the military levy, especially when troops were being dragged off to fight in Spain, from which they did not soon return (unlike their commanders). The benefits of conquest could be seen in the fortunes of others, but were not enjoyed by the average peasant or city-dweller. The distribution of the goods of empire was precisely the issue that Gracchus raised.

Slavery

The issue that Tiberius Gracchus raised was land. In a series of brilliant speeches—assuming that our much later source for his statements, the biographer Plutarch, is correctly reporting a second-century BC tradition—he argued that the peasants whose virtues had won the empire had been driven from their land. Rome was no longer what it had been, and the only way to restore its moral virtue was by returning a self-sufficient peasantry to the fields of their ancestors. The peasants' land had been taken from them by rich profiteers who had filled the countryside with gangs of slave laborers. Tiberius's brother, Gaius, later wrote that Tiberius was moved to propose the redistribution of public land by his journey to Spain a few years earlier. Gaius claimed that Tiberius had not seen a single free farmer the whole way through Etruria.

Tiberius Gracchus must have been lying (if this is indeed what he said). Etruria was sufficiently well stocked with peasants to provide numerous armies for the civil wars that convulsed the Roman world in the first century BC (see pp. 108–10). That said, impressions are often far more important than reality, and Gracchus's claim that Rome was no longer what it once was resonated throughout Roman society. He had first-hand experience that may have led him to think this way, for he had negotiated the surrender of a consular army to the inhabitants of the Spanish city of Numantia in 137 BC, and Numantia was still resisting Roman armies under the command of Gracchus's brother-in-law, Scipio Aemilianus, who had been responsible for the destruction of Carthage. How could it be that the great power that had humbled the mightiest kingdoms of the Greek world, defeated Hannibal, and destroyed the naval power of Carthage, was now incapable of taking a single city in the hills? The actual reason has a great deal more to do with military incompetence than anything else, but that is beside the point. Gracchus had transformed the issue of the war in Spain into one about Rome's national character. The images that he employed—the virtuous free peasant versus the slave—may owe something to Greek philosophy, in which the self-sufficient farmer was held to be particularly virtuous, and a society dominated by slaveholders had destroyed the class to which it owed its strength.

Even if Tiberius Gracchus was overstating his case, was there not some fire behind all his smoke? If so, then the most important result of the acquisition of empire was to transform Italian society into one of the few in history that may be described as being based on a "slave economy," one where slave labor is the basic means of production. Was Italy during the second century BC a place where slave labor was the basic means of production? In a world where some 80 percent of people lived in the countryside, producing a surplus that could support the remaining 20 percent of the population that lived in cities, this would mean that slaves made urban life possible. Such an extreme view is probably not valid, though slaves did play a role in a reformed rural economy that was beginning to be dominated by very large landholdings. The most likely structure of these landholdings was that a villa belonging to a wealthy family occupied the best land on the estate, and farmed some of it directly. The rest of the land was then rented out to tenant farmers. Slaves would staff the villa in sufficient numbers to maintain productivity throughout the year, while free seasonal laborers would be employed at critical times, such as during the harvest.

The decline in the status of the peasantry was thus arguably from freeholder to tenant, rather than, as Gracchus would have it, from freeholder to homeless person. But even this view of earlier conditions may have been a little rosy, for we know that there were large classes of subordinate tenant farmers in areas of Italy (Etruria, for example) before the Roman conquest, and the history of the early Republic is filled with crises arising from rural debt. The big change was probably not so much in the status of peasants, but rather in the size of the estates held by individuals, and this might have given the impression of a rural economy dominated by slaves. At the same time, a decline in the size of the Roman army was leaving more young men on the land, quite possibly creating a sense of underemployment.

Slavery was intimately connected with the aristocratic lifestyle. The slaves who lived on country estates represented only a portion of the slaves held by a wealthy family. The majority were most probably held in cities. They provided the staff in

TIBERIUS GRACCHUS AND LAND

The poor, having been driven from their land, no longer showed themselves eager to serve in the army, and had no care for raising children, so that soon Italy appeared to suffer a dearth of free men, and was filled with barbarian slaves, through whose labor the rich cultivated the land.

(Plutarch, *Lives of Tiberius and Gaius Gracchus* 8.4)

the great houses of the wealthy, and performed important services within the urban economy. It was not uncommon for a Roman master to use slave agents to engage in various commercial activities, ordinarily on terms that would permit the hardworking slave to purchase freedom after a period of years. The Romans appear to have freed a large proportion of their slaves. This was a highly effective method of control, as it gave the slave some hope that good conduct and obedience would lead to freedom. Freed slaves became Roman citizens, though they were expected to remain clients of their former masters, and the urban population of Rome appears to have had a high proportion of ex-slaves as a result of this habit. Slaves who possessed special skills or could be taught to do interesting things were especially valued as investments: they might become actors, secretaries, confidants, cooks, business managers, or teachers.

The lot of the Roman slave might therefore be quite comfortable, leading to freedom and a decent income. It could also be absolutely appalling. Slaves who worked in the countryside were little valued, possessed minimal skills, and were readily replaceable. Their diet was poor, and it seems that they were often kept in chains. The slaves who occupied favored positions in the household were a minority. Slaves were sexually available to their masters at any time, and we have no reason to think that rape was an uncommon experience. Slave punishments were brutal. Slaves whose masters were displeased with them could be flogged, tortured, or crucified. It was generally assumed that the only way to get the truth out of a slave was to beat him or her, and when slaves were called upon to give evidence in court, it was always under torture. No matter how much influence a slave might have with a master, that influence could suddenly vanish forever. The threat of brutal treatment and general uncertainty about one's standing in the household was made even more psychologically traumatic by the fact that attempts by slaves to please their owners were interpreted as markers of a "slave nature." This was, in the eyes of the Roman master—who had inherited the Greek notion that a slave was a "tool that talked"—a sign that a slave could never truly be a real person. A freed slave was still a slave at heart.

The only constraint upon a master's conduct towards slaves was concern for the opinion of other free people, male and female. A man or woman who showed too much anger at slaves, who willfully mistreated them, was somehow flawed. But of course it did slaves little good to imagine that the person responsible for their torment would be less well liked by someone as a result of their flogging or crucifixion. The slave had no legal recourse, no actual protection from a master's whims. This basic fact of slave existence may have prompted some Romans to realize that slavery could corrupt the character of the master every bit as much as it did that of the slave. It may be that such notions, also current in Greek moral philosophy of the second century BC, made the rhetoric of Gracchus resonate with the force that it did.

The ideas and career of Tiberius Gracchus reveal a society that was beginning to be at war with itself. The unity of the Roman community was disintegrating in the later second century BC. The Romans had acquired an empire; some had learned to profit from it, but the effective government of that empire was beyond the structures that had served the Roman community in the past. The destruction of the Roman form of government and the transformation of the Mediterranean community under the rule of a monarchy were the consequences.

SLAVERY AND THE RURAL ECONOMY

Be a good neighbor; do not let your slaves commit offenses. If the neighborhood sees you as a decent soul, you will sell your produce more easily, you will make your contracts more easily, you will hire seasonal workers more easily; if you build, the neighbors will help with their work, their teams and material …

(Cato, *On Agriculture* 4.2)

Others divide the tools of cultivation into three parts: articulate tools, inarticulate tools and non-verbal: the articulate are slaves, the inarticulate are oxen, the mute are items like the plow.

(Varro, *On Farming* 17.1)

Summary

● Roman expansion in Italy had its roots in diplomatic structures that emerged in the course of dealing with its Latin neighbors—especially the revised system of alliances that emerged after the crushing of a Latin revolt between 340 and 337 BC. The new structures included bilateral treaties between Rome and cities that had surrendered, and the creation of new forms of semi-citizenship that enabled the spread of Roman communities. These changes enabled Rome to better exploit the manpower resources of defeated states.

● Another important factor in Rome's successful conquest of Italy was a major reform in the Roman army in the mid-fourth century BC. Earlier hoplite tactics were abandoned in favor of new formations of more lightly armed infantry. These made the army both better on the battlefield and better able to use the available manpower.

● The question of why Rome fought is a complex one. The Mediterranean world as a whole was extremely violent. Rome did not initiate all the wars it fought, but as in many other states, internal factors drove Rome towards aggressive responses, including simple greed, an aristocratic culture in which men sought validation through warfare, and a powerful sense of self-righteousness.

● Three wars in the course of the third century BC mark the emergence of Rome as a Mediterranean power: the war with King Pyrrhus (281–275), and the two Punic Wars with Carthage (264–241; 218–201). In all three the Romans faced serious disadvantages. Pyrrhus was a professional soldier with an experienced professional army. Carthage at the time the first war began had a massive war fleet, Rome had none; and in the Second Punic War, Hannibal was a military genius. Rome's ability to exploit the superior resources of Italy enabled it to overcome these difficulties.

● As the Roman empire expanded around the Mediterranean, it did not have a well-developed administrative system. Only in areas where the Romans feared that Carthage might return did they establish new administrative structures—in Sicily, Sardinia, and Corsica after the First Punic War, and Spain after the second. Even the small number of provinces created in this way strained Rome's administrative resources.

● To control their empire the Romans tended to rely on the sorts of patronage relationships that existed in Italy. Although they succeeded in destroying their enemies, the Romans failed to create cohesive structures to replace those they had demolished. At the same time, patronage greatly enhanced the influence of the most powerful groups within the senate at the expense of others. Economic expansion also tended to be uneven, benefiting the most powerful and leaving the less powerful almost as they had been.

● The third and second centuries saw significant changes in Roman literary culture, with new poetic forms being borrowed from the Greeks and the earliest histories to be written by Romans appearing first in Greek and then in Latin. This was also the golden age of Roman comedy, represented by the works of Plautus and Terence.

● The end of the second war with Carthage established Rome as the most powerful state in the Mediterranean and embroiled it in conflicts with eastern Mediterranean states. Rome defeated the major powers of this region, including Philip V of Macedon, in a rapid series of conflicts, but did not establish new provinces in the East. Instead it maintained its traditional diplomatic stance of returning territory to defeated peoples in return for their continued loyalty. Only after 146, when Rome destroyed both Carthage and Corinth (the latter as part of wars in Greece begun in 149), did Rome begin to expand provincial administration to the east and south, creating provinces in north Africa and Macedonia, and in 133 in western Turkey.

● Unrest began to develop after 146 in both Italy and other areas: Rome provided no ideological replacement for the destroyed powers of the Hellenistic world, and people began to sense a decline in Roman society's well-being. Tiberius Gracchus blamed the malaise on slavery, whose growth and impact he grossly overemphasized.

The
Failure
of the
Roman
Republic

(133–59 BC)

TIMELINE III   THE FAILURE OF THE ROMAN REPUBLIC

The Beginning of the Crisis	**133 BC**	Tribunate of Tiberius Sempronius Gracchus; Scipio Aemilianus destroys Numantia
	123–122	Tribunates of Gaius Gracchus
	119	Scordisci defeat Roman army in Macedonia
	116	Jugurthine problems begin in north Africa
	114	Scordisci defeat Roman army in Macedonia
	113	Cimbrians defeat Roman army in Gaul
	112	Jugurtha massacres Italian community at Cirta
	111	Jugurtha defeated, brought to Rome, and released
	109–108	Metellus campaigns against Jugurtha
	108	Cimbrians defeat Romans in Gaul
The Age of Marius	**107**	Consulship of Marius, who takes command against Jugurtha; Helvetians defeat Romans in Gaul
	106	Birth of Marcus Tullius Cicero; birth of Gnaeus Pompey
	105	Jugurtha captured; Cimbrians and Teutons defeat Roman army at Arausio
	103	First tribunate of Saturninus
	102	Marius defeats Teutons at Aquae Sextiae
	101	Marius defeats Cimbrians at Vercellae
	100	Second tribunate of Saturninus; birth of Julius Caesar
The Social War and Sulla	**91**	Tribunate of Livius Drusus
	91–88	Social War
	89–85	First Mithridatic War
	88	Sulla marches on Rome
	87 BC	Rome captured by the armies of Cinna

▼

I N 133 BC TIBERIUS GRACCHUS transformed the practice of politics at Rome, by asserting two basic principles. The first was that the Roman people controlled the *res publica*, and could pass bills governing the state even if the senate had not voted to support those measures. The second was that the property of the *res publica* should be used for the welfare of the Roman people as a whole. The crucial debate that would come to dominate Roman society would be the limits, if any, of popular sovereignty at Rome. The way Gracchus framed this question injected a new level of violence into the ways that Romans dealt with each other, and, ultimately, with the other inhabitants of Italy. It also began to change the stake that the Romans had in their empire. The empire in 133 was still an entity that had very little organization. By 59 BC, it had expanded enormously in size and complexity. It had also become the regular staging ground from which a series of ambitious politicians could dominate the state. The last in that series, Julius Caesar, would hold the office of consul in 59 BC, and in that year acquired the provincial command that enabled him to bring the traditional government of the Republic to an end.

The transformation of Roman politics was swift indeed. At the beginning of the period, in 133 BC, a relatively small number of noble families still feuded for influence with the people, as they had throughout the preceding centuries. By 100 BC, however, the situation had changed so that popular passions drove the agenda of an increasingly broad political class. The acquisition of the provincial empire had not only expanded opportunities for some Roman aristocrats to acquire vast personal fortunes, and caused resentment among others who felt that they were cheated out of their just rewards, but it had also expanded the range of potential adversaries.

The destruction of Carthage and the effective elimination of the Greek kingdoms of the eastern Mediterranean as powerful political entities meant that adversaries of Rome now tended to be the tribal peoples of Spain and western and central Europe, as well as residents of emergent states in Africa and Asia Minor. These groups had not participated in the urban culture of the Greek-influenced world and tended to be less amenable to the traditional mode of Roman control based on cities. At the same time they tended to engage in forms of warfare that rendered the traditional Roman "big battle" style of campaigning less effective. In an ideal world, this would have led the Roman army to change the way it fought, and its commanders would have learned how to command in new ways. But in the absence of any sort of centralized staff or command system there was no structural way to make sure that this happened, and it appears that by the end of the century each new general was training his army in the way that he thought best.

The coincidental result of the demise of "big enemies" was that the Roman state—again this is often the case with empires—created for itself new sorts of rivals. Some of these rivals existed in the first instance because they had become regional powers after supporting Rome against earlier enemies, or through filling political vacuums left by those enemies. Some of these new opponents came to despise the Romans for standing in the way of their regional ambitions; others would come into contact with Rome because the polities that would have stood as buffers between the Romans and these peoples had been so badly destabilized by the Romans that they could no longer resist the newcomers. It is scarcely surprising that in the decade after the Romans quashed the major Celtic powers along the Rhône valley of central France, powerful new enemies would move south from Germany, bringing destruction on a scale comparable to that caused by Hannibal.

In addition to changing conditions on the battlefield, the disappearance of old enemies had a number of other significant consequences, not least the shrinking of both the army and the navy (see box, below). The reduction in the size of the Roman military is important because the army was essentially a large public works project, capable of sweeping up excess population from the countryside and giving it employment elsewhere. Although military service was rarely a popular option—and became decidedly less so as wars in Spain seemed to drag along endlessly—it remains the case that the state was providing less employment than it had in the first half of the second century. Additionally, large-scale settlement of Roman citizens into new colonies around Italy appears to have come to an end in the course of the 170s. While such foundations had begun tapering off in the course of the third century, there had been an upsurge in settlements after the Hannibalic war and in the wake of campaigns in northern Italy. Since colonial projects had offered members of the Roman community a fresh start in new locations, they seem to have been generally popular both with potential colonists as well as with the *nobiles* charged with founding the new colony, which would be linked to their families through bonds of patronage. As with the reduction in the size of the army, the end of colonization does not appear to have been the result of any coherent long-term plan. Rather it may have been the case that vested interests around the Italian peninsula were working against such settlements for two reasons. Firstly because colonies seem to have been extremely unwelcome in the areas where they were founded—the Gallic wars in the 220s, for instance, had been sparked by the foundations of Cremona and Piacenza to the north and south of the Po river, which ran through the heart of Celtic northern Italy—and secondly, because members of the nobility were unwilling to grant an opportunity for their colleagues to exercise substantial patronage (each colony would be set up by a board of three men).

It is true that few Romans, if any, seem to have put their finger on the nature of the problem. But there is no doubt that discontent seethed, and that the focal point

THE DECLINE OF THE MILITARY

The decline of Rome's old adversaries had dramatic consequences for the Roman military. First, it eliminated the need for a significant fleet. In the course of the Second Punic War, the Roman navy had kept between 120 and 180 mainline warships in commission, requiring between 48,000 and 72,000 men each year. In the first half of the second century BC the fleet shrank to around 60 ships, and was essentially demobilized after the fall of Carthage in 146.

The second consequence was that the army also decreased in size. For the Second Punic War (218–201 BC) the Roman state had deployed somewhere around 120,000 men each year (half of them Roman citizens, the other half Italian allies). The number did not shrink in the course of the next half century, as the total annual employment of Romans and Italians (the latter now employed in a 2-to-1 ratio to Roman citizens) ranged from roughly 100,000 to 150,000. In the years after 146, however, average employment fell to between 100,000 and 120,000 each year, and the roughly 20,000 men employed by the fleet ceased to be employed at all. Since the average term of service approached 10 years for young men between the ages of 18 and 34, this meant that recruitment fell in proportion to the decrease in the size of the army.

of that discontent was in the younger male population. What did the state owe its people, and were they not, in theory, sovereign?

This changing economic situation was part of a broader problem facing the community of the Romans. Although the Roman empire had grown, for the purposes of administration it remained very much a collection of ad hoc administrative divisions, the governing officials of which changed on an annual basis. But methods of defining membership in the community had not changed. When describing the peoples of the world in an extortion law passed in 122 BC, the best that the legislator could do was to offer up a list of different legal statuses: people were either Roman citizens, Latins, allies of Italian origin, people outside Italy whose status was determined by treaty (either voluntary or the result of their surrender), or "foreign nations." This list of statuses emerges entirely unchanged from within the realm of Roman public law dating back to the beginning of the period of expansion in the fourth century, but what had once been a way of bringing people into a new relationship with the Roman community was now becoming a way of keeping them out of that community. Indeed, the land of Italy was now divided entirely between the *ager Romanus* (territory directly controlled by the Roman state) and the territory of the Latins and "allies." This was a problem, because it meant that the Roman state now encompassed a far greater population, that these people had minimal ability to affect the direction of affairs, and that the differential benefits of empire were becoming ever more evident.

The result of the disjuncture between membership and control generated increasingly bitter disputes in the course of the half century after 133. The failure of the Roman state to develop institutions of government that could win the loyalty of the vastly enlarged group of people connected to it would prove its undoing. Lacking government institutions, Romans turned to systems of patronage to address their needs, further undermining the power of the state as individuals came to control greater effective power than did the senate.

The Gracchi (133–121 BC)

Tiberius Gracchus

Later generations of Romans would follow the lead of Gaius Gracchus in seeing the tribunate of his elder brother, Tiberius, as a turning point in Roman history. They saw the year 133 BC as the point at which the clash between the interests of the traditional governing aristocracy and the people as a whole became the focal point of Roman politics. This view seems to be validated by the speed with which the nature of the political debate changed over the next ten years. Tiberius Gracchus looked only to landholding in Italy; Gaius looked to restructure the Roman state. At the same time, opposition to both brothers underscores the inherent unwillingness of the governing class to engage in coherent long-term planning. Long-term planning was at odds with the tradition of annually elected magistrates, and could be seen as a threat to the equilibrium that the Roman nobility required to maintain its dominance.

Tiberius himself might have seemed a most unlikely radical. Although his family was not patrician, it was unquestionably among the most distinguished and powerful in the senate. His father—also named Tiberius Gracchus—was a pillar of

Roman society, who had twice been consul (in 177 and 163) as well as censor (in 169), and his grandfather had been consul twice during the war with Hannibal. The elder Tiberius Gracchus had also forged intimate links with the family of Scipio Africanus, marrying his daughter. The link between the families was strengthened in the next generation when Tiberius and Gaius's sister married Scipio Aemilianus, who had been adopted into the Scipio family. Tiberius himself married the daughter of the consul of 143, who was a member of the extraordinarily aristocratic family of the Claudii. Even his own reform proposals had a distinctively conservative taste, as they were based upon the Licinian-Sextian laws, now some two centuries in the past; the alleged point of the law was to restore the virtues of a bygone era in language that was evocative of that used by Cato in his description of farmers (see p. 99).

It was shortly after Tiberius Gracchus took office on December 10, 134 BC that he introduced a proposal to the senate that seems to have eliminated the formal limitation on the total amount of property a person could possess (500 *iugera*, something that may have been widely ignored by this point even though the elder Cato had made a sly reference to the rule in a speech he gave in 167). The proposal vastly increased the amount of public land that a single family could hold, so that it was now twice what had been permitted under the Licinian-Sextian laws. The upper limit of public land was now set at 1,000 *iugera*, and the proposal stipulated that the rest should be divided up in plots of 30 *iugera* (around 20 acres or 8 hectares) and given to those Roman citizens who agreed to farm the land. The supposed necessity driving this change was the idea that the moral fiber of the Roman people had degenerated as they had been driven from the land by nobles who had replaced free Roman laborers with gangs of slaves (see pp. 101–3).

Much in this proposal was deeply misleading. It was misleading to assert that there were insufficient men to serve in Rome's armies (see p. 109). Within the next fifty years, rural Italy provided an unprecedented number of soldiers, eventually exceeding even the numbers that went to war against Hannibal. There is no reason to believe that this abundance of soldiers was a direct consequence of the Gracchan land policy, since many of the soldiers recruited in the 80s BC were descended not from citizens but from allies who had not benefited from the Gracchan land reform. Gracchus's approach was deeply traditional in so far as he had taken trouble beforehand to exploit his connections within the aristocracy to build up a group of extremely prominent supporters. Thus it was that, before introducing his proposal, he had taken advice from one of the principal jurists of the generation, secured the support of a consul, and proposed that the commission to be responsible for the actual division of the land would consist of a board of three (known officially as the triumvirs for the distribution of land) consisting of himself, his brother, and his father-in-law. To all appearances the bill might initially seem to fit the traditional model of Roman politics whereby groups of nobles promoted legislation as a way of enhancing their status. It was the behavior of Gracchus that changed everything.

It should scarcely have been surprising that the leaders of Italian communities throughout Italy objected to the Gracchan bill. The bulk of the *ager publicus* had by custom, it seems, been distributed not to Roman renters, but rather to the Italian upper classes in the cities that had once owned this land. Nor should it have been surprising that the majority of senators proved resistant to a bill so obviously designed to advance the standing of Gracchus's family, particularly since it gave the triumvirs charged with land distribution the power to adjudicate disputes arising from their own activity. What is not clear, however, is how obvious it may have been that Gracchus believed passionately in what he was doing.

It was passion that proved Gracchus's undoing, for he would stop at nothing to get his way. When the senate refused to vote in favor of the bill, he decided to bring the proposal to create the land commission directly to the people, in violation of the old tradition descending from the archaic *auctoritas patrum* (see pp. 49–51) that the senate should approve any motion put before the people. Unsurprisingly, the bill passed, and it might even then have been possible to justify what Gracchus had done by appealing to tradition, for this was scarcely the first bill that was passed in this way. But a second irregularity was considerably more grotesque: as he moved his proposal before the people, Gracchus responded to an effort to veto the bill by one of his tribunician colleagues, Marcus Octavius, by having the people vote to remove him from office. A third irregularity followed upon the first two, when Gracchus sought to make sure that the land commission was properly financed. Since Gracchus's original bill had not included details about how the commission should be funded, his enemies in the senate attempted to derail his plan by refusing to provide anything like enough money for it to function. It was at this point that news came that Attalus III of Pergamon had died, leaving the royal land that was in his possession to the Roman people. The senate hesitated over whether to accept the inheritance, which would involve the creation of a complex administrative structure by which a Roman governor would have to replace a king. Gracchus did not hesitate. He now moved another bill to accept the inheritance and use the money to fund his commission. This too passed.

Gracchus's assertion that all power was vested in the *populus Romanus*, and his coincidental assertion that he could dictate the policy of the Roman state without reference to the senate, were almost textbook examples of conduct expected of an aspiring tyrant, according to the Greek political philosophers whose work was coming to be known at Rome. When Gracchus then announced that he would seek re-election as tribune for the following year (yet another irregularity), a gang of senators decided they could abide him no longer. Publius Scipio Nasica, the cousin of Gracchus's brother-in-law, Scipio Aemilianus, led a group of his colleagues out of a meeting of the senate to break up a popular meeting that Gracchus was holding. A brutal fight ensued, in which Scipio and his colleagues scattered Gracchus's followers and beat the tribune to death, along with three hundred of his supporters, with pieces broken from the benches upon which these supporters had previously been seated.

The senate responded to the murder of Gracchus with studied ambiguity. Although Nasica was guilty of gross sacrilege, since the person of a tribune of the plebs was sacrosanct, he was sent on a mission to organize the lands received from Attalus, thus ensuring that he would only stand trial for his crime if he returned home. One of the consuls of the following year was told to investigate supporters of the murdered tribune (which he did, with considerable brutality). Scipio Aemilianus, when asked about his brother-in-law's death, said that he thought he deserved it, and that is likely to have been the majority view. Yet there was no move to rescind the two main pieces of Gracchus's legislation, and the investigation of his supporters seems soon to have been dropped. The board of three, in which Gaius

This coin depicts Attalus II, who became king of Pergamon, in what is now western Turkey, in 158 BC. Attalus had fought alongside the Romans in their war against Perseus of Macedon (see p. 91), and he remained a loyal ally of Rome. His nephew Attalus III, who succeeded him in 138 BC, continued this tradition.

Gracchus's father-in-law replaced Tiberius, duly went to work surveying the *ager publicus* and settled colonists in several parts of Italy, while the Roman state went to war to secure the inheritance from Attalus.

Gaius Gracchus

As the Gracchan land commissioners toured Italy, taking land from Italian communities and distributing it to Roman citizens, Gaius Gracchus, who was elected tribune for 123 BC, had the opportunity to appreciate what his brother had done. The laws proposed by Tiberius ten years earlier chiefly had the potential—which seems to have been realized—to alienate the Italians and acquire a new province. Gaius's legislative program aimed to fix the problems with the Italians, improve the administration of the empire, and generally transform the Roman state. For this to happen there would need to be greater involvement of the upper classes in government, while the common people would have to be rewarded for taking an interest in the affairs of state and the Italians rewarded for their patience. Even Rome's provincial subjects would benefit from greater scrutiny of the conduct of their governors, who would no longer be permitted to seek a particular province for their own personal reasons.

Unlike Tiberius, whose experience before his tribunate seems chiefly to have been defined by his participation in the spectacularly unsuccessful siege of Numantia in the early 130s, Gaius had spent the decade before his tribunate on the land commission. He seems to have listened to the complaints of the Italians, and experience as quaestor in Sardinia had given him some idea of provincial administration. A surviving section from one of his speeches details the outrageous treatment of Italian communities at the hands of Roman magistrates (see pp. 124–25); another section describes the corruptibility of senators when they were able to hear embassies and receive from kings behind the closed doors of the senate house; yet another treats the corrupt practices of provincial officials. All these themes would figure in the legislative scheme that Gaius would introduce while he was tribune.

Just as Gaius's interests were broader than those of his brother, so too his tactical instincts seem to have been better honed. Unlike Tiberius, who had moved from moderate to radical action when his initial proposal did not win the support he thought it should from the senate, Gaius started from the assumption that he would be working with the *comitia tributa*. So the first bills he introduced had a distinctively populist flavor, including one that banned a man who had been removed from office from ever holding another: the reference was plainly to Marcus Octavius, the tribune who had vetoed his brother's bill, even though, as far as we know, he never achieved higher office. Another stated that no magistrate should deny a citizen the right of appeal to the people in a capital case, something that might be taken as a reference to the murder of Tiberius, or the persecution of his followers in 132. Quotations from speeches that Gaius delivered at this time are laced with references to the murder of his brother, whom he attempted now to paint as a martyr to the cause of popular sovereignty, and the discussion of these bills (the first of which he withdrew) seems to have served to cow potential opposition.

The next group of Gaius's laws was very different. This package included: a law that subsidized the price of grain for the population of Rome; a significant revision to the agrarian law of 133; a law stating that soldiers would no longer have to pay for

THE LAWS OF GRACCHUS

Of the laws that he proposed, gratifying the people and overthrowing the senate, one was a land bill distributing public land to the poor, another was military, ordering that clothing be provided to soldiers at public expense, and that nothing be deducted from their pay for this, and that no one should be enrolled under the age of seventeen; a law concerned the allies, giving the Italians an equal vote to Roman citizens; another law concerned the grain supply, lowering the price for the poor, while the judicial law most reduced the power of the senators who alone had served on juries, and were for this reason an object of dread to the common people and the equestrians.

(Plutarch, *Lives of Tiberius and Gaius Gracchus* 25.1)

their clothing (the cost would be met from the state treasury); a law ordering that the collection of tribute from the province of Asia be transferred to corporations of equestrian *publicani*; and another stating that provinces for consuls would be selected before the consular elections. It is possible that he also proposed a bill to increase the number of senators by three hundred, though this seems not to have passed; it is also possible that the law is a phantom of the immensely complex tradition that later emerged to describe what Gaius Gracchus had done.

These Gracchan laws offer the first coherent effort to define the relationship between the provincial empire and the domestic structures of the *res publica*. Since Roman government was effectively whatever the Roman people decreed it should be, Gracchus's method inevitably involved legislation; his intentions, and thus perhaps his understanding of the issues of the day, may be gleaned from an examination of the affected parties. In this round of legislation the empire as a whole is seen as the possession of the Roman people: its revenues, which would now be raised in a more transparent fashion, would be used to support both the urban population, which benefited from the guaranteed price for grain, and the citizen peasantry. The group attacked as implicitly dishonest was precisely the group held responsible for the murder of Tiberius: the senate. The point of the law transferring the taxes of Asia to a corporation of *publicani* was to stabilize the annual income, since the *publicani* would have to guarantee the sum for which they contracted; while the law on the consular provinces should be read as an open suggestion that consuls sought to manipulate the situation of the empire to obtain the most profitable province for themselves while they were in office.

Re-elected to the tribunate for 122, Gracchus introduced a further set of proposals to refine or enhance measures from the previous year. The three most important of these laws (two of which were actually introduced by tribunician colleagues Acilius and Rubrius) were measures to establish a new procedure for trying magistrates charged with corruption under the old *Lex Calpurnia de repetundis* (moved by Acilius); the establishment of colonies at Corinth and Carthage (moved by Rubrius); and the extension of citizenship within Italy. The first of these laws, which is largely known through a contemporary inscription, reveals much of Gaius's political ideology. The jurors, who were to be selected from the equestrian order to try the magistrates, are not treated as though this is any great privilege. Rather it seems to be assumed that the duty will be onerous, and that it will only be undertaken by those who are not in a position to benefit directly from investment in the empire. Implicit in the proposal is the suggestion that the jurors will resent being selected, and that their service will be resented by others—they require the protection of the secret ballot—while their own service is guaranteed by the threat of fines and the publicity of their calling. The praetor, who will manage the trial, is ordered to provide assistance to the plaintiffs in the collection of evidence and the execution of a judgment, which would be that if found guilty magistrates would have to repay twice what they had stolen. The law reveals a fundamental aspect of Gracchus's approach to public life, and, by implication, that of other Romans of his time. Gracchus seems to have thought that the mechanisms of existing public law could be used to reform the state. He further added that no one should prevent a judge from carrying out his duty, listing what would seem to be standard abuses of the judicial system, such as summoning away or arresting the presiding magistrate; collusion between the prosecution and defense; or the presiding magistrate taking some action to prevent the trial from moving forward. The only thing in this law that can stop a trial is if the magistrate should be summoned to a meeting of the senate, or the people assembled to vote on a legally worded proposal.

The final clauses of this extortion law concern the grant of citizenship to successful plaintiffs who are either of Latin or Italian origin. Since this issue would soon become the most important domestic issue in Roman politics, these clauses are of particular importance. Two options are presented. One is a grant of full citizenship, including enrolment in the tribe of the person whom the plaintiff had convicted, with exemptions from military service; the other is a form of partial citizenship whereby the successful prosecutor would be given certain protections—*provocatio*—against the arbitrary actions of a magistrate, and exemption from both military service and compulsory public services within his home community. The presumption in this case is that it was possible to conceive of a class of successful, wealthy individuals who would be content to remain citizens of a subordinate state so long as a Roman official could not bother them.

Similar assumptions about government to those that may be inferred from the extortion law also appear in Gracchus's agrarian law (see box, p. 116). The dominant theory appears to be that if government was transparent, it would be honest.

That some Romans perceived there to be added benefits to being Roman under the Gracchan schemes may have doomed one of Gracchus's major legislative projects in 122—a bill to extend citizenship more widely throughout Italy. Although the details of this law are lost in the political spin of later years, it seems at the very least that Gracchus proposed that Latins and Italians would be allowed to become Roman citizens. (The fact that these groups are not distinguished in the extortion law makes it somewhat unlikely that the statement in one source—that he proposed making people with Latin rights Romans, while granting Latin rights to Italians—is accurate.) Possibly what he did was propose that the option to acquire citizenship should be open to Italians and Latins who wished to receive it in return for some action on their part. We can be reasonably sure that the law did not pass because the Roman people felt that expansion of the franchise would dilute the benefits they were now receiving. This argument would recur numerous times in later years.

Gracchus's successes won him few friends among the leaders of the senate, and that proved his undoing. Rivals urged another tribune, Livius Drusus, to introduce Gracchan-style proposals that went beyond those Gracchus himself had introduced, thus undermining his position. At the beginning of 121, the newly elected consul, Lucius Opimius, supported a proposal to repeal Rubrius's law establishing the colony at Carthage. Seeing this as a way of undermining his reforms, Gracchus took to the streets with thousands of supporters (including one former consul). Opimius had anticipated this, and the senate passed a decree urging the consuls, praetors, and tribunes of the plebs "to see to it that the state should suffer no detriment." The decree seems to have been modeled on earlier traditions (probably invented) by which the senate could declare individuals to be enemies of the state: passage of such a decree enabled magistrates to use violence against Roman citizens, who were thereby deprived of *provocatio* and other protections. The legal fictions surrounding this decree, known as the "ultimate decree," are significant, because they allowed the dominant faction within the senate to use force against rivals without having to get the people as a whole to agree that such a step was necessary, and to provide political cover to magistrates who acted in this way. In this case, Opimius was well prepared. With a force of soldiers at his back, he killed Gracchus and thousands of his supporters.

THE AGRARIAN LAWS OF THE SECOND CENTURY BC

Gaius Gracchus's agrarian law is known through references in a later law, passed in 111 BC. In his law, Gracchus certainly seems to have tried to score propaganda points by implying that the year 133 marked a turning point in Roman history: he makes constant references to land that had been *ager publicus* in that year, and thereby made available for distribution. But he also made a number of genuinely constructive changes. Among these were the exclusion of specific tracts of land from potential distribution, and the elimination of the power of the triumvirs—the board of three created in 133 to distribute land—to decide in disputes about their own activity.

A second law referred to in the law of 111 was passed on the motion of Gracchus's tribunician colleague, Gaius Rubrius. This established a colony at Carthage with much larger allotments of land than were provided in the original law—at 100 *iugera* (66 acres or 27 hectares) they were far bigger than a simple family farm—suggesting that there may have been some pressure from people of greater means to be included in the distribution schemes.

Appian says that three laws passed in the decade after Gracchus's death allowed recipients of the land to sell it. As a result the rich began to pressure the poor to sell, until the tribune Spurius Borius (or Thorius) passed a law saying that there would be no further distribution, that the land that had been distributed would belong to those who now held it, and that they should pay a rent on it that would be used for distributions to the people. The text of the law of 111, although badly damaged in many places, complicates this picture. Most significantly, while it does recognize that recipients of land from the Gracchan commissioners might have sold it, it does not grant title to those who purchased it (suggesting that the Gracchan ban on selling this land was still in force), and states that those who had received land from the commissioners would not pay rent on it under this law. It does, however, state that land that had not been

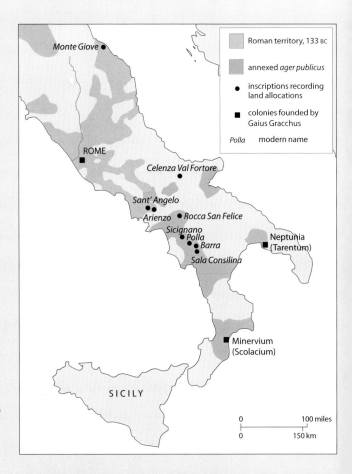

The activity of the Gracchan land commissioners can be traced through inscriptions on boundary stones, the locations of which are shown on this map. The commissioners' work appears to have been concentrated in areas where ager publicus had been seized after the Second Punic War.

distributed under the Gracchan laws would continue to be leased at rent. On the other hand, the law also makes provision for the protection of smallholders who had been ejected from their land by force, and states that no holding should exceed the Gracchan limits.

Popular Sovereignty and Senatorial Control

(121–100 BC)

The Suppression of Popular Sovereignty

Democratic institutions are often inherently unstable—a point noted by political theorists both ancient and modern. Ancient theorists saw democracy as unstable because of a tendency to degenerate into mob rule and tyranny. Most contemporary theorists tend to look instead at the tendency of democratic institutions to give way to domination by economically powerful groups that exploit their economic strength to assume control of the institutions of political power. Modern understanding is more acute on this point than ancient: the traditional aristocracy dominated life at Rome for fifteen years after the murder of Gaius Gracchus. Although people who wished to pass laws still had to put them before an assembly of the people, the fate of Gracchus was a powerful disincentive to anyone who might wish to place some measure before the people that had not already won approval from the senate.

The requirement that legislation be passed through the senate implied that it would be subject to the intervention of the relatively small number of men who had achieved the office of praetor or consul. More significantly, the implicit requirement that these people should have a voice in the shaping of legislation eliminated the threat that had been available to the Gracchi of simply ignoring them. This threat was an inherent check on the extent to which the dominant group within the senate could expect to influence a motion that might have widespread support.

The senate of the late second century consisted of three hundred men, all of whom had, at least in theory, completed ten years of military service. After the completion of that service the difference in experience among the members was striking. The harsh rules of ancient demography, when applied to the senate, meant that once a man had achieved the consulship—an office for which the minimum age requirement was thirty-four—he was likely to live only another fifteen to twenty years. (In practice the age of achieving consulship may have been closer to the ages—forty-one years for patricians and forty-two years for plebeians—established by later legislation; but at this point the only rule was that there had to be a two-year interval between offices after the age of thirty.) At any given time, therefore, there would be between thirty and forty living ex-consuls. There were six praetors each year, only two of whom could reasonably expect to rise to the consulship: this meant that at any given time there might be something like seventy former praetors in the senate who would not have been consul; descent from a family of *nobiles* (see p. 85) was often the crucial factor in determining if a man made this leap. Thus only about one-third of the senate's membership would have held any office grander than that of quaestor or tribune of the plebs. Indeed, it is one of the curious facts of Roman public life that in numerical terms the senate should be dominated by former tribunes—probably around 270 out of 300—few of whom had any hope of further advancement, and whose active participation in public life ended when it became clear that they would not advance to the praetorship.

According to the rules of the senate, the censors would select one man—a leader, or *princeps*, of the senate—who would speak first after any motion was introduced, and retained office for life (which might not be all that long, since such men were typically among the senate's most senior members). The order of speakers would then proceed according to the highest rank a person held—with magistrates-elect speaking ahead of former magistrates. The practical effect of this rule must have been that few former tribunes ever spoke at all: their primary function was simply to vote on measures by walking to one side of the senate chamber or the other, thus earning their title as *pedarii*—footmen—since virtually all they did was cast their votes, if and when they could be bothered to show up. The fact that the decree of the senate on the Bacchanalian cult specifies 100 as a quorum suggests that the majority of senators simply did not bother to go to meetings (see p. 98). There was little reason for them to do so, and, as a result, the interests of Roman society as a whole seem to have been subordinated to those of the roughly 100 men whose views might be thought to matter.

A much later observer—the historian Sallust—summed up the interests of the senate in this period as being "the revenue, provinces, office holding and the glories of a triumph" (*Jugurtha*, 41.7). Such benefits could accrue only to those who were in a position to govern provinces and command armies. Another development of the late second century that also worked in favor of a small elite was the passage of a number of agrarian laws—culminating with the law of 111, the text of which, partially preserved, survives to this day—that gradually eliminated one of the most important terms of Tiberius's law. This was that land given to colonists would continue, technically, to be the property of the Roman state. Those who received the land paid a nominal rent upon it and could not sell it. According to the law of 111 the land became the possession of those who had received it, and it had become possible for others to buy it from them. These changes worked entirely in favor of those who already had substantial estates and could use their economic power to convince poorer people to sell their land. Once again, this strengthened the power of the dominant group in the senate (see box, right).

The combination of the lack of opportunity to speak, and indeed lack of experience in administration, meant that effective control of the senate resided with the *nobiles*. In the years following the death of Tiberius Gracchus the situation was further complicated by the extraordinary demographic success of one particular family. The Caecilii Metelli produced six consuls in this period, and the women of the family married a number of others. So it was that, in the year 116, a Caecilius Metellus served as consul with his brother-in-law, Aemilius Scaurus. The attitude of the Metelli to outsiders—by which they meant people from families that had not produced a consul—was summed up by the well-publicized story of the conversation between one consular Metellus and a former praetor, Gaius Marius, who was not only the first man from his family to hold senatorial office, but also the very first man from his particular town—Arpinum—to be elected to public office at Rome. Metellus told Marius, who was serving on his staff, that he should wait until Metellus's young son was ready to run for the consulship, and, at that point, he would support his candidacy. Given that the son was in his teens, Metellus's point was that Marius should simply forget about standing for higher office.

In 108 Gaius Marius defied his commander and make a successful run for the consulship. He then dominated the political life of Rome for the next decade, won five more consulships, reformed the army, and, at least in the view of his supporters, saved the Roman world from the threat of imminent destruction at the hands

VICTORY OF THE *NOBILES*, 111 BC

The nobility made use of that victory according to its pleasure: it eliminated many through death or banishment, and made itself for the future more dreadful than powerful. It is this that often gives ruin to great states, when one side desires victory above all else and to take vengance more fiercely upon the defeated.

(Sallust, *Jugurtha* 42.4)

This coin type, minted in 101 BC by Gaius Fundanius, probably depicts Marius celebrating a triumph over the Cimbrians and Teutons. A Roman triumph was a family affair (see p. 49) and the child seated on the horse was probably Marius's eight-year-old son. If so, this was the first time a living Roman appeared on a coin.

of barbarian hordes from the north. Although the threat of imminent destruction might have been overstated, Marius was energetic, competent, and honest, qualities notably missing in the leadership of the state in the years after the murder of Gracchus. The failings of this period came to a head around Rome's dealings with tribes to the north and with Jugurtha, the murderous king of Numidia.

The Roman involvement with the Numidian kingdom in north Africa stemmed from the settlement that Scipio Africanus made after the defeat of Carthage in 201. In place of the former pro-Carthaginian ruler, Scipio had installed Massinissa, a Numidian prince who had defected in Spain. Massinissa, who died at the age of ninety in 148, proved a loyal ally, as did his son, Micipsa, who aided Scipio Aemilianus in the destruction of Carthage and sent men to help at the siege of Numantia in 133. One of those whom Micipsa sent was his nephew, Jugurtha, who evidently made friends with a number of Romans on Scipio's staff. Some of these staff, we are told, had grown into the leaders of the Roman state by 118, the year that Micipsa died. Micipsa had arranged to divide his kingdom between his two biological sons and Jugurtha, whom he had adopted. It was typical of the Republic's settlements with its territories that Rome was given a role guaranteeing that the terms of the king's will would be obeyed. Thus, when Jugurtha suddenly assaulted his kin in 116, killing one brother and driving the other into exile at Rome, it was necessary for the senate to intervene. Despite the fact that Jugurtha was plainly the aggressor, a commission under none other than the ex-consul Opimius decided to divide the kingdom between Jugurtha and his surviving brother.

The situation in Numidia continued to fester for the next few years as Jugurtha continued to scheme against his brother and rely upon the protection provided by his allies in the upper echelons of the senate. After an especially outrageous event—another invasion of his brother's territory—led to a trial by the senate at Rome resulting with the decision that yet another commission should be sent to Africa in 112, Jugurtha allegedly remarked that Rome was a city where everything was for sale.

Writing some seventy-five years after these events, Sallust claimed that the senate's failure in dealing with Jugurtha marked an important stage in the degeneration of Roman political society from civility to civil war, and that it ended a period of control by the senate that had begun with the death of Gaius Gracchus. It appears that Sallust was especially drawn to these events because Jugurtha's final destruction was accomplished by two of the leading figures in the civil wars of the 80s BC, who would become two of the leading symbols, respectively, of popular and senatorial control in his own generation. These men were Gaius Marius and his then lieutenant (and later sworn enemy) Lucius Cornelius Sulla. Sallust's view of the period is not entirely unreasonable, but his concentration on personalities—especially those of Jugurtha, Marius, and Sulla—obscures more general patterns of political behavior. The latter are of greater significance to the historian who prefers to understand historical developments in terms of the social trends that enable the careers of whatever leaders happen to come to the fore. Although he later wrote a history of the Roman world that appears to have been constructed around themes of personal and public morality in the era after the death of Sulla, Sallust's early works definitely display the Roman tendency to understand history through the contemplation of the examples offered by individuals.

The fact that Sallust's *Jugurthine War* has survived, while other works—chiefly the gigantic history of Rome that Livy composed in the generation after Sallust—have not, means that efforts to break free of his framework are to some degree speculative. That said, later summaries of the contents of Livy's history do provide just about enough detail—taken with anecdotes in other authors and the occasional document—to enable us to detect significant patterns of political behavior. These are, in fact, latent within Sallust's own narrative, and conform with concerns evident in the documents of the Gracchan age.

Two significant patterns emerge from the comparison of the summaries of histories of the period with the narrative of Sallust: first, military incompetence, and second, a predilection on the part of tribunes from families outside the charmed circle at the center of the senate to appoint commissions to investigate the misdeeds of the senate's leaders. This is an obvious echo of the Gracchan belief that publicity would enhance honesty.

While there were a number of successes by Roman armies in these years—indeed, more successes than failures—Rome suffered six major defeats in the thirteen years between the murder of Gracchus and Marius's election to the consulship. In an era when there was no other major military power, this is truly striking. Two of these defeats (in 119 and 114) were at the hands of a Celtic tribe, the Scordisci, whose lands were north of Macedonia; three were in southern France (113, 108, and 107); and one was in north Africa, where in 110 Jugurtha compelled the surrender of a Roman army to which he had previously surrendered.

The tribunician commission of inquiry, a tool once used to bring down Scipio Africanus, seems to have been rediscovered by enemies of the senate leaders at the very end of 114, following a scandal involving the Vestal Virgins. Three Vestals were accused of having sexual relations with men, but only one was found guilty. She was sentenced to the dreadful death of burial alive by order of the *pontifex maximus*, a death that was accompanied by the further sacrifice of a pair of Gauls and a pair of Greeks in the forum. At the beginning of 113, a tribune insisted on appointing a commission to discover why the other two girls had escaped punishment. All three of the Vestals were—as was required by custom—daughters of important patrician families, and the case was clearly intended to embarrass the *pontifex* (a Metellus) as the alleged lovers of the two girls who survived were both members of senatorial families, while the lover of the girl who had been executed had been an equestrian. Three years later a tribune named Memmius demanded that Jugurtha, who had recently surrendered, be brought to Rome to answer questions about his connections with the nobility, so as to explain how he had been allowed to make peace and keep his kingdom. The collapse of this investigation led to the renewal of the war and Rome's surrender to the king. In turn, this surrender occasioned yet another tribunician commission of inquiry, this one resulting in the condemnation of five leading members of the senate, including Opimius.

The power of the anti-Gracchan aristocracy, badly damaged by 110, was finally overthrown two years later when Gaius Marius defied his commanding general and won the consulship promising efficiency, competence, and an end to the war in Africa. Africa seems to have acquired a reputation as a sort of aristocratic playground that would only be closed by a man untainted by potential personal connections with Jugurtha. At the same time, the situation in southern France was going from bad to

This coin was minted in 56 BC by Faustus Cornelius Sulla, the son of the dictator, whose name appears on the obverse. The reverse is thought to reproduce a painting of the surrender of Jugurtha to Sulla that was erected by Bocchus of Mauretania on the Capitoline. Sulla is the seated figure, Bocchus kneels on the left holding an olive branch, and the bound Jugurtha is on the right. A similar image was engraved on Sulla's signet ring.

worse. The consul of 109 was defeated by the Cimbrians, a Germanic tribe that had moved south from its homeland north of the Rhine; and Marius's consular colleague of 107 was killed in battle by a confederation of Alpine tribesmen, the Helvetians, which then accepted the surrender of his army. Marius succeeded Metellus, who came home to face trial on a charge of corruption. Marius also finally accomplished the capture of Jugurtha, whom he had driven from his kingdom, through the negotiations of his quaestor—Sulla—with the king of Mauretania, into whose care Jugurtha had given himself. The end of the Jugurthine affair was overshadowed by a massive disaster in the south of France to which two consular armies—totaling eight legions—had been assigned. The commanders of these armies—the consuls of 106 and 105 respectively—quarreled about precedence in command, and refused to cooperate. Both their armies were destroyed completely by the Cimbrians and Teutons at Arausio, near the modern city of Orange in southern France.

The Restoration of Popular Sovereignty

The battle at Arausio in 105 BC, marking as it did the collapse of the conservative wing of the senate, heralded a new heyday for advocates of popular sovereignty. Marius, now regarded as Rome's only possible savior, was elected consul for the next five years in a row, while plebeian members of the nobility seem suddenly to have discovered an interest in assaulting the prerogatives of their class. Already in 107 there had been signs that the election of Marius reflected a sea change in the direction of the state. In that year, Quintus Lutatius Catulus—descendant of the man who defeated the Carthaginians at the end of the First Punic War—lost the first of the three elections he contested for the consulship before he finally won the office in 102. Also in 105, one member of the nobility, then a tribune, resorted to the populist tactic of summoning the people to deprive the consul Caepio (one of the commanders at Arausio) of his *imperium*, allegedly the first time that the people had done such a thing since the expulsion of Tarquin. More young nobles followed suit in 104, including Gnaeus Domitius Ahenobarbus, who unsuccessfully prosecuted the consul of 109 for his incompetence in battle against the Cimbrians, attacked Aemilius Scaurus for diminishing the religious rites of the Roman people (also unsuccessfully), and promulgated (successfully) a law mandating popular election to priesthoods. Another noble, Marcius Philippus, moved an agrarian law. These rebellious *nobiles* were overshadowed by two men of less exalted background— Servilius Glaucia and Lucius Appuleius Saturninus.

Saturninus burst upon the political scene as tribune in 103 after a rather bad term as quaestor, in which he had been removed, presumably for incompetence, from control of the grain supply through the Roman port of Ostia. Undeterred, he was determined to make a name for himself, and prove to Marius, who remained throughout these years in the south of France, that he was absolutely indispensable. Thus one of his first acts was to pass an agrarian bill guaranteeing Marius's veterans large-scale land grants in north Africa. Another was to bring the commanders at Arausio to trial before the people, and a third was to pass a new law defining the crime of high treason as one that could be tried before an equestrian jury. The tenor of Saturninus's rhetoric—the assertion that he was the heir to the Gracchi—may be gleaned from several facts: his claim that one of his followers, a man named Equitius, was in fact the illegitimate son of Tiberius Gracchus; that he is said to have broken the chair of a praetor (while the praetor was in it); and that he had a fellow tribune driven from the forum by a mob when he attempted to veto the agrarian bill.

Two years later Saturninus was joined by Servilius Glaucia, who passed a law reinstating equestrians on juries for extortion trials (from which they had been banished by a law carried by the consul of 106, one of the bunglers of the battle of Arausio), and ensured that Saturninus was re-elected to the tribunate when a rival was murdered. At some point in these years a legislator whose political inclinations were distinctively on the side of popular sovereignty introduced a novel clause into laws, requiring all members of the senate to swear an oath that they would follow that law. These clauses survive on a bronze tablet that probably preserves Glaucia's law on treason—although the surviving portion of the text is too short to permit certainty on this point—and in a law governing affairs in praetorian provinces for 100 BC. The oath clause in the first of these texts offers the best evidence for the ideal of popular sovereignty as practiced in the last few years of the second century BC:

> [Whatever consul, praetor, aedile, quaestor, triumvir for overseeing executions, triumvir for the granting and assigning of land,] is now in office, within five days next after any of them shall know that the people or the plebs [have passed] this statute, he [is to swear, just as is written below. Likewise, whatever] dictator, consul, praetor, master of horse, censor, aedile, tribune of the plebs, quaestor, triumvir for overseeing executions, triumvir for the granting or assigning of lands, judge [chosen] according to this statute or plebiscite [—(uncertain number of words lost) whoever of them] shall be chosen hereafter, within the five days next after any of them shall have entered upon his magistracy or *imperium*, they are to swear, [just as is written down below. They [—(uncertain number of words lost) in front of] the temple of Castor, openly, before the light of day, facing the forum, and they are to swear within the same five days, in the presence of the quaestor, by Jupiter and the [ancestral] gods, [that he] will do [what shall be appropriate according to this statute,] and that he will not act contrary to the statute knowingly with wrongful deceit and that he will not act or intercede [to the effect that this statute may not be, or be improperly, observed]. Whoever shall not have sworn according to this statute is not to stand for or hold or have any magistracy or *imperium*, nor is [he hereafter to speak his opinion] in the senate [nor] is anyone to allow (him) nor is a censor to enroll him in the senate.

(Roman Statutes 7)

The final clause quoted here, disqualifying a man from holding office if he did not swear obedience to this law of the people, is a powerful statement that all magistrates should be subject to the people's will, and that they were unfit for public life if they would not submit themselves to this will. The order that the oath should be sworn "before the light of day" and facing the forum is an implicit critique of senatorial actions carried out without public scrutiny. Finally, the oath contains the very interesting point that the law here supersedes an election, suggesting that in the theory of the legislator the laws represented the true will of the Roman people in a way that an election did not.

This sculptured relief, which depicts Roman citizens being formally enrolled for military service, offers a rare glimpse of the equipment of soldiers in the age of Marius. It is part of a longer frieze, traditionally known as the Altar of Domitius Ahenobarbus, which may have been created in commemoration of a census conducted by Lucius Domitius Ahenobarbus, father of the Gnaeus mentioned in the text.

Those who supported these laws adopted a particular oratorical style that was evidently distinct from that used in addressing the senate. We are told this by Marcus Tullius Cicero—destined for the consulship and the reputation as the greatest orator of his own time—who knew people who had heard such men as Saturninus speak. He described men whose style was "not worthy for the ears of a select audience, but extremely appropriate to boisterous public meetings" (*Brutus*, 223). Of them all he says that Saturninus was the best speaker, "though he captivated the crowd through his gestures and dress rather than eloquence," while Glaucia was evidently very amusing (*Brutus*, 224).

Entertaining and insistent though they might be, Glaucia and Saturninus were quite aware that their success depended on the support of Gaius Marius. They seem to have attempted to honor these interests by offering an agrarian bill that allowed Marius the right to grant citizenship as well as land in the additional provincial zones where they were proposing new veteran settlements. The issue was particularly significant in 100, because Marius had managed to destroy the Teutons at the battle of Aquae Sextiae in southern France towards the end of 102, and the Cimbrians at Vercellae in northern Italy during the latter part of 101, at which point he was sharing command with his former rival Lutatius Catulus. Catulus would later try to claim credit for the victory, despite the fact that it was his incompetence that had allowed the Cimbrians to get as far as they did. Both men's armies included large numbers of Italians, who may have been much irritated by the fact that they were offered utterly different terms at the end of a period of service from those offered to the citizen comrades with whom they had faced a ferocious enemy, undergone a stringent new training regime, and been treated as equals in the battleline. Marius seems to have taken their cause to heart, but the terms in the law of Saturninus reflect one of the profoundly significant facts of contemporary politics. The Roman people, increasingly inclined to see the empire as a possession to be exploited by themselves, were unwilling to allow others to share it. This attitude may have been reinforced by another law of 100, this one setting new (more generous) rules for the distribution of subsidized grain at Rome.

The real problem with Glaucia and Saturninus was that, whatever they might say about their devotion to popular sovereignty, their general conduct, and ready reliance on violence, made them deeply unpopular. A second issue was that whatever claims they might make about being the champions of the people, the real champion of the people was Gaius Marius. Although members of the traditional aristocracy continued to despise Marius and disparage his accomplishments, there could be no question that he had done his job. The army he had taken over in 104 had become very much his army, a process assisted both by victory and by the generous retirement benefits provided to Marius's soldiers through Saturninus's legislation. Marius's men continued to live as a community once the campaign was over, and there are signs that they retained enormous pride in their achievement—the eagles that Marius introduced as the sole symbol of a legion were brought out to evoke the memory of the old general in the next generation. The affection that Marius won with all ranks enabled him to send drafts to Rome in the wake of his victory at Vercellae, ensuring his election to the consulship for the next year; many of the men he sent were thus likely to have been from the officer corps, since they would have voted in the earlier centuries (see pp. 43–44), and we know that Marius was returned

at the head of the poll. The next year was less easy. Although he returned to celebrate a triumph, Marius found Saturninus and Glaucia difficult to deal with. When they tried to disrupt the consular elections, he sided with the establishment. The senate passed a decree modeled on the one that had been passed against Gaius Gracchus in 121. Marius brought troops into the city, driving Glaucia, Saturninus, and their supporters to take refuge on the Capitoline, and allowing their enemies to slaughter them even though it seems that he had given them some guarantee of their safety.

The Age of Sulla (100–78 BC)

The War with the Italians

Much of what we know about the history of the late second century BC is derived from the work of much later historians. As we saw in Chapter 2, the biographer Plutarch, writing early in the second century AD, is our prime source for Gracchus's views on Italian land. His biographies of Marius and Sulla are also the most important sources we have for their careers; the biography of Sulla is largely a summary of Sulla's memoirs, which also infect the later stages of the biography of Marius. Another second-century AD writer, Appian of Alexandria, wrote five books on Rome's civil wars from the time of Tiberius Gracchus to the 30s BC, and one on the wars that Rome would begin to fight with King Mithridates of Pontus in 89 BC.

Although both men used sources that were closer in time to their subject matter, they also wrote with the benefit of hindsight. The problem with hindsight is that it can often obscure what seemed important at the time, and is often corrected to correspond with contemporary realities. This problem affects Sallust's account of the wars with Jugurtha, which makes no reference whatsoever to immediately contemporary events in southern France. It also affects, to a much greater degree, the summaries of Livy, written long after Livy's lifetime, which simply reduced Livy's vast work to a convenient size.

If we wish to hear the unedited voices of second-century BC politicians we have to turn to a number of bronze tablets inscribed in the late second century by various Italian communities. These provide us with several laws of the period, including the extortion and agrarian laws—both known from a tablet found near the Italian city of Urbino—already mentioned in this chapter, while the document that provides the text of the oath clause quoted on page 122 was found at Oppido Lucano on the Bay of Naples. These are three of the best preserved of the eleven documents that have survived from these years. The desire to make these texts public seems to have been absent in the generations before 133, and would subside between the end of the 90s and the beginning of the imperial age after 31 BC. This suggests a new interest in actions specifying the duties of Roman officials, and perhaps in limitations placed upon their authority. At the very least, the publication of these texts in non-Roman communities shows that the doings of the Roman state had acquired a new relevance to leaders of such places. The surviving portion of a speech delivered by Gaius Gracchus offers a disturbing picture of that relationship as he describes how:

> The consul came recently to Teanum Sidicinum (a city in Campania).
> His wife said that she wanted to bathe in the men's bath house. The

task of removing the bathers from the bathhouse was assigned to the quaestor (in this case "quaestor" denotes a local office) of Sidicinum, Marcus Marius (no known relationship to Gaius Marius). The wife told her husband that the baths were not handed over fast enough, and were not sufficiently clean. Therefore a stake was set up in the forum and the most important man of his town, Marcus Marius, was brought to it, his clothes were stripped off and he was beaten with rods. The people of Cales (a city close to Teanum), when they heard this, decreed that no one should use the public baths when a Roman magistrate should be present. At Ferentinum (a city in Etruria), for the same reason, our praetor ordered the arrest of the quaestors. One threw himself from the walls, the other was captured and beaten with rods.

(Aulus Gellius, *Attic Nights* 10.3.3)

These expressions of sympathy for the plight of the Italian aristocracy might ring a bit hollow from the pen of the man who had spent nearly a decade taking land from Italian communities so that it could be distributed to Roman citizens. His account of the way the story spread from one town to the next, however, no doubt reflects the attention paid to the activities of Roman magistrates—which must rarely have seemed benign—on the part of Italian communities.

Despite what Tiberius Gracchus may have thought or said, the most substantial problem in Italy was not in the countryside, but at Rome itself. Rome was now the largest city in the Mediterranean with a population approaching half a million by 100 BC, and the focus for massive migration from all corners of the peninsula. The increasing wealth of the ruling class created new openings for workers in skilled trades and drew people to it—just as major cities do today in the developing world—while the movement of people into and out of Rome disrupted centuries-old patterns of life, and quite simply created resentment in all quarters. In 95 BC, anti-immigrant resentment may have boiled over when the censors ordered all Italians to leave Rome, a move that one Roman would describe as the principal cause of the war that broke out five years later. While there is no reason to think that this is literally true, it is likely that people were deeply disturbed by change, and that the reasons for the economic changes of the period were poorly understood by those who experienced them. This is perhaps unsurprising, as there had never been a city as large as Rome now was, and the social consequences of the emergence of such a city had never been studied.

It did not help, of course, that Roman politicians remained focused on power rather than policy, and that relations between various groups within the community of Roman citizens were more tense than they had been for years. The focal point of this antipathy was again the intersection between money and power. The immediate cause of the tension was equestrian control of the juries for extortion trials (see box, left). The Gracchan legislation establishing these juries appears to have envisioned the task as a burden. By 106, however, when the consul Servilius Caepio replaced equestrians with senators, the issue seems to have become one of class warfare, which is why Glaucia restored the Gracchan system four years later. Equestrian juries might be thought to be more willing to convict senators than panels filled solely with senators. That may well have been true, but equestrians were also more

THE COURTS AND CLASS WARFARE

The *equites* had taken power (over the courts) through the Gracchan laws and persecuted many famous and innocent men, and finally convicted Publius Rutilius, the best man not just of that age, but of all ages, who had, to the great grief of the state, been charged with extortion.

(Velleius Paterculus, *Short History* 2.13)

closely linked with the companies of *publicani* doing business in the provinces, and thus not exactly free from conflict of interest. There appears to have been a major scandal in 92 BC when equestrian juries found a senior member of the senate guilty of corruption in the province of Asia on grounds that seemed in later times to be rather nebulous—a view supported by the fact that the man who had been found guilty moved to Asia and lived with the people he had theoretically oppressed.

In 91 BC Livius Drusus, whose father had been the front man for senators opposed to Gaius Gracchus, became tribune, and declared an interest in promoting a major program of reform. There were four parts to his program: one was an agrarian law offering land in Italy and Sicily; another was a law proposing a technical change in the silver content of Roman coinage; the third proposed to return control of the courts to the senate, while adding 300 equestrians to that body and subjecting all jurors to a public review of their conduct; and the fourth was a bill proposing the extension of citizenship to every Italian community south of the Po.

Drusus's first three bills passed, and did so with prior approval in the senate. The bill extending citizenship to the Italians seems, however, to have brought public business at Rome to a standstill, just as Drusus clashed with Marcus Philippus, one of the consuls for the year and his bitter personal enemy. Things seem to have gone so badly against Philippus that he declared that he needed a new council, since he could not administer the state with the senate as it then was (the senate duly passed a motion condemning his statement). But when the matter of the extension of citizenship to the Italians came to the vote, support in Rome seems to have rallied around him. At the same time, the intense involvement of the by now highly organized leadership of the Italians stands in stark contrast with the period of Gaius Gracchus, whose proposal to extend citizenship received no organized support from Italy as a whole. Poppaedius Silo, one of the leaders of the revolt that followed upon the failure of Drusus's initiative, is even said to have stayed at Drusus's house, and a text exists that purports to be an oath sworn by leaders of the Italian peoples. Whether it is actually a sworn oath, or simply a document created to illustrate the passions of the period, we cannot now know, but whatever the case may be, it certainly reflects powerful emotions (see box, right).

Despite the pressure, the law concerning citizenship never actually came to a vote. One afternoon in the early autumn Drusus collapsed on his way home from the forum. According to one account he had been stabbed in the thigh, though we have no way of knowing if this was true. He died almost immediately. Philippus managed to convince the rest of the senate to cancel his earlier laws as being illegal, and the Italians declared war on Rome. According to the descendant of one who fought for Italy in this war:

> The cause was most just, for they sought the citizenship of the empire
> they had won in arms; every year and in every war they furnished twice
> as many infantry and cavalry, and yet were not admitted to the right to
> be citizens of the state which, through them, had come to that pinnacle
> of power that enabled it to treat with disdain men of the same blood and
> race and spurn them as foreigners.

(Velleius Paterculus, *Short History* 2.15)

SWEARING LOYALTY TO DRUSUS

I swear by Capitoline Jupiter, and Vesta of the Romans, Mars, her ancestral god, and by the Sun the founder, and the Earth, the benefactor of animals and growing things, and by the demigods who were the founders of Rome, and the heroes who helped extend Rome's rule, to have the same friends and enemies as Drusus, and to spare neither my life, nor that of my children nor my parents, unless it should bring aid to Drusus and to those who swear this oath. If I become a citizen by the law of Drusus, I will regard Rome as my homeland, and Drusus as the greatest benefactor. I will pass on this oath as best I can to as many of my fellow citizens as I can. May all good things come to me if I keep this oath, and the opposite if I break it.

(Diodorus Siculus, *Universal History* 37.11)

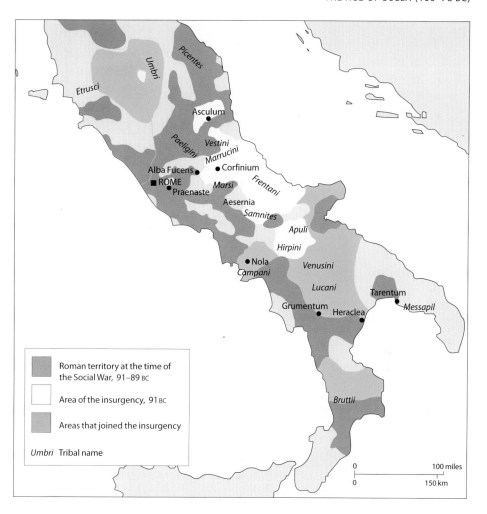

A map of Italy showing the areas that joined the revolt against Rome in 91 BC. With the exception of Campania, most of the regions that rebelled were among those that had experienced the least economic expansion in the previous half century.

The vehemence of this man, who was writing a century after the event and sixteen years after he had held the praetorship at Rome, is striking testimony to the profound importance of the war that coalesced out of a series of violent urban uprisings in the months after Drusus died. In a very real sense this war—subsequently known as the Social or Italian/Italic War—prepared the way for the emergence of the Roman monarchy. Indeed, Rome would be subjected to a pair of "proto-monarchies" within ten years, as the major campaigns that began in 90 BC mutated into a series of wars between various members of the Roman ruling class that reached ghastly proportions.

The reason the war between Rome and the Italian allies should be seen as marking the end of the traditional Republic is that Rome acted almost immediately to give in to the demands of its enemies. By the end of 89, citizenship would be offered wholesale to Italian communities that agreed to lay down their arms. The traditional structure of Roman Italy based on treaties of long standing thus came to an end, as did the notion that the voting assemblies of Rome could possibly reflect the will of the Roman people as a whole. When peace finally came to Italy, the number of citizens was something like two million souls, most of whom had only the most tangential relationship with the city. They would never vote for a law or for a magistrate or participate in any of the shared rituals, human and divine, that helped shape the collective identity of the majority of Romans who lived in the area of Latium before 90 BC. To the majority of new Romans the institutions of Republican government were unlikely to be seen as hallowed by antiquity; rather they would have been experienced as the engines of oppression. A Roman who lived through these years, and served as a junior officer in the army, later admitted as much when he wrote that the war started when "the laws and courts had been displaced" (Cicero, *On Duties* 2.75).

The level of frustration that the leadership of the Italian confederacy felt with Rome became thoroughly evident as soon as the war broke out and the Italian confederation selected the city of Corfinium in the central Apennines to be their capital, renaming the place Italica as they did so. The creation of a central capital, and the name selected for it, reflect a strong desire to eliminate Rome altogether as the political and metropolitan center of the peninsula. At the same time leaders of various communities gathered their local armies to do battle with the Romans.

Velleius Paterculus, who obtained a praetorship in AD 14 and whose family flourished under the first two emperors, lists a group of Italian leaders as if they were heroes (see box, right), and to some degree they may well have become such to later generations for whom their struggle would bear fruit. None of these leaders had any experience of high military command, however. The two critical advantages that Rome possessed were that its legions had an inherently more stable internal command structure than did the Italian units, and that Rome's generals were experienced in commanding large bodies of men. Although Velleius's claim that the Italians contributed twice as many men to Rome's wars as did Rome itself seems to be essentially true for the latter half of the second century, these troops had always been raised as cohorts rather than legions. In the field, the legions of allies were actually no more than a collection of diverse Italian contingents serving under the overall command of a Roman. No Italian general who took the field in 91–90 BC had ever commanded a unit as large as a legion in battle. Initially this may not have seemed a great disadvantage, as Italian forces scored a number of successes against scattered Roman units, but as the year 90 wore on Roman superiority began to tell. Among the men returning to hold subordinate commands under the consuls Lucius Julius Caesar and Publius Rutilius Rufus were the highly experienced generals Gaius Marius, Lucius Cornelius Sulla, and Quintus Lutatius Catulus. Others in similar positions are likely to have held high commands either under Marius and Catulus in the war with the Cimbrians and Teutons, or as praetorian governors in the intervening years. Indeed, the direct result of the death of the consul Rutilius in battle was that command of his army fell to Marius, who achieved successes in the course of the year. At the same time, one of the praetors of the year, Gnaeus Pompeius Strabo, achieved notable successes largely in the area of his home district on Italy's east coast. He had on his staff not only his own son, also called Gnaeus, but also a young man from Arpinum by the name of Marcus Tullius Cicero. In the southern part of Italy, such success as the Romans achieved seems largely to have been due to the leadership of Sulla.

Although Roman armies stabilized the military situation in the course of 90, it was clear that the central issue was citizenship, and that offers of citizenship were needed both to shore up support among those Italian states that had not joined the alliance against Rome, and to undermine the opposition. The consul Caesar duly

OUTBREAK OF THE SOCIAL WAR, 91 BC

The most illustrious leaders of the Italians were Popaedius Silo, Asinius Herius, Insteius Cato, Gaius Pontidius, Marius Egnatius, and Papius Mutilis. For my part, I will not detract from the glory of my own family through false modesty. Indeed I must pay a great tribute to Minatus Magius of Aeculanum, who, as the grandson of Decius Magius, a most famous and faithful man, showed such great faith to the Romans in this war that, with the single legion that he raised amongst the Hirpini, he captured Herculaneum with Titus Didius, attacked Pompeii with Lucius Sulla and occupied Compsa.

(Velleius Paterculus, *Short History* 16)

proposed a law granting citizenship to every Italian community that had not joined the rebellion, as well as to every community that agreed to lay down arms, while also allowing individual generals to grant the franchise to individuals or units that had distinguished themselves in war. Those given citizenship under this law would be enrolled in eight new tribes, so that their numbers would not swamp those of the Romans in the traditional thirty-five tribes. This final provision reflects, albeit in a somewhat creative way, the rhetoric of those who had opposed granting citizenship to the Italians on the grounds that it would rob existing Romans of the control of the state. At the same time, since the law had the desired effect of securing the loyalty of allied states and convincing some rebels to stop fighting, it underlines the fact that what Italians most desired from citizenship was protection from the sort of arbitrary actions that Gracchus had so eloquently described.

Sulla: The Reactionary Revolutionary

Although by the end of 90 BC Roman armies were operating well into the territories that had declared allegiance to the Italian cause, and many communities had been accepting peace in return for citizenship, Rome's obvious problems were inspiring a ruler in a very different part of the world. King Mithridates VI, ruler of a kingdom that included the northern rim of modern Turkey and some significant territory on the central Anatolian plateau, had long resented the restraint that Roman officials placed on his ambition to become a truly powerful figure. The immediate cause of the war that he launched in the summer of 89 was a boundary dispute with Nicomedes, the ruler of the kingdom of Bithynia, immediately to his west. The governors of what were now two Roman provinces in Turkey—Asia (west central Turkey) and Cilicia (southern Turkey)—attempted to rally what forces they had, including many troops from the cities of their provinces, but to no avail. Mithridates had a powerful army, and his generals swept all before them. As Asia fell under his control, he ordered the officials he implanted in the newly subject cities to oversee the killing of all Romans and Italians who could be found in his territory. It is said—doubtless with great exaggeration—that 80,000 people perished in the massacre. At the end of the year Mithridates prepared to expand the war into mainland Greece. He dispatched one army overland into the Roman province of Macedonia, and another force to Athens in company with a pair of Athenian politicians who had previously fled to his court: they now urged all Greeks to rise up against those who were, as Mithridates himself put it, "the common enemies of mankind" (C. B. Welles, *Royal Correspondence of the Hellenistic Period*, 1934, n. 74).

The war in Italy had gone well enough in 89 for the senate to decide that it could dispatch a consular army to deal with Mithridates in 88. The assignment fell to Sulla, who had campaigned successfully for the previous two years in the Samnite highlands of the south central Apennines and been elected to the consulship for that year. We can never be certain why what then happened took place. All we know is that a tribune, Sulpicius Rufus, who surrounded himself with a group of thugs whom he called his "anti-senate," forced through two bills over the objections of the consuls in the course of the summer. One abolished the new tribes for the Italians and redistributed them throughout the traditional thirty-five tribes. The other transferred the command against Mithridates to Marius. (In the thoroughly one-sided account that we get from Plutarch, based upon Sulla's *Memoirs*, we are

This bust has been identified as one of Sulla, on the basis of parallels with coin portraits that depict the dictator with a matching hairstyle. If this attribution is correct, it suggests that Sulla wished to be depicted in a way that echoed the royal portraiture of Eastern kings.

told that Marius was motivated by jealousy of his former subordinate.) One of the consuls, Quintus Pompeius, whose son was murdered by Sulpicius's "anti-senators," seems to have been cowed by the violence. Not so Sulla. He rejoined his army outside the city of Nola in Campania and convinced his men to march on Rome to reclaim the command against Mithridates for their general. The question for us is whether the decision to march on Rome was as significant as the decision on the part of other generals, any of whom might have marched to defend the city, to allow Sulla to have his way. Seen in this light, Sulla's march on Rome is not so much the act of an individual as it is part of a statement by the most powerful Romans of the time that Sulpicius's behavior was intolerable.

Encountering minimal opposition, and that only from men rapidly recruited by Marius and Sulpicius rather than from the other armies of the state, Sulla occupied the city and passed a law declaring Sulpicius, Marius, and ten of their leading confederates public enemies (Sulpicius was killed, and Marius escaped under dramatic circumstances to north Africa). In a further spate of legislation, Sulla sponsored bills rescinding Sulpicius's laws and passed some new ones of his own, including the enrollment of three hundred new men in the senate and two laws that effectively summed up the anti-populist agenda of the previous thirty years. One banned the introduction of legislation before the people without prior senatorial approval (a restoration of the old *auctoritas patrum*); the second ordered that all legislation had to be passed through the *comitia centuriata*, on the basis that it would be a bastion of conservative common sense. Sulla seems to have believed that the archaic *comitia centuriata* was a great deal more conservative, and radical tribunes a good deal more powerful, than seems actually to have been the case in the fifth and fourth centuries (see pp. 53–55).

Given his use of the legislative process, the violence previously employed by Sulpicius, and the fact that he had not fought a set battle in the course of his occupation of the city, Sulla might actually have believed that his actions would bring peace. Before leaving Rome to take up the war against Mithridates he conducted the consular elections, and allowed the election of Lucius Cornelius Cinna, a man he knew to be his enemy, asking only that he swear an oath not to upset his arrangements. Sulla might even at this point have seen himself as a consul acting in the tradition of Opimius; he had most likely killed fewer people than Opimius had when he crushed Gaius Gracchus's people on the Aventine. But that was not the point that people were willing to take from his military occupation of the city, and trouble was plainly brewing before Sulla left town.

Cinna had served with Pompeius Strabo, the consul of 89, who had arguably been Rome's most successful general in the course of the Social War. Although he had done nothing to defend Rome from Sulla, Pompeius Strabo clearly saw that his personal power was intimately linked to his continuing control of the army he had been leading. The army seems to have felt kindly disposed to him as well. When Quintus Pompeius, Sulla's colleague as consul and staunch ally, arrived in Strabo's camp to take command, the soldiers murdered him, and Strabo resumed command. Few doubted that he had arranged the consul's murder, but Sulla, who must have known of the murder before he left for Greece, did nothing about it (see box, opposite).

The peace that Sulla may have thought he was leaving behind him collapsed almost immediately when Cinna proposed, like Sulpicius, to distribute the newly enfranchised Italians throughout the thirty-five tribes. When Sulla's supporters drove

Mithridates VI of Pontus was Rome's most formidable adversary in the first century BC. He exploited seething tensions throughout the Mediterranean region, drawing support for his struggle against the Romans from other dynasts of Iranian heritage, contemporary Greeks, and even, in Spain, the Roman general Sertorius.

him from the city, Cinna took control of an army around Nola, recalled Marius from exile, and marched on Rome, gathering support as he did so from the newly enfranchised. The government at Rome had few resources, and needed to depend on the goodwill of Pompeius Strabo. Pompeius delayed until it looked as if total victory was at hand for Cinna, at which point he lent just enough aid to the government in Rome to keep it going; but then, in 87 BC, he died. Rome fell. Cinna ordered a thoroughgoing massacre of his opponents and dominated the affairs of Italy for the next several years. These years proved immensely important, for having achieved power with the aid of the newly enfranchised, he made good on his promise to spread them throughout the thirty-five tribes, a gesture that seemed at the time to be of considerable symbolic, and perhaps practical, significance. Marius was elected consul at the end of 87 for the year 86. He survived long enough to hold office for a short period of time, setting a record for the most consulships in Roman history. Cinna, who managed his own re-election to the office for every year down to 84, when he was killed in a mutiny of the army, set a precedent for using traditional offices as the basis for a nascent Roman monarchy.

Sulla could do nothing about Cinna. He had a major war on his hands with the generals of Mithridates in Greece, and had started a very difficult siege of Athens, which had been taken over as the advanced base for Mithridates's armies. Sulla managed to crush his enemies, and subjected Athens to an especially brutal sack by

PERSONAL LOYALTY

In 88 BC Pompeius Strabo, the consul of the previous year and arguably the most successful general in the course of the war with the Italians, arranged the murder of his successor—the consul of that year—by his troops. This enabled him to retain a major army to serve his own ends, in the wake of Sulla's use of his army against Sulpicius. These facts establish the crucial point that the men who made up the rank and file of these armies did not see themselves so much as soldiers of Rome as they did the soldiers of their particular general.

Sulla had been able to lead his army to Rome because the rank and file felt that they had been cheated, like their general, out of a potentially lucrative war. The emotions of these men were perhaps not so different from those of the men they had recently been fighting—the soldiers who fought for Italy had done so under the command of officers from their home districts, whom they knew. Although the leaders on both sides might proclaim that their goal was the defense of the Republic or the establishment of a new Italy, these higher aims seem to have meant far less to the average soldier than loyalty to their fellows and to a general whose interests would be linked to their own.

Soldiers who saw themselves as clients of a general naturally had a vested interest in making their patron as powerful as they could. One of the notable facts about Sulla's march on Rome is that his soldiers followed him even though all but one of his legates refused to do so. That too suggests that abstract ideals of government were more firmly held by members of the aristocracy than by the people they were trying to rule.

Certainly over the course of the following two years, no major military force seems to have been motivated by loyalty to the abstract ideal of the Republic. Instead, the events of these years seem to underline the tendency of Roman armies to become a general's personal following rather than an army of the state. This is in part a result of the fact that legions might be recruited from particular areas for particular armies—the area of Picenum, for instance, seems to have been a recruiting ground for the family of Pompeius Strabo. It also reflected the aristocratic tradition—believed by the Romans to stretch back at least to the earliest days of the Republic—whereby aristocrats undertook campaigns at the head of personal war bands. This was a process that had certainly continued throughout the second century, as exemplified by the conduct of both Scipio Africanus and Scipio Aemilianus (see pp. 72 and 119).

the end of 86. A year later, when an army sent by Cinna reached Asia Minor ahead of him for a final push against Mithridates, Sulla corrupted the senior staff, so that they brought their men over to his side as their own general committed suicide. Sulla had already made a treaty with Mithridates that allowed the king to retain control of his ancestral lands in return for massive payments and the gift of a large fleet to support Sulla's planned invasion of Italy.

When Sulla landed back in Italy at the beginning of 83 BC, the opposition was in some disarray. Cinna was dead, and neither consul had experience of senior command. Men who had withdrawn from public life, or had yet to enter it, rallied to Sulla's side. The most notable of these was Gnaeus Pompeius, son of Pompeius Strabo, who would become better known to history as Pompey the Great. At this point, still in his early twenties, he raised two legions from his own district, out-maneuvered Quintus Sertorius, the only experienced general of the post-Cinnan regime, and joined forces with Sulla. By the end of the year, Sulla was closing in on Rome. As he did so, he promised the Italians that he would not take from them the rights of citizenship that had been granted by Cinna.

The civil war in Italy ended in a trio of military actions fought in the course of 82: the defeat of Cinna's colleague, Carbo, at Clusium in Etruria; the defeat of an army of Samnites outside Rome's Colline Gate; and the capture of Praeneste in the hills south of Rome, long defended by the son of Gaius Marius. The latter two victories were accompanied by horrific massacres of prisoners. The screams of the Samnite prisoners as they were being killed were said to have been audible in the Senate House where Sulla was giving a speech (he seems to have presented their defense of what was then arguably the legitimate government of Rome as an effort to destroy the state). In the course of the fighting, Sulla's strength had increased to something like 130,000 men, an army that was roughly the same size as that raised by his enemies,

(Opposite) The Roman empire in 60 BC. As can be seen, the wars of Marius, Sulla, and Pompey had ranged across the Mediterranean world. Pompey's career is especially remarkable. From Spain to Turkey he was victorious against vastly different enemies in a series of campaigns that demanded meticulous planning and complex logistics.

SULLA'S RUTHLESSNESS

As he took control of Rome following his successful invasion of Italy, Sulla acted brutally to suppress his many enemies. His savagery was calculated, for he seems genuinely to have believed that his enemies were incorrigible and that Rome could not thrive if they retained the capacity to influence the state. It did not matter if these enemies were common soldiers or generals; one leader of the Cinnan cause, the nephew of Gaius Marius, was horribly tortured by a lieutenant named Lucius Sergius Catilina (or Catiline as he is better known in English). Land was confiscated throughout Italy from communities that had supported the Cinnan cause and distributed to colonies of Sulla's veterans—justifying the client army's loyalty towards its patron general. A program of destruction was launched in Samnium that was described by Appian in terms that make it sound like

the "ethnic cleansing" that has become a tragic feature of modern conflicts.

In addition, Sulla posted a list of men in the forum who were thereby "proscribed." To be proscribed was to be sentenced to death: anyone could kill one of the proscribed and receive a reward upon presentation of the head to Sulla or one of his agents. The property of a proscribed person was immediately confiscated to the state, and his children were forbidden ever to take part in public life. The list of the proscribed, which initially contained eighty names, continued to expand until it included those of more than 1,600 members of the equestrian and senatorial orders, as well as leaders of communities throughout Italy. The extension of the lists was only ended on June 1 of the following year. Apart from the simple carnage caused by the proscriptions, the fact that the law encouraged family members to turn upon each other, and slaves to turn over their masters, meant that it was seen as undermining fundamental principles of Roman society.

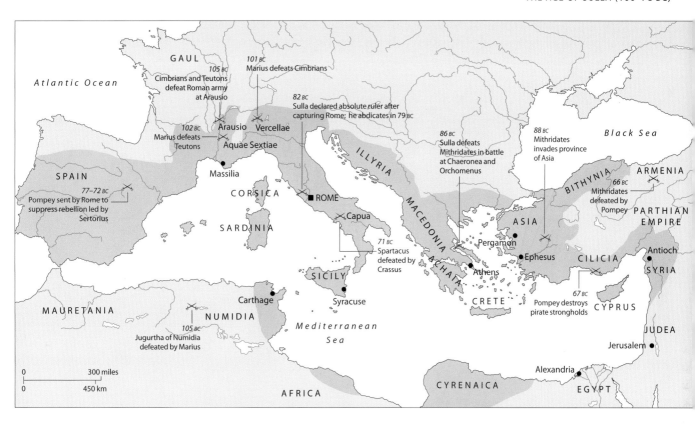

GAUL

105 BC
Cimbrians and Teutons
defeat Roman army
at Arausio

101 BC
Marius defeats Cimbrians

82 BC
Sulla declared absolute ruler after
capturing Rome; he abdicates in 79 BC

86 BC
Sulla defeats
Mithridates in battle
at Chaeronea and
Orchomenus

88 BC
Mithridates
invades province
of Asia

Atlantic Ocean

Black Sea

102 BC
Marius defeats
Teutons

✕ Arausio   ✕ Vercellae

Aquae Sextiae

ILLYRIA

BITHYNIA

ARMENIA

66 BC
Mithridates
defeated by
Pompey

PARTHIAN
EMPIRE

● Massilia

SPAIN

77–72 BC
Pompey sent by Rome to
suppress rebellion led by
Sertorius

CORSICA

■ ROME

✕ Capua

MACEDONIA

ASIA

Pergamon

● Ephesus

CILICIA

● Antioch

SYRIA

SARDINIA

71 BC
Spartacus
defeated by
Crassus

ACHAIA

Athens

SICILY

CRETE

67 BC
Pompey destroys
pirate strongholds

CYPRUS

MAURETANIA

● Carthage

Syracuse

JUDEA

NUMIDIA

*Mediterranean
Sea*

Jerusalem ●

105 BC
Jugurtha of Numidia
defeated by Marius

0   300 miles
0   450 km

Alexandria ●

AFRICA

CYRENAICA

EGYPT

and roughly equivalent to the armies that had been mustered during the civil wars of the early 80s.

Sulla was now proclaimed dictator, and advertised his fortune by taking the additional *cognomen* of Felix, or "the Fortunate." Besides treating his enemies with calculated ruthlessness (see box, opposite), he completed his victory, as he had done in 88, with a thoroughgoing legislative program. Although the major political elements of this program did not last a decade after Sulla's death, its administrative aspects laid the bureaucratic foundation of the empire for the next three hundred years. The principle of Sulla's reform was simply that magistrates should spend their year in office at Rome doing actual jobs, and the next year(s) governing a province. In order for this to work there would have to be both more magistrates and more jobs. He also seems to have felt that Drusus's notion of expanding the senate was a good one—especially if this enabled him to pack its ranks with loyalists to his regime. Thus he passed laws expanding the senate from 300 to 600 and provided for a new entering class of twenty men each year. In the past, senatorial status had depended upon the censors. Now it depended upon holding the office of quaestor. Aside from changing the way that people became senators, the most significant change that Sulla engineered was with the praetorship. He increased the number of praetors from six to eight, and provided that each praetor—other than the man who was returned first in the polls, who continued to hold the traditional office of praetor *urbanus*, or administrator of Rome in the absence of the consul—would be in charge of one of the new standing jury courts that were created at the same time. The jurors would all be senators, and the fact that each jury would consist of thirty men meant that more than half the senators in Rome would be on one every year.

133

The major political elements of Sulla's legislative program included the restoration of the restrictions he had placed on tribunician activity in 88, with the added proviso that no tribune could aspire to higher office. This measure would have been impossible with a senate of three hundred, but was now feasible with an entering class that included twice as many potential officeholders as there were tribunes. His other major reforms involved rewriting the law governing treason to specify that no governor could lead his army past the border of his province without express instructions from the senate; and setting out firmer rules governing the ways that magistracies could be held. (These rules left the minimum age for the quaestor at thirty, and made thirty-eight the minimum age for the praetorship, forty-one the minimum age for a patrician to be consul, and forty-two the minimum age for a plebeian consul.) The particular provision that proved decisive in the later history of the Republic was one banning a man from succeeding himself in office and establishing a minimum ten-year interval between consulships: there would be no more Gracchi, and no more Mariuses, in the reformed Republic. The unintended impact of this law was that it created pressure to invent extended commands that would substitute for repeated consulships.

Perhaps as important as his constitutional reforms—or more so, since some of the most significant (those concerning the tribunate of the plebs) would be abolished within a decade—was the example Sulla set of how to go about running an empire out of one's house. Sulla's extensive entourage had many of the qualities often found in royal courts, in that it served to integrate people from different classes, creating its own strata of authority that could be quite different from those of the state itself. Sulla himself was now the wealthiest person in the Roman world: he left an estate valued at 200 million sesterces, enough to produce an annual income sufficient to fund an army—and this was after having spent several times that sum between the peace he struck with Mithridates in 84 and the end of the civil wars. In so doing he massively enriched his closest associates. What had been the most expensive house in Rome when Sulla was a boy was now a relatively insignificant mansion, as vast new houses were built to accommodate the victorious elite not only in Rome but also in new villas throughout Italy (especially in the vicinity of the Bay of Naples). Notably, many of the commanders of Sulla's armies were technically too young for the job, meaning that the new elite would be around for some time. The most significant of these characters, Pompey, was in his twenties when he became the head of his legions. Another important officer was Lucius Licinius Lucullus, Sulla's quaestor in 88, who was well below the minimum age for the praetorship while leading Sulla's legions. Marcus Licinius Crassus, another man who raised his own troops on Sulla's behalf, was likewise below praetorian age—he would not be eligible to be consul until 70 BC—while Lutatius Catulus, the son of Marius's dyspeptic colleague at Vercellae, was old enough to become consul only in the year of Sulla's death. Sulla advanced all their careers even though it would soon become clear that they had little other than his patronage in common—their mutual detestation was a crucial factor in the politics of the next two decades, enabling the astonishing rise to prominence of Marius's nephew, Gaius Julius Caesar.

In addition to senators, Sulla was surrounded by members of his household whose power came from their ability to be useful to him. Some, especially famous actors, catered to his cultural tastes; others oversaw basic administrative tasks, something that caused some tension within the victorious party as a whole. The earliest speech delivered by Cicero—who served with Sulla at the siege of Nola before the march on Rome—was in defense of a man accused of murdering his own father. Cicero convinced a court to find him innocent, even though the man had been included on the proscription list (see p. 143). Although Cicero would later admit the man had been guilty, he won the case by making the trial not about his client (Roscius of Amerina) but rather about the power of Sulla's freedman, Chrysogonus, who had become very wealthy. In attacking Chrysogonus, Cicero touched on the distaste that even Sulla's supporters felt for people from outside the traditional governing class who exploited their connections with the dictator for personal gain. This is not to say that the people to whom and for whom Cicero was speaking had many qualms about profiting on their own account, but they did not like sharing their wealth with people they considered déclassé. By focusing attention on a person as unpopular as Chrysogonus, Cicero was able also to avoid direct criticism of Sulla.

Sulla's proto-court could not develop into a real court because Sulla had no succession plan: nor could he make one. His son was too young, and Rome was not yet ready to tolerate anything that smacked of hereditary monarchy. It was perhaps in recognizing that he had done all that he could—once he had reformed the constitution, slaughtered his enemies, and impoverished swaths of territory throughout Italy—that Sulla laid down his power as dictator. He then withdrew to Cumae in Campania, where he completed his memoirs (they ultimately filled twenty books) and drank heavily. He was dead within the year, and was granted a public funeral, the terms of which he had evidently dictated in his will. The funeral procession resembled a triumph, and when the two life-sized images of Sulla made from incense were lit upon his pyre, the odor of his passing must literally have filled the streets of Rome. His statue remained on the rostrum in the heart of the forum as a symbol of his impact. His tomb was inscribed with the words that he had ordered to be placed there: "No man ever did more good for his friends or harm to his enemies."

Life after Sulla (78–59 BC)

The Professionalization of the Roman Army

If Sulla thought that he had brought peace to the Roman world, he was deeply mistaken. In the last years of his life, the survivors of the Cinnan regime rallied around Quintus Sertorius, a man who had served Marius in the northern wars and fought hard against Sulla's forces in Italy. He now continued the struggle from Spain. In Italy itself, the Sullan confiscations brought on a new war almost as soon as the dictator's ashes were laid in their tomb. The outbreak began in the territory of Faesulae, near modern Florence. The two consuls were sent, each with his own army, to suppress the revolt, which appears to have dissipated rapidly in the face of overwhelming force. But then the consul Lepidus refused to return to Rome and began to stir up revolt anew.

Lepidus's effort failed in the face of determined resistance on the part of his former consular colleague, Lutatius Catulus, and further forces commanded by Gnaeus Pompey. Lepidus's five legions ultimately ended up in Spain, joining with

Sertorius. More significant, however, was the action of Pompey, who refused to disband his army at the end of 77 BC, marching instead into southern France. There he received news that the senate had conceded him a command in Spain. By the end of the year there were again something like 130,000 men under arms, a number that remained remarkably consistent over the course of the next fifteen years, save only for the last few years of the 70s, when the total may have reached 200,000.

While the overall size of the Roman army remains largely stable from the end of the third century BC to the middle of the first century BC, the overall level of professionalism appears to have increased enormously between the lifetime of Marius and the end of the decade following Sulla's death.

In the century between the adoption of the manipular legion and the outbreak of the war with Hannibal, the most significant tactical change the Romans made was to adopt the Spanish thrusting sword (*gladius*) as the principal infantry weapon (see pp. 64 and 71). In the course of the next century, no significant tactical innovation appears to have taken place, other than some generals' preference for grouping maniples into larger tactical units that they called cohorts. The series of military failures that culminated in the disastrous defeat of the Roman army at Arausio in southern France in 105 BC appears to have convinced some people that change was needed. The problem was that without a staff college, or any institutions that even vaguely resembled a general staff, reform depended upon the tastes of individual generals; and since these generals were annually elected magistrates, none of them could necessarily influence the behavior of any other general. It was only the fear inspired by the Cimbrians and Teutons at Arausio that caused the repeated re-election of Marius to the consulship after 105 and so allowed for substantial change.

Marius does not seem to have been inherently radical. When he took command of the army in Africa, for instance, there is no evidence to suggest that he changed the tactical operation of the army. The one alteration for which he was allegedly responsible was in the recruitment of his army, but even here both the novelty and significance of his action are easy to overstate. Marius's reform was to enroll men who did not have the property qualification that allowed admission into the regular centuries of the *comitia centuriata* (see pp. 43–44)—the so-called *proletarii*—into the legions. This had been done before—in the depth of the war with Hannibal, for instance—and did not involve a very large number of men, since Marius's recruits were for a *supplementum* or "fill-up" for the army already in Africa. Sallust's later assertion that this action packed the army with indigent beings, who had no care but for their general, does not mean that this was Marius's intent—Sallust admits that contemporary authors did not know why he took this action—or that Sallust's analysis is particularly accurate. Marius's army in 100 BC included men who could swing the vote in consular elections (hence anything but *proletarii*); and the armies with which Gnaeus Pompey and Julius Caesar later dominated the *res publica* were notable not so much for the poverty of their recruits, but rather the fact that very high percentages of them came from specific areas. In Caesar's case this was northern Italy; in Pompey's it was Picenum. Indeed, what little evidence we have for recruitment in the years after the Social War suggests that the traditional Roman *dilectus*, which theoretically swept people up from across the thirty-five tribes, gave way to a system that more closely resembled the recruiting pattern for Italians before the war. According to this system, local officials were required to send specific numbers of recruits according to a set formula (see also p. 62). Thus it is likely that legions enrolled after the Social War were assembled from sub-units formed of people whose civilian lives were spent in close proximity to each other.

Far more serious army reforms than those concerned with recruitment followed the battle of Arausio, and at this time we hear nothing more about Marian "reforms" in this area. In fact, Marius did not even recruit the army of which he assumed command in 104. Rather he took over the force that had been commanded in the previous year by the consul Publius Rutilius Rufus, on the grounds that it had been well trained. As part of his program Rufus had imported gladiatorial trainers to work with his men, something that seems to have become institutionalized: at one point Julius Caesar is explicitly compared with a gladiatorial trainer while giving instructions to new recruits. Marius supplemented this regime with important tactical reforms: he reorganized the legion, and in 102 introduced a major change in the nature of the basic missile weapon (see box, p. 138).

Marius's tactical reforms, hallowed as they were by his successes at Aquae Sextiae and Vercellae in 102–101 BC, were evidently taken up by all subsequent generals. It is quite possible that Marius was merely formalizing changes that had been taking place over the course of time, which may have made the process of adopting them easier. Whatever the case, on the battlefield itself, Marius appears to have been a very traditional commander. He might use some elements of deception (at Aquae Sextiae he imitated Hannibal's tactics at Trebia in deploying a force that attacked the Cimbrians from ambush), but on the whole he relied on the superior training of his men. The generals of the next generation were very different, and the model for their conduct of war appears to have been Sulla. In the course of his campaigns against the armies of Mithridates, Sulla made extensive use of field fortifications to control the battlefield, especially at the decisive battle of the Greek campaign at Orchomenos in 86. In the civil war, he drew the armies of his enemies into battle against his entrenched forces outside Praeneste. Although Sulla was not at all averse to fighting a head-to-head battle in the traditional manner (this is what he did in the struggle outside the Colline Gate), his innovative use of the entrenching tool seems to have made a profound impression on his staff officers. They had many, many opportunities to put his tactics to the test during the next fifteen years.

One area where Sulla can be said to have learned from Marius was in the use of his army after retirement. Thanks to Saturninus, Marius had managed to acquire generous grants of land for his troops, beginning with the men who had served in north Africa and continuing through the end of the war with the Cimbrians and Teutons. Although more than a decade past their fighting years by the time of the civil war, these Marian settlements appear to have remained devotedly loyal to their old general.

Sulla used the settlement of his own veterans to try to assert control over the Italian peninsula. In total something like 80,000 men were settled in some twenty colonies on land confiscated from the communities upon which they were imposed. The roughly 4,000 colonists in each place were granted a special status. This remains visible in some spots a century or more later, where inscriptions or other texts mention such groups as the "old inhabitants of Arretium" or the "new inhabitants of Clusium"(which in itself implies a group of "old inhabitants") or an even more offensive title such as the "more faithful people of Arretium," which served as a

THE REFORMED ROMAN ARMY

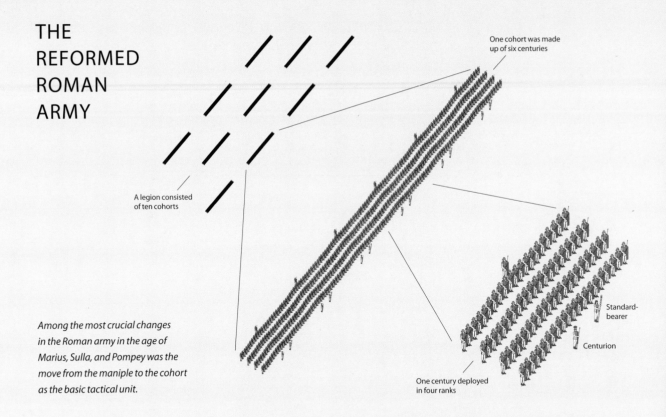

A legion consisted of ten cohorts

One cohort was made up of six centuries

Standard-bearer

Centurion

One century deployed in four ranks

Among the most crucial changes in the Roman army in the age of Marius, Sulla, and Pompey was the move from the maniple to the cohort as the basic tactical unit.

Marius encouraged wide-ranging reforms of the Roman army after the shock of the Roman defeat at Arausio in 105 BC. One of these was the reorganization of the legions. The new Marian legion was no longer divided into four sections deployed by maniples (see p. 64). It now consisted of ten cohorts, all armed in the same way, and expanded from about 4,200 infantrymen to roughly 6,000. The standard for all men was now to be an eagle, with which each cohort and each legion was equipped. In battle, the ten cohorts would be drawn up in a triple line, with four cohorts in the front rank and three in each of the next two in a staggered formation, so that the second line could move into gaps between cohorts in the first rank. The third line was evidently retained as a tactical reserve in case of emergency, much as the *triarii* had been under the old system.

The Marian reforms also introduced a new basic missile weapon. This was a redesigned *pilum*, a heavy javelin that seems to have already come into use during the second century to replace the throwing spears of earlier generations. The redesigned *pilum* had a new head that would break off from the shaft, making it hard to remove if it became stuck in a shield, and thus rendering the shield useless.

At the same time that he changed the *pilum*, Marius may have eliminated the old light infantry who had been part of the legion since the fourth century. (This is assuming that they had not already been dispensed with, which is something we cannot now know.) Henceforth a typical engagement involving the legions would fall into four parts (a point that Caesar and other sources make very clear). These elements were: the raising of the war cry, the advance into *pilum* range, the hurling of *pila* by (at the very least) all men in the first rank of cohorts, and finally the attack with the *gladius*.

reminder that the new inhabitants were there because they were "more faithful" to Sulla. What is more, even though Sulla's decision that the "old" inhabitants of some of these places should lose their citizenship was annulled very soon after his death, the "old" and "new" communities seem often to have remained at odds with each other, so much so that violent quarrels might be expected even twenty years later.

As a memorial to their victory, it also seems that the new groups constructed large public buildings that would be evocative of their success. The sudden upsurge in stone amphitheaters—the prime venues for watching gladiatorial combats throughout Italy in the middle of the first century BC—years before such a building was constructed at Rome, may be attributed to Sullan veterans, who would sit in the stands recalling their days of martial glory as they watched the gladiators fight.

The result of Sulla's colonial scheme was that soldiers seem to have come to expect that such rewards might be theirs, even though the senate, loaded as it was with Sullan partisans, resisted such requests as staunchly as they resisted anything. Even when the senate did allow a bill to be promulgated during the 70s that would have granted land to veterans of the war with Sertorius, no land seems actually to have been distributed. The underlying problem was that the state had no regular method of demobilizing soldiers, who were left dependent upon the political clout of their generals for whatever bonus they might receive as a reward for loyal service. The example of Sulla suggested that they might dream of quite enormous rewards, even though the government of the *res publica* had no intention of granting them.

The failure of the senate to create a coherent and mutually satisfactory way to demobilize troops became ever more problematic as new armies had to be raised to face a wide range of challenges. The war with Sertorius continued until 72, the year after he was murdered by former associates of Lepidus, who rapidly proved themselves as militarily competent as they were personally honorable. Pompey's triumph was secure by the end of the year, and that was none too soon, because by then two other wars had erupted. One was in Italy, the other in the Eastern provinces. The first war was occasioned by the rebellion of some gladiators near Capua at about the same time that the Spanish war was drawing to a close. The leader of these gladiators was named Spartacus. The other war broke out at the beginning of 73, when Mithridates assailed the kingdom of Bithynia, whose king, Nicomedes, had died, leaving his estates to Rome.

Just one year before these wars broke out the senate had passed a bill conferring a special command on one of the year's praetors, Marcus Antonius (who would subsequently take the additional *cognomen* Creticus to celebrate victories on Crete a few years later). Antonius was fighting around Crete because it was a notorious home to pirates, whom the senate's bill commissioned him to hunt down across the Mediterranean. In order to make his task easier, he was granted a new kind of *imperium*, "imperium without limits" (*imperium infinitum*), equal to that of a proconsul. Interestingly, the senate could not count on its own governors to support the operation of their own free will; granting *imperium infinitum* probably seemed a practical thing to do at the time, since a naval campaign would, of necessity, touch upon many provinces, and Antonius would need to be able to give orders to supply his ships wherever he landed. Despite his success, Antonius developed quite a reputation for greed and corruption, and he was perhaps fortunate to have died before he could return home and face the consequences.

The wars with Spartacus and Mithridates are a study in contrasts. In the former, the armies of Rome were led with such arrant incompetence that what should have been a minor police action turned into a major rural revolt; in the latter, Roman armies were brilliantly commanded and fought with genuine distinction. The commander against Mithridates was Sulla's former lieutenant, Lucius Licinius Lucullus, who was one of the consuls for 74 (his colleague, Marcus Aurelius Cotta, had been sent east ahead of him and had been heavily defeated by Mithridates). Although he had made an alliance with Sertorius—under the terms of which Sertorius had sent men to retrain his army in Roman combat tactics—Mithridates soon found that he could make no headway against Lucullus. When Mithridates laid siege to the city of Cyzicus, southeast of modern Istanbul, Lucullus encamped across his line of communications, making able use of field fortifications to control his enemy as Sulla had done. By the end of 71 Mithridates was in full flight from his kingdom. Two years later Lucullus was leading Roman armies beyond the Taurus mountains into northern Mesopotamia, then the capital district of the kingdom of Armenia, whose king had expanded his dominion after the collapse of the Seleucid kingdom in Syria, and offered refuge to Mithridates. Here again, Lucullus's superior operational ability enabled him to win a relatively easy victory, although in the course of 69 BC he was operating in territory where no Roman had ever fought, and at the end of a very long supply line.

Ultimately, however, Lucullus's army got tired after two more years of what seemed like an endless series of marches; inspired by a deeply problematic staff officer named Publius Clodius, the army, which was now at Nisibis near the River Euphrates, mutinied. Lucullus had to withdraw while Mithridates re-emerged as a threat to Roman control of his former homeland. As he did so, command of the entire war passed to Gnaeus Pompey.

Pompey

Pompey's arrival in the East, with a grant of powers stemming from the action of a tribune before the *comitia tributa*, was the culmination of a series of events that began with the senate's failure to control the revolt of Spartacus. Spartacus himself is difficult to fathom. As an active gladiator when, in 73 BC, he led his comrades out of a training ground where they had been imprisoned—the imprisonment of gladiators was highly irregular and, in this case, actually described as an "injustice" by Plutarch—he must have been in his early twenties. Furthermore, since he was a gladiator, he would never have been trained in even small unit command, much less the technical aspects of logistical control needed to maintain any sort of armed force. How then did a man with no training or experience in military affairs manage to hold the armies of Rome at bay for two years?

The two main sources for information about Spartacus's career—the account in Appian, who treats the outbreak as a civil war, and the account in Plutarch's biography of Marcus Licinius Crassus, the former lieutenant of Sulla who played a major role in the years to come—contain shadowy suggestions that Spartacus's armies were able to engage Roman forces in head-to-head encounters. The point becomes explicit when Crassus made extensive use of field fortifications to set the scene for the final battle (not something that would have been necessary against disorganized troops). Moreover, we are also told that the final battle took place in southern Italy because some "Cilician pirates" who had promised to transport his army to Sicily had betrayed Spartacus. We may never know what really happened, but the details that we have do suggest that Appian was right to see the events of these years as a feature of the civil wars. Spartacus must have drawn support from free men with military experience, quite possibly victims of Sulla's confiscations, in order

Pompey aspired to be the Roman Alexander, even taking for himself the cognomen magnus ("the Great"). This bust, now in Venice, reflects these ambitions, depicting Pompey in a style that echoed contemporary portraits of Alexander.

to face Roman legions in battle; he must also have been able, during the two years when he maintained an army of many thousands of men, to draw upon technical experts in military supply. (The very large numbers given for his followers—around 100,000—are almost certainly false, implying that he was able to lead a larger army than Hannibal; the fact that 5,000 men were crucified at the end of his revolt might, however, imply that his forces could have included 20,000 fighting men.) Finally, of course, the impact of the ongoing wars with Sertorius and Mithridates may well have played to Spartacus's advantage by removing the majority of trained officers and men from Italy for foreign parts. If his army was filled with survivors of the Sullan civil wars, he may well have had more men with experience of battle in his forces than did the praetors who were shipped out to hunt him down in the course of 73 and 72 BC. If these officials had had the wit to realize that they were facing a determined adversary, they might have behaved more cautiously from the start and avoided much of the trouble that followed. It was simply caution, and the willingness to take the time to train his men, that enabled Crassus to win the final victory in 71.

One thing that Crassus always resented was the fact that while he had defeated Spartacus, Pompey claimed credit for ending the war, since, returning from Spain with several legions, he had rounded up Spartacan supporters who had escaped the final battle. Pompey and Crassus were thus barely on speaking terms when they assumed the consulship in 70. That year, however, saw the virtual end of Sulla's political reforms: first, Pompey and Crassus supported a measure to restore the rights of the tribunes; and second, one of the praetors of the year, Lucius Aurelius Cotta, put forward a successful bill to replace the senatorial juries imposed by Sulla with juries drawn in equal parts from the senate, the equestrian order, and a group known as the *tribuni aerarii* ("tribunes of the treasury"), presumably members of the first census class who lacked the money to be included in the equestrian order. Sulla's vision of a Roman state run solely by members of the senate had failed. The fact that the measures proposed by both the consuls and Cotta passed through the senate also suggests that the majority of senators had come to realize that the state could not function without the active involvement of other orders.

Although Pompey and Crassus agreed not to take up provincial commands, the gradual deterioration of the army under Lucullus and an alleged crisis at sea soon opened opportunities for Pompey. Mithridates had evidently reached some sort of agreement with the independent states of southern Turkey that they would raid the Aegean to support his war efforts. In the absence of a regular Roman fleet, communities bordering the sea (especially on the island of Crete) had often taken advantage of their proximity to sea lanes to seize shipping as it went past. This situation was virtually as old as sea trade itself in the Mediterranean, where any merchant might decide to turn to raiding in areas where the writ of his state did not run. Such people were not, in their own terms, pirates, but they certainly were in the eyes of the Romans. The inhabitants of Cilicia seem to have been emboldened by Mithridates to raid more widely than in the past (hence their potential intervention in the revolt of Spartacus) and in the course of 67 they held for ransom a couple of praetors whom they had kidnapped on the coast of Italy. In response, a tribune named Gabinius proposed that Pompey be given command of the entire Mediterranean, and authority over any other Roman magistrate up to fifty miles (eighty kilometres) inland, in order to suppress the pirates.

Although the notion of unlimited *imperium* seems to have its roots in the grant of *imperium infinitum* to Antonius Creticus a few years before, there was an important difference in that Pompey was not now given the power of a proconsul, but rather *imperium* that was greater (*maius*) than that of any magistrate he might encounter. He appears also to have been given the right to raise at state expense whatever troops he needed (it otherwise appears to have been standard practice to make governors who raised new troops in an emergency pay for those troops themselves, unless the senate agreed to take up the cost).

The passage of Gabinius's law was an extraordinary moment in Roman history, since in previous emergencies either dictators had been appointed for a short term, or serving magistrates had been assigned the task of ending the problem, or the mission had been assigned to ex-magistrates whose terms in office were extended and who were technically subordinate to magistrates. Now, for the first time, a private citizen would be given a grant of *imperium* that was not only superior to that of a sitting magistrate, but also not connected with any office. The fact that the bill was moved through the *comitia tributa* against the will of the senate was a sign that the spirit of popular sovereignty had returned with a vengeance.

Pompey proved stunningly efficient in the suppression of piracy. So, with Mithridates resurgent in his old homeland and the army of Lucullus in a state of chaos, a new bill was passed in 66, granting Pompey even greater powers to bring the war with Mithridates to an end. This he did, again with great efficiency (and the astute use of field fortifications). He went on a tour of the East, not only bringing all of Anatolia under Roman rule, but also making treaties with rulers on the eastern end of the plateau, and moving south of the Taurus into Syria. With the collapse of the Seleucid regime under pressure from the Parthians (see p. 89), the area of the former kingdom in what is now southern Turkey and Syria had fallen into chaos. In 64 BC Pompey created a province there, and in so doing opened the traditional Semitic world of the Near and Middle East—with its distinctive traditions, often with roots stretching back for many centuries before Alexander's conquest in the fourth century BC—to direct Roman control. All that remained, when he learned of Mithridates's death in 63, was for the senate to confirm his actions. This would prove a most complex operation; more so than Pompey could have imagined when (to the relief of all) he dismissed his army after landing in Italy. Pompey was now the wealthiest man in the world, and he had financial agents busy both in the provinces and in the lands of kings whom he had confirmed on their thrones. These rulers needed money to support their royal ambitions, and this Pompey was only too happy to lend them—at high rates of interest. After years in the field he had built up a loyal cadre of Roman nobles, some of whom would be completely reliant upon him for their political futures. One of these men was consul in 62, another would get that office in 58 (neither seems to have been very bright, though both give evidence of substantial ability to behave in thug-like ways). And then there were the provincials. Theophanes, Pompey's closest associate in many ways, was not a Roman citizen when Pompey came to Rome. His influence with Pompey did, however, mean that his townsmen would celebrate this man as a god (they did the same for Pompey). Being much younger than Sulla, with growing children, Pompey could expect to dominate Roman politics for the rest of the generation, and was building the infrastructure that might allow that dominance to pass on to the next. Unfortunately for him, his near total lack of experience in domestic politics led him into traps that a more natural politician might have anticipated, and created dependencies upon others that undermined his position.

Cicero and Caesar

One of the men who spoke in favor of granting exceptional powers to Pompey for the war with Mithridates was one of the praetors of 66 BC, a man from Arpinum named Marcus Tullius Cicero. Cicero, who was born in 106, had moved to Rome in the 90s, and had there frequented the houses of famous orators to learn his trade. After his service in the Social War under Sulla and Pompeius Strabo it appears that he lay low in the years of Cinna, reemerging into public life with his spirited defense of Roscius of Amerina (see p. 135). After this he headed east for a couple of years to polish his education by listening to Greek intellectuals, before returning to Rome, where he was elected quaestor in 75 and served in western Sicily. The time in Sicily gave him the contacts that he would exploit in his next great public moment: in 70, when he further enhanced his reputation by opening a prosecution of Gaius Verres, recently returned from three years as governor of Sicily. So spectacular was Cicero's advocacy of the Sicilian complaint that Verres went into voluntary exile midway through the trial.

The fact that Cicero could aspire to the consulship is an important indication of the resurgence of the principles of popular sovereignty. He had no significant military service, and no significant connection to members of the Sullan nobility (or any other collection of long-term power brokers in the senate). He had achieved notoriety simply because he was the greatest orator of his age (see box, below left), and his most notable cases had a slightly anti-establishment edge to them. When he stood for the consulship of 63 his brother wrote that he needed not only to recall that he was a "new man," but also that he had "elevated the novelty of his name through extraordinary renown in speaking" (Quintus Cicero, *Handbook on Electioneering* 2). As a "new man" he could count on the support of the equestrian order (especially those who were members of corporations of *publicani*), people from nearby towns, and, as a successful advocate, the many people he had defended in court. Notably absent from this list is any member of the traditional aristocracy; on the other hand he had already "won over the city crowd and the support of people who attended public meetings by honoring Pompey, taking up the case of Manilius and defending Cornelius" (*Handbook on Electioneering* 51). The trial of Manilius, who had proposed the bill conferring the command against Mithridates on Pompey, had been engineered by Pompey's enemies. Cicero, after some extremely complex maneuvering, appeared to defend him, but, after rioting by Manilius's friends disrupted the courtroom, Manilius decided to leave town. The Cornelius whom Cicero defended, as tribune in 68, had moved a number of bills that might have made the ghost of Gaius Gracchus grin with approval—including one forbidding members of the senate to take loans from foreign ambassadors, and another requiring a quorum of two hundred at meetings of the senate. He was something of a populist hero, and the fact that Cicero showed up on his behalf obviously endeared him to those who disliked the status quo. These supporters of Cicero were therefore not simply the poor and downtrodden of Roman society: they included enough equestrians and others in the top census classes for Cicero to sweep to the consulship

This bust, now in Apsley House, London, captures the image of Cicero as a senior statesman, a role that he very much took for himself in the years after his consulship. It contrasts strongly with the perpetually youthful image that Pompey, who was born in the same year as Cicero, preferred to project.

CAESAR ON CICERO

First of all men to triumph in a toga, you (rightly) claim the prize for language and eloquence, and equally that for Latin literature—as the Dictator Caesar, once your enemy wrote—a prize greater than that of all other triumphs, as much better it should be to have moved the boundaries of Roman genius than to have moved those of the Roman empire.

(Pliny, *Natural History* 7.117)

at the top of the poll. One of his opponents that year, indeed the man who finished third, was the Catiline who was responsible for the horrific murder of Marius's nephew in the civil wars.

Catiline was badly hurt by his defeat and decided to seek election in the very next year. At the same time he seems not only to have gathered around him a group of nobles who were profoundly dissatisfied with the state of affairs, but also to have discussed a conspiracy to murder Cicero and throw the state into some sort of crisis from which Catiline might emerge as a dominant figure. The plot included a rural revolt in Etruria that began to gather steam under the leadership of a man named Manlius in the late summer. We can have no idea what might have transpired had Catiline been elected consul—the situation that he was engineering might be somewhat similar to the crisis around Faesulae in 78—but he wasn't. When Cicero charged him with plotting against the state in October he decided to join Manlius. On December 2, 63 BC the ambassadors from a Gallic tribe with whom they had been conspiring exposed confederates of Catiline in Rome leading to their arrest. After a prolonged debate on December 5, the senate passed a motion initially proposed by Cicero that the conspirators be put to death, and the sentence was duly carried out under Cicero's personal supervision. Catiline died, along with virtually all of his supporters, in battle a few months later. It is more than a little ironic that his men carried into battle an eagle that had once been borne before a legion serving Marius. As a measure of the misery that subsisted in the land of Italy, Manlius had managed to raise nearly two legions without allowing slaves to join up for fear that his rebellion would be compared to that of Spartacus.

The man who most vigorously opposed Cicero's motion to execute the Catilinarian conspirators on December 5 had recently been elected praetor for 62, and, in a separate election in 63, *pontifex maximus,* in a stunning upset over Sulla's old henchman Lutatius Catulus. This man was the nephew of Gaius Marius, and the descendant of a patrician house the members of which had accomplished virtually no act of distinction since their legendary progenitor, Anchises, had fathered a child with the goddess Venus. His name was Gaius Julius Caesar. (The consul of 90 who may have been another uncle was the only other member of the clan to obtain distinction.)

Gaius Caesar owed his prominence to championship of the cause of popular sovereignty. Born in 100 BC, Caesar barely managed to avoid execution at the hands of Sulla, who is alleged to have remarked that there were "many Mariuses" in the young man. (Had he really thought this, it is impossible to imagine that he would have allowed Caesar to live, and the story fairly clearly descends from Caesar's carefully cultivated personal mythology.) He went on to complete his education in the province of Asia, where he won an award for valor in the early stages of the third war with Mithridates. Still, when Lucullus arrived, Caesar went home, where he rapidly established himself as an anti-establishment figure of the first order. His private life was routinely tinged with scandal involving women of the highest nobility; he wore frilled togas and notably didn't drink. One enemy called him the "only sober man who ever tried to wreck the Republic;" another called him "every woman's husband and every man's wife" (the latter was a reference to the sexual relationship that Caesar was alleged to have had with King Nicomedes of Bithynia, a story that he vigorously denied). In public life he consistently supported enemies of the establishment, while carefully steering clear of any direct involvement in actions that might be deemed treasonable. At the same time he also appears to have spent money well beyond his means, and to have depended heavily upon the generosity of Crassus. It was almost certainly not with his own money that he funded the games he planned to give as aedile in 65, which would have set a record for the number of gladiators involved. When the senate forbade him to use all the gladiators he had hired, the matter simply redounded to his credit, and in the same year he struck a significant symbolic blow by restoring memorials to the victories of Marius.

Much of Caesar's early success depended upon his ability to deal with the supporters of Sulla; the fact that his mother, Aurelia, was sister to some of Sulla's most prominent followers may have eased his way. He seems to have played down his connection with Marius sufficiently well that he was able to marry Sulla's granddaughter, Pompeia, after his first wife, Cornelia (Cinna's daughter, whom he had married in the 80s and persisted in staying with despite pressure from Sulla that he divorce her), died in or around 70. The marriage with Pompeia proved to be a disaster, however (Caesar's most notable extra-marital affair took place in these years), and Caesar now sought to identify himself with the cause of Sulla's victims. By 63 he was not only firmly identified with opponents of the Sullan regime, but also linked with Marius's memory, having restored trophies celebrating Marius's victories over the Cimbrians and Teutons that Sulla had removed from the Capitoline. Caesar's election as *pontifex maximus* was a sign that he was rapidly becoming an irresistible force in domestic politics, and for the next couple of years he continued to dodge both the increasingly vigorous demands of creditors other than Crassus for repayment of his debts, and direct involvement in squabbles from which he could not possibly benefit. His favored tactic was to take a stand that would gain him praise while making an opponent look foolish, even if he did not win an outright victory. This was true of his resistance to Cicero's proposal to execute the associates of Catiline. It was also manifest, earlier in 63 BC, in his sponsorship of a bizarre show trial of the elderly senator Rabirius, who was accused of treason for murdering Saturninus: the trial employed an archaic statute and ended, after much abuse of senatorial excess, when a praetor raised a red flag on the Janiculum, an ancient symbol for the approach of an enemy requiring all public business to stop. It also characterized Caesar's swift exit from a scandal involving his wife Pompeia and Publius Clodius. Clodius had tried to meet Caesar's wife at a ceremony celebrating a female divinity at the end of 62, an act of sacrilege that outraged conservative opinion. Rather than become involved, Caesar simply divorced his wife, saying that she needed "to be above suspicion," and took off to govern the province of Further Spain. He did not return until the summer of 60, just in time to stand for the consulship.

The situation to which Caesar returned was chaotic. Pompey had arrived back from the East at the beginning of 61 and promptly dismissed his army, presumably thinking that the senate would not make trouble about confirming his settlement of the East, or retirement benefits for his men. If that was the case he was sadly mistaken. By the summer of 60, nothing had been done. The same senators who resisted confirmation of Pompey's acts were also resisting an effort by *publicani*, whose representative in the senate was Crassus, to reduce what they owed on the contract they had taken out for taxes from the province of Asia. Cicero appears to have been a voice of reason, especially after having alienated Clodius by appearing as a witness

POMPEY'S EASTERN CONQUESTS

Pompey fundamentally transformed the eastern portion of the Roman empire, extending its boundaries far to the east after his annexation of Pontus along the Black Sea (which now became part of the province of Bithynia-Pontus). In the region that is now central Turkey, Pompey created a group of client states, including Galatia and Cappadocia, the rulers of which were dependent upon his favor. Territory that had once formed part of the Seleucid kingdom was incorporated as the province of Syria, and the Euphrates river now marked the eastern boundary of the Roman empire.

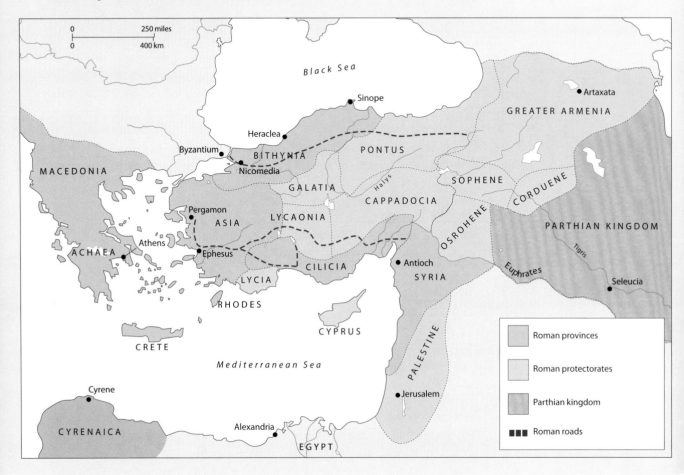

against him in his trial for sacrilege the previous year (which ended with a verdict of not guilty): but to no avail. Cicero's main hope simply seems to have been that the senate would do what Pompey wanted it to do. By this point, he seems to have come to see himself as a domestic version of Pompey: as a figure who could dominate politics at Rome in the same way that Pompey—whose own skills as a domestic politician were weak at best—dominated his enemies in the field. The old nobility despised Cicero, and appears to have disliked Pompey with equal intensity. Their leader was Marcus Porcius Cato, the great-grandson of the conservative politician of the second century BC (see p. 99). Born in 95, Cato's ability to project an image of personal incorruptibility had enabled him, by this point, to achieve a position of genuine significance among those who opposed the likes of Pompey and Crassus (see also pp. 165–66). Also, unlike many who shared his dislike of Pompey and Crassus, he was absolutely untainted by the massacres of the Sullan era.

At the end of 60, Caesar, who had been elected consul for the coming year, changed his typical conduct, suddenly becoming far more decisive and refusing to back down; his aim was now, it seems, to dominate the state. In order to do so, however, the master of popular politics would have to become a general, and for this, he needed to form an alliance with those who, for their own reasons, needed change. Pompey and Crassus agreed to support him, and Cicero was invited to join a clique whose avowed aim was to shift the business of the state out of the senate and into the *comitia tributa*. This was more than Cicero was prepared to do, for he retained a desperate hope that reasonable government could follow if the mutual respect of the different orders of society could be cultivated. Within a decade, many Romans would see this as a decisive moment marking the end of traditional government.

In the first month of the year 59, Caesar moved bills supporting Pompey and Crassus through the *comitia*. Probably in March, Caesar was granted a five-year tenure as governor of Cisalpine Gaul ("Gaul on this side of the Alps," or northern Italy) and Illyricum (the region of ancient Illyria, which was assigned to Caesar as a zone of operation; it was not yet an organized province, despite the presence of communities of Roman citizens there). Several months after that, Transalpine Gaul ("Gaul on the other side of the Alps," in this case southern France) was added to his administration. The bills confirming the acts of Pompey, reducing the liability of the Asian *publicani*, and granting Caesar his provinces were all triumphs for the principle of popular sovereignty over senatorial control.

Summary

● Contemporary Roman historians traced the origin of the civil wars that led to the emergence of the Roman monarchy and the end of the Republic to the tribunate of Tiberius Gracchus in 133 BC. Gracchus's land reform program seemed to set the governing aristocracy against the people, and his determination to brook no opposition led to his murder later that year. His land reform bill actually did little to address the causes of economic stress in Italy.

● Tiberius's brother Gaius's reform platform in 123–122 BC was far more extensive, looking fundamentally to alter the way the empire was exploited. Even more clearly than Tiberius, Gaius advocated popular sovereignty based on the concept of openness in administration. His reform program was undermined by a fellow tribune in 122, and he and his followers were slaughtered by the forces of the consul Opimius, on the basis of a decree of the senate ordering magistrates to act to protect the state.

● During the fifteen years after Gaius Gracchus's death, popular sovereignty had little support against the dominance of the senate, particularly the elite group of ex-consuls. This domination fell apart, however, after a series of military defeats, and embarrassments connected with the war against the north African king, Jugurtha. In 107 BC Gaius Marius, a man without senatorial ancestors, became consul and eventually captured Jugurtha. A massive victory by Germanic tribes at Arausio (in southern France) in 105 BC led to Marius's repeated re-election as consul to save Italy from invasion by these tribes. Marius introduced major tactical reforms into the army and defeated the Germans. At the same time, the tribunes Saturninus and Glaucia reasserted the cause of popular sovereignty, until Marius, alarmed by their violent tactics, condoned their murder.

● The communities of Italy had become increasingly alienated from the Republican government. In 91 BC the tribune Livius Drusus proposed a bill granting citizenship to the Italians. When the bill failed and Drusus mysteriously died, a rebellion broke out against Roman control. Through a combination of superior command, and conceding citizenship to Italian communities that remained loyal or surrendered, Rome gained the upper hand.

● In 88 BC the tribune Sulpicius proposed putting Marius in command of the army being sent to the eastern Mediterranean to fight King Mithridates, who had invaded Roman territory, instead of the consul, Sulla. As a result, Sulla, who was unopposed by the commanders of other Roman armies, marched on Rome, killed Sulpicius, drove Marius into exile, and reformed the constitution, before setting out to fight Mithridates.

● The consul Cinna overthrew Sulla's settlement the following year, after a bloody civil war. In 83 BC, after defeating Mithridates (and after Cinna's death), Sulla invaded Italy, overcame his enemies and became dictator. He brutally killed many of his enemies and imposed new reforms on the state. The decade after Sulla's death in 78 BC was marked by further violence and the rapid dismantling of his most significant political reforms.

● The leading figure in the next generation was Gnaeus Pompey. He supported Sulla and ultimately obtained commands that enabled him to win glory and vast wealth for destroying the kingdom of Mithridates. Pompey received his military commands by vote of the people rather than as the result of holding office (he was to be consul in 70 BC). In the late 70s BC, while Pompey campaigned against pro-Cinnan survivors in Spain, Italy was rocked by the revolt of Spartacus, which drew strength from those displaced by Sulla.

● Campaigns to suppress piracy led to the creation of new forms of *imperium*, granting the holder broad powers unconnected with provincial boundaries or tenure of a specific office; especially significant are the Gabinian and Manilian laws of 67 and 66, which created distinct commands for Pompey, first against piracy and then against Mithridates.

● The 60s BC saw the rise of such politicians as Cicero and Caesar. Cicero gained fame as an orator and—as consul in 63 BC—for his role in suppressing a rebellion engineered by Catiline. Caesar drew strength from anti-Sullan groups within the state, and in 59 BC he acquired the provincial command, as governor of Gaul, that would prove key to his future ambitions.

IV

The
Transition
from
Republic
to
Principate

(59 BC–AD 70)

Caesar from Consul to Dictator

59 BC	Consulship of Julius Caesar; Caesar given five-year command in Gaul
58	Caesar defeats Helvetians and Ariovistus in Gaul
55	Second consulship of Pompey and Crassus; Caesar given five-year extension of his command
53	Battle of Carrhae and death of Crassus
52	Third consulship of Pompey, who becomes sole consul; defeat of Vercingetorix in Gaul
49	Caesar invades Italy
48	Caesar defeats Pompey at Pharsalus; Pompey murdered in Egypt
46	Battle of Thapsus; Younger Cato commits suicide
45	Battle of Munda
44	Julius Caesar murdered on March 15

The Civil Wars

43	Formation of the triumvirate for a five-year term; murder of Cicero
42	Battle of Philippi
41	Civil war at Perugia between Octavianus and Lucius Antonius
40	Meeting of Antony and Octavianus at Brundisium; marriage of Antony and Octavia
38	Marriage of Octavianus and Livia
37	Meeting of Octavianus and Antony at Tarentum; renewal of the triumvirate for a second five-year term
36	Defeat of Sextus Pompey; removal of Lepidus from the triumvirate; Antony invades Parthia, is defeated
31	Octavianus defeats Antony and Cleopatra at the battle of Actium
30	Death of Antony and Cleopatra at Alexandria

The Reign of Augustus

28	Restoration of constitutional government by Octavianus
27	Octavianus receives the title Augustus
23	Augustus receives *imperium maius* and *tribunicia potestas*
19	Augustus recovers standards captured by the Parthians from Crassus and Mark Antony; renewal and expansion of Augustus's powers; death of Virgil; publication of the *Aeneid*
18	Augustus introduces laws governing marriage
17 BC	Augustus adopts his grandsons Gaius and Lucius Caesar, sons of Agrippa and Julia

THE PERIOD BETWEEN 59 BC AND AD 70 is marked by the gradual change of Roman institutions to include a *princeps*. This word, which in Republican times was applied to one principal statesman, such as Pompey, came to mean a man endowed with extraordinary legal powers that enabled him to govern the state. The form of government that came into being as this happened was known in Latin as the *principatus*, or, in English, the principate.

The law granting Caesar his five-year command in 59 BC is but one of a series of exceptional moments in the process of transition from the traditional Republican form of government to the principate. Another was the election of Pompey as sole consul in 52 BC. Yet another was the passage of a law in AD 37 conferring the powers that had defined the "principate" of Tiberius on his adoptive grandson, Caligula, who had no official position at that time. This law is the precedent for the law passed at the end of AD 70 listing the powers that would define the position of Vespasian as *princeps*.

The theme of this chapter will be the process by which the Romans went from creating ad hoc extra-magisterial positions for individuals to institutionalizing such positions as a regular feature of government. The Republic did not die: it evolved.

Explaining the Change

How did later historians view this transition from Republic to principate? Much of what we know of this period comes from Cornelius Tacitus, the greatest narrative historian of Rome, who was also an immensely successful politician. He was consul in AD 97 and governor of the province of Asia in 112–13, a position that was the pinnacle of a senatorial career in his time. The fact that he achieved such distinction indicates that he was well regarded by the *princeps*, a man named Trajan, who was born in Spain (probably in AD 53) to the descendants of Italian immigrants who had moved to the area sometime in the first century BC. Trajan's father had been the leading general for another *princeps*, Vespasian, who had seized the position through civil war in AD 69. The accession of Vespasian, whose father had not been a senator, marked the end of the political dominance of the old aristocracy of the *nobiles*, who had dominated the senate since the defeat of Hannibal in 202 BC.

The institutions that supported the existence of a *princeps* and the impact of various *principes* on the Roman state were the primary topics of Tacitus's two great historical works, the *Annals of Imperial Rome* and the *Histories*. Through these accounts it is clear that Tacitus viewed the rise of the *princeps* as an inevitable consequence of a series of experiments in increasingly autocratic government. In the opening lines of the *Annals*, after describing the early history of the Roman constitution, he wrote that:

> The domination of Cinna was not long, nor was that of Sulla, the influence of Pompey and Crassus rapidly gave way to Caesar, the armies of Lepidus and Antony gave way to Augustus, who received the whole world, worn out by civil discord, under his power with the name of *princeps*.

> *(Annals of Imperial Rome* 1.1)

In the *Histories*, he had already written that:

> The ancient and innate desire of mortals for power matured and erupted with the magnitude of the empire; for when the state was not powerful, equality was easy. But, when the world was subdued, when rival cities and kings were annihilated, there was time to desire secure wealth. The first struggles broke out between the senators and the people. Afterwards turbulent tribunes sometimes held sway, at other times the consuls; the first steps of civil war appeared in the city and forum. Soon Gaius Marius, emerging from the lowest order of the people, and Lucius Sulla, the most savage of the *nobiles*, turned freedom, conquered by arms, into autocracy. After these men, Gnaeus Pompey was less obvious, but no better, and nothing was afterwards sought other than the principate.
>
> (*Histories* 2.38.1)

While we may quibble about some of Tacitus's facts here (Marius was certainly not from the lowest order of the people), the most fascinating point is that he sees Pompey as a precursor to Augustus, Rome's first emperor (31 BC–AD 14). Likewise, in a discussion of the history of law, he wrote that:

> Pompey, chosen consul for the third time to correct the morals of the state, was harsher with remedies than the problems justified; he was at the same time both the author and subvertor of his own laws, and what he held through force of arms he lost through force of arms.
>
> (*Annals of Imperial Rome* 3.28.1)

Interest in the institutions of the Roman state drew Tacitus's attention to Pompey: for Tacitus the principate arose not in opposition to the Republic, but directly out of the institutions of the Republic. Others took different views, looking to make a clean break between the time of the emperors and what had gone before. Tacitus's immediate contemporary, Gaius Suetonius Tranquillus, wrote of the "twelve Caesars," from Julius Caesar to Domitian, as if Julius was the first in the line. Cassius Dio stated explicitly that autocratic government began with the victory of Augustus over Mark Antony at Actium in 31 BC, again in an effort to find a specific point at which it was possible to say that the Republican form of government had come to an end.

The Domination of Caesar (59–44 BC)

Culture in the Age of Caesar

When later Romans sought to identify a point at which their cultural traditions achieved maturity, they would invariably pick the decades after the death of Sulla in 78 BC. Cicero was the central literary figure of this age.

Cicero was not only a spectacular orator, but he was also the author of significant handbooks on the practice of oratory, on political theory, and on philosophy (his efforts to write poetry commanded less respect, largely because his favorite subject was the celebration of Ciceronian courage and genius). Much of the theory that he brought to bear on Latin oratory was adopted from contemporary Greek theory—as was all his own philosophical speculation—but he gave this theory a distinctively

Roman touch. Throughout the three books of his dialogue *Concerning Oratory*, Cicero has his speakers (all leading figures of his youth in the 90s BC) debate the fine points of rhetoric, not only acknowledging debts to Greek theory, but also displaying a profound confidence in their own achievements. The speakers draw examples from the politics of their time, showing how the art of rhetoric is crucial to the man of affairs. By implication, the era of Greek originality has passed. In his own youth, Cicero had translated the popular poem on astronomy, the *Phaenomena* of Aratus of Soli, into Latin, revealing an excellent command of contemporary theory that governed the adaptation of Latin to Greek; and after his consulship he treated various intellectuals of the Greek world to a history of what had by then become Cicero's favorite subject (his own consulship) in Greek.

Romans of Cicero's status were, in his generation, thoroughly bilingual. His closest friend, Titus Pomponius, added the *cognomen* Atticus to his name from his affection for Attica, that part of Greece that included Athens, where he spent his teenage years. Much of what we know about Atticus comes from the biography of him composed by one of Cicero's younger contemporaries, Cornelius Nepos. In addition to this life, he composed numerous biographies of famous men, both Greek and Roman, as well as his own chronicle of world history (in Latin) that exploited recent Greek work. Nepos's interest in biography—and chronology—was an extension of Atticus's own and represents a distinctive effort to produce Latin works in distinctively Greek genres that, as yet, had had no significant Latin practitioners. At the same time, it seems, Greeks were finding new ways to write Rome into their own histories of the world. Diodorus Siculus, for instance, was hard at work on his history of the world even as Cicero wrote. One of Diodorus's major accomplishments was to synchronize the events of Greek history with those of Rome, a task that had recently been attempted for the first time by a Greek from Rhodes named Castor, who wrote a brief chronicle of world history.

Cicero was not alone in his interest in Greek philosophy, and in his lifetime we find Romans openly identifying themselves with specific Greek philosophical sects. To judge from the contents of Cicero's *Concerning Oratory* and other works, Romans of his generation were inclined to identify themselves as adherents of various Greek philosophical schools as a sign of their personal sophistication. Cato, for instance, openly sought to present himself as an adherent of Stoicism, whose founder, Zeno, had lived at the end of the fourth century BC. Cato's point was that through strict adherence to Stoic teachings he could present himself to the world as the one honest politician in Rome. Even as he did so, the stereotype of the dour Stoic seems to have been sufficiently well established in the mind of the Roman public for Cicero to satirize it brilliantly when he defended the consul-elect for 62 BC against a charge of electoral corruption (*ambitus*), a charge brought by Cato along with the noted jurist Servius Sulpicius Galba, one of the unsuccessful candidates.

Cicero tended to identify himself with the "Academic" school descended from Plato, while Lucius Calpurnius Piso, who was one of the consuls of 58 BC, was renowned as a patron of the Epicurean school. The remains of his library at Herculaneum were buried in the great volcanic eruption of AD 79 that also destroyed Pompeii. Generations of scholars working with the carbonized remains of the papyrus rolls that filled this library have managed to decipher many works of Philodemus, the noted Epicurean philosopher who is believed to have been

Unrolled and rolled papyri. The pyroclastic flow that descended on the city of Herculaneum in AD 79 carbonized the library in a villa once owned by Lucius Calpurnius Piso, a former consul and the father-in-law of Julius Caesar. Using increasingly sophisticated techniques, including multi-spectral imaging technology first developed by NASA, we are able to read ever more of the works that have been discovered at this site.

maintained by Piso in this house. Another notable Roman politician, Lucius Memmius, also seems to have had an interest in Epicureanism, and patronized an extraordinary Latin poet, Lucretius, who wrote a poem *On the Nature of Things* in which he sought to explain Epicurean doctrine to a Roman audience in Latin verse. Throughout the six books of this remarkable work he laments the poverty of his native tongue to render Greek philosophic concepts adequately in Latin. The result does not justify the author's professed modesty: the poem was rapidly established as a work that any Roman aspiring to a literary career had to know. Cicero himself wrote that it displayed both genius and technical skill.

One of the important tenets of Epicurean thought was that the gods took no direct interest in the world, and that the wise man should withdraw from direct involvement in politics. Memmius, like Piso, did not heed this advice, and in 53 BC he disgraced himself through a corrupt deal to fix the consular elections. When Memmius withdrew into exile in Athens he bought Epicurus's house and proposed to tear it down (Cicero intervened to prevent him from doing so).

Another poet known to Memmius was Gaius Valerius Catullus, arguably the greatest non-epic poet in Roman history. The poetry of Catullus is important not only because of the author's genius, but also for what it reveals about the intellectual world of a young man of his generation. The one piece of genuine evidence we have for the life of Catullus that is independent of his own poetry—Catullus himself writes that it would be foolish to assume that he is the person he portrays in his poems (Poem 16)—comes from Suetonius's biography of Julius Caesar. There it is clear that Caesar befriended Catullus's father, who was a figure of some importance in northern Italy. The fact that as the father of an adult son he was still active in public life suggests that he was roughly Caesar's own age, and thus that Catullus was in his twenties in the 50s BC. In addition, the fact that Suetonius placed the father in northern Italy allows us to believe that Catullus's references to his northern Italian homeland are not fabrications.

This is extremely important, for it shows just how cosmopolitan the culture of Italy had become. Catullus's poetry reflects intense, creative engagement with the literature of contemporary Alexandria as well as contemporary Asia Minor. He was particularly influenced by the standards of the third-century Alexandrian poet

Callimachus, who had urged others not to write epic poems in the style of Homer, the Latin equivalent of which would be not to write like Ennius (see p. 96). The surviving corpus of Catullus's work is littered with references to Callimachus: one work (Poem 66) is a translation of a poem that Callimachus wrote praising Queen Berenice of Egypt (the wife of King Ptolemy II, his patron); and, displaying a very much more independent take on the master, one of the most remarkable of his works is a poem describing the self-castration of Attis, a devotee of the goddess Cybele in the region of the Troad (Poem 63). In this case, though, Catullus has taken what seems to be a Greek model and used it as a vehicle to explore his own interest in the effect of passion. Elsewhere, in keeping with his interest in northwestern Turkey, Catullus writes of a stint on the staff of Memmius when the latter governed Bithynia in 58, claims that his brother died near Troy, and portrays himself as a member of a group of similar Romans who travel with ease between the metropolis and the towns of Italy. One of the people he identifies as a friend is a young man from Teatina (on the east coast of central Italy) named Asinius Pollio, the grandson of one of the Italian generals in the Social War; another friend is Cornelius Nepos, and yet another is Licinius Calvus. Calvus was the son of Licinius Macer, who had agitated against the Sullan restrictions on the citizenship while he himself had been tribune in 73 BC, and then taken to writing a massive history of Rome from the foundation of the city to (we think) his own time. The format adopted by Macer looked back to a format that had developed in the later second century, largely under the influence of Gnaeus Calpurnius Piso, who wrote a monumental history of Rome organized by annual magistrates that he called the *Annals*. Macer's work evidently won the admiration of another contemporary of Catullus, Sallust, who later included a speech by Macer denouncing the Sullan regime in his own histories. Yet another character who appears in Catullus's poetry is Marcus Caelius Rufus—also a friend of Cicero, and infamous for an affair he had with a sister of Publius Clodius—the man who attempted to seduce Caesar's wife and disrupted the campaign of Lucullus. The same sister of Clodius may appear, under the name Lesbia, as the object of Catullus's affections in many of his poems.

Although it is impossible to reconstruct the affair between Catullus and Clodia, we know that Catullus described his love for Lesbia as turning him into a person who was the very antithesis of the ideal Roman male of his generation. Both the image he sought to convey and the depth of engagement with Greek literature that he expected of his audience emerge perhaps most clearly from his version of a poem by the sixth-century BC Greek poet Sappho (see box, opposite).

Although Catullus's poems are filled with references to his immediate contemporaries, there are few mentions of the older generation. There is one reference to Cicero in a poem (see box, right). Given that Catullus's description of himself is plainly ironic, we can only take his description of Cicero the same way. Nonetheless, it is more generous perhaps than his one overt reference to Clodius (who he suggests committed incest with his sister, also a theme of Cicero's—Poem 79); while he twice makes fun of Publius Vatinius (Poems 52 and 53), a well-known supporter of Pompey, and suggests that Cato could benefit from developing a sense of humor (Poem 56). Pompey appears only in a reference to the great stone theater that he dedicated in 55 BC (Poem 113). When it comes to Caesar, Catullus is scathing, accusing him—in what appears to have become an extremely well-known poem—of

CATULLUS TO CICERO

Most learned descendant of Romulus, as many as there have been, there are, and will ever be, Marcus Tullius, Catullus, the worst of all poets, gives you thanks, he who is by as much the worst of all poets as you are the best patron of all.

(Catullus, Poem 49)

SAPPHO AND CATULLUS

Catullus's poetry displays a remarkably sophisticated handling of earlier Greek verse; we can readily see its Greek antecedents and so appreciate the way that Catullus transformed the meaning of the original text for a Roman audience. A good example is his handling of the poem known to us as Sappho fragment 31 in his own Poem 51. (Since no book of Sappho's poetry has survived from antiquity, the surviving passages are referred to as "fragments" in modern editions, while the numbers of Catullus's poems refer to the order in which the poems appear in the one surviving manuscript.)

Sappho writes in fragment 31:

> He seems to me to be the equal to the gods, that man,
> whoever he who sits opposite you and listens,
> close by to your sweet speaking
> and sweetly laughing; it puts wings on the heart in my chest,
> for as I see you, even briefly,
> no power of speech is left to me,
> but my tongue shivers and a light fire races under my skin,
> there is no sight in my eyes, drumming fills my ears,
> a cold sweat takes me, shaking grips me all over,
> I am greener than grass; I seem dead to myself, or almost so.
> But all things must be dared, even by a poor person.

Catullus's version runs:

> He seems to me to be the equal of a god, he,
> if it is permissible to say so, seems to be better off than the gods,
> who sitting opposite you, sees and hears you,
> sweetly laughing, which takes every sense from me,
> for as soon as I see you, Lesbia, there is nothing left to me …
> but my tongue stops in my mouth,
> a slender flame runs through my frame,
> my ears ring with their own sound, my eyes are covered in dark.
> Leisure, Catullus, that is bad for you;
> you run riot in leisure and play too much:
> leisure has already destroyed kings and beautiful cities.

To make sense of Catullus's poem, the reader must not only notice the subtle variations introduced in the course of the translation—especially the last stanza, which translates the poem entirely into the moral world of contemporary Rome—but also realize that the persona Catullus has adopted is that of Sappho herself! Like the Attis of whom he had written, he has quite literally emasculated himself in his passion.

Much of our knowledge of Sappho's poetry depends on papyri, such as this one from Oxyrhyncus in Egypt, which dates from the third century AD. This particular fragment offers a poem inspired by myth—the marriage of the Trojan prince Hector to Andromache.

having passive sexual relations with one of his lieutenants under the guise of "King Queer" (Poem 29), and writing two lines later regarded as utterly rude:

> I have no interest in pleasing you, Caesar, and I don't give a damn who you are.
>
> (Catullus, Poem 93)

The first of these poems allegedly caused Caesar to seek out Catullus's father so that he could arrange a lunch with the poet, where the two were said to have been reconciled.

Caesar could afford to be generous. Catullus's poem was written sometime around 55 or 54 BC when Caesar was already moving from one success to another. Besides, ostentatious displays of good humor might distinguish him from men like Cato, and, more pointedly, Sulla. Indeed, Caesar might have looked to the style of Sulla for what would become the most famous of his own literary accomplishments: his *Commentaries Concerning the Gallic War*. The "commentary" was scarcely a novel genre by the time that Caesar began to write the annual accounts of his victories in France, southern Germany, and Britain from 58 to 52 BC. In Caesar's own generation, not only had Cicero treated the world to one on the subject of his consulship, but Lucullus had also written of his campaigns (he had a Greek poet named Archias write an epic poem about them as well); and at the end of the second century Lutatius Catulus composed "commentaries" to explain why he, rather than Marius, deserved much of the credit for their joint victory at Vercellae (see p. 123).

All these works, however, pale in comparison to the torrent of self-praise unleashed by Sulla in the twenty volumes of his memoirs, which included reference to divine visions that had inspired him as well as extensive denigration of his foes. Caesar's prose is marked not only by his tendency to refer to himself in the third person—possibly a feature of his personal style—but also by the complete absence of divine machinery. Where Sulla had been verbose, Caesar would be succinct; where Sulla appears to have been overt, Caesar would be implicit; and where Sulla spoke of the "Senate and People of Rome," Caesar would imply that his deeds brought glory to the "Roman people."

Caesar and Pompey

By the time he completed the seventh book of his *Commentaries*, detailing difficult campaigns fought in the course of 52 BC, Caesar had proved that he was the greatest general in Roman history. While his enemies had hoped that Caesar—lacking serious experience of command—might fall victim to one of the tribes north of the border, Caesar rapidly demonstrated an ability to transfer the skills that had made him a successful politician to the battlefield. Behind the often deceptively simple narratives of his campaigns there resides an immense capacity for advance planning, an ability to understand the psychology of his opponents, impressive flexibility when confronted with new challenges, and a profound sense of his own ability. Time and again a chance comment reveals supplies laid up in advance, detailed and accurate intelligence operations, and the ability to take advantage of changing circumstances or to react to unexpected challenges. Caesar knew, above all else, that absolutely no faith should be placed in intelligence offered by people who sought to gain from the information that they provided; that wars are won not on the

Julius Caesar is shown here in a bust that was completed well after his death. Like most later images it depicts Caesar as an older man. There is no hint here of the extremely risqué private life that Caesar enjoyed in defiance of popular morality during the 70s and 60s BC, when, according to one of his enemies, he "was every woman's husband and every man's wife."

battlefield so much as at the conference table; and that the enemy was watching and reacting to his every move. He never fought the same tactical battle twice, and spent a great deal of his time before and after the campaigning season building a network of supporters among the Gauls.

For all the impression of order that Caesar offers in his own account, the Gallic campaigns appear to have begun almost by accident; when Caesar laid down his consulship at the end of 59 BC, the bulk of his army was in the area bordering the Balkans, and Caesar was monitoring a bizarre political situation at Rome into the spring of 58. It was only then that he learned that the Helvetian peoples who lived in what is now Switzerland had begun to move towards the Rhône valley.

The Helvetian threat seems to have been genuinely unexpected, for Caesar had to leave Rome even before the political situation he had been watching played itself out. This situation had its origin in the trial of Clodius for his attempted seduction of Caesar's wife in 62 (Caesar seems to have forgiven Clodius, but Cicero had testified against him). After Cicero delivered a speech that was heavily critical of Caesar and Pompey, Pompey and Caesar had supported the patrician Clodius's adoption by a plebeian so that he could stand for the tribunate of the plebs. Duly elected in 59 BC, Clodius introduced a broad-based legislative program. Measures included the legalization of neighborhood associations of lower-class Romans within the city and a massive new grain distribution program, for which he planned to pay by taking over Cyprus (Rome's dubious claim to the island stemmed from the will of a deceased member of the Egyptian royal house nearly thirty years before). This grain bill is a characteristic example of legislative behavior in these years, since it created an obligation for the state without creating the necessary bureaucracy to run it efficiently. Finally, Clodius introduced a law stating that any man who had put a Roman citizen to death without a trial should be exiled. This applied only to Cicero, who had personally overseen the execution of the Catilinarian conspirators in December 63. Pompey and Caesar refused to intervene; members of the traditional aristocracy (who largely loathed Cicero as an upstart) refused to help; Cato, their spiritual leader, sided with Clodius by accepting the task of annexing Cyprus; and Cicero went into exile. He would return in triumph some eighteen months later, once Pompey and Caesar had found Clodius even harder to control than Cicero had been. At the same time, Pompey was given control of the grain supply, as the state once again looked to an individual to solve a problem that arose from lack of the necessary public institutions.

While Clodius occupied center stage at Rome, Caesar manipulated the Helvetian situation to his advantage. Declaring the Helvetians a threat to the security of his province, he broke Sulla's law on treason (see p. 134), as well as a law on corruption that he himself had sponsored in the previous year, by leading his army into the tribal lands of the Rhône valley where he destroyed the Helvetian army. Having done that, he professed profound surprise that the Gallic tribe in whose territory the Helvetians had been defeated (this tribe had arranged supply depots for Caesar's men at very short notice) was "oppressed" by a German king, who had taken control of lands to their north and defeated them in battle. Although he had named this king—Ariovistus—a "friend and ally of the Roman people" in 59 BC, Caesar now provoked a war that ended in another total victory. This victory, he claimed, required his army to winter near the Rhine! Victory followed upon victory as Caesar conquered the Belgic tribes of northwestern Gaul in the course of 57, and tribes along the Atlantic coast in the summer of 56. In 55 he annihilated two German tribes that sought to move across the Rhine, and launched a brief invasion of Britain. This was repeated in 54, and after a serious setback in the winter of that year (the destruction of fifteen cohorts by a Belgic tribe called the Eburones), he spent 53 avenging his losses. In the year 52 a massive uprising took place among the tribes of central Gaul under the leadership of the chieftain Vercingetorix. This revolt ended, after considerable stress, when Caesar compelled Vercingetorix to surrender in an epic struggle around the city of Alesia, in central France (see box, p. 162).

During these years Caesar acquired a massive fortune and built a network of dependants throughout Italy. Young men, and men whose prospects were otherwise limited, were drawn into his service as the best way of advancing their careers—just as they had been to Sulla, and were still to Pompey. Caesar also assembled what was arguably the best army in Roman history. There seems little question that his men were devoted to their general, and willing to undertake labors on his behalf that might have caused others to mutiny; the only mutinies that Caesar faced were after he invaded Italy, and both proved remarkably easy to quell. We will never know what end he envisaged from all this, but it may well be that he never looked beyond the issue that would spark the civil war in 49: that he should be allowed to continue to dominate Roman political life through continued provincial commands.

At the same time, there can be little doubt that Caesar's impact on Gallic society was devastating. Reading between the lines (and Caesar's assertion that it was inspired by the murder of Clodius in the year 52 BC), revolts such as that of Vercingetorix were caused by Caesar's ruthless handling of Gallic leaders, and the disruptive results of his victories. The immediate cause of the revolt of 52 BC was the infliction of the Roman penalty of flogging and beheading upon a chieftain. Claims both by Caesar and others about the total number of people he killed are wildly exaggerated, reflecting the Roman audience's delight in tales of massive barbarian bloodshed (peoples Caesar claimed to have annihilated tended to reappear with large armies rather rapidly after initial defeats). There can be no doubt, however, that hundreds of thousands died and were displaced in these years. Brutal as he could be, Caesar seems to have recognized that he could not build a successful base of support through terror alone. He was more than willing to accept those who would submit into his service, providing an alternative to resistance for Gallic nobles, many of whom would serve him well as commanders of auxiliary forces in later years. In so doing he laid the foundation for the growth of a provincial society in which Gallic leaders gradually adopted forms of Roman culture that enabled ever greater communication with, and ultimately membership of, the Roman governing class.

Despite his overall record of success, setbacks revealed that even Caesar was not without his faults. He was too quick, at times, to assume that his solutions were acceptable to everyone. In the winter of 54–53 he divided his legions into many camps so that no one tribe alone would have to try to feed tens of thousands of soldiers after a bad harvest. He may well have assumed that this concession was satisfactory, since no tribe would be foolish enough to revolt on its own. But he was wrong, and nearly 8,000 men paid the price for Caesar's failure to leave their commanders orders on how to deal with trouble. In 52, he claimed that his men exceeded their instructions during the siege of a Gallic city, panicked, and were driven back

The forum of Julius Caesar, pictured above, was paid for with the spoils of his Gallic campaign. Centered on the temple of Caesar's ancestor Venus Genetrix, construction began in either 55 or 54 BC. Pompey meanwhile dedicated his new temple complex for Venus the Victorious, which included Rome's first stone theater, in 55 BC. The coincidence of these two projects reflects both men's desire to use the wealth they had acquired to dominate the urban space of Rome.

with heavy losses. This may be true, but he also notes that there were issues with the terrain that made it difficult for people to know what his orders would have been in a specific tactical situation. Although he spent a great deal of time trying to communicate his strategic and tactical vision to his subordinates, he seems to have felt, at times, that people ought to be able to read his mind and know what he wanted.

During Caesar's years in Gaul the political situation in Rome changed. Opposition to the effective control of the political system by Pompey, Crassus, and Caesar had coalesced in the course of 56 (the year that Pompey demonstrated his continuing clout by arranging Cicero's return from exile), which led to an agreement that Pompey and Crassus should be consuls together in the following year. It was also agreed that as consuls, they should equip themselves with five-year provincial commands. These were modeled on Pompey's earlier commands, under the Gabinian and Manilian laws, and his passing of a new law that seems to have granted similar powers to Caesar. The most important of these provisions would prove to be the one allowing him to raise whatever troops he thought necessary, and—in what turned out to be the worst drafted piece of legislation in Roman history—the one that extended his command for five years. The evident problem with the drafting of the law was that Caesar's command in Gaul still had a year to run, and the law was written in such a way that Caesar could argue that it was extended for five years from the end of his previous mandate; equally, those who disliked him could claim that it ended five years after the passage of the new law.

The wording of the law perhaps seemed of little relevance as Pompey took control of the Spanish provinces, which he governed through officials he appointed as his legates (deputies), and as Crassus decided to take advantage of his new governorship in Syria by launching a blatantly illegal invasion of the Parthian empire (without a formal declaration of war he was only supposed to take military action in self-defense). The Parthian empire, which included modern Iraq and Iran, was the one great power remaining on the border of the Roman state. Crassus had nothing but contempt for its power and in 53 led a large army to destruction outside the city of Carrhae, the modern Harran in Turkey. Ignorant of enemies whom Rome had never fought, he paid for his folly with his life, and the lives of thousands of his men. The Romans were lucky that the Parthians lacked the organization to be a genuine threat to the Eastern provinces.

Taken together with Caesar's operations in Gaul, Crassus's attack on the Parthian empire was a sign that the government of the Republic was losing control of its own foreign policy. An even more serious indication of this appeared the year before Crassus arrived in Syria, having been cursed by a tribune of the plebs on his way out of Rome since it was clear that he was planning to start a war and that no one would be able to stop him. Similarly to Pompey and Caesar, Crassus was somewhat of a special case because his wealth and network of supporters set him apart from the average Roman. This was not true of Aulus Gabinius, Crassus's predecessor as governor of Syria. The author of the law giving Pompey command against the pirates in 67, Gabinius owed his tenure of the consulship in 58 to Pompey's influence, and even if we discount most of what we know about him—which comes from some vitriolic speeches by Cicero, who held him partly responsible for his exile—he was not one of the more impressive specimens of his generation. As it happened, the actions of Gabinius in restoring King Ptolemy XIII to the throne of Egypt against the

CAESAR'S WARS

(Right) Caesar's campaigns in Gaul lasted from 58 to 50 BC. From 58 to 56 he campaigned in the Rhône valley against the Helvetians and Germans, and then in northern France against the Belgic tribes and the peoples of Brittany. In 55 Caesar defeated some German tribes that had moved into Gaul, and launched a brief invasion of southern Germany and an equally brief invasion of Britain. A second invasion of Britain consumed the summer of 54. In the winter of 54/3 Caesar suffered a serious setback when a legion and a half were destroyed by the Belgic Eburones. The year 52 saw a massive effort to destroy the Roman presence, led by the Gallic chieftain Vercingetorix, which ended with the latter's surrender at Alesia. In the next two years Caesar put down further revolts and prepared to confront his rivals at Rome.

(Below) The civil wars began in January 49 BC with Caesar's invasion of Italy. After four years, and campaigns in Spain, Greece, and north Africa, they ended in 45 BC with the final defeat of Pompeian forces at the battle of Munda.

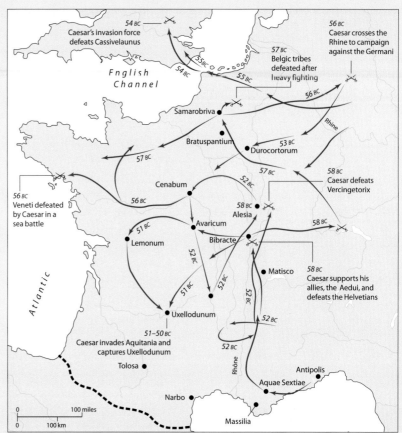

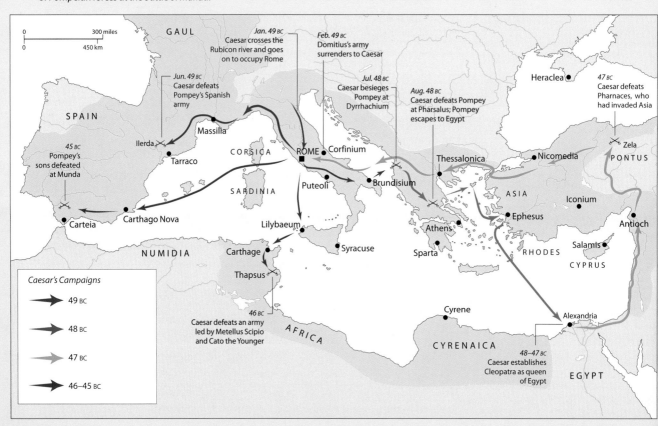

express wishes of the senate were more scandalous than anything Crassus would do. Although Crassus and Caesar had not been given permission to start the wars they did, at least they were not defying a direct order.

The case of Ptolemy XIII was complicated insofar as he had only become king of Egypt after he had promised massive bribes (which it seems he did not actually pay) to Caesar and Pompey. After one of Clodius's laws resulted in the Roman annexation of Cyprus, an Egyptian possession, in 58, a well-organized mob in Alexandria had driven Ptolemy into exile. Coming to Italy in 57 and soon enmeshed in colorful scandals, he asked the senate to restore him to his throne. Throughout the next year and a half the senate engaged in desultory debate as to who might do this—obvious choices were Pompey or the governor of Cilicia in southern Turkey—since it was clear that whoever it was would be likely to have open access to the royal treasury. That was too much for many people to stomach, and Pompey, with his eye on the consulship of 55, did not press his case with vigor, as the king was becoming a toxic commodity. The whole business seemingly blew over by the end of 56, when the senate decreed that the king could be restored, but not with the aid of a Roman army. This caused Ptolemy to leave Rome in disgust. What people may not have counted on was that his fallback plan was to pay Gabinius to help him back to the throne, which Gabinius did, leaving two legions of his men behind in the king's service. This was so outrageous that Gabinius was put on trial and exiled; it is possible that a timely flood, suggesting the gods were angry with Rome, helped the jury reach this decision. Otherwise, the invasion was also said to have been the point at which the king's eldest daughter, Cleopatra, first met an aristocratic young Roman officer named Mark Antony.

Even before Crassus's death, the union between Caesar and Pompey had suffered a serious blow. A year before Crassus's disaster, Julia—Caesar's daughter and Pompey's wife, once the strongest bond between the two men—died, just as Pompey was becoming jealous of Caesar's rise to power. The death of Julia became a serious issue in the wake of another death—that of Publius Clodius—in January of 52. Thanks to the political chaos that reigned in the city, no consuls had been elected for the new year. A greater crisis ensued when massive riots broke out, including one on the day of Clodius's funeral in the forum, which resulted in the burning of the senate's meeting house. Pompey was made sole consul: an event that Tacitus saw as marking a turning point on Rome's path to autocracy. Pompey could only have assumed this position with Caesar's agreement, and that came at a high cost. Caesar demanded that Pompey allow for the passage of a bill moved by all ten tribunes giving Caesar the right to stand for the consulship without entering the city of Rome. The usual requirement was for a man to make a personal declaration of his interest—professio—before the presiding magistrate within the city, but to do so Caesar would have to lay down the imperium that protected him from prosecution for illegal acts in Gaul (such as his assault on the Helvetians and Ariovistus). Pompey agreed, but then supported a law imposing a comprehensive change in the nature of provincial government, which required a five-year interval between holding office and governing a province. The point of this was to prevent such deals as that attempted by consular candidates in 54, in which the successful candidates guaranteed that the outgoing consuls would get provinces where there was a high probability of profit. Pompey also passed a law imposing new courtroom procedures, and another stating that a man must make *professio* in person. Suetonius says that Pompey amended this law, which would have superseded the law of the ten tribunes, by entering the treasury—where the bronze tablets upon which Roman laws were inscribed—with a scribe who added a clause stating that this law did not apply to Caesar. At the same time, Pompey brought troops into the city to quell the rampant violence, using them to surround the courts where the trials of those involved were being held. Cicero was said to have been so frightened by the scene that he could not deliver the speech he had written in defense of Milo, a long-term political ally whose bodyguards were responsible for Clodius's death.

Pompey capped off his term as sole consul, which lasted several months, by marrying the daughter of one of Caesar's sworn enemies and elevating his new father-in-law to the consulship. War now became virtually inevitable, despite rounds of fruitless negotiations over both the terminal date of Caesar's command in Gaul, and Caesar's demand that he should be allowed to stand for the consulship without entering the city of Rome. Caesar was confident of two things: that he would win an election, and, if he laid down his command before he took up the consulship, that his enemies would bring him to trial and prevent him from standing. In the meantime he appears to have been building up his army so that it included more than ten legions in the wake of the victory over Vercingetorix, and continued to expand, even though, with major combat now drawing to a conclusion in Gaul, there was no obvious justification for such a course of action. With his army mustered and now largely concentrated in southern France and northern Italy, Caesar was ready for what the new year would bring. He would not have to wait long, as the crisis came to a head in early January 49 BC when the senate passed an "ultimate decree," along the lines of that first passed against Gaius Gracchus (see p. 115), and asked Pompey to raise an army. The senate also drove the tribunes who supported Caesar out of the city, an action that gave Caesar exactly the pretext he desired to launch what was, by January 11, a carefully planned invasion of Italy. As Caesar crossed the Rubicon river that divided his province from Italy, it is alleged that he said simply: "the die is cast."

In Pompey Caesar faced an able adversary of genuine ability who understood the realities of warfare as well as he did. The first of these realities was that Pompey could not possibly face Caesar with the forces that could be raised in Italy while Caesar was already on the march. Despite howls of protest from members of the senate who did not see the situation the way he did, Pompey withdrew as fast as he could to the port of Brundisium in southern Italy. From there, whatever troops he could raise—and he did raise more than 20,000 men as he withdrew—could be taken to Greece to join the armies he was marshalling in the Eastern provinces. Pompey's problem was that he could not get his subordinates, who tended to see themselves as his equals, to agree to his plan: one of them, Lucius Domitius Ahenobarbus, ignored a series of letters from Pompey, and was cut off with 10,000 men at Corfinium in central Italy. The texts of these letters reveal just how well Pompey understood his rival (see box, right), and in the end, virtually as Pompey had predicted, Domitius was imprisoned by his own men, who surrendered, en masse, to Caesar.

Corfinium was the defining moment of the war. When the garrison—which included many leaders of the political opposition—surrendered, Caesar took the soldiers into his service and released the rest. This act of mercy, so unlike anything seen in previous civil wars, was a tremendous stroke of propaganda. The force of

POMPEY WARNS DOMITIUS

It would ill befit your foresight to consider only how many cohorts Caesar has against you at the present moment without regard to the size of the forces, both horse and foot, which he will shortly muster … If these forces are concentrated at one point, with part of the army sent against Alba and part advancing on you, Caesar not offering battle but repelling attacks from favorable positions, you will find yourself in a trap.

(Cicero, *Letters to Atticus*, trans. Shackleton-Bailey, 8.12c)

Caesar's action was underlined by a ridiculous statement by Pompey, who was heard to declare: *Sulla potuit, ego non potero?* ("Sulla could do it, why can't I?"). The reference was to his strategy of invading from the East, but it was taken as a reference to proscription, an interpretation supported by the insistence of Pompey and his supporters that people were either with them or against them. Caesar, by way of contrast, was writing:

> I had on my own accord decided to show all possible clemency and
> to do my best to reconcile Pompey. Let us try whether by this means
> we can win back the good will of all and enjoy a lasting victory, seeing
> that others have not managed by cruelty to escape hatred or make their
> victories endure, except only L. Sulla, whom I do not propose to imitate.
>
> (Cicero, *Letters to Atticus,* trans. Shackleton-Bailey, 9.7c)

Although Pompey's diplomatic skills were limited, Caesar recognized that he was still a formidable adversary. Indeed, as he left Italy to take apart the armies that Pompey's officers had been building up over the previous few years in Spain, he is said to have remarked that once he had dealt "with the army without a general, he would take care of the general without an army" (Suetonius, *Life of Caesar* 34). His judgment in both cases was reasonable, for he had minimal difficulty in forcing the excellent army in Spain to surrender in the late summer of 49, and came close to disaster against the poor army that Pompey had assembled in Greece. Once Caesar had evaded the fleet that Pompey had hoped would keep him in Italy, Pompey did the best he could to avoid direct confrontation on the open battlefield, where the superiority of Caesar's veterans would win the day. He was at first successful, defeating Caesar in what was virtually an ancient version of trench warfare near the city of Dyrrachium in Illyria in 48 BC. Unfortunately for Pompey, the victory emboldened the numerous senators who had accompanied him, and they ultimately compelled him to offer battle on the plain of Pharsalus in Thessaly on August 1. Caesar's victory was total, and once Pompey had seen that the one attack he had hoped might prevent a Caesarian victory had failed, he did not wait for the end of the battle before withdrawing to his tent. Having lost his army, Pompey fled to Egypt, where agents of its king, Ptolemy XIII, murdered him later that year.

After Pompey's defeat, and professing great shock at the assassination of his former friend, Caesar became embroiled in the civil war then brewing between the Egyptian king and his sister, Cleopatra. The war proved easy enough to win, but Caesar was plainly enamored of Cleopatra, who bore a son she named for him shortly after his departure. The affair was a scandal, for it suggested an unhealthy interest in royal power on Caesar's part; not surprisingly, it is entirely obscured in the writings of Caesar's partisans, as well as those of Caesar himself.

The civil war had not ended with the death of Pompey. As was the case with the Sullan civil war, pockets of resistance remained throughout the Mediterranean. Caesar's dalliance in Egypt, and a further delay occasioned by the invasion of northern Turkey by a son of Mithridates—defeated rapidly enough for Caesar to claim *veni, vidi, vici*: "I came, I saw, I conquered"—gave surviving supporters of Pompey time to build an army in north Africa. This army was only beaten after hard fighting at the battle of Thapsus in 46. Following the defeat, Cato, who had played a shadowy role in the military aspects of the campaign, committed suicide rather than surrender to Caesar, setting off a literary war over his memory that, despite Caesar's best efforts to discredit him, established Cato as an example of principled courage in the imagination of later generations.

The Pompeian cause did not die with Cato. A year later it was resurrected in Spain under the nominal leadership of Pompey's two sons and the actual leadership of Titus Labienus, who had once been Caesar's chief lieutenant in Gaul, before he deserted to Pompey when Caesar crossed the Rubicon. Caesar's victory came only towards the end of the summer of 45 after a brutal struggle at Munda, which claimed the lives of both Labienus and Pompey's older son. One moment of particular importance during this campaign occurred when Caesar was accompanied from Italy by his grandnephew, Gaius Octavius, who seems to have impressed him profoundly.

Although the Spanish campaign ended immediate resistance to Caesar, there were, within the year, glimmerings of yet further trouble. Sextus, the younger son of Pompey, who had survived the Spanish campaign, began to rally support based on the fleet that he had salvaged from earlier losses; while in Syria, legions that had once been recruited by Pompey were showing signs of discontent.

While Caesar's military skills showed little sign of deterioration, his political skills had plainly become rusty. After years of giving orders and expecting them to be obeyed, years of being proven right time and again, he had lost the ability to listen and govern as part of a group. Thus although he retained a good sense of what the poor of Rome and his own soldiers desired, he failed to take account of the impression that his extraordinarily centralized style of government made on other members of the ruling class. One of the most potent symbols of this style was Caesar's decision to regularize the calendar, now badly out of alignment with the seasons (the August date given for the battle of Pharsalus masks the fact that it actually took place in what would have been May). As the reform of the calendar took place in the summer of 46, sixty-seven days were added to the year between November and January, in addition to an intercalary month added after February 24; by the new calculation, 46 BC had a total of 445 days. In a symbolic sense, Caesar was asserting his control over nature and using the latest Greek science to do so, as the new calendar was based on the workings of the mathematician Sosigenes of Alexandria.

Cicero made jokes about Caesar's new calendar and attempted to comfort himself with the thought that things would not have been much different if Pompey had won. In Cicero's view, Pompey had behaved in a high-handed, autocratic style, listening to the wrong advisers. Caesar was no different.

Others appear to have cared little that Caesar's arrangements to settle many poor Romans were practical; or that his model for a reformed grain distribution system at Rome worked; or that, when he released thousands of soldiers with grants of land, the land was purchased rather than confiscated. What they noticed was that he simply announced policies without debate. A document from the last two weeks of Caesar's life shows him personally conducting business that was properly that of the senate; signs of conflict with the senate suggest that the chief grievance the members of the ruling class had with Caesar was that he ignored them. Most troubling perhaps, was that Caesar—who had set up a structure that would permit him to ignore standard procedures while the civil war was raging—showed no interest in dismantling that structure once the war looked as if it might end. The structure was

CAESAR'S OFFENSE

Another incident occurred which very much spurred on the conspirators. Caesar was undertaking the building of a large, magnificent forum in Rome, and, having gathered together the builders, he was selling off the contracts for its construction. While he was doing this, the noblest of the Romans approached him carrying the honors that they had just then unanimously voted him. The consul, Caesar's colleague at the time, preceded these men carrying the record of the honors voted, while the lictors went in front and kept back the crowd on both sides ... While they were approaching, Caesar remained seated, and because he was paying attention to the men on one side, he did not turn and face the procession, nor did he pay them any attention, but, without a change in posture, he dealt with the business at hand. At this one of his friends standing nearby said "Look at the men opposite approaching." Caesar then put aside his papers, turned to them, and gave ear to why they had come. Because of this insult, the conspirators present with the leading men were incensed and filled the others with hatred of Caesar.

(Nicolaus of Damascus, *Life of Augustus*, trans. Bellemore, 78–79)

based on the Office of Dictator, and looked back to when Sulla made the office the basis for his power after the civil war. Notably, Sulla laid down the dictatorship after the consular elections of 79 as a sign that life had returned to normal. Caesar's experimentation took a very different course. He briefly took the office in late 49 (when he also secured the consulship for a second time) and again, for a longer spell, after Pharsalus. During a short stay at Rome in 46, he took a new approach to the dictatorship, accepting the office for ten years and then, two years later, in perpetuity. He also held the consulship in 46, 45, and 44. Caesar was critical of Sulla's decision to give up the dictatorship, instead insisting that the regime would include a dictator operating as he saw fit alongside the traditional institutions of the state.

One incident that takes pride of place in all accounts of Caesar's death, whether produced to justify the assassination, or to criticize the murderers for misinterpreting what had really happened, involved Caesar's failure to rise from his seat to meet a senatorial delegation. The severity of the offence may be seen in the sensitivity with which it was treated in a life of Augustus, composed two decades after the event by a Greek historian named Nicolaus of Damascus (see box, opposite). Other actions, even Caesar's acceptance of divine honors on the model of a Greek king (see pp. 247–48), and his renaming of Sulla's games in honor of "the Victoria (goddess of Victory) of Sulla" for July 44 as the games in honor of "the Victoria of Caesar," do not figure so prominently (or at all) in the debate over whether it was right to kill him. The divine honors were evidently modeled upon honors that had been given to many Roman governors in the Eastern provinces (including several who may have voted on the measure concerning Caesar), and, while "un-Roman," were not unheard of.

Discontent continued to mount as Caesar offered no model for government other than that of the new-style dictatorship, and looked to depart from Rome

This temple, built by Quintus Lutatius Catulus on the Campus Martius in 101 BC, sits in what is now the Area Sacra di Largo Argentina. It faces what was once the end of the great portico attached to the Theatre of Pompey, in which the senate met on the day Caesar was assassinated.

for several years in order to avenge the defeat of Crassus by invading the Parthian empire. To many senators Caesar's style smacked of *regnum*, the evil power of a king that was opposed to the principle of *libertas* (the freedom from a single master) that was theoretically the characteristic of the Republican regime. In addition, a bizarre incident at the Lupercalia festival in February, when Mark Antony three times offered Caesar a crown (which he refused), strengthened the belief that some day he would take it. Caesar may have thought that he could solve his difficulties by going to war with the Parthians. He intended to leave Rome on March 18, 44 BC, and he certainly seems to have believed that other Romans realized that "if something happened to him, the *res publica* would not have peace, but would be plunged into civil war" (Suetonius, *Life of Caesar* 86). But the Ides of March came first. On the morning of March 15, a group of some sixty senators stabbed Caesar to death at a meeting of the senate convened in the theater that Pompey had built. Caesar fell dead at the feet of a statue of Gnaeus Pompey.

Octavianus and Antony (44–31 BC)

Caesar's Heir (44–43 BC)

Thirteen years separate the assassination of Caesar from the battle of Actium in 31 BC, the point at which Cassius Dio asserted that the Roman monarchy began (see p. 153). The tale of these years is dominated by two men whose backgrounds were very different. One was Mark Antony, a member of a family that had seen many men enter public life, and whose own father, Antonius, had been given special *imperium* to pursue pirates on Crete in the 70s BC, nineteen years before the death of Caesar. The other was Gaius Octavius. Octavius's father was a moderately distinguished senator whose principal claim to fame was that his own father had married Caesar's sister.

The relationship between Antony and Octavius falls into roughly three phases. The first, which saw Antony as the dominant partner, lasted from the moment of Caesar's assassination to around 37 BC. In the course of the next three years the two men were roughly equal in power, while in the three years before Actium, Octavius became ever more the dominant member of the pair. Antony's problem throughout these years was that, although capable of great achievement on the battlefield, the fame that he won was inevitably undermined by his scandalous conduct in private. Octavius, on the other hand, while deeply lacking in ability on the battlefield—he tended to become violently ill when danger threatened—proved to be a brilliant and innovative politician. One quality that both men shared was utter ruthlessness.

Octavius owed his career to the fact that Caesar had surrounded himself—as did Pompey and Sulla before him—with a court-like structure at the heart of which was a group of long-serving and close associates. Some of them were provincials, including the Spanish multi-millionaire Cornelius Balbus, who was recognized in the fifties as one of Caesar's most important spokesmen; Gaius Matius (a member of the equestrian order) to whom he was very close; and Aulus Hirtius, the consul designate for 43, who was at work completing Caesar's account of the Gallic wars in the course of 44 BC, adding an introductory letter to Balbus in which he stated that he could see no end to civil strife. These men formed a powerful group that soon found itself in opposition to the men who were formally in charge of Rome after Caesar's death.

Marcus Lepidus is here shown on a coin of 43 BC, struck by Antony to commemorate the formation of the triumvirate. The fact that Antony's head appeared on the other side of the coin—and that further coins depicted Antony and Octavianus— shows that this pairing was intended to indicate equality among the members of the triumvirate.

On the day of his death Caesar was both Dictator for Life and consul. His assistant as dictator, or Master of Horse, was Marcus Aemilius Lepidus, son of the revolutionary consul of 78. His colleague as consul was Mark Antony. It fell to Antony and Lepidus to decide how to deal with the assassins, and what to do about the legacy of Caesar. Their first steps after the murder were uncertain—they even dined with the assassins on March 18, and allowed the senate to pass an amnesty for the killers on the same day that it voted to confirm decisions made by Caesar that had not yet been made public. At this point there were already signs of tension between Antony and Caesar's inner circle. Calpurnius Piso, Caesar's father-in-law, had insisted on the public reading of Caesar's will, wherein it was discovered that Caesar was leaving lavish gifts to the Roman people and that he was adopting Octavius as his principal heir.

The political situation in Rome changed radically on or about March 20 at Caesar's funeral, the last major event at which Antony and members of the inner circle worked closely together. It was Calpurnius Piso who led the funeral procession, but it was Antony who gave the funeral oration—a speech that remains famous to us today mostly because of the brilliant version Shakespeare invented for Antony in *Julius Caesar*. The actual event was more dramatic even than Shakespeare allows us to imagine. Antony did deliver an incendiary funeral oration, and displayed the bloodied garment that Caesar had been wearing when he was murdered, but it was the image of Caesar himself that seems to have driven the crowd into a fury. After Antony finished, an actor dressed as Caesar spoke a line from Pacuvius—"Oh that I should have spared these men to kill me"—at which point a wax effigy of Caesar was lifted up, its body displaying his wounds. The crowd rioted, burning the body in the forum and attacking the assassins' houses. This riot showed that the sympathy of the Roman people was with Caesar's partisans.

The split between the inner core of Caesar's supporters and Antony grew rapidly after the funeral, as Antony's behavior—both in his personal life and in his exploitation of the decree giving legal force to Caesar's unpublished decisions (which enabled Antony to claim that decisions he was making were actually Caesar's)—offended them as much as his failure to deal with the assassins. It soon became clear that Antony's primary interest was himself. In June, Brutus and Cassius were allowed to depart for the Eastern provinces, where Pompeian sympathies ran deep, where they overthrew Caesar's administrators, and where they began the process of assembling a substantial army of their own. Lepidus, who had been in the background during these months, assumed Caesar's title of *pontifex maximus* and took off to take command of armies in Gaul. Octavius, who had been at Apollonia in Greece, awaiting Caesar's arrival on the way to Parthia, came to Rome in April; immediately his own relationship with Antony became problematic.

Not the least significant sign of the problem was that Antony blocked confirmation of Octavius's adoption, which required action by the *pontifices* because he was being transferred from a plebeian to a patrician family. (For the sake of clarity, from this point until 28 BC when he assumed the name Augustus, I will refer to Octavius as Octavianus, a standard *cognomen* formed from the former *nomen* of a man who had been adopted, rather than as Caesar, even though after the adoption his name was in fact Gaius Julius Caesar.) At the same time, Cicero emerged from the semi-retirement into which he had retreated after supporting Pompey during the civil war and to mourn the death of his beloved daughter. In doing so Cicero displayed enormous courage, and seems genuinely in the course of this year and the next to have rallied opinion against Antony through a series of speeches known as the *Philippics*: the title was derived from the famous speeches given by the fourth-century Athenian orator Demosthenes against King Philip II of Macedon, the father of Alexander the Great.

By the beginning of the summer of 44 Antony realized that he needed troops to secure his position, and began to summon Caesarian veterans from their farms. He also transferred four legions from Macedonia. In November, two of these legions suddenly declared their loyalty to Octavianus (who had offered 2,000 sesterces, more than two years' pay, to each man). Realizing that there was nothing he could accomplish in Rome, Antony now took the forces at his disposal (five legions) north into the province of Cisalpine Gaul, which was then governed by Decimus Brutus, one of the assassins, who (unlike Marcus Brutus, one of the leaders of the conspiracy and a former supporter of Pompey) had been one of Caesar's favored officers. Brutus's forces were weaker than Antony's and he shut himself up in the city of Mutina, to which Antony promptly laid siege.

The consuls for 43 BC were two of Caesar's trusted generals, Aulus Hirtius and Gaius Vibius Pansa. When the senate declared Antony a public enemy, Octavianus was given the rank of praetor, although he had never held any office. He was sent with the consuls to confront Antony. Two battles were fought outside Mutina in March and April at which Antony was defeated, and in each of which one of the consuls died. Octavianus was now left in command of the army as it pursued Antony towards Gaul. Decimus Brutus, to whom Octavianus refused to speak even though he had ostensibly been sent to rescue him, soon took flight for his life (he was later killed). In the late summer, as Antony joined forces with Lepidus and others in southern France, Octavianus turned back to Rome, extorting the office of consul from the senate, although he would not ordinarily have been eligible for the office for another twenty-two years. Several weeks later he met with Antony and Lepidus near Bononia. Their troops refused to fight, saying that they should instead be pursuing Caesar's killers. The three men then agreed that they would assume joint leadership of the Caesarian cause. On November 23 the tribune Marcus Titius carried a law that established a board of "Three Men for setting the state in order" (*tresviri rei publicae constituendae*). The triumvirs, essentially a board of three dictators, were Antony, Lepidus, and Octavianus. Their term was initially set at five years.

The Era of the Triumvirs (43–31 BC)

The next six years were, in many ways, a continuation of the previous civil war. The issue at stake was not so much whether the traditional government of the Republic could ever be restored—even the assassins of Caesar, who thought that this was a possibility on the day they did their deed, seem rapidly to have realized that it was an impossible dream. Rather, it was which of the factions should provide the replacement for Caesar. One thing that does seem clear is that both sides soon abandoned the notion of one-man rule in favor of a limited collective style of leadership that was less offensive to Roman tradition. Marcus Brutus and Gaius Cassius commanded the party of the assassins, while the Caesarian side was now led by the triumvirs.

This famous coin was struck by Brutus after his conquest of territory in Macedonia. In one of the few discussions of the significance of a coin type from antiquity, Cassius Dio described how Brutus had depicted on his coins: "a freedman's cap and two daggers, showing by this and by the inscription (the date of Caesar's assassination) that he had liberated the fatherland."

As soon as they took office the triumvirs found that they had a serious problem on their hands. Each man led his own army, with the result that they collectively controlled something like 100,000 men under arms, and there was simply no money to pay the troops. The solution of the triumvirs was to reinstitute a Sullan-style proscription. We will never know for certain which of them came up with this idea, and to some extent this is unimportant, since all three agreed that this is what they would do. In the long run, once control of the historical record fell to Octavianus, Antony received the bulk of the blame. This may not be entirely unjust. Antony was the most powerful member of the group, and Sulla evidently provided a far more powerful model for him than did Julius Caesar. Like Sulla, Antony drank to excess, enjoyed the company of actors, and saw the Eastern part of the empire as an area from which it would be possible to control the rest.

The triumvirs' proscriptions were even more ghastly than those of Sulla. More than three thousand members of the upper classes were summarily executed, including Cicero. The execution of Cicero was an explicit act of revenge for his role in rousing opposition to Antony, and indeed for the vitriolic tone of his *Philippics*. More than that, however, the brutal slaughter of the most distinguished member of the senate by men Antony sent specifically to kill him proved that no man was safe. The experience of less distinguished Romans—the constant fear that beset those who were not intimate with the regime—is perhaps best seen in the words of a man who managed to survive, although he had been proscribed, because of the support he received from his family. Many others like him died after their family members or slaves had betrayed them: the breakdown in normal human relationships, and the sense of mutual obligation that had been at the heart of Roman social relations for centuries (see pp. 35–36), was one of the most horrific aspects of these years. The text that preserves these words is an inscription bearing the speech that he delivered to honor his deceased wife. Of their experience in 43 to 42 BC he wrote:

> Why should I now reveal our intimate and hidden plans, our secret conversations, since I was snatched from sudden announcements and imminent dangers, and saved by your advice so that you did not allow me to run risks, and when I had thought of more reasonable alternatives, you prepared for me sure refuges, and you chose as allies in plans to save me your sister and her husband Gaius Cluvius, who were joined to us in every peril. I would never finish if I tried to list all that you did. It is enough for you and me that I hid safely. I will, however, speak of the bitterest moment of my life with you, when I had been restored as a useful citizen through the beneficence and judgment of the absent Caesar Augustus, when you approached Marcus Lepidus, his colleague, who was present, about my restoration, you threw yourself on the ground at his feet, and then, not only were you not raised up, but rather, hoisted up like a slave, your body battered, you told Lepidus about the edict of Caesar concerning my restoration—with his compliments—and you forced it openly upon him despite insults and blows, so that the man responsible for my peril took note of it.
>
> (*Elegy for a Roman Matron*, also known as the *Laudatio Turiae*, ii.4–18)

The absence of Octavianus (referred to here by his later name, Caesar Augustus) occurred in the course of 42 when he joined Antony to fight the assassins in Greece. The gratuitous brutality was as familiar to inhabitants of the East as it was in the West. Brutus and Cassius were as vicious as their rivals in their treatment of communities deemed slow to provide support for the armies that they were assembling. The core of Brutus and Cassius's army was provided by legions that Pompey had once raised for the war with Caesar, and that Caesar had left in the East, hoping to gain their loyalty in the Parthian war. Since the war had never taken place, the memory of Pompey had remained strong with these men, and greatly helped the cause of the assassins.

In the late summer of 42, Octavianus and Antony defeated Brutus and Cassius in two battles near Philippi in northern Greece. The credit went to Antony, while Octavianus disgraced himself in the first of the two actions by taking to his tent with an illness, barely escaping when Brutus's soldiers defeated his part of the army and captured the camp. Antony now took the army of the assassins into his service, dampening the memory of Pompey, and beginning the creation of an Antonian empire in the East. Meanwhile other Pompeians now emerged in the West. Sextus Pompey (see p. 166), having rallied various fleets raised to fight the Caesarians over the years, began a war off the coast of Italy that lasted until the summer of 36 BC.

The key events between 42 and 36 BC included a civil war in Italy that broke out as Octavianus was settling veterans from the Philippi campaign on land that had been confiscated, again as Sulla had done, from the communities of Italy; a pair of meetings among the triumvirs in 40 and 37 to reconfirm their authority; a seesaw struggle with Pompey; and striking failure by Antony in the course of an invasion of Parthia. For Octavianus the greatest of these challenges, other than the war with Sextus Pompey, was the civil war of 41, in which he opposed Antony's younger brother Lucius Antonius, who was consul for that year. Octavianus's success was guaranteed only when several armies commanded by allies of the elder Antony failed to support the younger. The elder Antony had given no clear instructions, having, it seems, failed to foresee clearly what might happen, and only decided after the fact to intervene personally. When Antony finally did show up, Perugia, the focal point of the struggle, was in ruins (see box, right); his brother was in Spain, and the troops that were with him joined with those of Octavianus to urge reconciliation. Antony sealed the agreement with Octavianus by marrying his sister, Octavia, and sailed home.

When the two met again three years later, the situation was somewhat different. Although the prestige of Octavianus had suffered a serious setback following two defeats at the hands of Pompey, Antony's prestige was likewise challenged by a recent defeat in the East. Giving Octavianus the ships he needed for a fresh campaign the following year in return for the promise of troops for a renewed war in Parthia, and agreeing to a renewal of their powers as triumvirs, Antony returned to the East.

In 36 BC Octavianus defeated Sextus Pompey and, in a dramatic move, rode into the camp of Lepidus, who was dithering after having moved into Sicily to support the naval campaign. Lepidus's army, unimpressed by his lack of activity, stood by as Octavianus stripped its general of his authority as triumvir, and sent him off for a long, undistinguished retirement in Italy. He retained his position as *pontifex maximus* until his death in 12 BC.

Antony was in trouble. Although he and Octavia had two daughters, their relationship was problematic. Even as he married Octavia, Antony had been deeply in

CIVIL WAR IN ITALY

Tullus, you ask in friendship whence my rank and race. Where is my homeland? Is the Perugian grave of our country known to you, the graveyard of Italy in dark times, whence Roman discord drove its own citizens (thus are you, Eturia, the special cause of grief to me, you who are pressed down by the cast out corpse of my friend, you do not cover his unfortunate corpse with any earth)? Where Umbria, abundant in fertile fields touches the plain that is below it, there was I born.

(Propertius, *Poems* 1.27)

Such coins as this one, which depicts Antony and Cleopatra, are evidence of a severe lack of judgment on Antony's part. While Julius Caesar concealed his affair with Cleopatra in his own writings and refused to acknowledge their son, Antony advertised an equality between himself and Cleopatra that was unpalatable at Rome.

love with Cleopatra of Egypt: in the years that followed, his passion for her, and for life in her capital of Alexandria, became a scandal. Antony dressed and partied as a Greek. Sources infected by Octavianus's propaganda paint a lurid enough picture of debauched behavior. But they are tame compared with a solitary contemporary text, carved in stone, found at Alexandria: a dedication to "Antony the Great" from a local drinking club, and positive proof that stories of Antony's conduct are not pure invention. Antony had long been known for overindulgence—one of the more memorable moments in the course of one of Cicero's attacks upon him was a description of the hungover Antony vomiting while attempting to attend to public business in the forum. Now Octavianus and his supporters returned to the attack, suggesting that his vice was infecting other Romans. Stories were spread of wild parties, including one in which a senior officer—Munatius Plancus—stripped naked, painted himself blue, and flopped around on the floor wearing a fish tail in imitation of a sea god.

Antony attempted to respond by composing a book, *On his Own Drunkenness*, the precise contents of which we can now only imagine, though he may well have pointed out that Alexander the Great had imbibed all night and still managed to conquer the world. If so, it would have been an unfortunate point: historians of Alexander tended to point out that Alexander had been a nasty drunk who had killed a close friend during a particularly intense drinking bout. People recalled that Alexander's last years could be seen as a descent into tyranny, and Antony's devotion to life in Alexandria, as well as his passion for the queen of Egypt, suggested that his vision of Rome's future involved the establishment of a most un-Roman style of tyranny.

Octavianus, in the meantime, managed to bring a semblance of order to the government of Italy. He stopped settling veterans on confiscated land, improved public services at Rome, and made sure that the people had enough to eat. In one particularly striking display of public service, Marcus Agrippa, Octavianus's chief lieutenant and the architect of the victory over Sextus Pompey, accepted a reduction in rank—he had already been consul—to serve as aedile and carry out a personal inspection of the public sewers. As for Octavianus himself, he now attempted to project an image that was in accord with the dignity of a traditional Roman male. It is hard to imagine that anyone seriously believed his claim to have given up sex in his late teens for the good of his health, or the somewhat contradictory claim that he only indulged in adulterous relationships with the wives of his enemies to learn their secrets. In 38 BC, however, he settled into a stable marriage with Livia, a woman of impeccable aristocratic heritage. The marriage began with a first-rate scandal, including Octavianus's divorce from his first wife (the mother of his daughter Julia) and Livia's divorce, although pregnant at the time, from her current husband; but they became a model couple—at least as compared to Antony and Octavia or Cleopatra.

The legal authority of the triumvirs, renewed at the end of 37 (retroactively to the end of 38), was due to expire on December 31, 33 BC. In February 32, after one of the consuls attempted to read a letter from Antony to the senate, Octavianus entered Rome at the head of an armed guard, marched into the senate house, seated himself between the consuls, and proclaimed his continuing authority as head of state. Shortly thereafter he produced what he claimed to be a copy of Antony's will, proving that Antony intended to move the capital to Alexandria. The consuls fled to Egypt, and Octavianus took advantage of the crisis that he had engineered to obtain a further grant of supreme authority for the war that was now declared against Antony. He evidently called himself *Dux*, or "leader," in these years, reflecting this grant.

Antony had expected something like this to happen, and by the late summer of 31 had marched into western Greece at the head of a mighty army. He intended now to do as Sulla had done. The parallel would win few friends, and neither would the fact that Cleopatra had accompanied him on his campaign. He had also underestimated his foe; Octavianus may still have sickened at the prospect of physical danger, but he now knew how to delegate. Antony found that he had isolated himself with an army he could no longer feed near the bay of Actium. Octavianus's army, commanded by Statilius Taurus, proved superior in a preliminary skirmish, and Octavianus's fleet, under the command of Marcus Agrippa, dominated the sea lanes. On September 2, 31 BC, Antony attempted to break out of the trap into which he had so rashly inserted himself. Nothing went right, and as the battle turned against him, Antony saw Cleopatra's squadron take sail to flee the scene. He followed suit, while what remained of the fleet joined the entire army in surrender within the next couple of days.

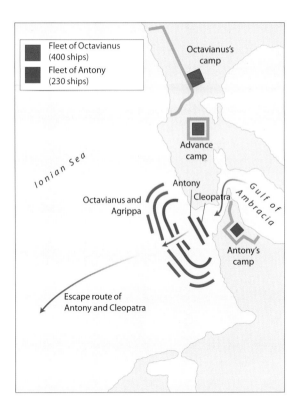

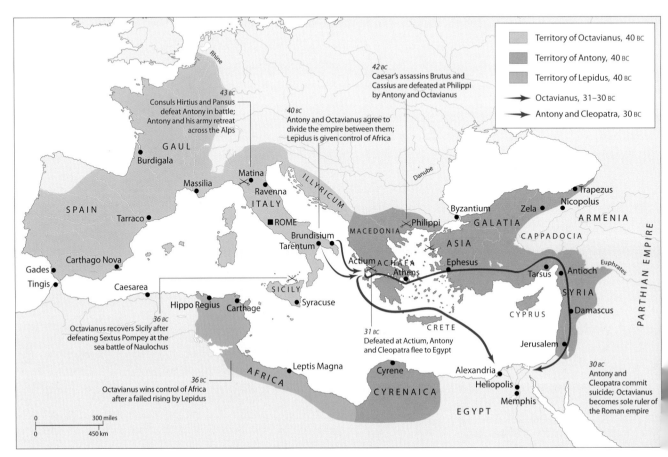

(Opposite) All surviving records of the battle of Actium stem from sources controlled by Octavianus. This makes it hard to reconstruct the battle itself reliably, and to answer the crucial question of whether Antony intended to fight or flee. As the plan on the left suggests, however, Antony was fighting from a position of great inferiority with little room for maneuver. It was this, rather than cowardice, that probably sealed his fate.

(Opposite) The rise and fall of the triumvirate, 43–31 BC. Into the mid-30s, Octavianus and Antony were roughly equal in power. In 36 Octavianus achieved two notable successes with the defeat of Sextus Pompey and the removal of Lepidus from office, which gave him control over Sicily and north Africa. In 31 Octavianus defeated Antony at Actium. He then traveled through the Eastern provinces to shore up support before the final capture of Alexandria in 30 BC.

The gold aureus of Octavianus, as described in the text. This coin was probably minted in 28 BC in Asia Minor (modern Turkey).

Octavianus was now the ruler of the Roman empire. Victory was finalized a year later when his armies marched into Alexandria as Antony committed suicide and died in the arms of Cleopatra. The queen did not long survive her capture. We are told that servants assisted her suicide by slipping an asp into her quarters, and that she died from the poison of its bite. Had the guards been told to ignore suspicious packages?

The Fall of the Republic

A gold coin minted sometime after Actium, illustrated below, depicts Octavianus on the obverse (front); on the reverse (back) is an image of a Roman magistrate sitting on his chair of office with a scroll extended in his right hand. The legend reads, from the obverse to the reverse: "the Imperator son of the divinity Caesar consul for the sixth time / restored laws and statutes." Even though this coin was probably minted for distribution to only the richest Romans—who alone used gold coins—it nonetheless carried with it an important message: the extra-constitutional authority of the triumvirs was at an end now that the power of Antony was no more. Many years later, Octavianus—now Augustus—inscribed this account of his deeds on two bronze tablets before the massive tomb he had erected for himself and members of his family near the banks of the Tiber:

> In my sixth and seventh consulships, after I had extinguished civil wars, when, through the agreement of all people, I was in complete control of affairs, I transferred the *res publica* from my power to the domination of the Roman senate and people … After that time, although I excelled all influence, I had no more power in my several offices than others who were my colleagues.
>
> (*Deeds of the Divine Augustus* 34.1, 3)

The moment of victory was described as follows by the man whose sufferings in the time of the proscriptions were so eloquently recorded in the epitaph he composed for his wife:

> When peace had been restored to the world, when the *res publica* was restored, when fortunate and peaceful times touched us.
>
> (*Elegy for a Roman Matron*, also known as the *Laudatio Turiae*, ii.25–26)

And finally, a man who grew up in the years after Actium wrote:

> Twenty years of civil war ended, foreign wars were buried, peace was recalled, the madness of arms was silenced everywhere, force was restored to the laws, authority to the courts, majesty to the senate, the *imperium* of magistrates was restored to its pristine form … that old and ancient form of the *res publica* was recalled.

(Velleius Paterculus, Short History 2.89)

The crucial point that emerges from all these passages is that Actium ended the civil war, and that the trappings of the traditional constitution were no longer burdened with the additions of triumviral authority. The world is divided between "Restored Republic," which meant that there was peace between Romans, and "civil war." Indeed, Augustus, who now incorporated many of his former enemies into his regime, and ostentatiously showed mercy to those who asked, might be seen as being far more agreeable to surviving aristocrats than Sulla. In so far as a number of his subordinates were able to achieve great dignity on their own—there were more triumphs celebrated in the 30s BC than any other decade of Roman history, largely by allies of Augustus over tribal peoples in central and northern Europe—Octavianus might well seem a good deal more agreeable than Caesar. It took the long perspective of Tacitus to identify a fundamental change (see box, opposite); in his words "the situation had changed so there could be no Roman state unless one man ruled" (*Annals of Imperial Rome* 4.33.2).

Why the situation had so changed remains one of the fundamental questions of European history. There is no simple answer, and in the case of Augustus the question may in fact be mis-stated. Augustus ruled as the head of a victorious coalition. Without his group of loyal subordinates he could not have won, and he would remain remarkably loyal to these supporters. In the course of the civil wars he had depended heavily upon two close friends, Agrippa and Maecenas, to help him. They were a study in contrasts. Maecenas, who never held public office, was a patron of the arts and enjoyed a life of luxury. Agrippa, a masterful soldier, had been consul in

The mausoleum of Augustus in Rome, constructed while Augustus was still alive as a collective tomb for his family. Two bronze tablets, inscribed with the account of his deeds, which he had composed, were displayed in front of the tomb (see p. 188).

37, and shared the consulship with Augustus when the structure of government was reformed in 28 and 27. It was widely believed that Agrippa and Maecenas, with their very different personal styles, disliked each other, and that the contrast between them was of the greatest importance: it made the emergent Augustan regime still look much more like a collective arrangement than it did a monarchy, even though there could be no doubt who had the greatest power. In addition, a number of other men retained very powerful positions within the senate. These included Asinius Pollio, who had won the friendship of Augustus when he did not bring his army to support the younger Antony in 41; Messalla Corvinus, who had served both Cassius and Antony before declaring his undying support for Augustus in the early 30s; Statilius Taurus, who had commanded the land army in the Actian campaign; and Munatius Plancus, who had abandoned Antony just before the battle of Actium.

Augustus's ability to reconcile various members of the aristocracy was matched by his realization that he needed to take an approach to reconciling diverse elements within Roman society, an approach that was unparalleled among his predecessors. On the inscription in front of his tomb, Augustus makes it very clear that he respected the traditional status of the senate, took care to entertain and feed the people of Rome, looked after the army, defended the provinces from outside attack, ensured that the laws had force, and honored the gods. Some of this may well be self-serving, but the significant point is that the most successful Roman politician of his age identified these quite different constituencies as ones with which he had to deal. Still, the question remains: why did the Republican form of government need to change? In simplest terms the answer might be because a government where office-holders changed every year was incapable of building institutions that would satisfy the various groups within Roman society.

When the failure of the Republic is considered as Tacitus considered it, in institutional terms, it is clear that to see the change in government as solely a feature of the age of Caesar and Augustus would not be correct. As early as the Social War of 91–88 BC it was apparent that the bonds linking the senate and people of Rome with the army were very weak. The bulk of the army was made up of men who never came to Rome and who were more likely to be loyal to their generals, and to their fellow soldiers and officers—many of whom were their compatriots in peacetime—than to the civil institutions of the state. The result of the Social War was to overturn the system of alliances that had supported the traditional Republic. The institutions of government at Rome were then clearly insufficient to accommodate the enlarged citizen body. In this regard, at least, those who had opposed the extension of citizenship to all Italians were right in seeing that the Rome they grew up in could not endure a massive change in the number of citizens. The fact that the government of the Republic never developed institutions that could promote widespread loyalty to itself was a sign of the inherent weakness of a senatorial administration whose tendency was to oppose any sort of change that could upset the status quo at Rome.

The growth of the empire had made it necessary to have some mechanism for creating longer-serving officials than had been previously the case. The state had been saved from Hannibal largely because the same men had held office on a regular basis in the years after Cannae, while Scipio had been given a free hand against the Carthaginians in Spain from 210 to 206 BC and in Africa from 205 to 201 BC. The war with Philip and subsequent settlement of Greece had occupied Flamininus from

198 to 194 BC. Once the Cimbrians, Teutons, and Mithridates emerged to challenge the rickety structure of provincial government in the late second and early first centuries BC, further long commands were needed, and long commands meant that generals were able essentially to privatize their armies. The Roman Republic fell because the self-interest of the governing class prevented it from adapting fast enough to the changing environment that stemmed from the acquisition of empire. With the exception of Cinna and Sulla, the men who dominated the politics of the last seventy years of Republican government did so because they were able to exploit the traditions of popular politics and doctrine of popular sovereignty to create extra-constitutional positions with which to deal with the empire. At the same time, outside the senatorial class, the idea of government simply by the senate and people could find few champions. This government did nothing for the average Italian—before or after the grant of citizenship—and little or nothing for the average provincial. If Italians or provincials wanted something from the state, they required powerful patrons: ultimately, that is what Marius, Sulla, Cinna, Pompey, Caesar, and Octavianus became.

The House of Augustus (31 BC–AD 14)

The Creation of a New Order

Octavianus returned to Rome in 29 BC and laid down the power he had been granted to command the armies of Rome in the war against Antony. In January of 27 BC he assumed a new identity. By vote of the senate he was granted the name Augustus, or "exalted personage," completing a transformation that had been going on for a number of years. In 42, when Julius Caesar had been declared a god, Octavianus had become Gaius Julius, son of the divinity, Caesar. Five years later he had changed his *praenomen* from Gaius to *imperator*, or "victorious general," around the time of his victory over Sextus Pompey. Henceforth he would be known as imperator, son of a divinity, Caesar Augustus.

This statue of Augustus was discovered at Prima Porta near Rome in 1863. The emperor's breastplate depicts the recovery of standards lost by Antony and Crassus to the Parthians, suggesting that the statue was probably made some time after Augustus's return from the Eastern provinces in 19 BC. The figure of Cupid riding a dolphin may be intended to recollect the supposed connection of the Julian family with the goddess Venus (see p. 144).

The new name, while acknowledging a debt to the older Caesar, proclaimed to the entire world that his achievement exceeded that of any other mortal. He was not, however, a god. Although people throughout the empire now offered sacrifice on his behalf, and although his adoptive father was now divine, he remained very much a part of the human race. He went to dinner parties with his friends, made sure that he consulted the senate about matters of importance, and took care to seem generally accessible to the average Roman; and while others might now begin to refer to him as the *princeps*, he himself called the collection of duties that the senate delegated, and the people confirmed, his *statio*, a term that evoked the image of a man on guard duty to protect the state from chaos.

Augustus's accomplishments in the years after Actium were extraordinary. Unlike Caesar and Sulla, who had marched on Rome from the provinces and never fully succeeded in ending the wars they had started, Augustus operated from an established position at Rome. The fact that he defeated Antony as the head of a functioning government made it possible for him to integrate the former supporters of his rival into his regime. At the same time, his difficult early years had taught him how best to deal with the seemingly intractable problem of demobilizing massive armies that were no longer needed. It was plainly impossible to find enough land in Italy; but now many of the soldiers, especially the men who had served under Antony, had been abroad so long that their connections with the Italian homeland were tenuous indeed. Augustus therefore seems to have met little resistance from the troops to their settlement in military colonies throughout the empire. Hundreds of thousands of men were successfully settled in this way. The army was reduced by more than 50 percent to a permanent force of twenty-eight legions—roughly 150,000 men—with supporting "auxiliary" units consisting of cavalry, archers, and other more lightly armed infantrymen who were recruited from the provinces in roughly equal numbers to the legionary force.

At the same time that the senate conferred on Octavianus the name of Augustus, it also made him, as consul—a position he would hold every year until 23 BC—governor of a number of provinces, the direct control of which was given over to legates, who were either former praetors or former consuls depending on the importance of the province: they would technically serve with the rank of "former praetors," and thus be subordinate to Augustus with his power as consul or "former consul." At the same time, he retained two important powers associated with the tribunes of the plebs: personal sacrosanctity (awarded in 36 BC) and the right to veto legislation (awarded in 30 BC). Since the provinces Augustus was given tended to be the ones that also had garrisons, the effect was to make Augustus the commander of the vast bulk of the Roman army. The extensive governorship made it possible for Augustus to justify long absences from Rome, and offered an opportunity to swamp the memory of civil war under a deluge of foreign conquests. The result of this policy was ultimately to transform the Roman army into a permanent frontier force. Retaining Marius's structure, based on legions, the army was physically separated from Rome: its soldiers were no longer settled in Italy, and, in time, would largely be recruited from outside the peninsula. Since each provincial army was relatively small (the largest no more than four legions) no individual commander could pose a threat to the political order, and it seems fairly clear that the threats the army was expected to counter were regarded as readily containable. Larger armies would be necessary only if Augustus chose to go on the offensive, which is something that he would do only to promote either his own political position, or that of a prospective heir.

Politically useful conquest required foes that would not be very dangerous—a consideration that ruled out the Parthians for now—but respectable enough to justify Augustus's presence with the armies. He therefore fixed his attention upon Spain, where a long history of resistance made the independent tribes ideologically respectable targets. With great pomp and ceremony, Augustus declared war upon them in 27 BC, and, even though the tribes proved tougher than he might have expected—Augustus fell ill in the course of the campaign, which was never a good sign—his generals won sufficient victories by 25 BC for Augustus to claim that he had solved a problem that was more than a century and a half old. There was less ostentation when further armies, and more experienced generals, including Agrippa himself, had to be dispatched to Spain in the course of the next fifteen years. But, in the end, Spain was firmly brought within the provincial system.

In 23 BC Augustus decided to make some changes. He had held the consulship every year since 31, and this seems to have been causing some discontent. Even though he began to regularize a system by which replacement, or suffect, consuls would take up office in the course of the year, ambitious members of the aristocracy still yearned to be one of the pair who opened the year in office, and thereby give their names to that year. People might also have begun to wonder at the nature of the Republican government, which Augustus claimed he had "restored" in 28, when one man kept holding office while asserting that there was no crisis. After a serious illness in 23, Augustus laid down the consulship halfway through the year. He retained his collection of provinces, however, and allowed the senate to vote him further honors, including the powers of a tribune (*tribunicia potestas*) that he still lacked: the right to bear aid to a Roman citizen who felt oppressed by the actions of the state. So that he could govern his province without the consulship, Augustus was granted a new power, the *imperium maius*, or "greater imperium," which was technically described as "greater than that of any governor in a province," and modeled on the power Pompey had received to fight the pirates and Mithridates. As a power that was technically valid only in the provinces, the *imperium maius* could not, in theory, be used in Rome or Italy. The totality of the *tribunicia potestas*, however—which included the right to summon assemblies of the people to vote on laws, the veto, and the right to summon meetings of the senate—now gave Augustus all the legal power he needed to administer Rome itself, and became the symbol of his civil authority. Within a few years, Augustus's reign would be measured in terms of the number of years that he had held this power.

This one fact underlines the extraordinary nature of the position that Augustus had created: an office designed to protect the Roman people from the arbitrary acts of a magistrate had become the defining power of the emperor. Words do matter, and the two words used to connote the power of a tribune—*tribunicia potestas*—were vastly more palatable to Roman sensibility than "dictator," the word used by Sulla and Caesar. While the effective power of the dictatorship was concealed behind the *imperium maius*, *imperium maius* could, unlike the office of dictator, be shared. Unlike Caesar's dictatorship for life, it was—up until the very end of Augustus's life—only ever granted with a fixed-term limit. Use of *tribunicia potestas* proclaimed to all the world that Augustus would remain part of a group: there were, after all, still ten other men, every year, who held this same power, and from 18 BC onwards he would routinely associate others with him in that power. As if to underscore this point, Augustus refused the dictatorship at the end of 23 when the senate offered it to him to help solve a threatened grain shortage. Instead he agreed merely to accept the care of the grain supply, and, miraculously it seems, the threatened grain shortage failed to materialize. This may all have been political theater, but it was at least consistent political theater that made a coherent point.

Political theater of another sort, enacted the following year (see box, opposite), turned Augustus's thoughts to who would succeed him, and a system of succession took shape that was based upon the familiar Roman principle of collegiality. During his illness in 23 BC, Augustus had indicated that Agrippa should succeed him, and now arranged that he should marry his daughter Julia, while also promoting the careers of his own two stepsons, the products of Livia's first marriage. The elder of these two, Tiberius, who was quaestor in 23, was given some high profile tasks in the course of the coming campaign in the East.

Whereas previously Augustus had considered Parthia too dangerous an enemy, for the last couple of years it had been riven with dynastic controversy, with the

THE PLOT OF 22 BC

In the course of 22 BC a group of senators plotted to kill Augustus. We will never know exactly what happened, but several of the conspirators were very well placed—one was the brother-in-law of Augustus's close associate Maecenas—and the whole business threw the system into shock. The immediate cause of the conspiracy seems to have been the testimony that Augustus gave at the trial of a former governor of Macedonia in 23, stating that the man had fought a barbarian tribe without his authority. Augustus had stated that the governor had fought without his order, thereby guaranteeing that he was convicted of treason under Sulla's law (see p. 134). Although the conspiracy of 22 was unmasked before any assassination attempt was actually made, it served to warn Augustus that he could not take senatorial opinion for granted. It also underscored what had recently emerged as a very serious problem: the lack of an obvious successor should Augustus die.

Augustus himself was now forty-one, Agrippa was a year older; most Romans did not expect to live much past fifty. In the previous year Augustus's eldest nephew—who had been marked out for succession through his marriage to Julia, Augustus's only daughter—had died, suddenly. Two things needed to be done: Augustus had to start looking for heirs who were younger than him, and he had to remind people how much they really needed him.

result that one claimant to the throne was now in Roman territory with two sons of his rival as Roman hostages. Agrippa headed east in 23 BC, Augustus and Tiberius followed him a year later. In 19 BC, after much diplomatic maneuvering, the Parthian king officially recognized the Euphrates as the border between the two empires; agreed that the king of Armenia (whose realm occupied much of what is now eastern Turkey) would be appointed by the Romans in a ceremony over which Tiberius presided; and returned military standards captured from Crassus and Antony in return for the restoration of his sons. Augustus proclaimed the result a victory of tremendous importance, and to some degree he was justified in doing so. A Roman army could not possibly have occupied Iraq and Iran, or even a significant portion of that territory. There were simply not enough soldiers to control an area that was culturally and politically too complex for the Romans to manage. Indeed,

An important theme of the Augustan regime was that the relationship between Rome and its gods, damaged by the impiety of the previous generation, had been restored by Augustus himself. This detail of the south frieze of the Augustan Altar of Peace (see p. 186) links this theme with Augustus's designated successor, his son-in-law Marcus Agrippa. It depicts a collection of priests proceeding to sacrifice followed by Agrippa. The child who grasps Agrippa's toga may be his son, Gaius Caesar.

181

Augustus still avoided direct Roman administration in many Semitic borderlands of the empire where traditions of Greco-Roman government, based upon city-states, were foreign, and local traditions resistant to their imposition. The return of the standards was a suitable symbolic acknowledgment of Roman power that cost the Parthians little, but meant an enormous amount to Romans, who still regarded the losses of the previous generation as a profound embarrassment.

Augustus and Roman Culture

Returning to Rome in 19 BC, Augustus opened a new phase of his reign. Although he would continue to spend the bulk of his time outside of Italy, winning further military glory for himself, he now began to highlight plans for the succession. In doing so he gave titular command of armies to his stepsons, Tiberius and Drusus, so that they could build suitable reputations for themselves. Even as armies under the command of Tiberius and Drusus moved into Switzerland and southern Germany, Augustus asserted that the moral regeneration of Rome must become a priority. In 19 and 18 BC he introduced legislation to expel "unworthy" men from the senate and create new rules to govern the marital and the reproductive habits of the upper classes. One of these laws was intended to encourage members of the upper classes to have more children. Men whose wives managed to bear three or more children were given various advantages in the pursuit of public office. Men who refused to marry at all suffered various penalties, including a ban on their receipt of inheritances. His other law concerned adultery, imposing stiffer penalties on both men and women. One of the more striking clauses of the new law was that a man who did not divorce a wife who was having an affair could be charged as a pimp.

The new laws reflected the Augustan version of the period of the civil wars: that they arose from the anger of the gods at the immoral conduct of the Roman people. He marked the end of the war with Antony by restoring "eighty-two temples of the gods in the city on the authority of the senate, neglecting none that required restoration at that time" (*Deeds of the Divine Augustus* 20.4). Through these and other construction projects to repair temples and other buildings damaged in earlier years, people could be reminded again of the fact that in the past personal immorality had run rampant, the cults of the gods had been ignored, and personal splurges on private luxury had replaced proper expenditure for the common good. This continued a trend that had begun much earlier for proper expenditure: Asinius Pollio had opened the first public library at Rome in 39; Agrippa had built a new portico in 25, in which he encouraged members of the Roman elite to display their art collections; and Augustus famously spent money on public spectacles (see box, opposite).

Augustus's reign also saw the completion of two major building projects in the heart of the city. The first of these was the completion of the forum begun by Julius Caesar, centered on a new temple to Venus as the generative power in the universe, a clear reference to Caesar's supposed ancestry (the temple itself was dedicated in 46, even though the forum as a whole was unfinished). The forum was designed to back upon the new senate house that Caesar had also begun before his death, to replace the one burnt down in the riots of 52 BC (see p. 163): this, too, might be seen as symbolizing the link between the family of Caesar and return of an orderly society. The senate house, as appropriate to its symbolic purpose, was dedicated on August 28, 29 BC, just a few weeks after Augustus celebrated his triumphs over

AUGUSTAN SPECTACLES

Augustus paid for some extraordinary spectacles for the Roman people at various points in his career, and encouraged extensive construction of new venues for shows. These spectacles provided crucial opportunities for contact between the *princeps* and the people of Rome. By this point the political use of the spectacle was well established in Roman tradition: Cicero himself had said that the theater was the best place to go if one wanted to gauge the true feelings of the Roman people.

Augustus made sure that they would take place in proper venues. To this end, a huge new theater was built in the name of his deceased nephew Marcellus; the Circus Maximus, from which spectators could now look up and see the house of Augustus himself on the Palatine, was enhanced; and Statilius Taurus constructed the first permanent amphitheater for gladiatorial shows. On the west bank of the Tiber, Augustus also excavated an enormous pool in which, as his grandson set out on a mission to the East in 2 BC, he staged a naval battle intended to recall the Greek victory over Persia in 480 BC.

(Below left) Gladiatorial duels were emblematic of the military virtues of Rome and individual gladiators could become popular heroes, which may explain the market for figurines such as this one.

(Below) Augustus's improvements to the Circus Maximus included the addition of new lap counters in the form of seven dolphins (one for each lap in a race) to the central barrier, commemorating his victory at Actium.

Antony and Cleopatra. The second great project, which abutted the forum of Caesar on its eastern side, was a new forum centered on a temple to Mars the Avenger (Mars Ultor). The symbolism again was quite obvious: this massive project initially commemorated Augustus's role as the avenger of Caesar, since construction began after the victories over Brutus and Cassius at Philippi of 42 BC; and, as time went by, his role as avenger of the disasters of the previous generation more generally (the standards that Augustus recovered from the Parthians were housed in this temple). The porticoes of colored marble that defined the east and west sides of this new forum were bowed out at the north end to contain portrait galleries: on one side were members of the Julian dynasty, extending back through Romulus to Aeneas to stress the connections of Augustus's family to both of Rome's founders; and on the other were portraits of the "best men," whose deeds had ensured the growth of the empire.

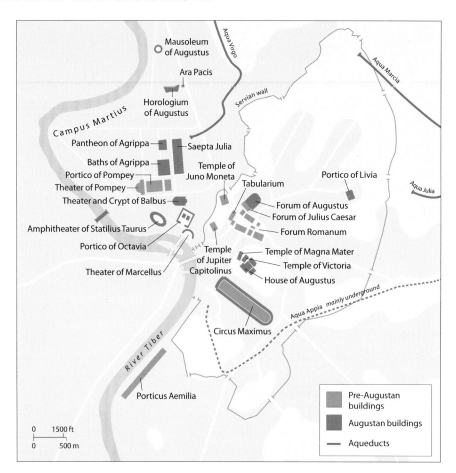

Rome in about AD 14. The landscape of the city was transformed by Augustus. Among the most important projects he sponsored were the completion of the forum of Julius Caesar, the construction of the forum of Augustus (pictured below), and the erection of a number of public buildings on the Campus Martius.

Map labels:
- Mausoleum of Augustus
- Aqua Virgo
- Aqua Marcia
- Ara Pacis
- Horologium of Augustus
- Servian wall
- Campus Martius
- Pantheon of Agrippa
- Saepta Julia
- Baths of Agrippa
- Temple of Juno Moneta
- Portico of Livia
- Portico of Pompey
- Tabularium
- Theater of Pompey
- Aqua Julia
- Theater and Crypt of Balbus
- Forum of Augustus
- Forum of Julius Caesar
- Amphitheater of Statilius Taurus
- Forum Romanum
- Portico of Octavia
- Temple of Jupiter Capitolinus
- Temple of Magna Mater
- Temple of Victoria
- Theater of Marcellus
- House of Augustus
- Aqua Appia mainly underground
- River Tiber
- Circus Maximus
- Porticus Aemilia

- 0   1500 ft
- 0   500 m

Legend:
- Pre-Augustan buildings
- Augustan buildings
- Aqueducts

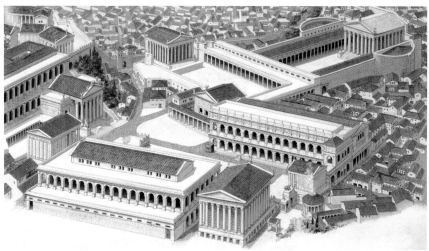

The Curia Julia, as the new senate house would be called, was just one of a number of new buildings that were constructed in the old Roman forum. One of these was a temple to the Divine Julius, begun, like the temple of Mars Ultor, in 42, but built much more rapidly on the spot where Caesar's body had been incinerated (its dedication took place ten days before that of the Curia in August of 29). Other buildings included a triumphal arch for Augustus (initially to celebrate Actium, later expanded to include commemoration of the recovery of the standards from Parthia);

HORACE AND THE SECULAR GAMES

When the sacrifice was finished it was announced that 27 boys whose fathers and mothers were alive and as many girls would sing a hymn in the same way on the Capitol. Quintus Horatius Flaccus composed the hymn.

(Acts of the Secular Games of 17 BC)

Goddess, may you bring forth children, and hasten decrees of the Fathers about the joining of women and the offspring of new abundance from the marriage law; so the fixed cycle of eleven times ten years will bring back the games we crowd three times under the clear light of day and as many times by blessed night.

(Horace, *Sacred Hymn* 16-24)

A TRIBUTE TO VIRGIL

Tityrus, the crops, and the arms of Aeneas are read and will be read as long as Rome is ruler of the conquered world.

(Ovid, *Loves* 15.25-6)

porticoes for Gaius and Lucius (Augustus's grandsons); and a basilica commemorating Caesar. These and numerous other projects transformed the space from a focal point for expressions of the popular will to a celebration of the new order.

If the building programs that continued throughout Augustus's reign were intended to give physical expression to the ideology of Augustus, they were not the only vehicles of ideological expression. Thus, of all the spectacles of the Augustan age, none, perhaps, equaled the one that Augustus celebrated in 17 BC to commemorate his work in restoring the relationship between Rome and the gods. This was no less than the 800th birthday of Rome itself.

For this celebration, Augustus commissioned a special hymn by a poet named Horace (see box, left). Horace was one of a number of brilliant poets whose careers had begun in the years after Caesar's death. Alone of these, Horace served on the losing side at Philippi, but he rapidly won the patronage of Maecenas in the course of the 30s, during which time he wrote mainly satires. In the wake of Actium, the bulk of his work took the form of poems adapting a wide variety of Greek meters to Latin, and often addressed to leading figures of the regime. Another significant poet of these years was Propertius, whose first book of elegies took as its themes his love for a woman named Cynthia and the desire to evade the demands of Roman militarism—a powerful response to the tenor of an age devoted to civil war—and included, at its end, a epitaph on the destruction of Perugia in 41 BC (see box, p. 172). As a whole the book stands with the career of Horace as an example of Augustan "tolerance" of dissenting opinions—a tolerance so pronounced that "dissent" appears to have been part of the ideological program of the regime, so long as it stopped well short of the scurrilous freedom with which Catullus had expressed his views. Propertius produced three further books of elegies, the last of which handled a number of specifically public themes (Actium included). In the work of both Horace and Propertius, apologies in the manner of earlier poets for the poverty of the language have been banished, along with the sense that appears in some of Cicero's work that Latin culture lagged behind the achievement of the Greeks. For both Propertius and Horace, Greek literature is part of the cultural heritage of the Roman present.

This more confident relationship with the Greek past is especially evident in the work of the greatest of all Augustan poets, Publius Vergilius Maro—known in English as Virgil—who died just two years before the celebration of Rome's birthday. Virgil's first major work, written under the patronage of Asinius Pollio, consisted of ten poems set in a mythical world of shepherds. It was an imitation of a well-known Greek form, but in the course of these poems Virgil had dwelt, with great delicacy, on the sufferings of the present, and in one case on hopes for a better future. His second work, a poem ostensibly on farming, had exalted the virtues of life in the countryside as the implicit antithesis to a corrupt society. His third and greatest poem was the *Aeneid*, published in 19 BC. Recognized immediately as a work of astonishing genius (see box, left), the *Aeneid* told the story of the mythical foundation of Rome by Aeneas; of his long, hard struggle to find the right path to the future; and of the various obstacles that his own humanity placed in the way of future glory. Throughout, the audience is reminded of Rome's mission, and the pain demanded of a people if they were to win through in the end: "so great a struggle it was to found the Roman race" (*Aeneid* 1.33), as Virgil writes at the end of the preface to the first book. In the sixth book, as Aeneas is treated to a vision of Rome's future, he is told:

Other people will cut breathing bronze more softly (so I think), and they will draw living faces from marble, they will argue cases in court better, and they will better describe the course of heaven, and announce the rising stars. You Roman, remember to rule people with *imperium* (these are your arts) and impose the habit of peace, spare the humbled and wear down the proud in war.

(Aeneid 6.847–53)

For all these reminders, Aeneas often seems lost in the vastness of his mission. Without knowing what he is doing, he commits his descendants to the huge death-struggle of the Hannibalic wars when he has an affair with Dido, the legendary founder and queen of Carthage, who dies cursing him as he abandons her to carry on his mission. Likewise, once he has seen the future of Rome, he does not always seem to realize its implications. In book eight he is given a shield decorated with scenes of Rome's future: he "admired it and, ignorant of the events, he reveled in the image, bearing the fame and fate of his descendants on his shoulder" (*Aeneid* 8.730–31). Like the Romans of Virgil's time, Aeneas is trying to find his way to the brighter future that must be out there somewhere.

Poets were not the only people seeking to recover the distant past of Rome. Throughout the decades after Actium, Livy labored on his massive history of Rome—and he was not alone. The Greek rhetorical theorist turned historian, Dionysius of Halicarnassus, produced his own mammoth history of early Rome to prove to Greeks that the Romans were really Greeks, and a new generation of scholars followed the path blazed by Terentius Varro, the greatest scholar of the previous generation, whose *Human and Divine Antiquities of the Romans* was said by Cicero to have saved his contemporaries from wandering like children lost in the dark, ignorant of what lay about them in their city.

One last remnant of the bad old days departed in 12 BC. After many years of internal exile, Lepidus finally died, freeing up the office of *pontifex maximus*, to which Augustus was duly elected. The event may be commemorated in the frieze on the massive new Altar of Peace (Ara Pacis), construction of which had begun the year before on the banks of the Tiber near the spot where Augustus built the huge mausoleum in which he planned to be buried. Rome was now much altered. New public buildings had transformed the cityscape, the empire had been enlarged by conquests in the Alps and Germany, and Augustus presided over a state reinvigorated by refurbished traditions where nonconformity was viewed with increasing suspicion.

The Succession (12 BC–AD 14)

As Rome changed, so too did the regime. Agrippa died in March of 12 BC, leaving the new generation as heirs apparent. To mark this, Julia was remarried to her step-brother Tiberius, who was forced to divorce Agrippa's daughter, whom he seems genuinely to have loved. The new marriage was not a success: the grim Tiberius was a poor partner for a younger woman who enjoyed an active social life. In 9 BC, his brother Drusus died from an accident while on campaign, and Augustus now promoted the advancement of Julia's two sons from her marriage to Agrippa, whom Augustus had adopted in 17 BC. Tiberius, to whom the burden of military command now fell with particular weight for new campaigns in the Balkans and the East,

The eastern face of the Ara Pacis, which was dedicated in 9 BC. The panels on this face depict a goddess (her identity is in dispute). Panels on the west side depict the myth of Romulus and Remus, and Aeneas offering sacrifice. The north and south panels offer a sacrifice scene that includes images of Augustus's family (see p. 181).

became increasingly restive. In 6 BC he announced that he was retiring to Rhodes. It was the beginning of a tough decade.

Augustus seems to have become very difficult to live with. A man of ostentatiously simple tastes, he wandered the palace uttering homey expressions about things being quicker than boiled asparagus, and delighting in dice games that the profoundly academic Tiberius disliked. He doted on his grandsons, and was openly critical of Drusus's son Claudius, who had a clubfoot and whom Augustus did not want to be seen in public. He also believed that a woman's place was at home with the spinning wheel, and while it is not at all clear that this stricture was applied to his wife Livia—with whom he seems to have communicated by letter even when they were both in Rome—it certainly seems to have applied to Julia, who grew to hate him. In 2 BC, just after the grandsons were dispatched on campaign, Julia was suddenly found to have been involved in very dubious activities with several members of the aristocracy. One of these activities seems to have been an orgy in the forum; another may have been a nascent plot to kill her father. She was sent into exile.

The exile of Julia was followed by the sudden deaths of her two sons in AD 2 and 4. Tiberius was recalled to Rome and sent to live in his house on the Palatine. Two years later he reemerged as the heir apparent, formally adopted Drusus's eldest son, Germanicus, and departed Rome to fight first in Germany and then in the Balkans, where recently conquered tribes had risen in revolt. In AD 8 scandals again shook the house of Augustus, involving the daughter of Julia and Agrippa, also named Julia, and her brother, known as Agrippa Postumus (he was born after Agrippa's death). This younger Agrippa had already been sent into internal exile for allegedly deranged behavior (open criticism of his grandfather seems to have been part of it); he was now sent to an island. Julia was found to be pregnant by a man other than her husband. Augustus saw to it that the child was killed and that she was exiled. At the same time Augustus lashed out at Rome's most brilliant living poet, Ovid, among whose works was a poem on the art of love, which Augustus now claimed was offensive. We don't know why Augustus should suddenly have noticed a poem that had been in circulation for several years, but that poem did contain some wonderfully witty send-ups of contemporary propaganda—recommending, among other things, that imperial processions provided excellent opportunities to meet lovers. It may be that Ovid was also connected with Julia's problems: he admits in poems written during his exile at Tomis, a city on the Black Sea, that he had made some sort of mistake.

So far dynastic disturbances had made little impact on the regime's ability to govern, and indeed these years would see important change as Augustus moved the state away from Republican reliance upon individual benefaction to what would become imperial reliance upon institutions. The two most important innovations took place in AD 6 and 7, and involved the grain supply of Rome and the army. Augustus wrote:

> Four times I assisted the treasury with my own money so that I gave those in charge of the treasury 150,000 sesterces … From the consulship of Gnaeus and Publius Lentulus (18 BC) onwards, whenever the taxes that are collected in money fell short, I made distributions of grain and money from my own estate and granaries, sometimes to 100,000 people, sometimes to more.
>
> (*Deeds of the Divine Augustus* 17–18)

Germanicus Caesar, the son of Drusus Caesar and Antonia (Augustus's niece), assumed an important place in Augustus's plans for dynastic succession. He is seen here in a coin minted in the reign of his son Caligula.

Distributions of this sort, and such offices as the charge of the grain supply, which Augustus was offered in 23 BC, were a typical "Republican" response to a crisis—the charge of the grain supply offered to Augustus appears to have been very similar to the one that Pompey took up in 57 BC. But following grain crises in both AD 6 and 7 Augustus created permanent positions for two ex-consuls to oversee the distribution of grain within the city and the importation of grain from abroad. Within a couple of years these positions had been turned over to equestrian officials: the *praefectus frumenti dandi* (prefect for distributing grain), who operated out of the porticus Minucia on the banks of the Tiber, and the *praefectus annonae*—prefect to the grain supply—whose precise headquarters are unknown, but who ranked as one of the three most important non-senatorial officials in the Augustan regime. The other two were the prefect of Egypt (Augustus had always retained the right of appointing equestrian governors) and the prefect to the imperial guard, the *praefectus praetorio* (praetorian prefect). A fourth equestrian prefecture, ranking just below the others, was also created in this year. This was the *praefectus vigilum*, or "prefect of the watchmen."

Traditionally, the maintenance of public order in Rome had been under the control of the aediles, who were notoriously ineffective in dealing with the sorts of crises that arise in large urban areas, especially those connected with fire and everyday criminal activity. In 26 BC there had been something of a scandal when Egnatius Rufus, then aedile, had formed his own fire service, resulting in his early election to the praetorship. Augustus responded by telling the aediles to make sure they put out fires, and in 22 he gave them the wherewithal to do so, by placing six hundred public slaves at their disposal. In AD 7, after reorganizing Rome into fourteen districts, Augustus had given responsibility for firefighting to the officials in charge of the new districts (*vicomagistri*), and, at some point, he created three "urban cohorts" of five hundred men each, which he placed under the command of the urban prefect (the only senator to control soldiers in Rome itself) to act as a police force. This did not work, however, and the previous few years (as well as

Towards the end of his life, Augustus composed an account of his deeds for display in front of his tomb in Rome (see p. 176). This extensive copy of the inscription survives on a temple in the Turkish capital of Ankara, built to honor Augustus and the goddess Roma.

AD 6 itself) had seen significant public unrest. Augustus's next move was to create the *praefectus vigilum*, which would command a force of seven cohorts of freedmen, the *vigiles*, totaling thirty-five hundred men (in addition to the urban cohorts) stationed throughout the city, with salaries paid from a new tax on the manumission of slaves. Taken together with the reform in the grain supply, the creation of the watch marks the formal imperial takeover of the administration of the city of Rome.

Also in AD 6, Augustus set up a new treasury, the *aerarium militare* (military treasury), to guarantee retirement bonuses to soldiers who had completed twenty years of service. Funded initially by a large gift from Augustus's private fortune, and thereafter by a tax on goods sold at auction, and—from a senatorial point of view—by a deeply unpopular tax on inheritances, this measure was the final step in creating a professional structure for the career of private soldiers and ensuring the loyalty of the army to the imperial house. The importance of these arrangements is that they created structures both to separate soldiers from their generals, making them beholden to the emperor for their retirement packages (which were specifically set in cash terms), and to feed the urban populace. Since grain was transported to Rome by independent contractors who negotiated with the *praefectus annonae*, a substantial body of merchants entered into a more stable relationship with the state.

The new treasury created to handle the retirement pay for soldiers was entrusted to a pair of ex-praetors, and is emblematic of another crucial development of these years. This was the emergence of a senatorial career, with real jobs that people would hold once they had completed their year in a magistracy. The more developed career pattern that gradually emerged in these years was particularly important for ex-praetors: they would now be employed commanding legions, governing provinces, or doing other necessary tasks, thereby creating a framework through which people might win imperial support with which to advance their careers.

The new institutions were created even as Tiberius, supported by a cadre of able generals, was on the verge of crushing a serious revolt in the Balkans. The string of military successes was interrupted by news of a catastrophe in Germany, where Quinctilius Varus lost all three legions under his command at the battle of the Teutoburg forest (see box, p. 190). The disaster struck the regime hard. Augustus supposedly wandered the palace banging his head against the walls and crying "Quinctilius Varus, give me back my legions!" He seldom appeared in public thereafter, and his health began to fail. Tiberius restored the situation to a degree; he ensured a new frontier could be maintained on the Rhine, before giving way to his nephew Germanicus, who was tasked with recovering the standards that had been lost with Varus. The three legions were not replaced, however, and elaborate efforts to develop a German society that would be more amenable to Roman control were abruptly cancelled. This is apparent at the site of Waldgrimes (in the modern German state of Hesse, north of the Rhine), where the Roman-style city in the process of development at the time of Varus's disaster was abandoned within a few years. Despite the retrenchment, Augustus evidently hoped to recover the lost territory, and, although content that the empire should remain within boundaries marked by the River Danube, the Euphrates in the East, and the Sahara in north Africa, he ordered attacks along the Rhine.

Five years after the disaster in Germany Augustus departed on a journey to Naples. He fell desperately ill, and died on August 19, AD 14 at the age of seventy-six.

DEFEAT AT TEUTOBURG FOREST

The battle of Teutoburg forest was a crushing defeat for the army led by Publius Quinctilius Varus. A distant relative of Augustus, he commanded the army garrisoning the province that Drusus had carved out between the Rhine and Elbe rivers. In AD 9 Varus allowed himself to be tricked by a German chieftain named Arminius, who advised him to withdraw to the Rhine lest he be cut off for the winter by a rebellion among the tribes. When Varus began his retreat, Arminius, the author of the entire conspiracy, sprang a trap, ambushing and destroying all three legions under Varus's command in the Teutoburg forest, now known to be near Kalkriese in modern Germany.

Initial discoveries of shattered Roman equipment at the site revealed a spot where Germans, fighting from behind field fortifications, evidently ambushed the Romans. There was also some evidence to suggest that the Roman army was badly beaten at this point. Further work has allowed us to begin to trace the army's route and see that ancient accounts of a three-day battle in which the army was gradually destroyed are likely to be accurate. On the third day, seeing his army in ruins, Varus committed suicide.

Although a less bloody defeat than that of Cannae or Arausio, the battle near Kalkriese may have been more decisive, since Augustus and Tiberius decided to abandon efforts to transform the area between the Rhine and Elbe rivers into a province.

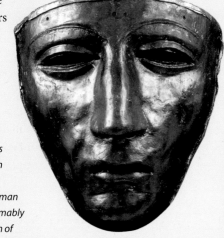

This silver face mask was excavated at Kalkriese in Germany. It would once have been worn by a Roman cavalryman, who presumably fell victim to the ambush of Varus's column.

Tiberius, whose power had been made equal to that of Augustus everywhere but Rome a year earlier, now succeeded to his *statio*.

For all his personal failings, Augustus remains an extraordinary figure. He is hardly the only political leader who could not, in the end, balance private happiness with public success, but it is for the public success that he is remembered above all. He brought an end to civil war, ensured the basic comfort of his people, and, in the course of the forty-five years after Actium, settled the point that the Roman state would run better with a chief executive than without. Through his extraordinary longevity he outlived direct memory of his murderous early years and offered the average inhabitant of the Roman empire both the image and reality of stability that they desired.

The Empire at the Death of Augustus

One of the documents that Tiberius revealed to the senate after the funeral of Augustus was a testament that Augustus is said to have written in his own hand, which included a statement of:

> The resources of the state, the number of citizens and allies under arms, the number of fleets, allied kingdoms and provinces, the sums receivable from taxes on land and persons (*tributa*), as well as from taxes on goods for sale (*vectigalia*), mandatory expenses and sums given annually as gifts … and he added the advice that the empire should be contained within its current boundaries.

(Tacitus, *Annals of Imperial Rome* 1.11.4)

The period of imperial expansion did indeed end with Augustus. Although some territory was added in the course of the next several centuries—most significantly the island of Britain, the area of Jordan, and a portion of modern Romania—the empire continued to be defined essentially in Europe by the Rhine and Danube rivers, and in the East by the River Euphrates. In Africa, the empire continued to extend as far south as Elephantine in the Nile valley and the Saharan sub-desert elsewhere.

In terms of economic power the only state comparable with the Roman empire at this time was Han China, which, like the empire, controlled about one-fifth of the world's population (see box, below). The Roman armies stationed along the Rhine and Danube were strong enough to control raiding on the part of the neighboring tribes, which suggests that their manpower was roughly equivalent to that of their anticipated adversaries: the military forces of the German tribes amounted to something like 200,000 men, so if we allow that this amounted to 10 percent of the adult male population, this suggests a population for Germany and west central Europe beyond the empire's frontier that was somewhere in the order of eight million people. The population of the Parthian empire was likewise about eight million. There was no way, then, if its armies were competently led and its resources properly disposed, that the Roman empire faced any actual threat from its neighbors; what defeats there might be should all have been retrievable through the mobilization of Rome's vastly superior resources.

Within the empire itself, two fundamentally distinct modes of organization existed for the basic rural economy, depending on whether one looked east or west from what is roughly the area of modern Hungary (and north of modern Greece). Looking west and south as far as modern Libya, the basic pattern of landholding tended to follow a model of aristocratic exploitation that had begun to predominate in Italy by the mid-first century AD. The basic feature of the "Italian" pattern was the division of rural territory into very large estates dominated by villas—in some cases extremely luxurious villas—the territory of which tended to be leased out to tenant farmers (at no point did large-scale slaveholding ever become a significant feature of this rural economy). There is enormous regional variation in the effect of the villa system, and indeed, variation within regions: in Etruria, for example, the villas that grew up around the city of Volterra seemed to be status symbols owned by local aristocrats, while in the city of Luna, new villas were connected with specialized production of olive oil and wine. Elsewhere, we find Roman aristocrats engaging in specialized production of other luxury goods for use in the capital's festivals. The large-scale development of Rome's grain supply system may have encouraged similar

THE POPULATION OF THE EMPIRE

The resources of the Roman empire depended, above all else, upon its population. It is likely that when Augustus died there were some 45 million people living within its frontiers. This number is somewhat on the low side for the "carrying capacity" (the number of people who could be supported by farming with the available technology) of these lands.

It seems a likely estimate for the population at this period, however: archaeological evidence from both cities and the ancient countryside suggests that there was a considerable increase in the population between the time of Augustus and the late second century AD. At that point it is plausible to think that the population reached the limit of the carrying capacity of the land, and that the total population amounted to about 60 million people. This was something like one-fifth of the total population of the planet.

developments in some provinces. North Africa, for instance, was dominated by the huge estates of a very few landholders by the middle of the first century AD, and was by then supplying two-thirds of Rome's requirements; while at Pompeii we can see how what was once a series of small-scale local manufacturers of *garum* (the fish sauce that was an essential condiment in Roman cuisine) began to change into retail outlets during Augustus's time. The local *garum* industry was being transformed by the mass-production methods developing in Spain. At the same time, the products of potteries that had flourished in the late Republic were beginning to be replaced by the products of larger potteries along the River Rhône in Gaul. Such developments, which emerge through excavation, reveal that Rome's dominant class was engaging in commerce on a much broader basis than it had before. These changes seem to have occurred slightly earlier than the reorganization of Rome's grain supply, suggesting that the economically savvy aristocrats of Cicero's generation were setting the direction that the government of the empire would follow.

Whatever the impact on government, the basic pattern of villa production and broader trade networks represented the aspirations of the upper classes. To be an aristocrat now meant that one would split time between the quiet life of the country and the more active life of one's city. The style of the local aristocrat thus imitated the style of the super-rich in the senate and equestrian order, whose patronage local notables still sought to attract to their town. To be worthy of such patronage, a city had to have sufficient amenities: thus, in the first century, local building programs mimic the building programs of Augustus, tending towards infrastructure (including aqueducts), temples, and entertainment venues.

The pattern that emerged in Italy spread throughout the Western provinces in the course of the next century, and seems to have led to the complete subordination of the peasant farmers who worked the land that these villas controlled. Indeed, even if they lived in their own villages, few of these villagers would have been independent of either an aristocratic landowner or of the emperor, whose ever-expanding estates might encompass large swathes of land within the provinces, and on occasion be delivered to a favored member of the senate to enhance his wealth. The cities that began to emerge throughout Western Europe in the course of the first century BC that were not directly connected with the system of imperial redistribution (see p. 251) developed from earlier tribal centers as centers of display for local aristocrats, who sought to prove that they were worthy of inclusion in the imperial aristocracy.

The pattern of landholding and aristocratic exploitation in the East was rather different. From Greece through Egypt, the fundamental organizational unit was the village. Large-scale landholding did exist in the East, but the landholder, even if he or she owned estates that included entire villages, remained very much an urban creature. The massive luxury villas that dominated the rural landscape in the West never became a significant feature of the Eastern provinces, where the highly urbanized Aegean coast of Turkey backed onto a largely rural hinterland dominated by villages: these often retained a strong sense of independent identity even when they were attached to the territory of cities or bordered the estates of the wealthy. Outside the urban rim, most cities, such as they were, developed out of the dynastic centers of sundry rulers of the region, and were thus exceptions to what was otherwise an economy based on village life. This was true even in Syria, where great centers of the

The city of Aphrodisias, in western Turkey, was renowned in antiquity for the quality of its marble quarries and the skill of its sculptors. One of the most remarkable monuments in the city is a large stoa attached to a temple of the imperial cult, decorated with sculptures commemorating the Julio-Claudian house. The example here depicts Nero with his mother, Julia Agrippina.

former Seleucid regime, such as Antioch, remained bastions of Greek culture in a sea of villages where the main language was Aramaic.

Nonetheless, where there were cities in the East, they inevitably needed to be improved. Here too there tended to be quite substantial variation. Herod the Great built up Caesarea as a symbol of the "Hellenic" aspirations of his realm, and filled his palace at Masada with luxuries from Italy as a sign of his close connections with his patrons in Italy. But the most important city in his kingdom was Jerusalem, which continued to be dominated by the great temple that had been reconstructed in the early fifth century BC. Some areas of southern Turkey, where Augustus had settled veterans in colonies, took on aspects of Western style, while other cities in the area looked to their own traditions. Typical buildings here would be temples—often celebrating the imperial family—theaters, and infrastructure. One example is the new market place that two freedmen of Augustus constructed at Ephesus in western Turkey; another is the stoa or colonnade (pictured left) erected in his own honor at Aphrodisias, also in western Turkey, by Gaius Julius Zoilus, a freedman of Augustus who had helped the city to negotiate the treacherous waters of the triumviral period. Another of Zoilus's projects was a new theater, while in the generation after his death the city undertook the construction of a massive shrine in honor of the imperial house: this included an extraordinary double colonnade decorated with sculptures linking the deeds of the imperial house with the traditions of local history.

Despite various efforts at urban embellishment, the Eastern countryside always contained far more villages than the West, and in some of these people who had acquired reasonable wealth would aspire to raise their villages to the status of cities. In the very long run, the greater diversity of landholding in the Eastern provinces offered a flexibility that was lacking in the West (see p. 346); but in both East and West the basis of aristocratic wealth was, and would remain, the income derived from land.

The most important aspect of the economy of the empire at the time that Augustus died, however, was simply that peace reigned across the vast bulk of imperial territory. With the armies stationed on the frontiers, and no natural enemies with the strength to do more than cause occasional irritation, the Roman empire was set upon a period of unparalleled economic growth, despite the manifest and manifold failings of Augustus's immediate successors.

Eccentric Stability: The Successors to Augustus (AD 14–69)

Tiberius (AD 14–37)

The pillars of the Augustan regime were the loyalty of the army to the *princeps*; the care and feeding of the population of Rome; and the promise of dignified jobs for loyal members of the governing class, with some respect for their opinions. The overarching ideological principle was domestic tranquility. People remembered that the years before the battle of Actium were filled with violence and uncertainty. Rome without a *princeps* was Rome with civil war.

Augustus's success in selling himself as the antidote to civil war resulted in profound fear that civil war would break out upon his death. In the absence of any actual threat that war would break out, since Tiberius was already securely in power, people made up stories. Some wondered if Agrippa Postumus might break free from his island prison to challenge the new regime (the rumors persisted even after Postumus was executed in AD 14, an act of gratuitous brutality for which Tiberius refused point blank to take either responsibility or blame). Others looked to his nephew and adoptive son Germanicus, now commanding the army on the Rhine, and wondered if he would wait his turn to succeed to the top spot.

Then the army got in on the act. All eight legions on the Rhine and four legions stationed in the Balkans mutinied almost as soon as they heard that Augustus had died. The ostensible cause of the mutinies was anger over conditions of service. Men were being held beyond their proper retirement point, officers were brutal, pay was lousy, and so forth. All of these may have been legitimate complaints, but the way the mutinies developed suggests that the root cause was uncertainty about the future. The Danubian mutiny ended quickly thanks to competent action by Tiberius's son Drusus, dispatched with Aelius Sejanus, the recently promoted praetorian prefect, to deal with the problem. The mutiny in Germany turned out to be far more serious, exacerbated by the histrionics and ineptitude of Germanicus. At one point, when there were mutterings in the ranks that he should seize the throne, Germanicus pulled out his sword and threatened to commit suicide unless the men returned to their proper loyalty. One soldier was sufficiently unimpressed by this display that he offered his own sword, saying that it was sharper. It was a few days later that these same men were so moved by the sight of Germanicus's wife and children leaving the camp that they agreed to return to service if Germanicus agreed to allow them to punish abusive officers. He did, and after some further acts of violence (including a massacre of the mutineers in another camp), the insurrection came to an end.

This sardonyx cameo of the emperor Tiberius offers an idealized portrait of an emperor who was fifty-six years old and completely bald when he succeeded Augustus.

Germanicus's performance at the time of the mutinies was not impressive. Equally, rational assessment (largely missing from our sources) of his campaigns in southern Germany during the next couple of years suggests that he was not an especially able commander. Any success on the battlefield was balanced by problems moving men back to their bases. In AD 15 a major column was barely saved from destruction in an ambush by the courage of its commanding general, and in AD 16 the fleet transporting the army back from north central Germany was wrecked in a storm. Germanicus's reputation was probably enhanced in later years by the fact that he had become the crucial figure in the dynasty. The simple reason for this was that his wife, Vipsania Agrippina, Augustus's granddaughter, was exceptionally capable of bearing healthy children. No fewer than six survived infancy, including one future emperor—Caligula—and the mother of another, Nero.

After the problems at the end of the campaign of AD 16, Tiberius extracted Germanicus from the Rhine armies and prepared to send him on an expedition to the Eastern provinces. There he was to negotiate the succession to the throne of Armenia with the Parthians and take on a number of other tasks, including the transformation of the independent kingdom of Cappadocia (eastern Turkey) into a province. Germanicus seems to have done as he was told, only exceeding his instructions when he decided to visit Egypt in the summer of AD 19.

Germanicus's success had come in spite of the astonishing conduct of the person whom Tiberius had appointed governor of Syria to assist him. This man, Gnaeus Calpurnius Piso, was a member of one of Rome's most aristocratic and complex families. One branch of the family had been intimately linked with the Caesarian cause through Calpurnia, Caesar's third wife; the other branch, from which Piso descended, had sided with Pompey, then with Caesar's assassins, only becoming reconciled with Augustus in the later twenties. He was closely connected with Roman leaders: Piso's father had shared the consulship with Augustus in 23 BC, and Piso himself had shared it with Tiberius in 7 BC. Married to the daughter or granddaughter of Munatius Plancus, another major figure of the Augustan age, Piso had a reputation for independence, ambition, and a really bad temper. In a series of actions evocative of the worst sort of aristocrat squabbling in the last century before Actium, he was openly insubordinate and seems to have gone so far as to have promoted the cause of an alternative candidate to the one Germanicus placed on the throne of Armenia. Not surprisingly, the relationship between the two men completely deteriorated by the time Germanicus returned to Syria from Egypt. In around late September, Piso, angry and alienated, left the province, at which point Germanicus suddenly fell ill, dying at Antioch on October 10, AD 19. Both he and his followers seem to have believed that Piso had poisoned him. Piso did not help matters when he celebrated the news of Germanicus's death and tried to retrieve Syria by force of arms from the members of Germanicus's staff.

News that the heir apparent had died shocked the empire; the matter was complicated not only by the fact that Germanicus was a great deal more popular than Tiberius's son Drusus, but also by the fact that people found Tiberius unsympathetic. His opaque manner of speech made many feel that he was trying to hide something, and when Tiberius failed to display adequate public grief, suspicion rapidly arose that he secretly rejoiced in Germanicus's death, which some also believed he had ordered Piso to bring about.

The actual impact of Germanicus's death on the political order is revealed by an extraordinary pair of documents that flesh out Tacitus's description of the honors voted to Germanicus after his death. Arches were ordered for Rome, the Rhine, and Syria to represent the prince's travels on behalf of the Roman people; centuries in the *comitia centuriata* were renamed in his honor; games offered to the memory of Augustus were rescheduled so as not to coincide with the day of Germanicus's death; the urban plebs erected a statue in his honor; Drusus and Tiberius published memoranda on his virtues; and the senate ordered that the record of the commemoration be published throughout the empire. In its decree the senate tells us:

> [That scroll] which Tiberius Caesar Augustus had read out before the senate on the seventeenth day before the Kalends of January [and] had published [under] his [edict,] be inscribed on bronze and fixed in a public place, [wherever] it please [—]; and that the senate regarded that as all the more appropriate to come to pass, because the innermost [thoughts of Tiberius] Caesar Augustus indeed contained not so much a panegyric of Germanicus Caesar, his son, as the course of his entire life and a true witness to his virtue, to be handed down to eternal remembrance, and (because) he himself, in that same document, did not dissimulate his desire that he wished not to present matters other than as they were and judged it useful to the young of the next generation and those of our posterity.
>
> (*Roman Statutes* 37–39, slightly adapted)

The words of the senate seem to reflect a need to insist that Tiberius really did grieve, that he really did care, and that he was aware that people might think he was dissimulating. Piso returned to Rome and committed suicide while his trial for treason was still ongoing in the senate (interestingly, the suicide followed a visit from the praetorian prefect Sejanus). Several months later the senate issued another decree, directed to the empire as a whole, to publicize what had happened. Here, too, concerns for openness and the succession appear, perhaps nowhere more plainly than where the senate says that:

> since the senate judged that Ti. Caesar Augustus our Princeps had surpassed the sense of duty of all parties, <indications of> a grief so great and so constant having so often been witnessed, by which even the senate was deeply moved, (the senate) earnestly asked and sought that all the care he had previously divided between his two sons he devote to the one he had; and the senate hoped that the one who survives would be all the more an object of the immortal gods' concern insofar as they understood that all future hope of his father's *statio* was now placed in one man, for which reason he ought to end his grief and restore to his fatherland not only the frame of mind but also the countenance befitting public happiness.
>
> (*Senatorial Decree Concerning the Pisonian Affair* lines 124–32)

This coin from Bibilis in Spain is datable to AD 31. The obverse of the coin depicts Tiberius; the reverse has the letters COS (short for consul) in a wreath surrounded by an inscription that refers to Sejanus. The coin was obviously minted before the events of October that year, when Sejanus was removed from power and executed.

The "one man" left of this decree was Drusus, and he did not long survive Germanicus, dying in AD 23. Things soon got a great deal more complex. Sejanus, who was having an affair with Drusus's wife, seems to have seen himself as a potential Agrippa figure. Everyone knew that Agrippa might have succeeded Augustus, and Sejanus seems to have felt that, if he made himself indispensable, Tiberius might see him in the same light. This would be especially true if he married Drusus's widow (a sister of Germanicus and thus a blood-relative of Augustus), and if other potential heirs to the throne—in this case the two teenage sons of Germanicus—made themselves obnoxious to Tiberius, who had already conceived an intense dislike for their mother Agrippina. Moreover it appears that Tiberius was getting tired of governing. In 26 Tiberius left Rome, and in the following year took up residence in a villa on Capri and ran the state from there, or, rather, left day-to-day affairs in Sejanus's hands while retaining trusted subordinates for long terms in command of the armies. In subsequent years, irritated by Sejanus's reports of Agrippina's annoyance with him, and similar stories about her two sons, he threw all three into prison. The succession now looked as if it must fall to either Germanicus and Agrippina's third son, Gaius, nicknamed Caligula, or the young son of Drusus, who stayed at Capri with Tiberius.

In AD 31 Sejanus, whose request to marry Drusus's widow had been refused, seems genuinely to have plotted the murder of Tiberius and the surviving male members of the imperial house. The details of this conspiracy, which was uncovered by Germanicus's mother, emerged only because members of her household later achieved immensely important positions, and told their stories to others. The key figures here were a slave girl named Caenis (see p. 214) and a freedman named Antonius Pallas (later a virtual prime minister when Germanicus's brother Claudius, against all reasonable expectation, became emperor) who conveyed the news of the

plot to Tiberius. Tiberius responded by ordering the execution of Sejanus and as many followers as his network of informers could reasonably bring to trial.

The last years of Tiberius's reign were bitter. Members of the senate feared that they might be suddenly charged with treason, and some long-serving provincial governors lapsed into incompetence. One of these men was Pontius Pilate, the governor of Judea, who was finally dismissed in AD 36, a few months after he had executed a teacher from Galilee at the behest of the religious authorities in Jerusalem. It was one of the few times that he seems to have been willing to go along with what they wanted, but Jesus of Nazareth was the sort of independent religious leader who had caused him trouble at various points during his years in office. Pilate's brutal response to the actions of another holy man, whose name is lost to us, in the course of the year would finally convince the governor of Syria that he had to go.

Tiberius had never been lively company. Deeply intellectual, his idea of a good time seems to have been quizzing academics on obscure mythological facts over dinner. He could be bitterly sarcastic, was a terrible public speaker, and seems never to have recovered emotionally from having been forced to divorce his first wife. Yet sad though he was, Tiberius was still a symbol of stability, and no one questioned, even after ten years of absence, that his symbolic presence was crucial to the public welfare. Would the next generation do as well? Sitting on Capri, the old emperor began to have serious questions about the fitness of his grandson, especially as the alternative, Caligula, was in his mid-twenties, making him the obvious choice over the much younger son of Drusus. As the questions became more serious, Tiberius seems to have publicized some horoscopes suggesting that Caligula should not be the next ruler, but then became convinced through further study of the stars that there was nothing he could do about it. In March 37 he fell ill and died (though stories were spread that he was actually smothered by Macro, Sejanus's successor as praetorian prefect).

Caligula and Claudius (AD 37–54)

When Tiberius succeeded Augustus he had a very long track record, and a legal position nearly equivalent to that of his predecessor. Caligula had held precisely one junior office, and had no official position when Tiberius died. The result was that the senate and people now took it upon themselves to define the legal position of the emperor by passing a bill to confer that position on Caligula. To those who did not know him, Caligula seemed the perfect choice: his father, Germanicus, had been very popular, he was young, and he gave every sign of liking to party. Crowds greeted the new emperor with enormous enthusiasm and cursed the memory of Tiberius. Caligula rewarded them with an extraordinary series of chariot races, plays, and gladiatorial shows, making up for all the years that had passed without special imperial events while Tiberius was away.

It soon became clear that the initial response was considerably overstated. The formative period of Caligula's life had been spent in Tiberius's house, and there his chief companions were the sons of Eastern client-kings whose attitudes towards power were very different from those of the average Roman. Kings were used to giving orders, and Caligula seems to have imbibed this view in the course of his stay on Capri. His closest friends were his three sisters, and it was rumored that he had incestuous relations with at least one of them (others said it was all three).

Contemporary portraits of Caligula, such as this bust now in the Getty Villa in Malibu, appear to have deliberately sought to evoke memories of the emperor's much-loved father, Germanicus.

It was probably in response to these stories and rumors of Tiberius's doubts about Caligula's ability that details were made public about the way that Tiberius had spent his waning years. It was said that he had suddenly developed a taste for watching young people have sex: the image of the grim, academic ex-general gave way to that of the septuagenarian voyeur. His character had been overthrown by the delights of "secret vice," rendering his judgments unworthy of respect. Propaganda and smear campaigns cannot, however, change essential truths. Tiberius was right: Caligula lacked experience of collective decision-making, and thought that power was exercised by telling people what to do, while doing whatever he liked.

Bizarre things began to happen. The praetorian prefect Macro was executed on a charge of treason within a year. People tired of his influence may have been glad to see him go, but there was now no voice to control the emperor. Caligula began to suggest that he was a god, and his parties were said to involve routine sexual assaults upon upper-class female guests. It took less than a year before the first conspiracy against him was uncovered, and that revealed yet another undesirable characteristic of the new ruler: he liked to watch people being tortured. Torture was a routine feature of Roman life: masters tortured slaves, and such slave punishments as crucifixion were widely used for all but members of the upper classes. But that did not mean that proper Romans enjoyed watching it administered: that would be cruelty, while the willingness to impose such penalties, if done with justification and without joy, was the virtue of severity.

Soon after the first conspiracy, Caligula left Rome to visit the armies in Germany, where yet another conspiracy was uncovered, and his behavior became even more erratic. What seems to have been a planned invasion of Britain—intended as a public relations stunt to prove that the emperor was a competent leader—fell apart, and Caligula returned to Rome. On January 17, AD 41, Cassius Chaerea, a tribune of the praetorian guard whom Caligula had insulted, stabbed the emperor as he left the temporary theater that had been erected on the Palatine for the performance of plays.

The officers of the guard who had been aware of Chaerea's plan knew that they were going to need an alternative to Caligula, and the obvious choice was Caligula's uncle Claudius. It was later said that he had no idea what was happening—that members of the guard found him hiding behind a curtain in the palace and took him to their camp for his protection. This story was a convenient alternative to one that has also come down to us—that Claudius joined the praetorians in their camp as soon as he learned that Caligula was dead, a story that makes it seem as if he connived in his nephew's demise.

Sejanus had built the praetorian camp to concentrate the guard, previously stationed throughout Italy, in one place and to provide an armed force with which to control the occasionally unruly population of the capital city. At this moment, however, the camp played a very different role: it was the senate that needed to be controlled. The senate met after the assassination, and some men seriously proposed that they should have no more emperors. The response from the street was not encouraging and reveals the extent to which the principate remained the legacy of earlier arguments for popular sovereignty against the rule of the senate. The narrative of the Jewish historian Flavius Josephus, who came to Rome with the later emperor Vespasian, provides an echo of conversations that took place on the subject

Caligula celebrated his three sisters in this bronze coin, having them represented in the form of the three Graces (goddesses believed to embody such virtues as beauty, charm, and creativity). The name of his eldest sister, Drusilla, appears at the top of the coin.

(Opposite) Claudius survived the dynastic upheavals of Tiberius's later years and the peculiarities of Caligula to reign for thirteen years. He can reasonably be said to have exceeded the expectations of his enemies, who regarded him as a fool. This bust shows the emperor wearing a diadem: a white browband set with pearls.

REACTIONS TO THE ASSASSINATION OF CALIGULA, AD 41

A clear difference had emerged between the attitude of the senators and that of the people. The aim of the senators was to regain former dignity; they owed it to their pride to free themselves, now that it was possible at last, from the slavery imposed on them by the tyrant's insolence. The people on the other hand, resented the Senate; they saw the emperors as a curb on its rapacity and a protection for themselves.

(Josephus, *Antiquities of the Jews*, trans. Wiseman, 19.227–28)

of imperial government in January of AD 41: he included in his own history of the Jewish people material about the assassination of Caligula that he found in a Roman history of the time (see box, left). The deadlock was broken when the guard made it clear that Claudius was their man. After a day of intense negotiation, the senate welcomed the new emperor, and shortly afterwards the people would have voted him all the powers of the imperial *statio*.

Claudius is a curious figure. Augustus had kept him out of public life because he had been born with a clubfoot, and (possibly) suffered cerebral palsy, and he had remained in the background throughout the reign of Tiberius. As part of his anti-Tiberian reaction, Caligula had shared the consulship with him in 37, but thereafter had more often humiliated than respected him. They were very different characters. Claudius had spent his years in the palace reading widely and writing. History was his particular love, and he developed a genuine interest in Roman antiquities. But, like Caligula, he had no real experience in collective decision-making, and seems to have found the company of senators, many of whom seem to have despised him as an imbecile, difficult. He turned naturally for advice to the freed slaves who administered the increasingly complex affairs of the imperial household, which controlled vast territories throughout the empire. In modern terms, Claudius might be seen as a technocrat, valuing the company of other people who knew how to get things done. His weakness was that he did not realize that men served him not only for his advantage but also for their own, and he was easily duped by those who said they loved him.

In the early years, the weaknesses that would prove his undoing were yet to manifest themselves. After surviving a poorly organized revolt by a governor in the Balkans, his staff organized a highly efficient invasion of Britain, an attractive target because Julius Caesar had failed to conquer it, and because it seemed unlikely that the Britons could stand up to a Roman army. The invasion was launched in AD 43 and proved successful, up to a point. Aulus Plautius, who commanded it, was an excellent soldier and ensured that Claudius could safely appear with the armies to claim success, but there was no effective end game. The Romans could not go home again, and there were not enough troops to occupy the island. Effective administration would take nearly fifty years to establish, and cost many thousands of lives, both British and Roman (see box, p. 200).

Although it created a long-term problem, the invasion had satisfied short-term political goals. Claudius had demonstrated military ability, and could settle down to years of generally effective government. He kept the army happy, and improved the welfare of the people of Rome by reconstructing the port at Ostia so that it could serve as an entry point at the mouth of the Tiber for the grain supply. Also in these years, as he served as censor, Claudius directly addressed the issue of expansion of the citizenship, applying rules that looked to the tradition of a "cultural" rather than "biological" definition of who might be Roman. In this case, the emperor's own words are preserved on a bronze tablet found at Lyons (see p. 201). With the age of civil war now safely in the past, it was becoming more plausible to propose a more open Roman society. There would always be bigots who opposed such moves, but the balance of opinion was now moving in the other direction.

THE CONQUEST OF BRITAIN, AD 43–84

The Roman conquest of Britain began in AD 43 with Claudius's successful invasion and occupation of the southeast of the country. It took the Romans another fifty years to firmly establish their ascendancy over the majority of the country, however, and to quell opposition from native tribes.

Around AD 47, two major revolts against the Romans took place, and there was heavy fighting between the Roman governor Ostorius Scapula and the British chieftain Caratacus. These revolts were suppressed, Caratacus was captured, and Roman control expanded into the Welsh marches. Another large-scale revolt took place in AD 60, this one led by Boudicca, the widow of the deceased king of the Iceni, in the modern English county of Norfolk. The rebels attacked Camulodunum (Colchester), Verulamium (St. Albans), and Londinium (London). Archaeological excavations have revealed that these towns were almost completely destroyed. The revolt was effectively ended by Suetonius Paulinus, the Roman governor who defeated Boudicca's army in a battle west of London.

The twenty years after Boudicca's revolt saw the consolidation of Roman rule. In this period, imperial officials—most notably Agricola, the governor from AD 77 to 84—were able to shift Roman operations gradually northwards, reaching the Scottish lowlands by the early 80s.

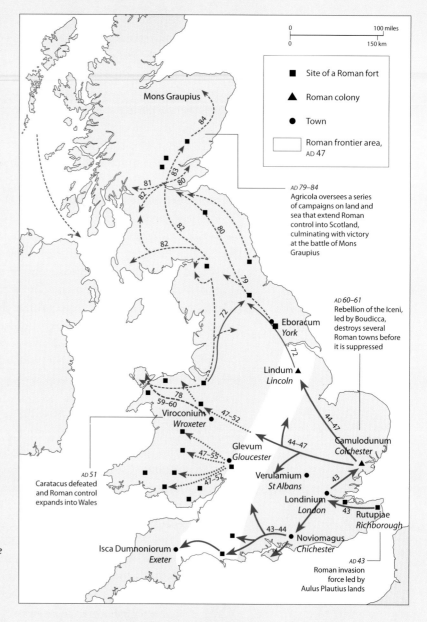

Site of a Roman fort

Roman colony

Town

Roman frontier area, AD 47

AD 79–84
Agricola oversees a series of campaigns on land and sea that extend Roman control into Scotland, culminating with victory at the battle of Mons Graupius

AD 60–61
Rebellion of the Iceni, led by Boudicca, destroys several Roman towns before it is suppressed

AD 51
Caratacus defeated and Roman control expands into Wales

AD 43
Roman invasion force led by Aulus Plautius lands

As time passed, however, problems within the emperor's household began to overshadow the administration as a whole. Claudius became estranged from Messalina, his much younger wife. He took slave mistresses, and she took lovers of her own. Although we cannot verify the story that she spent an evening in a brothel seeing if she could outperform an experienced prostitute, it is clear that she had many partners. In AD 48, while Claudius was out of town, she even went through a mock wedding ceremony with one of them, and that proved more than Claudius could stomach. Messalina and a number of her lovers were summarily executed.

Tacitus tells us that the freedmen who administered the palace realized that Claudius could not remain a bachelor, and there was the additional problem that Britannicus, his son by Messalina, was too young to succeed to the throne. They

This bronze tablet records Claudius's speech on the admission of Gallic aristocrats to the senate (an extract from which is translated in the box below). As a colony, Lyons was a center for Roman culture in the region; Claudius had been born there in 10 BC, and it is likely that this tablet was made by the local elite in grateful acknowledgment of his efforts to improve their status in the empire.

CLAUDIUS SPEAKS

I anticipate the first complaint that you will make, bear with me, lest you complain that some new thing is being proposed. But, before you do that, think about how many innovations there have been in this society, and, indeed, into how many forms our *res publica* has been led … Of course, it was thanks to some new idea that the divine Augustus, my granduncle, and my uncle Tiberius Caesar wished the whole flower of the municipalities and the colonies everywhere, that is to say men of worth and wealth to be in the senate house … I do not even think that provincials, provided that they can be an ornament to the senate house should be rejected.

(*Select Latin Inscriptions* no. 21)

selected Claudius's niece, Agrippina "the Younger," as his new mate. The match was plainly incestuous under Roman law, but no matter. A law was passed granting an exemption, and Agrippina moved into the palace with her son, Lucius Domitius Ahenobarbus, who was three years older than Britannicus. Agrippina made sure that Claudius adopted her son, thereby changing his name to Nero Claudius Drusus Caesar (Nero for short), while gathering enormous power for herself. In AD 54, so the story goes, she decided that it was time to take succession issues into her own hands, allegedly killing her spouse with a serving of poisoned mushrooms. Some, especially senators who had been unable to penetrate the charmed circle of freedmen and the few senators with whom Claudius was at ease, greeted the news that Nero was available to become emperor with delight.

Nero (AD 54–68)

It took some time for Nero to prove to be a catastrophe. At seventeen, he had little interest in governing, and left effective control of the state in the hands of competent people chosen for the job by his mother Agrippina. As long as Seneca, a famous man of letters who was Nero's former tutor, and Burrus, an effective bureaucrat, controlled appointments, the state could function well enough. The best indication of their preference for efficiency came when they decided that a real soldier, Domitius Corbulo, was needed to handle a dispute with the Parthians over control of Armenia that had arisen in Claudius's last years: he was granted enormous authority over the Eastern provinces for as long as it would take to solve the problem.

While Nero seems to have been amenable to having other people run the empire, enabling him to devote himself to things in which he was more interested—he fancied himself a poet and actor—he was not at all happy when these same people tried to tell him how to live his life. He had been obliged to marry Claudius's daughter Octavia as part of the succession scheme, and he did not like her. As emperor he began to take concubines. His mother disapproved. As he entered his early twenties,

Nero tired of his mother's constant interference, and communication between them seems to have broken down almost completely. It was at this point that Nero found Poppaea Sabina, the granddaughter of one of Tiberius's generals, and a woman of powerful personality. He wanted to divorce Octavia and make her his wife. Agrippina and the senior advisers counseled against this: Octavia was a symbol of stability and continuity. Nero turned to other advisers and devised a plot to kill his mother.

In 59 AD Nero did the unthinkable. He had Agrippina take a trip on the Bay of Naples in a boat so designed that its back end, where she would be riding, would break apart. It is a sign of how little Nero knew of his mother that he did not realize she was a strong swimmer, and had the ability to make it back to shore. The dripping empress was an object of pity to the crowd that assembled as she dragged herself on to the beach, but not to her son. He sent a detachment of the guard to kill her.

The murder of Agrippina changed everything. Seneca and Burrus disapproved intensely, and their influence waned even as Nero devoted himself ever more to amateur dramatics and displays of his skill as a charioteer. Burrus died in 61 AD, and Seneca retired a year later; their replacements realized that the emperor's eccentricities were linked with a craving for applause, and that their own power was linked to their ability to provide that applause. Octavia had been charged with adultery, divorced, and executed at about the same time that Seneca was let go. Poppaea was installed as empress, and Tigellinus, who had gained an entrée to the powerful as a supplier of chariot horses for the circus, became praetorian prefect, joining an inner circle that now looked very much like Claudius's last cabinet, in that Nero was otherwise coming to rely heavily on freedmen.

The affairs of the empire began to totter not so much because any specific crisis was actually Nero's fault, but rather because Nero's response in each case seemed inadequate. In AD 60, for instance, a violent revolt broke out in Britain: it was led by Boudicca, the queen of the Iceni—a tribe in the area of Norfolk—who had been flogged, and her daughters raped, by agents of the imperial household. Although the governor soon crushed Boudicca's army, three cities, including London, lay in ruins and the casualty rate was enormous. The victorious general, Suetonius Paulinus, was then fired for brutality, an unusual fate for a successful soldier. Furthermore, even if the dismissal was justified, the fact that it was done by an imperial freedman, Polyclitus, did not sit well with other senators. Four years later disaster struck closer to home: in AD 64 a fire destroyed most of Rome. The Roman version of disaster planning was unclear, and relief efforts needed to be directed by the emperor, who had allegedly reacted very badly to the initial news: people said that he had recited a poem on the fall of Troy, even though he claimed that he had been vigorously involved in fighting the fire.

Nero's rebuilding plan was no more satisfactory than his conduct during the fire. The centerpiece was a gigantic new palace for Nero himself, the Golden House: an extraordinarily luxurious space that seemed a virtual wonderland, but that is likely to have created problems for people trying to get from one place to another, because it blocked the heart of downtown Rome. Furthermore, realizing that people blamed him for the fire, Nero tried to push responsibility onto a group of which few people had ever heard: the Christians. Nobody much liked the Christians, who seemed strangely interested in the end of the world and a man who had been crucified by a Roman official, but Nero's treatment of them passed the boundary of the

Nero is said to have taken a personal interest in his image on coins. This portrait certainly marked a break from the allusive "Germanicus" style of his two predecessors—stressing instead the emperor's descent from Lucius Domitius Ahenobarbus, who had surrendered Corfinium, and his son, who had commanded the fleet of Brutus and Cassius.

grotesque, and people sympathized with their plight. Much later tradition holds that among those killed at this time were the two men who were largely responsible for the spread of the Christian message outside the Jewish community. One of these men—Peter—had been one of the original followers of Jesus, while the other—Paul—joined the movement after the execution of Jesus and a brief stint persecuting the followers of Jesus before he himself converted.

The regime staggered from crisis to crisis. A year after the fire, a conspiracy, involving members of the senate and the guard, was formed to kill the emperor and install a new man in his place. Their candidate was Lucius Piso, a former consul who was the grandson of Germanicus's *bête noire* and once the harassed participant in a bizarre *ménage a trois* including his wife and Caligula. As often happened when members of the senate were involved, people could not keep silent, and the conspiracy was discovered. A round of executions followed, and a group of men around Tigellinus took advantage of the emperor's considerable fright to sweep up additional targets. Seneca was forced to commit suicide, and within the year other men were charged with what amounted to little more than "conduct unbecoming a loyal subject." Important people were nervous, and Nero's advisers made a huge mistake in the course of the following year. Domitius Corbulo, sent early in his reign to deal with problems in Armenia, finally completed his dealings with the Parthians and headed home. No sooner had he landed than he was charged with treason and executed. He was, however, a man with many friends. As Nero took off for Greece to demonstrate his skill as a charioteer in the famous athletic contests of the Greek world (all of which were rescheduled to accommodate his visit), a conspiracy formed among various generals and governors.

In AD 67, the same year that he had Corbulo killed, Nero kicked Poppaea in the stomach while she was pregnant, causing a miscarriage and her death. The trip to Greece may have helped him recover from this domestic tragedy. Indeed, Greece proved a great success in providing him with a distraction: despite falling out of his chariot during his race at the Olympics, Nero was crowned victor in all the events he entered.

Nero could not have been pleased to be summoned home in the midst of this enterprise by a letter from Helius, the freedman he had left in charge at Rome, warning of an enormous conspiracy. It proved too late to do anything about it. In March 68 the governor of one of the Gallic provinces proclaimed his loyalty to the government of the Roman people rather than to Nero. Vespasian, the governor of Judea and commander of a powerful army assembled to suppress the revolt that had broken out there a few years before, halted military operations—an act, given the murderous efficiency that he had been displaying, suggesting advance knowledge of the revolt. And Galba, the governor of one of the Spanish provinces, had himself proclaimed emperor. Although Verginius Rufus, governor of Lower Germany (the more northerly of the two German provinces on the Rhine) initially marched to suppress the revolt, he soon declared in favor of Galba. Within Rome itself a fifth column was at work, and it appears it acted with the support of the guard. On June 9, AD 68 the guard declared for Galba, and the senate declared that Nero was a public enemy. Nero fled the palace, making for the house of a freedman named Phaon, not knowing that Phaon had tipped off his pursuers. As he heard them approach, Nero stabbed himself to death. His last words were, allegedly, "how great an artist dies with me."

Nero's Golden House, construction of which began after the great fire of AD 64, was a marvel of contemporary design, and occupied an enormous amount of space on the slopes of the Palatine, Esquiline, and Caelian hills. Nero's successors dismantled parts of the Golden House, but not all. Pictured below is what was once the palace's octagonal dining room.

The Year of the Four Emperors (AD 69)

The eighteen months following the death of Nero saw the Augustan system put to a test like no other in the previous century. There would be four emperors—Galba, Otho, Vitellius, and Vespasian—two palace coups (one resulting in Nero's death, the other in Galba's), and two civil wars (between Otho and Vitellius and then Vitellius and Vespasian). All of this, however, occurred within the institutional framework that grew up after the battle of Actium. All the claimants to the throne were senior senators with significant office-holding experience; their armies were the regular armies, not the mass agglomerations of men recruited for a campaign or two as had been the case in the civil wars before Actium. At no time was the continuation of the principate as a form of government in doubt.

Galba was already far along the path to self-destruction before he was welcomed into Rome as Nero's successor in September 68. Nero, while he was contemplating resisting the rebellion, had raised a legion from marines serving in the fleet based on the bay of Naples, granting these men pay equal to that of regular legionaries. Galba refused to honor this arrangement and executed a number of men who protested. At the same time, he alienated the army of Lower Germany by removing its popular commander, Verginius Rufus. Soldiers took the removal of Verginius as an insult, were enraged that Galba had not seen fit to reward them with generous gifts, and were offended by the appointment of a nonentity named Hordeonius Flaccus as governor. The situation with the army in the other German province was even more complex. One of the senior officers in the army murdered the governor in the hope that he would be appointed to the position himself. Instead he found himself subordinated to Aulus Vitellius, whose father had been Claudius's closest associate.

Vitellius was remembered as an idle pleasure seeker: such was the fate of the loser in civil war. The facts of the matter appear rather different. He seems immediately to have perceived that Galba was terribly weak, and that the armies in the provinces of Germany felt that they had been insufficiently rewarded for their break with Nero. Even before he left Rome he had checked a sword that had once belonged to Julius Caesar out of the temple of the Divine Julius. As soon as he arrived in Upper Germany, he began to ingratiate himself with his new general staff. The fact that he was allowed to leave Rome with a powerful symbolic trophy is a sign of just how badly organized Galba's government was.

Vitellius was not the only man with an interest in demonstrating the disorganization of Galba's regime. In December a statue of the god Jupiter on the island in the middle of the Tiber at Rome miraculously turned around and pointed east. The day this miracle occurred was the day that Galba presided over his election as consul for the following year, and it was a reminder that he had yet to deal with Vespasian. The Tiber island "miracle" suggests that Vespasian thought he deserved a reward for his support of the revolt against Nero; and the dispatch of his elder son, Titus, to Rome suggests that he might have thought that Galba should adopt him, thereby making him the next in line for the throne. The fact that Titus's uncle, Titus Flavius Sabinus, held the office of city prefect is unlikely to have been a coincidence: the office was of largely symbolic importance, but it had a staff and could be used to promote Vespasian's interests as Titus departed Judea for Rome. Arranging miraculous events, and assisting Titus's claim in other clandestine ways, would not have been difficult. By the beginning of January Titus was already in Greece.

This coin of Galba is inscribed with the words Libertas (freedom) on the front and Restituta (restored) on the reverse; its design echoes that of a famous coin minted after the assassination of Caesar (see p. 170).

Vitellius was the son of Claudius's closest senatorial associate. Until Nero's death he had a relatively quiet career, but his rapid organization of the revolt against Galba suggests considerable ability.

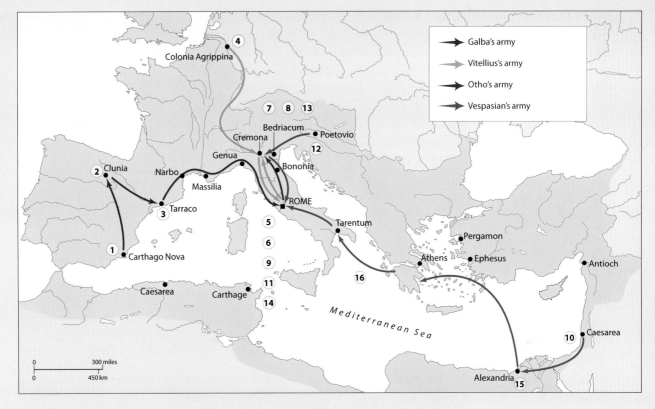

THE YEAR OF THE FOUR EMPERORS: KEY EVENTS

AD 68

1 April Galba proclaimed emperor at Carthago Nova.
2 June Galba learns of death of Nero at Clunia.
3 late-summer Galba leaves Tarraco for Rome.

AD 69

4 1 January Rhine legions declare for Vitellius.
5 15 January Otho proclaimed *princeps* by the praetorian guard; murder of Galba.
6 14 March Otho leaves Rome.
7 14 April Vitellius's army defeats Otho's army at Bedriacum.
8 16 April Otho commits suicide at Brixellum.

9 19 April Vitellius recognized as *princeps* by the senate.
10 1 July Vespasian proclaimed emperor in Judea.
11 17 July Vitellius enters Rome.
12 mid-August Danube legions declare for Vespasian at Poetovio.
13 24–25 October Vespasian's army defeats Vitellius's forces at Bedriacum and advances on Rome.
14 20–21 December Vitellius surrenders at Narnia and commits suicide; Vespasian confirmed as emperor by the senate.
15 Vespasian winters at Alexandria.

AD 70

16 Summer Vespasian sails to Italy and travels overland to Rome.

Galba's response was to dither, and to ignore the demands of yet another potential successor, Salvius Otho. Otho had once been involved in a wife-swapping arrangement with Nero—he had allegedly married Poppaea Sabina on the understanding that Nero would sleep with her until he could get rid of Octavia—and supposedly instructed Nero in the art of foot perfuming. All the same, he had proved an able supporter of Galba during the revolution, joining up as soon as he could from his own province in Portugal and endearing himself to the troops on the march.

By the end of December it should have been clear to Galba that he needed to ally himself with either Vespasian or Otho to keep his throne; but Galba was a snob, and neither Vespasian nor Otho came from one of the "right" families. When news came that Vitellius had claimed leadership in a well-organized coup whereby both Rhine armies swore allegiance to him in the first days of January 69, Galba selected Lucius Piso as his heir. This Piso was not from the branch of the family that had produced the failed assassin of Nero, but rather the great-great grandnephew of Julius Caesar's wife, whose immediate ancestors had married into the families of both Crassus and Pompey, and represented an effort on Galba's part to reassert the importance of the old Republican aristocracy. Sadly for Galba, Piso brought nothing but social distinction to the regime, and the appointment sent Otho into high-speed plotting, something at which he seems to have excelled. Working with a small number of carefully chosen supporters (and encouraged by his personal astrologer), he rapidly suborned the loyalty of several officers and enlisted men serving in the praetorian guard. Shortly after dawn on January 15 Otho engineered his declaration as emperor by the praetorian guard and other troops stationed in Rome; Galba was killed in the middle of the forum.

Like Vitellius, Otho gets rough treatment from the sources, but—also like Vitellius—he seems to have had a great deal more energy than the later tradition gives him credit for. Vitellius's army was first-rate, but Otho managed to rally a sound force from Nero's former troops, gladiators, and the praetorian guard to mount a credible defense, in the hope that he could hold Vitellius's advance long enough for reinforcements to come in from the Balkans. The holding action failed when Vitellius's army defeated Otho's men in a hard-fought battle at Bedriacum outside Cremona in northern Italy. When he learned of the defeat, Otho committed suicide on April 16 to spare Rome further violence.

Vitellius himself reached the capital by the beginning of June and had begun the process of forming his own regime, when news came that, on July 1, Vespasian had been proclaimed emperor by the garrison of Egypt, followed rapidly by the armies in Judea and Syria. The Balkan legions, fearing retribution for their support of Otho, and, in some cases, commanded by men with links to the Eastern commanders, soon declared for Vespasian. Vitellius did what he could, sending his main force to northern Italy, while at the same time keeping open lines of communication by not arresting either Vespasian's brother, Sabinus, or his younger son, Domitian. It was only as Vespasian's army—after crushing Vitellius's army on almost the same spot where Vitellius had earlier defeated Otho's forces—approached Rome that Domitian and Sabinus faced arrest. They fled to the temple of Capitoline Jupiter, Rome's greatest temple, which was burnt to the ground as Vitellius tried to take them into custody (Domitian escaped, but Sabinus died). Within days, Vespasian's men were in Rome and Vitellius was dragged through Rome's streets, beaten, and killed (December 20).

In the wake of Vespasian's victory the senate met to propose the law granting the powers of a *princeps* to Vespasian. It was the third time in less than twelve months that it had done so, and that the people had assembled in the *comitia centuriata* to vote in favor of those portions that conferred *imperium*; and it was the third time they had voted tribunician power to a new ruler in the *comitia tributa*. We have one bronze tablet (there was at least one more) containing a portion of the law concerning the *imperium* of the emperor (see box, opposite). This reveals what the position had become in the century after Actium, while providing a list of those emperors whose legacy was officially "approved"—a list that began with Augustus, while omitting Caligula, Nero, and Vespasian's immediate predecessors.

Tacitus's assertion that Otho, who is depicted in this coin, did nothing in his life as noble as his leaving of it may underestimate his talent. From the family's origins in Etruria, Otho's grandfather had risen to hold the praetorship, and his father was consul in AD 33. This history was typical of many families that rose from the municipal aristocracy to the senate on the strength of their effective service of the emperors, and there is evidence that Otho was himself a competent administrator capable of inspiring loyalty.

LAW CONCERNING THE *IMPERIUM* OF THE EMPEROR VESPASIAN

[—] or that it be lawful (for him) to make a treaty with whomever he shall wish, just as it was lawful for the divine Augustus, Tiberius Julius Caesar Augustus [Tiberius] and Tiberius Claudius Caesar Augustus Germanicus [Claudius];

And that it should be lawful for him to convene the senate, to report business, to transmit (business), to pass decrees of the senate by report and by division, just as it was lawful for the divine Augustus, Tiberius Julius Caesar Augustus and Tiberius Claudius Caesar Augustus Germanicus;

And that when the senate shall be convened according to his wish or authority, by his order or mandate or in his presence, the law in all matters should be maintained and observed, as if the senate had been summoned and was being convened according to statute;

And that whomever, when they seek a magistracy, power, *imperium*, or care of anything, he shall have commended to the senate and people of Rome, or to whomever he shall have granted or promised his support in canvassing, account be taken of them in any elections not held at the usual time;

And that it be lawful for him to advance and extend the line of the *pomerium* when he shall deem it to be according to the public interest, just as it was lawful for Tiberius Claudius Caesar Augustus Germanicus;

And that whatever he shall deem to be according to the custom of the *res publica* and the "greatness" of divine and human, public and private matters, there be right and power for him to undertake and to do, just as it was lawful for the divine Augustus, Tiberius Julius Caesar Augustus and Tiberius Claudius Caesar Augustus Germanicus;

And in whatever statutes and plebicites it is written down, that the divine Augustus, or Tiberius Julius Caesar Augustus, and Tiberius Caesar Augustus Germanicus should not be bound, the *imperator* Caesar Vespasian should be released from those statutes and plebiscites; and that whatever it was appropriate for the divine Augustus or Tiberius Julius Caesar Augustus, or Tiberius Claudius Caesar Augustus Germanicus to do according to any statute or *rogatio*, it will be lawful for the imperator Caesar Vespasian Augustus to do these things;

And that whatever before the proposal of this statute has been undertaken, carried out, decreed or ordered by the imperator Caesar Vespasian Augustus or by anyone according to his order or mandate, they be lawful and binding, just as if they had been undertaken according to the order of the people or plebs.

Sanction

If anyone in implementation of this statute has acted or shall have acted contrary to the statutes, rogations, or plebiscite, or decrees of the senate, or if in implementation of this statute he shall not have done what is appropriate for him to do according to a statute, *rogatio*, or plebiscite or decree of the senate, that is not to be a matter of liability for him, nor is he to be obligated to give anything to the people on account of that matter, nor is anyone to have action or right of jurisdiction concerning that matter, nor is anyone to allow there to be action before him concerning that matter.

(*Roman Statutes* 39, slightly adapted)

This bronze tablet, now in the Vatican Museum, contains the final few clauses of the Lex de imperio Vespasiani, which are translated above. Similar laws had been passed since the time of Tiberius.

The terms of this law are striking confirmation of Tacitus's view that the imperial autocracy grew from within the framework of the Republic. Here the emperor is seen as an add-on to the old institutions of the state to enable them to function. Even a man who derived his power from an army, and won power through civil war, would have that power confirmed by the people, just as it had been since the time of Sulla.

Summary

- Ancient authors offered two views of how and why the Roman monarchy emerged in the mid-first century BC. Some thought it evolved from the politics of the previous fifty years; others saw a sharp break with the victory of Augustus over Antony at Actium in 31 BC. The most prominent exponent of the first view is Tacitus, the great historian of the imperial regime who wrote in the early second century AD.

- Caesar achieved dominance in the state first through his conquest of Gaul, and then by defeating his enemies, led by Pompey, in civil war. Following in the footsteps of Marius and Cinna, Caesar based his power on a combination of military might and support from the urban plebs. He tended to ignore the senate, which came to regard him with distaste, resulting in the successful conspiracy to assassinate him on March 15, 44 BC.

- Chaos followed Caesar's assassination, with his supporters splitting into different factions depending on their views of Mark Antony. After a few months Antony succeeded in making life in Rome untenable for the party of the assassins, at which point they seized control of a number of provinces.

- Supporters of Caesar who disliked Antony coalesced around Caesar's adopted son, Octavianus. He and Antony fell out very quickly, and fought a civil war in 43 BC. The soldiers of their armies forced a reconciliation, which included their sharing power with a third party, Marcus Lepidus, and the three were granted dictatorial powers as triumvirs later that year. As triumvirs they ordered proscriptions of their own, with Cicero the most prominent victim. Antony and Octavianus then led their armies against Caesar's assassins, whom they defeated at Philippi in 42 BC.

- Octavianus removed Lepidus from the triumvirate in 36 BC, and in 32 BC declared war on Antony, who was defeated at Actium the following year. Octavianus, who was given the name Augustus by the senate in 27 BC, set about establishing a new regime. This was based on the support of an army that was rapidly dispatched to the frontiers; appeals to the common people of Rome through improvements in public services; and appeals to members of the upper classes for whom he created many new offices. He thereby laid the groundwork of a system of government that would last, essentially unchanged, for nearly 300 years. He stressed continuity with the past, the end of civil strife, and the new regime's tolerance of self-expression.

- The economic impact of the empire was felt ever more strongly, enriching members of the senatorial class, whose influence expanded well into the provinces, where new industries developed: in some cases replacing earlier Italian centers of production or forcing them to change their focus. Peasants were generally subordinated to large landowners throughout the empire.

- The mid-first century BC saw the coming of age of Latin literature. This was exemplified in the generation before Augustus in the careers of Cicero and Catullus, and in his own time by a number of major literary figures, the greatest of whom were Virgil and Livy.

- The Roman empire at the death of Augustus in AD 14 was far more powerful than the areas that surrounded it. The population was vastly greater, and internal peace allowed for significant internal development, though this took very different forms in the West and East.

- The strength of the Augustan system was revealed in the half century after his death. None of his immediate successors had strong administrative skills. As the system took hold, however, diverse groups within Roman society developed their own reasons for wishing to maintain it. Significantly, when Nero was driven from the throne in AD 68 there was little desire for a return to the days before the emperor. Each of the four new emperors in AD 69 was confirmed in office through grants of power moved through the traditional assemblies of the Republican period.

V

The
Age
of
Stability

(AD 70–238)

The Flavians	AD 70	Defeat of the Batavian revolt; Titus captures Jerusalem, where the temple built by Herod the Great is destroyed
	79	Death of Vespasian; Titus becomes emperor; Vesuvius erupts, destroying Pompeii
	80	Dedication of the Colosseum
	81	Titus dies; Domitian becomes emperor
	96	Assassination of Domitian; Nerva becomes emperor and adopts Trajan
	98	Trajan becomes emperor
	101–2	First Dacian War
	105–6	Second Dacian War
	107	Probable completion of Tacitus's *Histories*
From Nerva to the Death of Hadrian	113–17	Trajan's Parthian War
	115	Capture of Ctesiphon
	117	Death of Trajan in Cilicia; Hadrian becomes emperor at Antioch
	121–25	Probable completion of Tacitus's *Annals*
	122	Construction of Hadrian's Wall in Britain
	131–35	Bar-Kochba revolt in Palestine
	138	Death of Hadrian; Antoninus becomes emperor; adopts Marcus Aurelius and Lucius Verus
	161	Death of Antoninus Pius; Marcus Aurelius becomes emperor and awards the title of co-emperor to Lucius Verus; Parthian invasion of Cappadocia and Syria
	162–66	Lucius Verus commands Roman armies against the Parthians
The Antonine Age	164	Probable date of the birth of Cassius Dio
	167–75	First phase of the Balkan wars
	AD 169	Death of Lucius Verus

	AD 177	Commodus made co-emperor with Marcus Aurelius
	178–80	Second phase of the Balkan wars
The Antonine Age	180	Death of Marcus Aurelius at Sirmium; Commodus becomes sole emperor
	192	Commodus renames Rome *colonia Commodiana* after himself and appears as a public combatant at the *ludi Romani*; Commodus murdered on December 31
	193	War of succession follows death of Commodus; Severus emerges victorious and is recognized as emperor in June; Severus proclaims Clodius Albinus Caesar
	194	Severus's armies defeat Niger at Issus
Septimius Severus	197	Severus defeats Clodius Albinus at Lugdunum; Severus invades Parthia
	207–11	Severus campaigns in Britain
	211	Severus dies in Britain at York; Caracalla and Geta are co-emperors; Caracalla murders Geta
	212	Caracalla issues the *Constitutio Antoniniana* granting Roman citizenship to most free inhabitants of the empire
	217	Caracalla murdered at Carrhae; Macrinus proclaimed emperor
	218	Elagabalus leads revolt at Emesa and defeats Macrinus; Macrinus executed
	219	Elagabalus arrives at Rome as emperor; he proclaims the Emesene god Elagabalus the chief god of the Roman pantheon
The Later Severans	222	Praetorian guard murders Elagabalus; Severus Alexander becomes emperor
	223	Ulpian murdered by the praetorian guard
	225	Ardashir defeats Artabanus, initiates Sasanian dynasty in Persia
	231–32	Severus Alexander 's indecisive invasion of Persia
	235	Severus Alexander murdered; Maximinus becomes emperor
	236	Ardashir invades northern Mesopotamia
Maximinus	AD 238	Gordian I and II proclaimed co-emperors in Africa and recognized by the senate but are both killed in north Africa; Pupienus and Balbinus proclaimed emperors by the senate; Gordian III proclaimed Caesar; Maximinus murdered; Pupienus and Balbinus murdered; Gordian III sole emperor

O N JANUARY 1, AD 70, ROME WAS A MESS. The temple of Capitoline Jupiter had recently been incinerated and the streets had been littered with the dead bodies of soldiers fighting for mastery of the city. The situation outside Rome was worse. Italy was filled with troops whose ordinary posts were on the Danube, on the Rhine, and in Syria. Those from the Rhine had lost to the Danubian and Syrian troops at the decisive battle outside Cremona in northern Italy (the city had been left a smoldering ruin by the victorious soldiers) in October. The soldiers of the losing side remained disgruntled even as tensions rose between leaders of the victorious forces; and hatreds were openly vented among influential non-combatants in the senate, now dealing with its fifth emperor in eighteen months. Outside Italy, the legions that were left on the Rhine were falling victim to a revolt by the Batavi and other tribes, centered among the auxiliary cohorts who had once been their colleagues. The long-running revolt in Judea was heading for a tragic denouement in the massacre that would accompany the Roman capture of Jerusalem and destruction of the great temple on August 29/30. In an even more bizarre turn of affairs, the first of three men to capitalize upon rumors that Nero had not really died appeared in the Aegean, playing a lyre and claiming to be the emperor.

Tacitus saw this state of affairs as the consequence of the moral collapse of the governing class. In his view, the ideal state was one in which the governing class—including the emperor—united to provide guidance to their subjects. Instead, the would-be leaders of society had allowed themselves to be corrupted by the despicable habits of their monarchs. In one of the most stunning scenes of his *Histories*, Tacitus shows how the leaders of Otho's armies in the first civil war—including Suetonius Paulinus, arguably recognized by his contemporaries as the greatest soldier of his age for his suppression of Boudicca's revolt in Britain—disgraced themselves before Vitellius by stating that they had deliberately placed their armies in a position to lose. Earlier they had fled their own soldiers by jumping from the window of the house in which they had been staying. Yet according to Tacitus this is all that might be expected, given the rulers with whom they had to deal. Vitellius himself he saw as virtually incapable of independent action other than ordering dinner (a false characterization, but one designed to further Tacitus's interpretation of the facts), and his generals were devoted to self-enrichment. Otho had done nothing so worthy in his life as his leaving of it (his suicide was to prevent further bloodshed); Galba was a man judged "capable of ruling" by his contemporaries, until he actually tried to do so. As one member of the senate put it: "We pray for good emperors but deal with the ones we get." Still, things did not have to be that way. "It is possible to be a good man under a bad emperor" is something that Tacitus also wrote in describing his father-in-law, a long-serving governor of Britain. Of another man, Aemilius Lepidus, he had learned that he was:

> a wise and serious person for he transformed many things proposed by others in brutal displays of loyalty to the better, but he acted respectfully and thus lived with equal influence and goodwill with Tiberius. From this I am compelled to wonder whether it is fate or the stars at our birth, as in other things, that determines the favor of *principes* towards some and their hatred towards others, or whether it should be permitted to

ourselves to travel a path between outspoken insolence and appalling
flattery that is free from ambition and peril.

(Annals of Imperial Rome 4.20)

In framing the question as he did, Tacitus was far from eccentric. Many younger
men of his generation flocked to the city of Nicopolis (on the site of the battle of
Actium) to study philosophy with a freed slave named Epictetus. One of the major
tenets of Epictetus's teaching was that men of affairs should be content with their lot,
accepting what came to them and retaining a sense of their own humanity.

Tacitus's views might accord with those of Epictetus, but not with those of other
members of the ruling classes, who defined their opposition to the imperial system
as a whole in purely moral terms. These men looked back to the example of Marcus
Porcius Cato, who had preferred death to the mercy of Caesar (see p. 165); and now
they could look to Thrasea Paetus, who committed suicide on Nero's order in AD 65,
as an example of a man who put principle above self-advancement (although others
might have thought that his bloody-minded rudeness and tendency to waste time in
senatorial meetings by debating minutiae might have justified Nero's antipathy). Other
members of Thrasea's extended family would follow his example of principled and
suicidal opposition to imperial rule in the course of the next couple of decades. In so
doing they served to define the point that there were good emperors and bad emperors, a point that was also enshrined in the law granting imperial power to Vespasian
(see p. 207), which cited examples only from senatorially "approved" predecessors.

The point that most would agree upon was that the system worked for the best
when the *princeps* provided worthy leadership. Could you really, Tacitus asked,
blame young members of the Neronian nobility who fought as gladiators, or
appeared on the stage, when the emperor urged them to do so? (Both were activities
that in earlier times, as well as in Tacitus's own, would have resulted in expulsion
from the senatorial and equestrian orders.) Rome emerged from the mess that it was
in because Vespasian "alone of all the *principes* before him changed for the better"
(Tacitus, *Histories* 1.50.4). Vespasian, who lived a moderate lifestyle and worked
hard seemingly every day of his life, set an example for others to follow. At the same
time, Tacitus noted that the governing class itself was changing. Under the Julio-
Claudian *principes* (as the emperors from Augustus to Nero tend now to be known)
men might compete with the emperor in ostentation but:

> After massacres by savage emperors and after greatness of reputation
> had become perilous, many turned to a wiser course. At the same time,
> new men from the municipalities and colonies and even the provinces
> were frequently taken into the senate. They brought the thrift of their
> ancestors with them, and, although many came through fortune or hard
> work to wealthy old age, there remained nonetheless something of the
> prior inclination. Vespasian was the particular author of more moderate
> habits, being himself a man of old-fashioned habit and lifestyle.

(Annals of Imperial Rome 3.55)

For the most part, Vespasian set an example that many successors were willing to
follow in the course of the next 130 years. With the exception of two emperors (both
of whom were murdered), the rulers of the Roman world would be mature men when

they took the throne, and men who were capable of working with the governing class in the administration of the empire. It was not only senators who needed to learn the limits of their behavior: the emperor had to do so too. The result was a period of peace and order without parallel in the history of the Mediterranean world.

New Dynasties (AD 70–180)

The Flavians (AD 70–96)

From the moment he accepted the acclamation of his legions as emperor in July AD 69, it was obvious that Vespasian knew how to delegate authority. Command of the invasion of Italy had been given to his ally, the governor of Syria, and he had left his elder son, Titus, to deal with the revolt in Judea while he went to Alexandria in Egypt. There he advertised his ability to perform miraculous cures of the sick, to convince people that the gods had indeed ordained that power should be his (on a more mundane level control of Egypt would also enable him to cut off the grain supply to Rome if the war should drag on). Vespasian did not return to Rome until the spring of AD 70, by which time Titus was well launched on the final approach to Jerusalem, and Petilius Cerealis, his nephew, was on his way to suppress the revolt on the Rhine, a task he accomplished in the course of the following year.

Vespasian was an odd emperor. The first man with actual military experience to occupy the throne since Tiberius, he was a first-rate soldier who had proven himself as a legionary commander during Claudius's invasion of Britain and brought order to the previously chaotic Roman response to the Jewish revolt in 67. He was also the first emperor since Tiberius to have mature sons as heirs apparent. Within the palace, some might titter that he lived in a stable relationship with an elderly freed slave—the very Antonia Caenis who had joined in revealing the plot of Sejanus (see p. 196)—or complain that such a person had risen to become the most influential woman in the world; but none could suggest that his lifestyle was anything but austere. Another person to arrive in the palace, a man who some may have found a little different, was Vespasian's Jewish prophet. Flavius Josephus, who was born in Jerusalem in AD 37 or 38, had been entrusted with the defense of Galilee by the leaders of the Jewish revolt. Captured by Vespasian in 67 after surviving a suicide pact at Gamala, he had immediately predicted that Vespasian would become emperor: this thought was seemingly very much on Vespasian's mind, so he tossed Josephus in chains but kept him alive, presumably in case he might really be privy to divine inspiration. Once he arrived at Rome when Titus returned from Jerusalem in 71, Josephus wrote a history of the revolt in his first language (Aramaic) before completing a new version in Greek. His basic thesis was that the rebels were enemies of God, who was in fact on the side of the Romans, and that it was the fault of the rebels that the temple had been destroyed. For all its intensely partisan tone, *The Jewish War* remains one of the two most important views of Roman administration from a provincial perspective that has survived. The other is also by Josephus—his twenty-book *Antiquities of the Jews*, which recounts the history of the Jewish people from the Creation to the outbreak of the revolt in 65.

Josephus's explanation of the destruction of Jerusalem may be somewhat self-serving, and more than a shade unfair to his former colleagues, but it was a very

The new style of leadership Vespasian brought to the imperial palace was reflected in contemporary images of the emperor. This bust is typical in emphasizing Vespasian's age, knotted neck and brow, and the determined set of his lips; the intention was perhaps to evoke his long career of military service.

useful way of relieving the pain. Jewish communities had been expanding through-out the eastern Mediterranean ever since the refoundation of the temple in the fifth century BC, and in recent years they were also becoming well established in the Western portions of the empire—there was a large community in Rome, for instance, that had attracted the patronage of Nero's wife, Poppaea. It was clearly important to be able to state that there was nothing inherent to Judaism that was opposed to Roman rule. Even if the Jews could not worship the gods of the Roman pantheon, they could still pray to their own God on behalf of the emperor's well-being. Similarly, the customs that set Jews apart from other people—their dietary laws, the observation of the Sabbath, and circumcision—could be seen as interesting rather than threaten-ing, and non-Jews could be invited into various forms of associate membership in local synagogues. This was also a point worth making once Vespasian had imposed a special tax—payable to the newly created Jewish treasury or *fiscus Judaicus*—on Jews, defined according to cultural practice (the observance of the law).

Although Josephus's analysis might assist the process of reconciling non-Pales-tinian Jews to Roman rule, it did little to explain the root causes of the trouble in Palestine, and the failure to address those concerns would contribute significantly to two further catastrophes in the second century AD. This is all the more strik-ing because indigenous revolts against Roman rule virtually ceased in the same period. The basic cause of revolts under the Julio-Claudians—a point that Tacitus stressed—was Roman misgovernment. Although this view seems to fit very neatly into his basic thesis that everything that went wrong in Rome was the consequence of poor behavior by the ruling class, there is some reason to take him seriously. The basic problem experienced by peoples in newly conquered areas was that they did not have ready access to the patrons who could support their interest. The rise of the *principes* did not fundamentally alter the place of patronage in Roman political society (see pp. 84–85): to become important, people still needed dependants, but it took time to develop these relationships, which, in provinces, were often with out-going governors. It is inconceivable, for instance, that in Britain in AD 60 Boudicca would have been abused on the orders of the imperial procurator Decianus Catus, if he had felt that a powerful senator at Rome might have close links with the Iceni. But, since Britain was a place where governors spent a good deal of time fighting (and the previous governor had died in office), these links had not had much opportunity to develop. The situation in Judea was even more problematic: the region had essen-tially become a playground for various descendants of Herod the Great, alternatively subject to procurators subordinate to the governor of Syria, or attached to kingdoms ruled by one or another of these men. The local upper class, of which Josephus had been a member, simply had not had the opportunity to develop the links that leading groups in other provinces had with powerful people at Rome.

The problems of provincial government were but one of many issues confronting Vespasian. From his point of view, probably the highest priority was to establish a relationship with the people of his capital, distinguishing himself from Nero and his immediate predecessors. Perhaps the most obvious sign he could offer of a desire to make changes that would benefit the Roman people was his decision to set in motion the progressive rededication of Nero's Golden House complex to the pleasure of the Roman people rather than their ruler. To this end he tore down the fountain that Nero had built in place of the unfinished temple of Claudius, and

completed the temple. At the same time he opened the parks within the house to the people. Finally he replaced the artificial lake that Nero had built within the house with a massive amphitheater. Although the official name of this building was the Flavian amphitheater, it would be known to later generations as the Colosseum. The building's purpose was to commemorate the capture of Jerusalem. Somewhat later in the reign, Titus demolished another portion of the Golden House and constructed a massive public bath house that was dedicated, along with the Colosseum, just after Vespasian's death.

The Colosseum was one of two major victory monuments marking the end of the Jewish revolt, even before the final act was played out when Flavius Silva, governor of Judea, captured the last stronghold of the rebels at Masada in 74. The second monument was the Temple of Peace, which dominated a new forum opposite the Forum of Augustus. The colonnade around this forum contained sculptures that once stood in the Golden House, as well as spoils from Jerusalem, and housed a public library. Since the new forum also seems to have become a center for the administration of Rome, it looks very much like Vespasian's version of the Augustan

(Above left) The Flavian amphitheater—the Colosseum, as it was later known—was an architectural marvel. Incorporating the latest design techniques, and capable of holding as many as 55,000 spectators, it set the fashion for later amphitheaters around the empire.

(Above) The Arch of Titus, in the Roman forum, was constructed by Domitian in AD 81 to commemorate the suppression of the Jewish revolt ten years before. The inscription reads: "The Roman senate and people (dedicate this arch) to the divine Titus, son of the divine Vespasian, Vespasian Augustus."

(Left) Masada is an isolated plateau that rises some 1,500 feet (450 meters) above the western shore of the Dead Sea. To capture the citadel there, in AD 74 the Romans built a ramp (visible on the left of this photograph) against its western face. According to Josephus, the 960 defenders committed suicide when the Romans breached the walls of their fortress.

message that success in war brought peace and good government to the city. Also in the tradition of Augustus, Vespasian avoided government through favorites drawn from the palace staff. His closest advisers came from the senatorial and equestrian orders, and he was not afraid to promote people of genuine ability. One of these was his marshal Ulpius Traianus, commander of a legion during the Jewish revolt, who was soon left in overall charge of the Eastern provinces.

Vespasian died after ten years of generally successful rule in AD 79, to be succeeded by his son Titus. It was Titus who opened the new amphitheater with one hundred days of spectacular games just before a horrific disaster: the eruption of Vesuvius, which buried the cities of Pompeii and Herculaneum under volcanic ash and lava, respectively. For us these two events define the reign of Titus, whose style seems to have been close to that of his father throughout the mere eighteen months that he ruled before succumbing to an illness.

His successor and younger brother Domitian was a very different sort of person. Although he retained many of his father's advisers, and celebrated the memory of his brother with the triumphal arch that still stands on the Via Sacra at the eastern end of the Roman forum, his relationship with both court and senate was strained by an acute sense of imperial self-importance combined with a profound streak of self-righteousness. The former tendency was manifest in his preference for being addressed as "master and god," an extreme variation on the use of the word *dominus* in polite address (in English, *dominus* might best be understood as the equivalent of "sir," but to use *deus*, "god," in this way was beyond normal discourse). Self-righteousness was manifest in the fact that he took the title Censor for Life in 84, and engaged in several high-profile investigations of sex scandals, including one that resulted in two Vestal Virgins being buried alive when it was found that they were no longer virgins. It is also reported that he liked torturing insects.

Domitian's style endeared him to few, but he retained the loyalty of the military, and his reliance upon men who had risen to prominence under Vespasian protected entrenched interests. This army soon had a lot to do along the northern borders, where Domitian annexed fresh territory north of the Rhine and began a series of wars that would continue for nearly twenty years with the powerful Dacian kingdom in roughly the area of modern Romania. That said, serious tensions began to emerge before the end of the 80s, manifesting themselves in what remains a murky assassination attempt, followed by a major revolt by the governor of Lower Germany at the end of 88. The revolt was rapidly and brutally suppressed, but Domitian now began to be ever more suspicious of men outside his immediate circle. These problems were compounded in 92 when the army suffered a serious defeat at the hands of the Dacians: this may have resulted in the destruction of two entire legions and left the Balkan provinces open to attack, until a fresh expedition managed to crush the invaders. The Balkan crisis was accompanied by a series of executions of perceived critics of the regime that profoundly upset many in the senate, and by the late summer of 96 the situation within the palace had become intolerable to many of the staff. On September 18, the chief of the domestic staff murdered the emperor.

Nerva, Trajan, and Hadrian (AD 96–138)

The senate greeted the death of Domitian with joy; the guard was decidedly less enthusiastic. It was only through the intervention of the praetorian prefects, and the

(Below) Titus served with distinction on his father's staff in Judea, and he was left in charge of the siege of Jerusalem when Vespasian departed for Egypt in AD 70. Prior to his accession, Titus maintained an erotic liaison with Berenice, the sister of the king of Galilee, but opposition at Rome prevented their marriage.

(Bottom) Domitian stayed in Rome while his father and brother campaigned in Judea, and he was fortunate to escape with his life during the civil war of AD 69. Both these coin portraits make the Vespasian family resemblance clear.

promise of a massive "gift," that the guard could be convinced to support the acclamation of an elderly senator, Nerva, as the next *princeps*. Unlike Galba, Nerva understood that his first job was to find an acceptable successor. Having no son of his own, he realized that he needed to adopt a man whom the army would respect, and acted swiftly when the guard took to the streets demanding the execution of Domitian's murderers. He acceded to their demands for vengeance, and at the same time adopted Trajan, the commander of the army in Lower Germany and son of Vespasian's old marshal, Ulpius Traianus. The adoption of Trajan satisfied the guard, and brought a measure of stability to the political scene for the remaining year of Nerva's life.

Trajan was a spectacularly good choice. Like Vespasian he had worked his way up through the ranks, and knew the business of government. So it was that when Nerva died on January 18, AD 98, Trajan was still in Lower Germany, and in no hurry to return to Rome, a signal that he placed "imperial security" ahead of his own self-interest. He did not go to Rome until 100, and then started to work making his mark on the urban landscape, following the example of Nerva in taking over a project begun under Domitian. Nerva had dedicated the forum built by Domitian between the fora of Julius and Augustus and Vespasian's massive complex around the temple of Peace, as the Forum Transitorium. It fell to Trajan to complete Domitian's second project (much less far along than the first), a forum that extended to the west of the fora of Julius and Augustus, which became the Forum of Trajan. Trajan also began work on a major reconstruction of the Circus Maximus, expanding the marble seating that Augustus had installed to include the entire structure. He also tore down yet another section of the Golden House to build a great public bath house of his own. These three grand projects supplemented the Colosseum and had the effect of ringing the traditional heart of Rome with buildings for the benefit of the Roman people—a physical sign of continuity with Vespasian's regime and of the emperor's devotion to the welfare of his people.

Trajan's personal conduct seems largely to have coincided with his public persona. Although he was given to drink, and enjoyed the sexual company of boys, he was hard-working and imbued his staff with a sense that the "spirit of his age"—a phrase that appears several times in letters he exchanged with a governor in

(Above) Nerva was born into a family that had risen to prominence during the civil wars. Despite his senatorial status, he was very much a palace insider, and had been a friend of Nero.

(Below left) The Forum of Trajan, here shown in a computer reconstruction, had five main elements: a 100-foot-high column (30 meters) celebrating the conquest of Dacia, two libraries (one Greek, the other Latin), the massive basilica Ulpia, and the temple of the divine Trajan. These elements stressed the military virtues of Trajan, and his devotion to the unity of Greco-Roman culture.

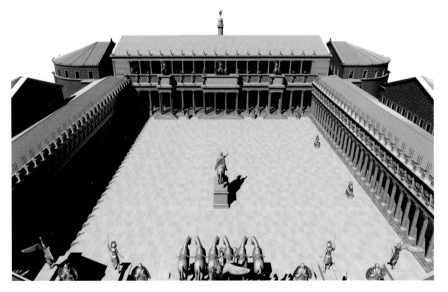

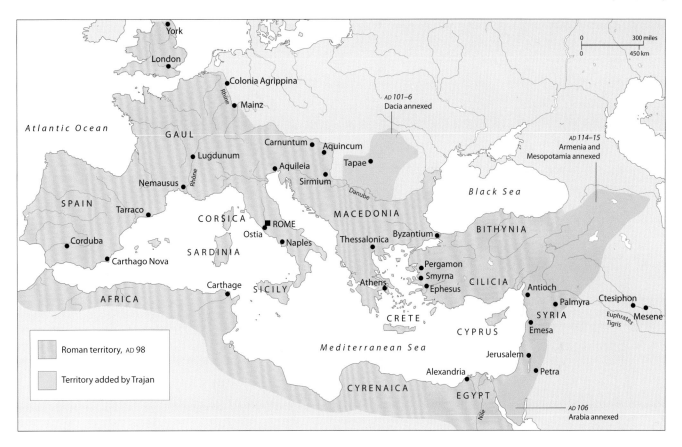

Roman territory, AD 98

Territory added by Trajan

AD 101–6
Dacia annexed

AD 114–15
Armenia and
Mesopotamia annexed

AD 106
Arabia annexed

(Above) The Roman empire reached its greatest extent in the reign of Trajan as a result of the emperor's successful military campaigns, but sustaining these conquests soon proved problematic.

(Opposite) Trajan was probably born in AD 53 at Italica in Spain, making him the first emperor whose ancestors had migrated from Italy during the period of the Republic. This marble bust, now in the British Museum, suggests a tall, powerfully built man, which accords with several contemporary descriptions of the emperor.

northwestern Turkey—required sensible behavior on the part of officials. In return he gave them a great deal of latitude, recalling Augustus's management of the empire as a collective operation. Within the palace, Trajan balanced the interests of senior officers with those of his family, which seem to have been dictated by Plotina, the most powerful empress since Livia. Her aim appears to have been to ensure that Hadrian, Trajan's nephew and the husband of her niece, Sabina, received sufficient experience in government for him plausibly to succeed to the throne if—as seemed likely, because she was now in her forties—she should have no son.

Peace seems to have been Trajan's aim when he took the throne, but peace was not to be. Decebalus, king of the Dacians, attacked Roman territory in 101, possibly to test the new emperor's resolve. He must have been sorely disappointed by what he found: his armies were so badly beaten by the end of 102 that he was forced to accept terms making him a subject of Rome. In 105 he broke the treaty, with devastating results for himself and his people. Within two years Dacia was transformed into a province, and Decebalus killed himself to avoid capture by a detachment of Roman cavalry. Meanwhile, in the East, the king of the Nabataean Arabs died, and Trajan decided that it was time to incorporate this long-term client state directly into the empire. The creation of the province of Arabia (roughly the area of modern Jordan) in 106 completed yet another process begun under Vespasian, who had incorporated remaining client states around Syria into the provincial structure of the empire. A century of contact with Roman imperial structures appears to have enhanced the process of urbanization in these regions so that they became plausible as areas where direct Roman rule might work.

Trajan's column, which still stands in Rome, is the only part of the emperor's forum to have survived to the present day. A sculptured frieze that extends up the length of the column depicts scenes from Trajan's Dacian campaign. In this detail, Decebalus, the king of Dacia, is shown committing suicide to escape capture by Roman scouts.

Throughout the first decade of his reign, Trajan was cautious in his dealings with neighboring peoples. Dacia became a province because Decebalus had refused the role of client king; Arabia became a province because it made sense. Something (we will never know what) made Trajan take a different view of the Parthian empire. In 113 he launched a massive invasion of Iraq. Following a plan of campaign inherited from the last days of Julius Caesar, Trajan began in Armenia and moved south, capturing the Parthian capital of Ctesiphon (near modern Baghdad) in 115. It was a massive triumph, but short-lived. To the rear, inspired it seems by messianic visions of the world's end, the Jewish population of Cyrenaica, Egypt, Palestine, and other border regions suddenly rose against Rome. In Iraq itself, the outbreak of fierce insurgencies a year after the Jewish revolt convinced Trajan to create puppet governments in enough formerly subsidiary Parthian kingdoms so that whatever regime won out when he left would be too weak to pose a threat to Rome. He then began a fighting withdrawal, crushing rebels where he found them, and sending large forces West to smash the Jewish revolts with extreme brutality.

As Trajan returned to the West in 117 he suddenly fell ill in Cilicia, on the southeastern coast of Turkey. He died on August 9, and Hadrian, then governor of Syria, succeeded to the throne. While he was the only possible heir from within the family, it appears that Trajan had toyed with the notion that the succession might lie elsewhere; Hadrian's adoption as his son, solidifying his claim, only occurred as Trajan lay dying, if then. There were many who believed that Plotina had slipped a servant into Trajan's deathbed to make the announcement after the emperor had died. The rumor, if it was such rather than a statement of the truth, reflects serious tensions that were on the verge of erupting between senior generals and the palace staff. What went wrong we cannot know for certain, but before Hadrian returned to Rome, four of Trajan's leading generals were executed.

The executions shocked the political establishment, but Hadrian immediately made it clear that he would not tolerate dissent. A man of powerful intellect, he seems to have viewed officials as subordinates rather than colleagues and to have dealt firmly with anything that he perceived as dissent. The palace staff received warning of his habits when he fired two senior officials—a praetorian prefect and the biographer Suetonius, then his chief secretary for correspondence in Latin—for excessive familiarity with his wife. The firings came while Hadrian was in Britain, and it may well be that he detected tendencies in Sabina to play a role similar to that of Plotina. Sabina herself was publicly embarrassed when Hadrian declared, in the context of the dismissals, that he would have divorced her if he had the freedom permitted to private individuals. Similarly, when a poet recited some lines suggesting that he was thankful not to be following the emperor on what he portrayed as lice-ridden journeys around the empire, Hadrian responded with a poem of his own suggesting that the poet was a lazy slob. The firestorm that had erupted after the execution of the Trajanic marshals in AD 117 seems to have made Hadrian realize that further executions were politically unpalatable, and that he could more effectively achieve his aims through public humiliation.

Another sign of Hadrian's impatience with the political establishment was his desire to be away from Rome as much as possible, and, even when he was in Italy, to reside in the massive villa he built for himself at Tivoli (see box, p. 222). The overt intellectualism and dislike of senatorial life that Hadrian manifested recall, to some degree, the conduct of Tiberius, a parallel reinforced by his evident interest in astrology. Another characteristic that he shared with Tiberius was a strong desire to avoid aggressive imperial policies. The great wall that he ordered to be built across northern Britain in AD 122 was a symbol as much to his own people as to the peoples north of the wall that Roman rule would expand no further. Other walls were constructed, of wood and turf rather than stone, along the frontiers of the German provinces, and it was in Hadrian's time that the empire came to be envisioned as a fortress that protected civilization from the barbarian world.

Unlike Tiberius, however, Hadrian seems to have felt that he should know as much as possible about the empire he was ruling. It was in the course of his travels that he began what seems to have been the most important personal relationship of his mature years, with a young man from Bithynia named Antinous. We cannot be entirely certain when the relationship began, but in 130 it came to a sudden and tragic conclusion when Antinous drowned in the Nile. Hadrian's celebration of his beloved—which included the refoundation of the town closest to the place where he had died as Antinoopolis, and permission being granted to a number of cities to offer divine honors to Antinous—seemed excessive to some, but Hadrian persisted. Such was the power of his personality that his ability to control the empire seems to have been unchecked by what would have seemed a major domestic scandal in the case of a ruler who commanded less respect. Respect for Hadrian was perhaps compounded with a healthy dose of self-interest. His favor to men who wished to enter the

Antinous, who was born in the northern Turkish city of Bithynia around AD 110, was deeply loved by Hadrian. The emperor deified Antinous after his accidental death in Egypt, and statues, such as this one, celebrating his masculine beauty, subsequently appeared across the empire.

HADRIAN AND TIVOLI

The villa Adriana in modern Tivoli, some twenty miles (32 kilometers) from Rome, was designed not only as a grand pleasure villa, but also as a place from which Hadrian could govern. An inscription found at Delphi in Greece makes it clear that Hadrian was already receiving embassies there as early as AD 125, and the grand reception hall was plainly intended as a place for the conduct of official business. Construction of the villa took place in two phases. The first, largely complete by 125, included the throne room, library, theater, stadium, and several elaborate porticoes. The second phase, which lasted until 133, added pavilions and further porticoes, many named for famous places throughout the empire. Not surprisingly given Hadrian's love of Greek culture, names from Athens were common. One group of buildings was called the Academy, after Plato's school, and there was also a "Lyceum," "Painted Stoa," and "Prytaneion." One of the best preserved sections of the villa, an artificial pool surrounded by colonnades and statuary (pictured right), was named for the Canopus, the waterway that ran alongside the city of Alexandria in Egypt.

imperial ruling class from the outside began to change the senate from a predominantly Italian and Western body into one that more closely reflected the population of the empire as a whole. The acceleration of the process by which people from many different regions came to govern the Roman empire was perhaps Hadrian's greatest contribution to the success of the empire as a whole.

Of all the regions of the empire, those that interested Hadrian most were the Greek homelands of mainland Greece and western Turkey. At Athens he completed the massive temple of Olympian Zeus that the Athenian tyrant Pisistratus had begun in the sixth century BC but no one had managed to finish. On an arch that separated the zone of the Olympeion, as the temple was known, from Athens, he compared himself with the city's legendary founder, Theseus: on one side the inscription read "This is Athens, once Theseus's city," and on the side of the arch facing the temple were inscribed the words "This is Hadrian's, not Theseus's city." Hadrian's passion for Greece is linked with a flowering of Greek culture that would become known, thanks to the work of the third-century historian Philostratus, who may have coined the phrase, as the "second sophistic": the term implied that this was a second flourishing of Greek rhetoric, the first being in the fourth century BC. The point that Philostratus was trying to make—rightly or wrongly—was that command of the traditions of Greek culture was now a path to actual political power at Rome, enhancing the tendency of this period towards the use of cultural criteria for inclusion in the extended "Roman" community. (This tendency was also evident in Vespasian's definition of the Jewish community as a cultural entity through the creation of the *fiscus Judaicus*.) Certainly one of Hadrian's friends was Arrian, originally from Bithynia, who is not only the source for much of what we know about the thought of Epictetus, but also the author of books on hunting, military tactics, and travel in the Black Sea, and the best biography of Alexander the Great to survive from antiquity.

Arrian is but one of a number of significant Greek authors whose work helps shape our understanding of the Roman empire in the generations after the death of Tacitus. Among these writers is Pausanias, whose account of Greece, stressing what were already in his time its ancient monuments, has long guided modern recovery of the Greek past. Another was Appian, whose massive history of Rome's conquests from earliest times to the reign of Augustus is often the best surviving source for the history of the generations before Augustus. Another historian, somewhat later in date, was Cassius Dio, whose father entered the senate towards the end of Hadrian's reign (see p. 14). Finally, a very different writer, whose career would begin under Hadrian's successor, was Lucian of Samosata, a brilliant satirist.

While generally successful in his dealings with his subjects, Hadrian had a serious blind spot for the emotions of one particular group: the Jews. He had no interest in their traditions, and felt that they should rejoice in being shown attention like that given to others when he refounded Jerusalem as a Roman city, named Aelia Capitolina. The result, however, was quite the opposite. Inspired by the Rabbi Achiva, and led by Simon Ben-Kosiba (who assumed the name Bar-Kochba, or "Son of the Star," in response to a prophecy by Achiva), the countryside of Judea rose in arms against the Romans. The revolt lasted from 131 to 135, ending only after massive and merciless military intervention. Hadrian had no pity for those who refused to accept that he knew what was best for them.

(Opposite left) Hadrian's affinity for Greek culture was reflected in his appearance. This bronze statue, now in the Israel Museum, shows the emperor in military dress, but with the beard of a philosopher: a style that would be adopted by several of his immediate successors.

223

In the early 130s it was clear that Hadrian was neither going to live forever nor have a son. The obvious successor was Pedanius Fuscus, the son of his uncle, the incredibly aged Julius Severianus, who was then in his mid-eighties; but Hadrian, who appears to have had a very difficult relationship with Severianus, would have none of it. In 136 he ordered both Fuscus and Severianus to commit suicide and adopted Lucius Ceionius Commodus. Commodus was the stepson of one of the men whom Hadrian had executed after Trajan's death, and his sudden adoption may have been a sign of remorse for an earlier injustice. It also had the advantage of ensuring that the throne would fall to a mature man with children of his own. Commodus had a young son, Lucius Verus, and one of his daughters was betrothed to a youth, Marcus Annius Verus, whom Hadrian seems also to have liked. Then disaster struck. Commodus died within months of his adoption, and Hadrian cast about for an heir whom he could trust to look after the interests of Commodus's children. In February 138 he adopted Aurelius Antoninus, the elderly uncle of Annius Verus, evidently on the condition that he would in turn adopt both Marcus Verus and the son of Commodus, for he had none of his own. On July 10, 138 Hadrian died in a villa in the resort town of Baiae on the Bay of Naples.

Simon Ben-Kosiba not only styled himself Bar-Kochba, but also—as this document reveals—called himself "Prince of Israel," dated his regime according to the years "of the Liberation of Israel," and divided the territory under his control into districts under military governors.

The Antonines (AD 138–80)

Aurelius Antoninus, known to history as the emperor Antoninus Pius, could not have been more different from his predecessor. He earned the name Pius through his strict adherence to the wishes of Hadrian, and by forcing an unwilling senate to declare Hadrian a divinity. For the next twenty-three years Pius did not stir from Italy, all the while entrusting his regime, as might be expected of a man who had enjoyed an extremely successful senatorial career, to experienced administrators. Marcus Aurelius, as Marcus Annius Verus became known after his adoption, later wrote of his adoptive father as the model emperor: kind, diligent, polite to subordinates, unwilling to decide in haste, and always looking to the good of the community ahead of anything else. Aside from Marcus's very personal recollection, little else is known of the man who ruled Rome at the height of its prosperity, partially because there were no major wars, scandals, or executions of prominent men, other than one who had openly incited a rebellion, without success, in Spain. At the end of Pius's long life it might also appear that perhaps more attention should have been paid to events outside the empire, but it is difficult to find grounds for criticism of a ruler who did his best, and maintained the peace.

(Below) Antoninus Pius had a distinguished senatorial career before his adoption by Hadrian. As can be seen in this marble bust, as emperor Pius sought to imitate his predecessor's appearance.

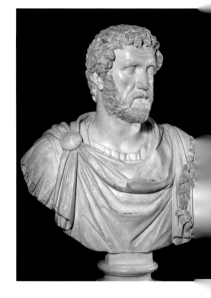

Long before Pius died, Marcus Aurelius had been marked out as the heir apparent, while Commodus's son Lucius Verus had lived in the palace "as a private citizen." This had been Pius's choice, but Marcus understood the terms under which he had been placed into the line of succession. Hadrian had intended Lucius to be emperor as well, and Marcus acknowledged his wishes. When the senate met to vote him the few powers of an emperor that he did not already have, he refused to accept them unless the senate voted the same powers to Lucius.

Marcus Aurelius continued the dynastic style of appearing with a full beard. Although his reign was dominated by wars and a catastrophic plague epidemic, Marcus's personal style was such that he was ever after regarded as a model emperor.

Although the simultaneous election of two emperors looks like a radical break with the past, it was actually the logical extension of practices that reached as far back as the early years of Augustus. For nearly twenty years after the battle of Actium in 31 BC, Agrippa had been co-emperor in all but name, and in the last years of Augustus's life so too had Tiberius. Before their deaths in AD 19 and 23 respectively, Germanicus and Drusus had played similar roles for Tiberius; and Titus had been virtual co-ruler with his father Vespasian, as Trajan had been in the few remaining months of Nerva's life. Marcus himself had held both *imperium maius* and tribunician power since November 147, an award that had marked the birth of the first of the fourteen children his wife Faustina would bear in the course of their long marriage. It is also notable that, with the exception of Tiberius, all the emperors who had advertised a close associate in their administration were regarded as very good rulers, and that even in the case of Tiberius, people felt that his regime began to deteriorate only after Drusus's death. Domitian had alienated people by insisting on his sole prerogatives, and Hadrian's insistence that he was the sole decision-maker had not endeared him to his subjects.

Pius and Marcus may reasonably be forgiven for accepting peace as they had it, avoiding preemptive strikes that might well cause more trouble than they solved. Still, major changes had been taking place in Iraq, where a new Parthian regime had taken hold in the late 150s under King Vologaeses, who seemed determined to reverse the political effects of Trajan's victories. The timely withdrawal of Roman troops, before they could suffer the effects of contending with endless insurgencies, had left Rome with considerable influence in southern Iraq. The region was especially important because it was the midpoint of a major trading route with east Asia: goods unloaded at the ports of Mesene, near modern Basra, were transshipped up the Tigris and across the desert to Syria in a network of traders based at the desert city of Palmyra, which was formally within the Roman provincial system. In 157 Vologaeses took control of Mesene, and even as Pius lay dying was preparing a massive invasion of the Eastern Roman provinces.

The fact that Vologaeses was making a huge mistake was not immediately evident when Parthian armies defeated a badly led provincial garrison north of Syria, and moved into Syria itself in 161. Marcus responded by sending a very large army and a number of highly competent generals to the East, with Lucius in titular control of the operation. While Lucius remained at Antioch—he lacked experience of direct command—the newly arrived forces drove the Parthians back into their own territory. In 163 these armies began to retrace the expedition of Trajan, and in 165 once again sacked Ctesiphon as Trajan had fifty years earlier. Vologaeses disappears from the historical record at this point and Roman control over the border regions was strengthened. In 166, after a further Roman campaign in northern Iraq, the armies withdrew to the West.

The Roman withdrawal was accompanied by a disaster. Some form of epidemic illness, possibly smallpox or the bubonic plague, had been raging in Mesopotamia while the Romans were completing their victories. As they returned to their posts throughout the empire, the legions brought the sickness with them. The result was catastrophic, with roughly 10 percent of the empire's population—as many as six or seven million people—succumbing to the illness. Ancient medicine had no cure for catastrophes of this sort, so Marcus turned to the gods. Apollo, speaking from his oracle at Claros in western Turkey, evidently prescribed some rites to avert the demons who were blamed for the outbreak, and Marcus circulated the response throughout the empire. He also consulted a second oracle, which a man called Alexander had established in the city of Abonuteichos in northwestern Turkey in the reign of Antoninus. We are reliably informed not only by his enemies, but also by the many who believed that a miracle had occurred, that Alexander had a snake named Glycon that was thought to respond to questions put to him by the faithful. Marcus asked Glycon's advice not only about the plague, but also about a new problem that threatened the empire's Danubian frontier in the wake of the catastrophe.

The nature of the threat from the north is not immediately clear: it does not seem as if there was any threat of large-scale invasion as opposed to the sort of long-distance raiding that these tribes beyond the Danube routinely indulged in when the Romans appeared to be distracted. The real problem was perhaps not so much that the tribes were doing anything especially new, but that the initial Roman response was inept, requiring years of campaigning to restore Roman prestige—largely in the eyes of the Romans themselves. The man responsible for all this was Marcus himself, since Lucius died of a stroke in 169. In response to an oracle from Glycon, Marcus tossed two lions into the Danube, possibly as a form of sympathetic magic to make the river impassable. If that was his intent, it did not work. The lions simply swam the river; the tribes launched a raid that reached Aquileia in northern Italy, where Marcus himself was besieged; and at least one Roman army was heavily defeated

This sculptured relief shows the "Rain Miracle" of Marcus Aurelius, who summoned a great storm to overwhelm the barbarian forces that had surrounded one of his legions. The story emphasizes the notion that the emperor could perceive things at a great distance, with virtually divine foresight. There are other versions of this story, which was very widely advertised at the time; this particular one, however, is from the column of Marcus Aurelius, which stands in the Piazza Colonna in Rome.

in the central Balkans. Again, Marcus turned to the gods for help, and he asserted that they now heard his prayers. In one case, possibly during the siege of Aquileia, he is said to have summoned a thunderbolt from heaven to destroy a siege engine; in another, it is alleged that the emperor's prayers (or the intervention of a favored Egyptian magician) brought a thunderstorm to the rescue of a legion that was in terrible difficulty.

By 175, the combination of prayer (as Marcus might have had it) and simple military skill had turned the tide. At the same time, Marcus began to groom his only surviving son, the fourteen-year-old Commodus, for the succession, while relying on a powerful coterie of experienced generals for day-to-day control. Not all of them seem to have been pleased by the promotion of Commodus. As soon as the advancement of Commodus became known, Avidius Cassius, supreme commander of the Eastern provinces, declared himself emperor. It was a foolish act that garnered minimal support, and Cassius was soon murdered by one of his own men.

Warfare on the northern borders filled Marcus's declining years, but now there was more success than failure, with campaigns designed to enhance the reputation of the young Commodus, just as Augustus's wars in Germany served once to enhance the reputation of his possible heirs. Certainly Marcus seems to have had no strategic aim other than getting the Danubian tribes to admit the superiority of Rome. It was as he engaged in these campaigns that he fell ill and died on March 17, 180. The nineteen-year-old Commodus succeeded to the throne as sole emperor. Surrounded as he was by experienced men, it may have seemed that there was little to fear from the fact that Rome, for the first time since Nero, had a teenage emperor who lacked experience of government. But this proved not to be the case, and Cassius Dio said simply that, after Marcus's death, the empire passed from an age of gold to one of rust and iron.

Imperial Culture

The Contemporaries of Tacitus

The reinterpretation, recovery, and reconfiguration of Augustan institutions that emerged after the round of civil wars in AD 69 were not features confined to political life alone. The period also saw a profound renewal and flourishing of high culture. The lifetime of Tacitus (c. 57–c. 120) extended from the reign of Nero to that of Hadrian, and his was scarcely the only voice to win the admiration of later generations. This was also the age of the great satirist Juvenal, of Martial, the author of potent epigrams, of the biographer Suetonius, and a number of epic poets whose work set ancient myth and history firmly in the context of the post-Augustan political system. It was also the time of Quintilian, the teacher of rhetoric whose work on the education of an orator showed fresh confidence in the emergence of a distinctive Latin voice that drew from a literary heritage that was both Roman and Greek. A similar view of the world appears in the astonishing work of the polymath known now as the Elder Pliny (Gaius Plinius Secundus). In his letter of dedication to the emperor Titus for his massive *Natural History*, he moves with ease through authors whom he assumes that Titus will know well—beginning with Catullus—and places his work in the context of both Greek and Latin literature. He also points out that he has collected no fewer than 20,000 facts on thirty-six scrolls, to which he has added an additional scroll giving the contents of the work as a whole, and listing his authorities, both Greek and Latin. For such a man as Pliny, the literature of his time was the culmination of all earlier traditions.

Similarly, a man of culture knew that there was nothing odd in quoting liberally from works of the generation before Augustus when writing to the emperor. Like Tacitus, the Elder Pliny regarded the present system of government as a continuation of the old rather than the result of a radical break. Pliny was himself the author of a major narrative history (now lost) continuing the work of another writer, Aufidius Bassus (also now lost), who may have died around AD 60. His choice of Aufidius is significant, because Aufidius was famous for the description he provided of the death of Cicero: a history beginning where Aufidius left off thus stressed the continuity between the generation of Caesar and his own. In describing his effort in the letter of dedication to Titus, Pliny wrote:

> I have dealt with all of you—your father, yourself and your brother—in a regular book, a history of our times beginning from the end of Aufidius. Where is it you ask? It has been finished now for some time; and, in any event, I have entrusted it to an heir so that no one might think that my career was owed to flattery. Thus do I do a good turn for those who hold the position (of *princeps*) and for those of future generations, who I know will contend with us just as we contend with those of earlier times.
>
> (The Elder Pliny, *Natural History*, preface, 20)

The sense of competition with earlier generations did not simply involve attempting to create works of equal merit with those of the past, but also attempting to make old stories relevant to the modern era. Lucius Annaeus Seneca owed his reputation in later generations as much to voluminous productivity as to his career as Nero's tutor and adviser. His *Moral Epistles*, which date to the years after his dismissal, are fictitious correspondence with a man named Lucilius on points of Stoic philosophy, and include many examples derived from Roman history: his brand of Stoicism seems to have been thoroughly adapted to the moral world of a Roman aristocrat. Similarly, his *Natural Questions*, a work of the same period in his life, takes on aspects of the natural world in a way that was attuned to Stoic understanding of the physical world (see also p. 237). Otherwise his literary output included a number of treatises on topics ranging from good government to the benefits of Stoic thought (e.g. books on fate, anger, grief, the constancy of the wise man, and such like); a spectacular satire on the deification of Claudius (whom he hated) called the *Apocolocyntosis* or "Transformation into a Gourd" (of Claudius); and tragedies. Seneca's tragedies, which may have been written for recitation rather than full-scale performance, tend to project contemporary concerns with the nature of power onto a Greek mythological canvas, often with truly gruesome results. For instance, Thyestes, the brother of King Atreus of Argos, realizes that he has been fed his own children for dinner when he hears them speaking from within his stomach (see box, right).

The interest in the gruesome that is evident in Seneca's plays resonates with spectacles based on myth that were enacted in the contemporary amphitheater. There condemned criminals were put to death in tableaux evocative of some of the more

STOMACH TROUBLE

What riot now attacks my
  guts?
Why do my innards shake?
  I sense an unbearable
  burden
My breast groans with a
  groan that is not its own!
Come children, your
  unfortunate father calls,
Come! Grief will leave him
  once he sees you.
Whence come their voices
  to me?

(Seneca, *Thyestes* 999–1004)

LUCAN AND NERO

He took it badly that Nero called a meeting of the senate and walked out while he was giving a reading for no other reason than to throw cold water on the performance, and afterwards did not refrain from words and actions that were hostile to the emperor; so much so that one time, relieving himself with a very loud noise in a public toilet, he recited half a line of the emperor's verse—"you would think that it thundered beneath the earth"—so that the others who were there for the same purpose, fled.

(Suetonius, *Life of Lucan*)

unpleasant aspects of myth: such executions were not confined to the age of Nero, but equally celebrated as aspects of the games with which Titus, generally regarded as a good emperor, opened the Colosseum. This interest is also apparent in the form of dance called pantomime that became hugely popular during the time of Augustus, an avid fan. Pantomime, also known as "rhythmic tragic dance," developed in the eastern Mediterranean in the generations after Alexander the Great. Its themes were all from myth, while the performance involved a single dancer whose dance was choreographed to a script sung by another soloist, and accompanied by a percussion band. (In the pre-Augustan age it seems that the dancer may also have sung, while lip-syncing was a feature of the Augustan period.) The preferred themes included such stories as the madness of Hercules—who was prone, before becoming a god, to fits of insanity during which he murdered family members—or the intercourse of the Spartan princess Leda with the god Jupiter, who had assumed the form of a swan.

One man who, like Seneca, was able to move between different genres with considerable ease was the poet Statius, whose career spanned the reign of Domitian. Statius himself seems, at least once, to have made an enormous amount of money for providing the script for a pantomime entitled the *Agave*, named for the queen of Thebes who, under the influence of Dionysus, joined with other women to tear her son, Pentheus, apart. Statius's father was a teacher around the Bay of Naples and his own first language was Greek; however, for a member of the Roman elite at this period, first language was irrelevant, for by adulthood all were bilingual. Statius proved to be an extraordinarily skilled poet, whether in the composition of epic or the occasional pieces (several praising Domitian to the skies) that he collected in five books entitled the *Silvae* (*Groves*). The range of his imagination is best seen, however, in the remarkable poem that he wrote about the mythological civil war fought between the sons of Oedipus, the *Thebaid*. Here he draws upon the themes associated with civil war in Latin literature to transform the Greek myth into a story that would have resonated with the interests of a contemporary audience, as the action moves from the world of mortals to the gods above the world and, occasionally, to those below. His models are equally poets of the Latin tradition and the Greek, and whose potential for the absurd or grotesque he is expert at depicting.

One of the models to whom Statius often looked was a poet of the previous generation, the nephew of Seneca, Lucan, whose death Nero ordered for complicity in the plot of Piso (see p. 203). Lucan was by all accounts as colorful a character in life as he appears to be in his poetry. He was originally a close friend of Nero, but the two parted ways, quite possibly because Nero became jealous of his extraordinary talent. The issue was not helped by the fact that Lucan openly insulted the emperor's talents when, for instance, he recited a line from a poem of Nero while defecating in a public toilet (see box, above left). The place emptied out as people recognized Lucan's suggestion that this was where the emperor's poetry should reside. In the end Nero barred Lucan from performing in public, an act that seems ultimately to have driven him to join the Pisonians; and defiant to the last, he is said to have named his mother as a co-conspirator. The point was not to get her killed, but rather to suggest that, by putting her in peril, he was truly Neronian.

Lucan's great work, probably incomplete at the time of his death, was a poem on the civil wars that began in 49 BC. In its surviving form, the poem tells of the period from the crossing of the Rubicon to Caesar's arrival in Egypt. Distinctively anti-Caesarian in tone, Lucan's stance is in keeping with the spirit of the Augustan and post-Augustan age. Virgil had criticized Caesar for starting the civil war, and Nero had far closer links with the losers of civil wars than with victors. His great-great-grandfather was the Domitius Ahenobarbus, who had surrendered to Caesar at Corfinium (see p. 164) and died at Pharsalus; his great-grandmother was Antonia, daughter of Octavia and Mark Antony. For Lucan virtue could not survive civil war, which was by far the worst of all evils in the ideological system of the Julio-Claudians, as it was for the Flavians. What is most striking about Lucan, however, is that unlike Statius, who reverted to the usual epic device of countless interventions by the gods, he included no gods at all. The poem has plenty of allusions to the divine—prophecies and a vision of the underworld that Sextus Pompey gets from a corpse, animated for that purpose by a witch—but no gods. They had no role to play in civil war.

Statius and Lucan were not the only poets who experimented with the traditions of epic. Valerius Flaccus composed a new version of the adventures of Jason and the Argonauts with a distinctively Roman cast (including the development of a civil war for Jason and his companions to participate in while they were retrieving the fleece), and Silius Italicus, the last consul of Nero's reign, devoted his later life to a seventeen-book poem on the war with Hannibal. Perhaps the most interesting message to emerge from Silius's massive work is that nostalgic visions of the third-century BC senate were not in the least incompatible with loyalty to the imperial system, the future glories of which are revealed to Scipio Africanus when he visits the underworld in the thirteenth book.

Among the associates of Silius was a poet from Spain named Martial, whose time in Rome appears to have spanned the period roughly from the death of Vespasian (AD 79) to the accession of Trajan (AD 98), at which point he returned to estates in Spain that had been augmented by gifts from wealthy friends. Martial's specialty was the epigram, and his poems, which span the gamut of upper-class life, allow us a glimpse into the psychology of his audience. A constant theme in his poems is the way that appearances can be deceptive. Frequent targets are chinks in the armor of the upper class: he picks holes in the image of the elite Roman as a person who remained in thorough control of his or her emotions, acting at all times as a person of unflappable dignity. Likewise, to judge from Martial's poetry, members of the aristocracy liked to imagine that virtually everyone was sleeping with someone to whom they were not married. Life is unlikely to have been anything like as lively as this, but a society built upon the appearance of stable propriety had a tendency to be fascinated with the ancient version of tabloid culture.

Such a fascination is also evident in a radically different sort of work, the *Satyricon* of Petronius. The author is likely to have been the senior senator known informally as Nero's "overseer of elegance," whose death Nero ordered on the false charge of complicity in the Pisonian conspiracy of AD 65. The *Satyricon*, most of which has been lost in transmission (of what may once have been sixteen books, we have portions of the last three), chronicles the misadventures of a pair of male lovers, Encolpius and Giton, whose problems stem from some offense that Encolpius, who is also the narrator, has committed against the god Priapus (a fertility god whose principal attribute was a gigantic penis). Various topics in the surviving section include the decline of oratorical standards, the poor quality of contemporary poetry,

(Opposite) A reconstruction of what ancient Pompeii may have looked like just before it was buried by volcanic ash in AD 79. The city was rediscovered in 1748, and since that time excavations have revealed about 100 of the 163 acres (65 hectares) that it once occupied. Discoveries there have given us a vivid picture of every facet of urban life in a Roman city.

(Above) Priapus, the god of fertility, was thought to protect doors and gardens from unwelcome intruders. In this painting from the entrance to the house of the Vettii—a wealthy family whose villa was among the most spectacular at Pompeii—he weighs his penis against a sack of money, a reflection of Priapus's common association with good fortune.

lousy art, the gross manners of rich freedmen, the habits of people who seek to get themselves named in other people's wills, and sex. Among these discussions, all of which have a very sharp edge, Petronius's masterpiece is the description of a banquet held by Trimalchio, a fabulously wealthy freeman whose ignorance of true culture is matched only by his taste for garish extravagance. If there is a theme that links any of the events in this book together it seems to be the inversion of the proper order of society, and the folly of assuming that things are as they seem.

Martial's themes, and those of Petronius, resonate very well with what is written on the walls of the city of Pompeii, which abound in poems about people's sexual preferences, and indeed with what was painted there. The reason we know so much about Pompeii is of course because the city was buried by the eruption of Mount Vesuvius in AD 79, but there is no reason to think that the tastes that emerged from the volcanic ash are anything but typical. The art on the walls of the houses, ranging from abstract patterns and naturalistic scenes to scenes from myth and (quite often) of copulation, reflects the diverse tastes of the average Roman, and a range of views on sexuality appreciating its role at the heart of relationships, from the affectionate to the abusive. Other aspects of this art, depicting people going about their daily lives, stress the tendency for Romans to define their place in terms of their public actions. A fascination with the correspondence (or lack of it) between public persona and private individual remained one of the most basic in Roman life.

It is one thing to identify this intrigue with the dissonance between public and private as a passionate interest of Romans in the age of Vespasian (and just about any other era). It is another to determine where the norm might lie on the continuum of conduct between that implied by Martial and the graffiti poets of Pompeii, and that implied by, for instance, Roman funerary monuments, which stress long-standing affectionate relationships, while at the same time revealing a variety of

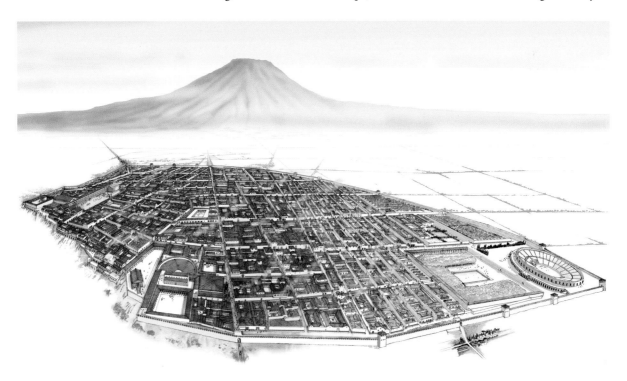

marital experiences. Thus Gaius Livanius Acutus presumably intended to live to old age with his first wife when he had a joint memorial made for them. Things did not go as planned, so the stone was recarved for his second wife. Luccius Mindius Dius seems to have been devoted to his first wife, Tryphaena, with whom he lived for twenty-three years; to his second wife, Lucceia Ianuaria, who is also in the tomb that he built; and finally to his mistress Annia Laveria. Verria Zosime, who was buried at Isola Sacra, the huge cemetery outside Ostia, in a sarcophagus with her husband Verrius Euhelpistus, once planned to be interred with her first husband Verrius Eucharistus (they were all freed slaves from the same family). One interesting aspect of Verria's career is that the tombstone attached to the tomb of her first husband says that she will be buried there too. It is a reminder of the fact that the language of such texts tends to be stunningly lacking in originality, which is why the language used to describe family relationships is a fairly reliable indicator of socially accepted norms. Ideal women tend to be thrifty, faithful, good at weaving, chaste, and avoid quarrels. Husbands tend to exist in a more restricted zone of virtue that includes such qualities as being "dear" and "incomparable," while mention of personal chastity and domestic arts do not tend to figure for them, which may suggest a double standard with regard to sexual relations (women may have serial partners, but multiple partners might be admitted for men). That said, when a man writes that he wishes either that his wife would return from the underworld or that he may die so that they are no longer separated, or that he wishes he could still go to the baths of Apollo with his wife, it is reasonable to think of these as monogamous matches. The crucial bond between adults often appears to be children, whose loss is invariably a tragedy, and the grief seems not to have lessened by awareness that death was commonly the lot of the young.

In addition to tombstones, letters from one of Tacitus's contemporaries—the nephew of Gaius Plinius Secundus, Gaius Plinius Caecilius Secundus, or, more simply, the Younger Pliny—paint a picture of reasonably close-knit family groups in which adultery is not to be mentioned. Pliny married two (possibly three) young teenage girls, one after the death of the other, and seems to have taken both to bed immediately despite medical advice suggesting that this was deeply unhealthy: the attested habit of other Romans who contracted marriages with young girls was that they did not consummate them for years. But aside from Pliny's personal taste, there is some reason to think that his attitudes on monogamous union might be nearer to the norm than those of Martial, who was nonetheless included in his circle of friends. Suetonius, another friend of Pliny, presents the sexual excesses of emperors he did not like as signs of poor character, suggesting again that marital life from his point of view might not routinely have involved mistresses. At the same time, there is yet other evidence suggesting that there was regular tolerance for a "third person" in marriages, usually slave concubines: their presence may be detected in Roman wills where inheritances are provided for what are plainly the offspring of these liaisons.

One of a number of paintings on mythological themes found in the house of the Dioscuri at Pompeii, this depiction of the mythological Medea brilliantly captures her emotions as she contemplates murdering her children to take vengeance upon her husband, Jason, who has abandoned her.

The existence of these children in households where there was also a wife suggests that wives—especially those who were much younger than their husbands—might not always object. The basic facts of Roman marriage—that divorce was easy, and that women could control property (see p. 35)—make it unlikely that women were trapped in marriages that they could not stand. Indeed, the positive obsession with the sex lives of independent women that appears not only in Martial, but also in various other works of fiction, such as Apuleius's *Golden Ass*, strongly suggests that many of the male authors of these works were projecting their own fantasies upon women whom they could not control.

The inability to control women informs one of the more extraordinary works of this same period, the sixth *Satire* of Juvenal, which is an attack on the women of Rome. What little we know about Juvenal suggests that he entered the literary world of Rome before the death of Domitian—Martial mentions him as a friend in three poems—and that he continued to live there into the reign of Hadrian. He produced five books of *Satires* (the sixth *Satire* comprises the whole of the second book). Arranged as a sort of anti-handbook on marriage (the gist of which is, why bother, since women will never do what you like?) it reads at least initially—and perhaps on several further readings as well—as an astonishing outburst of misogyny. In fact, it is testimony both to the freedom that women could enjoy in Roman society, and to male discomfort with that freedom. Elsewhere Juvenal assails the wasteful lifestyle of the extremely wealthy, their lack of intellectual engagement, the fate of literature in his age, and the vanity of human ambition. The range of his subjects and the vehemence of his tone presumably amused precisely the class that was the object of the *Satires*. Some of these people might have been fans of Statius, whose work he parodies in his fourth *Satire*, which describes a fictional meeting of Domitian's council, summoned to discuss how to cook an enormous fish. Other members of his audience would have been familiar with Tacitus, whose histories seem often to lie behind the examples from nearly contemporary history that appear in the *Satires*. We also owe to Juvenal the lament that the Roman people, who used to determine the fate of the world, were now solely interested in bread and circuses. His dismissal of the importance of such spectacles is perhaps unfair.

Spectacle and Culture

Roman aristocrats, the Younger Pliny and Tacitus, for example, tended to express contempt for popular culture; we are fortunate that the same is not true of Martial, one of whose books was devoted to the spectacles of the amphitheater. The world of public entertainment as a whole was central to the creation of a shared culture across the empire. It was at public spectacles that people could come together for mutual enjoyment at events that stressed common values.

These public spectacles came in three basic forms: theatrical events, athletic contests, and public combats. Theatrical events included full productions of plays, usually plays that were part of the educational curriculum; solo performances of "greatest hits" from famous plays, sometimes set to musical accompaniment; poetic recitations, musical performances, and choral acts; and mimes, a generic term for "low-brow" performances that ranged from sitcoms and clown routines to dancing displays and pantomime. On some occasions these could be supplemented with performances that were intended to illustrate an important event in the history of

The Roman empire helped establish the popularity of Greek-style sports across the Mediterranean world. This mosaic from Thyna in modern Tunisia shows wrestlers in action; the table at the top of the image displays the prize money for which they fought.

This mosaic from Lyons in France depicts the basic components of a chariot race. These include the drivers wearing the colors of their factions, the central barrier around which seven laps were run, the assistants to the charioteers (mounted and on foot) in the arena, and the starting gates.

the empire—we have, for instance, part of the script for a depiction of Hadrian's ascent to the gods that was put on in an Egyptian town after his death. Athletic contests descended from the festivals of pre-Roman Greece, and involved naked athletes engaging in a variety of running events, the pentathlon, and the triumvirate of "combat" sports: boxing, wrestling, and pancration—a brutal combination of the other two events. They might also include some equestrian events, including horse races and races involving chariots drawn by two- or four-horse teams. These chariot races were distinguished from circus chariot races at Rome—very few other cities could afford to build their own circuses—by the fact that the tracks were of varying dimensions and could admit a large number of contestants. Circus chariot racing, which evolved in Rome's valley of the Circus Maximus, involved a set track where a maximum of twelve teams ran seven laps around a central barrier. A further peculiarity of the Roman races was that they were dominated by four professional factions—known according to the colors worn by their drivers as the Blues, Greens, Reds, and Whites—that had organized the sport since, probably, the fourth century BC. Finally, public combats included bouts between pairs of gladiators, hunting exhibitions, and the execution of criminals, when they were not simply tortured, exposed to wild beasts, or forced to fight to the death in duels against each other, but instead put to death in the course of mythological tableaux (see box, opposite).

The rules governing ancient sports suggest that audiences had little patience. When they gathered for a sporting event, they expected to see close contests, to be thrilled by rapid changes of fortune, and not to be surprised if one or more contestants failed to make it out of the arena in one piece. Unlike modern fans, who are willing to tolerate championship events that stretch out for weeks or months, ancient fans looked for instant gratification. In combat sports, for instance, all the rounds of a championship event took place on a single day, so that the ultimate victor had to win a series of decisive victories with almost no time between bouts. In boxing, for example, the victor had to win by an equivalent of a technical knockout each time, so the final was as much a test of endurance as it was of technical skill.

The rewards for success in this world were also immediate, and in many cases substantial. Professional athletes who won at the major festivals—the Olympic Games, or the games that Augustus founded to commemorate his victory at

ROMAN GLADIATORS

Gladiatorial combat originated in central Italy. The earliest evidence comes from literary references to gladiatorial events in Campania in the fourth century BC and from depictions of men engaging in single combat in tomb paintings of the same period. The original context for these fights was evidently funeral games at which the military virtues of society were celebrated, and it was as part of funeral celebrations that gladiatorial combat was introduced in Rome in the third century BC. It rapidly became identified with the militaristic culture of Rome, and began to spread into the provinces.

Although it was enormously dangerous, gladiatorial combat was still a sport. Gladiators only ever fought in duels where two men were matched against each other, and with officials present. Events where groups of people fought each other or were required to kill each other involved criminals. Gladiators only fought to the death under special circumstances—usually at Rome when the emperor was present, or in the provinces during an imperial visit or by special dispensation from the government. The fact that a fight could be to the death, however rarely this was required, set gladiatorial combat apart from other sports, including chariot racing and the Greek pancration, which could also result in the death of a contestant. Given the rarity of actual fights to the death, however, when gladiators did die as a result of combat it was usually either because their wounds were poorly treated, or because of incompetent officiating. In the provinces, the imperial authorities tried to restrict the danger of the games, and even supported fights in which gladiators fought with wooden weapons.

Several crucial aspects of gladiatorial combat are shown in this mosaic from the fourth century AD, including pairs of gladiators with different weapon types, and the referees who were charged with controlling the match. In the top half of this mosaic a fight is stopped as one gladiator surrenders.

Gladiators could be either freed men or slaves (and occasionally women, either slave or free). They were highly trained, and, as they gained experience, highly compensated. The appearance money for a gladiator in the time of Marcus Aurelius was as much as twelve times the annual salary of a legionary. Much of our information about gladiators comes from tombstones erected by family members or friends, revealing that people were proud of their profession.

Actium—would receive pensions from the city of which they claimed citizenship upon entering the competition (many athletes belonged to a number of cities). They were also eligible for membership in the professional association of champion athletes (the actual name of this group changed at various points in imperial history), which granted them valuable privileges, including exemptions from taxation and public service that would otherwise have been compulsory. In this way some men could acquire incomes that were certainly the equivalent of important senators. No athlete, however, could do so well as a successful charioteer at Rome. The most successful of these competitors, Diocles, enjoyed a twenty-four-year career in which his annual income was around 1.5 million sesterces. The huge sums of money involved in these cases reflect the enormous enthusiasm people had for their sports, and the sense that the athletes truly were exemplars of the qualities regarded by society as important.

It was not only in sport that endurance, the ability to deal with pain, and risk-taking were celebrated—these were also important themes in contemporary fiction. Deriving from the tradition of such traveling heroes as Aeneas and his great Greek forebear, Odysseus, whose trip home from the Trojan war took ten years, the novels that emerged as the one new literary genre of the imperial period were often tales of people separated from home, wandering through exotic locations before they could be reunited in the love that they desired. The stories were often intended to reflect the character of the upper-class heroes and heroines as they were subjected to the threat or actuality of intense suffering on the way. The anxieties of the audiences of these books are well summarized in a remarkable astrological text of the second century AD by the astronomer and geographer Ptolemy, which reads:

> If Jupiter and Venus are the rulers of the places which govern travel … they make the journeys not only safe but also pleasant; for the subjects will be sent on their way either by the chief men of the country or by the resources of their friends, and favorable conditions of weather and abundance of supplies will also aid them … If Saturn and Mars control the luminaries … they will involve the subject in great dangers, through unfortunate voyages and shipwreck if they are in watery signs, or again through hard going and desert places; and if they are in solid signs, through falling from heights and assaults of winds; in the solstitial and equinoctial signs, through lack of provisions and unhealthy conditions; in the signs of human form, through piracy, plots, and robberies; in the terrestrial signs, through the attacks of beasts, or earthquakes, and if Mercury is present at the same time, through the weather, dangerous accusations, and, furthermore, through the bites of reptiles and other poisonous creatures.

(Ptolemy, *Tetrabiblos*, trans. Robbins, 4.8)

The famous Laocoön statue group, now in the Vatican Museums, was probably the work of a Greek artist at Rome in the reign of Augustus. In its vivid depiction of the moment when the gods exacted their horrible vengeance upon the Trojan priest and his family, this sculpture exemplified the perils of challenging the will of the gods.

The people for whom these books (and predictions) were written were most unlikely actually to meet a pirate in real life, fall from heights, or get bitten by a reptile. That did not, however, make the prospect any less interesting. Indeed, one of the characters who fascinated a Roman audience was the ultimate victim of reptilian assault, the famous archer Philoctetes, who had accompanied the Greeks to Troy, been bitten by a serpent, and sent by the Greeks to live on a deserted island when they could no longer tolerate his cries of pain and the stench of his suppurating wound. Equally these audiences were intrigued by the image of Laocoön, the Trojan priest who had attacked the wooden horse and was devoured by serpents for the affront.

A fascination with pain is yet another aspect of Roman culture that stands in stark contrast to the equally powerful fascination with outward displays of intense calm. The outer facade was not only threatened by sexual passion, but it could also be upset by illness. Marcus Aurelius seems to have been typical of the age in his willingness to write letters to friends detailing the illnesses he suffered and the pain that he overcame. Aelius Aristides, an important rhetorician from western Turkey whose career spanned the reigns of Antoninus Pius and Marcus Aurelius, recorded a series of medical conditions that might strike modern readers as deeply psychosomatic. But the audiences for the diary—the *Sacred Tales*—in which he recorded these illnesses, and the years he spent seeking treatments from the priests of the god Asclepius, presumably felt otherwise. Aelius seems to have thrived by projecting the image of a man who could function despite the debilitating illnesses that also brought him closer to his god.

Not surprisingly, the second century AD was also the great age of the performing medical man, whose demonstrations of new techniques and lectures on health drew large audiences. Sometimes they were genuinely competent: as in the case of the great Galen, doctor to (among others) Marcus Aurelius himself. Others may have been less so, but concern on the part of the audience was what drew them to medical performances in the first place; and it was concern with the world around them that often drew the inhabitants of the Roman empire to speculate about their own relationship with the gods.

Religion and Culture

Marcus Aurelius was representative of his age in turning to the gods when disaster struck in the form of plague, earthquake, storm, or dearth. His belief that the gods would speak through oracles, and that they might respond to his prayers, stemmed from the Stoic philosophy that he strove to have govern his dealings with others. It was the basic tenet of Stoicism that fate was identical with the will and body of Zeus; this made it possible for the gods to communicate with mortals, and for mortals to think that they could live in accord with nature. The issue that distinguished Marcus's belief in fate and the gods, as it would distinguish the beliefs of many intellectuals—whether they were Stoics or followers of the other significant philosophic movements—was the notion that the gods represented the will of a single divine mind. For many others, the gods tended to be considerably less well organized. The Roman empire was filled with shrines and temples to gods of all sizes and shapes, and people sought the ones who could help them with their specific concerns.

Belief in the gods continued to be sanctified by tradition, and often by extensive records of direct divine action. The temples of Asclepius, for instance, kept records of the way that Asclepius healed the sick within their walls; oracular shrines kept records of the responses that the gods had given at their sites; cities recorded moments when the gods had averted disaster or revealed new rites to them to heal what seemed to be breaches in their relationship. Traditional cult, wherever

In this marble relief, which may once have adorned an arch at Rome, the emperor Marcus Aurelius makes an offering to the gods in front of the temple of Jupiter Optimus Maximus. The contrast between this representation of the proper religious order, and the terror and confusion of the Laocoön statue, is striking, and serves to symbolize the contrasts that were characteristic of Roman religion and culture in the imperial period.

and however practiced, asserted the profoundly logical observation that the continued existence of the world was the result of demonstrable acts of intervention by the immortals.

The most basic act of belief in the Roman empire remained the offer of sacrifice. People gave what they could, either burning it on an altar if they were trying to reach a god thought to dwell in the heavens, or pouring it on the ground, to reach one of the gods thought to dwell beneath the earth. For some people, however, this was simply not good enough, and many of them sought ways to reach the gods outside the established limits of cult. As cult tended to celebrate existing relationships, it may be seen as an essentially passive religious activity, if we allow "passive" to mean satisfaction with existing norms. But, as society changed, so the system of traditional cult required mechanisms by which it could be brought up to date—ways in which new revelation could be obtained and integrated within the existing system. Divination was the most basic of these mechanisms: since the traditional system reflected earlier revelation, the best way to update the system was by seeking new revelation. Divination may be seen therefore as an "active" element of worship that helped keep the system relevant. As the empire expanded, the process of integrating different traditions within the Roman experience continued (see pp. 40 and 98), albeit, as in earlier years, with some tensions; this was particularly the case with the many and varied forms of divination that were now available (see box, below).

Although prophets through whom the gods communicated were highly valued, the Roman state, at this point as in the distant past, frowned upon those prophets who operated outside the parameters of state cult, and magicians who claimed to be able to compel supernatural visitations. They were potentially very dangerous people, and every emperor from Augustus onwards issued edicts against unauthorized contact with the divine. People who used magic to attack their neighbors, as well as the magicians who served them, were liable to death sentences. The problem was that people could not be stopped from appealing to them, and even emperors were known to consult independent experts when they needed them. Hadrian gave

DIVINATION AND THE GODS

Attempts to obtain relevations from the gods took many and varied forms. Some involved direct approaches to oracles, where the gods were thought to speak directly through inspired prophets. By and large, at these shrines the gods only spoke directly to people who were socially important enough to merit direct communication.

Other mortals might approach the gods more indirectly by consulting oracles that worked by a system of lot. A classic form in Egypt was to place two inquiries with responses to them in an urn and assume that the one drawn forth represented the god's answer. Others involved rolling dice and matching the number rolled against a list of predetermined responses, while yet others could involve

the observation of fish feeding in a sacred pool, of the eating habits of sacred chickens, or the way that a cheese floated. At sacrifices the victim would be inspected after it had been killed to see if some sign was written upon its entrails, while the behavior of the animal would be closely watched to make sure that it behaved properly on the way to its death.

For some this was still not good enough. They sought the wisdom of the gods through people who were thought to be capable of having visions on their own, from others who could command information from the gods through their skills as magicians, or those who possessed sacred writing from the sages of the distant past. Some of those who were thought to be able to command visions of the gods through their magical powers were also believed to be able to command the actions of the god against people whom one wished to control.

great rewards to an Egyptian magician named Panchrates, while Marcus appears to have announced that another Egyptian magician, Harnouphis, caused the miraculous rainstorm that saved his soldiers in the war with the northern tribes. Hadrian also seems to have publicized the horoscope of a senator whom he executed as a way of proving that he had done the right thing: the man was destined to be a traitor. Many people seem to have been impressed with the record of Apollonius of Tyana, who was thought to have saved Ephesus from a plague demon, to have healed the sick through his innately divine nature, and who described the murder of Domitian in AD 96 as it was taking place in Rome, even though he was more than a thousand miles away in Ephesus at the time. Objects he was thought to have created as a protection against demons seem to have been spread throughout the Eastern provinces for centuries after he departed from the earth, and there was a strong body of opinion that he had ascended to live with the gods. The enormous gulf that opened between what the law said and what people did with regard to these practitioners is a sign of the abiding fascination with the search for divine revelation.

Those inhabitants of the empire whose primary cultural background was either Greek or Roman had the sense that their culture was relatively young compared with those of Egypt and Mesopotamia. Tourists—not the least of them being Hadrian himself—were drawn to Egypt as a place to see genuinely ancient books of wisdom, and talk to people connected with cults who knew things that others did not. Egyptian temples were repositories of texts that reached as far back in time as the Pharaohs, and Egyptians responded to market forces by peddling books of ancient wisdom that had been rendered into Greek (usually with the wisdom thoroughly "modernized" as well). Likewise the ancient Persian sage Zoroaster was felt to have been the discoverer of magic and the author of all manner of books (all in fact very different from the actual Persian texts that seem to contain an authentic record of his visions). Interest in the greater wisdom of the East was emblematic of the feeling of cultural superiority that many educated Romans came to believe: their world rested upon the collected wisdom of sages from all eras and all places.

The fascination with the prospect of new learning about the gods, and the admission that this information might come from outside the Greco-Roman tradition, lie behind the stunning success of a variety of cults that came into widespread circulation during the first century AD, and continued to expand in the course of the next few centuries. One of these was the cult of Isis and Serapis, originally invented, it seems, by the first of the Ptolemaic kings of Egypt in the early fourth century BC. With a relatively stable mythology, and a relatively stable body of texts—especially in the form of hymns in praise of Isis—the cult took hold throughout the Roman empire. Another movement, this one resulting from a reinterpretation of the mythology of the Persian god Mithras, seems to have arisen in the later first century AD. With a powerful liturgy that stressed service and secrecy on the part of the initiated, it looks as if the Roman form of Mithraism was the product of an inspired group in Commagene (now in southeastern Turkey), which adopted traditions of Persian worship that had existed there in the centuries after Alexander destroyed the first great Persian empire.

Both the cults of Isis and Mithras, which promised salvation to the devoted followers of their respective divinities, parallel yet another cult—that of the Christians—that emerged in the course of the first century AD, and was much less

readily absorbed within the bonds of conventional society. Although the cult of Isis had occasionally been repressed in the first century—it was shut down altogether for a while in Rome during the reign of Tiberius, after its priests facilitated a notorious sex scandal involving people of senatorial status—it was not exclusive, and it did not fundamentally question the norms of ancient society. The cult of Mithras, which likewise allowed its members to worship in conventional ways and make offerings to other gods, could even be seen as being openly supportive of the status quo. The same could not be said of the cult that held that a Jewish teacher executed in AD 36 by a Roman magistrate had risen from the dead, was the son of God, and promised salvation to those who believed in his revelation when the world ended, an event that he seems to have thought was imminent.

The fervent belief of the first followers of Jesus in the corruption of the world around them, and the rejection by many of them, though not all, of the existence of any true god other than the God of Jewish scripture, set the new movement at odds with all its neighbors. Christianity, as it emerged from the teachings of the first generation of preachers after the execution of Jesus, appealed to people as a genuine alternative to the religious practices of their time, and an alternative to conventional morality. Unlike the cults of Isis or Mithras, its message was based not only on the marvelous actions of a god (though the miracle stories connected with Jesus in the Gospels were surely important), but also on the suffering of a human being who had protested against established authority. Within a couple of generations, Christians had begun to produce a literature that had no parallel in terms of its complexity and modernity, for this literature addressed not some mythic past, but the conditions of life in the here and now. Even when some splinter groups produced their own books of revelation that made the message of Jesus a great deal more mystical than did the four Gospels and letters from first-generation teachers, they remained in touch with a basic narrative that took place in the reign of Tiberius. The Gospels themselves may

(Above left) The centerpiece of a Mithraeum, on its northern wall, was an image of Mithras's slaying of the bull, which symbolized the sun's victory over the moon. This example is from a third-century fresco in Marino, central Italy.

(Above) Followers of the cult of Mithras worshipped in distinctive chambers that they called "caves," such as this one, preserved beneath the church of San Clemente in Rome. These caves had a north–south orientation, and were supposed to provide an image of the universe, with depictions of Saturn, Venus, and Mars on the eastern walls, and those of Jupiter, Mercury, and the moon on the west.

have been littered with contradictions, but they still provided a model for an alternative lifestyle. People were fascinated with messages that came from outside the power structure of the state, and it was this, as well as the insistence on a strict moral code as the path to salvation, that seems to have drawn people to the new religion.

The awkward and often brutal response of the Roman government to the new faith helped publicize its message. Nero had blamed Christians for the great fire of AD 64 at Rome (see p. 202), and later emperors came to regard the new faith as subversive enough to be banned. But just as bans on magic did not quell interest in magic, so a ban on Christianity, which was only enforced erratically, did little beyond encouraging people discontented with the world around them to have a look. The rise of Christianity in the course of the first two centuries AD was not the result of weakness in the existing belief system, but rather a result of the fact that it offered a profoundly different vision of the way that people ought to live their lives.

Running the Roman Empire

Emperors and Their Officials

Roman emperors preferred the company of people like themselves. In his *Meditations*, Marcus Aurelius sometimes tries to see himself in terms of general humanity—it is not easy being the most powerful man on earth—but when he reflects on people he knows, they tend to be members of the political elite or slaves in the household. Dealing with officials defined the parameters of his existence, and Cassius Dio says that he routinely worked late into the night so that he could finish his day's work. The work included hearing petitions from subjects or reports from officials, managing state finance, the dispositions of the army, and finding the right people to work for him (see box, below).

Whatever social group they came from—senate, equestrian order, or freedmen—the quality that all officials needed was the ability to deal with finance. With the exception of some senior imperial secretaries who were recruited directly into their positions on the basis of their rhetorical or legal skills, the people who made

OFFICIALS AT THE IMPERIAL COURT

The officials who surrounded the emperor at court were a microcosm of the government as a whole. They included members of the senate, members of the equestrian order, and freedmen. In general terms, senators were employed in areas linked to the command of armies and the government of provinces. Members of the equestrian order were generally found in jobs connected with the financial management of the state or of areas directly controlled by the emperor—especially the vast network of estates throughout Italy and the provinces that now

formed the *patrimonium*, or property passed from emperor to emperor. (By the second century AD the distinction between the finances of the state and those of the emperor had become essentially meaningless.) A favored few members of the equestrian order obtained positions close to the emperor as secretaries, legal advisers, or overseers of the grain supply of Rome, a position that was often a prerequisite for holding one of what were ordinarily two praetorian prefectures.

Freedmen tended to be entrusted with fiscal positions in the household and a variety of tasks connected with special areas of imperial concern, such as the quality of entertainment in the palace or for the people of Rome.

their way into the upper echelons had proved that they could be trusted with money. That fact alone might have been sufficient reason to recruit officials both from the landholding classes, where young men might be expected to have learned from their parents how to manage estates and relatively large staffs, and from men who had proved their competence as a way of earning their freedom. Less obvious, but equally important, was that the members of all three groups were trained to work within a hierarchical structure. Almost all senators and equestrians who made their way into the imperial service had to spend at least a year or two as mid-grade army officers. In the course of their service they moved fairly rapidly from unit to unit, gaining experience in dealing with entrenched subordinates.

Good people skills and a head for finance may have been prerequisites for advancement in the emperor's service, but they were not the sole factors in determining the success or failure of a career. Although the chances of becoming consul now were far better than in the Republic, when only one in ten aspirants had a realistic chance of obtaining the office, it was still the case that fewer than one-third of the men who began a senatorial career would reach the consulship, and it seems that fewer than one-third of equestrians reached the highest paying jobs at the top of the ladder.

The additional qualities needed for success stemmed from a man's ability to make and exploit useful connections. It obviously helped to have family members who could lubricate the early stages of a career through friendship with the emperor. But "interest" of this sort could only take a person up the first few rungs on the ladder of promotion. One of the notable features of the recommendations that have survived in the collections of the Younger Pliny and Fronto, Marcus's tutor, is that they are overwhelmingly for people at the beginning of a career. To succeed in the later stages of a life, a record of actual accomplishment and a proven ability to mix well in society were both necessary. Thus, for instance, the skills demonstrated by Tacitus's father-in-law seem to have been on the military side, while those of Tacitus himself, who had a considerable reputation as a lawyer, were in civil administration. The demonstration of legal ability was a test of judgment: each case had to be chosen with care so that people could see that a man was devoted to justice. To prosecute a fellow senator who had behaved badly and contribute to his ruin might win the favor of the emperor—he needed senators to undertake these prosecutions—but alienate one's peers. When not in court, such a man as Tacitus was expected to attend meetings of the senate, where he would continue to build his reputation through displays of wisdom and tact: drawing out a meeting by arguing minor points (a specialty of Thrasea Paetus) was irritating; offering sensible suggestions to improve a proposal from the emperor showed wisdom and independence. In general terms, the successful man knew how to balance the interests of his class against the interests of the emperor, showing independence without arrogance.

If senators required ways to demonstrate their skills, emperors also needed to have their own ways of deciding whom to trust. Thus an emperor often invited important subjects to dinner, or to join him for a few days to decide legal cases. In a letter preserved by Suetonius, Augustus reveals to Tiberius that he has been dining and playing dice with a couple of senior generals; he also maintained a council of senators that changed every six months so that he could get to know the men who served him. Nor were senators alone on these occasions. The Elder Pliny, when not writing books (see p. 227), routinely visited Vespasian at home, while letters from emperors to communities include reference to the notable men of the senatorial and equestrian orders who sat with them and heard the business that was put before them. Good emperors followed Augustus's example by revolving invitations to participate, so that they could take the measure of as many members of the upper classes as possible. In such sessions the emperor could form his own impression of a person's judgment, allow potential appointees to learn his approach to various issues, and demonstrate his general decency. As the Younger Pliny put it on the one occasion that he joined Trajan, "what could be more pleasant than to witness the justice, wisdom and grace of the emperor in a quiet place where these qualities were easily revealed." The extent to which Trajan used these sessions as training meetings may be reflected in some things he later wrote to the Younger Pliny when the latter was serving as governor in Bithynia (northern Turkey) in AD 110–12. Trajan reminded him that he knew "very well that it is my fixed position that reverence for my name may never be sought from fear or terror or through charges of treason." Elsewhere he praised Pliny for recognizing the need to consult him on issues where there could be no fixed rules or where the laws might be ambiguous; only once does he seem to show some frustration at being consulted on a matter that he thought Pliny should have been able to figure out for himself.

Since—as Trajan often said—there were no fixed rules that could be invoked specifically to solve the myriad problems that arose throughout the empire, it was crucial that subordinates knew the way his mind worked. His willingness to take the time to pay attention to the details of government without micro-managing his officials made Trajan a success. He understood that there were occasions when an emperor had to rely upon the judgment of men he trusted. Marcus Aurelius displayed the same abilities. Thus, for instance, Marcus listened when his brother-in-law, Claudius Pompeianus, championed the cause of Helvius Pertinax (the son of a freedman, who showed great talent in war) and defended him against critics who may have thought that his lowly birth disqualified him from the highest offices. Pertinax obtained both the consulship and the governorship of an important province. In a very real sense, Roman government depended upon the ability of senior officials to work with the emperor. There could be no such thing in government as the socially maladjusted technocrat; equally, given the amount that people learned about each other in the course of long years of social and administrative interaction, the possibility that a complete fool would be found in an important task was also minimized.

The conduct of emperors from Vespasian to Marcus was a reaction against the inward-looking administrative style of the Julio-Claudians, who had a tendency to promote from within the palace rather than to advance men who had proved themselves through careers in senatorial administration. During the reigns of Claudius and Nero, for example, freedmen had occupied publicly prominent positions: such figures as Narcissus, Claudius's chief secretary, Pallas, virtually his prime minister, or Polyclitus and Helius, who served under Nero (see pp. 202 and 203), all alienated senators. Freedmen who had risen high were not so evident in the second century AD, but that does not mean they had vanished from the face of the earth (see box, p. 244). Vespasian lived with a freedwoman who had grown up in the house of Augustus's niece; Marcus gave thanks to the gods that he slept with neither

THE CAREERS OF FREEDWOMEN AND FREEDMEN

There is some evidence to suggest that men, and some women, who stood outside the elite might actually choose a career as an "imperial freedman or freedwoman." A papyrus letter from Egypt mentions a man who decided to go to Rome to become a freedman of Caesar and take up "offices," while a *cubicularius* of Hadrian named Aelius Alcibiades was honored by his home city in western Turkey as a benefactor. At the end of the second century, the immensely powerful freedwoman Marcia, mistress of Marcus Aurelius's son Commodus, and one of the effective heads of government, also gave substantial sums to her homeland. She had begun her career as a freedwoman of Lucilla, the daughter of Marcus who had married Lucius Verus.

Strictly speaking, to become a freedman or freedwoman a person had first to be a slave, and thus he or she should not have a home city—slaves were solely the possession of the masters in whose households they served. There is,

however, considerable evidence in literature and in Roman law codes for the practice of self-sale into slavery, and that such transactions could be seen as a path to economic advancement. The jurist Ulpian, for instance, mentions places in cities where people would go to put themselves up for sale, and there is ample evidence for a practice by which men might sell themselves into slavery and keep the money (which they might then use to buy themselves back out of slavery) (*Digest* 21.1.17. 12; *Codex Justinianus* 7.18.1). The evidence for self-sale suggests that there was a mechanism through which the palace staff recruited servants who possessed the attainments needed to participate in government. Some of these attainments may have been sexual, others may have been cultural—the author of several important books, including one on marvels and another on chronology, was yet another freedman of Hadrian with an identifiable homeland, named Phlegon of Tralles—and some were more obviously fiscal. The important point is that these freedmen and freedwomen were present at court, and represented a group with very different experience from senators and equestrians.

Benedicta nor Theodotus, both non-elite members of the palace staff; while the man who stabbed Domitian was the freedman Stephanus, who was his *cubicularius* (in charge of intimate access to the emperor), and Trajan's *cubicularius* appears to have helped Hadrian to the throne. One of the cases that the Younger Pliny heard with Trajan involved the role of Ulpius Eurythemus, an imperial freedman who held a procuratorship. He was charged with helping an equestrian procurator, Sempronius Senecio, to forge the will of a senator, Julius Tiro. Having laid the charge, the aggrieved heirs said they were afraid to appear, leading Trajan to exclaim that he was not Nero, and neither was Eurythemus a Polyclitus. Pliny liked the line well enough to quote it, but the case was postponed and evidently dropped. Later, Pliny himself trod lightly around the freedman procurator of Trajan who managed imperial estates in Bithynia. As the link between Senecio and Eurythemus suggests, freedmen who were procurators socialized with equestrians, while the *cubicularius* was effectively on a level with the praetorian prefects, the most senior equestrian officials in the realm.

Second-century emperors had to be able to work with these different groups of officials, set boundaries between them, and recognize that all had something to offer. Even the Younger Pliny had to admit that it was right for Trajan to have influential freedmen, so long as they shared the essential values of the governing class: a frugal lifestyle and willingness to work hard. Yet behind all this praise of hard work lies an implicit but powerful threat. The emperor who shared the values of his subjects would live long and prosper. The emperor who did not would inevitably succumb to those around him.

IMPORTANT CITIES

IMPORTANT CITIES

It must be recognized that certain *coloniae* have the *ius Italicum*, as is the case with the most splendid *colonia* of Tyre in Syria Phoenice, from whence I come, which is ennobled by its territories, most ancient according to the passing of ages, powerful in war, most observant of the treaty that it struck with the Romans; for the deified Severus and our own emperor [Caracalla] gave it *ius Italicum* because of its outstanding loyalty to the Roman state and empire.

(Ulpian in *The Digest*, 50.1.1)

A GOVERNOR ARRIVES

If he (the governor) arrives at some famous city, or the leading city of the province, he should tolerate the city's commendation of itself to him and ought not to look bored when hearing its praise of itself since provincials hold that as a point of honor for themselves.

(Ulpian in *The Digest*, 1.7.1)

Emperors and Their Subjects

"When were there so many cities on land or throughout the sea, and when have they been so adorned?" So asked the rhetorician Aelius Aristides in a speech he delivered to praise Rome during the reign of Antoninus Pius. His stress upon cities as a measure of prosperity reflects not only the urban bias of his own outlook, but also that of the Roman government. The same observation is made, albeit somewhat differently, by his contemporary, the Greek historian Appian, who noted that when barbarians applied to be taken under Roman rule, the emperor might refuse their application because they would not be profitable to rule. Barbarians were, virtually by definition, people who lacked cities. To live in an area influenced by the lifestyle of a Greco-Roman style city mattered a very great deal in a world where, by and large, cultural attainment was more important than biological origin in providing definitions for membership in the larger community. Nevertheless, the demand that people share in an urban lifestyle was not particularly restrictive in a world with room for local interpretations of what this meant. There was no way, given the ecological diversity of the Roman empire, that any "one size fits all" definition of "Roman-ness" could be applied.

At first glance, the use of cities as a basic way of defining the cultural and administrative structures of an empire in which three-quarters of the population lived on the land may seem a little odd. But in fact almost all the land where these people lived—if not owned by the emperor or the *res publica*—was attached to cities. From an administrative point of view, a province remained a collection of civic territories interspersed with tracts of imperial or public land.

The cities of a province were, broadly speaking, of two varieties: stipendiary and free. Stipendiary cities were liable to tribute, while free cities had an independent relationship with the Roman state. The precise nature of this relationship varied according to the history of the region: some free cities had stood by Rome during past crises and been rewarded with a special treaty (see box, above left); others had been settled by Roman citizens, and, as *coloniae*, were exempt from the tribute assessed on subjects. The vast majority of *coloniae* were created by the settlement of veterans from the armies of the civil wars of the first century BC: they were intended to serve as centers of Latin culture and sources of men who could be recalled to service in times of emergency. In the Western provinces there were also many *municipia*, organized in a manner that descended from the mid-Republic, and where inhabitants, though of provincial descent, obtained full citizen rights if elected to a civic magistracy (the situation addressed by Claudius in his speech to the senate—see p. 201). *Municipia* simply did not exist in the eastern part of the empire. In the East, where the Romans were willing to accept that the values of Greek civic life were in sufficient accord with their own, there was no great interest in spreading specifically Latin culture.

The job of the governor was to make annual tours of his province to settle legal problems and make sure that cities were properly managed. Since, in most cases, it was impractical to expect him to visit every city, provinces were divided into judicial districts, or *conventus*, each one with a leading city where the governor conducted his business for a few weeks each year (see box, left). Since a good profit could be realized from a governor's visit—because people had to come from throughout the district to do business with him—there was considerable competition between the cities to be recognized as one of these centers. This competition ordinarily took

245

the form of expenditure on civic amenities, such as theaters, market places, and fountains; and in the Western provinces, amphitheaters for gladiatorial combat. Much of the evidence for imperial administration in these years reflects conflicts, either internal or external, where the imperial government was expected to act as a referee in the struggle for status. Thus, for example, when Gaius Julius Demosthenes, a former procurator, wished to establish a self-commemorative festival in his home town of Oeonanda in southwestern Turkey, and found that either the city council or the governor (or both) was acting with less speed than he would have desired, he wrote directly to Hadrian asking for his consent to the event. Hadrian duly gave it, and Demosthenes appears to have agreed to a festival in his honor that gave more space than originally intended for self-display on the part of local aristocrats. In another case, also from the reign of Hadrian, the international association of professional actors wrote to the emperor asking him to set forth their privileges so that all would know what they were, and Hadrian's three surviving letters of AD 134 in response reveal an extraordinary willingness to micro-manage the timing of games across the empire (see box, opposite).

From the same collection of letters it is clear that many cities had come at the same time to Hadrian to discuss issues connected with the games, and that Hadrian had decided to take the opportunity to issue a set of principles governing these events. Sometimes he answered specific questions about poor behavior in a single city, and at other times set out general rules about how to handle prize money, or even the preferred way of flogging a contestant who misbehaved so as not to harm him unduly. This is an extreme level of intervention from the very top, and a manipulation of a system based upon petition to issue a general policy statement. Such statements are a feature of imperial government that we see in other documents, including the decree concerning the punishment of Gnaeus Piso (see p. 196), which mentions imperial "letters" as vehicles for the communication of general policy. Still, interventions tend to stem from requests by local provincial officials who make it clear that there is something wrong with the current system. Such policy statements are thus part of a dialogue between the central government and its subjects: while the central government was capable of micro-management, it only stepped in if local efforts at conflict resolution failed. The people responsible for making the system work were, in the first instance, the leaders of local communities.

Such questions as the one that Hadrian dealt with in his letter to the artisans of Dionysus arose out of conflicts between groups within the province. In some cases such conflicts were actually inspired by the imperial administration as a way of focusing local energy on the task of seeking rewards from the imperial authority. One way of doing this was to make it clear that *conventus* centers might change. In the East, from the time of Hadrian onwards, cities could also compete to be recognized as the *metropolis*—literally "mother city"—of the province. Recognition as a *metropolis* was one way that a city could be recognized as a provincial center for the imperial cult, and as such also the center for the provincial assembly, an organ of local government that was independent of the governor. Another way was to be recognized as a "temple warden" for the cult, and this too could result in a city becoming a place where all the stipendiary cities of the province sent representatives to celebrate the annual festival of the emperor—the festivals at Pergamon, Ephesus, and Smyrna mentioned in Hadrian's letter are all festivals of this sort.

HADRIAN AND THE ARTISANS OF DIONYSUS

When Hadrian agreed to set down in writing the privileges of professional actors (the "artisans of Dionysus") in AD 134, the dossier that emerged reveals just how important the system of public entertainment was to the imperial government. It also demonstrates the extent to which the imperial government was able, when it felt like it, to micromanage the affairs of its subjects. Hadrian wrote:

> Imperator Caesar son of the divine Trajan Parthicus, grandson of the divine Nerva, Trajan Hadrian Augustus, pontifex maximus, in the eighteenth year of tribunician power, consul three times, father of the country, to the travelling theatrical association of artisans of Dionysus who are crowned international victors. Greetings:
>
> It seems to me that I should make clear to you the organization of the games, concerning which speeches and petitions were made, in my presence, at Naples, and write to the provinces and cities, from which embassies came to me on this topic. I will set the beginning with the Olympic games, which are the oldest contest, and the most famous of the Greek games. The Isthmian games will be after the Olympics, the contest in honor of Hadrian will be after the Isthmian games, so that these games begin on the day after the end of the Eleusinian festival. This is the first day of the new month of Mamakterion amongst the Athenians. The contest in honor of Hadrian shall last forty days. The contest at Tarentum after the contest in honor of Hadrian will begin in January, the games in Naples will be held, as is currently the case, after the Capitoline games; then the Actian games will be held nine days before the Calends of October (September 23) and last for forty days (the games are thus moved from September 2, the anniversary of the battle to Augustus's birthday). According to the passage of ships the contest at Patras, then the Heraia and the Nemean games will be held between November 1 and January 1. The Panathenaia will be held after the Nemean games on the same day that they are currently held according to Attic reckoning. The people of Smyrna will hold their contest after the Panathenaia with the contestants having fifteen days to sail after the race in armor at the Panathenaia. The games will begin immediately after the fifteenth day, and last for forty days. Leaving two days after the race in armor at Smyrna, the Pergamenes will begin their games immediately and celebrate them for forty days … From there the contestants will go to the Pythian games, and then the Isthmian games, which occur after the Pythian games, and then to the joint games of the Achaians and Arcadians at Mantineia, and the Panhellenic games are celebrated in this year.
>
> (*Second Letter of Hadrian to the Artisans of Dionysus,* lines 57–71)

In these lines the voice of the emperor himself, lover of both Athens and Antinous, comes through with extreme clarity. The use of dates from Athens's civic calendar for Athenian festivals in place of the dates from the Roman calendar bespeaks the first love, as does the fact that the cycle of games comes to an end with the games that he had founded at Athens. The exaltation of the joint games of the Achaians and Arcadians, from whose people, according to legend, the ancestors of Antinous had sprung, bespeaks the second. The assertion that the three great cities of the province of Asia (Ephesus, Pergamon, and Smyrna) will all have games of equal length reveals a diplomatic side, while the experienced traveller speaks in the setting of dates according to how long it takes to get from one place to another.

Although the attitude towards cult offered to a living emperor remained deeply ambivalent at Rome, it was generally recognized as a singularly important provincial focus for expressions of loyalty to the state. So it was that Augustus agreed that the assembly of the three provinces of Gaul could offer sacrifices on his behalf (this was the standard form in all ruler cults, and distinguished the rites for rulers from those of the immortal gods, to whom the sacrifices were offered). In the wake of the death of Augustus, and the symbolic ascent of his soul to the heavens that was staged at his funeral, a feeling seems to have developed that the decision to create a cult in honor of an emperor could act as a sort of judgment on his reign. When Tiberius refused to allow a cult for himself in Spain, Tacitus commented that this showed insufficient ambition to be regarded as a great ruler; while the senate's reluctance to deify Hadrian reflects its feeling that the emperor should be aware that his posthumous reputation depended upon the goodwill of his subjects.

There was a simple difference between the understanding of ruler cult at Rome and in the provinces. At Rome, emperors were deified after their death, while in the provinces they tended to be deified during their lifetime. Emperors received divine honors as soon as they took the throne, and provincial assemblies took the opportunity, each year, of sending a delegation to the emperor to tell him how they had honored him. In the course of those delegations contacts could be made, careers advanced, and complaints laid against the governor. In a purely practical way, allowing for the fact that people knew perfectly well that the emperor was not a god, ruler cult came to act in a way that was very like traditional cult, in that provincials could use it to reach out to the distant power that could actually make their lives easier.

The imperial cult bound the cities of the provinces together, and thence the provinces to the emperor. Since cities represented the effect of government and its cultural values, they also played an important role in extending the values of government to the vast mass of people who lived in the countryside. Here again, the major difference between East and West—the presence of villages of independent peasants rather than tenant farmers—makes itself powerfully obvious. Villages in the West did not aspire to city status or even seem to have much corporate identity. This was not so in the East, where even villages that were attached to cities had a recognizable identity. Thus when Gaius Julius Demosthenes's festival finally came into being, a decree from the town council listed all the surrounding villages and the sacrifices that they should offer (see box, right). The procession joined together people from the countryside, living in villages with distinctively non-Greek names, with the leaders of the civic community. The villagers were there to see and to hear—to learn about Demosthenes and the wider world. Indeed the very fact of Demosthenes's existence in their area meant a sudden, and large, injection of money into the local economy, thanks to the large salary he received as an imperial official.

Before a place could hope to have a Demosthenes in its midst, however, it had to be a city with enough wealth to support such a person's rise to influence. In the East, villagers therefore sought—so far as they were able—to equip themselves with structures that imitated those of cities, in the hope that someday they too might attain full civic status (see pp. 302–3). We also find villages on the fringes of the Arabian desert calling themselves "mother villages," to distinguish themselves from lesser spots by imitating the nomenclature of cities. There are villages with public baths, council houses, fountains, and market places; and there are villages where some inhabitants reached a level of personal prosperity well beyond that of subsistence farmers—so great in fact that it could, on occasion, become personally perilous. Some wealthy villagers appear in the historical record because they were kidnapped and held for large ransoms by Roman soldiers working for imperial procurators, who were trying to feather their own nests by stealing from those whose oppression they felt the emperor would never notice. In many cases they may well have been right, but in others we know that the villagers were able to organize themselves, find a patron, and get the emperor to address their grievances.

THE FESTIVAL OF DEMOSTHENES

The agonothete (official in charge of the festival) himself (will offer) one bull; the civic priest of the emperors and the priestess of the emperors (will offer) one bull; the priest of Zeus (will offer) one bull; the three panegyriarchs (officials in charge of other festivals) (will offer) one bull; the secretary of the council and the five prytaneis (executive officials of the town council) (will offer) two bulls; the two market supervisors (will offer) one bull … of the villages, Thersenos with Armadu, Arissos, Merlakanda, Mego Oros, […]lai, Kirbus, Euporoi, Oroata, […]rake Valo and Yskapha, with their associated farmsteads (will offer) two bulls.

(*Supplement of Greek Epigraphy* 1988 no. 1462 c. 70–73)

For his subjects who lived in the countryside, the emperor was not the master of oppression who imposed the rents or taxes that they had to pay, appointed the officials who tormented them, and ruled the army whose members were an object of terror. He was an abstract symbol of justice who was supposed to listen to even the most lowly, as a famous story of Cassius Dio's exemplifies (see box, below). In another example of the prevalence of this notion, two authors, telling the story of a man magically transformed into an ass by a slave-girl with whom he wished to continue an erotic liaison, have the character call out to Caesar for aid when he is oppressed. The notion of an ass trying to utter the name of Caesar while being beaten may have seemed a comic touch to these authors, but it still reflects an attitude towards the imperial office that was widely held. So widely was it held that when Paul of Tarsus insisted that the emperor—not his representative in Judea—should hear his case, he was packed off for Rome. Paul also claimed that he was a Roman citizen, an issue that may not have been independently verifiable without writing to Rome, but that is beside the point. The story of Paul as Luke tells it in the Acts of the Apostles represents the view that no matter was so insignificant that the emperor might not find out about it.

Whoever it might be—an old woman, a transformed ass, or an itinerant preacher—the emperor was supposed to care. All these stories were written down in the years after Vespasian, and reflect the profoundly important perception that emperors took a direct interest in what happened in the provinces. Although the reality perhaps did not match the perception, it was not unreasonable to believe that it did, in light of three observable factors that thrust the existence of the emperor into the lives of most people: the all-encompassing nature of the tax system, highly publicized moments of successful communication that linked corporate entities—most often cities—with their ruler, and a system of public entertainment in which the emperor was consistently represented.

The imperial tax system was the single most obvious symbol of Roman control. There were two significant changes in this system between the generation of Cicero (to the mid-first century BC) and the death of Augustus in AD 14. The first was the elimination of the equestrian *publicani* (see p. 86) from the collection of the two main taxes on land and people (they retained a role in the collection of excise taxes on sales). The second was the fact that the two basic taxes would now be collected on the basis of a provincial census. In most of the empire these reassessments fell once a decade, in Syria once every twelve years, and in Egypt once every fourteen years.

The census defined the most basic, and intrusive, relationship between the government and its subjects. All the inhabitants of the empire were subject to a tax on their persons and a tax on their property (Italy alone remained outside the system).

THE OLD WOMAN SEEKING JUSTICE

A well-known story related by Cassius Dio, the third-century Greek historian, illustrates the widespread perception of the emperor as a symbol of justice. According to the story, an old woman approached Hadrian to complain of an injustice, and when he told her that he did not have time to hear her, she replied: "then cease to be ruler." He stopped in his tracks and bade her speak.

In point of fact this story, which was also told about at least three Greek kings, is probably false, but it made the point that "nothing so befits a ruler as the work of justice."

The full extent of each person's liabilities was recorded in registers maintained by local officials, who were ultimately responsible for making sure that everyone paid what they owed. To assist them these local officials tended to maintain gangs of thugs, and if the thugs weren't effective enough, they could call in some troops from the governor. It was a system that ultimately depended on the threat of violence—a threat that seems to have been perceived as real by the vast majority of the empire's people. No wonder they imagined that somewhere above it all there resided a beneficent emperor who could intervene to save them. And sometimes the emperor was motivated to help, since peasants who were too badly treated fled the land, reducing revenues, while officials whose activities went unchecked were likely to pocket as much of the state's potential income as they thought they could get away with. For this reason it was important for senior officials to have some feel for what went on at the local level; to have personal experience of the conflicts that could, if unchecked, tear a community apart; and to have a sense of how to balance the interests of the local administrative class with the interests of those who were governed by them.

By the beginning of the second century AD, the period of peace that began with the reign of Augustus and the organization of the state were beginning to have a significant impact on the shape of the empire. In economic terms, the imperial tax system created a superstructure that was supported by a group of relatively autonomous zones, each centered on what was, in ancient terms, a huge city or other large collection of non-productive personnel. In the West, where landholding was still centered on villas, these zones included the two main areas of military occupation along the Rhine and Danube rivers, each with a garrison of around 80,000 men, and Rome. In the East, where the countryside continued to be dominated by villages, the principal zones were the highly urbanized region of western Turkey—which included Ephesus, Pergamon, and Smyrna, as well as a host of smaller places—and the area around Antioch in Syria. Rome, with a population of around a million people, now required the excess agricultural resources of north Africa, Spain, and Egypt to support its existence. At the same time, the requirements of shipping this surplus to Rome meant that a rebuilt Carthage emerged as a major city, as did Alexandria in Egypt: through it were funneled the resources of the Nile valley, along with a high proportion of the trade in luxury goods—chiefly spices—from east Asia.

The excess production of Gaul supported the garrison on the Rhine, while the army on the Danube was supported by the development of agriculture throughout the Balkans. In both areas a number of major cities developed along or near the river. In terms of buildings, it seems that eyes were still fixed on fashions at Rome, at least in the West where, for instance, new amphitheaters modeled on the Colosseum were built, along with bath houses, market places, and basilicas. Many of these cities also played a direct role in support of the imperial infrastructure. In Germany, Bonn, Trier, Mainz, and Cologne were such cities, with significant development further south in Gaul on the route leading up the Rhône valley at Lyons and in the ancient city of Marseilles. Along the Danube, major cities developed at Aquincum and Sirmium, as well as Siscia on the major east–west road to the south, and Thessalonica. In Britain, London became a major trading city, while in Spain Corduba emerged as the center of the highly productive Guadalquivir valley. By providing a redistribution network for excess production, and in fact inspiring the production of surpluses in areas that could manage them, the Roman empire

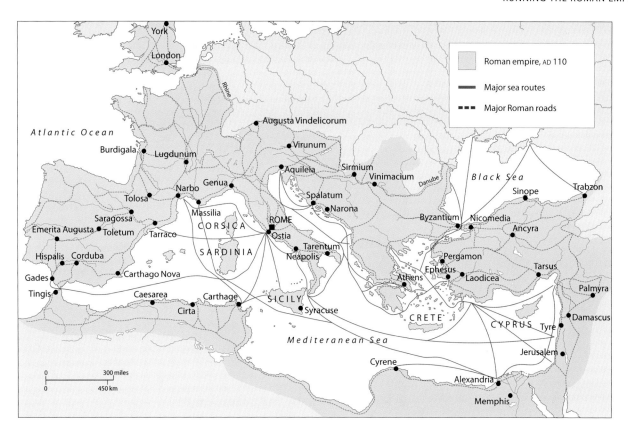

The major trade routes of the Roman empire in the second century AD. The roads and sea routes that connected Rome with the frontiers of the empire, where armies had been implanted in areas with previously underdeveloped economies, served to channel grain, wine, olive oil, metals, and other goods back to Italy.

brought a level of prosperity to its territory that simply had not existed in the past, even if the benefits of this prosperity were enjoyed vastly more by the aristocrats who controlled the bulk of the land than by the peasants who worked it.

One further aspect of this economic development is that, even though there was some technological development—as represented, for instance, by the turbine-driven water wheels that have been found in both Gaul and north Africa, dating to the second century AD—the economy tended to expand by creating more jobs in industries, rather than by making those industries more efficient. Places where there is evidence for large-scale manufacture of pottery or fish sauce in north Africa tend to be agglomerations of smaller businesses rather than massive "corporations." This might reflect a general belief on the part of the wealthiest Romans that risk should be spread across a number of activities rather than exposed to the success or failure of a single estate or operation.

The striking feature of the imperial redistribution system is that all roads did not lead to Rome. Although grain fleets regularly sailed from north Africa and Egypt to Rome's port at Ostia, much trade flowed elsewhere. Most tax revenue, either in agricultural produce (required of the land tax) or hard currency (deriving from the head tax and various taxes on the transshipment of goods), was used to support the administration in the areas where it was collected, or in the areas serviced by the local redistribution network. Similarly the ships that carried grain to Rome also carried cargoes that their captains could trade on the open market, which meant that a wide-ranging exchange economy, based on long-distance trade, supplemented both the tax system and the regional economies. This is the reason why, for instance, products from Gaul tended to reach Britain along a route that involved shipment down the Rhine. Fourth-century AD legal texts, plainly reflecting the practice of earlier times, stated that the captains of merchant ships did not have to produce receipts for the tax cargo in the port where that cargo had been loaded until two years had passed since their sailing.

These captains are a rather specialized group within the overall merchant community, and the tax ruling is significant chiefly because it indicates that they might reasonably be expected to be away from home for long periods of time, looking for the best markets for their cargoes, dropping off one load, and picking up another. Sometimes, of course, they did not make it to port: more than 900 shipwrecks from the Roman period have been located. Although the vast majority of these shipwrecks come from shallow water near modern tourist attractions, suggesting that we have anything but a random sample, they nonetheless give us some idea of what the long-distance trading economy looked like. A principal cargo in a large ship might consist of several thousand amphorae of wine, along with less bulky items, such as crates of both fine and coarse dinner ware and various forms of local produce (in one case this was pine cones). Such cargoes as these reveal that trade was not simply for the rich, since the coarse dinner ware, for instance, was likely to end up on the table of a person of quite moderate means. Excavations throughout the Roman empire show that on sites of all sorts there was simply a lot more stuff around.

The merchants who carried this traffic lived very different lives from their consumers. As might be expected of what was largely a peasant society, people tended not to move very far from the place where they were born. Even if, as seems to have happened in Egypt, they might move from their village to seek employment in Alexandria, their roots remained in the village of their birth. Similarly, the city of Lyons may have had a population of some 30,000–35,000; but if we assume that the relatively small number of tombstones that record a person's place or origin as being other than at Lyons is a representative sample of the population, then it is possible to state that the vast majority of people who moved to Lyons had not moved very far— they are mostly from Gaul and the Rhineland. It is only in such a city as Mainz, which developed around a legionary camp, that a very large number of outsiders (almost all Italian) can be found. But that was in the first generation or so of the occupation. By the time Marcus Aurelius died, most soldiers served in legions that were stationed near where they were recruited, and retired in the provinces where they had served.

The trade networks that grew up alongside the redistribution network of the tax system are a significant new development in the centuries after Augustus. It is also immediately apparent, however, that increased trade is a direct consequence of the willingness of the imperial government to allow the communication systems it had created to be used in this way. It appears that the imperial government was remarkably generous in another way, for the system of exchange was astonishingly under-taxed. The standard tax rate on goods traded across provincial boundaries appears to have been 2.5 percent. The commerce stimulated by the distribution of the land and head taxes therefore remained largely untouched by the tax collector, even though individual cities could impose their own taxes on goods entering their territory.

One result of the inability to levy effective taxes on trade was that the emperors seem to have been chronically short of cash. Although they could alleviate shortages by redirecting surpluses, their fiscal condition remained dire. The tax system, based as it was on the relatively inelastic system of ten- to fourteen-year censuses, could not be counted on to produce massive new revenues when they were needed. Otherwise, one option to raise extra silver was to reduce the quantity of pure silver in the basic silver coin, the *denarius*, which was reduced to roughly 60 percent in the course of the first two centuries after Augustus. At the same time, rampant inflation was staved off by maintaining a ratio of 25:1 in the relationship between the *denarius* and the basic gold coin, or *aureus* (inflation in this period remained relatively stable at about 0.25 percent a year). Shortfalls that could not be solved in this way had to be made up by the emperor, who, from the time of Augustus onwards, diverted surpluses from his own income to the state treasury. But that was not always enough: Marcus Aurelius actually had to auction off palace furniture to meet his expenses during his northern wars.

Still, for three centuries this system worked because the empire offered, if nothing else, one thing that contributed above all else to the prosperity of its subjects: peace. It also offered a vision of a world that should be united under the rule of a single man governing from Rome. Neither peace nor unified rule were obvious or natural conditions of life before the time of Augustus, and they should be seen as the product of imperial government in the two and a half centuries after the battle of Actium in 31 BC. The government of the Republic, such as it was, had not been inclined to such a vision of the world; and the imperial government would also find different priorities in the course of the century after the death of Marcus Aurelius.

The Roman Army

One of the most important developments of the Augustan age was the transformation of the Roman army from a force with roots deep in the Italian soil to an institution based in the provinces. As this happened, the function of the army changed from being a group that represented the will of the people to a force devoted to protecting the reputation of the *princeps*. It was the quintessential institution of the governing power.

The process of reform was gradual under Augustus, whose first task was to reduce the size of the military—about half the men in service in 31 BC had been released by 27 BC. His second priority was to find a task for an army that at 28 legions was still 25 percent larger than the 21 legions that had existed in 50 BC, and that was also responsible for a great deal more territory. The best estimate of the population of the Roman empire in AD 14 is that there were 45 million inhabitants. At that point in time there were 25 legions each with a theoretical strength of 5,600 men, for a total of 140,000 legionaries; the recently constituted imperial guard, stationed in Italy, numbered 4,500 men, and it is probable that there were around 170,000 soldiers serving with the *auxilia* (the ratio of auxiliaries to legionaries seems to have been slightly more than 1:1). Assuming that there were roughly 20,000 men serving with the main battle fleets, which would henceforth be based at Ravenna and Misenum, the total military establishment of the Augustan age amounted to around 335,000 men, or roughly 2.5 percent of the male population over the age of 18. In the reign of Marcus Aurelius, the best estimate is that there were around 60 million inhabitants of the empire (see p. 191). At this point the praetorian guard had grown to a total of 10,000 men, the number of legions had expanded to 30 for roughly 168,000 legionaries, and there were around 200,000 auxiliaries and about 30,000 men serving in the guard and fleets. The military establishment under Marcus—just before the radical but temporary reduction in the population resulting from the great plague of the 160s—exhibits a lower ratio of serving soldiers to civilians than the Augustan establishment (roughly 2 percent of the adult male population).

In considering the size of the army we also need to think about its cost. Interestingly, the proportion of the total budget spent on defense did not decrease in accordance with the decline in number of the male population under arms. Assuming that the imperial budget had expanded at the same rate as population—which makes sense, since the bulk of taxes were derived from cultivatable land and population—the cost to the treasury would have been proportionally higher than it was in AD 14. The reason for this was twofold: Domitian granted a 33 percent salary increase to soldiers in AD 84; and, in the course of the second century, food and equipment now came to be included in legionaries' salaries (when previously the individual covered the cost). As we have already seen, the depression of the denarius' silver content suggests that income was not keeping up with expenditure even as population increased. It is perhaps a sign of the army's role in domestic politics that emperors chose to increase the compensation of their soldiers rather than their numbers. Such a decision also bespeaks a fundamental decision to limit the manpower needs of the empire: emperors were not, by and large, looking to expand in these years. An estimate of the overall cost of army salaries under Augustus would put them at roughly 58 percent of the total budget—71 percent when retirement bonuses are figured into the mix. In order to test the authenticity of these figures we must measure them against real numbers attested for other pre-modern societies. For instance, during the Ottoman empire in 1595/6, expenditure on wages and pensions amounted to 62 percent of the budget. In Elizabethan England, military expenditure ranged from 73 percent to 80 percent of the budget. While such data cannot confirm to us the true situation in the Roman empire, it does at least suggest that our calculations are within a reasonable range for such a state. In this way comparative data acts as a check on speculation: if results for Roman expenditure fell outside the parameters established by measurable budgets of other pre-modern states, then the model that I have suggested here would not be a valid method of estimation.

The imperial system of service evolved gradually in the course of Augustus's reign, and it was only after the conquest of the Balkans in the penultimate decade of Augustus's life that a regular disposition of legions as garrisons in different parts of the empire became clear. The bulk of the army began to settle in the areas that at this point had borne the brunt of Augustan military activity: the Rhine and Balkan lands. Augustus's establishment of the *aerarium militare* in AD 6 stabilized a much longer period of military service than had been the norm in previous centuries: now twenty years for members of the legions, twenty-five for soldiers in auxiliary cohorts. He also guaranteed that men who survived their term of service would become people of standing in whatever community they joined. In cases where a soldier did not retire to the community where he was born, he often settled somewhere in proximity to the camp in which he had served most of his career.

Several trends became clear in the course of the first century. The first is that Italian recruits were increasingly rare. It is striking that when a levy was held after the massacre of Varus's legions in the Teutoberg forest in AD 9, poor soldiers were

THE ARCHAEOLOGY OF THE ROMAN ARMY

The Roman army can be studied on both a macro level (as it is discussed in the text) and a micro level. In fact, it is usually best to look at it—as with any institution—from both perspectives. On a macro level, we tend to consider the army through the eyes of the emperor or one of his close associates; on a micro level we try to understand the experience of soldiers stationed in different parts of the empire. This sort of study is made vastly more possible because of the documents that have become known to us through excavation at various sites. In some cases we can see distinct patterns: for example, the peacetime tendency for a high proportion of soldiers to be dispatched from their unit's main base to various other parts of a province; and the tendency for auxiliary units to expand over time. In individual pay records we can observe the way the state relieved its soldiers of basic costs—including their uniforms and food—that they had born from the Republic into the early imperial period.

At the fortress city of Dura Europus (in what is now Syria), where a unit from the great mercantile city of Palmyra was recruited into Roman service, we can observe that the administration was run in Latin; though the soldiers used their native Palmyrene (an Aramaic language) in their private lives. This same habit was observed in another Palmyrene unit stationed in Egypt's eastern desert, patrolling the region between the great port city of Berenice on the Red Sea—to which much of the trade across the Indian Ocean was carried—and Coptos, on the Nile, where Indian goods were taken by caravan to be shipped down the river and from there around the empire. Other soldiers in this region—whose actions are revealed by writing on broken pots, known as ostraca—appear to use Greek on a regular basis in their official duties. Ostraca from Bu Njem, in modern Libya, show us life in another auxiliary desert base. The camp here was established in the early third century, and the soldiers—despite their very Roman names—seem to have functioned in an environment dominated by speakers of a Semitic dialect (this being the Punic language the Carthaginians had brought with them from Phoenicia many centuries before). At Vindolanda, where the writing material that survives is the bark of trees, we meet the officers and men of a group of Roman auxiliary units, all raised from the areas that are now Belgium and the Netherlands. It is through such documents that we are able to hear Roman voices: women who wrote to their friends as "sisters," men who called their friends "brothers," slave owners who complained about the clothing for their "boys" (slaves), and one person who seems to have liked oysters a lot.

These remains are from a second stone fort on the site of Vindolanda, dating to the early third century; they include a bathhouse and a guest house for travelers.

said to have been drafted even from the city. The statement that Rome provided recruits only in emergency situations plainly implies that it was rarely a source of soldiers in normal times. It also suggests that recruits from the capital were almost guaranteed to be sub-standard. The evidence of inscriptions also suggests that Italy became consistently less important as the point of supply for the roughly 8,000 men required each year to keep the legions up to strength. Other inscriptions suggest that men tended to go into service from specific areas of the empire when others from their district had done so before. The garrison of Britain, for instance, seems to show a disproportionate number of men from Spain and southern France; the north African garrison appears largely constituted from men who had grown up in the area; the Danubian legions were mostly from the Balkans; and the Eastern legions reveal very few members of Western extraction. The majority were volunteers rather than recruits, and a third-century jurist noted that "in the past" men who resisted the levy were enslaved, but that in his time punishment was unnecessary because the number was made up by volunteers.

Although the men who served in the legions were increasingly local, their officers were not. In the time of Marius and Caesar, centurions had largely been drawn from the local ruling classes in the areas from which their men had been recruited. This seems to have no longer been the case by the end of the reign of Augustus, when, in the mutiny of AD 14, there is evidence of considerable hostility between enlisted men and centurions. As "normative" equestrian careers came into being during the first century, the centurionate often appears as the first rung on a ladder. Centurions also tended to move from legion to legion. The result was to create an administrative class of officer that was distinct from the common soldier.

Tacitus's discussion of the motivation of armies in the course of the civil war of AD 69 offers vivid evidence for the change in the army between the late Republican civil wars and the end of the Julio-Claudian era. In the civil wars after Nero's death, Tacitus shows that the soldiers often had quite different motivations from their officers. Vitellius, he says, rebelled because he wanted to be emperor; the soldiers followed because they were angry with Galba, who they felt had not treated them with respect. The legions on the Danube joined Vespasian not because they were devoted to his cause, but rather because they felt dishonored by Vitellius's summary execution of a number of their officers. Julius Caesar's men followed him because they believed that their best interests were directly served by his success.

The soldiers of the imperial period, then, though typically stationed close to the areas where they were born, do not seem to have viewed themselves as representatives of the local population. Papyri from Egypt, along with inscriptions from various provinces, reveal that soldiers tended to act as a privileged class distinct from civilians, whom they saw themselves as ruling; a distinction that, at least symbolically, was enhanced in the early third century by the fact that soldiers were not allowed to contract legal marriages before they left the service. Military administration as a whole appears as two marginally intersecting spheres of interest between officers and men. The average soldier seems to have viewed himself as a member of an elite group that ruled the area in which he served, even though he did not necessarily regard himself as a member of the local aristocracy. The officer corps, from the rank of centurion upwards (all of whom were allowed to marry), saw appointment to individual units as a series of stepping stones that would either lead to a lateral move into an

THE VINDOLANDA WRITING TABLETS

Vindolanda was a fort that guarded the road from the River Tyne to the Solway Firth, just south of Hadrian's Wall in Roman Britain. The first garrison, which arrived around AD 85, was the 1st cohort of the Tungrians (an auxiliary unit from what is now Belgium); its fort was made of wood. It was replaced around AD 95 by the 1st Batavian cohort, a mixed group of 1,000 infantry and cavalry (a unit of this sort was also known as a *cohors milliaria*), which built a larger wooden fort for itself and remained for about ten years, demolishing the structure when it left. The 1st Tundrian cohort then returned, building another wooden fort, and remained there until about AD 122, when it joined the garrison of Hadrian's Wall (again destroying the fort upon exit).

One of the most fascinating discoveries at Vindolanda is the writing tablets, most of which were found in a waterlogged trash heap near the commander's house in the Batavian fort, though more have now been discovered in other parts of the site. The number of texts now totals more than 400. All are made from thinly cut slivers of wood, between 1 and 3 mm thick. The surviving texts include private letters and some official documents. Of these, the letters are perhaps the most interesting, as they allow us to hear directly the voices of real Roman people. The majority of letters appear to have been written by scribes, taking dictation from the author, who in some cases would then add a few lines in his or her own hand. A letter from a woman named Claudia Severa, to the wife of the cohort commander, reads:

> [Scribe's handwriting] Claudia Severa to her Lepidina greetings. On 11 September, sister, for the day of the celebration of my birthday, I give you a warm invitation to make sure that you come to us, to make the day more enjoyable for me by your arrival, if you are present (?). Give my greetings to your Cerialis. My Aelius and my little son send him (?) their greetings. [Claudia's handwriting] I shall expect you, sister. Farewell, sister, my dearest soul, as I hope to prosper, and hail. [Back, scribe's handwriting] To Sulpicia Lepidina, wife of Cerialis, from Severa.

This is the earliest known writing by a woman in Latin. Other correspondence is less genial, as in the case of this somewhat-difficult-to-read petition, written by a civilian:

> …he beat (?) me all the more … goods … or pour them down the drain (?). As befits an honest man (?) I implore your majesty not to allow me, an innocent man, to have been beaten with rods and, my lord, inasmuch as (?) I was unable to complain to the prefect because he was detained by ill health I have complained in vain (?) to the *beneficiarius* and the rest (?) of the centurions of his (?) unit. Accordingly (?) I implore your mercifulness not to allow me, a man from overseas and an innocent one, about whose good faith you may inquire, to have been bloodied by rods as if I had committed some crime.

The Roman occupation of Vindolanda did not end with the departure of the Tungrians. A stone fort was built on the site by the next garrison, the 3rd Nervian cohort (also from Gaul), which arrived in the middle of the second century. Two more stone forts were built here in the course of the next century, the last of which housed another Gallic cohort, which remained in place until the late third century. There was no subsequent fort after this garrison departed.

equestrian civil service position or to a more significant social position altogether. Given such attitudes, it is impossible to postulate any specific military agenda; officers and men reacted to events in terms of what they understood to be in their best interests, a point Tacitus makes very clear in his account of Vespasian's invasion of Italy.

When soldiers were not engaged in war (which was more often than not), they might spend their time oppressing civilians. This seems to have been a regular practice, with soldiers demanding bribes, requisitioning property, stealing, kidnapping local worthies whom they thought could pay ransom, or compelling people to cart things around—the Biblical expression "to go the second mile" derives from a Roman soldier's right to compel a civilian to carry kit for him. Otherwise, they might be employed in major public works projects, such as the great transportation system that connected the entire empire through new roads and bridges: a system that would be the marvel of Europe for more than a thousand years after the empire in the West came to an end in the fifth century AD. Soldiers also occupied themselves in elaborate training exercises during times of peace. All Roman units were evidently supposed to master specific maneuvers, no matter how irrelevant they might be to the areas in which they were garrisoned. The image of the army that appears in the great works of art commemorating the campaigns of Trajan in Dacia and, later, of Marcus Aurelius north of the Danube, sum up an idealized vision of the soldier's role. These works show men listening to their rulers, engaging in construction projects that symbolized the extension of Roman power and their emperor's control of the natural world, and slaughtering their enemies. Ultimately, the success of the rest of the imperial enterprise depended upon the loyalty and effectiveness of the army, and that would be seriously challenged in the years after Marcus's death.

An Age of Rust and Iron (AD 180–238)

Commodus (AD 180–92)

The twelve-year reign of Commodus, during which the emperor did his best not to govern, mingled moments of extraordinary theatricality with murder, while various of his lieutenants did their best to undo the fragile balance achieved by the emperors of the previous century. In the end, this balance collapsed into civil war, which saw the rise of a new regime in which the tensions unleashed at the end of Commodus's reign were never fully reconciled.

The fundamental problem with Commodus was that he was not very bright. Lacking native ability, and naturally inclined to sloth, he left the basic business of government to a series of favorites who in turn alienated and appalled those who wished for a continuation of the Antonine style of governance. The first crisis of the reign arose out of Commodus's insensitivity to the feelings of his sister Lucilla, who felt that Commodus's wife threatened her own prerogatives as the widow of Lucius Verus. Her response to perceived slights was to gather a group of discontented younger senators in a plot to assassinate her brother. The plot might even have worked, if the designated assassin had not chosen to shout "the senate sends you this" as he drew a dagger on the emperor. Although the announcement alerted the emperor's guards and doomed the plot to immediate extinction, Commodus was profoundly shaken. One of the praetorian prefects, Perennis, saw in the emperor's fear an opportunity to eliminate various rivals to his own power. The government descended immediately through a brief reign of terror, designed to eliminate potential rivals, into five years of government by the most powerful official since Sejanus (see p. 196).

Although he was brutal, Perennis was at least efficient. The image of Commodus was generally positive in the provinces, and the generals whom Perennis selected seem to have been able to maintain order on the frontiers. The problem was that, as he concentrated on public affairs, Perennis could not control what was going on in Commodus's inner circle, where the chief *cubicularius*, Cleander, was beginning to plot. When a delegation of soldiers arrived at Rome in AD 185 from mutinous legions in Britain, Cleander convinced Commodus that Perennis was conspiring against him and arranged for the legionaries to murder the praetorian prefect. Cleander, who realized that his servile background made it impossible for him to claim the praetorian prefecture for himself, now managed the state under the title of *a pugione*, which may be translated as "dagger man," or perhaps more accurately "chief of security."

Cleander's influence remained unchecked for a number of years until the prefect of the grain supply, working in tandem with other figures in the court—including Commodus's sister, Fadilla, and his mistress, Marcia—arranged for a riot to begin in the Circus Maximus. The trouble began when a gigantic mime actress entered the arena and told the crowd that Cleander was planning to starve them; when the crowd took to the streets, Commodus ordered Cleander's immediate execution. Effective government now fell into the hands of Marcia, Eclectus—the new *cubicularius* with whom she had a long-standing romantic liaison—and the new praetorian prefect.

This bust of Commodus, the last of the Antonine emperors, was discovered in the ruins of an imperial palace on the Esquiline hill. He is shown holding the apples stolen by Hercules from the Garden of the Hesperides in his left hand, as if he had accomplished the labors of Hercules.

The most serious issue facing the new coalition was that Commodus was becoming very hard to restrain. He began to present himself as Hercules, wearing a lion-skin in public, and ordered that Rome be renamed in his honor. In the fall of AD 192 he took to the floor of the amphitheater. Having trained extensively as a public combatant—he may even have moved into a gladiatorial dormitory—he treated the Roman people to a display of his skills as a gladiator and a beast hunter. In the beast hunt, which was supplemented by the slaughter of deformed Romans dressed as mythological enemies of the gods, he seems to have wanted people to see him as Hercules on Earth. By the time this was over, the staff had had enough. On New Year's Eve 192, Marcia fed him some poisoned beef; when it looked as though he might recover, she found a professional wrestler named Narcissus in the palace and had him strangle the emperor.

The conspiracy against Commodus had been organized so rapidly and secretly that the conspirators had not arranged the succession. So it was that in the middle of the night, the elderly Helvius Pertinax, twice consul and one of Marcus's best generals, was approached by the assassins and offered the job.

On New Year's Day 193 he became emperor. The result was a disaster—not because Pertinax was the son of a freed slave, but because he was a stern disciplinarian. The praetorian guard resented the fact that the palace staff had killed an emperor whose eccentricities had worked in its favor, and was instantly restive when presented with a fait accompli. In March a group of guardsmen left their camp and stormed the palace. When Pertinax tried to face them down, he was killed.

The day and night after the death of Pertinax witnessed one of the most bizarre events in Rome's long history. The guard was asserting that no man could be emperor without its prior approval, but doing so without a candidate in mind. One of the prefects had gone to the camp to negotiate on his own behalf when a wealthy senator, Didius Julianus, suddenly appeared outside the walls. Supported by followers chanting slogans in favor of Commodus, he won admission to the camp and, having promised that he could pay a much larger accession "donative," or gift, than his rival, won the support of the guard. Accession gifts had a long history going back to the time of Tiberius, and the amount offered by Julianus was roughly what Marcus had given, but the circumstances were poisonous. In doing what he did, Julianus effectively asserted that the army should have the deciding role in selecting a new emperor. The lesson was immediately taken to heart outside Rome.

(Above left) Pertinax, who succeeded Commodus in 193, was of humble origins and had risen to prominence as a general under Marcus Aurelius. The portrait on this coin is evidence of his adoption of aspects of that emperor's dynastic style—a mark of abiding respect for Marcus, at least among the senatorial aristocracy.

(Above) Didius Julianus succeeded as emperor after Pertinax's murder in March 193. Although the two men had been colleagues, their backgrounds were very different, Julianus having been raised in the household of Domitia Lucilla, the mother of Marcus Aurelius.

Septimius Severus (AD 193–211)

In his account of the civil wars of AD 69, Tacitus had written that the secret of empire was that it was possible to make an emperor elsewhere than in Rome. This was very true, though no one had tried to do so for more than a hundred years since the accession of Vespasian. Still, one did not need to be a reader of Tacitus—even though his *Histories* could be read as a guide to ancient *coups d'état*—to know that there were three ways to overthrow a Roman emperor. The first two methods—the plot within the household (the cause of death for Claudius and Domitian), and the revolt by the imperial guard (used against Caligula and Galba)—had already been demonstrated in the course of 192–93. The third mode of replacement required the coordination of several provincial armies behind a single candidate. Galba had succeeded in overthrowing Nero once the garrison of Upper Germany had joined the legion he was bringing from Spain. Vitellius required the support of the garrison of Lower Germany before he allowed himself to be proclaimed by the garrison of his own province, while Vespasian secured the loyalty of the garrison of Egypt as well as that of Syria before announcing his rebellion against Vitellius.

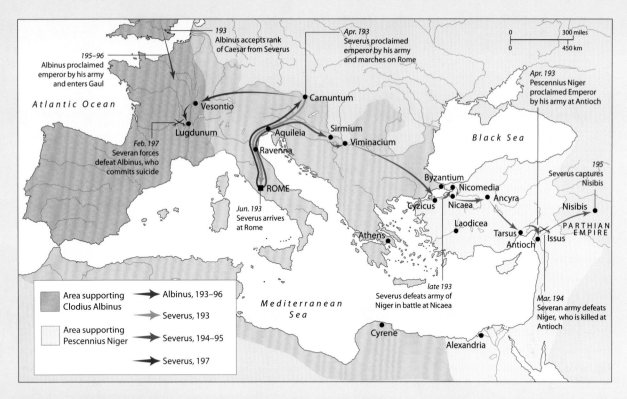

THE WARS OF SUCCESSION: KEY EVENTS

After the assassination of Commodus the Roman empire descended into civil war, and two emperors were proclaimed and assassinated at Rome before Severus arrived at the city in June 193 (see right). After establishing his authority at Rome, Severus moved east to confront Niger. He then invaded the western provinces of the Parthian empire, to punish them for allying themselves with his enemies. Severus returned to Rome in 195. In 196 he declared war on Clodius Albinus, who was defeated in battle the following year.

AD 193

1 January	Pertinax proclaimed emperor by the praetorian guard.
28 March	Praetorian guard murders Pertinax.
29 March	Didius Julianus proclaimed emperor by the guard; proclamation ratified by the senate.
April–May	Septimius Severus in the Balkans, Pescennius Niger in Syria, and Clodius Albinus in Britain are all proclaimed emperor by their troops after learning of the murder of Pertinax.
2 June	Didius Julianus murdered by the guard.
10 June	Severus leads his troops into Rome.

In the wake of Pertinax's assassination, three provincial revolts broke out almost immediately. One involved Clodius Albinus, governor of Britain; another, Pescennius Niger in Syria (with support from other Eastern provinces); and the third was led by Septimius Severus, who had support from all the Balkan armies (followed swiftly by those on the Rhine). It is entirely likely that all three men, aware that Pertinax was in a weak position, had already planned some sort of intervention: his murder simply provided the excuse they needed.

Of the three new claimants to the throne, Severus was in the best position. The central European armies, totaling nine legions, were the strongest in the empire, and the closest to Rome. Proclaimed on April 9, Severus was in Rome by mid-June.

A member of the guard killed Didius Julianus, who had realized that resistance was futile as Severus was closing on the city. The betrayal of Julianus did the guard no good: Severus dismissed its members and appointed troops drawn from his own army in their place. He then departed to attack Niger and made a deal with Albinus, trading the position of heir apparent, or Caesar, in return for his loyalty.

War in the East was already under way. Niger, heavily outnumbered, realized that his only hope for victory lay in the speedy invasion of Severus's territory and early victories before the enemy could concentrate his forces. For his part, needing few men to take Rome, Severus had sent a portion of his army to face Niger, and soon transferred the seat of action eastward through Turkey into Syria. Winning the final battle at Issus—previously famous as the site of a great victory by Alexander the Great—in May 194, Severus spent the rest of the year punishing supporters of Niger, rewarding those who had deserted his opponent, and launching an expedition against the western provinces of the Parthian empire. The reason given for this act of aggression was that the Parthian king had aided Niger; the actual reason might better be sought in the Roman tendency to use foreign wars to enhance an emperor's reputation. At the same time, since he had elevated Caracalla, the elder of his two sons, to the rank of Caesar in 195, Severus was also effectively declaring war on Albinus, who was crushed after bloody fighting in the course of 197 culminating in the battle of Lugdunum (Lyons).

Between his return to Rome in 195 and departure to Gaul for the war with Albinus, Severus had taken the remarkable step of retroactively adopting himself into the family of Marcus Aurelius, claiming that Commodus was his brother. Despite what might be read as a salute to the traditions of more ancient history, Severus rejected the merciful moderation of his new Antonine ancestors. His model came from an earlier age: when senators protested against the deification of Commodus, Severus lectured them on the wisdom of Sulla, whom he thought more astute than the merciful Caesar. He backed up the threat implicit in such a statement with large-scale executions of men believed to have been sympathetic to his rivals. Mass murder did not, however, make him particularly comfortable in his capital, even though he filled Rome with monuments to his success. In 197, immediately after defeating Albinus, Severus took off for a further campaign in the East, sacking the Parthian capital at Ctesiphon, and adding new provinces between the Euphrates and Tigris in what is now south-eastern Turkey. It was the first significant addition of new territory since the time of Trajan, and it soon proved to be a serious problem: the new province, known as Mesopotamia, became a magnet to later Persian kings, once the Parthians had given way to the Sasanian dynasty from Iran (see p. 268), who saw the Roman presence there as a threat to their security.

In the years after his invasion of Parthia, Severus continued to traverse the provinces, visiting Egypt and then his north African homeland, reconstructing his home city of Lepcis Magna to make it appear a suitable place of origin for an emperor. At the same time, much of the daily administration of the empire was turned over to a relative, Plautianus, who was now sole praetorian prefect. Such was his perceived importance that his statues were erected along with the members of the household, to which he was further linked through his daughter's marriage to Caracalla. When unfounded rumors of his demise swept the empire—so Cassius Dio tells us—civic officials tore down the statues and were then executed for treason.

(Top) Pescennius Niger enjoyed a distinguished career under Marcus Aurelius and Commodus, rising from equestrian rank to the consulship. Like Pertinax before him, Niger sought to emphasize his connection with Marcus by adopting elements of that emperor's dynastic style.

(Above) Clodius Albinus was perhaps the most aristocratic of the three claimants to the throne of Didius Julianus. He seems to have held important military positions under Marcus, but rose to senior rank under Commodus.

The great basilica, shown here, was part of the new forum that Severus built in his home city of Lepcis Magna, in modern Libya. The internal colonnade was constructed from columns of pink Egyptian granite, and images of Bacchus and Hercules (the Roman equivalents of Shadrap and Melqart, the chief gods in the local Punic pantheon) stood at the entrances at either end.

In the course of 205 the relationship between Severus and Plautianus cooled significantly. The agent of the change may have been Caracalla, who hated both his wife and father-in-law, leading to the sudden execution of Plautianus in the palace. Effective control of the state now passed to others, including Papinian, the greatest jurist of the time, and several of Severus's associates in the civil war. Also included in the charmed circle was Severus's wife, Julia Domna, a woman related to the formerly royal house of the Syrian city of Emesa, whom Severus is alleged to have married because he learned that she had a horoscope that predicted she would marry a king. Severus was yet another emperor who had a profound interest in astrology: Cassius Dio says that he kept a false version of his own horoscope painted on the ceiling of the palace, while the true one adorned his bedroom. It would be interesting to know if this horoscope told Severus that he would not die in Rome, and if that played any role in his decision to take personal command in northern Britain during 209 to punish tribes that had broken through Hadrian's Wall. He may also have hoped that by taking Caracalla and his younger son, Geta, with him, he could convince them to get along. Geta seems to have been his mother's clear favorite, and Severus had now determined that he would leave the two boys as joint rulers when he died.

Severus may, however, have recognized that neither of his sons was yet capable of ruling alone, and may also have hoped to imbue both with some of his own wisdom. On his deathbed at York in February 211, he summed this up by advising them to get along with each other, pay attention to the soldiers—whose pay he had doubled without improving the tax base of the government—and not to give a damn about anyone else. These words, if true, betray a fundamentally problematic view of power.

Septimius Severus, his wife, Julia Domna, and their sons, Caracalla and Geta, are depicted in this portrait. Severus's hair is shown tinged with grey, suggesting his advancing age at the time he took the throne. Geta's face has been erased, presumably after Caracalla had him killed in 211. This circular painting on a wooden panel, called a tondo, is probably of Egyptian origin, and is one of the few such works to have survived from the Roman period.

In order to be effective, emperors needed to have a certain amount of distance from any individual interest group. The army especially, while obviously a key to power, needed to be kept at arm's length and used as a tool to enhance the imperial office, rather than as a principal pillar of the regime. An emperor who took direct command of the troops in battle was an emperor who might also be personally responsible for a defeat. The more closely an emperor became identified with the interests of his soldiers, the harder it was to entrust significant commands to others; there should have been no need for the elderly Severus to command in Britain, and subsequent years saw emperors who had little business accompanying armies on campaign doing so with catastrophic results.

The Successors of Severus (AD 211–38)

Severus's hope that his sons would learn to get along was seriously disappointed. By the time they returned to Rome, the two new emperors had ceased speaking to each other, and when they arrived in the capital, they divided the palace between themselves, walling off direct access points between the two zones. Government was split between advisers, such as Papinian, who were devoted to trying to make dual government work, and partisans on either side. In this contest, despite the affection of his mother Julia, Geta—who was younger, less well connected, and possibly less vicious—was at a severe disadvantage. On December 25, 211, Caracalla felt that he had gained enough of an upper hand to call a private meeting with Geta. It was a trap. Centurions of the guard who had been concealed in the room butchered Geta as he sought the protection of his mother, who had come to mediate the encounter. A wholesale massacre of his supporters ensued, including Papinian and others who had simply tried to make the system work, and, as in the case of Pertinax's son and Marcus Aurelius's grandson, those who were simply too prominent. It is alleged that the casualty list rose to as many as 12,000.

For all his ferocity, Caracalla seems to have wanted to be loved. He spent much time at the circus, while giving private exhibitions of his skill as a hunter and charioteer so that he could let the people of Rome know that he shared their pleasures, while expressly avoiding the excessive display of Commodus. Early in 212, Caracalla also took the remarkable step of inviting his subjects to share his joy at having escaped the alleged plots of his brother through an edict that conferred citizenship upon all but a very few of them (and of course excluding all slaves). The surviving portion of his edict, as preserved on a badly damaged papyrus, runs as follows:

> I give thanks to the immortal gods, because [when that conspiracy occurred] they preserved me, thus I think that I should be able, [magnificently and piously], to make a suitable response to their majesty, [if] I were able to lead [all who are presently my people] and others who should join my people [to the sanctuaries] of the gods. I give to all of those [who are under my rule throughout] the whole world, Roman citizenship, [(with the provision that) the just claims of communities] should remain, with the exception of the [*ded*]*iticii*. The [whole population] ought [—] already to have been included in the victory. [—] my edict will expand the majesty of the Roman [people—].
>
> (*Giessen Papyrus* 40 col. 1.1–12)

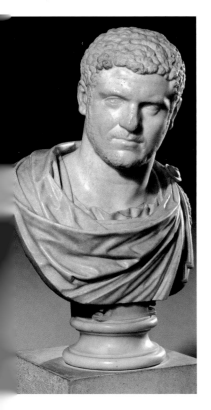

With his trimmed beard and furrowed brow, Caracalla's image in this bust reflects his conscious abandonment of the dynastic style of his immediate predecessors. By murdering his brother, he also emphatically rejected his father's plans for the succession.

Although the majority of people in the empire were not citizens, the impact of this edict may have been more symbolic than real. In fact, strictly legal distinctions between citizen and non-citizen had long since been eroded, especially in the area of the legal system: the protections that Roman citizens had once enjoyed from brutal punishments now only applied to locally important people, and by the early third century even high social status was not always sufficient protection from a horrible death if a governor was angry enough. Cassius Dio asserted that Caracalla's edict merely reflected a desire for money. One result of the edict was that all people now became liable to inheritance taxes previously limited to Roman citizens; and in practical terms, that may be what it principally meant to the masses of new Romans who all took the formal family name of Caracalla, which, as a result of Severus's self-adoption into the line of earlier emperors, was Antoninus. The fact that Cassius Dio, who disliked Caracalla intensely, did not react any more strongly than he did to this measure shows that he, too, regarded a definition of Roman-ness based on law (or biology) as less important than one that was based on culture. Indeed, the most remarkable point about Dio's response is that he asserts that becoming a Roman citizen under this edict was a disadvantage!

Whatever he hoped to achieve, Caracalla plainly did not succeed in winning the love of the Roman people; instead he took off for the provinces, traveling from the

Rhine to the Danube and then to the East. In the course of these travels he seems to have become fascinated with the character of Alexander the Great, presenting himself as a new version of the conqueror and even rearming some legions in the style of the ancient Macedonians. At the same time, he showed an extreme interest in antiquities, especially those connected with the mythological past or the actions of the gods, while failing all the while to endear himself to anyone beyond the soldiers whose salaries he increased significantly, and with whom he seems often to have marched on foot. His ability to appreciate what the common soldier liked may have been matched only by his inability to understand what the civilian population could endure. His problems in this regard reached a new low at Alexandria in 215, when he responded to insulting chants from the crowd as he entered the city by ordering his soldiers to massacre those who offended him. At the same time, his conduct in council was becoming increasingly intolerable to those around him (see box, right).

Disliked by those around him, and having failed time and again to win the love of the people whose cities he visited, Caracalla resolved upon a serious military adventure. He would follow the footsteps of Alexander into Iraq. In 216 he stood on the plain of Gaugamela, where Alexander had won one of his greatest victories, before withdrawing to winter in his own territory. As he prepared for the following year's campaign he decided to spend the first week of April visiting antiquities around Carrhae, one of the oldest inhabited sites on earth as well as the scene of Crassus's disaster centuries before (see p. 161). As he journeyed out from the city to visit a nearby temple he dismounted from his horse to relieve himself, and, as he was so engaged, a man who had been bribed by Opellius Macrinus, one of the praetorian prefects, ran him through with his sword.

After several days of intense negotiation, the general staff agreed to make Macrinus emperor. It was not a job that Macrinus appears to have sought with any great eagerness, as the situation confronting him was dangerous. The Parthian king was advancing at the head of a substantial army, while the rank and file of the Roman army was discontented. After an indecisive encounter with the Parthians, who agreed to make peace in return for a substantial payment, Macrinus withdrew the army to spend the winter in Syria.

Never popular with the army, Macrinus made the situation worse when he declared that he would cancel the additional pay granted by Caracalla to new recruits. Although existing soldiers kept their new pay packages, they felt threatened by the move. Moreover, though Julia Domna, who had accompanied her son to the East, died in the early months of Macrinus's reign, her sister, Julia Maesa, fearful that she would lose the prerogatives that went with being an imperial aunt, withdrew to the family homeland of Emesa. There she found her teenaged grandson, who was chief priest of the local god Elagabal. He looked a little like Caracalla, and she convinced soldiers of the legion stationed near the city that he was in fact Caracalla's illegitimate son. Unhappy as they were with Macrinus, and offered a substantial bribe when the boy was brought to their camp, the soldiers proclaimed him emperor. After a botched attempt to suppress the revolt in its early stages, and displays of panic, Macrinus finally managed to pull an army together to face his rivals. The battle near Antioch in June 218 was evenly matched until Macrinus lost his nerve and fled. He got as far as Asia Minor before a centurion who had been sent in pursuit caught up with him and cut off his head.

THE CHARACTER OF CARACALLA

He made many mistakes because of his obstinacy; for he wished not only to know everything, but to be the only one who knew anything, and he alone wished to hold power, and because of this he made use of no adviser, and he hated people who had useful knowledge. He never loved anyone, and he hated those who excelled in anything.

(Cassius Dio 77.11.5)

The young emperor Elagabalus, portrayed on the left, brought his god—in the form of a huge black meteorite—with him from Emesa. On at least one occasion, as depicted in the coin on the right, the emperor staged an event in which it appeared that the god was driving his own chariot.

Although his formal name as emperor was Aurelius Antoninus, the young man from Emesa is generally known by a Latinized form of the name of his god: Elagabalus. The reign of Elagabalus is one of the more unusual in Roman history, despite the best efforts of the rather effective palace staff that he had inherited from Caracalla. This staff was quick enough to recognize that the recent civil war was essentially a struggle for control between itself and the more bureaucratic elements that had supported Macrinus, and that, even though victorious, they needed to reconcile their former opponents. The ascendant palace group therefore made genuine efforts to include members of the senate and senior equestrian bureaucracy in their new regime.

Contemporaries, such as Cassius Dio, later described the men of the palace as a collection of sexual deviants who had no merit whatsoever. That is unfair, and Dio himself accepted an appointment as an overseer of financial affairs in his home province of Bithynia (a post that might well be described as a last stop before retirement). He was not alone, and the administration of the provinces seems to have been decent enough during the next few years. In fact, the issue that divided Dio and others from their patrons had nothing to do with how they managed things, and everything to do with what no one seemed able to control: the behavior of the emperor. Elagabalus believed passionately in the power of his god, and liked to dress up in the robes appropriate to a priest of the god and lead dances around his image. His piety struck conventional Romans as transvestism, and Roman senators had limited tolerance for such expressions of difference. Nor was that all: the emperor asserted that the gods of the Roman pantheon were all servants of Elagabal, and appears to have expressed a great deal of concern for his god's emotional welfare. Elagabal, who took the form of a meteorite, was "married" first to the goddess Vesta, and then to a fellow meteorite, the goddess Urania from Carthage. Elagabalus himself was even more troubled—he married and divorced four women in the course of twenty-four months.

As Elagabalus became more erratic, the previously united staff was riven by factionalism: his mother, Julia Soaemias, was on poor terms with her sister, Julia Mamaea, and the matriarch of the clan, Julia Maesa, was hard pressed to hold them together. She may also have sensed that Elagabalus's eccentricities were becoming intolerable, and that she needed to be in a position to control the direction of the violent change that seemed likely. In 221, Elagabalus adopted his cousin, Severus Alexander, and then realized that by naming a rather conventional, if very young, man as his heir, he had prepared his own death warrant. At the beginning of 222 he went to the praetorian camp, asking the guard to murder Alexander. After a long and confusing night, the guard killed both Elagabalus and Julia Soaemias, and proclaimed Severus Alexander emperor. The senate confirmed the decision of the guard and returned the god Elagabal to Emesa.

Although Severus Alexander, who was eleven, could no more run the empire than his cousin, he did have a much smarter mother. Julia Mamaea moved rapidly to make members of the traditional aristocracy feel important. Men who might reasonably have thought that their careers were over—including Cassius Dio—were brought back into positions of prominence. In many ways the new regime looked very much like a vision of the age of Marcus Aurelius, when experienced statesmen advised an emperor who acted according to knowledge gained from experience. The problem with this vision was that the emperor was in fact incapable of acting as a chief executive, and the government defaulted into a deeply conservative, reactive mentality. Under ordinary circumstances this might not have been fatal. But circumstances were not ordinary. In AD 225 Ardashir, the Sasanian ruler of a southern Iranian principality, overthrew the king of Parthia, Artabanus, and initiated a new regime marked by religious fanaticism and military competence. The Roman state had no evident ability to understand the forces unleashed by the Iranian revolution, especially the power of Ardashir's belief that he was doing the will of Ahura Mazda, the god of Light and Truth, by destroying the servants of Ahriman, the god of the Lie and Darkness; so it supported survivors of the old regime. It was only when Ardashir began to raid the province of Mesopotamia, and the garrison mutinied, that the central government decided to act. Eventually Alexander himself went East with his mother to oversee the operations. The result was a disaster: the best that could be said when the campaign ended was that the Ardashir stopped attacking Rome for a while.

Alexander's prestige was badly damaged, and now he needed to stay with the armies to gain some success to offset the failure against the Sasanians. After returning to Rome he departed, again with his mother, for the German frontier. In early March 235 the two of them were murdered at Mainz in a mutiny led by a relatively junior officer, Julius Maximinus. Maximinus took the throne for himself and set about securing his position by launching a series of attacks against the tribes north

A marble bust of Severus Alexander, in which the emperor's lack of beard and close-cropped hair underline his youth. Unlike portraits of Elagabalus, which had emphasized his resemblance to the young Caracalla, depictions of Alexander distanced him from his relatives.

(Far left) The strong, mature image of Maximinus on this coin is quite different from the youthful portraits of the Severan emperors, reflecting the new emperor's interest in distancing himself from the regime he had overthrown.

(Left) An elderly senator, whose family came from Asia Minor, Gordian I was an unlikely man to lead a rebellion in North Africa. This coin portrait is one of the few depictions to have survived from his three weeks as emperor.

Pupienus, portrayed on this coin, was proclaimed emperor with Balbinus after the deaths of Gordian and his son became known at Rome. Almost nothing is known about his earlier life, though he had presumably been consul and must have impressed his colleagues to be chosen for this task.

of the Rhine and Danube. He never went to Rome, and offended the populace by cutting back on expenditure for the grain supply. The traditional aristocracy plainly resented an upstart, and in February 238 the senate declared its support for an elderly senator, Gordian, who declared himself emperor in north Africa.

The initial phases of the revolt of 238 did not bode well for the success of the enterprise. Gordian and his son, also Gordian, who had been declared emperor alongside him, were killed by soldiers under the command of the governor of the neighboring province of Numidia. Realizing that Maximinus was unlikely to be a merciful victor, the senate then elected a board of twenty men to undertake the defense of the state against the emperor, whom it declared a public enemy. It was the ultimate statement of the value that was attached to collegial government, especially as two men, Pupienus and Balbinus, were now declared co-emperors. When friends of the deceased Gordians started a riot among the Roman people because their family had been cut out of the succession, Pupienus and Balbinus agreed to add the eleven-year-old nephew of the younger Gordian to their imperial college as heir apparent (Caesar). It is a sign of the deep discontent with Maximinus that declarations of loyalty to the unlikely coalition arrived from many parts of the empire even as the emperor led his army into Italy.

Despite the genuine lack of enthusiasm for Maximinus, the events of the late winter and early spring of 238 must have astonished the world. When Maximinus entered Italy, his army came to a halt before the city of Aquileia; weeks passed without his being able to capture the city. The army, which may not have been properly provisioned, became restless, and at the beginning of April murdered its emperor. Pupienus and Balbinus did not long survive their remarkable triumph. The praetorian guard, which had been besieged in its camp when it tried to quell the initial revolt in February, seems to have surrendered: it then worried that it would be replaced as the emperors looked to reward those whose disloyalty to the former emperor had saved their necks. In April the guard murdered Pupienus and Balbinus, declaring for Gordian III, whom they said the people wanted anyway. Since Maximinus had made his own son co-emperor when he invaded Italy, the young Gordian officially became the seventh person to hold the position of Augustus in the course of 238.

Summary

● The Flavian dynasty ushered in an age of more professional government. The period from the accession of Vespasian in AD 69 to the death of Marcus Aurelius in 180 is generally considered as the high point of the Roman empire, when Rome dominated its neighbors and provided peace for most of its subjects.

● Senior senators disliked Vespasian's younger son, Domitian, and rejoiced in his assassination. The military and imperial guard liked him, however, and nearly a century passed before there was another imperial assassination. Generally the emperors after Vespasian were hard working and used their staffs effectively. Trajan (98–117) was a very able general. Hadrian (117–38), also regarded as rather difficult by those who worked with him, was more concerned with internal development and, especially, the promotion of Greek culture. Antoninus Pius (138–61) seems to have been a cautious administrator, while Marcus Aurelius (161–80) spent much of his reign at war with either Germanic tribes to the north or the Persians to the east.

● The economy of the empire expanded throughout this period. The empire was divided into a number of economic zones—Western Europe, Italy and north Africa, the Balkans, and the Eastern provinces—that differed from each other in terms of basic structures and cultural history. The imperial regime stimulated economic development in each of these regions, which were linked together by the overarching structures of the imperial tax system. Insofar as there was a common Greco-Roman culture, it spread outwards from cities, where it appears that the entertainment industry, including gladiatorial combat, athletics, and the stage, established a degree of continuity across the empire.

● The administrative classes of the empire were divided into three groups—senators, equestrians, and freedmen. In each case, administrators needed to be able to deal with money, get along with their peers, and understand the implications of working within a hierarchical system. Emperors tended to make policy in dialogue with subject communities, in some cases engaging in detailed micro-management, and at times issuing broad policy statements in response to specific queries.

● The Roman army was transformed from a force with roots deep in the Italian soil to an institution based in the provinces. As this happened, the function of the army changed from being a group that represented the will of the people to a force devoted to protecting the reputation of the *princeps*. Soldiers were now mostly recruited from the provinces, but saw themselves as members of an elite group, ruling the area in which they served. The army expanded somewhat in the two centuries after Augustus, but remained limited to around 2 percent of the male population.

● Many saw Marcus Aurelius's death as the end of Rome's golden age. He was succeeded by his son Commodus, who was murdered in 192. Commodus was dominated by a succession of favorites, who took advantage of his weakness to control the government. The assassins failed, however, to establish a stable regime under Pertinax, the general they selected to succeed Commodus. He too was murdered, and civil war ensued, in which Septimius Severus ultimately proved successful.

● Severus changed the balance of government by stressing the dependence of the emperors on the army; his successors were expected, like him, to lead their armies in the field in person. After his death in 211, power was split briefly between his sons, Caracalla and Geta, and then held by Caracalla (who murdered Geta).

● Caracalla proved an objectionable ruler: after his death in 216 there was another civil war in which the bureaucratic candidate, Macrinus, was defeated by the court candidate, Elagabalus, seen by the imperial staff as weak and therefore preferable. Government by committee followed under Elagabalus's successor, Alexander, which failed to respond adequately to the rise of a new power—the Sasanian dynasty—in Persia. After a botched invasion of Persia, Alexander lost face with the army and was murdered by his men in Germany in 235.

● Maximinus, an equestrian officer who led the revolt against Alexander, succeeded him. His brief reign was ended in 238 by the only senatorial military revolt in Roman history. After a year in which seven people held the position of emperor, power eventually passed to the pre-teen Gordian, grandson of one of the first rebel leaders. The balanced government with a strong executive in the emperor that had characterized the period from Vespasian to Marcus was now seriously compromised.

The Transformation of the Roman World

(AD 238–410)

TIMELINE VI   THE TRANSFORMATION OF THE ROMAN WORLD

Gordian to Gallus

AD240–70	Sapor I becomes king of Persia
244	Gordian III murdered by his soldiers; Philip proclaimed emperor
249	Revolt of Decius in the Balkans; Philip killed and Decius becomes emperor
251	Goths sack Philippopolis; Decius killed at Abritus; Gallus proclaimed emperor
252	Sapor defeats Roman army and sacks Antioch; German/Gothic raiders ravage Asia Minor
253	Aemilianus leads revolt against Gallus; Gallus killed

The Empire Divided

253	Valerian revolts; Aemilianus killed; Valerian proclaimed emperor; his son, Gallienus, becomes co-emperor
256	The Persians sack Dura Europus
257–60	Valerian issues persecution edict against the Christians; it is later rescinded by Gallienus
260	Valerian captured by Sapor; Sapor defeated by Macrianus and Callistus, aided by Odaenathus of Palmyra; Macrianus and Quietus proclaimed emperors in the East; Postumus establishes *imperium Galliarum* (empire of the Gauls)
262	Macrianus defeated in the Balkans; Gallienus appoints Odaenathus commander in the East
268	Odaenathus murdered at Emesa; Postumus murdered by his army; Gallienus murdered and Claudius II proclaimed emperor
269	Claudius defeats barbarian raiders at Naissus; Zenobia claims Odaenathus's position for Vabalathus

Reunification of the Empire

270	Palmyrene conquest of Egypt; death of Claudius; Aurelian proclaimed emperor
271	Aurelian begins construction of a new wall for Rome; Trajanic province of Dacia abandoned
272	Aurelian captures Palmyra
273	Imperial silver coinage reformed
275–76	Aurelian murdered at Perinthus; Tacitus proclaimed emperor but murdered the following year; Probus becomes emperor
282	Carus revolts against Probus; Probus murdered; Carus becomes emperor; begins invasion of Persia; Carus appoints Carinus co-emperor
283	Carus dies (or is murdered) in Mesopotamia; Numerian succeeds as co-emperor with Carinus

The Reign of Diocletian

284	Numerian murdered and Diocletian proclaimed Augustus; Diocletian defeats Carinus; Maximian appointed Caesar; revolt of Carausius in northern Gaul and Britain
286	Diocletian elevates Maximian to the rank of Augustus
293	Constantius and Galerius made Caesars
296	Constantius recovers Britain
296–99	War between Rome and Persia; Galerius defeats the Persians and a treaty is made
303	Diocletian promulgates persecution edict against Christians
AD 305	Diocletian and Maximian abdicate; Constantius and Galerius become Augusti; Severus and Maximinus Daia become Caesars

	AD 306	Constantius dies at York (July 25); Constantine proclaimed Caesar by the army in Britain; Maxentius claims the title "Leader of the Youth" at Rome (October 28) and imprisons Severus
	307	Marriage of Constantine and Fausta; Constantine issues edict restoring confiscated Christian property; Galerius fails to suppress revolt of Maxentius; Severus murdered
	308	Maximian flees to Gaul, is received by Constantine; council at Carnuntum; Licinius appointed Augustus by Galerius
	310	Maximian commits suicide after his revolt against Constantine fails
	311	Death of Galerius; death of Diocletian
Constantine	**312**	Probable date for conversion of Constantine to Christianity; Constantine invades Italy, defeats Maxentius at Milvian Bridge; Maximinus Daia ends persecution of Christians
	313	Licinius defeats Maximinus Daia; issues "Edict of Nicomedia"
	316	Constantine attacks Licinius
	317	Licinius makes peace; Crispus, Constantine II, and Licinius II recognized as Caesars
	324	Constantine deposes Licinius; Byzantium (Constantinople) selected as new capital
	325	Council of Nicea
	326	Execution of Crispus Caesar; Fausta removed from public life
	330	Dedication of Constantinople (May 11–12)
	337	Death of Constantine (May 22); Constantine II, Constans, and Constantius II become Augusti
	339	Death of Constantine II
	350	Constans murdered
	351	Constantius II defeats usurper Magnentius at Mursa
	353	Constantius II reunites empire
	355	Constantius II appoints Julian as Caesar in Gaul
	360	Revolt of Julian in Gaul
	361	Death of Constantius II; Julian proclaims allegiance to traditional gods
	363	Julian dies in battle in Persia; Jovian selected as Augustus by the army
	364	Jovian dies; Valentinian I selected Augustus; Valentinian selects Valens (his brother) as co-Augustus; empire divided between Valentinian and Valens
From the Death of Constantine to the Sack of Rome	**375**	Death of Valentinian; Gratian succeeds as Augustus in western Europe; Valentinian II proclaimed Augustus in the Balkans, Italy, and Africa; Goths admitted to the Roman empire
	378	Battle of Adrianople; death of Valens
	379	Theodosius I becomes Augustus in the East
	383	Gratian murdered
	392	Valentinian II commits suicide
	395	Death of Theodosius I; Arcadius becomes Augustus in the East, and Honorius becomes Augustus in the West
	408	Death of Arcadius; Theodosius II becomes Augustus in the East
	AD 410	Sack of Rome by the Goths under Alaric

WHEN GORDIAN III EMERGED as sole emperor from the carnage of 238, the Roman empire stood on the brink of a crisis greater than any since the emergence of the principate. The immediate cause of this crisis was the imperial government's sudden loss of the ability to control its own frontiers. The imperial response, which like that of the first century BC was located firmly in the governing class and army, brought about a massive reshaping of the empire. A comparison between the empire in AD 338 with that in AD 238 reveals changes almost as great as a comparison between the empire in AD 50 and 50 BC: while the empire in that earlier period acquired a new emperor, new frontiers, and a new ideology of government, so did the empire in this later century acquire a new governing structure, a new ideology, and a new form of internal organization. The most obvious changes at the end of the fourth century AD were that the emperor no longer resided at Rome, that the emperor was a Christian, and that the provinces of the empire, now subdivided into numerous smaller units, were gathered into regional prefectures.

The consequences of the changes that took place during the fourth century were profound. The division of the empire into four prefectures led to the development of four distinct bureaucratic structures, with the result that it began to be possible to envision one part of the empire moving in a very different direction from another. This is exactly what began to happen in the middle of the fourth century, leading to a permanent split between the areas comprising the Western prefectures from those of the East.

The organization of the empire into prefectures had been hinted at in the age of Marcus Aurelius. Marcus had authorized large military commands encompassing several provinces in both the East and the Balkans. These are natural geopolitical divisions. They existed before the rise of the Augustan empire, and they still do today—Western Europe differs from central Europe and the Middle East differs from both. In a geopolitical sense the Augustan empire might therefore be seen as an aberration doomed to inevitable failure. The span of 290 years from Augustus's capture of Alexandria in 30 BC to Sapor's seizure of Valerian in AD 260 (the low point of Roman fortunes in the third century) is, however, a long one. If the Augustan experiment is viewed as "unnatural" it must also be viewed as proof that a state could be successfully assembled that did not accord with geopolitical fault lines. So again, what had changed?

The most important factor leading to the split between the Eastern and Western portions of the empire was the emergence of a new, far more aggressive imperial bureaucracy and the consequent reduction in the power of an individual emperor. The constant negotiation of authority between the emperor and his subjects that was typical of government during the first three centuries after Augustus gave way to the concentration of power in the hands of regional authorities that could dictate policies to imperial courts, which depended upon their loyalty for their own survival. As the power of individual emperors began to diminish, so too did the power of the state as a whole. By the end of the fourth century, although the problems of over-powerful regional bureaucracies, increasing inability to control the frontiers, and economic challenge had not yet proved fatal, the stability of the imperial regime was fatally compromised.

Gordian III was in his early teens when he acceded as sole emperor in 238. This portrait echoes those of Alexander Severus in emphasizing the emperor's youth and innocence.

Third-century Crises (AD 238–70)

Bureaucrats and Emperors

Why did the imperial government lose control of its frontiers? Was this the result of the sudden rise in the military power of its neighbors, was it simply the result of a series of accidents, or was it the result of a systemic failure on the part of the government? Or was it some combination of luck (largely bad), new enemies, structural flaws, and military incompetence? In order to answer these questions we must ask how the government was functioning. The thirty years after the death of Caracalla in AD 217 were notable as a time when the emperor was almost invariably a very young man. This may, at least to some degree, have been a reaction by senior members of the administrative classes against the pig-headed and brutal style of Caracalla, but it also meant that the empire was effectively run by groups of senior officials (a reaffirmation of the tendency of Roman government to default towards oligarchy).

The characteristic administrator of the Severan age was the jurist. One such person—Opellius Macrinus—became emperor; one of the most important figures in the last years of Severus's reign was the jurist Papinian; and one of the dominant figures in the first few years of Alexander Severus's reign was Ulpian (also a praetorian prefect before his murder by members of the guard in 223).

These jurists were not just politically important people. Ulpian, Papinian, and their contemporaries were members of a group of legal thinkers whose accomplishments mark the culmination of the "late Classical period" of Roman law. Their work provided the vast bulk of the material that was later taken up in the sixth-century AD compendium of juristic thought known as the *Digest*: half of all the material in the *Digest* derives from either Ulpian (one-third of the whole) or Papinian (about one-sixth) (see p. 335). In addition to their administrative eminence, the sheer volume of their surviving work makes Papinian and Ulpian two of the most significant thinkers in Roman history.

The reason that jurists became so influential is that emperors had long since tended to shunt some of the most important work that came their way onto equestrian secretaries who oversaw their correspondence. It was Augustus, whose reign corresponds with the first rise of professional jurists, who gave certain distinguished legal experts the power of issuing legally binding "responses" on questions of law. According to a jurist who wrote in the time of Hadrian:

> To clarify the point in passing: before the time of Augustus the right of stating opinions at large was not granted by emperors, but the practice was that opinions were given by people who had confidence in their own studies. Nor did they always issue opinions under seal, but most commonly wrote themselves to judges, or gave the testimony of a direct answer to those who consulted them. It was the deified Augustus who, in order to enhance the authority of the law, first established that opinions might be given under his authority.

> (Pomponius, as preserved in the *Digest*, trans. de Ste. Croix, 1.2.2.49)

Hadrian further refined this power by stating that when the responses of authorized jurists agreed, judges had to follow them. In cases where they disagreed, the judge should follow whichever one he thought best (although, significantly, he was not free to act independently of them). Jurists developed their reputation through command of legal precedent, and expanded their reputation by writing on questions of law in ways that demonstrated this learning. Typical juristic books included text-books for beginners, commentaries either on individual statutes or other books by lawyers, and books containing their responses to questions about the law.

Successful jurists therefore tended to be men who were excellent at arguing detailed points, and deeply interested in tradition. Although it might be tempt-ing to see the rise and style of the jurists as an alternative to the autocratic, and at times irrational, conduct of their rulers, this would be to stretch the evidence too far—especially since the greatest of these jurists were in fact employed by emperors of the Severan age. Instead of seeing jurists as alternatives to the "spirit of the age" it is more reasonable to see their style as a function of an age where there was a general tendency to create specialized bodies of learning, accessible only to initiates who devoted themselves to long years of study.

This seems also to have been a feature of military thinking in these years, which mingled some deeply practical study with an almost fetishistic reverence for the past. Two inscriptions are extremely revealing about the nature of Roman military thinking. Septimius Severus erected one of them on two columns at Rome, listing the legions according to province. The fact that this text lists the legions accord-ing to the provinces in which they served, until it reaches the two legions formed by Marcus Aurelius and the three formed by Severus, reveals that it is based on a list that was possibly some fifty years old by the time that Severus had it inscribed. That, however, is as nothing compared to the fact that the military organization it describes goes back to the age of Augustus. In terms of training and equipment, the legions were little different from those of the first century AD, which were them-selves essentially the same as those of Marius in the late second century BC.

The other significant inscription is from north Africa, and contains a series of speeches that Hadrian delivered to squadrons whose maneuvers he reviewed, telling each unit what he thought best about its performance. Thus, in addressing one cavalry unit he says:

> It is difficult for the cavalry attached to a cohort to win approval even on their own, and more difficult still for them not to incur criticism after a maneuver by auxiliary cavalry; they cover a greater area of the plain, there are more men throwing javelins, they wheel right in close formation, they perform the Cantabrian maneuver in close array, the beauty of their horses and the splendor of their weapons are in keeping with their pay. But, despite the heat, you avoided boredom by doing energetically what had to be done; in addition you fired stones from slings and fought with javelins; on every occasion you mounted speedily.
>
> (*Select Latin Inscriptions* no. 2487, 9133–5; trans. Campbell, 19–20)

The Cantabrian maneuver, which is described in detail by Arrian (see p. 223) in a work on tactics, involved the main body of the units holding a close order forma-tion while hurling first javelins and then spears at members of the unit who were riding past and supposedly warding off the weapons with their shields. Its name is derived from a tribe in north central Spain that had long since been brought

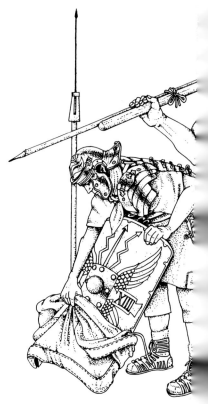

The typical equipment of a Roman soldier of the first century AD, illustrated here, was virtually no different from that of Roman soldiers two hundred years later. In its arms as well as its tactics, the Roman army had become a virtual fossil.

within the imperial system. The striking thing about the drill, in this context, is that Hadrian did not ask the troops to demonstrate any skill directly connected with the desert warfare with which they were most often involved. The principal training exercises of the Roman army appear instead to have prepared the men admirably to fight another Roman army. The nature of these drills underscores the fact that the primary purpose of the army was to support the emperor. After 400 years in which no enemy had been able to stand up to the fury of its warriors, there was no impetus within the military for change, and no institution, such as a staff college, where the art of war could be systematically studied. Institutionally, as well as tactically, the army had not developed since the age of Marius, Sulla, and Caesar.

The impetus for reform that was provided in the course of the twenty years after AD 238 arose in part because some of Rome's enemies may have gotten better, but also because the role of "imperial support vehicle" meant that the army was often commanded in battle by emperors who were not necessarily the best men for the job. The biggest problem that the Roman empire faced in 238 was that senior officials were trained to advance into the future with their eyes fixed firmly on the past.

New Enemies?

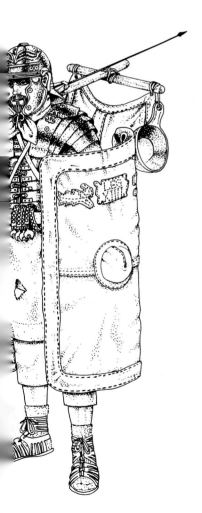

There is some evidence for the appearance of "new" enemies on the northern frontiers in the early third century AD. The problem is that we don't know whether these were really "new" enemies or simply "old" enemies with new names, and, in any event, whether this really matters all that much: there is no reason to think that the demographic balance obtained in the first century AD had changed in any significant way (except perhaps in favor of Rome, with the likely increase in population during the first two centuries AD: see also p. 191). Thus, for instance, Cassius Dio mentions a group called Alamanni in southern Germany. Alamanni was a collective term adopted by German tribes between the Elbe and Oder rivers to the north and east from Mainz along the Rhine, which probably meant something like "the tough guys," and is similar to another tribal name that appears around this time among the Germans of this area, the Juthungi or "young fighters." At roughly the same time we also get the first evidence for a group of people occupying the area from the mouth of the Rhine to roughly the area of Mainz: called the Franks, their name probably meant "the bold ones." The similarity between these names—the fact that they all claim some valued quality for a group of people—and the absence of any archaeological evidence for migration into the area suggest that these names reflect political reorganization rather than substantial change in the population north of the Rhine. Along the Danube, while we still hear about traditional tribes, such as the Quadi, Marcomanni, and Sarmatians, the reign of Severus provides the first direct evidence for people calling themselves Goths—albeit in the form of a Latin inscription identifying a unit of "Goths" serving in the garrison of Arabia.

Whenever northern peoples fought Rome rather than taking service in Roman armies, they continued to do so by launching raids as deeply as possible into Roman territory to seize plunder and return home. The typical Roman response, when it was not possible to wipe out the raiders before they could get home, was to retaliate by destroying whatever villages they could, and then establish treaties with the people closest to the border, who would (in theory) keep their more boisterous neighbors at bay, in return for some sort of payment or privilege from the Romans.

This was the pattern evident in Marcus Aurelius's wars, and repeated on numerous occasions in the course of the third century. On very rare occasions there would be a different sort of interaction, when a tribe lost out particularly badly to its neighbors and had to leave its lands. If they were in proximity to Romans they might ask Roman permission to settle in Roman territory. Sometimes the Romans would grant them permission, probably settling them on land belonging to the emperor (there is no direct evidence for what actually happened). Thus the appearance of "new people" north of the frontier does not really indicate any significant change in the situation.

In Persia, on the other hand, there was a very significant change when the Sasanians replaced the earlier Arsacid dynasty of the Parthians. The Sasanians proved deadly foes—but not because they brought with them any new technology, or even a new birthrate to equalize the disparity in economic power between the two empires. Sasanian armies appear to have looked very much like Parthian armies in that their great strength lay in the combination of horse archers with heavily armed cavalry. It was this combination that had defeated Crassus at Carrhae in 53 BC (see p. 161) and had yielded occasional victories in later years, for instance at the beginning of Vologaeses' war with Rome in 161 (p. 225). The main difference between Parthian and Sasanian armies seems to have been in terms of command rather than tactical structure. The Sasanian kingdom appears to have been much more tightly organized than its predecessor, especially in the first fifty years, as the possession of high office seems to have been linked with a virtual requirement that the holder be a blood relative of the High King (or King of Kings) at Ctesiphon. The regime as a whole was evidently informed by a strong sense, descended from the revelations of the holy man Zoroaster more than a thousand years earlier, that its purpose was to assert the superiority of the sky god Ahura Mazada over the servants of the god Ahriman, readily identifiable as all the regime's opponents.

On the military front, a possible sign of the improvement in efficiency that stemmed simply from the improved command structure is the fact that Sasanian armies appear to have been very good at siege warfare, something that is unattested for the Parthians. The technology and methods they used—catapults, siege towers, and the undermining of walls—were nothing new, but did require a high level of discipline and logistical organization to make them work. The other main difference between the old and new regimes is that the first two Sasanid kings, Ardashir and Sapor, were soldiers of immense ability. Ardashir had begun his career as the ruler of a single principality in the area of Fars in southern Iran, and managed to conquer the entire Parthian realm. Sapor, his son and successor, may have been the ablest soldier encountered by the Romans since Hannibal.

The problems that beset Rome in the course of the forty-five years after the death of Maximinus in 238 cannot therefore be credited to the arrival of new peoples along the northern frontier. To some degree they can be attributed to the increase in the power of Persia, but most of all, explanations for Roman failure must be sought within the governing class of the Roman empire. Two problems appear to be foremost in this regard. The first was that the emperor increasingly tended to take personal command of armies committed to battle, rather than offering overall strategic direction from within a secure base. Personal command was dangerous because it exposed the emperor if his army should mutiny (something it was more likely to do if recently defeated), because it limited strong responses to wherever an emperor might appear in person, and because it delayed response when trouble broke out on multiple fronts. The second was the conservative mindset of imperial administrators: indeed, the two emperors most closely associated with the catastrophes of the next twenty years were both consuls before 238, having risen to power when the cult of tradition was extremely potent within the imperial administration. The recovery of the empire at the end of the third century is connected with a new generation of officers who were willing to think in new ways. Finally, it must be stressed that the crisis that took place in the next twenty years was political. It involved neither great social or economic shift, until a radical reform of the coinage system during the 270s. Aside from the fact that emperors were changing at an alarming speed, there was little reason to think that the average inhabitant of the empire, so long as he or she was not in an area visited by Germanic raiders or Persian armies, would necessarily have thought that life was any worse now than it had been in earlier generations. For anyone living along the Danube or in Syria, however, the experience of these years may well have seemed quite horrific.

Barbarian Ascendancy (AD 238–70)

Problems connected with the desire to maintain tradition, the necessity for direct imperial command, and the problem of warfare on multiple fronts become immediately obvious in the years after 238. Plainly conscious of the chaos that was gripping the empire after Alexander Severus's assassination in 235, Ardashir had seized Carrhae and Edessa in the province of Mesopotamia. Maximinus, who was in no position either to respond in person or to appoint another to such a powerful command, had done nothing about the Persian attack. It was not until 241 that the leaders of Gordian III's regime, led by the praetorian prefect Timesitheus (the young emperor's father-in-law), felt able to respond. It took two years to get the army in a position to attack, but when it did, the Persians (now led by Sapor) were driven from Mesopotamia. At this point Timesitheus dropped dead, and the surviving praetorian prefect—Julius Priscus, the effective head of the government—elevated his brother Philip to be his colleague. They remained in office as the army invaded Iraq during the winter of 244, now with Gordian in titular command. When the army reached a spot on the Euphrates from which to launch an attack across Iraq in the direction of Ctesiphon, Sapor struck. The Romans were defeated and shortly afterwards Gordian was murdered in the camp. He was succeeded by Philip.

Philip was the first equestrian emperor to govern from Rome—neither Macrinus nor Maximinus had gone near the capital—and he appears to have been willing to take a proactive approach to deep-seated problems of imperial finance: papyri from Egypt reveal a number of measures designed to enhance the efficiency of tax collection. At the same time, he burnished his imperial credentials, with two projects in particular. One was the celebration of the 1,000th anniversary of the foundation of Rome in 248; the other was the reconstruction of his native city in Syria as a model homeland for an emperor. The remains of Philippopolis, as the new city was called, are remarkable for the prevalence of Roman architectural types that mark this as a city with a particular link to Rome. The millennial games were likewise produced on a scale appropriate to such a momentous anniversary. In terms of the overall

This famous bust of Philip, now in the Vatican Museum, presents a very different image from the idealized portraits of Gordian III, and suggests a man deeply concerned with the weight of his task.

administration of the empire, Philip seems to have realized that centralizing authority around the person of the emperor was unworkable, and might be counteracted by appointing men who could in effect serve as deputy emperors in various regions. The fact that his first two choices for such positions were family members—Julius Priscus in the East, and Severianus for a brief while in the Balkans—suggests that he had a limited entourage from which to draw senior officials, rather than that the basic conception was wrong. Indeed, it proved all too correct. In the absence of a relative, when a revolt broke out on the Danube (where Severianus had not remained in office for long) soon after the millennial games, Philip sent Decius, a senator who had sided with Maximinus during the civil war of 238, to suppress the trouble. No sooner had Decius done so than he turned on Philip and won a brief civil war, during which Philip was killed, to make himself emperor.

Decius seems to have been passionately attached to the traditions of the imperial past. One of his most notable acts was to issue an edict, almost as soon as he had defeated Philip, ordering all the inhabitants of the empire to sacrifice for the welfare of the state. Another was to issue a series of coins commemorating the "good emperors" of the past, as part of what seems to have been a broadly based effort to rewrite the history of the early third century. Unfortunately for both Decius and the empire as a whole, neither of these actions did much to address the issue of how to handle fresh raids into the Balkan provinces. In 250 what must have been a very large raiding party swept across the Danube, ambushing Decius and destroying an army that he was accompanying, before laying waste to the great city of Philippopolis (this one named for Philip II of Macedon, rather than the recently deceased emperor) in the Balkans. When Decius caught up with the raiders in 251, they lured his new army into a swamp and destroyed it at Abritus; Decius was killed in the battle.

Trebonianus Gallus, one of the governors of the Danubian provinces, now succeeded to the throne. Having paid off the northern tribes that had defeated Decius,

(Above) The remains of a Roman theater at Philippopolis in modern Syria. Like Severus before him, Philip rebuilt his native city to make it a homeland worthy of an emperor.

(Below) Decius, who was born in one of the Danube provinces, had first held the consulship under Alexander Severus. He was a firm believer in the "old time" virtues of Rome, and this is perhaps reflected in the rather traditional depiction of the emperor in this coin.

(Above) Valerian (top) and his son, Gallienus, had very different styles of leadership. Valerian appears to have been deeply conservative, while Gallienus was far more open to change. The contrasts between them are reflected in these quite different coin portraits.

(Right) This stone relief depicts the triumph of Sapor I over the Roman Emperor Gordian III, whose dead body lies beneath the hoofs of Sapor's horse. The figure standing next to the horse has been identified as Valerian; the kneeling figure may be Philip. This relief was carved into the rock at the gorge of Tang-e Chowgan, near Bishapur (in modern Iran).

he planned some sort of war with Persia—only to find whatever strategy he might wish to have employed thoroughly preempted in 252, when Sapor advanced up the Euphrates rather than across northern Mesopotamia (the expected route for a Persian attack). He crushed a Roman army at Barbalissos on the Euphrates, ravaged Syria, and sacked Antioch. At the very same time a group of Germanic/Gothic tribesmen constructed boats along the coast of the Black Sea and burst through the Dardanelles into the Aegean, sacking many cities, including Ephesus.

The years 251–52 rank as the two worst in Roman imperial history: three major cities were sacked, two armies were destroyed, and the emperor was seemingly powerless to do anything. When the Danubian army managed a victory in 253, it proclaimed its own general, Aemilianus, emperor. Aemilianus defeated Gallus in central Italy before falling prey to Valerian, an ally of Gallus who had arrived too late to help the former emperor. Valerian, another deeply committed traditionalist, was devoted to defending the frontiers, while eliminating those who did not subscribe to the cultural unity of the empire. It was Valerian who in 257 issued the first empire-wide edict ordering proactive persecution of the Christian church, the seizure of Christian property, and the execution of Christians who did not recant their beliefs. At the same time, he understood that he could not secure the empire on his own. As soon as he became emperor, Valerian raised his son Gallienus, then a man of mature years, to be his colleague, and appointed various sons of Gallienus to the rank of Caesar.

In 260, after failing to defend western Turkey effectively from yet another naval assault from the Black Sea, Valerian found himself threatened by a fresh Persian invasion. Sapor crossed into the Roman province of Mesopotamia, where he found Valerian's army weakened by disease and on the verge of mutiny. When, after a defeat south of Edessa, Valerian agreed to negotiate a peace treaty, Sapor threw him in chains and sent him off as a captive to Persia while his armies ravaged the Eastern provinces. Later Roman tradition held that Sapor used Valerian as a footstool when mounting his horse. Later Persian tradition held that he was assigned to bridge construction in southern Iran.

In the grand colonnade at Palmyra, statues of local notables once stood on the pedestals that can be seen in this picture. Inscriptions connected with these statues are a vital source of information about the city's ruling class, while the grandeur of the structure is evidence of Palmyra's immense wealth.

Within months of the unprecedented embarrassment of the capture of an emperor, the empire itself seemed on the verge of dissolution. In the East, the most senior official to survive the disaster, Macrianus, rallied what was left of the army and, receiving significant help from Odaenathus, ruler of Palmyra in central Syria, drove the Persians back. He then had his sons, Macrianus and Quietus, declared emperor and invaded the Balkans, where two rebellions had already greeted the news of Valerian's disaster. At the same time, the provinces north of the Alps broke loose and formed a new realm—the *imperium Galliarum* or "Empire of the Gauls"—under the leadership of Postumus, the former governor of one of the Rhine provinces.

Although Gallienus defeated both the two earlier Balkan revolts and the invasion of Macrianus in 262, he realized that he could not restore direct control over the East without the help of Odaenathus, whom he now recognized as commander of Roman forces in the region. The creation of a considerable Palmyrene army in the previous few years may have stemmed from frustration with newly aggressive Persian dominance of traditional trade routes. It proved to be surprisingly effective. Palmyrene armies defeated Sapor on several occasions, and Odaenathus proclaimed himself King of Kings while dressing in a style that was evocative of a Persian king rather than a Roman official. Despite this, Odaenathus remained loyal to Gallienus, never challenging the emperor's authority to appoint his own officials to provincial commands. It is also a matter of some interest that the two men agreed in taking a very different line towards the Christians. Gallienus issued an edict of toleration, and Odaenathus (or his wife, Zenobia) had an evidently friendly relationship with a bishop at Antioch. The relationship between Gallienus and Odaenathus as a whole, combining as it did local initiative with central government approval, reveals that there remained much strength in the traditional Roman policy of allowing locals to develop their own relationship with the central government.

The situation in the West was much worse for Gallienus than the situation in the East. Although he was able to regain control of the Balkans, Gallienus could not reverse the effects of the revolt on the Rhine. Postumus more than held his own until he fell victim to a mutiny in 269. That was the year after Gallienus fell victim to a plot by his own senior officers while trying to end yet another rebellion, this time by a senior commander in northern Italy.

The eight years after the capture of Valerian presented a possible model for a new Roman empire that would, with refinements, reemerge repeatedly during the two centuries before the Western empire ceased to function altogether. The Eastern provinces from Egypt through what is now Turkey formed a natural unit, as did the central European provinces with Italy, and, for now, north Africa, the surplus grain from which was crucial for the survival of Rome. The provinces north and west of the Alps could look after themselves.

The death of Gallienus accompanied yet another crisis. The central European tribes launched another attack in 268, this time by both land and sea. The emperor

This third-century relief from Palmyra was once thought to depict Queen Zenobia and an attendant, but it is more likely that it shows two goddesses. The goddess on the left sits with a water divinity beneath her feet, which may represent the spring of Palmyra; the woman with the turreted headdress could be the city's patron goddess. In its combination of Greek symbolism expressed in a Mesopotamian style, this sculpture is emblematic of the mixed culture of Palmyra.

who succeeded Gallienus, a Balkan general named Claudius, did an able job the following summer, defeating his barbarian foes at Naissus (in present-day Serbia), but thoroughly fouled up relations with both Palmyra and Gaul, even as those regimes experienced radical transformations. Odaenathus had fallen prey to an assassin from within his own entourage in 268, while the Gallic regime had fallen into temporary chaos after Postumus's murder in the summer of 269. Claudius proved unable to take advantage of the situation in Gaul and caused a complete breakdown in relations with Palmyra when he evidently insisted that Odaenathus's position as general had died with him. After the defeat of a Roman expeditionary force in western Turkey, Palmyrene armies took over direct control of Arabia and Egypt. The moving force behind the operation was Odaenathus's young widow, Zenobia.

Claudius did not live to deal with the situation in the East. He died of disease in the early part of 270, to be remembered ever afterwards as a great hero for his victory in 269. After a brief period of conflict, power passed to another of Gallienus's former marshals, again a man from the Balkans. His name was Aurelian.

The Restoration of the Empire (AD 270–305)

Aurelian and His Successors (AD 270–84)

Aurelian faced daunting challenges. The deaths of 268–69 had upset the equilibrium between the three parts of the empire, and the northern tribes were still raiding well south of the frontier. Throughout the summer of 270 and into 271 Aurelian was fighting in Italy, both against raiders and his own people (he had to suppress a revolt in Rome itself) before he could clear the enemy from his western sector of the empire. With victory in hand, however, Aurelian sought to stabilize his relationship with the Roman people, adding pork to the subsidized food supply and surrounding the city itself with massive new walls that seemed to symbolize the continued power of the capital. At the same time he took the bold step of renouncing Roman control over Dacia (see p. 219).

Aurelian, depicted here in military dress, appears to have spent his entire career in the army, and it is unlikely that he was ever a senator. After he took the throne, Aurelian's military leadership was key to reuniting the Roman empire, as was his willingness to negotiate with his rivals.

Having settled Italy and begun the abandonment of Dacia, Aurelian launched a multi-pronged invasion through Egypt and Asia Minor to defeat the armies of Zenobia and capture Palmyra. Once again he sought reconciliation over revenge. Zenobia was taken to Rome, where her descendants were identifiable members of the senate more than a century later. Various officials, possibly as a reward for timely betrayal of the Palmyrenes, continued in office, and Aurelian seems to have tried to make the transition back to direct control as painless as possible. But however well-intentioned his policies may have been, they did not work: as soon as he began his return to the West a faction in Palmyra seized control of the city, and defended it with extreme vigor. This time Aurelian showed no mercy. Palmyra's career as one of the great trading cities of antiquity ended with the sack of 273; what was left of the trade that it had once controlled now shifted northwards to the cities of Mesopotamia.

The victory in the East had one other quite remarkable result, since one of the decisive battles had been fought near Emesa, and in the course of the battle Aurelian determined that he had received aid from the local sun god, Elagabal. In the wake of the victory, Aurelian reintroduced the cult of this god to Rome, now renamed as "Invincible Sun," and with a more acceptable cult image. No one seems to have objected to the cult in this form, and it set an important precedent for the close identification of an emperor with a non-Roman divinity. The rationale for the new cult—some sort of divine vision—was used several decades later to introduce the worship of a quite different divinity, likewise temporarily Romanized to an almost unrecognizable degree by another emperor (see p. 298). As the actual personality of the emperor began to be subsumed within increasingly homogenized imperial propaganda, the choice of a guardian god could now become a symbolic expression that extended beyond a specifically Roman context. Aurelian and his successors, all men from the provinces, were perhaps more deeply attuned to messages that made sense to an empire-wide audience than many of their predecessors. At the very least, the introduction of Invincible Sun was a dramatic retreat from the Romano-centric religious activity of Decius and Valerian.

Aurelian now turned his attention to the empire of the Gauls. Tetricus, the most recent claimant to the Gallic throne, realized that he had no chance, and surrendered after allegedly deploying his legions in positions where they could not effectively defend themselves. He was given an undemanding governorship in southern Italy. Within four years Aurelian had achieved the seemingly impossible task of restoring unity to the Roman empire. Success was, however, fleeting. Many parts of the empire had become freshly militarized in the years of chaos and were, as yet, not fully reintegrated within the imperial system, including parts of Gaul, Syria, Egypt, and southern Turkey. Aurelian's own officers seem to have been divided over the wisdom of some of his acts, and Aurelian compounded the problems of the empire by issuing a "reformed" coinage that destroyed the existing tariff relationship between gold and silver, causing rampant inflation that was not cured for generations.

In the late summer of 275 Aurelian was murdered by members of his staff. Although his record as an administrator would forever be marred by his "coinage reform," his other achievements had endeared him to the rank and file. The army buried him with great ceremony near Perinthus in Turkey, where he had died, lamenting him as the savior of Rome.

The assassins seem to have realized that whatever designs they had for the future would not work in light of the army's response. As they retired to the deserts of Jordan, loyalist officers searched for a new ruler who would satisfy the troops. Their candidate was a general named Tacitus (no relation to the historian), who proved incapable of dealing with the tensions that still seethed within the high command. Aurelian's assassins actually penetrated the main camp of the army while he was in central Turkey and slew him too.

Problems did not end with the murder of Tacitus. He had intended that the throne should pass to his brother Florian, but that too was unacceptable to the army in Syria, which promptly proclaimed its own general, Probus, as emperor. When Florian failed to suppress the revolt in the East, Probus became ruler of the whole empire, and summoned a "reconciliation" meeting with Aurelian's assassins. The meeting ended with a dinner party at which Probus put an end to their dispute by murdering his guests.

Having taken the throne as a revolutionary and confirmed his power with murder, Probus spent most of his reign trying to control other revolutionaries in areas as diverse as southern Turkey, Egypt, and Gaul. These uprisings may be connected with the need that people throughout the empire had found to provide for their own safety. The evidence for these acts of self-defense is largely from chance finds of inscriptions or archaeology, but the aggregate is enough to reveal definite patterns of conduct. Among these pieces of evidence is an inscription from Augsburg (in southern Germany) mentioning a provincial militia. At Emesa in Syria, coins and an oracular text show that in 253 a local aristocrat, Uranius Antoninus, repulsed some Persian raiders; while a contemporary inscription from a nearby location mentions an unnamed "hero" who called upon a local god to repel the enemy. In 268 the cities of Greece assembled an army to repel invaders from the sea, who sacked Athens despite the best efforts of its citizens (who evidently rallied in the countryside and inflicted some sort of reverse on their enemies). The efforts of the larger Greek contingent are reflected in an inscription that says: "they fought in the front rank of the Greeks, they repulsed the enemies of the Athenians with our ships and our infantry, we died at sea under the swords of the barbarians. My brother prepared this tomb for me. I am Epaphrys, I lived twice ten years and twice six years" (*Greek Inscriptions* 5.1 no. 1188). In cities where walls had not been maintained, they

Like Aurelian, both Tacitus (below) and Probus (bottom) were from the Balkans. Tacitus was a compromise candidate placed on the throne after Aurelian's murder, but he did not long escape the assassins himself. Probus seized the throne from Florian, Tacitus's brother and intended successor, in 276.

were repaired. It is thus likely that the revolts that Probus dealt with were aspects of this phenomenon. The repeat of another phenomenon, however, cost him his life. In 282 the praetorian prefect, Carus, decided that he could overthrow Probus, and promptly did.

After years in which emperors had concentrated on domestic foes, Carus attempted something completely different. Sapor had died in 270, his immediate successors had been weak, and civil war now plagued the Sasanian kingdom, enabling Carus to invade Iraq with some success. Then something went terribly wrong. Tradition has it that his tent was struck by lightning. This may be true, or it may be a metaphor for mutiny. We will never know: but we do know that Carus's younger son, who had accompanied him east with the title of Caesar, now became Numerian Augustus; Numerian's elder brother, Carinus, who had remained in the West, had received that title a year earlier. Neither option seems to have pleased powerful elements in the Eastern army. Numerian was murdered after the army left Antioch in the summer of 284, though it appears that, unable to decide on a successor, the general staff transported his dead body in a litter, claiming that an eye ailment prevented him from appearing in public, until the stench of decomposition reached a point where they could no longer maintain the fiction. Forced to act, the general staff halted just outside Nicomedia in western Turkey and selected a mid-grade officer named Gaius Aurelius Valerius Diocles as emperor. Standing before the army, Diocles accepted the acclamation of the soldiers, drew his sword, and split the praetorian prefect, a leading contender for his job, in two. Shortly thereafter Diocles took the Latinized name Gaius Aurelius Valerius Diocletianus, and is hence commonly known as Diocletian.

Carus was unique among the emperors in the period after Gallienus in having grown sons to whom he hoped to leave the empire. This idea was unacceptable to members of the general staff, who murdered one son and supported Diocletian against the other.

Diocletian (AD 284–305)

When Diocletian set out to contest the throne with Carinus in the spring of 285 few could have predicted any great change. The contenders were typical third-century emperors who based their claims to power as much on their ability to undermine their opponent's authority as on the ability of their army to defeat those of rivals. Indeed, when Diocletian triumphed, his victory was achieved largely through treachery and desertions.

Much had changed over the previous fifty years, not only the character of the army (see box, opposite) but also the institutions of Rome itself. Gallienus was the last emperor to reside regularly at Rome in the 260s. Aurelian may have given the city new walls and a new god, but he had spent most of his time on the march. So had his successors, and that had consequences for the composition of the governing class. The most obvious of these was that senators were rarely found near the emperor's inner circle. As emperors no longer spent much time at Rome, senators no longer had ready social access, and while there were a few who achieved prominence under the new emperors, only one of these new emperors (Tacitus) was a senator before taking office. The people who had chosen Claudius, Aurelian, and Tacitus were generals with the army, while Probus and Carus were both victors in civil war. Faced with the prospect of a reign spent fighting on the frontiers until some northern barbarian, Persian, or other Roman managed to kill him, Diocletian decided to change the way the game was played.

This marble bust, now in the Istanbul Archaeological Museum, has been identified as depicting either Diocletian or Maximian. It suggests the more exalted style of dress that had become standard at the imperial court by the end of the third century AD.

THE ROMAN ARMY IN THE THIRD CENTURY

The armies that Carinus and Diocletian led against each other in AD 285 were radically different from the legionary forces of earlier years. These earlier armies had largely been destroyed in the disasters of the previous half-century: Decius's defeats by the Goths in 250–51, Sapor's destruction of the Syrian garrison in 252, and Valerian's capture by Sapor eight years later.

Although there were still many units called legions, these were no longer units of some 5,500 heavily armed and armored infantrymen. Legions now tended to number no more than 2,000 men, were more lightly armored, and were trained in new tactics. The main strike force of the army, which was gradually being separated from units that were primarily assigned to frontier protection, contained higher proportions of cavalry than had been the rule before 250. In many ways it was a better army, capable of a wider range of tactical maneuvers, and capable of adapting to a variety of enemies. Perhaps most significantly, the new army had been uniformly successful since the opening year of Aurelian's reign.

Changes in the tactical organization of the Roman army are reflected in this illustration, which depicts the equipment of legionaries in the time of Constantine. Most troops now carried oval shields, and the infantry and cavalrymen were usually equipped with the long-bladed spatha sword that can be seen on the hip of the soldier on the right.

A new era dawned in the summer of 285 when Diocletian married one of his daughters to a relatively junior officer, Maximian, raised him to the position of deputy emperor, or Caesar, and sent him off to the Western provinces. A year later he promoted Maximian to the rank of Augustus, with the proviso that important decisions be made in consultation with him, as befitted his rank as senior Augustus. Maximian justified the faith that had been placed in him by quelling rebellions in Gaul. These probably involved local leaders of military forces who had grown powerful in the years of the independent Gallic regime, though imperial propaganda now dubbed such people as "brigands," based on what seems to have been a Celtic word, Bagaudae.

Diocletian was not content merely to reshape the outward image of government. In the course of the next decade he transformed the administrative system from the ground up. Gone would be the notion that the emperor was a friend rather than a boss, and gone would be the notion that the empire had a single capital. Diocletian plainly did not find Rome agreeable: in twenty-one years as emperor he spent, in total, less than six months there. The center of power would now be wherever the emperor chose to reside. There was already something of an imperial residence at Sirmium in the Balkans; it was soon joined by the development of imperial residences at Aquileia and Milan in northern Italy, Trier in Germany, and other significant administrative complexes at Antioch (perhaps too close to the Persian frontier to be a primary residence), Carnuntum on the Danube, and Thessalonica in northern Greece. Most importantly, Diocletian decided that his main residence would be at Nicomedia in northwestern Turkey. The establishment of the imperial seat there indicates that Diocletian thought he should reside in an area whence he could move with relative ease to the frontier armies along the Danube and in Syria.

Diocletian's decision to govern away from Rome was accompanied by a gradual, but thorough, reshuffling of the way the government was organized. The tradition of dividing offices according to social class had largely ended in the mid-third century. Most offices were now in the hands of men who, though technically equestrians, had little in common with the officials of the Antonine age of the previous century. The catastrophic inflation that followed upon Aurelian's currency reform meant that the traditionally high salaries of these officers were now relatively modest—a lower level equestrian, who had not received the large salary increase that had gone to regular soldiers in the early third century, now made twelve times the salary of an infantryman, not sixty, as had been the case in the second century. These changes had a leveling effect, placing imperial office within the reach of men who would, in the past, have remained local dignitaries, or have had little chance to advance beyond the level of a unit commander. People who disliked Diocletian claimed that he was little better than a barbarian of peasant background; the claim reflects the fact that government was no longer the preserve of multi-millionaires.

Diocletian's reorganization of the empire in AD 294. The division of older provinces into new, smaller ones was something that had begun before Diocletian became emperor, although he accelerated the process. More radical was Diocletian's grouping of the provinces into twelve administrative units called dioceses.

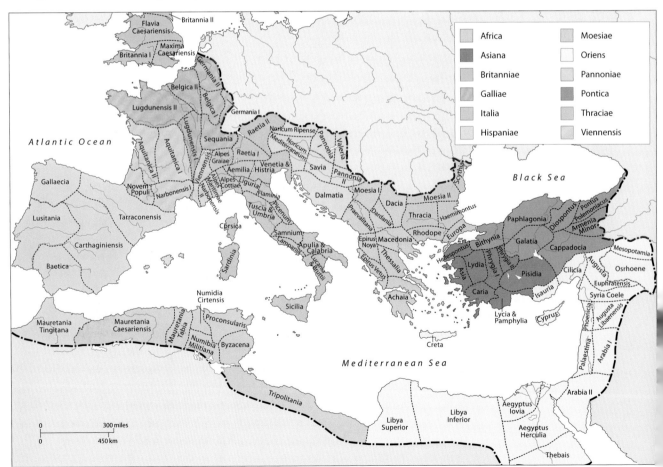

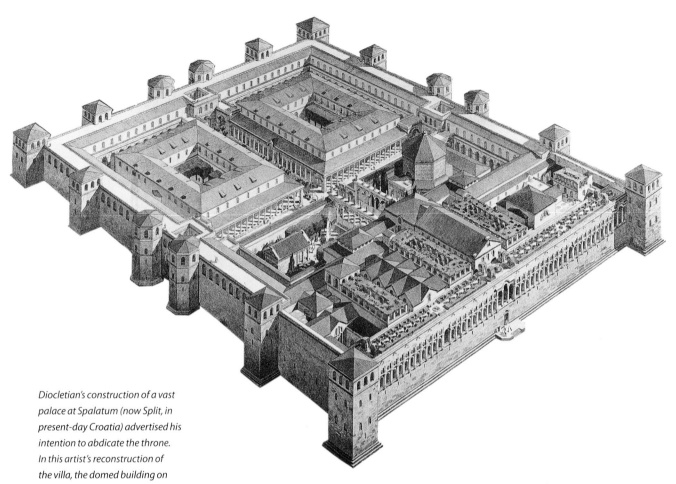

Diocletian's construction of a vast palace at Spalatum (now Split, in present-day Croatia) advertised his intention to abdicate the throne. In this artist's reconstruction of the villa, the domed building on the right is the emperor's tomb, and the building opposite it on the left is a temple of Jupiter. The imperial living quarters were entered through the colonnade that separated these structures.

The new civil administration had four principal elements. Provincial governors reported through the praetorian prefects, and were responsible for the administration of justice and the delivery of taxes in produce. The office of the *res privata*, the descendant of the old *patrimonium*, took over the collection of all taxes paid in coin, the production of mines, and the minting of coinage. The equestrian secretariats of the old empire were now collected, along with the legal staff, under the authority of the *magister officiorum*, master of offices, while the operations of the various palaces continued to be under the control of *cubicularii*, now more numerous than in the past and more likely to be eunuchs. For the present, the army was under the direct command of each Augustus, with *comites* or *duces* commanding larger formations of men within the army.

The inflation of the late third century may have made it difficult for the imperial government to count on its tax revenues. Reform was plainly needed, but it was also likely to be difficult since the tax system remained a fundamental point of intersection between the average person and the state. Over the years people had developed strategies for avoiding taxes, and local officials has learned what the limits of their power to control those evasions might be. To change the system would inevitably upset these practices. Nonetheless, in 296 Diocletian issued an edict that initiated a new fourteen-year census, or indiction, cycle: this would enable the state to gauge its revenues more accurately, since it would impose uniform taxes across all the

PAYING TAX IN EGYPT

The flavor of Diocletian's tax reforms, designed to levy uniform taxes throughout the empire, is well caught in a letter that the prefect of Egypt dispatched to introduce the edict to the people of the Nile valley:

> Our most provident emperors Diocletian and Maximian, the Augusti and Constantius and Maximian (Galerius), the most noble Caesars ... having learned that the levies of the public taxes were being made capriciously so that some persons were being let off lightly while others were overburdened, decided in the interest of their provincials to root out this most evil and ruinous practice and to issue a salutary rule to which the taxes would have to conform.
>
> Thus it is possible for all to know the amount levied on each aroura (the basic division of land in Egypt, measuring 0.68 acres or 2,767 square meters) in accordance with the character of the land, and the amount levied on each head of the rural population, and the minimum and maximum ages of liability, from the imperial edict which has been published and the schedule attached thereto, to which I have prefixed for purposes of public display the copies of this edict of mine.
>
> Accordingly, since in this too, they have been treated with the greatest beneficence, let the provincials take care to make their contributions with all speed in conformity with the imperial regulations and in no wise wait for the collector to exercise compulsion. For it is fitting that each person discharge most eagerly the full burden of loyalty, and if anyone should be detected doing otherwise after such great beneficence he will risk punishment.
>
> (*Archive of Isidorus*, trans. Youtie and Boak, document 1)

The people of Egypt reacted predictably to this change: serious revolts broke out in the next two years that required the presence of Diocletian to suppress them. Their fears that the new system would raise taxes seem to have been thoroughly justified. The tax burden on the average Egyptian—about whose taxes we are comparatively well informed, because so many tax records have been preserved on papyrus—doubled in the course of the next century.

provinces, and make it possible for the state to raise taxes, empire-wide, on an annual basis. Unsurprisingly, the reform was not met with universal joy: serious revolts broke out in Egypt (see box, above), and in later years, when the new system was introduced in Italy—which had previously been exempt from the land and head taxes imposed on the rest of the empire—the result was also intense anger (see p. 296).

Another feature of the new administrative system that became increasingly prevalent in the course of the next century was the notion that people were required to follow their parent's occupation. In practical terms, this changed little: very few children of tenant farmers ever grew up to be anything other than tenant farmers. It also proved impossible to enforce such regulations—surviving laws stressing this obligation are mirrored by documents, for instance one written by a landowner in the late fourth century wondering what the legal basis was for his claim that his tenants had to stay his tenants. These regulations, however, reflect the fact that the imperial government still saw itself as representing, primarily, the interests of the landowning class. Even if imperial officials could do little to prevent oppressed peasants from running away from oppressive landlords, they could make it harder for peasants, and others, to negotiate with landholders by constraining their freedom of action.

One final aspect of the new system that began to take shape in this period was that the central government was vastly more proactive than the government of the second century. A characteristic document of the Diocletianic age, well reflected in the quoted letter concerning the change in the tax system, was the imperial edict.

Edicts through which the emperor announced some new policy had always, of course, been a feature of government—Caracalla's decision to extend the citizenship in 212 (see p. 265) is a classic example of this—but in these years they seem to have been used more than ever. The result was that perhaps the strongest points of the Augustan and post-Augustan administrative systems—the freedom of individual communities to take their own initiatives, and the way in which general policy was stated in the course of a dialogue between the emperor and his subjects, taking some account of local concerns—began to give way to a system where the central administration prescribed the actions of its subjects with a great deal more precision. This was problematic in that it might often overlook specific local situations that would not be improved by a new rule. The issue is not so much that Diocletian was doing something radically new, but rather that the cumulative effect of his decisions was to shift the balance of initiative in government away from local to central authority.

Diocletian was able to take a personal role in suppressing the taxation revolts in Egypt in 297, despite the fact that a war had recently broken out with Persia, because of yet another important transformation. Dating to 293, this change is evident in the opening lines of the letter to the Egyptian prefect. It came about as a result of a series of catastrophes suffered by Maximian while he was attempting to suppress a revolt that broke out along the Rhine and in Britain under the leadership of Carausius, formerly the senior commander in the area. Carausius's rebellion had begun in 286 and Maximian had driven him from most of Gaul by 291; but when he attempted to follow up his successes with an invasion of Britain, his fleet was destroyed in a storm. Carausius took advantage of the disaster to reoccupy portions of the mainland, and in 293 Maximian appointed a deputy emperor to take charge of the campaign. Diocletian, who had less need of help, did the same, with the understanding that the two deputies, or Caesars, would some day succeed the current Augusti. The new Caesars were Flavius Constantius and Gaius Galerius Valerius Maximianus (known more succinctly in English as Galerius). Both Constantius and Galerius were experienced soldiers, and their appointments relieved the Augusti of the need to take personal control of risky military operations, thus breaking with the Severan tradition whereby the emperor needed to take personal command of the army on campaign.

To celebrate their new offices, the two men married into the families of their patrons. Constantius married Theodora, daughter of Maximian, and Galerius married Valeria, daughter of Diocletian. At the time of his promotion to the rank of Caesar, Constantius already had a son by a woman named Helena. The son, Constantine, then around ten years old, would soon be dispatched to Diocletian's court, where he would witness some of the most dramatic events in Roman history and learn lessons from Diocletian that he would never forget.

Appointed as Caesar to Maximian, Constantius rapidly drove Carausius's forces out of Gaul, invaded Britain,

The four tetrarchs—Diocletian and Maximian in front, Constantius and Galerius behind them—embrace, the uniformity of their clothing and pose emphasizing their physical and spiritual unity. This sculpture of the two emperors and their deputies, which dates from c. 300, would once have stood atop two columns. At some point it was removed from its original location to Constantinople, and from there it was carried to Venice in the thirteenth century, where it now stands in the facade of St. Mark's Basilica.

and brought the breakaway state back under the control of the central government. Galerius's record was initially more checkered. After years of internal turmoil, the Sasanian regime in Persia had recovered its sense of purpose under the leadership of Narses, a son of Sapor who had seized the throne in a *coup d'état* during 293 and objected strongly to Roman support for a ruler from the rival Arsacids in part of Armenia. In 297 Narses advanced across northern Mesopotamia and, after a bitterly fought campaign, defeated Galerius outside Carrhae, which now had the unique distinction of being the only city to have witnessed three major Roman defeats.

Diocletian was not impressed. He went in person to Antioch, where he made Galerius march before his chariot for more than a mile before the assembled army—a powerful statement that emperors were responsible for military failure, even if this show was for the army only. Other people in the empire may simply have had the idealized view of the new college of emperors, possibly even decked out with mythological finery, which is reflected in a contemporary poem from Egypt (this sort of language is used in other texts of the same period):

This medallion was issued to commemorate the Roman recovery of Britain in 296. The personification of London greets Constantius, who is described as the "restorer of eternal light."

> Other kings would have rushed to his aid from Italy, if Iberian Ares (a rebellion in Spain) had not restrained one [emperor] (Maximian), and the din of battle on the island of Britain had not flared up around another (Constantius). Just as one god comes from Crete, another from sea-girt Delos … the throng of Giants trembles as they put on their armor: so did the elder king (Diocletian), bringing an army of Ausonians (Italians), come east together with the younger king (Galerius).
>
> (*Select Papyri* 135)

Of more practical value was a new plan of campaign to draw Narses into the Armenian mountains, where Galerius was able to win a massive victory in 298, forcing the Persians to surrender five provinces east of the Tigris, and with them direct access to the Armenian highlands. It was perhaps the most decisive victory won by a Roman army over a foreign enemy since the time of Marcus Aurelius.

The strength of the new collegial system of government was further demonstrated, even as Galerius marched on Narses, by the fact that Diocletian and Maximian were able to devote themselves to quelling local disturbances in Egypt and Spain, while Constantius established himself at Trier to launch repeated assaults upon the Franks. It was with some justice that the propagandists of the regime trumpeted the restoration of the Roman world. It was also at this time that Diocletian turned his attention to domestic policy.

Throughout the 280s and 290s a pair of jurists, Gregorius and Hermogenianus, had tried to bring some order to the mass of Roman law. In 291 Gregorius produced a collection of the legal opinions of previous emperors that were still valid sources of law, while Hermogenianus updated the collection in 298 to include the rulings of Diocletian. The urge to set the legal record straight was but one part of a concerted effort to change the way that the reformed imperial administration dealt with its subjects. In 301 Diocletian introduced a new system of coinage, followed by an edict that fixed maximum prices for goods and services across the empire. The edict on

Fragments of Diocletian's edict on maximum prices, such as this one from the Pergamon Museum in Berlin, have been found at sites across the Eastern empire. Goods and services are organized into columns according to type, followed by their cost.

maximum prices was a failure, but, like Diocletian's other fiscal measures, represents his belief that the government could reform the conduct of the empire's subjects to make them more efficient servants of the regime.

By the end of 301 Diocletian had survived longer than any emperor since Septimius Severus, but he was also in his sixties. What would happen next? Diocletian was indicating clearly that he did not intend to die in office, having constructed a palace at Spalatum near his homeland of Salonae (in present-day Croatia) to which he intended to retire. But what of Maximian, and what of the Caesars? Constantius, who had been appointed a few weeks before Galerius, would naturally succeed to the post of Augustus that Diocletian intended to vacate, while Galerius might be expected to wait until Maximian, who had one less year in power than Diocletian, decided that it was time for him to step down. There never seems to have been a clear plan of succession, though, at some stage, Maximian's son Maxentius, who married Galerius's daughter, may have been in view. Diocletian had not seen Maximian in more than a decade, and there is no evidence that he ever met Constantius after appointing him Caesar; and neither of the Western emperors appears to have enforced the edict on maximum prices, which they may rightly have seen as deeply impractical. To complicate matters further, Galerius's wife (Diocletian's daughter) gave birth to a son: how would Diocletian's much younger grandson fit into the mix if the twenty-something children of the Western emperors were allowed to succeed?

On February 24, 303 Diocletian introduced a further strain into the relationship between East and West. On the day that he posted an edict at Nicomedia ordering all Christians to sacrifice to the traditional gods, their communal property was seized, and those who refused to recant faced the loss of civil rights and even capital punishment (see box, below right). Up until this edict—more than forty years after Gallienus had ended the persecution instituted by his father Valerian (see p. 283), and some thirty years after Aurelian had referred the resolution of a dispute among the Christians of Antioch to the bishops of Italy—the relationship between Christians and others had ceased to be a burning issue. There were Christians in the army, the court, and even in the higher education establishment at Nicomedia, where the North African rhetorician, Lactantius, may have taught Constantine. Lactantius was a curious sort of Christian in that he openly stated that the truth of Christian revelation was proved more obviously from works of traditional literature than from the Old Testament. But he was also representative of the discourse that had developed between Christian and non-Christian as the new religion had grown in the course of the third century and lost much of its earlier anti-establishment edge. Diocletian's edict brought this coexistence to an end: it fuelled the fire of Christian fundamentalism in some areas, and alienated such men as Lactantius. He later composed a grisly treatise, *On the Deaths of the Persecutors*, proclaiming that emperors who persecuted his faith had all met hideous deaths, and illustrated his point with the imagined fates of Diocletian, his colleagues, and several earlier rulers.

The rationale behind the edict, which upset long-established relationships, is difficult to fathom, but in his treatise Lactantius asserts that Galerius pushed Diocletian into action. The fact that the edict ceased to be enforced within eighteen months of its promulgation—only to be renewed with especial vigor by Galerius when he stepped into the role of Augustus—suggests that Lactantius was right in presenting it as a matter of politics more than of faith, and in suggesting that the bigotry inherent to the measure was particularly Galerian. Since Constantius seems largely to have ignored the edict, and Maximian's enforcement seems to have been less than enthusiastic, the measure highlighted differences between the Eastern and Western rulers on the eve of the journey that Diocletian planned to Rome, where he and Maximian would celebrate twenty years of shared power.

Maximian could not have been pleased to learn that, in 304, he would be celebrating this occasion, or that a year had been artificially added to his count of years as emperor. Now that they had the same number of years in power, Diocletian made it clear that he and Maximian would both retire on the same day, and that he had selected the new Caesars, one being a general named Severus, and the other Galerius's prospective son-in-law, Maximinus Daia. The principle then declared, looking back to earlier pronouncements, was that emperors made emperors. Inheritance was not to be considered a decisive factor in the succession.

Maximian and Constantius may have been enraged by Diocletian's decision but there was little they could do about it. After twenty years in which he had effectively restored Rome to a position that was every bit as dominant as it had been in the time of Severus, Diocletian's personal authority was enormous. Although not every action he took was especially wise—the edicts on maximum prices and Christian persecution are cases in point—and although the pomposity of imperial rhetoric in these years may owe something to his personal style, Diocletian possessed genuine wisdom. He was modest enough to realize that he could not govern on his own; willing to entrust great power to a man (Constantius) who was not part of his own inner circle; and consistent enough in his belief that the nature of the imperial office

PERSECUTION IN ACTION: AN OFFICIAL REPORT

Whereas you gave me orders in accordance with what was written by Aurelius Athanasius, *procurator privatae*, in virtue of a command of the most illustrious *magister privatae*, Neratius Apollonides, concerning the surrender of all the goods in the said former church and whereas I reported that the said church had neither gold nor silver nor money nor clothes nor beasts nor slaves nor lands nor property either from grants or bequests, excepting only the unworked bronze which was found and delivered to the *logistes* to be carried down to the most glorious Alexandria in accordance with what was written by our most illustrious prefect Clodius Culcianus, I also swear by the genius of our lords the emperors Diocletian and Maximian, the Augusti, and Constantius and Galerius, the most noble Caesars, that these things are so and that I have falsified nothing or may I be liable to the divine oath.

(*P Oxy.* 2673, trans. J. Rea)

needed to be changed to do what no other emperor had dared to do: he walked away. On May 1, 305 Diocletian went out to:

> a high point about three miles (five kilometers) distant from the city, on the top of which Galerius himself had assumed the purple, and there a column had been erected with an image of Jupiter. There was a procession to that place. An assembly of the soldiers was convened, in which the old man spoke, with tears in his eyes, to the soldiers. He said that he was weak, that he sought a respite from his labors, that he would hand power over to others, that he would appoint new Caesars … Then, suddenly, he proclaimed Severus and Maximinus Caesars…In plain view of everyone, Galerius, extending his hand behind him, brought Maximinus forward, and placed him, having removed his civilian garb, between himself and Diocletian.… Diocletian put his own purple cloak, which he had taken from his shoulders, on Maximinus, and was made again Diocles. Then he descended. The old king was carried through the city on a cart, and sent back to his homeland.
>
> (Lactantius, *On the Deaths of the Persecutors* 19.2–6)

At the same time, just outside Milan, Maximian conducted a similar ceremony with the new Caesar Severus, while Constantius became Augustus at Trier.

Constantine and His Empire (AD 306–37)

The Rise to Power (AD 306–12)

Even as Diocletian began the long journey to his retirement palace outside Salonae, and Maximian retired to a villa outside Rome, the succession plan began to fall apart. The reason was simple: Constantius was now senior Augustus, and he was not happy. He also saw a way to take advantage of the new administrative structures that emerged at the time of his accession to the highest office.

Although there were four courts in the time of Diocletian, the empire had not formally been divided into administrative districts, since no one would challenge Diocletian's authority over the empire as a whole. With the tensions that followed upon the succession, the empire was now split into four praetorian prefectures, with each prefect controlling three dioceses. Each of these was under the control of a *vicarius*, a title derived from the fact that he acted "in place of" (*vice*) the praetorian prefect for the purposes of day-to-day administration. Under the new system, while all prefectures were theoretically subordinate to Constantius, Galerius and his prefect administered the three dioceses that made up the Balkan provinces; Maximinus ruled the three from the Dardanelles to Egypt; Severus ruled Italy, Africa, and Spain; and Constantius held sway in Gaul and Britain. The four prefectures roughly mirrored the natural tax distribution zones of the second-century empire with one major exception: the transfer of Egypt to the Eastern administration. The inclusion of Egypt with the East rather than with Italy marks a significant diversion of resources towards Syria and the new capital district in northern Turkey. Rome still received grain from Egypt, and was still linked to the luxury trade that passed through Egypt to the Far East; but other areas had grown in importance.

The administrative joining of Egypt to the East reflects the fact that the natural economic and cultural divisions of the empire were beginning to shape the formal administrative structure, and this, in the long run, proved an important factor in the decline of the Western Roman empire.

Neither the fall of the empire in the West, however, nor the empire's permanent division—less than a century away—could have been foreseen by the members of the new college as the imperial system began to show signs of strain. Constantius demanded the return of his son Constantine, effectively a hostage in the court of Galerius. He had other children, several of them boys, but the child of his early romance evidently held a special place in his heart. Constantius now intended him to become emperor. Even if Galerius suspected the designs of his colleague, he could not refuse him. Since Maxentius, who had been in the court of Diocletian, had been returned at some point to his father Maximian and now dwelt outside Rome, there was no logical reason to keep Constantine from his father. With his son in hand by the end of 305, Constantius left to campaign in northern England. On July 25, 306 he died at York, and, evidently at his behest, the army declared Constantine emperor.

Galerius was furious, but there was nothing he could do—especially as Maxentius, inspired by developments in Britain, claimed the throne at Rome later that year. His rebellion was aided by the resentment caused by the extension of Diocletian's new system of tax registration to Italy (see p. 290) and by the fact that Maximian came out of retirement to assist him. When Severus attempted to suppress the revolt he found that the army, which had served for years under Maximian, was unreliable. Before the year's end he was imprisoned in a villa near Rome. Both factions now courted Constantine, who was recognized as Caesar by Galerius even as he contracted a formal marriage with Maximian's prepubescent daughter, Fausta. (Constantine, who already had a son by a previous marriage, evidently postponed the commencement of marital relations for the better part of a decade until Fausta could safely bear children.)

In the summer of 307 Galerius invaded Italy. Constantine remained formally neutral, which probably guaranteed the failure of the expedition. The problem was that, with the forces at his disposal, Galerius did not have enough men to lay siege to Rome, surrounded as it now was by Aurelian's massive wall. Maxentius, who plainly anticipated this turn of events, refused to engage in open battle. Faced with an impossible siege and a shortage of supplies, Galerius had to withdraw. The fact that he got out of Italy alive (in contrast to Severus, who was murdered at about this time on the orders of Maxentius) is testimony to his own force of character, and to the loyalty of the troops he had led for many years in the Balkans. It is also testimony to the fact that Diocletian's reforms had reinforced the tendency for the Roman army to divide along regional lines. The paradox of Diocletian's reforms was that, while he sought to concentrate all power in the college of emperors, he effectively created a group of central governments that could operate on their own. Diocletian's dominant personality had held the system together; in the wake of his failure to defeat Maxentius, Galerius turned again to his mentor.

Diocletian emerged from retirement in 308, making it clear that he did so to help Galerius. What would happen if he decided to take the field? Would any army fight against him? It is perhaps fortunate for all involved that Diocletian seems

This bust of Constantine, now in the Metropolitan Museum of Art in New York, was probably created in the 320s. It reveals that Constantine had abandoned the uniformity of tetrarchic imagery of Diocletian's era for a portrait that echoed earlier rulers, in this case Trajan (see p. 218).

to have abhorred civil war. During an immensely complex spring, Constantine exchanged aggressive gestures with Galerius while Maximian quarreled with Maxentius, tried to remove him from power, failed, and fled to Gaul. A meeting was summoned at Carnuntum on the Danube. While Maxentius was excluded from the conference and subsequent settlement, Galerius agreed that Constantine could call himself Augustus in the regions he controlled already, and Caesar elsewhere. This made it possible for Galerius to appoint a new Augustus, an experienced general named Licinius. With the principle of collegiate government reestablished, and with Galerius recognized as the senior member of the college, Diocletian retired once more to his palace, where he lived in peace for the three years remaining to him.

It is one of the ironies of these years that Galerius, who tried so hard to maintain Diocletian's system—even constructing a massive retirement palace of his own at Romuliana (Gamzigrad) in the Balkans—actually died a few months before his former mentor. He had, at least, managed to keep the peace between his fractious colleagues. Constantine took advantage of this time to hone his skills as a general, while Maximinus seems to have developed a profound loathing for Licinius, who had effectively been promoted over his head. Maximian lived with Constantine until 310, when he suddenly tried to seize power for himself in southern France while Constantine campaigned on the Rhine. The effort failed, and Maximian committed suicide (whether he did so with or without the active participation of his son-in-law Constantine is unclear).

As soon as Galerius died in 311, the survivors split into two factions: Maximinus allied with Maxentius, and Constantine with Licinius. The war that loomed in 312 certainly looked ominous: the two sides had roughly equivalent armies, and neither had a clear strategic advantage. The threat of Maximinus constrained Licinius from lending significant aid to Constantine, while Constantine could not help Licinius until he had dealt with Maxentius.

The Conversion of Constantine (AD 312)

The invasion of Italy was a daunting task. Maxentius's army was supported by a series of fortified cities in the north, and Rome had so far proved unassailable. It was most likely at this point that Constantine set out upon a spiritual odyssey that would transform the history of Europe.

While in Gaul Constantine had followed what by then was a traditional pattern of suggesting that he had a guardian divinity, the Sun God. This may have been more than propagandistic assertion, for Constantine seems to have been a deeply pious individual who felt that the gods should indeed talk to him. But what if they were misleading him? Galerius, he may have noted, had been devoted to the traditional gods and failed utterly. Perhaps the old gods were not strong enough: did the one god Galerius despised, the god of the Christians, have something to offer that Galerius might have missed? In the spring of 312, Constantine announced that he reposed confidence in *mens divina* (divine mind). Who was this god? Contemporary polytheistic propagandists writing immediately before and after the invasion do not tell us, and it is likely that, with an army of traditional believers behind him, Constantine did not wish to be more specific. Thus the author of a speech in 313 describes the crucial moment as follows:

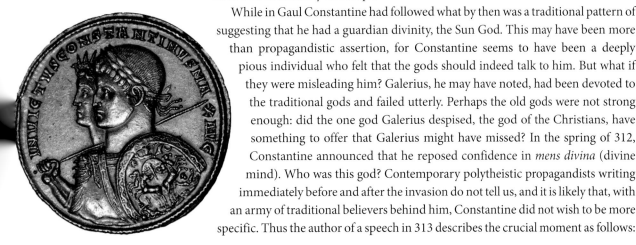

In this gold coin, minted at Ticinum in northern Italy in 315, Constantine appears alongside the sun god Sol Invictus (Invincible Sun), who is described as the emperor's companion. Such images were commonplace on coins in the decade after the emperor's conversion to Christianity.

What god, what majesty so immediate encouraged you, when almost all of your comrades and commanders were not only silently muttering but even openly fearful, to perceive on your own, against the counsels of men, against the warnings of soothsayers, that the time had come to liberate the City? You must share some secret with that Divine Mind, Constantine, which has delegated care of us to lesser gods and deigns to reveal itself to you alone.

(*Latin Panegyrics* 12.2.4–5; trans. Rodgers, minimally adapted)

It was not until many years later that Bishop Eusebius of Caesarea, the author of an influential biography of the emperor, told a very different story. He wrote:

If someone else reported it, it would perhaps not be easy to accept; but since the victorious Emperor himself told the story to the present writer a long while after, when I was privileged with his acquaintance and company, and confirmed it with oaths, who could hesitate to believe the account, especially when the time that followed provided evidence for the truth of what he said? About the time of the midday sun, when day was just turning, he said he saw with his own eyes, up in the sky and resting over the sun, a cross-shaped trophy formed from light, and a text attached to it which said, "By this conquer." Amazement at the spectacle seized both him and the whole company of soldiers which was then accompanying him on a campaign he was conducting somewhere and witnessed the miracle.

He was, he said, wondering to himself what the manifestation might mean; then, while he meditated, and thought long and hard, night overtook him. Thereupon, as he slept, the Christ of God appeared to him with the sign which had appeared to him in the sky, and urged him to make himself a copy of the sign which had appeared in the sky, and to use this as protection against the attacks of the enemy.

(Eusebius, *Life of Constantine* 1.28–29, trans. Cameron and Hall)

Peter and Paul were arguably the two men most responsible for the promulgation of Christ's teachings outside of the Jewish community in the years after the crucifixion of Jesus. By the third century, the tradition had been established that they were killed in the persecution of Christians that Nero initiated in AD 65. This fourth-century depiction is from the catacomb associated with the church of St. Ippolito in Rome.

As Eusebius of Caesarea says, the story of the vision of the sign in the sky appears perhaps to have been created by Constantine himself. At the time Constantine made it clear that his encounter with his new divine guide was a very personal one; in a letter he wrote to a council of bishops in 314 he describes the experience as follows:

> For there were of old things in me that seemed to be lacking in justice, nor did I think that the heavenly power could see those secrets that I bore within my breast. Verily what should have been allotted to these things? Plainly one abundant with all evils. But the all-powerful God who sits in the watchpost of heaven gave me what I did not deserve; truly I cannot say nor can those things be enumerated which heavenly benevolence granted to me its servant.

For a more general public, when Constantine was not discussing the favor that he enjoyed of the "Highest God" he advertised his devotion to the "Invincible Sun": the same divine power celebrated by Aurelian after his defeat of the Palmyrenes. But for Constantine there was an important twist, in that the imagery associated with the "Invincible Sun" also held a particular Christian meaning. Solar imagery had long been adopted in some Christian communities, and Christ was already equated with the sun god; some Christians understood the rising and setting of the sun as a metaphor for the resurrection, and others saw the sun as their god, facing east when they prayed. Lactantius himself would observe "the east is attached to God because he is the source of light and the illuminator of the world and he makes us rise toward eternal life (*Divine Institutes* 2.9.5)." On his way to Rome Constantine seems to have had four bishops in his entourage, which suggests that he had come to an important decision about his faith before crossing the Alps, and quite possibly that his new spiritual advisers were comfortable with his somewhat ambivalent expressions of faith. What difference did this make? We cannot know, for Constantine remains an enigmatic combination of many powerful qualities. He could be rash or patient; he had the ability to listen, and to change course when he recognized errors; while all the time reposing enormous confidence in his own judgment. He could be passionate, kind, deeply superstitious, and completely practical. He was no intellectual, but he was profoundly bright; he was capable of loving others, and of killing those who had once been closest to him. He could be subtle or utterly ruthless. He was also a great general. Although for Constantine his conversion was highly personal, involving his relationship with the god who had set him on the path to victory, the fact that he routinely advertised his debt to the Christian god (attributing his success to his piety, which encouraged others to follow the new faith) ensured that the Roman empire would also be a Christian empire. The speed with which the conversion happened—most of the empire's inhabitants were Christians before the end of the fourth century—may be connected with Constantine's willingness to allow his citizens to choose their own religious paths. He had learned from the example of Diocletian that persecution was a poor way of getting people to obey the emperor's commands.

Constantine's invasion of Italy in 312 was a brilliant military operation. Sweeping aside Maxentius's northern armies, by the early autumn he was advancing on Rome. The effect of the defeats in the north was that Maxentius could not retire behind the walls of Rome and wait for Constantine to exhaust his supplies. His reputation in tatters, he had to risk all in one final encounter. So it was that Maxentius led his army out of Rome on October 28 to a place called Saxa Rubra, north of the Tiber near the Milvian Bridge. The final battle was swift and decisive. Maxentius died in the rout. Constantine entered Rome in triumph.

Licinius (AD 313–24)

Within weeks of the victory over Maxentius, Constantine was on his way back north. Meeting Licinius at Milan, he spoke to him of the power of his new god, and cemented their alliance by giving him his half-sister, Constantia, in marriage. It was now up to Licinius to deal with Maximinus.

Maximinus crossed the Dardanelles in April 313, thereby saving Licinius the trouble of waging war in hostile territory. So thorough was Licinius's victory near the city of Adrianople (some 150 miles or 240 kilometers west of modern Istanbul) that Maximinus could mount no serious resistance when Licinius pursued him into his own territory. As Licinius closed in on his stronghold at Tarsus in southern Turkey, Maximinus, recognizing that he had no chance, committed suicide. One of his last acts had been to issue an edict declaring that the Christians in his part of the empire, against whom he had organized a rash of persecutions, could practice their religion in peace. Licinius, whose wife was a Christian, followed this with an edict of his own restoring property that had been confiscated in the persecutions. The combination of these edicts with earlier edicts of Constantine restored Christianity to the position of equality with other religions that it had enjoyed in the years after Gallienus.

Although Licinius and Constantine both believed that Christians should be given freedom to worship, there was little else upon which they seemed to agree. Although decrees of one emperor might be recognized as having the force of law in the territory of the other, the tendency was increasingly for the two to go their separate ways. Significant documents have survived, for instance, showing that Licinius's army enjoyed slightly different benefits from that of Constantine, and the bureaucracies of the Eastern and Western empires had little interchange with each other. There were now effectively two Roman empires, each consisting of six of the twelve dioceses.

Despite the effective division of the empire, neither man took a step to mark a decisive break until the wives of both emperors bore sons in 315 and 316. It was then that both emperors prepared for war. Constantine attacked in the autumn of 316, driving Licinius out of most of his territory in the Balkans, but then overreached himself, enabling Licinius to position his army across Constantine's supply lines and negotiate a treaty. Under its terms Constantine agreed to be content with the permanent acquisition of only one of the three Balkan dioceses, while recognizing three Caesars: Constantine's eldest son, Crispus, his infant son Constantine, and Licinius's infant son Licinius. The treaty was finalized on March 1, 317, and lasted for seven years.

Constantine spent much of his time after the treaty with Licinius with his army and wife (Fausta produced three more children, two daughters and a son, in these years) in the Balkans. By 324, with a household full of potential heirs, Constantine decided that it was time for Licinius to go. Declaring war in the summer, he drove Licinius out of the Balkans by the early autumn, and forced him to surrender at Nicomedia in November. Licinius was promised his life and sent into exile at Thessalonica. Shortly thereafter, Constantine "discovered" that he was at the center of a conspiracy and ordered his death.

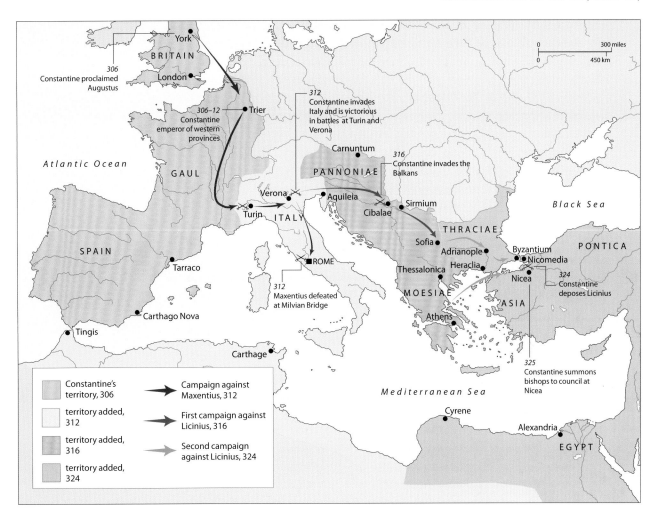

After the death of Galerius in 311, the empire was divided between Constantine, Maxentius, Licinius, and Maximinus. This map illustrates the sequence of military campaigns in which Constantine, who was unprepared to share power, defeated his rivals and unified the empire.

Constantine and the Empire (AD 324–37)

Soon after the defeat of Licinius, Constantine found that he had a problem with the Christians of the Eastern empire, who could not agree on the nature of God. The dispute divided communities between rival leaders, and sections of the empire against each other. The crux of the problem was the position taken by the bishop of Alexandria that all three members of the Christian Trinity—the Father, Son, and Holy Ghost—were of the same "essence." This view ran counter to what was by that time the more typical view, which was that the Father was superior to the Son and Holy Ghost. In Alexandria the traditional position came to be associated with the priest Arius, who drew considerable support from bishops outside Egypt.

Constantine had some experience of disputes within the Christian Church, for he had dealt with an extremely unpleasant schism in the Christian community during the great persecution of north Africa that had landed on his doorstep as soon as he defeated Maxentius. The split, stemming from a quarrel over whether it was better to humor the persecuting authorities or spark further persecution through resistance, had been complicated by disreputable behavior on both sides—the bishop favored by one faction had probably helped the persecutors under Diocletian, but the bishop who opposed him had accumulated an impressive record of fraud. The result was that when Constantine's officials arrived in north Africa to restore property seized in the persecution they found themselves confronted by groups that were essentially defined by their hatred for each other. To determine which groups had the better claim, Constantine had referred the matter to a series of church councils, all of which ruled against the party claiming that resistance to the authorities was in accord with God's will. The defeated faction—known as Donatists after Donatus, their leader in the time of Constantine—had refused to abide by the decisions of the councils, and after a brief bout of persecution Constantine had essentially washed his hands of the situation, having learned that he could not rely on third party arbitration to get Christians to stop fighting with each other. He needed to sit the two sides down with him and agree on a resolution to their differences.

Thus it was that in 325 Constantine summoned the bishops of the East to a grand council at Nicea, and there, after a show of listening, delivered a new creed laying out the nature of God. It was an important moment simply because, as had not been the case in early councils dealing with the African schism, Constantine asserted that he could propose theological solutions to the bishops, and also, thanks to the presence of some Western bishops, claim to legislate for the Christian community as a whole. The result was the so-called Nicene Creed, the first document to lay out a definition of the Trinity that all Christians were supposed to follow. The original version may be translated as follows:

> We believe in one God, Father, ruler of all, maker of all things seen and unseen; and in one Lord Jesus Christ, the Son of God, begotten from the Father as unique—being of the same essence as the Father—God from God, light from light, true God from true God, begotten not made, of the same essence with the Father, through whom all things arose—both those which are in the heavens and those that are on the earth—who, for the sake of us mortals and for our salvation came down and was made flesh, and became mortal, suffered, and rose on the third day, ascended into the heavens, and is coming to judge the living and the dead. And in the Holy Spirit. The Holy Catholic and Apostolic Church declares those to be accursed (anathema) who say that there was a time when he was not, and that "before he was begotten he did not exist," that he was made from that which did not exist and those saying that he is of another essence or substance or made liable to change or different from the Father.

(Socrates, *History of the Church* 1.8)

Even as he contemplated the nature of his God, Constantine was determined to construct a new capital in the East. Nicomedia would not do—perhaps because of its association with earlier regimes—and, after considering a number of other sites (allegedly including that of Troy), he picked the ancient city of Byzantium to be refounded as Constantinople. The design of the new capital was to mirror Constantine's own attitudes towards both government and religion. The bulk of the new construction program was centered on the palace, with a massive new circus attached so that the emperor could meet his people. There is no record that temples constructed in earlier years were shut, but a massive new church was constructed at the emperor's behest. Christianity was visibly presented as a faith that could supplement and enhance the regime without necessarily requiring repudiation of the

A CITY RESTORED

The inhabitants of Orcistus, which is already a city and a state, have offered us the material for our munificence, most dear and beloved Abablius. To those who desire either to found new cities, or to enhance those that have existed for a long time or to repair those which are on the point of death, that which is sought is most acceptable. They say that their village flourished with the splendor of a city in earlier times, and that it was decorated by the fasces of annual magistrates … It is unworthy of our age that so splendid a place should lose the name of city, and it is prejudicial to those who live there that they should lose all of their benefits and advantages through the ravages of a more powerful people. To all of these considerations, there may be added as a sort of pinnacle that all who live there are said to be followers of the most sacred religion.

(*Select Latin Inscriptions* no. 6091)

old ways. Constantine's method of moving forward while also looking firmly at tradition is also evident in the way that he decided to populate his new city. He did not force people to come to the city, but rather rewarded those who chose to move; he did not create a new senate that might offend the old one in Rome, but rather rewarded senior officials who chose to establish a new domicile in his capital with various privileges. He could create a new world without destroying the old, because the new world was not about Rome: it was about Constantine.

In some ways the most revealing statement of Constantine's method of linking tradition with novelty is revealed in a letter sent to an imperial official, which explains that the emperor has decided to grant civic status to a place called Orcistus in north-central Turkey (see box, left). The point is that Orcistus would have achieved its desire of having its status as a city restored for traditional reasons—that it had all the amenities that cities had—and it is just chance that it is also filled with Christians. That makes the decision easier, but in no way alters the fact that the decision is based on old-fashioned principles. In Constantine's world, radical change had to be made by asserting respect for the past.

What might be true of the new religion or a town in Turkey was no less true of the new capital, whose foundation was presented as a peaceable gesture rather than openly offensive. Nonetheless, the development of the new city raised questions about how the Western empire would now be run. Would Constantine remain in the East? What would be the status of his son Crispus, who had distinguished himself during the war with Licinius, and returned to Trier? We will never be able to explain what happened next, but by the end of 326 Crispus had been arrested, tried for treason, and executed. Fausta appears to have been sent into internal exile where she died within a couple of years. A later pagan writer created a lurid story of how Fausta had lusted after her stepson, and when he refused her advances, claimed that he had attempted to rape her, causing his execution; her plot was then exposed by the emperor's mother, causing an enraged Constantine to lock her in an overheated bath house until she died. Nothing in this story seems to be true: its existence merely illustrates the mystery that ever after shrouded the tragic events of 326. A likely explanation, which takes account of the fact that other sources report a series of executions accompanying that of Crispus, is that there had been a major split over the direction that the regime should take. Constantine seems to have interpreted the split as potentially treasonous and acted accordingly. That he may have regretted what happened is perhaps revealed by the fact that he never remarried, while turning to his mother to play the role of empress.

In the wake of the trauma of 326 the aged Helena was sent on a grand tour of the East, where she visited Palestine and was present as a massive new program of church building was undertaken in the Holy Land. Her participation in these events gave rise to the legend that she found the fragments of the cross upon which Jesus had been executed at Jerusalem. In truth, however, what her time in Palestine seems to reveal is that Constantine was willing to commit serious resources to celebrating the traditions of his new faith only where they did not overtly conflict with important survivals of polytheist tradition. For Constantine religion should help unite rather than divide the empire.

Constantine may have sensed that the empire required some force that could create a shared community in the face of the ever-deepening divisions that were

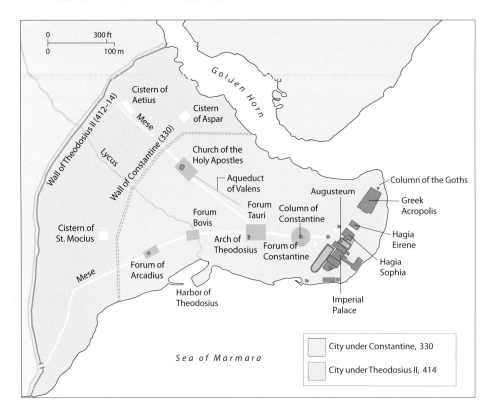

Constantinople, or Byzantium as it was previously known, was already an ancient city when Constantine adopted it as his capital. The emperor had a wall built to make the city more defensible, and oversaw the construction of forums and public buildings that reshaped the urban landscape in a manner appropriate for a Roman city. Many of the churches and the imperial palace depicted in this map were built or completed under Constantius I.

imposed by the government itself. As the central government asserted more control over local affairs—an inevitable consequence of Diocletian's policy of smaller, more numerous provinces—each region had less freedom to define its own relationship to the center. On the other hand, the more extensive government structures had the effect of enhancing the tendency of regional bureaucracies to function on their own. Constantine's administrative divisions varied over time: it seems that he often used five praetorian prefects in the decade after his defeat of Licinius: one based at Trier, another in Italy, a third in Africa, the fourth and fifth in the Balkans and the East respectively. His army was now firmly divided between frontier units, the *limitanei*; and units attached to mobile reserve formations, the *comitatenses*, a system begun by Diocletian. In addition to this functional division, the army was also divided into three main commands—the West, the Balkans, and the East—with each front under its own *magister peditum* (master of infantry) and *magister equitum* (master of cavalry). The different portions of the army, like the different bureaucracies, were increasingly regional in character: the Western sector was recruited heavily from Franks and Alamanni, the Balkan army increasingly included large numbers of Goths, while that of the East was recruited from the upland zones of the southern part of Turkey, Syria, and Armenia.

In the late 330s, as Constantinople grew into a great city around him, Constantine began to face up to the fact that he needed a succession plan. He still had three sons and two daughters by Fausta, and a number of nephews, the children of his half-brothers and sisters. Although he had spent much of his adult life eliminating rivals, Constantine seems to have felt that there was no obvious reason that the empire should have a single emperor, and even looked outside his immediate family to complete a new ruling group. In 335 he elevated his nephew Dalmatius to a position as Caesar equal to that of his own sons. He made another nephew, Hannibalianus, "King of Armenia," with the evident intent that he should rule a fifth prefecture as soon as it could be acquired. At the same time the number of domestic praetorian prefects seems to have been reduced to four, one for each of his intended heirs (with Italy and Africa combined under one prefect). The new fifth prefecture was to be in Iraq, and in 337 Constantine planned a massive invasion to take this region finally under Roman control. It would never happen. In the spring of 337 he fell gravely ill, and on May 22, after allowing himself to be baptized, he died. His body was taken to Constantinople, where it was interred in the great mausoleum that he had built for himself in his new city. Although he died a Christian, he intended to be buried an emperor. It was only later that his son, Constantius, transformed the mausoleum into the Church of the Holy Apostles. It was one of many signs that he misunderstood the importance of Constantine's belief that one could be both an emperor and a Christian, rather than simply a Christian emperor.

The Struggle for Control (AD 337–410)

Constantius II and Julian (AD 337–63)

At the end of a life spent unifying the empire, Constantine plainly felt that the empire could be divided up into prefectures and run by a college of emperors. The major difference between his scheme and Diocletian's was that Constantine's college consisted of blood relatives, while the Diocletianic system had ultimately stressed experience supported by marriage. Why did these two men feel that the Roman empire should have a collegiate government? Their feeling that it needed more than one emperor was accompanied by the strongly held belief, as evidenced by their own conduct, that the empire need not, and should not, be governed from Rome. It was the feeling that the empire could have capitals other than Rome that most sharply distinguished the shared governance schemes of the fourth century from those of earlier periods.

Although Constantine's plan for the succession recognized fundamental truths about the nature of the imperial government, it failed to account adequately for certain fundamental aspects of the human condition. These include emotions, such as hatred and jealousy, both of which Constantine's second surviving son, Constantius, possessed in ample quantity. To these feelings may be added considerable viciousness and fanaticism. The conduct of Constantius, followed by that of his equally objectionable cousin, Julian, had a profound influence on the development of the government in the second half of the fourth century. Once Julian was gone, senior imperial bureaucrats strove to ensure that their emperors would be more manageable.

Immediately after his father's death, Constantius began to dismantle his arrangements, while all the time offering public displays of devotion to the deceased. Six months passed with no formal announcement of the succession until, suddenly, Dalmatius was denounced as the murderer of Constantine. He was executed along with all other male members of the extended family save only Constantius's brothers Constantine II and Constans— now Augusti in their zones of the empire—and his two young cousins, Gallus and

Constantius II, the second son of Constantine and Fausta, is shown in this gold medallion. A devout Christian and a master of bureaucratic infighting, he became sole emperor in 353 after defeating the usurper Magnentius at the battle of Mursa Major.

Julian, who were sent to live in Nicomedia under the care of Bishop Eusebius (no relation to Eusebius of Caesarea).

Constantius may have acted without the full knowledge or agreement of his brothers (we will never know the truth here), for it seems that he very rapidly had to negotiate a settlement with them, according to which Constantine II was allowed to assert some sort of supremacy over Constans, who was still a minor. Constantius himself had a major problem on his hands, in that Constantine had started a war with Persia just before his death, and the Persian king Sapor II had now taken the initiative by attacking the Roman frontier. One result of the tripartite division of the empire was that Constantius could not now call upon obviously greater resources than the Persian king unless Constans and Constantine II chose to assist him. Constantine decided to do so, in part, it seems, as a way of asserting his superiority over the court of Constans by marching through his brother's territory. He never reached the end of the march, falling victim to an ambush or "hunting accident" (again certainty is impossible) that resulted in his death and the takeover of his portion of the empire by Constans, whose relationship with Constantius thereafter ranged from chilly to moderately hostile.

One of the major differences between Constantius and Constans was the degree of control that they tried to assert in matters of religion. Constans seems to have been quite interested in maintaining peace not only among Christians but also, as far as possible, between Christians and traditional believers. Constantius, however, summoned great councils of bishops throughout his reign to revise the Nicene Creed. One purpose of these councils, a purpose that followed in a long tradition of church councils dating at least to the second century, was to enforce church discipline by removing recalcitrant bishops from their sees. Under Constantius, the bishop who was most often affected by these changes was Athanasius of Alexandria, who was repeatedly expelled and recalled in the course of the reign. Athanasius tended, in his voluminous writings, to portray his treatment as the result of a vast conspiracy among the followers of the Alexandrian priest Arius, engineered first by Eusebius of Nicomedia (who had once supported Arius, but long since recanted) and later by Constantius (who was certainly no Arian). The issue at stake seems actually to have been control. Constantius was deeply interested in having "his people" in charge of one of the major cities of the East. In summoning these councils Constantius appears to have set a fashion—one that never became established in the West—whereby the emperor routinely summoned bishops to grand councils that he might himself address. The importance of such councils, even if they rarely (or never) resulted in complete agreement, cannot be overstated, simply because they created an avenue of communication between the emperor and his subjects that was independent of the bureaucracy.

Although relations between Constans and Constantius were never close, and Constantius never received the help that he needed against the Persians, their reign as co-emperors was nevertheless better than having the Western two-thirds of the empire ruled by someone from outside the family. Yet that is what happened after January 18, 350, when a senior officer in the army of Gaul, Magnentius, appeared at a dinner party in the garb of an emperor and ordered his agents to assassinate Constans, who was then on a hunting expedition (which they duly did). The immediate cause of the rebellion seems simply to have been that Constans made minimal effort to reconcile the military and bureaucratic establishment centered around Trier to his control. He spent almost all of his reign in the Balkans or Italy. In response to the rebellion of Magnentius, the Balkan bureaucracy and army put up an emperor of its own, one Vetranio, while members of the house of Constantine attempted to set up Nepotianus, a member of the family, as emperor in Rome (an effort that ended in a bloody failure). In 351 Constantius, now free of war with Persia, invaded the West, and received the surrender of Vetranio in a well-staged public meeting between the field armies of the East and the Balkans before moving West to take on Magnentius. As he did so he appointed his cousin, Gallus, as Caesar in the East. The primary purpose of this appointment appears to have been to have someone to show the banner of the dynasty in Antioch while Constantius was detained for some as yet indeterminate time in the West.

In 351, commanding the combined forces of the Eastern and Balkan armies, Constantius crushed Magnentius's army in a bloody battle near the city of Mursa, in present-day Serbia. (This is only a few miles from Cibalae, the site of Constantine's victory over Licinius. Both cities are in the area of Sirmium: battles had a tendency to occur near major transit centers.) Two years later Constantius ended the rebellion at a battle in central Gaul, at which point he began to exact a bloody revenge from the Western bureaucracy. This is the point at which the narrative history of Ammianus Marcellinus picks up, and it is through his pages that we can feel the intense resentment of imperial bureaucrats towards Constantius's regime. For instance, Ammianus deplored the dispatch to Britain of an official named Paul (whom he calls "the Chain") who extracted information from supporters of Magnentius through torture. It is clear that Ammianus's primary loyalty was to his own chief, an officer named Ursicinus, who, if Ammianus is to be believed, was a genius of the first rank. A later rebel against Constantius, the general Silvanus, whom Ammianus and Ursicinus were sent to murder, seems to have had the same sentiments toward Constantius: as Ammianus relates, Silvanus was duped because he felt that Ursicinus would agree with the view that:

> unworthy men were raised to the consulship and high offices while
> he and Ursicinus alone, having toiled through many and constant
> tasks, were despised, and that he had been cruelly harassed though
> the interrogation of his friends in a disreputable controversy, and
> summoned to a trial for treason, while he had been dragged from the
> east by the hatred of his enemies.

(Ammianus Marcellinus, *History* 15.5.6)

It does seem that Constantius controlled the bureaucracy through the use of informers, specialized in setting one branch of government against another, and, quite literally, tortured officials he did not trust—he also sent Paul "the Chain" to torture potential supporters of Silvanus (it is a pity that Ammianus does not tell us how he got their names). Just before Silvanus's revolt unfolded in the West, Constantius had to resolve conflicts in the East that were stimulated by his cousin Gallus: the latter was attempting to assert authority as Caesar that he did not have, since Constantius appears to have arranged that no senior official actually reported to him. Gallus was removed from office and executed in 354 in the very same place, Pola, where Crispus had met his end.

The execution of Gallus left Constantius with the question of how he was to govern the entire empire on his own. Again he chose to appoint a Caesar as a sort of figurehead. His choice this time was limited to his one surviving male cousin, Julian. A secret convert from the Christianity in which he had been raised to the worship of the gods, Julian had no intention of becoming another Gallus. Instead he seems to have come to visualize himself as a sort of Constantine in reverse, who would emerge from the Western provinces and spread the worship of the gods back across the empire. In order to accomplish this he would have to master the art of bureaucratic infighting. This he did by separating himself from the center of government at Trier and, in the course of the next couple of years, bombarding Constantius with news of a succession of military victories—of which the one over the Alamanni at Strasbourg in 357 was genuinely impressive—and complaints about the incompetence of senior officials. The result was that he was able to acquire actual power for himself, and by 359 had become the dominant political force in Gaul. At this point Constantius, who had spent much time in the previous few years on campaign along the Danube and bullying Western bishops to adopt his most recent views on appropriate Christian doctrine, seems to have become suspicious. He also suddenly had to confront a new Persian war, which broke upon his frontiers when Sapor II captured the fortress city of Amida.

Early depictions of Julian, from the period when he was Caesar, show a clean-shaven young man. As this coin reveals, Julian changed his image after he rebelled against Constantius, defiantly adopting a beard in the style of a philosopher.

If he was to have greater success against Sapor than he had enjoyed in the past, Constantius needed more men, and this meant taking troops from Julian. Perhaps in preparation for what he recognized might be an unpopular action, or because some rumor had reached him that Julian was already plotting rebellion (we know from Julian's letters that he was), Constantius began changing Julian's senior staff, and in February or March 360 he ordered him to send several legions to the East. Julian, whose habitual avoidance of Trier had taken him to Paris that winter, somehow arranged for several legions that had no obvious reason to be anywhere near Paris to pass through the city, mutiny, and proclaim him emperor.

Julian maintained an uneasy truce with Constantius throughout the next year, offering to use the title Augustus only in Gaul, while maintaining his position as Caesar elsewhere in the empire (an obvious echoing of Constantine's position after the council at Carnuntum in 308). There was not much that Constantius, still confronting Sapor, could do but deny the request. In the late summer of 361 Julian began a brilliantly conceived invasion of the Balkans, reaching Sirmium without a fight. On November 3, just as he was preparing to march against his cousin, Constantius died in southern Turkey.

Julian rejoiced not just at the news of his cousin's death, but at the fact that he could now worship the gods as he pleased: a view he expressed in a letter to his spiritual guru, a philosopher named Maximus (see box, right). The oddity of this letter lies not so much in the joy that Julian took in the ability to worship the gods, as in the fact that its recipient, Maximus, subscribed to a particular brand of philosophy known as theurgy. Literally "god-working," its core belief was that spiritual union with the gods could be attained by discovering their mystic names, which the gods could be compelled to reveal through oracles. Maximus's brand of polytheism held

JULIAN REJOICES

As you see, I pass over many great events, that you may know most of all, how, all at once, I have perceived the presence of the gods…. I worship the gods openly, and the great part of the army that follows me is full of piety. I sacrifice oxen in public; we have given thanks to the gods with numerous hecatombs. The gods command me to purify everything that I can, and I obey them with zeal. They say that they will give me great rewards if I am not remiss.

(Julian, *Letters* 26 [Bidez edition], 415a–d)

that animal sacrifice was useless. In his enthusiasm, Julian combined a variety of different traditions to such a degree that he put himself well outside the mainstream of contemporary pagan belief. It is this that may help explain why, as he tried to restore the worship of the gods—reopening temples and appointing provincial priests to oversee the renewed cults—he found that his reception by pagans was at best lukewarm.

As far as Christians went, contemporary evidence for the response to Julian is somewhat harder to gauge. He did not openly engage in persecution, preferring to cause distress by ordering the restoration of bishops whom Constantius had exiled for doctrinal nonconformity. He took direct action against Christian groups or individuals only when they did something to offend him—as Athanasius did when he oversaw the conversion of several rich Alexandrian women shortly after his own restoration to Alexandria—or engaged in acts of violence against each other in the wake of the return of exiles. His single most offensive action, which affronted the pagan Ammianus as much as it did Christians, was to forbid Christians from teaching Classical rhetoric, on the grounds that they could not teach such traditional texts as Homer if they did not believe in the gods they portrayed.

Perhaps more serious than his religious policy was the fact that he mixed badly with society. This was particularly noticeable to subjects who got to see him for a prolonged period of time, as did the people of Antioch from the summer of 362 through the spring of 363. Personal asceticism as a form of religious observation had become increasingly common in the course of the fourth century even among members of the upper classes. But Julian, who wore a beard so as to look like a philosopher, seems to have carried his version of this to an extreme and to have advertised his personal lack of interest in the common entertainments of his people, such as chariot racing. This, combined with his botched handling of a grain shortage around the city (possibly exacerbated by the presence of his army), his violent response to the accidental destruction of a famous temple, and his disrespect for a local martyr—whose bones he ordered to be moved from their resting place because he apparently thought they were interfering with an oracular site he was trying to restore—managed thoroughly to alienate the populace of the city. Julian responded to the expression of their hatred with one of the most remarkable documents ever issued by a Roman emperor, a satire on himself entitled the *Beard Hater*. In it he wrote that it was the fault of the people of Antioch that they could not understand his virtues, saying that:

> No, my temperament does not allow me to look wanton, casting my
> eyes in all directions in order that in your sight I may appear beautiful,
> not indeed in soul but in face. For, in your judgment, true beauty of soul
> consists in wanton life.
>
> (*Beard Hater* 351a, trans. Wright [Loeb edition])

In addition to the people of Antioch, Julian also seems to have alienated powerful groups within the bureaucracy. Immediately after his occupation of Constantinople at the end of 361, he ordered trials of some of Constantius's leading officials (all of which resulted in death sentences); and while many might agree that Paul "the Chain" was no loss, there were a number of others whom Ammianus thought were treated unjustly. Beyond this, Julian's appointees to various offices raised questions in people's minds. A contemporary orator says that he employed his prophetic powers to make these appointments, with the result that people who were expected to get them did not. Another way of seeing this is that people were not getting the promotions that they expected.

It was therefore against a background of considerable tension that Julian launched his attack on Persia in the spring of 363. Having at his disposal the army that he had brought with him from the West as well as the army of the East, he attempted to deceive Sapor by launching a diversionary campaign in northern Mesopotamia while he led a strike directly at Ctesiphon. Accompanied as he was by a Persian prince, it appears that the point of the campaign was to force some sort of "regime change." But he had not brought adequate siege equipment, so there was nothing Julian could do when he arrived in front of Ctesiphon and found that the Persians were unwilling to negotiate and that, as they had flooded the area behind him, he would have to withdraw up the valley of the Tigris. Through sheer force of personality Julian managed to hold his increasingly bedraggled and hungry army together as the main Persian army began to launch attacks designed to delay the retreat. Finally, however, on the morning of June 26, he was mortally wounded while trying to rally his men against an attack (see box, right). After a difficult council of war the general staff chose a relatively junior officer by the name of Jovian to succeed him, and to negotiate an end to the campaign. Jovian duly negotiated terms for the Roman withdrawal, which involved the surrender of all the territory that Diocletian had won from the Persians, together with the fortress city of Nisibis, which had resisted several attacks by Sapor in Constantius's time. Reflecting on his sight of Julian's body as it passed by Nisibis, the Christian deacon Ephraim wrote:

> A wonder! By chance the corpse of the accursed one,
> Crossing over towards the rampart met me near the city!
> And the Magus took and fastened on a tower
> The standard sent from the east,
> So that this standard-bearer would declare to the onlookers
> That the city was slave to the lords of that standard.
> Glory to the One Who wrapped the corpse in shame!
> I wondered, "Who indeed set a time for meeting
>   When corpse and standard-bearer both at one moment were
>   present?"
> I knew it was a prearrangement, a miracle of justice
> That when the corpse of the fallen one crossed over,
> The fearful standard went up and was put in place to proclaim
> That the evil of his conjurors had surrendered that city.
> For thirty years Persia had made battle in every way
> But was unable to cross over the boundary of that city;
> Even when it had been broken and collapsed, the cross
> came down and saved it.
> There I saw a disgraceful sight:
> The standard of the captor set up on the tower,
> The corpse of the persecutor laid in a coffin.

(Hymns against Julian 3.1–3, trans. McVey)

THE DEATH OF JULIAN, 363

The Persians, joined by some Saracen allies carrying lances, attacked him; one of them stuck a spear into Julian, striking him in the thigh near the groin; when the spear was drawn out it was accompanied by dung and blood. One of the emperor's bodyguards killed the Saracen and cut off his head; the members of his household, placing the mortally wounded Julian on shields, carried him to a tent. So sudden and unexpected was the blow, that many, being at a loss to know whence it came, thought that it came from his household. But the wretched Julian, taking the blood that flowed from his wounds in his hands, raised it to the sun saying "Take your fill," and called the other gods evil and destroyers. The Lydian Oribasius, the best of doctors, was with him from Sardis, but the wound defied all medical art for three days and carried Julian away from life.

(Philostorgius, *Church History* 7.15)

(Above) This gold coin, minted at Trier, shows co-emperors Valentinian and Valens seated on the same throne and holding a globe between them. This idealized vision of an united empire and a jointly held world was belied by events.

(Below) The emperor Gratian is depicted in this fourth-century medallion from Hungary, now in the Museum of Art History in Vienna.

Bureaucratic Backlash and Barbarian Invasion (AD 363–95)

The end of Julian's reign was a total catastrophe. With the disaster came a conscious decision on the part of senior officials that the next emperor should not be able to dominate the bureaucracy as Constantius and Julian had done. When Jovian died on February 17, 364, allegedly of asphyxiation from a coal fire in his bedroom, the leaders of the army met to choose his successor. As Ammianus tells it, they summoned the new ruler of the world, Valentinian, to come swiftly so that he could take up the job; while all this happened, "for ten days no one held the helm of state" (Ammianus Marcellinus, *History* 26.1.4–5).

The fact that the new emperor should be "summoned" to take up office reflects a profound alteration in the nature of imperial power. True, Diocletian had been a relatively junior guard officer at the time that he was placed on the throne, but he gained rapidly in stature, as he won the throne of the empire as a whole for himself in battle. There would be no such defining moment for Valentinian, or his brother Valens, whom he insisted on making his co-emperor. Valentinian went to Western Europe and Valens remained in the East. The empire was split into three prefectures, with Valentinian retaining control over the Western two, which included Gaul, Britain, and Spain in one, and Africa, Italy, and Illyricum in the other; Valens held the East in a vast semi-circle that extended from Thrace to Egypt.

Valentinian reigned until 375, rarely moving from his capital at Trier. He devoted a great deal of his energy to the security of the frontier, where monuments to his reign survive in the form of the forts he built to supplement the earlier Diocletianic and Constantinian defenses in the area. On November 17, 375 he died after falling into what appears to have been an apoplectic fit after hearing an embassy from the Germanic Quadi tribe: they had offended him the previous year by launching a raid that had nearly captured his future daughter-in-law while she was travelling from Constantinople to meet her new husband. This daughter-in-law was Constantia, the one surviving child of Constantius II, who had been an infant when her father died. Valens survived a serious rebellion at Constantinople led by Procopius, a distant (and Christian) cousin of Julian whom Julian had allegedly marked for the succession if he did not return from Persia. The revolt of Procopius lasted from the autumn of 365 into the early months of 366, after which Valens reigned without significant opposition or accomplishment until August 9, 378, when he died in battle at Adrianople against a Gothic army.

Valentinian was succeeded by his two sons, Gratian and Valentinian II. The latter's succession—as a young boy—was engineered by a group of officials who dominated the axis running from Africa through Italy to Illyricum, without, it appears, permission from either Gratian or Valens. In 379 Gratian agreed to the accession of Theodosius as emperor over the portion of the empire that Valens had ruled. Theodosius was the son of one of Valentinian I's generals who had been executed as a result of a palace intrigue just after Gratian acceded to the throne. He outlasted both Gratian and Valentinian II. The former was murdered during a military revolt in Gaul during 383; and Valentinian committed suicide when he could not enforce his authority over the officials with whom Theodosius surrounded him in 392, after he had "restored" Valentinian to the throne from which he had

been driven by a rebellious general named Magnus Maximus. Theodosius defeated his former associates in 394 and died a few months later on January 17, 395. He left the throne to his sons, Honorius and Arcadius. Theodosius was the last man ever to claim control over the entire empire while it still had something like the borders it had had in the time of Septimius Severus two hundred years earlier.

The fate of Valentinian II underscores one of the major developments of the period after Julian: the increasing loss of authority of the emperor, as opposed to that of the members of the administrative staff. It was often the case that, where Constantius might have been able to control a situation by manipulating or intimidating subordinates, the emperors in these years had to acquiesce in decisions made by others. The pages of Ammianus abound with instances that make it clear that Valentinian I and Valens had only the most tenuous control over their senior officials. Perhaps the two most striking instances that illuminate the lack of control involve the succession. In 369, when Valentinian I fell seriously ill:

> Julianus Rusticus, head of the secretariat charged with foreign affairs, was promoted for the imperial power by the Gauls who were with the court, a man who was, as if smitten by a blast of madness, eager for human blood, as he showed when he ruled Africa as governor (in 371–73). For as prefect of the city, in which office he died (in 387), fearful of the dubious circumstance of the tyrant, by whose choice he had

In this panel from an obelisk, which still stands in Istanbul, the emperor Theodosius is shown holding a wreath with which to reward a victorious charioteer. He is surrounded by courtiers and family, including his sons, Arcadius and Honorius, by his sides.

ascended that height, through a lack of better men, he was compelled to seem mild and softer. There strove, against these men, some with higher goals who favored Severus, then commander of the infantry, as a man fitted for the rank, since, although strict and feared, he was nonetheless more tolerable and preferable in every way to the man mentioned earlier.

(Ammianus Marcellinus, *History* 27.6.1–3)

When Valentinian I recovered, he immediately made Gratian his co-emperor, but the men who had been openly mentioned as potential heirs continued with distinguished careers—in Julianus's case, as Ammianus shows, in the civil administration, while Severus finished his career as commander-in-chief of the Western armies.

Similarly, when Valentinian I died it was a different group of officials who joined with his then wife, Justina, to place Valentinian II on the throne. The prime mover in this case was an official named Merobaudes, whose power was such that he not only survived this adventure, but also played a role in the overthrow of Gratian. A close associate of Merobaudes, the immensely wealthy senator Petronius Probus, also wielded effective power that an emperor might challenge with only the greatest reluctance. As such he was the subject of one of Ammianus's most memorable pen portraits:

> Like a type of fish expelled from its element that can no long breathe on land, thus did he wither away from prefectures, which he was driven to seek by the complaints of his vast family, on account of immense greed that was never free from guilt, so that they could accomplish much evil with impunity: although he was fortified by magnanimity so that he never, himself, ordered a client or slave to do something illegal, if he learned that any of them did something illegal, he would defend them, resisting Justice herself, without investigation of the matter, and without regard for right and honor.

(Ammianus Marcellinus, *History* 27.11.4)

As praetorian prefect of Illyricum, Probus was linked not only with the group that put Valentinian II on the throne but also with a scandal of spectacular proportions that gripped north Africa for many years. In this case, Romanus, the military commander in the area of modern Libya, was summoned to the aid of the city of Lepcis, which was being attacked by local nomadic tribesmen. After remaining in the city for forty days, demanding that he be provided with 4,000 camels, he departed without taking action against the raiders on the grounds that he had not gotten his camels. When the people of Lepcis tried to protest, Romanus exploited connections at court to insure that no action was taken, and that the plaintiffs were condemned to death even as the nomads renewed their raids. It was only when Theodosius's father, sent to north Africa to deal with another issue, began to intervene in this business that Romanus was charged with treason and executed.

In the East, too, officials seemed to be gaining increasing control in determining the succession. The situation in the East differed from that in the West chiefly because Valens had no son, a fact that was intimately linked with a bizarre and bloody event that took place in 371. In this case, a group of officials consulted a peculiar prophetic device—roughly an ancient version of a ouija board—to determine who the next emperor would be. The device offered the Greek letters theta, epsilon, omicron, and delta as the first four letters of the name of the next ruler, and the consultants decided that this indicated an official named Theodorus. It was an interesting choice, for Theodorus was a Gaul, and, according to Ammianus, once Theodorus was told of this fact he decided to share it with Valens. Before that could happen, the praetorian prefect, Modestus, who wished to secure the succession for an Easterner, launched an investigation of treasonous magical practices, leading to numerous brutal executions of senior officials (see box, right). Since Valens had no son yet, the succession issue was left open; but the point was made that the matter was not entirely his to decide.

The accession of Theodosius was likewise a matter of local initiative. Although Gratian appointed him to a command in the East, it does not seem that Gratian intended to make him an emperor. Theodosius apparently took this step himself when he managed to defeat some Goths, and felt secure enough to do so because he knew that he had support within the military establishment. He did not yet have support within the Eastern establishment, however: it is notable that he resided at Thessalonica for more than a year before going to Constantinople, moving on to the capital only after further victories had enhanced his prestige.

When Theodosius did arrive at his capital, observers noted that he too was surrounded by a close-knit group of officials. A charitable view of the situation describes it as follows:

> Since with equal kindness you wished to confer honors on more people
> than the number of places allowed, and since your means were more
> limited than your desires, and your power, however extensive, could
> not match your intentions, you consoled with your esteem whomever
> you had not yet promoted to some rank or other.… And so all who in
> your Principate have justly had confidence in themselves have either
> advanced in rank or found compensation in your kindly regard.
>
> (*Latin Panegyrics* 2. [12] 20.1–2, trans. Nixon)

A less charitable view (also in our extant sources) was that the state was for sale. Perhaps more significantly, although he was victorious in two civil wars, there is no evidence that Theodosius engaged in large-scale reprisals against the supporters of rival regimes. Some, as Ammianus suggested in his portrait of Julianus Rusticus (see pp. 312–13), might have deliberately steered clear of active service; more often, however, it seems that senior officials agreed to deal with whomever was in power and were ready to apologize profoundly when they picked the wrong side. The emperor was supposed to accept these apologies, as he was when things went badly wrong elsewhere. One notable case occurred at Antioch in 387 when a riotous crowd tore down statues of the emperor (an overtly treasonous act). After much negotiation, the city was forgiven. Three years later, Theodosius broke the rules when he ordered a massacre of the population at Thessalonica, where a mob had murdered one of his inner circle. After that, he allowed the powerful bishop Ambrose of Milan (who owed his see to the patronage of Petronius Probus) to publicly deny him communion while he was residing in the city after the defeat of Maximus. More notably, perhaps, he issued an edict stating that:

THE SUCCESSION OF THEODORUS, 371

To put it briefly, we all crept about as if in Cimmerian darkness, feeling fear equal to that of those at the banquets of the Sicilian Dionysius, who, when filled by banquets sadder than any hunger, shuddered to see swords hanging by mere horsehairs from the rafters of the rooms in which they reclined.

(Ammianus Marcellinus, *History*, 29.2)

If, in considering a particular case, we order a more severe penalty to
be inflicted upon someone than is our custom, we do not wish those
persons to suffer the punishment or receive the sentence immediately,
but for thirty days his fate and fortune with reference to his status will be
in suspense.

(*Theodosian Code* 9.40.13)

While bureaucrats might connive in the destruction of one another, the
emperor needed to be very careful. Valentinian I and Valens owed a great deal
of their unpopularity to their willingness to surrender to factional interests and
execute senior officials on the losing side of a dispute. Theodosius was far more
circumspect, as, perhaps, behooved a man whose own father had been a victim of
precisely this sort of infighting. Yet neither Valentinian nor Theodosius were truly
in command as emperor.

This weakening of control by the emperors and the increased power of administrative staff became even plainer after Theodosius's death, during the reigns of his
sons Arcadius and Honorius, both of whom were quite young when they took their
respective thrones. The situation they faced was compounded by another key factor
in this period: the progressive weakening of the army in relation to its enemies.
The imperial army was now in very poor shape. Ammianus, for one, was clearly
scared of the Persians, and does not seem to have thought that the imperial army
was categorically better than that of his foes. Similarly in the West, while there were
more victories over the tribes north of the Rhine and Danube, there were also more
defeats on many smaller fields, making it obvious that victory would not lie automatically with Roman forces.

Arcadius was only seventeen when, in 395, he succeeded his father as ruler of the Eastern portion of the empire. This bust, now in the Agora Museum at Athens, emphasizes the emperor's youth. Dominated by his courtiers, Arcadius had little influence over affairs. He died in 408 after falling from his horse.

The weakening of the imperial military regime took place as major changes
were occurring north of the frontier in central Europe. The key actors at this
time were the Goths and the Huns. At this point, the Goths had divided into two
main groups: the Tervingi, who occupied the region around the Dniester river,
and the Greuthingi, who held the lands bordering the Danube. The Goths had
developed a reasonably consistent relationship with Rome that involved less
long-distance raiding into the empire, more Goths taking service in the Roman
army, and an effort at Christianization launched by Constantine. The principal agent of conversion had been a priest named Ulfilas, who had translated
Christian scripture into Gothic and won some converts whose relationship
with their fellow tribesmen alternated between the hostile and the compatible:
one advantage was that the Goths could use Christian priests to open lines of
communication that might otherwise have remained closed.

It was the Huns who upset that status quo. The Huns were a semi-nomadic
people of the Eurasian steppe who, despite Roman accounts that suggest that
they appeared out of nowhere in the 370s, had probably existed in some sort
of mutually beneficial relationship with the Goths in the area of what is now
Ukraine. We cannot at this point know why that relationship changed, but it
is clear that the Huns began to raid the Tervingi with particular success in the
years before 376. This success was due to their adoption of a particularly powerful bow that enabled them to take down their opponents at such a great distance
that traditional Gothic tactics, which relied on spear-armed cavalry, were

ineffective. Several defeats threw the Tervingi into political chaos, leading a substantial number to leave their lands and seek refuge amongst the Greuthingi, who also now began to suffer raids from the Huns. A large number of Greuthingi now decided to abandon their lands and, like the Tervingi, asked for refuge within the empire.

Valens saw the Goths as a source of recruits, and hoped to manage the potential influx by allowing only the Greuthingi to enter his lands. It was not an illogical response, but it was one that required a great deal of advance planning to make it work. Although we cannot know for certain how many Greuthingi there were, the likelihood is that they numbered around 30,000–40,000 people, with a military strength in the vicinity of 10,000. With the bulk of the field army facing the Persians there were not enough troops to control the situation, and the supply network was simply insufficient, even if it had been properly managed (which it was not) to accommodate this many hungry people. Relations with the immigrants swiftly deteriorated, and, in 377, they broke down completely. The outbreak of war opened the frontier to other tribes, and by the summer of 377 the number of new arrivals swelled to something like 80,000. When compared to the overall population of the empire—still probably in the range of 60 million—this might not seem a large number. But it was indeed a large number to have in one place, and would have required a great deal of coordination on the part of the three governments of the empire to bring the situation under control. This coordination was simply lacking, and Valens seemingly could not make up his mind what he wanted to accomplish. When he led his army out of Adrianople to attack the Goths in 378, he waited to negotiate the possible surrender of his enemies rather than attack immediately. The delay contributed to the exhaustion of his army, and allowed a large group of Gothic cavalry, which had been away from the camp, to return. When the battle did begin, Valens was killed and the Goths won an overwhelming victory (see box, right).

It was initial success against the Goths that enabled Theodosius to take control of the Eastern government, but he soon found that his forces were inadequate to the task he set them of annihilating the invaders. Instead of culminating with a massive Roman victory, the war ended when Theodosius allowed the Goths to settle in an area of the Balkans under their own leaders, if they agreed to send troops to join his armies. Indeed, Gothic soldiers seem to have played a major role in Theodosius's victory over his Western rivals in 394. One of their leaders was a man named Alaric.

Stilicho and Alaric (AD 395–410)

The fifteen years after the death of Theodosius provide the ultimate case study in the role of bureaucratic infighting for the determination of imperial policy, and the immensely negative impact that this could have on the empire as a whole. Theodosius's leading general during his final campaign was Stilicho, the son of a German officer and a Roman mother. Present at Theodosius's deathbed in 395, he announced that he had been made guardian for both Theodosius's ten-year-old son, Honorius, and his elder brother Arcadius (see box, opposite). His first task as regent was to rebuild the Western field army, which seems to have suffered heavy casualties in the final campaign. The best way to accomplish its reconstruction would have been to draft a substantial number of troops from the East. This, despite Stilicho's claim to supremacy, could not happen, because Arcadius's ministers demanded the return of the Eastern army, and bureaucratic infighting rose to a new level.

DISASTER AT ADRIANOPLE, 378

The deaths of Trajan and Sebastian stand out in this vast slaughter of eminent men; with them fell thirty-five tribunes without special assignments and unit commanders as well as Valerian and Equitius, the one who was in charge of the stables, the other of the palace. Amongst the others was Promotus, the tribune of the Promoti, who died in the first flower of youth, honored by every good man both for his own service and for that of his father, Ursicinus, who was once magister of soldiers. It is established that barely a third of the army survived. History records no battle so destructive other than Cannae.

(Ammianus Marcellinus, *History* 31.13.18–19)

STILICHO: TWO VIEWS

During that time, count Stilicho, born from the race of the Vandals, a lazy, treacherous and grievous people, while ruling under a young emperor, strained to substitute his own son, Eucherius, whom most people believed had been privately planning a persecution of the Christians from a very early age, on the throne. For this reason he retained Alaric and the whole Gothic race, which asked humbly and without pretence only for an excellent peace and a place to live, encouraging them by a secret treaty, but officially refusing either war or peace, for the purpose of terrifying and devastating the state.

(Orosius, *History against the pagans* 7.38)

He was the most moderate of all those in power at that time. Although married to the niece of the elder Theodosius (Theodosius I) who had entrusted him with the empires of both his sons, and serving as magister for twenty-three years without ever having sold military commands for money or turned the provisioning of the army to personal profit. Although he was father to only one son, he promoted him only as far as *notarius tribune* (so called), without giving him any important office.

(Zosimus, *New History* 5.34.5–7)

Stilicho returned with the Eastern army as far as Thessalonica, where messengers from the Eastern government, then dominated by the praetorian prefect Rufinus, conveyed the message that if he personally came any closer to Constantinople, it would be viewed as an act of war. Stilicho let the troops continue under the command of Gainas, a Goth who had risen to high command under Theodosius. When the army reached Constantinople, Gainas promptly arranged for Rufinus to be murdered at a military review. With a loyal supporter in charge of the Eastern army, Stilicho might well have imagined that he had succeeded, at minimal cost, in making himself effective master of the empire. But that was not so. Gainas allied himself with Eutropius, the eunuch who dominated the court of Arcadius, and Arcadius refused to acknowledge Stilicho's claim to be his guardian.

The lack of cooperation between the governments of East and West in the face of a series of crises during the next seven years revealed that the empire was more firmly divided than ever. Stilicho received no assistance from the East in 397–98, when he had to quell a serious rebellion in north Africa. Equally he was given no support when Alaric—whom Theodosius had settled with his people on a reservation within the borders of the empire to end the war that broke out under Valens—burst forth to raid Greece in 399. Likewise, when the Eastern empire was wracked by a revolt that began with Gothic troops stationed in Asia Minor in 399, the Eastern regime looked to Uldin, king of the Huns, for assistance, since nothing was forthcoming from the West. In this case, after negotiations that can justifiably be called Byzantine, Gainas first negotiated an end to the revolt while he eliminated Eutropius, and then took command of the former rebels when they were transferred to Europe; but he now found that the Huns were more than he could handle. Despite having betrayed his former colleagues in the imperial administration, he believed that he could regain his position by negotiating the return of his Gothic troops to Asia Minor. As his men were placed on unarmed transports in the Bosporus, they were attacked by naval forces from Constantinople and destroyed. Gainas paid for his own treachery with his life, while Uldin withdrew beyond the Danube and awaited further employment by one government or the other.

In 401 Alaric launched an invasion of Italy: with no Roman army in his way, he entered northern Italy, drove Honorius from his palace at Milan to the city of Asta, and besieged the emperor for several months until Stilicho arrived in the war zone with a portion of the field army from Gaul. Stilicho defeated him twice in the next two years before making a treaty that allowed Alaric to return to his Balkan lands.

Stilicho's willingness to allow Alaric to return home contrasts markedly with his handling of the next group of invaders to cross his path, which makes it seem all the more certain that he felt Alaric might play a role in furthering his own ambitions. The same could not be said of the Alamannic chief Radagaisus, who led an armed migration from the region of the upper Rhine into Italy during the summer of 406. So large was the movement that Stilicho turned to Uldin: the help of the Hun enabled Stilicho to force the surrender of his enemies. Approximately 10,000 of Radagaisus's men were taken into the imperial service, while many thousands of others were sold into slavery.

Disaster followed upon victory. On December 31, 406 the Rhine froze over, enabling a second massive invasion, this time consisting of relatively new arrivals—the Vandals, Alans, and Suevi—all from central Europe. Stilicho still had the bulk of the field army in the south and there was nothing he could do to prevent the destruction of the Rhine frontier. The tribes that crossed the frontier would never leave the territory of the Romans. At nearly the same time, the commander of the Roman army in Britain, a gentleman with the name of Constantine, declared himself emperor and moved into Gaul.

Stilicho was unwilling to chance his own army, portions of which had come from Gaul, in open battle with Constantine. Instead he garrisoned the passes over the Alps. The situation was complicated by the fact that Honorius, now in his early twenties, seems to have detested his wife—Stilicho's daughter—and surrounded himself with courtiers who detested his father-in-law. In addition, there remained among the Romans a thorough distaste for Germans. Although much of the army was now in fact made up of Germans, this was not true of the civil administration. Tensions

This portrait of Stilicho in military dress is from an ivory diptych, or pair of tablets (diptychs, usually ivory, were often exchanged by members of the upper class to mark important moments). As magister militum (commander-in-chief) in the West and father-in-law of Honorius, Stilicho was the most powerful man in the Western empire between 395 and 408.

between civil officials and German soldiers had contributed mightily to the situation in Constantinople that had led to the demise of Gainas, and there had been occasional violent attacks on Germanic units in other cities of the empire. In the wake of Valens's defeat at Adrianople in 378 the *magister militum* of the East had ordered the massacre of Goths who had been incorporated into the Roman army and transferred to the East before the outbreak of the revolt. Now, with what could not have been worse timing, Arcadius died. The Eastern establishment replaced him with his seven-year-old son, Theodosius II, on May 8, 408.

Stilicho wanted to take an army East to "assist" in the establishment of the new regime, but at the same time, he had to watch Constantine and also find some way to deal with Alaric, who had advanced in the direction of northern Italy demanding a large sum of money. Alaric got his money, but when Stilicho suggested that he should be sent to Gaul to fight Constantine, he miscalculated the level of bigotry at court. Honorius's dislike of Germans spelled the end for Stilicho, who was arrested and executed on August 21. The new leader of the government, Olympius, then ordered a massacre of the "Germans" in the army, since they were thought to be especially loyal to the memory of Stilicho. Those who survived fled to Alaric. Realizing that there was now no Roman army of any strength between himself and Rome, Alaric made straight for the city. The senate voted to pay him an enormous bribe, and negotiated with Honorius to give Alaric new status within the Roman hierarchy. When Honorius refused, Alaric returned to Rome with an expanded list of demands—this time including a homeland for his people and the rank of *magister militum* in the Roman army. Honorius's officials were willing to grant this

INNOMINE
XPI·VINCAS
SEMPER·

HONORIOSEMP·AVG

This portrait of Honorius appears on the consular diptych of Anicius Petronius Probus. A diptych consists of two parts connected by a hinge, and in the later Roman empire these objects were carved in ivory to celebrate the assumption of consular office. In this case, the military and Christian aspects of the imperial office come together in the portrait of the emperor, which was included to thank Honorius for bestowing the office.

demand, but Honorius flatly refused. The reason was simple prejudice: he said that he would not grant such a title to a man of Alaric's race.

Honorius was as stupid as he was bigoted, and the management group around him was hopeless. The empire needed to find a way to deal with immigrants who could no longer be kept beyond the border by incorporating them constructively within imperial society. With many Germans serving in the army, even after the massacre of 407, and many still in the officer corps, it might have been possible to find a pragmatic solution, and many Romans were willing to try, including a significant portion of the senate itself. In 409, after a further siege of Rome, the senate proclaimed a new emperor, Attalus, who promptly joined Alaric with the senate's blessing.

Alaric's willingness to have his own emperor is significant in that it reveals his reading of the prevailing state of politics in the Roman West: in his view of the situation, important people had imperial offices and emperors of their own. But that proved insufficient, and so he deposed Attalus, and appeared once more before the walls of Rome. On August 24, 410 the Goths found that a gate had been left open. For the first time in 800 years, a man who was not part of the Roman hierarchy took control of the city. He left town after three days of highly organized, but relatively peaceful, looting.

The fall of Rome reveals many things. From one point of view, it reveals the effects of military decline and bureaucratic power in the course of the previous half century. From the viewpoint of the historian of Roman culture, the sack of Rome had deeper implications. Jerome, a leading Christian intellectual, then in Palestine working on biblical translations that would become standard fare for Western Christians until the Reformation, lamented the event as an unsurpassed catastrophe; while Augustine, the bishop of Hippo in north Africa, responded to pagan claims that the sack of the city was the result of the conversion of the state to Christianity by composing his massive *City of God*, in which he argued that political history was of little account when compared with the history of God's relationship with humanity. After all, he argued, far worse things had happened in the past, before the rise of Christianity. In support of his argument, a Christian from Spain, Orosius, wrote a seven-book *History against the Pagans*, the bulk of which recounts disasters before the birth of Christ. The city of Rome was a symbol of a world that was past, rather than of the world that was to come. It was eminently possible for there to be a civilized world that was both Christian and Roman, and that did not depend on any specific political order. For the Goths, the situation was perhaps even more problematic. Alaric had played his last card, but he had still not obtained the office he wanted or a homeland for his people. He died in 411 in southern Italy.

Summary

● By the beginning of the third century AD imperial government was stagnating. There is some evidence that the peoples beyond the empire's frontiers were more of a threat—the peoples to the north were better organized, and the new Sasanian regime to the East was vastly more efficient (and ideologically motivated). The empire's chief problem, however, was lack of imagination within the governing class. There had been no serious army reform for 300 years, and government as a whole was dominated by extreme devotion to the past.

● Between 244 and 260, Rome suffered a series of military defeats unparalleled since the late second century BC, or the time of Hannibal. Rapid change followed hard on the heels of disaster.

● The empire split into three parts after the Persian king Sapor captured the emperor Valerian in 260, though the Eastern portion of the empire remained nominally loyal to Valerian's son, Gallienus. This loyalty evaporated under Gallienus's successor, Claudius, but he reigned for only two years, and Aurelian restored the unity of the empire in the first half of the 270s. Aurelian, however, was murdered and his successors dealt—with little success—with the twin issues of division within the army and separatist tendencies in the provinces.

● Diocletian attempted a radical new solution to the empire's problems when he took the throne in 284. He shared authority with a co-emperor, Maximian, after 285, and, additionally, after 293, with two deputies, or Caesars—Constantius and Galerius. Diocletian also made significant changes in the structure of the empire, making provinces smaller, changing the taxation system, attempting to regulate prices, and persecuting the Christian Church. Not all these efforts were successful, but Diocletian's achievements outweighed his failures. Uniquely he determined to retire, forcing Maximian to do so too in 305 and pass power to the Caesars.

● The Caesars' regime was short-lived, as Constantius died in 306 arranging for his son Constantine to succeed him. When Maximian's son then seized power in Italy, a period of fractured government ensued. This only ended when Constantine defeated Licinius, the last of the emperors created by Galerius, in 324.

● Constantine continued a number of Diocletian's policies, including the movement of imperial authority out of Rome; he founded his own capital at Constantinople. He also promoted Christianity, to which he had converted in 312, by encouraging conversion rather than persecuting non-compliance. Christianity became the majority religion in the empire by the end of the fourth century.

● At the end of his reign, Constantine planned to revert to a divided government, leaving the empire to his three surviving sons and two nephews. His plan was upset by his middle son, Constantius II, who murdered the nephews and split power with his brothers. The powerful personalities of Constantius (who ultimately became sole emperor) and his cousin and successor Julian had a profound impact on the imperial bureaucracy, which thereafter sought to be ruled by less forceful men.

● Julian seized the position of Augustus while Constantius was still alive, and remained ruler of the whole empire after Constantius's sudden death. He attempted to restore pagan cult (with minimal success) and to conquer the Persians, dying in battle against them. After the brief reign of Jovian, Valentinian, a junior officer selected by the general staff, became emperor, and made his brother Valens co-emperor in the East. Their reign and those of their successors were characterized by bureaucratic infighting to control imperial policy.

● After Valens died in battle with Gothic tribesmen, Theodosius took power in the East (and later, briefly, over the whole empire). The Goths were seeking a new home where they would be protected from the Huns. Temporarily controlled by Theodosius, who gave them their own land within the empire, they sought greater influence once Theodosius died in 395. But when the Western emperor, Honorius, refused to deal with the Goths, their leader Alaric's ultimate response, in 410, was to sack Rome.

VII

The Endings of the Roman Empire

(AD 410–642)

AD 423	Death of Honorius
425	Accession of Valentinian III as emperor in the West
429	Vandal invasion of north Africa begins
431	First Council of Ephesus
435	Attila and Bleda take over leadership of the Huns
437	Promulgation of the Theodosian Code
439	Vandal capture of Carthage
444 or 445	Attila becomes sole king of the Huns
449	Second Council of Ephesus
450	Death of Theodosius II; accession of Marcian
451	Huns defeated at the battle of Châlons; Council of Chalcedon
453	Death of Attila
454	Murder of Aetius
455	Murder of Valentinian III; Vandal sack of Rome
457	Death of Marcian; accession of Leo
474	Death of Leo; accession of Zeno
476	Deposition of Romulus by Odovacer
477	Death of Geiseric
481	Clovis becomes king of the Franks
488	Ostrogothic invasion of Italy under Theodoric begins
491	Death of Zeno; accession of Anastasius
493	Establishment of the Ostrogothic kingdom in Italy under Theodoric
507	Clovis defeats Alaric II at the battle of Vouillé; establishment of the Franks as the paramount power in Gaul
511	Death of Clovis
AD 518	Death of Anastasius; accession of Justin

Barbarians and Emperors from Alaric to Geiseric

Eastern Emperors and Western Kings

▼

THE QUESTION OF WHEN the Roman empire fell is deceptively simple. To answer it, one must first answer the question of what it meant to "fall." By "fall" do we mean "ceased to rule the whole area once ruled by Septimius Severus," or "ceased to be the most powerful state in the Mediterranean," or "ceased to rule in Italy?" If we select the first of these answers it might be said that we have already passed that point, since it might mean that we should look to the surrender of territory within the empire to the Goths under Theodosius as the moment of "fall." To accept the third answer would perhaps be even more problematic, since the imperial government would give up its claim to Italy and north Africa in the fifth century, only to reassert control over both in the sixth century; but by the time it gave up its last foothold in Italy after that—in the eleventh century—the "Roman empire," such as it then was, was not a particularly powerful state. If we accept the second definition, we are left with selecting either 636 or 642, the dates respectively of the loss of Syria and of Alexandria, as the definitive date for the "fall." On balance the second date is probably better, since the loss of Egypt compounded the impact of the loss of Syria and ensured that the surviving empire could only be an Anatolian and Balkan entity, rather than one that could still aspire to Mediterranean dominance.

At this point it might simply be best to admit that selecting any one date is not a particularly rewarding activity, any more than attempting to pick a date at which the empire came into being is especially rewarding, since the rise of Rome, like the fall of Rome, was a gradual process. It might be reasonably said that the "rise" of the empire was completed some time in the reign of Augustus when the frontier system took shape, and that its "fall" was complete when the empire ceased being the dominant state in the Mediterranean world; but that in both cases, seeking a fixed point is of far less value than seeking to understand the reasons for and consequences of either the development of the imperial state or its failure.

Yet however unsatisfactory the quest may be, the search for an "end date" is still of some value, if only because it makes it clear that the "fall" of the empire was progressive, and that the impact of the "fall" was varied from region to region. It is against the background of the political events of these years that it is necessary to read the evidence (much of it archaeological) that might help to answer the central question connected with the decline of the Roman empire: what difference did it make? The answer to this question offers insight first into how the empire came apart in the West, and then into why the remaining portion failed to defend itself against the relatively small armies that emerged from the Arabian peninsula in the second quarter of the seventh century AD.

The Course of Events (AD 410–642)

Barbarians and Emperors from Alaric to Geiseric (AD 410–77)

The century after Alaric's capture of Rome witnessed the breakdown of effective Roman government in Western Europe, and the continuation of effective government in the East. In these years the Germanic tribes that had entered the empire between 376 and 410 began to form new states for themselves in France, Spain, and north Africa, while a vast new power emerged and imploded in the Balkans within the space of a single immensely destructive decade. This was the kingdom of the

Huns assembled by Attila. The long-term impact of Attila's regime was to destroy what was left of the imperial frontier system along the Danube. One observer, the historian Priscus, tells us that when he went on an embassy to Attila's court in AD 449, he traveled across an area of desolation south of the Danube that took five days to pass through.

In the course of his embassy to Attila, Priscus also makes it quite clear that he sees the interest of his emperor, Theodosius II, the son of Arcadius, as being quite distinct from those of "Western Romans," ruled at this point by Valentinian III, the son of Constantius III (see p. 326). These Romans, who also had an embassy at Attila's court, had issues with the Huns that were completely independent of those that took Priscus north of the Danube. When he speaks of his own people, he refers to them as "the Eastern Romans," and, as various sources preserve his words, he writes of Rome as a geographical area ruled by multiple "kings." His language is especially striking because it differs so much from that of Olympiodorus, the historian who grew to maturity and played a major role in events of the first quarter of the fifth century. Olympiodorus writes of the empire as if it is still a unified whole, with its two emperors ideally working in tandem with each other.

The different perspectives of Olympiodorus and Priscus reflect a change in attitude that set in between the time of Theodosius II and the 470s, when Priscus completed his history. Whereas Theodosius's court was deeply committed to maintaining the symbolic unity of the Roman world, even while admitting to the fact of bureaucratic division, by the 470s Eastern regimes seem simply to have given up on the West as a lost cause. It is also clear from Priscus's writings that he, at least, regarded territory ruled by German kings as now being independent of Roman authority altogether: at one point he says that the general Aetius defeated the Goths of Gaul who were "encroaching" upon Roman territory.

The Goths of whom Priscus wrote were none other than the descendants of the Goths who had sacked Rome in 410. Led after Alaric's death by his half-brother, Athaulf, they had arrived in western Gaul after wanderings of several years, having with them Galla Placidia, the sister of Honorius. These Goths seem at some point to have begun calling themselves the Visigoths, or "Strong Goths," a self-congratulatory self-description similar in form to that of the Franks and Alamanni (see p. 277). This group was indeed so far removed from the bands of Tervingi and Greuthingi, and now so intermixed with other Germanic peoples, that the adoption of a new tribal name was a logical act of community formation. A further logical act took place in 414 when Athaulf married Galla, with the intention of staking a claim to the throne (their son, who did not survive infancy, was called Theodosius). By this time Athaulf had long been alternately ally and foe of Honorius's regime, either fighting its forces or helping to suppress the tribes that had crossed the Rhine in 406, some of which had now moved into Spain.

In the course of the next twenty years the Visigoths more often than not took the side of the imperial regime, although some were deeply ambivalent about their relationship with Rome (Athaulf's successor, for example, immediately shipped Galla back to the imperial court). The result was that by the late 420s they had acquired a substantial kingdom that ran from central France through southern Spain. At this point they also seem to have ceased to regard the affairs of the central government as being of great import to themselves.

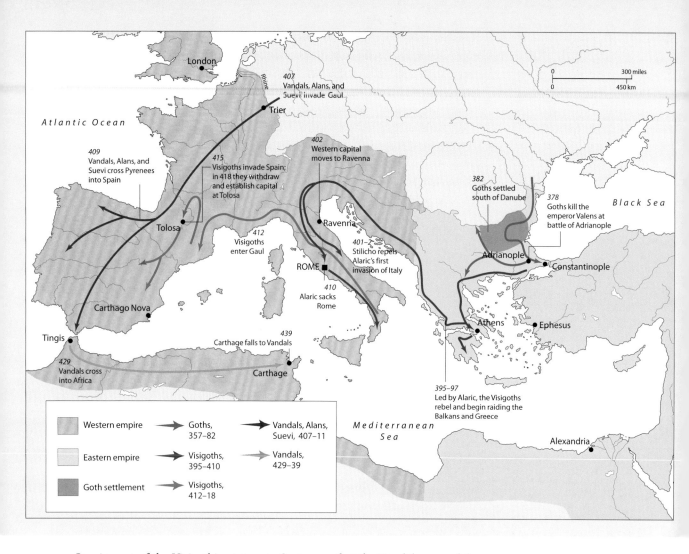

407
Vandals, Alans, and
Suevi invade Gaul

402
Western capital
moves to Ravenna

382
Goths settled
south of Danube

378
Goths kill the
emperor Valens at
battle of Adrianople

409
Vandals, Alans, and
Suevi cross Pyrenees
into Spain

415
Visigoths invade Spain;
in 418 they withdraw
and establish capital
at Tolosa

412
Visigoths
enter Gaul

401–2
Stilicho repels
Alaric's first
invasion of Italy

410
Alaric sacks
Rome

439
Carthage falls to Vandals

429
Vandals cross
into Africa

395–97
Led by Alaric, the Visigoths
rebel and begin raiding the
Balkans and Greece

London
Trier
Tolosa
Ravenna
ROME
Carthago Nova
Tingis
Carthage
Adrianople
Constantinople
Athens
Ephesus
Alexandria

Atlantic Ocean

Black Sea

Mediterranean Sea

Rhine

Western empire	Goths, 357–82	Vandals, Alans, Suevi, 407–11
Eastern empire	Visigoths, 395–410	Vandals, 429–39
Goth settlement	Visigoths, 412–18	

One impact of the Visigothic victory in Spain was that the Vandals, one of the groups of invaders in 406, were driven to seek a new home in north Africa. The staggering incompetence of Roman imperial officials in the western Mediterranean enabled the Vandals to acquire the ships needed to transport tens of thousands of people across the straits of Gibraltar into the one region of the empire that Rome had to continue to control if it were to survive.

The defense of Africa was hampered by dynastic infighting. Towards the end of his life, Honorius became deeply beholden to a general named Constantius, who had defeated the Visigoths and brought an end to the usurpation of Constantine; he was also peculiarly interested in the personal affairs of his sister. Very much against her will, Honorius married the now widowed Galla to Constantius, who was raised to the rank of Augustus and is thus known as Constantius III. When Constantius suddenly died in 421, Galla found that Honorius was expressing a desire for greater intimacy. In 423 she evaded her brother's clutches by fleeing to Constantinople, and Honorius promptly died. When Western officials tried to place a man named John on the throne, Theodosius II sent an army to place Valentinian, Galla's young son by Constantius, on the throne. The effort was successful, but the ill-will left behind continued to fester, especially the dislike Galla bore Aetius, one of three generals

FALL OF THE WESTERN EMPIRE

The immediate cause of the collapse of the Western Roman empire was a series of invasions by Germanic peoples from the north. This was a progressive process, with different groups carving out new homes for themselves at different times. The Goths, who had entered the Balkans in 375, began an attack on Italy at the beginning of the fifth century; they would eventually form a group that called itself the Visigoths, and settled in parts of Spain and Gaul. Also at the beginning of the fifth century, the Vandals, Alans, and Suevi crossed the Rhine into Gaul. The Alans and Suevi settled in Spain, while the Vandals conquered the north African provinces and settled there in the middle of the fifth century. The Ostrogoths, who like the Visigoths had emerged from groups that entered Roman territory from regions north of the Danube, eventually established a kingdom in Italy in 493.

who had risen to power in the last years of her brother's life. Even as the Vandals were advancing across Africa, Galla summoned the governor to her aid in a war with Aetius. There was thus no substantial garrison to defend Africa when the Vandals, led by their king, Geiseric, took Carthage in 439, and in one blow shattered the economic equilibrium that sustained the city of Rome. Appeals to Constantinople for aid in retaking the city were achieving some success when Attila, who had taken over the kingdom of the Huns with his brother Bleda a few years before, launched a devastating invasion of the Danubian provinces.

The long-term impact of the short-lived Hunnic empire in the Balkans was substantial. Unlike other tribal leaders, Attila recognized the need to command siege warfare, and the trail of destruction left by his several invasions of the Balkans is still evident in the archaeology of the region. The concern of the court of Theodosius II for the insecurity of the Balkans is reflected in the construction of a massive new fortification wall for Constantinople (see map, p. 304).

In 451, Attila (who had been sole ruler since Bleda's death a few years earlier) fabricated a series of complaints not only against the Western regime, but also against one of the successor states that had begun to emerge in northern Gaul—that of the Franks—and led his forces to crush them. He was defeated by an allied army comprised of German tribes that had occupied northern and western France, the Visigoths, and what remained of the Roman field army under Aetius. Defeated at the battle of Châlons in northeastern France, Attila returned home, only to launch yet another destructive raid into Italy the next year. Returning home at the end of that raid, in 453 he married a German woman named Ilico and died of a burst blood vessel on his wedding night. His kingdom collapsed in the course of the next few years.

A section of the walls constructed at Constantinople in 412–14 by the praetorian prefect Anthemius under Theodosius II. In 447, after an earthquake damaged this wall, it was repaired and another wall was built just beyond it.

Aetius was responsible for the Roman victory at Châlons, but that did nothing to ease the hatred for him at the palace. In September 454, Valentinian personally led a physical attack on him in the palace at Ravenna in Italy and killed him. A few months later some former officers murdered Valentinian, and a wealthy senator, Maximus, who had achieved considerable influence in these years, took the throne for himself. The result was an utter disaster. Emulating Attila (who claimed that he invaded the Western empire at the behest of Honorius's daughter Honoria) the Vandal king Geiseric asserted that Eudoxia, Valentinian's widow, had called upon his aid. In 455 the Vandal fleet sailed up the Tiber and sacked Rome.

Geiseric's sack of Rome, even more than Alaric's, reveals the fundamental weakness of late imperial government. The Western emperors actually controlled more territory at this point than the government of the Roman Republic had controlled when Appius Claudius crossed into Sicily to begin the First Punic War in 264 BC. That said, the power of the Western emperors was not remotely comparable to that of the mid-Republic. Roman power in the third century BC had been based upon a coherent system of alliances throughout Italy, and upon the power of the citizenry to make decisions about war and peace. For reasons of self-interest at the very least, the mass of Roman and allied peoples were capable of devoting themselves to broadly conceived social goals. The power of the fifth-century AD emperor, by contrast, was based upon an increasingly oppressive tax system, and the inhabitants of the empire had minimal impact on decision-making (protesting in the circus, rioting, refusing to pay, or fleeing being the most common responses to government action of which they disapproved). Moreover, rather than participating in their own defense as they had in the third century BC, the inhabitants of the empire were dependent for their security on a military establishment that was in the hands of such warlords as Aetius, who tended to put their own self-interest ahead of that of the state: hence the withdrawal of a substantial portion of the garrison to fight a civil war in Italy while Geiseric was advancing across Africa. No one in the Western command structure, it seems, had any interest or experience in sea warfare, and there was not even a fleet to defend the coastline of Italy: on the two occasions when an effort was made to retake north Africa, the fleets had to be supplied from Constantinople.

With no Roman fleet to contend with, the fleets of the Vandals reigned supreme in the western Mediterranean; and with no significant Roman military establishment left north of the Alps, the Frankish kings solidified their power in northern France, as did the Visigoths in southern France and Spain. The politics of the Western regime in Italy, dominated as they were from about 457 by a general named Ricimer, thus became increasingly irrelevant. A descendant of the royal lines among both the Suevi and Visigoths in Spain, Ricimer had entered imperial service under Aetius, and emerged as the "emperor-maker" in the West, placing a series of puppets on the throne (including one candidate sent West by the Eastern emperors) until his own death on August 18, 472. Three years later another general, Orestes, declared his son, Romulus, emperor. A year later, in 476, one of Orestes's generals, Odovacer, overthrew Romulus and declared himself the king of Italy (see box, right). Odovacer was very much a creature of the times. The son of one of Attila's leading henchmen, he had begun his career fighting the Franks in Germany before moving to Italy in the service of Ricimer and becoming a commander of the imperial guard. In keeping with the times, he established his court at Ravenna, and sent Romulus

GEISERIC

Geiseric, now most famous for the sack of Rome, was of moderate stature and lame as the result of a fall from a horse; a deep thinker who spoke rarely and despised luxury, he was fierce in anger, desirous of gain, skilled in negotiation, and ready to sow dissension to arouse hatreds.

(Jordanes, *History of the Goths* 33, 168)

A CONTEMPORARY ACCOUNT OF 476

(Romulus) Augustus, the son of Orestes, hearing that Zeno once again held the imperial power in the East having driven out Basiliscus, he forced the senate to send an embassy to Zeno saying that there was no need for their own emperor, and that one emperor would be enough for both regions. (They added that) they had chosen Odovacer as a suitable person to look after their affairs, as he had political and military experience, and asked Zeno to appoint him a patrician and grant him the government of Italy …

(Malchus fragment 14, (Blockley))

Romulus Augustus, depicted in this coin, was sixteen when he was declared emperor in 475 by his father, Orestes; he was deposed the following year. Romulus's reputation as the last of Rome's emperors in the West owes much to the irony of his sharing the name of the city's founder. Julius Nepos, who had been deposed by Orestes but continued to rule parts of Gaul and Dalmatia until he was assassinated in 480, may more reasonably claim this title.

into internal exile on an estate that looked out over the Bay of Naples. The Eastern emperor, Zeno, who was facing problems of his own, declined to name a new emperor, and another claimant to the throne withdrew into the Balkans.

Geiseric died in 477, a year after the deposition of Romulus. By separating north Africa from Italy, he had doomed the Western regime to irrelevance. In his sack of Rome he may have pretended that he was answering Eudoxia's prayer. In fact he might be seen as fulfilling the vision that Virgil placed in the mind of Queen Dido of Carthage as she died: that an avenger would come from Carthage to punish the descendants of Aeneas.

Eastern Emperors and Western Kings from Theodosius II to Justinian (AD 408–527)

The regime of Theodosius II, which survived rather than thrived, endured largely through the efforts of two enormously able women: the emperor's sister, Pulcheria, and his wife, Eudoxia. Although the two women appear to have entertained a quite profound hatred for each other, they both sought to extend their power (and, coincidentally, that of their brother/husband) through the expansion of links between the palace and the church. In doing so they followed in the footsteps of the first Theodosius, who introduced himself to his Eastern subjects by proclaiming his devotion to the Nicene Creed and summoning a council to Constantinople to condemn doctrines other than those held by the bishops of Rome and Alexandria.

The secular issue that seems to have dominated the thinking of Theodosius II (or his senior advisers) was the desirability of maintaining the integrity of the empire. To this end he (or his advisers) dispatched expedition after expedition to the West—an activity that Priscus for one thought was folly—and decided to promulgate a massive new law code. While the Theodosian Code, completed in 437, remains a stunning achievement, collecting and organizing thousands of texts around hundreds of headings, it may have been of more symbolic than legal value. Although governors were instructed in how to use the texts (the most recent trumping the older), new regulations continued to be issued, which tended to date the contents rather fast.

As a historiographic document—beginning with legislation issued by Constantine from 312 onwards, tending to omit texts bearing the name of Julian, and ignoring earlier material from the codes compiled under Diocletian—the Theodosian Code sent a clear message: the empire of Theodosius was a profoundly Christian operation. Furthermore, as the entire sixteenth book of the Code was devoted to regulations governing the Christian Church, the Code also made a clear statement about the relationship between the emperor and his faith. The opening section of book sixteen contains three laws of Theodosius defining Christian doctrine; the first according to the Nicene Creed as interpreted in Rome and Alexandria; the second stating that the doctrine promulgated by certain other Eastern bishops was in accord with Nicea; and the third stating that the creed of Constantinople in 360, which such enemies as Athanasius had held was essentially Arian (see p. 308), was in accord with the Nicene Creed. Section four of book sixteen contains six rulings against those who contend about religion, while section five offers no fewer than sixty-six rulings on heresy! Section six is concerned with the nature of baptism (which was not to be repeated—an important point in north Africa where Donatists insisted upon rebaptism); section seven is concerned with apostates (those who had rejected Christianity); while sections eight and nine contain a total of thirty-four rulings that disadvantaged Jews. Section ten offers a mere twenty-five rulings on the topic of paganism. It is surely not accidental that the very last text in the Code affirms the ban on Donatist practice in north Africa (see box, right), and it is a very interesting choice. By the time that the Code was presented in the West, most of Donatist north Africa was actually under Vandal control. Was Theodosius trying to suggest that, in an ideal world, neither the Vandals nor the Donatists would continue to exist for much longer?

Against the background of book sixteen of the Code, it is hardly surprising that the emperor's main concern when it came to religion was with imposing "orthodox" or "straight thinking" belief. From the point of view of domestic policy the most controversial moments in the reign of Theodosius were the councils convened at Ephesus in 431 and 449. The point at issue was, as always, the nature of the Trinity. The Council of Nicea had held that Christ was "The Word" of God incarnate, that He was absolutely of the same substance with God, and that the Virgin Mary was the "Mother of God." But Bishop Nestorius of Constantinople had revived a tradition not all that different from that of Arius (see p. 301) by stating that while the divine nature of Christ was identical to that of the Father, He was also endowed with a human nature. The council of 431 condemned Nestorius (who happened to be a favorite of Pulcheria whose power was, at that point, eclipsed by that of Eudoxia) as a heretic. The council of 449 essentially confirmed the doctrines declared in 431.

When Theodosius died, falling from his horse in 450, Pulcheria agreed to marry a general, Marcian, if he agreed to respect her virginity (which he did). The following year a council was summoned at Chalcedon (across the Bosporus from Constantinople) to produce a new creed, which was declared to be in complete accord with that of Nicea on the grounds that it was simply an "interpretation" of that creed. That was stretching the definition of "interpretation" farther than many were prepared to go, since this new creed involved the statement that Christ had two natures that became one after "he was made man." Although the doctrine of Chalcedon might have seemed to bridge the gap between Nestorius and hard-core Nicene believers, as well as the gap with the practice of the faith as defined by the bishop of Rome (who had vigorously protested the doctrines of Ephesus) it proved anathema to bishops in Syria and Egypt. Division over the doctrine of Chalcedon continued to split the church for more than a century.

LAST TEXTS IN THE THEODOSIAN CODE

The emperors Arcadius, Honorius and Theodosius to Diotimus the proconsul of Africa: We wish that the edict, which our clemency sent throughout the African regions, be posted in many places, so that all men will know the one true Catholic faith of the all powerful God, which, confessed by correct thinking, will be retained. Given at Ravenna on March 5 in the second consulship of Stilicho and the first consulship of Anthemius (405).

(Theodosian Code, 16.11.2)

The emperors Honorius and Theodosius to Marcellinus (an official dispatched to end the Donatist dispute): Greetings. We wish that those things, which, with respect to Catholic law, either antiquity once ordained, or the religious authority of our fathers established, or our serenity strengthened, be maintained safe and inviolate with new superstition removed. Given at Ravenna on October 14 in the consulship of the most noble Varanes (410).

(Theodosian Code, 16.11.3)

Although such councils as Chalcedon and Ephesus resulted in deep divisions, they nonetheless provided a venue for communication between the fringes of empire and the emperor. Bishops assembled in their hundreds, and the emperor appeared in person, speaking Greek rather than the Latin of the court. Bitter though the disputes would become, at this point it is arguable that the simple fact that such councils took place was of enormous importance for asserting the unity of the (Eastern) empire as a whole.

Marcian came to the throne as the threat from the Huns receded with the death of Attila, but the instability created by the collapse of Attila's empire sent ever more tribes on the move across the Danube. The absorption of the tribes that were now moving into Illyricum was to become one of the major issues of the next several decades, as the command structure of the Eastern army divided between those who originated from the Greek-speaking part of the empire—chiefly the uplands of the southern Taurus rim in Turkey, a region known as Isauria—and those whose origins lay outside the empire. The question of origin was inextricably linked with that of religion. The most powerful general at the time of Marcian's death was Aspar (an Alan), who could not take the throne himself because it was generally held that Goths and other peoples from north of the borders were Arian heretics, if they were even Christians at all. (This may also explain why, in the West, Ricimer never bothered to make himself emperor and Odovacer did not take the imperial title.) In formal terms the notion that Goths could be Arian is patently false. The creed of Arius was never official; Ulfilas, who spearheaded the conversion of the Goths, held beliefs that were in accord with those of Constantius II (see p. 317); and, to cap things off, Theodosius had even declared that Constantius II's final creed of Constantinople counted as orthodox. The official creed of Chalcedon, with its admission that there might be a separate human nature of Christ, was actually closer to Arianism than anything a Goth may have believed. The problem was that once ethnicity was linked with religion, to be "Roman" meant that one was "straight thinking," while to be "German" was to be "other thinking" or "heterodox."

Religion, masking racial prejudice, thus made it impossible for Aspar to succeed Marcian. His support was crucial, however, in securing the succession in 457 for an Isaurian general by the name of Leo, who, in a fascinating ceremony that reflected the dual power structures—Roman and German—of the capital, was first raised upon the shields of his soldiers and then crowned by the patriarch of Constantinople. Leo, who lasted until 474, was closely allied to another Isaurian officer, Zeno; and, once he had executed Aspar for treason, Leo arranged for Zeno's son to marry his daughter, Ariadne. When Leo died, the theory was that he would be succeeded by the child of Zeno and Ariadne, also called Leo. These plans were upset almost immediately after Leo's death by the death of the younger Leo, meaning that the throne fell to Zeno, who barely survived a major rebellion in the first year of his reign.

Aspar's sons, who survived the slaughter of their parent, joined forces with one of two Gothic bands that were then dominating the Balkans, both led by men named Theodoric. In the initial stages of the rebellion against Zeno, one Theodoric— Strabo—sided with the rebels, while the other—"the Amal"—had fought for the emperor (see box, left). Once Zeno had secured the throne, the two Theodorics, after briefly joining forces in an attempt to extract territorial concessions from the emperor in the Balkans, fell to fighting, with Theodoric Strabo tending to take the

THE TWO THEODORICS

Ambassadors came to Zeno from the Goths of Thrace who were bound by treaty— people whom the Romans called *foederati*—asking that Zeno make a treaty with Theodoric the son of Triarius, who wished for a peaceful life and not to engage in any war with the state. They asked him to compare how much harm he had done the Romans as an enemy with how much damage Theodoric the son of Valomar had done to the cities, although he was a friend and general.

(Malchus fragment 15, (Blockley))

imperial side until his death in 481. The death of Strabo seems to have left Theodoric the Amal supreme among the Balkan Goths, now (and possibly for some time before this) known as Ostrogoths. After a massive raid that nearly reached Constantinople, Zeno arranged with Theodoric that he would have imperial blessing if he would drive Odovacer—the deposer of Romulus—from his throne in Italy. After five years of bitter warfare, Odovacer surrendered in 493, only to be murdered at dinner by Theodoric, who claimed that he was avenging relatives killed either by Odovacer, or some relative of his in the past. Theodoric then became established as king of Italy.

The Ostrogothic conquest of Italy completed the division of the Western empire into four main kingdoms, with a number of minor ones around the fringes. In each kingdom it appears that the previous Roman aristocracy tended to represent the church and civil administration, while their new German kings saw themselves as primarily military figures. The alliance between—in traditional terms—highly cultured Romans and their new German rulers is well represented in the works of such figures as Sidonius Apollinaris, who served several of Valentinian III's successors, and Ennodius, who composed poems in honor of Theodoric. The massive collection of letters produced by the Roman aristocrat Cassiodorus offers important insights into the way that Roman and Ostrogoth could interact in a system where civil administration was largely in the same hands in which it had always been. The moving *Consolation of Philosophy*, written by his relative, Boethius, reflects the tensions that could exist between the two sides. Indeed, Boethius, who represents himself as being active in protecting Romans from oppression by Gothic officials, was brought down when three Romans charged him with treason against Theodoric in 525.

Aside from the replacement of Odovacer by Theodoric in Italy, the most significant change in the power structure of Western Europe occurred around the year 500. This change involved the development of the Frankish kingdom under King Clovis into a power that could aspire to rule not only most of Gaul, but also considerable territory east of the Rhine. In 507 Clovis defeated the Visigothic king, Alaric II, at the battle of Vouillé outside Poitiers. He killed Alaric, as he would many other rivals, with his own hand. Victory here was followed by the Frankish takeover of most Visigothic land in France, leaving the Visigoths as essentially a Spanish power.

Clovis continued to rule until 511, while Theodoric remained on his throne until 526. A year later, a new emperor took the throne in Constantinople, driven by a dream of restoring imperial power throughout the Mediterranean: Flavius Petrus Sabbatius Justinianus, known to us more simply as Justinian.

The Vision of Justinian (AD 527–65)

Justinian was born in Thrace, probably in 482. His uncle, Justin, had enlisted in the palace guard in the reign of Leo. By 492, now in the reign of Anastasius, an elderly court official who succeeded Zeno in 491, Justin had risen to a senior military command. At this point war broke out with the Persians. This war had a more bitter religious edge than previous conflicts with the Persians, as the Sasanians insisted upon the superiority of Zoroastrian revelation (see p. 278). The Sasanian attitude seems to have become progressively stronger as large numbers of their subjects in Mesopotamia converted to Christianity, and Roman emperors suggested that they had an interest in the well-being of fellow Christians. In 518, on the death of Anastasius, Justin was proclaimed emperor. Either at that point, or somewhat earlier, he adopted his nephew—who had already risen to a relatively senior position in the palace guard—as his son, and soon left the day-to-day management of affairs in his hands, making him co-emperor on April 1, 527. Justinian, who became sole emperor on August 1 of the same year, had already married a woman named Theodora, a former actress who had also, allegedly, been widely intimate with the young men of Constantinople (see box, left). Whether this is actually true, or simply a reflection of the belief that people in the entertainment industry lived scandalous lives, we cannot now know.

The unflattering picture of Theodora the prostitute comes to us courtesy of the *Secret History* of Procopius (see pp. 16–17), the major historian of the era. It is thanks to his principal historical works on the wars of Justinian that we have narratives of Justinian's efforts to restore imperial control over the western Mediterranean. Since, in his history of the wars, he also describes how the Germanic kingdom of Africa and Italy came into being, his work is also important for Western history from the mid-fourth century onwards. The other main source for the history of the previous half century also resided at the court of Justinian: this is the historian Jordanes, whose main work is a history of the Goths in Latin. Another figure of some importance at this time, also a Westerner who had come to the court, was a theologian known as Dionysius Exiguus (meaning either "the Short" or "the Insignificant"). It was Dionysius who popularized a system of dating based upon the notion that Jesus Christ had been born 490 years after the putative date of the foundation of the second temple at Jerusalem. This put the birth of Christ, in Roman terms, in the consulship of Cornelius Lentulus and Calpurnius Piso, at a date now known as 1 BC. The fact that it is irreconcilable with dates for the birth of Christ offered in either the Gospel of Matthew (before 4 BC when Herod the Great died) or Luke (in AD 6 when Sulpicius Quirinius was governor of Syria) did not prevent its gradual adoption as the chronological system by which most of the modern world numbers its years.

All intellectual projects of this time, however, pale into insignificance by comparison with Justinian's massive new codification of Roman law. At this point the issuance of a law code may have been more symbolically important than ever, for, in imitation of the Romans, the Germanic kings of the West were now issuing their own laws. In 506 (the year before his fatal encounter with Clovis), Alaric II had issued a law code for the use of his Roman subjects consisting of two parts: a collection of laws (mostly derived from the Theodosian Code and later legislation of that emperor that had been collected as the Novels of Theodosius), and a statement of "law" based on earlier works (including extracts from the two Diocletianic Codes). Similarly, another set of laws, *The Roman Law of the Burgundians*, was issued by King Gundobad. Gundobad had briefly assumed the mantle of Ricimer in 472 as imperial emperor-maker before leaving Italy to take regal office among the Burgundians, an east Germanic tribe who had remained in eastern Gaul ever since they crossed the Rhine after the breach of the frontier at the end of 406. Although Gundobad was as dangerous as any German king of the age—he murdered both brothers with whom he had originally shared power—his code is an interesting example of independent legal reasoning that sets out legal rules on the basis of a number of earlier Roman sources.

THE RAVENNA MOSAICS

These two mosaics, which appear opposite each other in the apse of the church of San Vitale at Ravenna, offer powerful images of the emperor Justinian and his wife, Theodora. In the first mosaic, Justinian, cloaked in purple and with a halo around his head, holds a paten (the golden bowl that held the bread of the Eucharist). The arrangement of figures around the emperor emphasizes the unity of the civic and episcopal hierarchy. The archbishop of Ravenna, Maximianus—the only figure identified by name in the mosaic— and other clerics are depicted on the emperor's left; court officials and the imperial guard appear on Justinian's right. In the second mosaic, Theodora is front and center. Like her husband, she is depicted with a golden halo and bears an offering (a golden cup containing the Eucharistic wine). The empress is surrounded by ladies of the court as they process together through a curtained doorway into the church. These mosaics were made soon after Justinian's troops had captured Ravenna in 540. Although the emperor and his wife never visited the city, such images as these were an important means of emphasizing Ravenna's unity with the Roman empire in the East, and of asserting Justinian's authority in Italy. The fact that Theodora should have featured so prominently is a sign of her unique position at the emperor's court.

Justinian's Code would remain the foundation for later law based upon that of Rome. The first effort at codification began in 528 and was completed a year later (the sole remaining passage from this code has come down through a papyrus). The next act was the collection of fifty decisions that seem to have been assembled in preparation for another code, which was being prepared even as a massive compilation of the work of earlier jurists, now known as the *Digest*, was assembled in fifty books. The *Digest* was officially completed on December 30, 533 and its publication was accompanied by a textbook (which was also to have the force of law) known as the *Institutes*. Our knowledge of Roman legal thought is largely derived from this astonishing undertaking. Finally, on November 16, 534, a new code, drawing upon the Diocletianic and Theodosian codes as well as later legislation, was issued in twelve books. Covering ecclesiastical law in book one, private law in books two to eight, criminal law in book nine, and administrative law in books ten to twelve, the *Codex Justinianus* presents the remains of imperial legislation from the second century AD onwards. Although many texts are very heavily edited (something that becomes immediately evident when texts that also appear in the Theodosian Code are compared with the versions included in the Code of Justinian) they are still crucial for our understanding of how emperors did their jobs throughout the many centuries of imperial rule. For Justinian the code represented his hope that he could stabilize the laws of his empire under the protection of God, but it may have remained a dream. Later legislation depicts the emperor seeking always for something better. In that case it is a fitting parallel for his efforts to recover land in the West.

Even as the great legal projects were in progress, Justinian had provoked a war with Persia by expanding Roman control along the eastern shore of the Black Sea and constructing new fortified bases in Mesopotamia, especially at a place called Dara, close to Nisibis, the key fortress surrendered by Jovian in 363. After a pair of

This map illustrates Justinian's attempt to reconquer the West, which began with the takeover of Vandal north Africa in 533. The invasion of Italy proved more complex, and was not fully completed until 562. The invasion of Visigothic Spain began in 551, after Justinian sent 2,000 men to support a rebellion against King Agila.

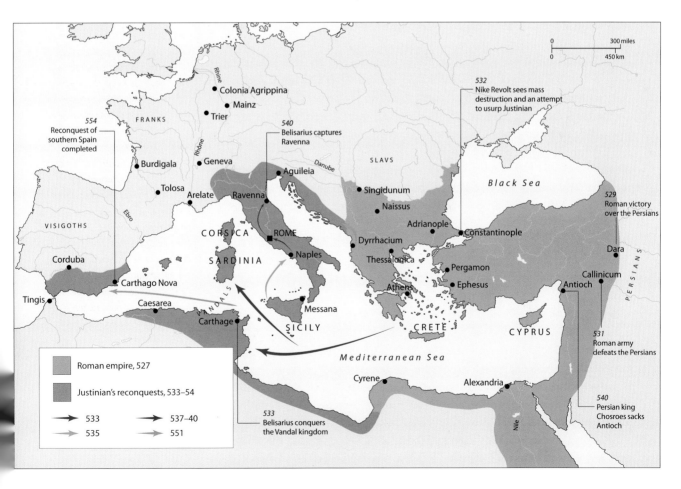

major battles—one (at Dara) an unequivocal Roman success, the other (at Callinicum on the Euphrates) at least a strategic success—and a succession crisis in Persia, peace was made in 532. That peace also followed a massive riot that broke out in the circus at Constantinople during January of the same year. Known as the Nike Revolt, since the mob used the circus cry of "Nike" or "victory," this riot exploded after a very badly managed effort on the part of the urban prefect to impose order after an earlier riot. The end result was massive destruction in Constantinople itself, an aborted coup against Justinian, and the massacre of tens of thousands of the rioters by Justinian's troops. One of the men sent to suppress the riot was the general Belisarius, recently recalled from command against Persia, and soon to be sent out as leader of the effort to restore imperial government in the West.

Justinian's plan mirrored the collapse of imperial authority: it was to begin with the recovery of Africa and Sicily (essential to support both military activity and reconstruction) and then proceed to the overthrow of the Ostrogothic regime in Italy. The first phase of the campaign went very smoothly. Belisarius landed in Africa in 533, routed the Vandal army, captured Carthage, and reinstituted Roman control within little more than a year.

The invasion of Italy seemed, at least initially, as if it would go as smoothly as the invasion of north Africa. Landing towards the end of 536, the armies of Belisarius occupied Rome, and, after withstanding a long siege, broke out to occupy the rest of the peninsula, capturing Ravenna four years later. The Ostrogoths were not, however, so easily beaten, and it seems that they retained the loyalty of a substantial proportion of the Italian aristocracy. War dragged on for the duration of Justinian's reign and well beyond, ruining the rural economy of Italy. At the same time a variety of natural catastrophes ensued. In the 530s some sort of disaster, presumably a massive volcanic eruption, blocked out the sun, leading to a series of abnormally cold winters and disastrous crop failures. Then, in 540, an outbreak of bubonic plague swept the Mediterranean. This outbreak, far more severe even than the great plague that swept the empire in AD 165–80, caused enormous loss of life. Although it is unlikely that the plague had such long-term effects on the population that the empire's economy went into permanent decline, there can be no doubt that the medium-term impact was enormous, meaning that Justinian's ambitious program simply lacked the economic infrastructure to make it work. One consequence may have been the failure to deploy a military force in Italy overwhelming enough to end the wars there.

At the same time that the war in Italy became bogged down, leading ultimately to a spectacularly unsuccessful intervention by the Franks, the Persians became vastly more aggressive. In 540 the Persian king Chosroes launched an attack on Syria, sacked Antioch, and extracted vast sums of money from other cities. He thus set in motion a tendency in these areas to accept foreign domination without resistance on the grounds that, once paid enough, the Persians would simply leave people to get on with their lives until the Roman regime managed to reassert itself. In this case, Chosroes left Syria relatively soon (in part, it seems, convinced by the outbreak of plague that it was an unhealthy place for his armies). Nonetheless war continued in various regions until 562.

Justinian died in 565. His dream of reconstituting something like the old Roman empire died with him. His legacy was a capital rebuilt in spectacular style after the

After the original church of Hagia Sophia (Holy Wisdom) in Constantinople was heavily damaged in the Nike Revolt, Justinian had a magnificent new church built on the same site. The nave of the Hagia Sophia, pictured right, is 260 feet (80 meters) long and its massive dome is more than 180 feet (55 meters) high, making it the largest open-vaulted interior constructed in the ancient and medieval periods. When the Ottoman Turks conquered Constantinople in 1453, the Hagia Sophia was converted into the Ayasofya Mosque; it is now a museum.

Nike Revolt, and imperial garrisons in Africa and in some portions of Spain (occupied in 551). But the war in Italy remained a constant drain on the economy; the population of Justinian's empire was shattered by the plague; the balance of power with Persia was turning in favor of the latter; and the Balkan frontier, whose defense had for some time relied on diplomacy rather than military power, was on the verge of collapse.

The World of Heraclius and Umar (AD 565–642)

The final collapse of the Balkan frontier was due to the movement of a new group of Turkic peoples, the Avars, out of the Ukraine and into the region north of the Danube. In 567 the Avars assisted the Lombards in destroying their long-term enemies, the Gepids (the safety of the Roman frontier had depended upon the Roman ability to play these two groups off against each other). The Lombards, however, recognizing that they were likely to be the next target for Avar expansion, headed south into Italy to continue the by now seemingly endless struggle for control of the peninsula. It is a mark of just how few troops the Romans state had committed to the Balkans that the Lombards were able to make their move without serious trouble.

Serious trouble was, however, on the cards for the Romans. The essential problem was that, even before the Avars arrived, the Slavs had moved into the area north of the mouth of the Danube. Once the Avars established themselves, the Slavs had a tendency to ally themselves with the Avars to raid Roman territory. On their own the Slavs, who seem to have been vastly less well organized than contemporary German peoples, were not a great threat. When linked with the Avars, they constituted a force that required powerful Roman armies to control it. From 572, with war raging in Italy and a new war breaking out with Persia, Justin II (Justinian's successor) had to concentrate on his Eastern enemy. The Avars seized the opportunity to launch a series of devastating raids across the Balkans that culminated in the capture of Sirmium—the long-time bastion of Roman rule on the upper Danube—in 582. That same year Tiberius, the short-lived successor of Justin, was replaced by the far more vigorous Maurice.

The reign of Maurice might seem to have stabilized the empire. A good soldier, he was able not only to drive back the Slavs and Avars, but also, through exploiting deep divisions within the Sasanian hierarchy, to impose what might have seemed at the time to have been a Roman client on their throne, Chosroes II. Impressive though they were, Maurice's victories could not reverse the effects of the disruption of the Balkan lands, and what seem to have been the knock-on effects in Asia Minor. It is in the second half of the sixth century in what is now western Turkey that we begin to see significant signs of the slowing of urban life, the movement of people out of city centers into the countryside, and a general decline in the upkeep of civic amenities. Of course this was not true in every place and to the same extent, but the trend is noticeable and suggests that the health of the Balkan economy had a direct impact on the economy on the far side of the Aegean.

Despite Maurice's successes and after a reign of twenty years, tensions surfaced within the imperial hierarchy. In 602, under the command of a general named Phocas, the Balkan army mutinied and marched on Constantinople. On November 25, 602 Phocas occupied the imperial palace. Maurice and his children were executed two days later in Chalcedon, or so it would seem. Shortly after the massacre, a man named Theodosius, claiming to be the son of Maurice, appeared in Ctesiphon asking that Chosroes restore him to the throne, just as Maurice had once respected the legitimate succession of Sasanian kings through the aid he gave to Chosroes. Whether this Theodosius really was the son of Maurice we cannot know. We do know that his appeal started a war between the Roman and Persian empires that would weaken them both so severely that they would both fall victim to a power, as yet unimagined, which would explode into being two decades later in northern Arabia.

From 603 to 610 the war with Persia went slowly but surely against the Romans, so much so that in the autumn of 610 the governor of Africa launched a fleet under the command of his son, Heraclius, to overthrow Phocas. On October 5 Phocas was dead and Heraclius was emperor. For the next fourteen years things went from bad to worse, beginning in 611 with the capture of Antioch; unlike the invasion

(see box, left)

VICTORY AT NINEVEH

Finding a plain suitable for battle he [Heraclius] set the army in order, making a speech to the soldiers. Razates, arriving there, drew up his army in three divisions and advanced upon the emperor. The battle was joined on the twelfth day of December, a Saturday. The emperor, advancing ahead of all the rest, fought with the commander of the Persians, and, through the power of God and with the aid of the Virgin Mary, he threw down his foe, and he routed those who had advanced with him, and immediately after that, the emperor fought with another man, and slew him. A third man assailed him, who struck him with his spear on the lip, and wounded him. The emperor killed this man, and when the trumpets sounded, both sides attacked each other, and as a fierce battle ensued, the tawny horse of the emperor, named Dorkos, was wounded, taking a lance in the thigh from the infantry; he also took many swords in the face, but, since he was wearing a helmet made of sinew, he was not hurt, nor were they effective. Razates fell in the battle, and the three divisional commanders of the Persians, and almost all their captains, and the greater part of their army.

(*Chronicle of Theopanes*, 318–19)

in the reign of Justinian, Chosroes had come to occupy not simply to loot. In 614, the Persians destroyed Jerusalem as an example to cities that might think of resistance rather than surrender, and in 619 they occupied Alexandria. The stage was set for the destruction of the empire, as Chosroes allied himself with the Avars and began a series of immensely destructive invasions of Asia Minor, culminating in a siege of Constantinople (assisted by the Avars) in 626. Heraclius, however, was not in the city. He had taken the bulk of his army into Armenia, and even as the siege of Constantinople fell apart, he advanced, at the head of an army that included a very large number of Turkish auxiliaries, into northern Iraq. On December 12, 627, Heraclius destroyed the Sasanian army in a battle at Nineveh, near Mosul in northern Iraq (see box, left). Chosroes was assassinated the next year and chaos ensued until the commander of Persian forces in what was still the Persian-occupied Near East negotiated the evacuation of all Roman territory so that he could claim the throne for himself. Peace was finally made in 630, and Heraclius entered Jerusalem in triumph.

The moment of Heraclius's triumph may not have been a matter of unmitigated joy for all. The churches of Syria, Palestine, and Egypt had never accepted the doctrine promulgated by the Council of Chalcedon of 451 as orthodoxy; they had responded to the notion that Christ had two natures by asserting a doctrine (now known as Monophysite) that he had "One Nature." Justinian had attempted to reconcile the Monophysites to the imperial regime at a council held at Constantinople in 553, where he issued a revised version of the Chalcedonian creed, stating that while there were two natures in Christ, there was only one will. However, this was no more acceptable to Monophysites than was original Chalcedonianism. As doctrine continued to be associated with a sense of community identity, and the imperial government whenever possible had tended to discriminate in favor of Chalcedonian leadership, it was often profoundly offensive to local sentiment. So, after nearly twenty years of rule by Zoroastrians who were disinterested in these issues, it would require a good deal of time before Heraclius's profoundly Chalcedonian regime could reestablish a viable relationship with the Christian establishment in newly liberated lands. The fact that one of Heraclius's most important appointments—a new head of the church at Alexandria—proved to be a violent persecutor of nonconforming clergy only aggravated the matter.

With the Sasanian empire collapsing into chaos, exhausted by the long war, it might have seemed that the imperial regime had survived the storm, and that some stability was returning. Although war continued in Italy, the Avars had submitted, securing peace along the Danube; the Frankish kings ruled Gaul and the Visigoths in Spain; and in Britain the first glimmerings were shining of a new Anglo-Saxon society. Real change was taking place well outside these areas, however, as a unique new product of the imperial world gave laws and revelation to a new community in northwestern Arabia. This was the prophet Mohammed.

The background for Mohammed's revelation is provided by the increasing penetration of Arabia by both Persians and Romans. One point upon which Christians of any denomination could agree was that it was better to be Christian than not, and thus that it was their duty to convert "infidels" (by definition people who lacked the faith) to their religion. Ethiopia had been converted in the time of Constantius II, and tribes along the frontier on the fringes of the Arabian desert had converted from the fourth century onwards, often serving as allies of Rome in the struggle with Persia.

Persia had responded with expeditions into Arabia and support for powerful pro-Persian tribal groups. Mohammed's revelation, asserting that Allah was the greatest of all gods, greater by far than the weak tribal gods who had been worshiped since time immemorial, urged the same tribes that had worshiped these gods to unite and become strong. By implication, the followers of Allah—a universal god whose first prophet had been Moses—would be able to rise up and subdue those who had taken advantage of their previous weakness.

The new message of Mohammed was powerful, if not immediately palatable. In 622 Mohammed was expelled from his homeland in Mecca, fleeing to the city of Medina where he established the first true community of Muslims. The flight from Mecca, the Hejira, is thus the first moment in the Islamic dating system, for it marks the beginning of history for the followers of the prophet. Within a decade, Mohammed had defeated his enemies in Mecca and forged a new tribal alliance that began to take in the desert Bedouin as well as the city Arabs who had been his original audience. The followers of the prophet then pursued Arabs who refused to accept the new revelation, and in the immediate aftermath of Mohammed's death in 632 Arab armies were already beginning to appear on the borders of the Roman and Persian empires. They were directed now by the first of Mohammed's successors, the Caliph Abu Bakr, who seems to have allowed a remarkably entrepreneurial system to take hold among his subordinates, which apparently allowed them to attack where opportunity offered. Given the weakness of both the Roman and Persian establishments in the wake of the war between them, those opportunities were readily available.

The Ka'ba at Mecca, in present-day Saudi Arabia, contains the Black Stone that embodies Allah and provides the directional focus for Muslim prayer; it is covered with a black veil, which is replaced annually. The holiest place in Islam, the Ka'ba has been the center of Muslim pilgrimage since the origins of the religion in the seventh century.

The Roman response to the sudden appearance of tribal armies from Arabia on the border of Syria was slow and ineffective. In 636 the army sent to repel the Arabs (ruled since 634 by the Caliph Umar) encountered their army at Yarmuk, near the Golan Heights. Thoroughly outmaneuvered, the Roman army was virtually annihilated. In the next several years, under constant pressure from the Arabs, Heraclius withdrew his defense to the line of the Taurus mountains. Communities in Syria and Palestine, left once again to their own devices, negotiated settlements with the new arrivals, expecting, at least in some cases, that the imperial government would at some point return.

When Heraclius died on February 11, 641 Egypt was under assault. The final act in this tale may be seen as the departure of the Roman garrison from Alexandria on September 17, 642. The fall of Alexandria effectively ushered in a new age in which the dominant force on the southern rim of the Mediterranean would be the new Islamic state. With the western Mediterranean long since lost to Germanic successor states, the Roman empire was now reduced to a regional power in the eastern Mediterranean, whose western outposts in Africa and Spain could not readily be supported. The Classical world had finally given way to the medieval.

Economic and Social Changes

There never was a single Roman economy. At the height of the empire in the second century AD, diverse local economies were linked by networks of exchange based on the imperial tax system, and on a system of redistribution that developed alongside, and extended beyond, the system of redistribution created by the tax system (see p. 249). The economic success of the empire stemmed from the ability of the imperial government to maintain the stability of this redistribution system. In the period from roughly AD 350 to 600 significant changes appear in the economic system, some of them directly attributable to political developments and others much less so, if at all. To explore these changes, it will be useful to examine broadly based structural issues: first, "environmental" changes that cannot necessarily be attributed to political and/or administrative changes; and second, issues of social organization that can be associated with administrative change (noting that failures of imperial administration do not follow a simple or unified pattern).

Among the most significant "environmental" changes are a decline in the smelting of metals, changes in health, and changes in diet. Studies of atmospheric pollution based on the Greenland ice-pack and Swiss peat bogs show that there was an overall decline in atmospheric pollution after AD 650. Other evidence suggests that production at major mining sites in Western Europe had declined much earlier. In Spain, for instance, where there were 173 mining sites before the fourth century, only twenty-one continued later; and of twenty-six iron-mining sites in Britain before AD 300, only three seem to have continued after that date. Similarly, iron works on the border between France and Spain that began operation in the first century BC ceased production in the fourth century AD. Iron mines in the Balkans, where imperial control became increasingly tenuous in the late fourth century (and when some miners are said to have sided with the Goths against Theodosius I), seem also to have ceased production around this time. On the other hand, mining activity in Armenia, southern Turkey, Cyprus, Egypt, and Attica, until at least the seventh century seems, if anything, to have picked up pace. The result for the Eastern government, which was still getting the metals that it needed, might not have been especially severe; it might, however, have hurt in the West.

Changes in the overall health of the empire might have had more serious economic consequences than changes in mining practice (see box, p. 342). At the same time, there is evidence of changing dietary patterns. These include a switch from the wheats typical of the earlier Roman period in Gaul to spelt, though in this case the switch may coincide with a change in villa ownership: more of the owners were now drawn from an increasingly Germanic upper class that was coming to dominate the military establishment at Trier. In Egypt there is evidence that tastes changed so that much less beer was consumed and a great deal more wine, while in Naples evidence for the consumption of pork, long a favorite of Romans, gives way to goats and sheep. The Vandals can be traced through their rather specific delight in eating horses.

In terms of economic and social issues, such as where people lived, how they were ruled, and how they made contact with the world beyond their immediate frontiers, the region of the empire most obviously affected by the departure of Roman government in the early fifth century was Britain. The Roman garrison largely departed with the usurper Constantine in 408, and Honorius appears to have renounced any interest in reestablishing direct imperial government on the

DISEASE IN THE SIXTH CENTURY

One of the environmental factors that may have affected the economic success of the empire was the overall health of its subjects. As we have already seen, in 540 there was a devastating outbreak of bubonic plague around the Mediterranean, which caused massive loss of life. Our sources provide evidence that there were other problems, however. There is, for instance, some reason to think that malaria was on the increase after the fourth century, especially in Italy, where growing inability to maintain earlier drainage efforts aggravated the problem. At the same time, in the East, Hansen's disease (leprosy), which had long been known in the empire, seems to have achieved virtually epidemic proportions in the course of the sixth century.

island in 412. Some sort of change, however, had already been in the air. As early as the 380s towns were beginning to fall into disrepair, as were some villas. After 402 it appears that silver coins ceased being shipped to the island, suggesting that the local imperial authorities were having trouble getting paid. Both Britain's link with the imperial tax system and the long-distance trading economy embedded within the tax system collapsed after the rebellion of Constantine. With the link to the broader economy broken, there was little to keep a local economy running as it had before. The removal of the bulk of the garrison to fight in Gaul, and the subsequent collapse of provincial administration, destroyed the basic mechanisms through which local hierarchies were joined, and through which local economies were held together. By about AD 430 town life had become seriously weakened, while in the countryside the mosaic floors of villas were covered in dirt, hearths were built inside rooms that had once been for display, and imports ceased. The indigenous British society was gradually being dominated by small groups of apparently highly militarized invaders from the other side of the North Sea, the Saxons. There are certain signs that an ancient urban society has collapsed. These include the fact that forum areas are no longer monumental centers, that there are fewer monumental buildings in general, that the spatial coherence of cities has broken down, that large buildings are divided into smaller ones, that construction techniques become simpler, that such public amenities as sewers cease to be maintained, that bodies begin to be buried within city walls, and that urban areas are transformed into rural. Britain pretty much fits this model.

In northern Gaul the situation was quite different. The decline of imperial society in the later fifth century brought to an end many centuries during which the Rhine had acted as a cultural dividing line between the Germanic tribes to the East and the Romanized regions of the West. The new Frankish regime straddled the Rhine, and as new cities began to develop at such places as Maastricht, what was once a frontier zone apparently started to develop into the center of a new economic system. In this case Frankish aristocrats tended to form alliances with earlier landholding elites, now often associated with churches as local bishops, to support their regime. A quite distinct division seems then to have grown up between urban centers that were heavily Christian, often supporting tourist sites based on the remains of a local saint (the most famous was Tours, and its fourth-century bishop, St. Martin), while the countryside remained a haven for unbelievers. That at least is the impression offered, for instance, by the biography of St. Martin, and by the new usage of the word *paganus* (whence our "pagan")—which means "outsider" or "country-dweller" in Classical

Latin—to mean "worshiper of the old gods." In the case of St. Martin, his crusade in the countryside involved, at one point, setting fire to an "ancient and famous temple" in "some village" and demonstrating his holy power by preventing the flame from spreading to neighboring houses. In another case, when he was initially stopped by the inhabitants of the isolated village of Leprosum from destroying their temple "made rich by superstition," he obtained aid from two angels in military dress who protected him in his work of destruction (Sulpicius Severus, *Life of Saint Martin* 14).

In the south of France, where more "Roman" regimes continued until the Frankish victory over the Visigoths at Vouillé in 507, change from earlier patterns was less obvious, both under the Visigoths and an essentially local emperor named Avitus. Trade networks with the eastern Mediterranean expanded in the course of the fifth century: by the third quarter of the century, amphorae found at Marseilles suggest that this trade was even more substantial than the continuing exchange with what was now Vandal north Africa. In the sixth century, possibly as a result of changes in the Vandals' relationship with their neighbors, patterns of trade revert to an earlier pattern where African wares predominate. Still, even as ships from Africa and elsewhere came to Arles and Marseilles, it appears that traffic was beginning to shift away from the Rhône, long the main line of communication between northern France and the Mediterranean. This was possibly because the weaker regimes in the area could no longer afford to keep the river navigable.

The situation in Spain was somewhat different from that of Gaul. The great expansion of Spanish agriculture in the first and second centuries AD, when southern Spain became one of the major providers of food and other goods to Rome, appears to have come to an end before the beginning of the fourth century: at this point Spanish pottery gives way to African in the great "amphora dump" of Monte Testaccio at Rome. That said, Spain does not seem to have entered into a period of obvious or significant decline (and it is always possible that Spanish produce was carried in African amphorae). A survey of villa culture in the fourth century shows that it continued to thrive in the areas that had always been especially rich—the Guadalquivir valley, the region around the Ebro, Catalonia in the north, and what is now southern Portugal. Evidence from local forms of Spanish pottery suggests that a well-established system of economic redistribution linked northern Spain with the Guadalquivir valley in the south.

Given the evidence for continued prosperity, it is perhaps not surprising that the arrival of the Goths and other German tribes in the early fifth century, which came as a shock to an area long insulated from violence, was seen initially as catastrophic (see box, p. 344); but the reality seemed quite different as time passed. Having driven the Suevi back into the mountains of Portugal, and made the land inhospitable even to the Vandals, the Gothic kingdom established increasingly close links with the existing aristocracy, which seems to have remained quite (if not immensely) wealthy. Spanish cities retain the architectural coherence of Roman cities, with new buildings tending on the whole to be churches. As in southern Gaul, the economy may have been simplified, but the Roman state had been replaced by a new state that still had the wherewithal to function. Only in the seventh century, starting at the fringes of the kingdom, is there evidence that some cities were completely ceasing to function; but even then, the kingdom as a whole was still a very rich prize for the Arab armies that began to arrive in 711.

THE GOTHS IN SPAIN: TWO VIEWS

The earliest chronicler of the arrival of the Goths and other Germanic tribes in Spain in the early fifth century viewed it as an unmitigated disaster:

> As the barbarians ran wild through Spain and the deadly pestilence continued on its savage course, the wealth and goods stored in the cities were plundered by the tyrannical tax collector, and consumed by the soldiers. A famine ran riot, so dire that driven by hunger human beings devoured human flesh; mothers too feasted upon the bodies of their own children whom they had killed and cooked with their own hands; wild beasts habituated to feeding on the bodies of those slain by sword, famine or pestilence, killed all the braver individuals and feasting on their flesh everywhere became brutally set upon the destruction of the human race. And this with the four plagues of sword, famine, pestilence, and wild beasts raging everywhere through the world, the annunciation foretold by the Lord through his prophets came to fulfillment.

(Hydatius, *Chronicle* 16, trans. Burgess)

The author here may, however, be overstating the case. The long-term effects of the arrival of the Goths (and, one suspects, the short-term as well) were considerably less dramatic. By way of contrast to the apocalyptic vision of Hydatius, Isidore of Seville's *History of the Kings of the Goths*, composed just as Syria was falling to the Arabs in the 630s, strikes a rather more positive note. Isidore concludes with such sentiments as:

> The Goths are agile by nature, quick to understand, with a strong sense of duty, robust in bodily strength, lofty in stature, of impressive carriage and demeanor, skillful with their hands and impervious to wounds ... All the peoples of Europe feared them. The barriers of the Alps gave way before them. The Vandals, widely known for their own barbarity, were not so much terrified by the presence of the Goths as put to flight by their renown. The Alans were extinguished by the strength of the Goths. The Suevi, too, forced into inaccessible corners of Spain, have now experienced the danger of extermination at the hands of the Goths.

(Isidore of Seville, *History* 67–68, trans. Wolf)

In north Africa, even though the Vandal conquest doomed the government of the Western empire to irrelevance, it does not appear to have doomed the peoples of the region to poverty. This is despite the fact that if any region might be expected to have suffered from the invasions, it would be north Africa, for the conquest effectively destroyed the principal market for its production. It is true that some, but not all, the signs of urban decline that appeared in Britain are evident, including the absence of monumental building (other than churches) and the transformation of public buildings into houses. This is even the case to some extent in Carthage, even though Vandal kings rebuilt baths and palaces on a substantial scale. Elsewhere, surviving mosaics from villas in north Africa provide intriguing visual evidence of how signs of continuity were mixed with those of discontinuity in the period after the Vandal conquest (see box, pp. 346–47).

The signs of economic weaknesses that appear under the Vandal kings—who were themselves very rich, and appear, along with their nobles, to have hoarded the goods they were no longer trading—do not continue in the wake of the imperial reconquest of 533–34. From the middle of the sixth century onwards, the province rejoined the Mediterranean world with genuine vigor, even though it seems that more of its trade might have been directed to the eastern Mediterranean than in the past. It remained a significant economic center through the first decades of the Arab conquest.

Turning to Italy, the most obvious change was in the status of the city of Rome. The population of Rome already seems to have declined by the end of the fourth century to somewhere around 800,000, a population still many times that of any other place. This decline was possibly because the loss of administrative relevance had drawn people to other imperial centers. The collapse of imperial government in the early fifth century led to a speedy and irreversible decline, with the population reaching perhaps 350,000 by the time of the Vandal sack (455) and dropping to perhaps 60,000 by the time of Belisarius's arrival eighty years later (536). At that point Rome was smaller than it had been at the end of the Regal period some 1,000 years earlier (see p. 53). The ravages of the invasions were felt elsewhere in Italy as well. In 418 Honorius ruled that:

> Campania shall have its lands made subject to tax equalization and with the exception of the tax dues, shall bear only the ninth part of the past amount of payments to the State, since a very heavy tax assessment of former times burdens its territory, and since that assessment it has been devastated by the incursion of the enemy.
>
> (*Theodosian Code* 11.28.12)

Scattered evidence for renewed stability in the wake of the Ostrogothic conquest of the late fifth century gives way to a very great deal of evidence for the ruin of urban Italy in the century after the arrival of Belisarius. With trade restricted and its lands a constant battleground, Italy was reduced to a situation that was worse than its circumstances before the rise of Rome in the later fourth century BC. One reason that the wars with the Ostrogoths may have continued was that the landed classes of Italy had come to identify their interests more strongly with those of the Ostrogoths than with those of Constantinople. A factor in this decision may have been the fact that the brand of Christianity promoted by the imperial court after 553 (see p. 399) was offensive to the church in Italy, especially as represented by the bishop of Rome who, ever since the reign of Gratian, had the right to style himself *pontifex maximus*. He began increasingly to assert that, as the heir of the apostle Peter, he had the authority to establish doctrine for the Western church.

The decline of the Balkans is perhaps more difficult to trace than that of other regions, since the archaeological record is not remotely as robust here as for other areas. Still, our literary sources do provide some clues. For instance, Theodoric Strabo is described as crossing "the central desert" (an area devoid of population in this case) in Thrace (Malchus, fragment 18.2), and various other accounts reveal that by 600 travelers from the West simply sailed to Constantinople rather than risk travel along the Danube or the ancient Via Egnatia, which had been the basic route across the Balkans since its construction in the second century BC (see p. 93). Histories of Roman campaigns against the Slavs and Avars seem to depict the struggle as being waged in a rural wilderness, and after the fall of Sirmium—which seems to have been an isolated outpost of imperial diplomacy for more than a century before its fall—in 582, there seems to have been little left of Roman rule. Indeed, descriptions from the fourth century already suggest serious depopulation resulting from Gothic raids; one reason that Gothic tribes could be settled in the central Balkans was presumably because they were not replacing significant tax-paying populations. It may be telling that from the middle of the fifth century,

NORTH AFRICAN MOSAICS

The mosaics that were created to decorate the floors of villas and public buildings offer an important window on the culture of Roman north Africa. One fourth-century mosaic from a villa in Carthage, pictured below, depicts an aristocratic estate. At the heart of the mosaic, reflecting its centrality in the life of the community, is the main building, which is surrounded by a wall. The estate owner is shown at the bottom right receiving his rents, while his wife adorns herself on the lower left. A peasant's hut is depicted in the upper right-hand corner of the mosaic.

These mosaics can offer important evidence of the continuity in the life and ambitions of the elite in the periods before and after the Vandal conquest. For example,

Scenes of harvesting and hunting predominate in this image, as they do in many north African mosaics. Agriculture was central to the continuing economic success of the region. Control of the African grain supply had been a vital aspect of political power at Rome in the final years of the Western empire, and the region remained a key source of grain for the wider Mediterranean world in the centuries after the empire's collapse.

imperial expeditions from Constantinople to the West tended to sail rather than march: this suggests that the infrastructure needed to support an army on the march had dissipated. Some counter-evidence to this view is offered by the acts of church councils, which reveal continuing organization within provinces for which there is otherwise little evidence. More telling, however, is that in other areas of the empire, the organization of successor states seems to bear some relationship to the existing urban structure. But this is not the case here. What excavations there are show such signs of shattered urbanism: closely packed houses, lack of respect for previously monumental areas, lack of new monumental building, and flimsy construction of newer dwellings.

The Eastern provinces are a completely different story, and continue to differ from the West well after the collapse of Roman control in Egypt. First, there remained a series of major cities aside from Constantinople, Antioch, and Alexandria. Such places as Thessalonica, Ephesus, and Aphrodisias remained distinctively prosperous until the early seventh century when it appears that the Persian invasions did them fatal harm. The most impressive evidence for not only continued prosperity but also

In this mosaic, the man at the top pursues a rabbit with hounds, and just below this a hunter is chasing a boar into a net; the next scene shows falconry, and at the foot of the mosaic partridges are being driven into a net.

a fifth-century mosaic from a villa in the town of Kelibia, pictured above, depicts scenes of hunting—suggesting that, even as the Vandals were taking control in north Africa, the traditional pastimes of the upper classes endured intact. Further evidence of continuity can be found in the fact that, even after the Vandal conquest, villas continued to be decorated with scenes from Classical mythology and depictions of the heroes of pagan antiquity. Although the people who commissioned these mosaics would almost certainly have been Christian, and were certainly subjects of a Vandal, they saw in the tales of Classical antiquity a symbol of their own authority rather than that of any specific state. Even if they did not know the stories very well, or were not well educated in Greek, they were aware that the narratives of the past conferred authority upon themselves.

Serjilla, pictured right, is one of the best-preserved examples of the communities that flourished on the limestone plateau in northwestern Syria from the beginning of the fifth century. The construction of substantial villas and a bath complex demonstrates that this region, despite its barren appearance today, was well enough watered in antiquity to support a diversified rural economy and a prosperous local elite.

actual economic expansion in the fifth and sixth centuries, however, comes from Syria and Egypt. This prosperity is despite the fact that these regions were now taxed at much higher rates than previously, and, with the Balkans in disarray, bore the main burden of supporting the military and administrative apparatus of the state. This new prosperity is perhaps most evident on the great limestone massif south of Antioch, which appears to have become a major exporter of agricultural produce right through the time of the Arab conquest.

At the same time that the economies of Egypt and Syria expanded, they gave rise to a significant new movement with Christianity. This was monasticism, which originally took two forms, anchorite and coenobic. Anchorite monks lived as individuals in the desert: the title comes from the Greek *anachoresis*, which, in Egypt, had the specific implication of "flight to the desert." Their existence is attested in the years immediately prior to the persecution unleashed by Diocletian. Coenobic monks begin to become significant in the reign of Constantine; the term derives from the Greek *koinos bios* or "common life," denoting the fact that they lived in organized communities. In both cases the impact of the monks was to add a significant new rural dimension to Christianity, which had developed as a largely urban institution in the first several centuries after the crucifixion. In the West, monastic communities, invariably coenobic, developed rather later, and largely seem to be a product of the lessening importance of cities as cultural centers.

The rural aspect of monasticism makes it especially important for understanding the nature of the relationship between cities and villages, as well as between emperors and their subjects. Although there had always been rural shrines, drawing interested tourists from cities into the countryside (or later, as in the case of such figures as St. Martin of Tours, incendiary reformist clergy), they were not linked in any profound, institutional way with religious practices in major cities. The relationship between monks and their rural sites, however, enabled them to assert considerable independence from cities, at a time when urban politics were increasingly dominated by the relationships between town councils and governors, which also led to a decline in the perceived status of people who served in (and paid for) local government. With provinces shrinking and governors more likely to participate in local politics, to be a town councilor was no longer to be the intermediary between a great and distant power, as it had been in the second century. Town councilors were more likely to have to act as audience to a self-promoting individual whose ability to dominate a city stemmed from his being somewhat richer and better connected. The complexity of the relationship between civic and imperial government may also help explain why by far the longest section of the Theodosian Code, containing no fewer than 192 entries, concerns the responsibilities of councilors.

Outside the cities, and possibly influenced by the increasing tension between local and imperial authorities, there seems to have been intense interest in finding ways either to exclude the agents of central administration, or to control their means of access. Thus peasants still paid their taxes (through their village authorities) and often paid rent to distant landlords, but tried to keep as distant from the imperial authorities as possible. It was often the monk who assumed the role of local authority figure to keep imperial officials at arm's length. Indeed, one thing that the anchorite St. Antony does, in the idealized life that Athanasius composed about him, is to consult with pagan philosophers who come into the country to debate with him;

another is to intervene in Alexandria to support Athanasius. Increasingly, with the passage of time, monks developed direct connections with bishops: on an ideological level, bishops might seek to exploit the reputations of specific individuals for particular holiness as allies in their causes; or, on a more mundane level, they would recruit monks as "muscle" to support a position during the endemic struggles over the nature of the Trinity. In both cases the greater power resided in the countryside. It was often the case that bishops sought to make famous monks into bishops who would side with them—and that some monks, such as Pachomius, who founded one of the most important coenobic communities in Egypt, actively avoided recruitment.

Evidence for the role of the monk in the countryside, providing not simply spiritual but also practical advice, appears throughout these centuries in both actual and idealized settings. Thus we can see one monk, named John, dealing with the problems of a man who clearly thought that John could act as arbitrator to solve some difficulty he had gotten into (see box, left). On a more idealized plane, there are various accounts of the activities of St. Symeon, who resided on a pillar near the village of Telanissos on the limestone plateau east of Antioch. This holy man had evidently resurrected (or repopularized) an old non-Christian form of Syrian devotion, according to which a person stood atop a pillar near a sanctuary. According to one of the witnesses to his career he could be seen as a mediator in disputes of all sorts:

> He can be seen sitting in judgment and handing down proper and just sentences. These and similar activities are dealt with after three in the afternoon, for he spends the whole night and the day up till three pm in prayer. After three pm he delivers the divine teaching to those present and then, after receiving the request of each and effecting some healings, he resolves the quarrels of the disputants.
>
> (Theodoret, *Life of Saint Symeon*, trans. Doran, 26)

Those who assembled for teaching, cures, or conflict resolution seem to have come from all over, since according to the same witness:

> It is not only inhabitants of our part of the world who pour in, but also Ishmaelites (Arabs), Persians and the Armenians subject to them, the Iberians, the Homerites and those who live even further in the interior than these. Many come from the extreme west: Spaniards, Britons and the Gauls who come between them. It is superfluous to speak of Italy, for they say that he became so well-known in the great city of Rome that small portraits of him were set up on a column at the entrances of every shop to bring through that some protection and security.
>
> (Theodoret, *Life of Saint Symeon*, trans. Doran, 11)

For another witness, the author of a life of Symeon in Syriac, the worldwide reach of the saint was equally impressive, for he managed to project his power great distances. For instance, he smote both a "Magus in the land of the Persians, head of all the Magi, that is to say, leader of all evil" who had convinced the Persian king to persecute Christians; and the town councilor of Antioch, "an evil and wicked man" who harassed many, including those who dyed skins red, with painful illnesses (*Syriac Life of Symeon*, trans. Doran, 56, 68). Somewhat more mercifully Symeon might also intervene, as he did when a ship at Cyprus, "loaded with much cargo and ready to sail

AN APPEAL TO A MONK

To my master, the beloved Apa (Father) John. I give thanks to God and whoever will assist me for your sake and through God; for all souls live through you because of your piety (towards) the Almighty. So help me now; write a letter to Psois from Taeto, ex-tribune, that I may be released—if I have not (by then) been released. For Psois's son has already demanded of me seven gold solidi and his assistant another gold solidus; for you took money from me so that I might obtain my release, and they [?] have not released me. I ask God that you either release me or hand over to me the eight gold solidi. For I am Psois, son of Cyllus from the village of Pochis in the Antaeopolite nome (district). Now then do not neglect this, master, for God's sake; for you have already given my children as securities to the moneylender on account of the gold. And I never go on active service, being unfit; for I have a complete excuse for this on account of my finger; it has not festered, nor has it healed either. [Address] Deliver to my master, the anchorite John.

(*Papyri from Hermopolis*, trans. Rees, no. 7)

for the West," was caught in a great storm (*Syriac Life of Symeon* 72). Perhaps most importantly, among all the acts of vengeance, healings of the sick, and conversions of pagans (occasionally smitten with pest-control issues) was the fact that his reputation enabled him to write to "the holy bishops, the clergy, and everyone according to his rank, even the Christian emperors and lovers of Christ, Mar Theodosius (II) and his sisters." On one occasion at least (much to the approval of his biographer) he got the emperor to reverse the tolerant action of an imperial official towards the local Jewish community (*Syriac Life of Symeon* 50, 121–22).

The point of the saint was thus to project power out from the hinterland and contain the resolution of disputes within it. This role may also be seen in the life of St. Theodore, bishop of Sicyon in central Turkey: he was not only very good at dealing with demons—who seem a virtual metaphor here for social unrest and disease—but also saw something of the world, purchased a silver chalice from Constantinople, and traveled to Jerusalem. Politically neutral, he exchanged letters with the Emperor Maurice, and healed Maurice's successor Phocas of disease. Likewise, St. Nicholas of Sion in southern Turkey (the prototype for Santa Claus) traveled widely through-

The cruciform church of St. Symeon, at Qal'at Sim'an, was constructed around an octagon (pictured above) at the heart of which stood Symeon's pillar. Part of a larger compound, which included a monastery, several other churches, and housing for pilgrims, the church was built in the late fifth century with the assistance of extensive patronage from the emperor Zeno. The project reflects the way that emperors had to negotiate their own authority around that of local religious figures.

out the East when not dealing with local survivals of pagan practice (especially the worship of gods in trees), healing the sick, and offering substantial banquets. For people who dealt with them, these religious figures are images of a world where people know how to keep outsiders at bay and gain respect for their communities.

Returning to the more mundane, perhaps the best evidence for the culture of avoiding interference by the government is offered by the text of an arbitration agreement from the village of Aphrodito in Egypt. This includes an oath to abide by the terms of the local arbitrator, while abandoning efforts to find a solution through the court system. Probably dating from 537, the terms of the oath include the following:

> And (I acknowledge) that I am not able at any moment or time to proceed against you or your heirs in court, be they local or elsewhere, or out of court, neither I on my own, nor through an authorized representative, nor through a man of straw, irrespective of whether this (acknowledgment) or part of it might become ineffective on the basis of an imperial act or an imperial decree or a rescript or an imperial will or a juridical argument or on whatever other basis … And for all this in general and for each one of the aforementioned items separately I took an oath by the holy and consubstantial Trinity and the piety and victory of the gloriously triumphant lord of the world, Flavius Iustinianus, the eternal august emperor, that I abide forever by the legal force of this agreement of settlement and to each of its parts and items and that I will not transgress it in any way.
>
> (*PMichAphrod*, 10, 57–66, 76–81, trans. Gagos and van Minnen)

Thus is the power of Justinian invoked as a guarantee for an agreement that specifically excludes the imperial justice system! The tendency towards self-help and self-governance evident in arbitration agreements of this sort, and idealized in the lives of saints, reflects an age-old process of negotiation that was so often at the heart of imperial administration. In Syria, Palestine, and Egypt, it also proved to be a habit that contributed in no small way to the sudden collapse of imperial authority. In the years of Persian invasion, only Jerusalem attempted to resist rather than negotiate a settlement with the invaders (and the result was a massacre of the population by the Persians). Similarly, in the years after the Arab victory over the Roman army at Yarmuk in 636, communities preferred to negotiate with the often very small armies of Arabia. No one could predict that they would never leave, or that the armies of the emperor would not come back. Indeed, so little did people understand the newcomers that contemporary texts do not even mention the fact that they were the bearers of a new religion. In exchanging one master for another, the communities of the East were not consciously exchanging one style of administration for another, nor would they be less prosperous as a result of their decisions.

In all of this the crucial point that emerges is that the decline of Roman power cannot be seen as the direct consequence of economic failure. Where economic decline is evident—in central and Western Europe rather than the Near East—it follows rather than precedes the decline of imperial control.

Explaining Decline

Just as there can be no single date for the "end of the Roman empire," so too there is no simple or easy explanation for the progressive decline. Indeed, more than 200 reasons—ranging from superstition, celibacy, imperial absolutism, two-front war, excessive taxation, and the consumption of water passed through lead pipes—have, at one time or another, been proposed to explain this. The fact that the declines of the Eastern and Western empire took place at different times, and in the face of very different circumstances, suggests that explanations that depend on "general truths" are best avoided. There is no actual evidence to prove, for instance, that the imperial government wrote its own death warrant by undermining the urban culture of the empire through excessive taxation; that urban decline preceded rather than followed the collapse of imperial administrative systems; that the state was more "superstitious" in the fifth century; that the weak rulers of the fifth century were especially "absolutist"; or that the imperial system had been poisoned by drinking water from lead pipes. There is no reason to think that there had been a long-term decline in the population of the empire—and certainly no reason to think that the population was approaching the sort of historical low point that has been plausibly postulated for the first century BC—though there is good reason to believe that the ability of the state to mobilize its population had declined dramatically by the end of the fourth century. Since the failure of imperial government was the cause rather than the effect of economic decline, it is likely that deliberate imperial policy decisions at various points in the course of the fourth through seventh centuries were factors in the weakening of the empire as a whole, and indeed that with each failure the consequences of further failure became more severe.

In discussing failure, the progressive weakening of the empire's military capacity also needs to be considered. For one thing, the division of the empire made it much harder to concentrate overwhelming force against any enemy. If Constantius II could not, for instance, summon extra legions from the Rhine to fight Sapor II on the Euphrates in the 350s (see p. 307), the demographic advantage enjoyed by the empire as a whole over the Sasanians evaporated. Later, the intense hatred of the Eastern court for Stilicho (see p. 317) meant that no help was forthcoming from the East until after his death, and it appears that by 420 nearly half the army that Honorius had inherited had been wiped out. In Gaul the situation was especially dire: of the fifty-eight units that comprised the army of the Rhine in 420, thirty-seven had been formed since 395 as replacements for units that had been destroyed.

Statistics, such as those for the army of Honorius, can be looked at in two ways. On the one hand, it is possible to stress the magnitude of the losses. On the other, it might also be possible to emphasize the fact that the losses had been repaired. Both are legitimate observations. Furthermore, it is clear that the fifth-century army in the West actually functioned reasonably effectively when it was well commanded. Stilicho did manage to beat Radagaisus and Alaric; the Romans under Constantius III managed to drive the Goths into Spain; and the army appears to have worked well in its last great battle at Châlons. Although suffering heavy losses in the wake of the Germanic invasion across the Rhine in 406, the army did recover, and in the end did not so much disintegrate as transform itself into the army of King Odovacer of Italy.

THE BATTLE OF YARMUK, 636

In this year the Saracens, leaving Arabia, came into the region of Damascus, being numerous beyond count. Vahan, learning this, sent to the imperial *sakellarios*, so that he would come to his aid with his own army, because of the number of the Arabs. The *sakellarios* joined Vahan, and, setting out from Emesa, they made contact with the Arabs, and the battle began, on the first day, which was the third day of the week, on the 23rd of July. Those with the *sakellarios* were defeated. The soldiers with Vahan mutinied, and proclaimed Vahan as emperor and denounced Heraclius. Those with the *sakellarios* withdrew, and the Saracens, seeing the opportunity, renewed the battle, a wind blew from the south into the face of the Romans, who were defeated when they were unable to resist the enemy because of the dust, and throwing themselves down the banks of the Yarmuk River were destroyed there. The armies of both generals amounted, in all, to 40,000 men.

(*Chronicle of Theophanes*, 337-8)

From the time of Julian through Heraclius, the Eastern army was more often the victim of displays of military ineptitude than the army of the West. Even when commanded by such incompetents as Vahan (the commander at Yarmuk), the army seems to have fought hard. The problem, however, was not so much that the army did not lose very often, but rather that an imperial army on the defensive could not really afford to lose at all. If Vahan had won at Yarmuk he would not then have gone on to crush the power of Islam by marching on Mecca; the infrastructure for long-term offensive actions no longer existed. The erosion of that same infrastructure meant that there were simply no troops left to contest further Muslim raids after Vahan's army was virtually annihilated, just as when Valens lost at Adrianople there were no troops with which to contest Gothic raiding, until Gratian showed up. Such major defeats as these, or the crossing of the Rhine in 406, or the capture of Carthage in 439, that were not answered by equally major victories, contributed to the inevitable weakening of the empire. But they still do not tell the whole story.

If neither economic decline nor military failure can be seen as decisive factors, how else might the failures of the empire be explained? In the third century AD, lack of imagination was certainly a significant factor in the weakening of the empire, and it may well be seen, in a different form, in the West during the fifth century. The sheer bigotry evident at the court of Honorius that prevented the enrollment of Alaric into the imperial service certainly caused immense difficulty. But so too did the failure to address the core reasons why anyone should have considered employing Alaric in the first place: the incapacity of the empire to raise large enough armies to serve its needs from internal sources. This was largely because of the concentration of power in the hands of people who would be disadvantaged if their tenants were drafted into the army. Men such as these could (and did) make their own arrangements with new rulers. In the end the issues confronting the government of the fifth century were very similar to those that Rome faced in the first century BC, in that the machinery of state was largely privatized by persons whose own power was such that the state could not control them.

The situation in the seventh century was, it seems, quite different. Here the imperial army's failure to control the frontiers led to the severe dislocation of authority, with the result that the tendency to devolve power onto local entities became ever more powerful, and had not yet been reversed by the time the armies of Caliph Umar began knocking on the gates of Syria. The fall of the empire beyond the Taurus was largely a voluntary operation, with cities that could have resisted the Arabs choosing instead to surrender on relatively generous terms. Religious antagonism may have played a role in the choices that people made—it certainly seems to have done so in Egypt—but more important may well have been the feeling that, after years of Persian occupation, one could do without the emperor if need be. The failure of the Eastern regime in the seventh century was largely a failure of ideology, in that the court could no longer convince its subjects that it was better off with Constantinople than without. The experience of the Persian wars had broken the essential social contract that had held an inherently fractious empire together. This was the promise of peace and prosperity, guaranteed by the emperor's military might.

To end this story with a vision of decline is at once inevitable and unreasonable. It is inevitable because, of course, the Roman empire is no longer with us. It is unreasonable because it is to devalue the astonishing accomplishment of the Roman people, in building a society from what was once a tiny town on the banks of the Tiber river into one that encompassed a truly enormous area, creating a unity never seen before or since over a large part of the globe. In so doing the Romans created a world that enabled people to communicate, to trade, to love, and to laugh in ways that would have been impossible otherwise. It was not a perfect world by any means—is there any such thing?—but without Rome our world would not be as it is today.

Summary

- When talking about the "fall of the Roman empire" we must first define our terms. The Western part of the empire "fell" nearly 200 years before the Eastern, and for very different reasons. In the West, imperial government ceased to function, and the territory once ruled by the emperors was divided into a number of successor states ruled by Germanic kings. In the East, the empire "fell" when Arab armies occupied Syria and Egypt in the second quarter of the seventh century AD. The Roman empire after that was a local power in Anatolia and the Balkans rather than a regional Mediterranean power.

- There was no single cause or date for the fall of the empire. This raises the question of what caused Roman power to decline and whether this stemmed from underlying economic problems, or whether political decline caused subsequent economic change as the imperial economic system devolved. In both East and West it appears that major economic change followed rather than caused the decline of imperial authority.

- The Western empire gave way to Germanic successor states mainly because state power was increasingly privatized in the course of the fourth and fifth centuries. This process made it impossible for the Western government to rally the resources needed to defend itself. Former Roman aristocrats are also found, quite often, acting in alliance with their new masters. In Italy during the sixth century, they apparently preferred their Ostrogothic rulers to the rule of the Eastern empire when Justinian attempted to reassert direct imperial rule.

- The Eastern government tended to display its ideology to its subjects in two ways. One was the composition of a law code (later imitated in the West by various Germanic kings), which represented temporal authority linked with religion. The second was through church councils. Neither seems to have succeeded in winning the ideological devotion of its subjects. Central efforts at defining doctrine were found deeply offensive by the "losing" side in controversies, especially in Egypt and Syria. Many communities developed mechanisms for distancing themselves from imperial control. This is typically reflected in the practice of arbitration that expressly excluded calling upon imperial officials and the new codes.

- In the course of the Persian and later Arab invasions, communities in Syria and Egypt often found they were better off negotiating their own terms with invaders rather than resisting them. These decisions were not always "anti-imperial"—people do not seem to have believed even during the Arab conquests that the emperor's armies would never return. Rather, they were pragmatic, stemming from existing tendencies to lessen outside intervention. They do, however, reflect the fact that the implicit contract traditionally binding communities to the imperial government—that the government would provide security in return for tax money—was broken by the military defeats of the seventh century.

- The two "falls" of the Roman empire stem from very different institutional failings, but were at heart both the result of the failures of the governing class. The falls did not stem from radical social change, though in the West major social change followed upon institutional failure. Instead they resulted from the failure of the imperial system to isolate the causes of its own weakness and correct them.

Glossary

aediles Originally plebeian magistrates charged with overseeing plebeian cults on the Aventine hill. The office was opened to patricians in 367 when the curule aedilship was created for them. Thereafter curule aediles were elected in alternate years to plebeian aediles (with curule aedilships falling in what were, in our terms, even numbered years), though in some years both plebeian and curule aediles were elected (e.g. in 65 BC). The duties of the aediles included the holding of certain games, overseeing the market place, and the maintenance of public order (a function that largely disappeared under the principate).

ager publicus Land owned by the Roman state.

ager Romanus The totality of the territory directly controlled by the Roman state.

agnatus The nearest relative on the male side.

ambitus The technical term for corrupt electoral practices. The word is the past participle of the verb *ambo*, *ambire*, to walk about; the connection with elections comes from the fact that Roman politicians "walked about" the forum collecting supporters for an election.

amphora A two-handled, oval-bodied vase with pointed base used for storage; large Greek amphorae tended to hold 9 US gallons (34 liters), Roman nearly 7 gallons (27 liters).

a pugione Title attested only for Cleander (d. AD 190) as the chief minister of Commodus; literally "at the dagger," though probably better understood to mean "chief of security."

Arian controversy/Arianism In Christian theology, a doctrine, expounded by Arius of Alexandria in the third and fourth centuries AD, which maintained that the Son of God, Jesus Christ, was not of the same "substance" as God the Father. The Council of Nicea in AD 325 affirmed that the Father and Son were coequal, coeternal, and "of one substance," thereby declaring Arianism a heresy.

auctoritas patrum The archaic formula by which the council to the magistrates (the *patres* or fathers; this council became the senate) gave approval to measures passed by the popular assemblies. It probably derives from patrician control of the *auspicia* since it seems that the justification for rejecting a measure would stem from a determination that the *auspicia* had not been properly conducted.

Augustus Literally "exalted one," the name conferred by the senate on Octavianus and adopted as the ruler's title by all subsequent emperors. In the course of time the title was used by senior imperial colleagues (and "Caesar" by the junior colleagues).

aureus Basic gold coin, worth roughly 300 sesterces before the traditional currency system collapsed in the third century. This was roughly one-third of the annual salary of a legionary in the first and second centuries AD.

auspicium/auspicia Literally "watching the birds," as the term is formed from *avis* (bird) and *spectio* (the act of observing omens). The augural art in fact came to involve the interpretation of five sorts of sign that, depending on the circumstances, constituted auspices or auguries: from the sky (e.g. thunder), from birds (from both their flight and behaviors while feeding), from the dining behavior of sacred chickens, from odd actions by quadrupeds, and from unusual natural phenomena. In the case of auspices, which could be taken by anyone, a sign—from whatever source—was good for only one day, and was thought to reflect divine approval of proposed human action. In the case of auguries, which required oversight from an augur, the sign did not have a time limit. The right to take auguries on behalf of the state was one of the most closely guarded privileges of the patrician order until 300 BC when plebeians were allowed into the college of augurs.

Caesar The family name (*nomen*) of Gaius Julius Caesar and his adoptive son Octavianus (Augustus), Caesar came to be used by all Roman emperors as an imperial title. When it was not used in conjunction with the title/name Augustus it signified the heir apparent.

censors The office of censor was established in 443 BC. Two censors were elected every five years for eighteen-month terms. Their chief function was to draw up lists of Roman citizens, which involved oversight of the morals of the community; they were also responsible for leasing revenue producing public property. Originally a patrician office, plebeians were allowed to hold the office after 339 BC. The office was occasionally assumed by emperors from Augustus onwards.

centuriae Centuries, or voting groups in the *comitia centuriata*. They had no fixed size, but were populated proportionally within each class; *centuriae* in the less numerous, but wealthier, first class were therefore smaller than centuries in the lower classes.

Circus Maximus The site of a large, oval race track in Rome, where various equestrian events and festivals were held. Chief among these were the popular chariot races, in which twelve chariots could race abreast around the track.

civitas sine suffragio Literally "citizenship without the vote," a formulation devised in the fourth century BC as a means of binding communities to Rome; it was typical of the constitutions of *municipia*.

cognomen The surname of a family or individual usually derived from some personal characteristic or achievement—e.g. Calvus (bald), Crassus (fat), or Africanus (conqueror of Africa).

cohort A military unit formalized as being one-tenth of a legion under the Marian army reforms (earlier cohorts had been understood to be groupings of maniples). Each cohort had six centurions and was the basic tactical unit of the legion. Auxiliary infantry units were also raised as cohorts even though they were not gathered into legions.

colonia/ae Originally a city founded from Rome, and settled by Roman citizens who retained full citizen rights; later, a free city in a province of the Roman empire that was exempt from any tribute payments to Rome.

comitatenses Units attached to the *comitatus* of the post-Diocletianic army.

comitatus   The mobile reserve forces formalized by Diocletian. The term derives from the participle of the verb *comitor, comitari*, which means to go along with or accompany. The *comitatus* was thus, in theory, the army that accompanied the emperor.

comites or **duces**   Commanders of large units in the army from the late third century AD onwards.

comitia centuriata   The Roman voting assembly, based upon the division of the Roman people into five classes and 193 *centuriae* (centuries). Since the bulk of the centuries were attributed to the members of the first two classes, this ensured that the wealthiest citizens had the strongest voice in public affairs. The *comitia centuriata* could only be summoned by a magistrate with *imperium* and could vote on the election of magistrates with *imperium*, declare war and peace, enact laws, and decide the fate of citizens who exercised the right of *provocatio*.

comitia populi tributa   An assembly, created on the model of the *concilium/comitia plebis*, probably in the course of the fifth century BC, in which the voting units were the tribes. Unlike the *concilium/comitia plebis*, patricians were admitted, and the presiding officer was a magistrate with *imperium*. The assembly could pass laws and elected curule aediles, quaestors, and special commissioners.

concilium/comitia plebis tributa   Originally formed as an assembly of plebeians only, and presided over by the tribunes. It elected tribunes and aediles of the plebs, and could pass motions—plebiscites—that were binding upon members of the plebeian order but not all citizens, until a series of legal reforms gave binding authority to plebiscites for the community as a whole in the course of the fifth and fourth centuries BC. The voting units were the tribes. Throughout the history of the Republic this was the venue through which laws proposed by tribunes were passed.

concilium/consilium   The difference between these two organizations emerges from their derivation. *Concilium* derives from the prefix meaning to gather together (*con-*) and the verb *calo, calare*, to call together, and denotes an assembly that was called together; *consilium* derives from the verb *consulo, consulere*, to consult, and can thus refer to any body that a person might apply to for advice. The significant difference is exemplified by the fact that the senate had its origin in a *consilium* while the *comitia tributa* had its origin in a *concilium*.

consul   The highest magistrate of the Roman Republic. Romans understood the term to be derived from the verb *consulo*, to take counsel, since the crucial aspect of the consulship was that there must be two at any given time (a consul who died in office had to be replaced by a suffect). The term itself probably came into common usage in the fourth century BC (see *praetor*). Consuls were elected by the *comitia centuriata*, and held the executive power of the earlier kings—command of the army in war, the right to summon assemblies, and the right to inflict punishment upon or otherwise physically coerce Roman citizens. The *imperium* of a consul was superior to that of every other magistrate unless a dictator was in office. Shorn of effective political power from Augustus onwards, the consulship still marked the pinnacle of a political career, and was the prerequisite for senior administrative positions, such as major provincial governorships and command of large armies. In the post-Diocletianic period, the office became entirely honorific.

conventus   Judicial division of a province.

cubicularius   A person, usually a freedman, who held the post of personal attendant to the emperor.

curia   Originally a voting assembly (see *curiae*), the word came, by extension, to designate a building in which a meeting took place, specifically at Rome, hence the building bordering the Roman forum where the senate held its meetings.

curiae   The earliest voting assemblies at Rome. There were thirty *curiae*, ten from each of the three early tribes. The sole purposes of the *comitia curiata* (voting assembly of the *curiae*) in the Republican period appear to have been to confirm grants of *imperium* to magistrates, and, when convened by the *pontifex maximus*, to confirm certain adoptions and wills.

daimon   In Greek thought, generally a spiritual or semi-divine being generally inferior to a god. The term could also be used to describe the power controlling the destiny of individuals, or the good or evil spirit that governed the lot of a family.

deditio   see *deditio in fidem*

deditio in fidem   Literally "handing over into faith," the standard diplomatic formulation of the mid-Republic. Defeated cities would be required to make a *deditio in fidem*, thereby handing all their property to Rome, which was then expected to return the bulk of it. A city that had made a *deditio* would then be given a treaty of alliance with Rome, imposing responsibilities to assist Rome in future wars. Not all acts of *deditio* were involuntary, however, as states could make a *deditio* to Rome as a way of placing Rome under a moral obligation to support them against their enemies, as happened in the case of Messene in Sicily in 264 BC. Rome was not obliged to accept a *deditio*.

denarius   The basic silver coin worth twelve sesterces in the coinage system of the late Republic and empire before Aurelian's reform in the AD 270s.

dilectus   The call-up of troops.

diocese   Under Diocletian and his successors, a group of provinces under the supervision of a *vicarius*.

domi   Locative case of *domus*, the Latin noun for "house." In technical parlance the term referred to the area within the *pomerium*.

duces   see *comites*

epic tradition   The tradition of epic poetry in archaic Greece, chiefly represented to us by the poetry of Homer and Hesiod.

Epicureanism   The philosophic movement founded by Epicurus in the fourth and third centuries BC in Athens. The central point of Epicurus's teaching was that the aim of philosophy was the happy life. He taught that all matter in the physical world consisted of atoms, that change resulted from the movement of atoms, and that happiness arose from the study of philosophy, which promoted freedom from disturbance. Since he also taught that the gods have no interest in the physical world, his teachings were widely regarded as atheistic.

epigram   Extensively used form of verse, developed in Greek and later adapted to use in Latin, consisting of couplets, the first of which was a dactylic hexameter, and the second a dactylic pentameter.

equestrian order Originally defined as the cavalry in the early army, by the mid-Republican period (if not before) the term was used to define the order that ranked just below the senate. From Augustus onwards the equestrian order was defined as being all Roman citizens of free birth who possessed property valued at 400,000 sesterces or more.

equinoctial Astrological term connected with one of the two periods in the year when the days and nights are equal in length all over the earth, owing to the sun's crossing the equator; described technically as the first points in Aries and Libra. The term is used loosely for the region of the ecliptic adjacent to these points.

evocatio The practice of calling the gods of a city at war with Rome to leave their native city and come to reside at Rome.

familia A group of people under the *potestas* of an individual. The term was used, in a domestic sense, of all persons subject to the authority of a *paterfamilias*, whether related by blood or not. It was also the term applied to juridically subordinate groups, such as gangs of slaves.

fasces The bundle of rods around an axe that symbolized the authority of a Roman magistrate with *imperium*. The fasces were borne by lictors whose number varied according to the *imperium* of the magistrate they served (a consul had twelve lictors, a praetor six).

fetial process see *ius fetiale*

fides Originally the condition of having trust placed in one; subsequently also a guarantee, a sense of duty towards others, and the quality of being worthy of belief.

first census class The first ninety-eight centuries in the *comitia centuriata* under the Servian system, which included the equestrian order as well as all men with the ability to provide themselves with hoplite armor in the early period. In the later period it was reduced to eighty-eight centuries and the property qualification for membership in the first class was increased.

flamen dialis The priest of Jupiter. He was always a patrician, chosen by the *pontifices*. His position was unusual in that it was bound by such an elaborate system of rules and taboos that it was virtually impossible for the *flamen* to have a political career. He was in many ways a living statue of Jupiter, representing the presence of the god in the community.

forum A market square or public space in Roman towns, usually colonnaded and surrounded by temples and public buildings.

genius Originally the male spirit of a *gens*, residing in the head of a family during his lifetime, and later the divine or spiritual part of every mortal.

gens/gentes Within the aristocracy, a group of individuals, probably all heads of individual *familiae*, who controlled the movement of property into and out of the group.

gladius Literally "sword," the term is normally used from second half of the third century BC onwards to refer to the Spanish thrusting sword adopted by the Romans at that time as the basic hand-to-hand combat weapon of the legionary.

hastati The second division of troops in the early Republican army (including the *velites*), whose task was to deliver the first attacks. The term is connected with the Latin word for spear (*hasta*), indicating that in the early period the *hastati* were envisioned as fighting primarily with spears.

hecatomb A sacrifice of one hundred animals.

hoplite An infantryman whose equipment was characterized by a large round shield (the hoplon) and a spear. The hoplite was the typical main line infantryman of Greece between the sixth and fourth centuries BC. The armament dictated tactics—typically a battle line drawn up eight men deep—and political structures that tended to favor men who could afford hoplite armor.

imperator Literally "victorious general," the title was granted to generals by the acclamation of their soldiers after a victory. Augustus adopted the term as a *praenomen*, and it afterwards became a standard feature of the titles of a Roman emperor.

imperium The legal power of a magistrate, by extension the area where that power was exercised (hence the *imperium Romanum*).

imperium maius ("greater *imperium*") One of the two key powers upon which the legal foundations of the imperial system were based (the other was *tribunicia potestas*). *Imperium maius* was power that was "greater" than that of other magistrates, who were therefore supposed to obey orders issued by one who held this power.

ius fetiale ("fetial process") Procedure according to which a city that felt that its territory or the rights of its members had been violated by members of another community could send an embassy to the offending state to declare its grievance, and proclaim the justice of its case before the gods.

lar/lares A class of protective divinities associated with places, most often with the hearth.

lemurs The evil spirits of the dead.

libertas Literally "freedom," in Classical Roman thought often defined as rational government through the consensus of citizens, as opposed to *regnum*, the tyrannical rule of an individual.

lictor The attendant of a Roman magistrate: a lictor carried the *fasces* that symbolized the magistrate's authority. (He also made use of them to flog and/or decapitate those whom the magistrate ordered him to treat in this way.)

limitanei Units based on the frontiers, in contrast to the *comitatenses*, in the post-Diocletianic army.

magister equitum Literally "master of the cavalry." In the Republican period it referred to the magistrate who was second in command to a Dictator (all Dictators appointed one); the title also represented the fact that the Dictator would be expected to command the main infantry force of the army in combat. In the later empire the term lost its connection with the constitution of the Republic and was used for a senior officer in the *comitatus*.

magister militum Literally "master of the soldiers," a new level of command, created in the late fourth century AD, above the master of infantry and master of cavalry.

magister officiorum Literally "master of offices," the position is first attested under Constantine (though it may well be Diocletianic), and was second in authority only to the *praefectus praetorio*. The *magister* controlled official communication, palace officials, munitions factories (by AD 390 if not before), and oversaw the bureau of secretaries that replaced the earlier equestrian secretariat.

magister peditum Literally "master of the foot soldiers," in the Roman army, the supreme commanding officer of the infantry units in the *comitatus*.

maiestas The Roman law on high treason was technically a *lex de maiestate populi Romani minutione*, or law concerning the lessening of the majesty of the Roman people. In the Republican period this tended to involve military disasters, major violations of religious scruple, or plotting to overthrow the Republican form of government. Under Sulla the definition was expanded to include such actions as a governor's leading his army outside the boundaries of his province without authorization from the people. From Augustus onwards statements insulting to the emperor could provide the justification for a prosecution *de maiestate*.

manes Those spirits of the dead that were regarded as generally well disposed.

maniple Primary tactical unit of the legion from the late fourth century to the second century BC, consisting of roughly 120 men.

metropolis An archaic Greek term indicating a city that had sent out another city as a colony (the founding city was thus the "mother city" of the colony). In the imperial period it denoted the "mother," or leading city of a province.

militiae Locative of the noun "militia" meaning "at war," in technical terms it defined the area outside the *pomerium*; the exercise of magisterial *imperium* in that area was less constrained than it was *domi*.

municipium/municipia An urban center that had been granted a civic constitution by Rome and whose citizens enjoyed the benefits of *civitas sine suffragio*, though some *municipia* ultimately attained the status of full Roman communities: one of these places was Arpinum, the homeland of Marius and Cicero. Introduced in the fourth century BC as a vehicle for expanding Roman power in Italy, it became a basic form of organization in the provinces under Augustus and later. Augustus created a standard charter for municipal government under a *lex Julia municipalis* (Julian law concerning municipalities).

nexum A form of binding obligation between a debtor and creditor by which in the case of non-payment the debtor (or a child of the debtor) automatically became the slave (*nexus*) of the creditor, until the debt was paid off. *Nexum* ended in the late fourth century BC.

nobiles Those members of the Roman aristocracy who came from families that had, at some point in their history, produced a consul.

nomen The second name after the *praenomen* and before the *cognomen*. Also known as the gentilician name, it identifies the *gens* to which a Roman was attached.

pancration A brutal combination of boxing and wrestling that developed in the Greek world by the end of the sixth century BC and remained the most popular of the three Greek "combat" sports (the others being boxing and wrestling).

paterfamilias The head of a Roman household (*domus*). Roman law granted the *paterfamilias* power of life and death (*patria potestas*) within his home over every member of his family and his servants.

patres The Latin word for father is *pater*. In earliest Rome, political structures (as elsewhere) made use of language connected with the family to define themselves. The *patres* in the archaic period were probably heads of *gentes* who formed a council for the king or magistrates. Memory of this institution is preserved in the Classical period by the description of senators as *patres conscripti* (fathers who had been enlisted).

patria potestas The authority of a *paterfamilias* over all individuals within his *familia*.

patrician A member of a ruling elite of Rome. The aristocratic families who made up the patrician order claimed descent from the city's original senators, who according to legend were appointed by Romulus. In the fifth century the title was used to designate a minister of immense importance.

patrimonium The portfolio of land and other property holdings under personal imperial control (largely acquired through seizures and bequests from citizens) and handed down from one emperor to the next.

pedarii A somewhat contemptuous term applied to senators whose sole importance was allegedly that they would vote by moving from one side of the *curia* to the other (the typical means of voting in the senate).

penates The protective gods of the Roman house (especially the store room) who were thought to govern the destiny of a household.

pietas An attitude of dutiful respect towards those to whom one is bound by ties of religion, blood relationship, etc.

pilum A heavy javelin that became the standard missile weapon of the Roman legionary from the third century BC to the third century AD.

plebeian Any Roman citizen who was not a patrician. Plebeians (or plebs for short) constituted the majority of the Roman populace, and could include people of very high social standing.

pomerium The sacred boundary of the city of Rome.

pontifex maximus The chief of the board of *pontifices*. Beginning with Julius Caesar, emperors held the post until AD 382.

pontifices One of the four major colleges of Roman priests, the *pontifices* oversaw actions connected with the state cult—sacrifices, festivals, and other rituals—and advised magistrates on matters of religious law. Originally consisting of three patricians, the college was expanded to seven in 300 BC as plebeians were added to the college.

populus Romanus The Roman citizen body.

portico A covered walking area consisting of a roof supported by columns, usually attached as a porch to a building, but sometimes forming a separate structure.

potestas Literally "power," in the case of magistracies it is modified by the title of the office or the person holding it—hence *tribunicia potestas*, *patria potestas*, etc.

praefectus annonae Praefect to the grain supply, who ranked as one of the three most important equestrian officials in the Augustan regime (the other two being the prefect of Egypt and the *praefectus praetorio*).

praefectus frumenti dandi Prefect for distributing grain, who operated out of the *porticus Minucia* on the banks of the Tiber. The position was created by Augustus.

praefectus praetorio The praetorian prefect, initially the commander of the praetorian guard. In the hands of Sejanus in the early first century AD the position expanded into that of a virtual prime minister, and, despite the execution of Sejanus, remained the single most influential position in the bureaucracy. Holders of the office had to be equestrians, and there were ordinarily two at a time in the first three centuries AD. Under Diocletian the number of prefects expanded to four, and the number varied thereafter according to the number of prefectures into which the empire was divided. The praetorian prefects of the fourth century onwards, though often less powerful than their predecessors, were nonetheless extremely influential as they controlled civilian provincial administration.

praenomen A personal name preceding the family *nomen*. There were seventeen male *praenomina*, while girls were given *praenomina* according to their birth order.

praetor/praetor maximus Roman magistrate. The title derives from the verb *praeire*, to go in front. The attestation of a *praetor maximus* makes it likely that this was the original title of the magistrates who replaced the king in 509 BC, and that *praetor maximus* was the title of the member of the college elected first. In 367 BC a praetor was added with *imperium* that was less than that of the previous two, who now came to be called consuls. A second praetor was added towards the end of the First Punic War and the number was raised to four around 228 BC and six in 198 BC to accommodate the demands of governing Spain. Sulla increased the number of praetors to eight and assigned them to the administration of standing courts at Rome, and Caesar to sixteen. The praetorship became the key position in the senatorial career after the time of Augustus, qualifying its holder for command of legions and minor provinces and a range of other positions.

praetorian guard Elite imperial bodyguard, formed under Augustus. Came to prominence under the influence of their prefect Aelius Sejanus during the reign of Tiberius, the praetorians increasingly wielded political power in the appointment of emperors until the guard was abolished by Constantine.

princeps Literally "leading man." In Republican times, the term could be applied, in a technical sense, to the leading senator (*princeps senatus*), or more generally to the leading men (*principes*) of the state; in the first century AD, this term became the most common designation for the emperor.

principes The third division of troops in the early Republican army, who were called into action if the attack by the *hastati* failed.

procurator Literally "a person appointed to perform business in the absence of another." In the imperial service procurators tended to be either equestrians or freedmen and filled basic roles in the imperial administration, including the civil and fiscal administration, governorships of minor provinces, and leadership of offices of government based within the imperial house.

professio Literally "an open declaration," in political life the formal declaration of intent to stand for public office, ordinarily made in person before a magistrate.

proletarii Literally "bearers of offspring," members of the lowest social class under the Servian constitution.

prorogation The extension of a magistrate's term in office as a "pro-magistrate" after the expiration of his term in office.

proscription Literally "to announce publicly in writing," and ordinarily used to announce that a property was for sale. Under Sulla the word came to mean a list of citizens who were sentenced to death as enemies of the state, by virtue of the special powers of jurisdiction asserted by Sulla as dictator and later the triumvirs,

Antony, Lepidus, and Octavianus, from which there was no right of *provocatio*.

provocatio Literally "an act of summoning," the term came to mean the right of any Roman citizen to appeal to the Roman people against the exercise of a magistrate's power of physical coercion. The *ius provocationis*, or right of appeal, was a basic tribunician power, allowing a tribune to intervene against a magistrate on behalf of a citizen.

publicanus/publicani A contractor for public works, especially, in the late Republic, tax collection; the term could apply either to the local collector of taxes who worked for a corporation of equestrians at Rome, or to the equestrian corporations themselves.

quaestor The lowest-ranking Roman magistrate. Quaestors had responsibilities for state finances and public works. Under the Sullan law governing the stages of the senatorial career, election to the quaestorship qualified a person to be a senator. From the fourth century AD onwards *quaestor* was a court office tending to be held by a distinguished jurist.

quinquireme The standard battleship of the third century BC, employing five oarsmen for each bank of oars.

regnum Literally "the office or power of a king," in the political vocabulary of the late Republic and imperial period it stood in opposition to *libertas* as signifying autocratic or despotic rule.

res privata The descendant of the *patrimonium*; after Diocletian the branch of the administration charged with the collection of all taxes paid in coin, the production of mines, and the minting of coinage.

res publica populi Romani The technical title of the Roman state, literally "the common possession of the Roman people," and thus, by implication, a state in whose governance all citizens participate.

rex sacrorum Literally "king of the rites." Although we know that this figure survived the expulsion of the *rex*, it is unclear whether the office was created to replace the king in religious rites or in the regal period as a leader of the state cult.

sacrosanctitas Literally "protected by religious sanction from harm." This was a crucial right of a tribune of the plebs, freeing him from the threat of violence at the hands of a holder of *imperium* while in office.

sesterces Anglicized form of the Latin *sestertius*, the basic Roman bronze coin.

Sibylline books At Rome, a collection of Greek prophetic books believed to have been compiled by the Sibyl, an ancient female prophet operating around the Bay of Naples. The collection may pre-date the formation of the Republic and would be consulted in times of national emergency by members of a board of priests, initially two patricians, then ten after 367 BC, and finally, after Sulla, fifteen. The title of this board—in its developed form—*quindecimviri sacris faciundis*, indicates that the college advised on public sacrifices, and the context of the Sibylline oracles from this collection seems to deal with sacrificial responses to problems. There were many Sibylline oracles in circulation beyond those in the official collection.

solstitial Astrological term indicating a movement of the stars connected with a solstice or the solstices (that is to say at one of the two times in the year, midway between the two equinoxes, when the sun, having reached the tropical points, is farthest from the equator and appears to stand still).

statio Originally the state of standing still, whence the usage of the word for military garrisons and guard posts. The aggregate of the powers of Augustus and Tiberius was described in their lifetimes as their *statio*, indicating that they presented themselves as being responsible for the military security of the state.

stipendiary cities Provincial cities that were liable to pay tribute to Rome.

stoa Greek term for a portico.

Stoicism Philosophy of which the basic tenet was that fate was identical with the will and body of Zeus. This made it possible for the gods to communicate with mortals, and for mortals to think that they could live in accord with nature.

suffect(us) The term derives from the perfect participle of the verb *sufficio*, to supply or provide. A magistrate who was *suffectus* was literally "supplied" in place of one who had died; Julius Caesar introduced the practice of inducing consuls to resign so that a *suffectus* could replace them, as a way of increasing the number of consuls. The practice continued throughout the imperial period.

triarii The fourth division of troops in the early Republican army (including the *velites*), who were only called upon to fight as a last resort.

tresvir *see* triumvirs

tribune Initially an official connected with the tribes (the word is derived from *tribus*), probably in a military context since military tribunes continue to be attested throughout the Republic. In 494 BC new tribunes were elected as representatives of the plebs—see *tribunicia potestas* and *comitia tributa*. The number was originally two, and varied (according to the tradition as it is preserved) until it stabilized at ten in 455 BC.

tribuni aerarii "Tribunes of the treasury," originally, in the early days of the Republic, an official who collected the tax to pay the army. Later the term referred to a member of an order below the equestrian from which one third of the membership of juries was selected between 70 and 46 BC.

tribunicia potestas Literally "tribunician power," though in effect the aggregate of separate powers that the tribunes had acquired in the course of the early Republic. These powers included the right to summon assemblies of the people to vote on laws, and

provocatio (the power to appeal the decision of a magistrate to the people): from these descend the *ius auxilii* (an extension of *provocatio* specifically allowing a tribune to protect citizens from the arbitrary actions of a magistrate) and *intercessio*, the power to halt any public action.

tribus Literally "tribe," the word derives from the number three (*tres*) and indicates the tradition that in earliest Roman society there were only three tribes.

tributum/tributa Probably derived from the participle of the verb *tribuo/tribere*, to share out, apportion, allocate, the term referred to a tax, originally a war tax, imposed on all Roman citizens through the tribes. It ceased to be collected from Roman citizens in 167 BC, and afterwards refers to direct taxes paid by subjects of Rome in the provinces.

triumvirs The term was applied to the informal political alliance between Pompey, Crassus, and Caesar in the 50s BC and, later, to the official board of three established in 43 BC "to set the state in order" that included Mark Antony, Octavianus, and Lepidus. The term derives from minor boards of magistrates that existed well before 59 BC, including, for instance, the *tresviri monetales* (the Republican board charged with oversight of minting) or the *tresviri capitales* (the board of three charged with carrying out death sentences).

vectigala Revenues accruing to the Roman state from public properties in the mid-Republic; the meaning expanded to cover revenues from such transactions as harbor and inheritance taxes.

velites The most lightly armed troops of the early Republican army, whose task was to open the battle as skirmishers.

Vestal Virgins The group of seven women who were servants of Vesta, the patron goddess of the Roman hearth and home. The Vestals were charged with keeping alight the eternal flame, symbolizing the enduring strength of the state, at the Temple of Vesta in the forum.

vicarius Literally "substitute, stand-in." The term was used in the early Roman empire to denote a deputy to a provincial governor. Following Diocletian's administrative reforms in the third century AD, the term denoted an officeholder who was responsible for the day-to-day administration of one of the three dioceses under the jurisdiction of each of the empire's four praetorian prefects.

Recommended Reading

General Introductions

For further insight into the period covered by this book, four volumes in the Blackwell Companion series and three from Cambridge University Press may be especially useful. These are A. Erskine, *A Companion to the Hellenistic World* (Oxford, 2003); H. Flower, *The Cambridge Companion to the Roman Republic* (Cambridge, 2004); N. Rosenstein and R. Morstein-Marx, *A Companion to the Roman Republic* (Oxford, 2006); D. S. Potter, *A Companion to the Roman Empire* (Oxford, 2006); N. Lenski, *The Cambridge Companion to the Age of Constantine* (Cambridge, 2006); M. Maas, *The Cambridge Companion to the Age of Justinian* (Cambridge, 2006); and S. Harrison, *A Companion to Latin Literature* (Oxford, 2005). The products of enormously long periods of gestation, volumes 7–13 of the second edition of *The Cambridge Ancient History* nonetheless contain many articles that retain their freshness even after many years. Although more focused, the importance of military history to Roman history makes P. Erdkamp, *A Companion to the Roman Army* (Oxford, 2006) broadly important for the subject.

In all cases, it must be noted that ancient history is an international discipline and that the concentration here on works in English obscures countless contributions of enormous value, especially by German, French, and Italian scholars. The survey articles in these companions will help readers gain a better sense of the importance of these contributions.

Introduction: Methods and Sources

For surveys of the sources of Roman history see the introductory chapters in N. Rosenstein and R. Morstein-Marx, *A Companion to the Roman Republic* (Oxford, 2006) and D. S. Potter, *A Companion to the Roman Empire* (Oxford, 2006), as well as D. S. Potter, *Literary Texts and the Roman Historian* (London, 1999). For the fourth and fifth centuries AD see D. Rohrbacher, *The Historians of Late Antiquity* (London, 2002), while for the later period see A. Cameron, *Procopius* (Berkeley, 1985).

Chapter 1: The Formation of the Roman Identity

The most important survey of early Roman history is T. Cornell, *The Beginnings of Rome* (London, 1995), though G. Forsythe, *A Critical History of Early Rome from Prehistory to Early Rome* (Berkeley, 2005) is an extremely useful book, written from a very different perspective. For the archaeology of the period (admittedly an ever moving target), C. J. Smith, *Early Rome and Latium* (Oxford, 1996) is invaluable. For the importance of Roman foundation myths see T. P. Wiseman, *Remus: A Roman Myth* (Cambridge, 1995) and *The Myths of Rome* (Exeter, 2004). For the significance of the myth of Romulus's asylum see E. Dench, *Romulus' Asylum: Roman Identities from the Age of Alexander to the Age of Hadrian* (Oxford, 2005). For patrician *gentes* see C. J. Smith, *The Roman Clan: The Gens from Ancient Ideology to Modern Anthropology* (Cambridge, 2006). For the significance of law-making in Roman society, see C. Williamson, *The Laws of the Roman People* (Ann Arbor, 2005). For the social

aspects of Roman citizenship, C. Nicolet, *The World of the Citizen in Republican Rome* (Berkeley, 1980) is fundamental.

For the Roman family, see R. Saller, *Patriarchy, Property and Death in the Roman Family* (Cambridge, 1994); for issues connected with Roman social history and religion see the essays by A. E. Hanson, M. W. Gleason, B. W. Frier, and D. S. Potter in D. S. Potter and D. Mattingly, eds, *Life, Death, and Entertainment in the Roman Empire* (Ann Arbor, 1999), as well as J. Scheid, *An Introduction to Roman Religion* (Baltimore, 2003). The discussion of Roman marriage in this chapter is heavily influenced by the views of Hanson. For a general introduction to the subject see also S. Treggiari, *Roman Marriage* (Oxford, 1991). For images of women in Roman society see K. Milnor, *Gender, Domesticity, and the Age of Augustus: Inventing Private Life* (Oxford, 2005). Finally, even those with no Latin will find enormous benefit from the balanced and intelligent analyses that fill the pages of S. Oakley, *A Commentary on Livy Books vi–x* (4 vols, Oxford, 1997–2005). The account of the Licinian-Sextian land laws in this chapter, which differs significantly from that of the previous edition, derives from S. T. Roselaar, *Public Land in the Roman Republic* (Oxford, 2010). H. Flower, *Roman Republics* (Princeton, 2010) is an important treatment of the way that the history of the Republic has been written and how the subject might be reconceived, while G. Woolf, *Rome: An Empire's Story* (Oxford, 2012), is a remarkably successful exercise in comparative history, showing how the Roman experience can be placed in the context of other empires. R. MacMullen, *The Earliest Romans: A Character Sketch* (Ann Arbor, 2011) is an important and original book that questions established orthodoxies and proposes new ways of looking at earliest Roman history.

Chapter 2: War and Empire

T. Cornell, *The Beginnings of Rome* (London, 1995), G. Forsythe, *A Critical History of Early Rome from Prehistory to Early Rome* (Berkeley, 2005), and S. Oakley, *A Commentary on Livy Books vi–x* (4 vols, Oxford, 1997–2005), are all invaluable for the first part of the period. For the second part, even those without Greek can benefit from the lucid discussions of countless issues in F. W. Walbank, *Commentary on Polybius* (3 vols, Oxford, 1957–79) and *Polybius* (Berkeley, 1972). For Roman literature, in addition to works listed under general introductions, see G. B. Conte, *Latin Literature: A History* (Baltimore, 1993) and E. J. Kenney and P. Easterling, eds, *The Cambridge History of Classical Literature*, vol. 2: *Latin Literature* (Cambridge, 1982).

The study of Roman imperialism has attracted an enormous amount of attention in the last hundred years, though for the account offered here the most important works (in English) are W. V. Harris, *War and Imperialism in Republican Rome* (Oxford, 1979); S. Dyson, *The Creation of the Roman Frontier* (Princeton, 1985); E. Gruen, *The Hellenistic World and the Coming of Rome* (Berkeley, 1984); and the chapters by P. S. Derow in *The Cambridge Ancient History*, vol. 8: *Rome and the Mediterranean to 133 BC* (2nd edn,

Cambridge, 1989). (See, however, the note above on the importance of contributions by writers in other languages, since this list is quite unbalanced.) As the Greek world becomes part of the Roman world there is a fresh perspective in R. J. Lane Fox, *The Greek World from Homer to Hadrian* (London, 2005). For the nature of "diplomatic" relationships in the Hellenistic world and the general belligerence of the period see also the splendid discussion in A. M. Eckstein, *Mediterranean Anarchy, Interstate War, and the Rise of Rome* (Berkeley, 2006). A. M. Eckstein, *Rome Enters the Greek East* (Oxford, 2008), offers a narrative to supplement the general analysis in Mediterranean anarchy, which is immensely stimulating and valuable, even if I do not always follow his conclusions. For the development of Roman historiography, U. Walter, "Annales and Analysis," pp. 265–90 in A. Feldherr and G. Hardy, *The Oxford History of Historical Writing: Beginnings to AD 600* (Oxford, 2011), is a valuable summary, drawing on the author's extensive work in German. For more on the Egadi rams, see S. Trusa and J. Royal, "The Landscape of the Naval Battle at the Egadi Islands (241 BC)," pp. 1–48 in *JRA* 25 (2012).

The fundamental study of the structure of the Roman aristocracy remains M. Gelzer, *The Roman Nobility* (Oxford, 1969), the English translation of a book first published in 1912.

The view on the question of slavery in second-century BC Italy taken in this book owes a great deal to M. W. Frederiksen, "The contribution of archaeology to the agrarian problem in the Gracchan period," 330–67, *Dialoghi di archeologia* 2–3 (1970–71) and D. Stockton, *The Gracchi* (Oxford, 1979). For an excellent exposition of the view that Italy became a "slave society" see K. Hopkins, *Conquerors and Slaves* (Cambridge, 1978). For a very different view of Roman slavery from the one presented in this book, largely because he feels that slavery was much more important to the productive economy of the countryside than I do, see K. Bradley, *Slavery and Society at Rome* (Cambridge, 1994), a book from which much can be learned. H. Mouritsen, *The Freedman in the Roman World* (Cambridge, 2011), is an exceptionally important analysis of the role of freedmen in Roman society. For a somewhat different take on agrarian issues, though one that shares the view expressed here about the prevalence of peasant agriculture, see N. Rosenstein, *Rome at War: Farms, Families, and Death in the Middle Republic* (Chapel Hill, 2004). For very different analyses of Roman control in Italy at the end of the second century BC see H. Mouritsen, *Italian Unification: A Study in Ancient and Modern Historiography* (London, 1998), who argues a minimalist position; and E. Bispham, *From Asculum to Actium: The Municipalization of Italy from the Social War to Augustus* (Oxford, 2007), who argues for more intensive Roman intervention. I have tended more often to agree with Bispham. At the same time the discussion of the cultural evolution of Italy owes a great deal to the essays collected in M. Torelli, *Studies in the Romanization of Italy* (Edmonton, 1995) and S. Keay and N. Terrenato, eds, *Italy and the West: Comparative Issues in Romanization* (Oxford, 2001).

Chapter 3: The Failure of the Roman Republic

The history of the late Republic is, above all, the province of P. A. Brunt, whose three books, *Social Conflicts in the Roman Republic*

(London, 1971), *Italian Manpower, 225 BC–AD 14* (2nd edn, Oxford, 1971), and *The Fall of the Roman Republic and Related Essays* (Oxford, 1988), are all fundamental. For the Gracchi see D. Stockton, *The Gracchi* (Oxford, 1979), and the chapter by A. Lintott in *The Cambridge Ancient History*, vol. 9: *The Last Age of the Roman Republic, 146–43 BC* (2nd edn, 1994). For two very different approaches to events leading up to the Social War see E. Gabba, *Republican Rome: The Army and the Allies* (Oxford, 1976) and H. Mouritsen, *Italian Unification: A Study in Ancient and Modern Historiography* (London, 1998). For the texts of late Republican laws see M. H. Crawford, *Roman Statutes* (2 vols, London, 1996). For a lucid account of the land laws and Gracchan extortion law see A. Lintott, *Judicial Reform and Land Reform in the Roman Republic* (Cambridge, 1992), while C. Williamson, *The Laws of the Roman People* (Ann Arbor, 2005) remains valuable for context. For the working of the constitution of the Republic see A. Lintott, *The Constitution of the Roman Republic* (Oxford, 1999).

The question of popular sovereignty and senatorial control is defined by the work of F. Millar, especially in *The Crowd in Rome in the Late Republic* (Ann Arbor, 1998) and the essays collected in F. Millar, *The Roman Republic and the Augustan Revolution* (Chapel Hill, 2002). For quite different views see R. Morstein-Marx, *Mass Oratory and Political Power in the Late Roman Republic* (Cambridge, 2004) and H. Mouritson, *Plebs and Politics in the Late Roman Republic* (Cambridge, 2001).

For the careers of Pompey, Caesar, and Cicero see R. Seager, *Pompey the Great: A Political Biography* (Oxford, 2002); M. Gelzer, *Caesar: Politician and Statesman* (Cambridge, MA, 1969); A. Goldsworthy, *Caesar: Life of a Colossus* (New Haven, 2006); D. Stockton, *Cicero: A Political Biography* (Oxford, 1971); and E. Rawson, *Cicero: A Portrait* (Ithaca, 1983). On the issue of M. Antonius Creticus see J. Linderski, "The Surname of A. Antonius Creticus and the Cognomina ex Victis Gentibus," pp. 157–164 in *Zeitschrift für Papyrologie und Epigraphik* 80 (1990), which is of general importance for understanding Roman commemorative practices.

Chapter 4: The Transition from Republic to Principate

For the literature of the period covered in this chapter, in addition to works listed under general introductions, see G. B. Conte, *Latin Literature: A History* (Baltimore, 1993) or E. J. Kenney and P. Easterling, eds, *The Cambridge History of Classical Literature*, vol. 2: *Latin Literature* (Cambridge, 1982), as well as E. Rawson, *Intellectual Life in the Late Roman Republic* (Baltimore, 1985) and C. Martindale, *The Cambridge Companion to Virgil* (Cambridge, 1997). For the thought of Tacitus, R. Syme, *Tacitus* (2 vols, Oxford, 1958) retains immense value.

P. A. Brunt, *The Fall of the Roman Republic and Related Essays* (Oxford, 1988), F. Millar, *The Crowd in Rome in the Late Republic* (Ann Arbor, 1998), and T. P. Wiseman's narrative chapters in *The Cambridge Ancient History*, vol. 9: *The Last Age of the Roman Republic, 146–43 BC* (2nd edn, Cambridge, 1994), offer a splendid introduction to the history of the late 50s BC. For Caesar see M. Gelzer, *Caesar: Politician and Statesman* (Cambridge, MA, 1969) and A. Goldsworthy, *Caesar: Life of a Colossus* (New Haven, 2006).

The fundamental study of the rise of Augustus, and indeed of the imperial system as a whole, remains R. Syme, *The Roman Revolution* (Oxford, 1939), though it must now be supplemented with G. Sumi, *Ceremony and Power: Performing Politics in Rome between Republic and Empire* (Ann Arbor, 2005); J. Osgood, *Caesar's Legacy* (Cambridge, 2005); G. Rowe, *Princes and Political Culture* (Ann Arbor, 2002); and P. Zanker, *The Power of Images in the Age of Augustus* (Ann Arbor, 1988). For later Julio-Claudians see A. R. Barrett, *Caligula* (London, 1989); B. M. Levick, *Claudius* (London, 1990); and M. T. Griffin, *Nero* (London, 1984); and for the civil war of AD 69 see K. Wellesley, *The Year of the Four Emperors* (3rd edn, London, 2000). For a broad overview of the imperial period see D. S. Potter, *Emperors of Rome* (London, 2007).

For demographic issues see B. W. Frier in D. S. Potter and D. J. Mattingly, eds, *Life, Death, and Entertainment in the Roman Empire* (Ann Arbor, 1999). On the economic development of the empire the argument in this chapter tracks that of C. Wickham, *Framing the Early Middle Ages: Europe and the Mediterranean, 400–800* (Oxford, 2005). The specific discussion of garum at Pompeii derives from S. J. R. Ellis, "The Rise and Reorganization of the Pompeian Fish Industry," pp. 59–88 in S. J. R. Ellis, *The Making of Pompeii: Studies in the history and urban development of an ancient town*, *JRA* suppl. 85 (2011). The estimate for the population of the Parthian empire is based on estimates of population of the portion of the Seleucid kingdom region later occupied by the Parthians offered by G. Aperghis, *The Seleukid Royal Economy: The Finances and Financial Administration of the Seleucid Empire* (Cambridge, 2004). The discussion of the army's economic role is based on calculations in R. Goldsmith, *Premodern Financial Systems: A Historical Comparative Study* (Cambridge, 1987); the method and outline established by Goldsmith is confirmed in later studies, such as W. Scheidel and S. J. Friesen, "The Size of the Economy and the Distribution of Income in the Roman Empire," pp. 61–91 in *JRS* 99 (2009); also important is M. Hendy, *Studies in the Byzantine Monetary Economy c. 300–1450* (Cambridge, 2008). The easiest access to finds of writing samples concerning the Roman army is through the admirable site for the Vindolanda bark tablets at http://vindolanda.csad.ox.ac.uk/

Chapter 5: The Age of Stability

For the Flavians and Trajan see B. M. Levick, *Vespasian* (London, 1999), and M. Griffin's chapters in *The Cambridge Ancient History*, vol. 11: *The High Empire, AD 70–192* (2nd edn, Cambridge, 2000). For the later years see A. R. Birley's *Hadrian: The Restless Emperor* (London, 1997), *Marcus Aurelius: A Biography* (2nd edn, London, 1987), and *The African Emperor. Septimius Severus* (2nd edn, London, 1988). For the social and administrative history of the empire see P. Brunt, *Roman Imperial Themes* (Oxford, 1990); F. Millar, *Government, Society, and Culture in the Roman Empire* (Chapel Hill, 2004); the chapters by W. Eck and B. Shaw in *The Cambridge Ancient History*, vol. 11: *The High Empire, AD 70–192* (2nd edn, Cambridge, 2000); and the essays in D. S. Potter and D. J. Mattingly, eds, *Life, Death, and Entertainment in the Roman Empire* (Ann Arbor, 1999). Funerary monuments of all sorts are well discussed in M. Carroll, *Spirits of the Dead: Roman Funerary*

Commemoration in Western Europe (Oxford, 2006). For the position of the emperor, F. Millar, *The Emperor in the Roman World* (2nd edn, London, 1992), remains central. On the literary history of the Flavian period see, in addition to works listed under general introductions, G. B. Conte, *Latin Literature: A History* (Baltimore, 1993) or E. J. Kenney and P. Easterling, eds, *The Cambridge History of Classical Literature*, vols 1 and 2 (Cambridge, 1982–85) (volume 1 contains a discussion of the Greek literature of the Roman empire); and especially A. M. Gowing, *Empire and Memory: The Representation of the Roman Republic in Imperial Culture* (Cambridge, 2005). For the ancient novel see S. Swain, ed., *Oxford Readings in the Greek Novel* (Oxford, 1999). For the history of religion see R. J. Lane Fox, *Pagans and Christians* (London, 1989), and more specifically for the rise of Christianity see R. Stark, *The Rise of Christianity* (Princeton, 1996). For discussions of acculturation in the Roman empire, very different approaches appear in E. Dench, *Romulus' Asylum: Roman Identities from the Age of Alexander to the Age of Hadrian* (Oxford, 2005), G. Woolf, *Becoming Roman: The Origins of Provincial Civilization in Gaul* (Cambridge, 1998), and C. Ando, *Imperial Ideology and Provincial Loyalty in the Roman Empire* (Berkeley, 2000). For a variety of approaches to the ancient economy see J. G. Manning and I. Morris, *The Ancient Economy: Evidence and Models* (Stanford, 2005) and R. Goldsmith, *Premodern Financial Systems: A Historical Comparative Study* (Cambridge, 1987). For a narrative of the history of the early third century AD see D. S. Potter, *The Roman Empire at Bay* (London, 2004).

Chapter 6: The Transformation of the Roman World

For a narrative from the third century AD though Theodosius I see D. S. Potter, *The Roman Empire at Bay* (London, 2004) and S. Mitchell, *A History of the Later Roman Empire AD 284–641* (Oxford, 2006). J. F. Drinkwater, *The Alamanni and Rome 213–496* (Oxford, 2007) is of general importance for relations between Rome and northern peoples. T. D. Barnes, *Constantine and Eusebius* (Cambridge, MA, 1981) puts forward a view of Constantine strongly influenced by Eusebius, while H. Drake, *Constantine and the Bishops* (Baltimore, 2000) and D. S. Potter, *Constantine the Emperor* (Oxford, 2013) offer alternative views. For a series of excellent discussions of issues connected with the age of Constantine see N. Lenski, *The Cambridge Companion to the Age of Constantine* (Cambridge, 2005) For the period after Constantine the fundamental works remain J. F. Matthews, *Western Aristocracies and the Imperial Court AD 364–425* (Oxford, 1975) and *The Roman Empire of Ammianus* (London, 1989; repr. Ann Arbor, 2007). See also A. H. M. Jones, *The Later Roman Empire, 284–602: A Social, Economic and Administrative Survey* (3 vols, Oxford, 1964; repr. in 2 vols, 1973). For the Gothic invasions see P. Heather, *The Fall of the Roman Empire* (Oxford, 2006).

For the Latin panegyrics, which provide important information on the period of the tetrarchy and Constantine (as well as Julian and Theodosius), see C. E. V. Nixon and B. S. Rodgers, *In Praise of Later Roman Emperors* (Berkeley, 1994). Although Eusebius's *Life of Constantine* is a deeply problematic document, designed to make Constantine out to be more aggressively Christian than he was and marred by numerous omissions, the translation and commentary by A. Cameron and S. G. Hall are immensely useful

(Eusebius, *Life of Constantine*, Clarendon Ancient History Series, Oxford, 1999). For the archive of Isidorus see A. E. R. Boak and H. C. Youtie, *The Archive of Aurelius Isidorus in the Egyptian Museum, Cairo, and the University of Michigan (P. Cair. Isidor.)* (Ann Arbor, 1960).

Chapter 7: The Endings of the Roman Empire
The view taken here of the fall of the Roman empires (or, as I prefer, falls of the empire) stems from certain basic assumptions—among the most basic of which is that people were better off before AD 400 than after it, and thus that it is viable to discuss the subject in this way at all. At the same time, as I hope I have suggested, life did not simply stop when the imperial government stopped collecting taxes. On the whole, the approach here aligns more closely with M. McCormick, *Origins of the European Economy: Communications and Commerce AD 300–900* (Cambridge, 2001), C. Wickham, *Framing the Early Middle Ages: Europe and the Mediterranean, 400–800* (Oxford, 2005), and B. Ward-Perkins, *The Fall of Rome* (Oxford, 2006), than with the approach found in the essays collected in G. W. Bowersock, P. Brown, and O. Grabar, eds, *Late Antiquity: A Guide to the Post-Classical World* (Cambridge, MA, 1999).

For overall narratives see especially P. Brown, *The World of Late Antiquity AD 150–750* (London, 1971), which is foundational for much modern research. For a good balance of East and West see S. Mitchell, *A History of the Later Roman Empire AD 284–641* (Oxford, 2006). In more detail, see the chapters in *The Cambridge Ancient History*, vol. 13: *The Late Empire, AD 337–425* (2nd edn, Cambridge, 1997), as well as M. Whitby, *The Emperor Maurice and His Historian* (Oxford, 1988); and for the end of the period, the careful analysis in W. E. Kaegi, *Heraclius, Emperor of Byzantium* (Cambridge, 2003) is invaluable. For the mid-sixth century, M. Maas, *The Cambridge Companion to the Age of Justinian* (Cambridge, 2005) offers an excellent starting point, as does, for the subsequent period, M. Whittow, *The Making of Byzantium 600–1025* (Berkeley, 1996). Fragments of the historians Priscus and Malchus are cited from R. C. Blockley, *The Fragmentary Classicising Historians of the Later Roman Empire: Eunapius, Olympiodorus, Priscus and Malchus* (Liverpool, 1981–82), while the discussion of arbitration (and the text quoted) derives from T. Gagos and P. van Minnen, *Settling a Dispute: Toward a Legal Anthropology of Late Antique Egypt* (Ann Arbor, 1994). The fate of the Balkans is now analyzed in A. G. Poulter, ed., *The Transition to Late Antiquity on the Danube and Beyond Proceedings of the British Academy* 141 (Oxford, 2007). The interpretation of early Islam offered here is borrowed from P. Crone, *Meccan Trade and the Rise of Islam* (Princeton, 1987), while the view offered of the Arab conquest derives from H. Kennedy, *The Great Arab Conquests: How the Spread of Islam Changed the World We Live In* (London, 2007).

In terms of sheer style and brilliance of exposition, E. Gibbon, *The History of the Decline and Fall of the Roman Empire* has no peer, and may most usefully be consulted through the edition of D. Womersley (3 vols, Harmondsworth, 1994), though J. B. Bury's notes to his seven-volume edition of 1909 retain genuine value.

Acknowledgments

This book is largely the product of twenty years of teaching Roman history in the Department of Classical Studies at the University of Michigan. I cannot begin to express my gratitude over the years to the countless students, both graduate and undergraduate, who have tolerated my teaching and put up with the evolving ideas that have come together in this book. It is also a pleasure to thank my colleagues in the department for creating an environment that simply makes it fun to come to work in the morning.

This book was originally conceived more than a decade ago, and assisted at that time by a generous award from the Earhardt Foundation of Ann Arbor (summer 1998). After the inception of the project, new administrative responsibilities supervened, and deadlines for other projects loomed. For many years this book remained buried deep within the file structure of various computers with little prospect of completion, until Ian Jacobs of Thames & Hudson generously offered to have a look at the first two chapters and found readers whose comments, both supportive and helpfully critical, relaunched the project. He has remained immensely helpful and supportive throughout the process of completion, which would never have happened without his intervention.

In finishing the book, I have benefited enormously from the help of Professors Garrett Fagan of Penn State, Maud Gleason of Stanford, and Celia Schultz, Nicola Terrenato, and Arthur Verhoogt of the University of Michigan, whose generosity with their time and detailed criticism of earlier versions have vastly improved the final product. The same is true of the anonymous comments provided by various readers for Thames & Hudson (especially on the Republican sections of this book), and Professor Craige Champion, who offered an extremely helpful series of corrections as I was preparing the new edition. I hope that these readers will recognize the impact they have had on the text, which they have greatly improved. All errors that remain are obviously my fault.

In considering the final product, readers may note that I have written before on the imperial period, but not on the Republic. Writing about earlier imperial topics and the Republic has proved both liberating and a pleasure, as I have been able to formalize ideas that have been developing through discussion with students over the years. My interests in this period indeed go back to my years as a graduate student, where my initial training was in Hellenistic history. My inspiration for continuing to teach in this area came from two dear friends, whose influence and friendship it is a pleasure to acknowledge despite their untimely passing. It is for this reason that the book is dedicated to the memory of George Forrest and Peter Derow.

It would simply not have been possible to write this book at all without the support at home of my wife Ellen and our two spectacular, if somewhat opinionated, daughters, Claire and Natalie.

Sources of Illustrations

l=left; r=right; a=above; b=below

akg-images **2–3, 178, 220, 237, 291, 334b**; akg-images/Bildarchiv Steffens **327**; akg-images/Hervé Champollion **160–61**; akg-images/Peter Connolly **184**; akg-images/De Agostini Picture Library **319**; akg-images/Suzanne Held **281b, 312**; akg-images/Erich Lessing **15, 194, 199, 240r, 315, 334a**; akg-images/Gilles Mermet **233**; akg-images/Pirozzi **186–87, 222br**; Adam Eastland Italy/Alamy **167**; Sona Halliday Photographs/Alamy **216ar**; Holmes Garden Photos/Alamy **255**; Peter Horee/Alamy **236, 286b**; Norma Joseph/Alamy **226**; Archivi Alinari **181**; Peter Phipp/Alamy **216al**; Art Archive/Jan Vinchon Numismatist Paris/Gianni Dagli Orti **308**; National Museum, Athens **100b**; bildarchiv preussischer kulturbesitz, Berlin **264, 293**; Fitzwilliam Museum, Cambridge **173**; Giovanni Caselli **28a, 67, 75, 77, 176, 231b**; © Jonathan Blair/Corbis **192–93**; Ali Jarekji/Reuters/Corbis **340**; Adam Woolfitt/Corbis **337**; National Museum of Damascus, Syria **283**; Museo Archaeologico, Florence **28b**; Niedersächsen Landesmuseum, Hanover **190**; Hirmer Fotoarchiv **73, 91**; Angelo Hornak **280a**; Israeli Antiquities Authority **224a**; Ian Jacobs **71**; Peter Inker © Thames & Hudson Ltd **276, 287**; Israel Museum, Jerusalem **222bl**; Giovanni Lattanzi **17, 81, 92–93, 183r, 202–3,** **222a, 298, 318**; Soprintendenza per i beni archeologici del Lazio **46–47, 62**; Jona Lendering **68**; British Museum, London **13al, 22, 23, 44, 72, 89, 112–13, 119, 120, 168, 170, 175, 187, 196, 198, 202, 204a, 214, 217b, 224b, 225, 237, 260, 265, 267, 281c, 284, 292, 329**; Musée Gallo-Romaine, Lyons **201, 234**; Museo Arqueológico, Madrid **235**; J. Paul Getty Museum, Malibu **197**; Antikensammlung Glyptothek, Munich **129**; Biblioteca Nazionale, Naples **155**; Museo Archeologico Nazionale, Naples **11, 78, 183l, 217a, 218a, 218br, 269, 274, 311a**; Metropolitan Museum of Art, New York **296**; Sally Nicholls **282, 347b, 350**; Bodleian Library, University of Oxford **157**; James Packer **218bl**; Bibliothèque nationale de France, Paris **130**; Musée du Louvre, Paris **122–23, 221, 268a**; David Potter **13ar–br, 29**; Josephine Powell **263**; Private Collection **206, 262, 268b, 280b, 281a, 285, 286a, 297**; Musei Capitolini, Rome **207, 259**; RPM Nautical Foundation **69**; Soprintendenza per i beni archeologici di Salerno e Avellino **62–63**; Photo Scala, Florence – courtesy of the Ministero Beni e Att. Culturali **240l**; Sites & Photos **100a, 216b, 231a**; Archaeological Museum, Sousse **97**; Bardo Museum, Tunis **346, 347a**; V&A Images **143**; Vatican Museums **158, 279**; Museo Archeologico, Venice **140, 204b**; Kunsthistorisches Museum, Vienna **305, 311b**

Index

Most Romans are listed by their *nomen*. Emperors are listed by the name most often used in the text. Page numbers in *italics* refer to illustrations and their related captions.